FREDERICK D.
PATTERSON
RESEARCH INSTITUTE
— OF THE COLLEGE FUND/UNCF —
A RESEARCH INSTITUTE ON AFRICAN AMERICANS AND EDUCATION

—————— T H E ——————

AFRICAN AMERICAN
EDUCATION

DATA BOOK

Volume II: Preschool through High School Education

Michael T. Nettles, Ph.D.
Executive Director

Laura W. Perna, Ph.D.
Research Scientist

©1997 Frederick D. Patterson Research Institute of The College Fund/UNCF

TESTIMONIALS

A sixth of the students in American public schools are African American but discussions of educational policy in recent years most often either ignore them or address their problems in terms of stereotypes and fads. This book continues the Patterson Institute's historic effort to assemble vast collections of clearly presented facts to inform the discussion and to provide a basis for much more thoughtful discussion and planning for educational change. Data that would otherwise be available only to those who obtain and analyzed huge federal data sets on their computers is readily accessible here.

The book provides a treasure chest of important data. It is not designed to make ideological points; it reports the bad news as well as the good and it will be relied on by people looking at a wide variety of issues from many perspectives. The book pays attention not only to the schools and the educational results but to the context within which the schools must function—a context of disproportionate poverty, less prepared teachers, and segregated schools. Its tables also reflect the great size and diversity of the African American community and its major presence in private as well as public schools. Although I have a large collection of studies of education and my office is in the midst of a library, this is one book that I will consult regularly. This is an essential reference book and the Patterson Institute is laying a strong foundation for its mission of providing the information needed to improve education for African Americans.

Gary Orfield, *Harvard University*

Prevailing policies and practices directed at improving the school success of African American students have often been guided by good intentions, conventional wisdom, and limited and sparse data sources that focus on single explanations of school achievement. Until the publication of this important volume, there existed no single resource that comprehensively compiled and described data on the many complex variables related to the school performance and experiences of African American students. The African American Education Data Book is a major contribution for educational researchers and policy makers in pre-school through high school education. I predict that this extraordinary book will be extensively quoted and referenced in the educational literature. More importantly, I predict that this seminal work will be a significant catalyst for reforms in K-12 education that will result in increased school achievement for African American children who continue to suffer from unequal resources and limited opportunities.

Jacqueline Jordan Irvine
Emory University

These data are invaluable. If we are ever to tackle the root causes of inequality in this country, we must understand the conditions of education for African American students. Anecdotes and hunches are not enough. We need to know with clarity and certainty what opportunities to learn students have available. This is a critical first step to creating sensible, grounded policies that have a chance of making a difference.

Linda Darling-Hammond
Columbia University

Foreword

We are proud to present Volume II of the educational status of African American preschool, elementary, and secondary school children. Like Volume I, Volume II records the African American educational progress that, heretofore, has existed in a multitude of places: as a part of research and census databases; inside testing companies; and inside schools, colleges, and universities. When the data and information about the education of African Americans are dispersed in this way, the picture of the educational status and condition of African Americans is incomplete and inaccessible for analyses, research, and policymaking. This volume retrieves and analyzes a vast array of data about the educational representation, distribution, and achievement of African Americans. It relies upon the most reliable national cross-sectional and longitudinal data sources; sorts the data on students, schools, and school personnel according to educational level; and presents comparisons based upon sex, race and ethnicity, socioeconomic status, and type of preschools and schools.

At this early stage in the history of the Frederick D. Patterson Research Institute, the data are largely descriptive, focusing exclusively upon presenting "just the facts." The explanations for the facts are reserved for future research. Here, Michael T. Nettles and the researchers at the Patterson Institute attempt to synthesize the educational experiences of African American preschoolers, elementary, and secondary school students in a way that will inform and serve as a powerful way of thinking about both the progress made and the challenges that we must confront. We hope this compilation of data will reveal information that has existed in isolation to allow for setting new research agenda, and to pave the way for improving educational opportunities and outcomes in the future.

How satisfying it would be, we think, if this can produce the compelling facts that would instantly suggest direction and development for lay leaders, as well as for those in the business and education fields who are attempting to improve the nation's preschools, elementary, and secondary schools. We invite policymakers, educators, legislators, media, and the public to examine the data and to set priorities and activities to address the many important and challenging issues that are revealed.

As a new Institute of The College Fund/ UNCF, the mission of the Frederick D. Patterson Research Institute is to design, conduct, and disseminate research to policymakers, educators, and the public with the goal of improving educational opportunities and outcomes for African Americans. The research conducted by the Institute focuses upon the educational status and attainment of African Americans from preschool through adulthood. The third volume of the Data Book will review the transitions students make from school to college and from school to work and will complete the three-volume set.

William H. Gray, III
President and CEO

Acknowledgments

The Frederick D. Patterson Research Institute has benefited from the support of some of the nation's leading corporate and philanthropic institutions and education organizations along with the most talented and committed professionals in producing this databook. To each one we are grateful. The Frederick D. Patterson Research Institute would like to extend its most heartfelt thanks to the following contributors: The Mott Foundation for contributing the initial funding that permitted The College Fund/ UNCF to establish the Frederick D. Patterson Research Institute as a permanent endowment; The Pew Charitable Trusts, The W.K. Kellogg Foundations, and Lilly Endowment, Inc., for providing grants used to design, produce, and disseminate the report; Sun Microsystems for donating a powerful state-of-the-art file server that permitted the Institute to store, process, and analyze large-scale databases and retrieve data and information electronically over the Internet; The IBM Corporation for providing the personal computers for the researchers at the Institute to use in analyzing data and writing the report; and both The Statistical Package for the Social Sciences Incorporated (SPSS) and The Microsoft Corporation for the software products required to write the reports and present the data in tables and graphs. The Institute would also like to thank The Rockefeller Foundation for providing part of the support needed for staff leadership at the Institute; and The University of Michigan for contributing the time and part of the salary of the Executive Director of the Frederick D. Patterson Research Institute along with the expertise of its faculty in the areas of population research and large-scale databases.

The time and proficiency of individuals are what transform valuable fiscal and material resources into valuable products. We are grateful to some of the nation's best talent for their involvement and support of this project, including Michael Fields, Chairman of OpenVision, for his assistance in designing the technology strategy and securing contributions from major corporations; Lester Monts, Vice Provost for Academic and Multicultural Affairs at the University of Michigan for championing the University's personnel and financial contributions to the project; and the staff of the Frederick D. Patterson Research Institute: Laura Perna, Mallery Hobbs, Erica Rhodes, Heather Herbert, Michael Fraser, Karen Warfield, and Monique Roberts for their tireless efforts in the production of this work.

Invaluable consultants to the project include: Mur Muchane from the University of Tennessee, who served as a software specialist and leading technology strategist; Nancy Robertson, who assisted in analyzing and producing sections of the report; and Susan MacKenzie, who provided editorial assistance throughout the project. Others involved in various aspects of the project were: Shep Roey of the Westat Corporation; Paul Ramsey, Eleanor Horne, and Eugene Johnson of the Educational Testing Service; Susan Hill of the National Science Foundation; Reynolds Farley of the University of Michigan; and Tom Satterfiel and Jim Maxey of the American College Testing Company.

The data and information included in this report are among the best and most voluminous collection and reporting of educational statistics in a single document. In the course of obtaining a license to operate restricted data collected by government agencies, the Institute received the support and assistance of Alan Moorehead and Cynthia Barton of the U.S. Department of Education, and Mary Reynolds and Carolyn Shettle of the National Science Foundation. The data that were not received from these two agencies were either contributed by or purchased from The American College Testing Company, The Defense Data Manpower Center, The College Board, The Educational Testing Service, and The National Assessment Governing Board. To these organizations we are extremely grateful, for the rich data provided on tests and assessments and other important indicators, and for the generous overtures of technical assistance on matters ranging from interpreting data to reviewing draft documents.

CONTENTS

CHAPTER I.

CHAPTER II.

CHAPTER III.

Characteristics of Schools Attended by African American Students 59

CHAPTER IV.

Attendance and Behavior Among 1988 8th Graders in 1988 and 1992 87

CHAPTER V.

CHAPTER VI.

CHAPTER VIII.

CHAPTER IX.

CHAPTER X.
Characteristics of Public and Private School Principals

CHAPTER XI.

CHAPTER XII.

List of Tables

CHAPTER II.
Enrollment at America's Public and Private Elementary and Secondary Schools

CHAPTER III.
Characteristics of Schools Attended by African American Students

CHAPTER IV.
Attendance and Behavior Among 1988 8th Graders in 1988 and 1992

CHAPTER V.
African American Student Performance on the National Assessment of Educational Progress

CHAPTER VI.
School Safety and Alcohol and Drug Use in America's Schools

CHAPTER VII.
Participation in Community Service by 1992 High School Seniors

CHAPTER VIII.
Characteristics of Public and Private School Teachers

CHAPTER IX.
Indicators of the Quality of Elementary and Secondary School Teachers

CHAPTER X.
Characteristics of Public and Private School Principals

CHAPTER XI.
Parents' Involvement in Their Children's Schools

List of Figures

CHAPTER III.
Characteristics of Schools Attended by African American Students

CHAPTER IV.
Attendance and Behavior Among 1988 8th Graders in 1988 and 1992

CHAPTER V.
African American Student Performance on the National Assessment of Education Progress

CHAPTER VI.
School Safety and Alcohol and Drug Use in America's Schools

CHAPTER VII.
Participation in Community Service by 1992 High School Seniors

CHAPTER VIII.
Characteristics of Public and Private School Teachers

CHAPTER IX.
Indicators of the Quality of Elementary and Secondary School Teachers

CHAPTER X.
Characteristics of Public and Private School Principals

CHAPTER XI.
Parents' Involvement in Their Children's Schools

CHAPTER I.
Characteristics of
African American Preschoolers

How well are African American preschoolers being prepared to enter elementary school? How do the lives and educational experiences of African American preschoolers compare with their peers of other racial and ethnic groups?

The future of the nation's preschoolers emerged as a high priority at the first National Education Summit in 1989, when President George Bush and the nation's 50 governors adopted six National Education Goals. Goal One of the National Education Goals states: "By the year 2000 all children in America will start school ready to learn." In 1994, Congress affirmed the six goals established at the first National Education Summit; added two more goals; and together with President Bill Clinton, Congress enacted the 1994 Goals 2000: Educate America Act.

The emphasis that Goal One places upon readiness to learn raises major questions for a study of African American educational progress. To address these questions, this chapter uses the National Household Education Survey, the National Longitudinal Survey of Youth, and the March 1995 supplement of the Current Population Survey.

The Early Childhood Education component, one of two components of the 1991 National Household Education Survey (NHES), provides data that describe progress toward achieving Goal One. In contrast to other national surveys sponsored by the U.S. Department of Education, National Household Education Survey data were collected from households rather than from teachers, students, schools, school districts, and state education agencies.

The Early Childhood Education Component focuses upon the experiences of children age 3 to 8, with attention to child care, primary and kindergarten school attendance, retention in early grades, parental involvement in education, the educational environment at home, and characteristics of the family. Extended interviews were conducted with 13,892 of the eligible 19,842 households for an overall completion rate of 77.0%. Separate survey instruments were used for students who were enrolled in preschool and those who were not.

CHAPTER ORGANIZATION

In this chapter, the focus is on 3-, 4-, and 5-year-old children, with emphases upon their economic status, health condition, preschool attendance, preparation and readiness for school, and performance on intelligence tests.

PART I — OVERVIEW

Because of low birth weights and other health problems related to income, many African American babies start life precariously. The majority of African American preschoolers are raised in low-income households (many below the poverty line) and are fed, clothed and sheltered at a subsistence level. The majority live in mother-led homes. Additionally, more of their mothers are employed than are the mothers of their White counterparts. Low levels of college completion by their parents suggest that few African American preschoolers live in households in which high levels of educational attainment are assumed or taken for granted.

Nonetheless, African Americans appear to recognize the need to provide their children with a strong preschool foundation. A higher percentage of African American 3- and 4-year-olds than of Whites and the overall population are attending some kind of preschool program. Not all African Americans are participating equally, however. Attendance rates are lower for African American children at lower levels of parental income. At the lower income levels, a higher percentage of children of working mothers appear to be taking part in these programs.

On most school readiness measures, African American children differ little from their peers in other racial and ethnic groups. African American 5-year-olds also exhibit positive attitudes toward their school experiences. Only on test performance do hints of future difficulties emerge. Although motor and social development scores are comparable to those of Whites, differences in group averages appear on vocabulary measures. Sex differences emerge at the preschool level, as evidenced by higher test scores for African American girls than for African American boys on the Motor and Social Development and the Verbal Memory tests.

Although educators may be encouraged by the relatively high rates of African American participation in Head Start and other preschool programs, current analyses are limited by the absence of impor- tant data. Important information about the quality of preschool experiences—including the curricula, the personnel and the educational focus of the preschool exposures—is missing from most discussions. Current national data and existing information about the lives of preschoolers do not fill in these blanks. Such background data and information are imperative for understanding why the academic progress and achievement of African Americans fall behind the levels of their White counterparts in subsequent years.

PART II — DETAILED DESCRIPTIONS AND TABLES

ECONOMIC STATUS AND HEALTH CONDITION OF PRESCHOOLERS

Household Income

Figure 1 shows that, in 1992, approximately one-fifth (18.2%) of all households with 3- and 4-year-old children had incomes of $10,000 or less.

- **Table 1** shows that 43.8% of African American preschoolers resided in households with incomes below $10,000, compared with 9.5% of Whites.

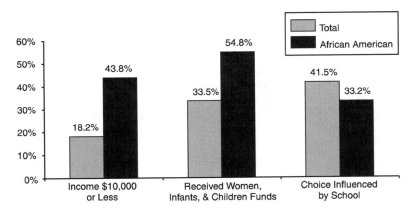

Figure 1. Economic Status of
3- and 4-Year-Olds: 1992

Source: National Household Education Survey, 1993.

Table 1. Economic Status of the Parents of 3- and 4-Year-Olds (as of 12/31/92) by Race and Sex
(weighted sample size in parentheses)

Characteristic	Total	Male	Female	White, Non-Hispanic			African American, Non-Hispanic			Hispanic			Other		
				Total	Male	Female	Total	Male	Female	Total	Male	Female	Total	Male	Female
Total Weighted Sample	100.0%	51.2%	48.8%	67.9%	34.1%	33.7%	15.3%	8.4%	6.9%	12.2%	6.3%	5.9%	4.6%	2.4%	2.3%
	(7,712,232)	(3,945,587)	(3,766,646)	(5,234,009)	(2,632,290)	(2,601,719)	(1,183,731)	(647,945)	(535,786)	(937,457)	(482,422)	(455,035)	(357,036)	(182,930)	(174,106)
Total Household Income * +**	100.0%	100.0%	100.0%	100.0%	100.0%	100.0%	100.0%	100.0%	100.0%	100.0%	100.0%	100.0%	100.0%	100.0%	100.0%
	(7,712,232)	(3,945,587)	(3,766,646)	(5,234,009)	(2,632,290)	(2,601,719)	(1,183,731)	(647,945)	(535,786)	(937,457)	(482,422)	(455,035)	(357,036)	(182,930)	(174,106)
$10,000 or Less	18.2%	20.1%	16.3%	9.5%	10.3%	8.8%	43.8%	46.4%	40.7%	33.0%	34.3%	31.7%	22.2%	30.5%	13.5%
	(1,406,789)	(791,968)	(614,820)	(498,655)	(269,934)	(228,721)	(518,947)	(300,655)	(218,292)	(309,758)	(165,535)	(144,223)	(79,428)	(55,844)	(23,584)
$10,001 to $25,000	28.0%	27.9%	28.1%	25.7%	25.6%	25.8%	31.0%	31.2%	30.8%	37.2%	35.4%	39.0%	27.4%	28.3%	26.5%
	(2,158,567)	(1,098,937)	(1,059,630)	(1,345,159)	(673,972)	(671,187)	(367,065)	(202,148)	(164,917)	(348,372)	(171,009)	(177,363)	(97,971)	(51,808)	(46,163)
$25,001 to $50,000	33.9%	33.6%	34.2%	39.9%	40.5%	39.3%	18.2%	16.2%	20.6%	21.0%	21.4%	20.5%	31.4%	27.1%	35.9%
	(2,612,659)	(1,324,472)	(1,288,186)	(2,088,296)	(1,066,538)	(1,021,758)	(215,619)	(105,095)	(110,524)	(196,697)	(103,217)	(93,480)	(112,046)	(49,622)	(62,424)
Over $50,000	19.9%	18.5%	21.3%	24.9%	23.6%	26.1%	6.9%	6.2%	7.8%	8.8%	8.8%	8.8%	18.9%	14.0%	24.1%
	(1,534,217)	(730,209)	(804,008)	(1,301,898)	(621,845)	(680,053)	(82,099)	(40,047)	(42,052)	(82,630)	(42,661)	(39,969)	(67,590)	(25,656)	(41,934)
Got Money From Women, Infants, & Children Program Since Child Born ***	100.0%	100.0%	100.0%	100.0%	100.0%	100.0%	100.0%	100.0%	100.0%	100.0%	100.0%	100.0%	100.0%	100.0%	100.0%
	(7,712,232)	(3,945,587)	(3,766,646)	(5,234,009)	(2,632,290)	(2,601,719)	(1,183,731)	(647,945)	(535,786)	(937,457)	(482,422)	(455,035)	(357,036)	(182,930)	(174,106)
Yes	33.5%	34.4%	32.6%	26.2%	26.6%	25.7%	54.8%	56.3%	52.9%	48.6%	47.6%	49.7%	30.8%	32.8%	28.7%
	(2,584,724)	(1,355,495)	(1,229,229)	(1,370,620)	(700,924)	(669,696)	(648,304)	(364,839)	(283,465)	(455,897)	(229,764)	(226,133)	(109,903)	(59,968)	(49,935)
No	65.1%	64.8%	65.4%	72.8%	72.7%	72.9%	41.8%	41.5%	42.3%	50.3%	51.7%	48.7%	67.2%	66.6%	67.8%
	(5,018,151)	(2,554,864)	(2,463,286)	(3,811,668)	(1,914,726)	(1,896,942)	(495,330)	(268,705)	(226,625)	(471,250)	(249,577)	(221,673)	(239,902)	(121,856)	(118,046)
Unknown (Missing)	1.4%	0.9%	2.0%	1.0%	0.6%	1.3%	3.4%	2.2%	4.8%	1.1%	0.6%	1.6%	2.0%	0.6%	3.5%
	(109,358)	(35,228)	(74,131)	(51,721)	(16,640)	(35,081)	(40,097)	(14,401)	(25,696)	(10,310)	(3,081)	(7,229)	(7,231)	(1,106)	(6,125)
Choice of Home Influenced by School * +**	100.0%	100.0%	100.0%	100.0%	100.0%	100.0%	100.0%	100.0%	100.0%	100.0%	100.0%	100.0%	100.0%	100.0%	100.0%
	(7,712,232)	(3,945,587)	(3,766,646)	(5,234,009)	(2,632,290)	(2,601,719)	(1,183,731)	(647,945)	(535,786)	(937,457)	(482,422)	(455,035)	(357,036)	(182,930)	(174,106)
Yes	41.5%	40.3%	42.7%	42.9%	40.9%	45.0%	33.2%	35.8%	30.0%	46.8%	47.7%	45.8%	33.5%	28.1%	39.1%
	(3,198,523)	(1,590,689)	(1,607,836)	(2,247,465)	(1,077,310)	(1,170,155)	(392,768)	(231,785)	(160,983)	(438,852)	(230,231)	(208,621)	(119,440)	(51,363)	(68,077)
No	58.5%	59.7%	57.3%	57.1%	59.1%	55.0%	66.8%	64.2%	70.0%	53.2%	52.3%	54.2%	66.5%	71.9%	60.9%
	(4,513,709)	(2,354,899)	(2,158,810)	(2,986,544)	(1,554,980)	(1,431,564)	(790,963)	(416,160)	(374,803)	(498,605)	(252,191)	(246,414)	(237,597)	(131,568)	(106,029)

Notes:
*** Test of statistical significance compares African Americans with Whites. *** p < .001, ** p < .01, * p < .05.
+++ Test of statistical significance compares White boys with White girls. +++ p < .001, ++ p < .01, + p < .05.
~~~ Test of statistical significance compares African American boys with African American girls. ~~~ p < .001, ~~ p < .01, ~ p < .05.
Tests of statistical significance calculated using adjusted sample weight to control for influence of large sample sizes.
Source: National Household Education Survey, 1993.

- Of African American 3- and 4-year-olds, 75.0% resided in households with annual incomes below $25,000, compared with 35.2% of Whites.

- More than half (54.8%) of 3- and 4-year-old African American children resided in families who received public support from the Women, Infants and Children's (WIC) program, compared with 26.2% of Whites and 33.5% of the overall population.

Less than one-half (41.5%) of all parents of 3- and 4-year-old children chose their residence based on a desire to have their children attend a particular school.

- A smaller percentage of African American parents than White parents considered the local schools when selecting their place of residence (33.2% compared to 42.9% of Whites and 41.5% overall).

Parents' Educational Attainment

Overall, one-third (35.1%) of all mothers and one-fourth (25.9%) of all fathers of 3- and 4-year-old children had high school diplomas as their highest level of education.

- **Figure 2** shows that only 8.1% of the mothers of African American 3- and 4-year-olds had a bachelor's degree or higher, compared with 17.2% for the overall population.

- **Table 2** shows that a lower percentage of African American fathers than White fathers had completed at least a bachelor's degree (4.8% versus 23.2%).

Family Composition and Employment Status

The family composition and the employment status of parents of African American and White preschool-age children are contrasted in **Table 3**.

- **Table 3** shows that 66.0% of African American preschoolers had no fathers in their household compared to 25.9% of the overall population and 15.8% of Whites.

- The full-time employment rate of African American mothers (37.6%) was slightly higher than that of White mothers (31.1%) and that of the overall population (31.7%).

- **Figure 3** shows that 16.4% of the mothers of African American preschoolers were looking for work, compared with 7.0% of all mothers.

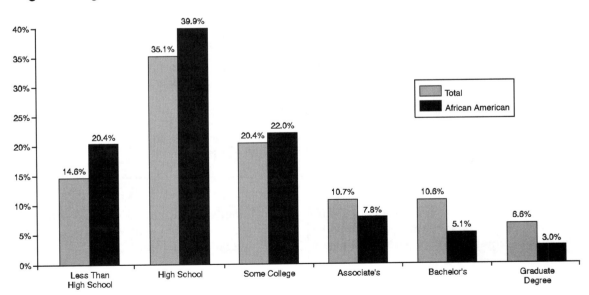

Figure 2. Highest Level of Education Attained by Mothers of 3- and 4-Year-Olds: 1992

Source: National Household Education Survey, 1993.

Table 2. Highest Level of Education Among Parents of 3- and 4-Year-Olds (as of 12/31/92) by Race and Sex
(weighted sample size in parentheses)

Highest Grade Completed	Total	Male	Female	White, Non-Hispanic			African American, Non-Hispanic			Hispanic			Other		
				Total	Male	Female	Total	Male	Female	Total	Male	Female	Total	Male	Female
Total Weighted Sample	100.0%	51.2%	48.8%	67.9%	34.1%	33.7%	15.3%	8.4%	6.9%	12.2%	6.3%	5.9%	4.6%	2.4%	2.3%
	(7,712,232)	(3,945,587)	(3,766,646)	(5,234,009)	(2,632,290)	(2,601,719)	(1,183,731)	(647,945)	(535,786)	(937,457)	(482,422)	(455,035)	(357,036)	(182,930)	(174,106)
Mother's Highest Level of Education***	100.0%	100.0%	100.0%	100.0%	100.0%	100.0%	100.0%	100.0%	100.0%	100.0%	100.0%	100.0%	100.0%	100.0%	100.0%
	(7,712,232)	(3,945,587)	(3,766,646)	(5,234,009)	(2,632,290)	(2,601,719)	(1,183,731)	(647,945)	(535,786)	(937,457)	(482,422)	(455,035)	(357,036)	(182,930)	(174,106)
Unknown (Missing)	2.0%	2.3%	1.6%	2.1%	2.3%	1.8%	1.8%	2.4%	1.1%	1.6%	2.1%	1.0%	1.8%	1.9%	1.6%
	(151,789)	(90,478)	(61,311)	(108,980)	(61,095)	(47,885)	(21,736)	(15,760)	(5,976)	(14,777)	(10,076)	(4,701)	(6,296)	(3,547)	(2,749)
Less Than High School	14.6%	14.2%	15.0%	8.2%	8.0%	8.4%	20.4%	18.4%	22.8%	43.3%	42.5%	44.2%	13.3%	13.5%	13.2%
	(1,123,534)	(559,375)	(564,159)	(429,009)	(210,802)	(218,207)	(241,029)	(118,908)	(122,121)	(405,838)	(204,926)	(200,912)	(47,658)	(24,739)	(22,919)
High School Diploma or GED	35.1%	36.4%	33.8%	35.6%	36.7%	34.5%	39.9%	41.0%	38.7%	25.5%	27.8%	23.1%	37.3%	38.4%	36.2%
	(2,708,910)	(1,436,219)	(1,272,691)	(1,863,689)	(966,477)	(897,212)	(472,804)	(265,526)	(207,278)	(239,156)	(133,939)	(105,217)	(133,261)	(70,277)	(62,984)
Some Vocational School or 1 to 2 Years of College	20.4%	19.4%	21.5%	21.4%	20.6%	22.1%	22.0%	21.2%	22.9%	16.3%	12.6%	20.3%	11.8%	12.8%	10.8%
	(1,573,964)	(764,172)	(809,792)	(1,118,769)	(542,623)	(576,146)	(260,155)	(137,486)	(122,669)	(152,747)	(60,578)	(92,169)	(42,293)	(23,485)	(18,808)
Associate's Degree or 3 to 4 Years of College	10.7%	10.7%	10.8%	12.5%	11.9%	13.2%	7.8%	9.6%	5.6%	5.5%	5.7%	5.3%	7.7%	9.5%	5.9%
	(827,357)	(420,254)	(407,103)	(655,900)	(313,095)	(342,805)	(92,249)	(62,484)	(29,765)	(51,604)	(27,345)	(24,259)	(27,604)	(17,330)	(10,274)
Bachelor's Degree	10.6%	10.5%	10.7%	12.7%	13.1%	12.3%	5.1%	4.2%	6.1%	4.3%	5.3%	3.3%	15.6%	10.7%	20.7%
	(819,039)	(415,871)	(403,167)	(663,000)	(343,895)	(319,105)	(59,852)	(27,051)	(32,801)	(40,506)	(25,336)	(15,170)	(55,680)	(19,589)	(36,091)
Graduate or Professional School	6.6%	6.6%	6.6%	7.5%	7.4%	7.7%	3.0%	3.2%	2.8%	3.5%	4.2%	2.8%	12.4%	13.1%	11.6%
	(507,643)	(259,220)	(248,424)	(394,665)	(194,305)	(200,360)	(35,906)	(20,730)	(15,176)	(32,830)	(20,222)	(12,608)	(44,243)	(23,963)	(20,280)
Father's Highest Level of Education***	100.0%	100.0%	100.0%	100.0%	100.0%	100.0%	100.0%	100.0%	100.0%	100.0%	100.0%	100.0%	100.0%	100.0%	100.0%
	(7,712,232)	(3,945,587)	(3,766,646)	(5,234,009)	(2,632,290)	(2,601,719)	(1,183,731)	(647,945)	(535,786)	(937,457)	(482,422)	(455,035)	(357,036)	(182,930)	(174,106)
Unknown (Missing)	25.9%	26.9%	24.9%	15.8%	15.4%	16.2%	66.0%	68.5%	63.1%	29.4%	31.4%	27.2%	32.0%	33.1%	30.9%
	(1,999,659)	(1,061,601)	(938,057)	(828,159)	(405,753)	(422,406)	(781,781)	(443,850)	(337,931)	(275,402)	(151,531)	(123,871)	(114,316)	(60,467)	(53,849)
Less Than High School	8.6%	7.5%	9.7%	6.5%	5.9%	7.1%	4.7%	3.5%	6.3%	27.2%	22.9%	31.8%	2.8%	3.0%	2.5%
	(660,001)	(294,133)	(365,868)	(339,096)	(155,643)	(183,453)	(56,169)	(22,662)	(33,507)	(254,837)	(110,319)	(144,518)	(9,899)	(5,509)	(4,390)
High School Diploma or GED	25.9%	26.2%	25.7%	30.5%	31.0%	30.0%	14.0%	13.8%	14.2%	20.8%	23.3%	18.0%	11.9%	8.5%	15.4%
	(1,999,446)	(1,033,042)	(966,405)	(1,597,199)	(815,599)	(781,600)	(165,297)	(89,299)	(75,998)	(194,601)	(112,605)	(81,996)	(42,350)	(15,539)	(26,811)
Some Vocational School or 1 to 2 Years of College	12.5%	12.8%	12.1%	13.7%	14.7%	12.7%	7.1%	6.3%	8.1%	10.7%	9.2%	12.4%	16.5%	17.6%	15.4%
	(961,960)	(504,552)	(457,408)	(718,016)	(387,048)	(330,968)	(84,224)	(40,834)	(43,390)	(100,729)	(44,491)	(56,238)	(58,991)	(32,179)	(26,812)
Associate's Degree or 3 to 4 Years of College	8.1%	7.7%	8.6%	10.2%	9.4%	11.0%	3.3%	3.6%	3.0%	3.3%	3.3%	3.4%	6.3%	8.2%	4.2%
	(627,646)	(302,649)	(324,997)	(534,640)	(248,631)	(286,009)	(39,391)	(23,197)	(16,194)	(31,280)	(15,762)	(15,518)	(22,335)	(15,059)	(7,276)
Bachelor's Degree	10.0%	10.0%	10.0%	12.2%	12.3%	12.2%	3.3%	2.6%	4.2%	4.4%	5.0%	3.9%	13.8%	16.1%	11.4%
	(770,979)	(394,994)	(375,986)	(641,123)	(324,808)	(316,315)	(39,077)	(16,732)	(22,345)	(41,543)	(24,013)	(17,530)	(49,237)	(29,441)	(19,796)
Graduate or Professional School	9.0%	9.0%	9.0%	11.0%	11.2%	10.8%	1.5%	1.8%	1.2%	4.2%	4.9%	3.4%	16.8%	13.5%	20.2%
	(692,540)	(354,616)	(337,925)	(575,775)	(294,808)	(280,967)	(17,791)	(11,371)	(6,420)	(39,064)	(23,700)	(15,364)	(59,911)	(24,737)	(35,174)

Notes:

*** Test of statistical significance compares African Americans with Whites. *** p < .001, ** p < .01, * p < .05.

+++ Test of statistical significance compares White boys with White girls. +++ p < .001, ++ p < .01, + p < .05.

~~~Test of statistical significance compares African American boys with African American girls. ~~~ p < .001, ~~ p < .01, ~ p < .05.

Tests of statistical significance calculated using adjusted sample weight to control for influence of large sample sizes.

Source: National Household Education Survey, 1993.

Table 3. Employment Status of Parents of 3- and 4-Year-Olds (as of 12/31/92) by Race and Sex
(weighted sample size in parentheses)

Characteristic	Total	Male	Female	White, Non-Hispanic Total	White, Non-Hispanic Male	White, Non-Hispanic Female	African American, Non-Hispanic Total	African American, Non-Hispanic Male	African American, Non-Hispanic Female	Hispanic Total	Hispanic Male	Hispanic Female	Other Total	Other Male	Other Female
Total Weighted Sample	100.0%	51.2%	48.8%	67.9%	34.1%	33.7%	15.3%	8.4%	6.9%	12.2%	6.3%	5.9%	4.6%	2.4%	2.3%
	(7,712,232)	(3,945,587)	(3,766,646)	(5,234,009)	(2,632,290)	(2,601,719)	(1,183,731)	(647,945)	(535,786)	(937,457)	(482,422)	(455,035)	(357,036)	(182,930)	(174,106)
Father's Work Status * +**	100.0%	100.0%	100.0%	100.0%	100.0%	100.0%	100.0%	100.0%	100.0%	100.0%	100.0%	100.0%	100.0%	100.0%	100.0%
	(7,712,232)	(3,945,587)	(3,766,646)	(5,234,009)	(2,632,290)	(2,601,719)	(1,183,731)	(647,945)	(535,786)	(937,457)	(482,422)	(455,035)	(357,035)	(182,930)	(174,106)
No Father in Household	25.9%	26.9%	24.9%	15.8%	15.4%	16.2%	66.0%	68.5%	63.1%	29.4%	31.4%	27.2%	32.0%	33.1%	30.9%
	(1,999,659)	(1,061,601)	(938,057)	(828,159)	(405,753)	(422,406)	(781,781)	(443,850)	(337,931)	(275,402)	(151,531)	(123,871)	(114,316)	(60,467)	(53,849)
Employed 35 or More Hours Per Week	64.6%	63.0%	66.3%	74.5%	74.1%	74.9%	26.8%	25.5%	28.5%	59.7%	56.7%	62.9%	57.3%	52.1%	62.7%
	(4,981,147)	(2,485,053)	(2,496,093)	(3,899,337)	(1,950,929)	(1,948,408)	(317,661)	(165,114)	(152,547)	(559,714)	(273,714)	(286,000)	(204,434)	(95,296)	(109,138)
Employed Less Than 35 Hours Per Week	3.7%	3.4%	4.1%	3.9%	3.4%	4.4%	1.8%	1.4%	2.3%	4.8%	5.4%	4.2%	4.5%	4.0%	5.0%
	(287,817)	(132,822)	(154,996)	(204,857)	(90,329)	(114,528)	(21,487)	(8,918)	(12,569)	(45,372)	(26,192)	(19,180)	(16,102)	(7,383)	(8,719)
Looking for Work	3.1%	3.5%	2.6%	2.9%	3.4%	2.4%	3.4%	3.1%	3.7%	4.0%	4.3%	3.6%	2.4%	4.7%	0.0%
	(237,183)	(139,631)	(97,552)	(151,284)	(89,928)	(61,356)	(40,098)	(20,268)	(19,830)	(37,285)	(20,919)	(16,366)	(8,516)	(8,516)	–
Not in Labor Force	2.7%	3.2%	2.1%	2.9%	3.6%	2.1%	1.9%	1.5%	2.4%	2.1%	2.1%	2.1%	3.8%	6.2%	1.4%
	(206,426)	(126,478)	(79,948)	(150,371)	(95,350)	(55,021)	(22,704)	(9,794)	(12,910)	(19,684)	(10,066)	(9,618)	(13,667)	(11,268)	(2,399)
Mother's Work Status * +**	100.0%	100.0%	100.0%	100.0%	100.0%	100.0%	100.0%	100.0%	100.0%	100.0%	100.0%	100.0%	100.0%	100.0%	100.0%
	(7,712,232)	(3,945,587)	(3,766,646)	(5,234,009)	(2,632,290)	(2,601,719)	(1,183,731)	(647,945)	(535,786)	(937,458)	(482,422)	(455,035)	(357,035)	(182,930)	(174,106)
No Mother in Household	2.0%	2.3%	1.6%	2.1%	2.3%	1.8%	1.8%	2.4%	1.1%	1.6%	2.1%	1.0%	1.8%	1.9%	1.6%
	(151,789)	(90,478)	(61,311)	(108,980)	(61,095)	(47,885)	(21,736)	(15,760)	(5,976)	(14,777)	(10,076)	(4,701)	(6,296)	(3,547)	(2,749)
Employed 35 or More Hours Per Week	31.7%	29.6%	33.9%	31.1%	28.1%	34.1%	37.6%	36.5%	39.0%	28.5%	28.3%	28.7%	29.3%	29.5%	29.1%
	(2,445,831)	(1,167,427)	(1,278,404)	(1,628,816)	(740,668)	(888,148)	(445,471)	(236,439)	(209,032)	(266,909)	(136,338)	(130,571)	(104,635)	(53,982)	(50,653)
Employed Less Than 35 Hours Per Week	20.6%	21.0%	20.2%	23.8%	24.9%	22.7%	11.2%	11.4%	10.9%	16.0%	17.6%	14.3%	17.2%	7.6%	27.2%
	(1,590,120)	(828,596)	(761,524)	(1,246,705)	(656,053)	(590,652)	(132,037)	(73,716)	(58,321)	(150,143)	(84,960)	(65,183)	(61,235)	(13,867)	(47,368)
Looking for Work	7.0%	6.5%	7.4%	4.2%	3.9%	4.6%	16.4%	14.8%	18.4%	11.1%	10.4%	11.9%	4.7%	4.1%	5.3%
	(537,683)	(257,193)	(280,490)	(222,092)	(103,517)	(118,575)	(194,533)	(95,900)	(98,633)	(104,267)	(50,247)	(54,020)	(16,791)	(7,529)	(9,262)
Not in Labor Force	38.7%	40.6%	36.8%	38.7%	40.7%	36.8%	32.9%	34.9%	30.6%	42.8%	41.6%	44.1%	47.1%	56.9%	36.8%
	(2,986,809)	(1,601,894)	(1,384,916)	(2,027,416)	(1,070,957)	(956,459)	(389,954)	(226,130)	(163,824)	(401,362)	(200,802)	(200,560)	(168,078)	(104,005)	(64,073)
Mother's Work Pattern * +**	100.0%	100.0%	100.0%	100.0%	100.0%	100.0%	100.0%	100.0%	100.0%	100.0%	100.0%	100.0%	100.0%	100.0%	100.0%
	(7,712,232)	(3,945,587)	(3,766,646)	(5,234,009)	(2,632,290)	(2,601,719)	(1,183,731)	(647,945)	(535,786)	(937,456)	(482,422)	(455,035)	(357,036)	(182,930)	(174,106)
No Mother in Household	2.0%	2.3%	1.6%	2.1%	2.3%	1.8%	1.8%	2.4%	1.1%	1.6%	2.1%	1.0%	1.8%	1.9%	1.6%
	(151,789)	(90,478)	(61,311)	(108,980)	(61,095)	(47,885)	(21,736)	(15,760)	(5,976)	(14,777)	(10,076)	(4,701)	(6,296)	(3,547)	(2,749)
Work Full-Time, Full-Year	24.1%	22.4%	25.9%	23.9%	21.3%	26.7%	29.2%	29.1%	29.4%	19.6%	20.1%	19.2%	22.0%	22.0%	22.0%
	(1,861,997)	(885,108)	(976,889)	(1,253,407)	(559,590)	(693,817)	(345,876)	(188,329)	(157,547)	(184,129)	(96,949)	(87,180)	(78,585)	(40,240)	(38,345)
Work Less Than Full-Time or Less than Full-Year	38.8%	39.2%	38.4%	41.1%	42.4%	39.8%	30.4%	29.6%	31.3%	38.7%	40.7%	36.6%	32.9%	22.4%	43.9%
	(2,992,826)	(1,545,638)	(1,447,189)	(2,153,391)	(1,116,711)	(1,036,680)	(359,529)	(191,928)	(167,601)	(362,604)	(196,109)	(166,495)	(117,303)	(40,890)	(76,413)
Not Employed	35.1%	36.1%	34.0%	32.8%	34.0%	31.6%	38.6%	38.9%	38.2%	40.1%	37.2%	43.2%	43.4%	53.7%	32.5%
	(2,705,620)	(1,424,365)	(1,281,254)	(1,718,231)	(894,895)	(823,336)	(456,590)	(251,928)	(204,662)	(375,946)	(179,288)	(196,658)	(154,852)	(98,254)	(56,598)

Notes:
"–" indicates sample size too small to estimate.
*** Test of statistical significance compares African Americans with Whites. *** p < .001, ** p < .01, * p < .05.
+++ Test of statistical significance compares White boys with White girls. +++ p < .001, ++ p < .01, + p < .05.
~~~ Test of statistical significance compares African American boys with African American girls. ~~~ p < .001, ~~ p < .01, ~ p < .05.
Tests of statistical significance calculated using adjusted sample weight to control for influence of large sample sizes.
Source: National Household Education Survey, 1993.

Figure 3. Employment Status of Mothers of 3- and 4-Year-Olds: 1992

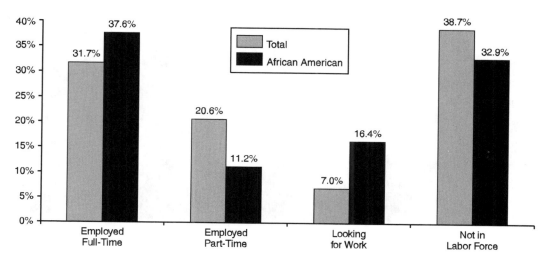

Source: National Household Education Survey, 1993.

Health Conditions

Figure 4 shows that 14.4% of African American 3- and 4-year-olds received intensive medical care when they were born, compared with 11.6% of all 3- and 4-year-olds.

- **Table 4** shows that twice the percentage of African American 3- and 4-year-olds as their White counterparts were reported to weigh less than three pounds at birth (0.7% compared to 0.3%).

- Twice the percentage of African American babies as Whites weighed less than 5.5 pounds at birth (10.4% versus 5.1%).

- A slightly smaller share of African American families than White families reported that their children had breakfast every day (86.8% versus 93.5%) and that they had a hot meal every day (82.5% versus 89.7%).

- About one-half (52.6%) of African American families reported that their 3- and 4-year-old children were in excellent health, compared with about two-thirds (65.5%) of White families.

- A slightly higher percentage of African Americans than Whites reported that their 3- or 4-year-olds had been to the doctor for a routine visit during the last year (91.3% versus 86.9%).

Figure 5 and **Table 5** show that only a small percentage of African American families reported that their 3- and 4-year-old children had chronic health problems or disabilities.

- The most frequent problem reported by all groups including African Americans was speech impairment. About 8.4% of African Americans and 5.9% of Whites reported that their children had a speech impairment at some time during their development.

PRESCHOOL ATTENDANCE

Figure 6 and Table 6 show that about one-half (52.5%) of African American 3- and 4-year-olds were attending or had been enrolled in preschool, compared to 44.6% of the overall population of 3- and 4-year-olds.

Figure 4. Health of 3- and 4-Year-Olds: 1992

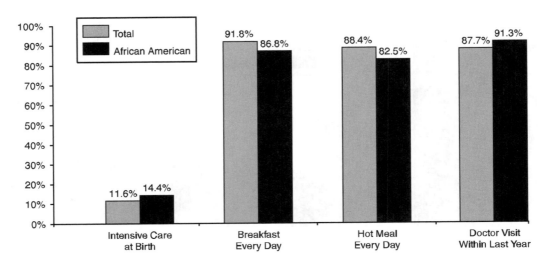

Source: National Household Education Survey, 1993.

- **Table 7** shows that 31.0% of African American 3- and 4-year-olds were either currently enrolled or had previously attended Head Start. Although this is somewhat higher than the rate of Head Start participation for the overall population, (12.7%), the majority (50.2%) of African American preschoolers attended some type of preschool other than Head Start.

Although national data describing the types of preschools, teachers, and curricula are not available, such data are very important for gaining an understanding of student readiness to learn when they start school.

A higher percentage of African American children than White children whose household incomes were below $50,000 attended preschool. In addition, for African Americans, Whites, and the overall population, the percentage of 3- and 4-year-olds attending some type of preschool increased with income.

- **Figure 7** shows that 54.1% of African American 3- and 4-year-olds, but 42.7% of all preschoolers, who lived in households with annual incomes of $10,000 or less attended some type of preschool.

- **Table 8** shows that, among families with annual incomes above $50, 000, 75.5% of African American and 65.0% of White 3- and 4-year-olds attended preschool.

At the lower income levels, the percentage of children attending preschool appeared to be somewhat higher for those whose mothers worked full time than for the overall population of 3- and 4-year-olds. But, at the higher income levels ($25,000 and above), the percentage of African American 3- and 4-year-olds with working mothers who were enrolled was higher than the percentage of Whites.

- **Table 8** also shows that, among families with incomes above $50,000 and with full-time working mothers, 83.2% of African Americans attended preschool, compared with 63.5% of Whites.

- About 60.5% of African Americans from families with full-time working mothers and in-

Table 4. Health of 3- and 4-Year-Olds (as of 12/31/92) by Race and Sex
(weighted sample size in parentheses)

Characteristic	Total	Male	Female	White, Non-Hispanic			African American, Non-Hispanic			Hispanic			Other		
				Total	Male	Female	Total	Male	Female	Total	Male	Female	Total	Male	Female
Total Weighted Sample	100.0%	51.2%	48.8%	67.9%	34.1%	33.7%	15.3%	8.4%	6.9%	12.2%	6.3%	5.9%	4.6%	2.4%	2.3%
	(7,712,232)	(3,945,587)	(3,766,646)	(5,234,009)	(2,632,290)	(2,601,719)	(1,183,731)	(647,945)	(535,786)	(937,457)	(482,422)	(455,035)	(357,036)	(182,930)	(174,106)
Birth Weight Under 3 Lbs.*** +++	0.6%	0.7%	0.6%	0.3%	0.1%	0.6%	0.7%	0.7%	0.8%	2.1%	3.5%	0.5%	0.8%	1.5%	0.0%
	(48,664)	(27,403)	(21,262)	(18,093)	(3,227)	(14,866)	(8,473)	(4,406)	(4,067)	(19,275)	(16,946)	(2,329)	(2,824)	(2,824)	–
Birth Weight under 5 1/2 Lbs.*** +++	6.4%	5.3%	7.5%	5.1%	3.3%	6.9%	10.4%	10.2%	10.7%	7.0%	8.2%	5.7%	10.7%	9.0%	12.6%
	(494,476)	(210,325)	(284,151)	(266,929)	(88,044)	(178,885)	(123,456)	(66,291)	(57,165)	(65,724)	(39,561)	(26,163)	(38,367)	(16,429)	(21,938)
Had Intensive Care When Born *	11.6%	13.0%	10.1%	10.9%	11.7%	10.0%	14.4%	16.4%	12.0%	11.0%	14.8%	6.9%	14.8%	16.5%	13.0%
	(894,189)	(514,629)	(379,559)	(567,899)	(306,721)	(261,178)	(170,621)	(106,334)	(64,287)	(102,849)	(71,436)	(31,413)	(52,819)	(30,138)	(22,681)
Ate Breakfast 7 Days in Last Week ***	91.8%	92.1%	91.5%	93.5%	93.5%	93.5%	86.8%	89.7%	83.2%	89.9%	88.5%	91.4%	89.3%	90.9%	87.5%
	(7,082,764)	(3,635,180)	(3,447,583)	(4,894,390)	(2,460,951)	(2,433,439)	(1,027,003)	(580,968)	(446,035)	(842,690)	(426,953)	(415,737)	(318,680)	(166,308)	(152,372)
Adult Made Child Hot Meal 7 Days in Last Week ***	88.4%	87.6%	89.2%	89.7%	89.7%	89.6%	82.5%	79.9%	85.6%	88.7%	87.8%	89.6%	88.1%	84.4%	92.1%
	(6,814,830)	(3,456,326)	(3,358,505)	(4,692,437)	(2,360,397)	(2,332,040)	(976,514)	(518,011)	(458,503)	(831,186)	(423,597)	(407,589)	(314,694)	(154,321)	(160,373)
Last Saw Dr. for Routine Visit Less Than 1 Year Ago **	87.7%	87.8%	87.6%	86.9%	86.2%	87.7%	91.3%	91.9%	90.5%	87.4%	88.4%	86.3%	88.7%	95.3%	81.7%
	(6,766,280)	(3,464,907)	(3,301,373)	(4,549,968)	(2,268,760)	(2,281,208)	(1,080,276)	(595,144)	(485,132)	(819,366)	(426,645)	(392,721)	(316,670)	(174,358)	(142,312)
Ever Been to Dentist	55.3%	55.2%	55.3%	57.2%	56.9%	57.4%	56.0%	59.3%	52.0%	43.4%	41.9%	44.9%	56.4%	51.3%	61.6%
	(4,263,328)	(2,178,520)	(2,084,809)	(2,992,733)	(1,498,232)	(1,494,501)	(662,726)	(384,236)	(278,490)	(406,636)	(202,120)	(204,516)	(201,234)	(93,932)	(107,302)
Child's General Health * ++ ~~**															
Excellent	60.7%	59.5%	61.9%	65.5%	65.2%	65.9%	52.6%	54.0%	50.9%	47.4%	40.2%	55.0%	50.8%	47.8%	54.0%
	(4,678,508)	(2,346,782)	(2,331,726)	(3,430,026)	(1,715,100)	(1,714,926)	(622,694)	(350,130)	(272,564)	(444,329)	(194,152)	(250,177)	(181,459)	(87,400)	(94,059)
Very Good	27.4%	26.4%	28.4%	26.5%	24.7%	28.2%	30.1%	28.9%	31.5%	28.0%	30.4%	25.4%	30.1%	31.0%	29.2%
	(2,110,491)	(1,041,237)	(1,069,254)	(1,384,485)	(650,810)	(733,675)	(355,926)	(186,943)	(168,983)	(262,479)	(146,737)	(115,742)	(107,601)	(56,747)	(50,854)
Good	9.4%	10.7%	8.1%	6.6%	8.2%	5.0%	13.4%	11.1%	16.2%	19.1%	23.2%	14.8%	12.6%	13.6%	11.6%
	(727,848)	(423,738)	(304,110)	(345,055)	(215,034)	(130,021)	(158,687)	(71,962)	(86,725)	(178,995)	(111,809)	(67,186)	(45,111)	(24,933)	(20,178)
Fair or Poor	2.5%	3.4%	1.6%	1.4%	2.0%	0.9%	3.9%	6.0%	1.4%	5.5%	6.2%	4.8%	6.4%	7.6%	5.2%
	(195,386)	(133,831)	(61,555)	(74,443)	(51,346)	(23,097)	(46,424)	(38,910)	(7,514)	(51,654)	(29,724)	(21,930)	(22,865)	(13,851)	(9,014)

Notes:

"–" indicates sample size too small to estimate.

*** Test of statistical significance compares African Americans with Whites. *** p < .001, ** p < .01, * p < .05.

+++ Test of statistical significance compares White boys with White girls. +++ p < .001, ++ p < .01, + p < .05.

~~~Test of statistical significance compares African American boys with African American girls. ~~~ p < .001, ~~ p < .01, ~ p < .05.

Tests of statistical significance calculated using adjusted sample weight to control for influence of large sample sizes.

Source: National Household Education Survey, 1993.

Figure 5. Percentage of 3- and 4-Year-Olds With Disabilities: 1992

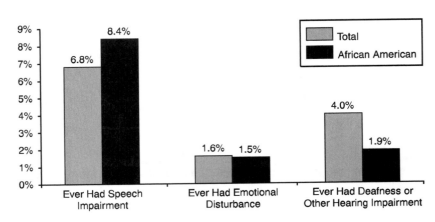

Source: National Household Education Survey, 1993.

comes between $25,000 and $50,000 attended preschool, compared with 37.7% of Whites.

- For families with incomes between $10,000 and $25,000 and working mothers, preschool attendance rates were comparable for African Americans and Whites (45.3% versus 46.8%).

Readiness for School

Three common criteria upon which children are assessed for school readiness include observations of their attitudes, their behaviors and their academic skills development. **Table 9** presents data on parents' assessment of their 3- and 4-year-olds' readiness for school along 16 different dimensions of behavior and motor skills (e.g., holding a pencil properly, recognizing colors and letters, counting to 50, and attention span). Parents generally rated their 3- and 4-year-olds favorably on most of these elements.

Figure 8 shows that, in cases where African Americans are not exhibiting readiness, such as recognizing all the letters of the alphabet and counting to 50 or higher, so too are students of other groups.

- One area in which there appears to be lower readiness for school among African Americans is the identification of colors. **Table 9** shows that 62.9% of African American 3- and 4-year-olds were able to identify all colors, compared with 83.7% of Whites.

- In addition, 12.6% of African American preschoolers stuttered or stammered, compared with only 6.2% of Whites.

Figure 9 presents the feelings that African American 5-year-old children express about kindergarten as reported by their parents. **Table 10** shows that African Americans' attitudes toward school generally appear to be favorable and similar to those of their White counterparts.

- In fact, 98.1% of African American 5-year-olds looked forward to going to kindergarten each day, 90.3% were highly enthusiastic about attending school, 93.1% liked their teacher, 95.6% had good things to say about their school, and 91.4% were reported to get along well with their peers.

Table 5. Percentage of 3- and 4-Year-Olds (as of 12/31/92) With Disabilities by Race and Sex
(weighted sample size in parentheses)

Characteristic	Total	Male	Female	White, Non-Hispanic			African American, Non-Hispanic			Hispanic			Other		
				Total	Male	Female	Total	Male	Female	Total	Male	Female	Total	Male	Female
Total Weighted Sample	100.0%	51.2%	48.8%	67.9%	34.1%	33.7%	15.3%	8.4%	6.9%	12.2%	6.3%	5.9%	4.6%	2.4%	2.3%
	(7,712,232)	(3,945,587)	(3,766,646)	(5,234,009)	(2,632,290)	(2,601,719)	(1,183,731)	(647,945)	(535,786)	(937,457)	(482,422)	(455,035)	(357,036)	(182,930)	(174,106)
Ever Had Learning Disability	1.8%	2.4%	1.2%	1.6%	2.0%	1.2%	2.6%	3.4%	1.6%	2.5%	3.6%	1.4%	0.8%	1.0%	0.5%
	(140,808)	(94,536)	(46,272)	(83,356)	(53,092)	(30,264)	(30,912)	(22,115)	(8,797)	(23,758)	(17,453)	(6,305)	(2,782)	(1,876)	(906)
Learning Disability Now * +	1.5%	1.8%	1.1%	1.2%	1.3%	1.0%	2.6%	3.4%	1.6%	2.1%	3.1%	1.1%	0.5%	0.5%	0.5%
	(114,367)	(72,532)	(41,836)	(61,669)	(34,475)	(27,194)	(30,912)	(22,115)	(8,797)	(20,054)	(15,115)	(4,939)	(1,733)	(827)	(906)
Ever had Speech Impairment + + +	6.8%	9.2%	4.3%	5.9%	8.7%	3.1%	8.4%	8.4%	8.4%	10.0%	13.5%	6.3%	6.6%	8.9%	4.3%
	(527,144)	(364,132)	(163,012)	(310,478)	(228,749)	(81,729)	(99,274)	(54,200)	(45,074)	(93,759)	(64,952)	(28,807)	(23,633)	(16,231)	(7,402)
Speech Impairment Now + + +	5.3%	7.1%	3.4%	4.8%	7.1%	2.5%	6.5%	6.1%	6.9%	6.4%	8.3%	4.3%	6.1%	7.9%	4.3%
	(409,000)	(280,347)	(128,652)	(250,817)	(186,081)	(64,736)	(76,666)	(39,553)	(37,113)	(59,604)	(40,203)	(19,401)	(21,912)	(14,510)	(7,402)
Ever had Emotional Disturbance	1.6%	1.8%	1.5%	1.6%	1.9%	1.4%	1.5%	1.4%	1.5%	2.0%	2.0%	2.0%	1.4%	0.6%	2.1%
	(126,317)	(69,812)	(56,506)	(85,487)	(50,037)	(35,450)	(17,391)	(9,108)	(8,283)	(18,530)	(9,487)	(9,043)	(4,910)	(1,180)	(3,730)
Serious Emotional Disturbance Now	0.7%	0.8%	0.6%	0.7%	0.9%	0.4%	0.2%	0.0%	0.4%	1.4%	1.2%	1.6%	0.6%	0.6%	0.5%
	(53,232)	(31,358)	(21,874)	(35,678)	(24,262)	(11,416)	(2,092)	–	(2,092)	(13,376)	(5,916)	(7,460)	(2,086)	(1,180)	(906)
Ever Had Deafness or Other Hearing Impairment *	4.0%	4.8%	3.1%	5.0%	6.0%	3.9%	1.9%	2.5%	1.3%	1.5%	1.9%	1.1%	1.8%	2.3%	1.3%
	(305,016)	(188,106)	(116,910)	(261,093)	(158,363)	(102,730)	(23,055)	(16,250)	(6,805)	(14,491)	(9,366)	(5,125)	(6,377)	(4,127)	(2,250)
Deafness or Hearing Impairment Now *	1.2%	1.6%	0.8%	1.5%	1.9%	1.1%	0.4%	0.8%	0.0%	0.6%	0.9%	0.3%	1.4%	2.3%	0.5%
	(93,990)	(64,470)	(29,520)	(78,480)	(51,047)	(27,433)	(4,965)	(4,965)	–	(5,512)	(4,331)	(1,181)	(5,033)	(4,127)	(906)
Ever Had Blindness or Other Visual Impairment	2.0%	1.9%	2.0%	2.3%	2.3%	2.3%	1.0%	0.9%	1.0%	1.8%	1.5%	2.0%	0.5%	0.6%	0.5%
	(150,467)	(74,262)	(76,204)	(120,545)	(59,733)	(60,812)	(11,273)	(6,056)	(5,217)	(16,693)	(7,424)	(9,269)	(1,955)	(1,049)	(906)
Blindness or Visual Impairment Now **	1.6%	1.5%	1.6%	1.9%	1.9%	2.0%	0.2%	0.4%	0.0%	1.7%	1.4%	2.0%	0.5%	0.6%	0.5%
	(121,485)	(59,779)	(61,706)	(100,896)	(49,365)	(51,531)	(2,410)	(2,410)	–	(16,224)	(6,955)	(9,269)	(1,955)	(1,049)	(906)
Ever Had Orthopedic Impairment * + +	1.8%	2.3%	1.2%	1.8%	2.6%	1.1%	0.8%	1.4%	0.2%	3.0%	2.7%	3.4%	0.9%	1.4%	0.4%
	(136,410)	(91,802)	(44,608)	(95,250)	(67,483)	(27,767)	(9,792)	(8,959)	(833)	(28,093)	(12,832)	(15,261)	(3,275)	(2,528)	(747)
Orthopedic Impairment Now +	0.8%	1.1%	0.5%	0.9%	1.2%	0.5%	0.5%	0.8%	0.0%	0.9%	1.1%	0.6%	0.7%	1.4%	0.0%
	(60,806)	(43,655)	(17,150)	(44,618)	(30,382)	(14,236)	(5,365)	(5,365)	–	(8,294)	(5,380)	(2,914)	(2,528)	(2,528)	–
Ever Had Other Health Impairment +	3.8%	4.7%	2.9%	3.8%	4.7%	3.0%	3.6%	4.2%	2.8%	4.4%	5.8%	3.0%	2.7%	3.3%	2.0%
	(293,468)	(184,380)	(109,086)	(200,308)	(123,132)	(77,176)	(42,043)	(27,116)	(14,927)	(41,588)	(28,050)	(13,538)	(9,527)	(6,082)	(3,445)
Other Health Impairment Now	2.2%	2.8%	1.6%	2.5%	3.1%	1.9%	1.8%	2.3%	1.3%	1.6%	2.7%	0.5%	1.3%	1.3%	1.4%
	(171,257)	(111,486)	(59,773)	(129,637)	(81,194)	(48,443)	(21,503)	(14,796)	(6,707)	(15,342)	(13,097)	(2,245)	(4,777)	(2,399)	(2,378)

Notes:

"–" indicates sample size too small to estimate.

*** Test of statistical significance compares African Americans with Whites. *** p < .001, ** p < .01, * p < .05.

+++ Test of statistical significance compares White boys with White girls. +++ p < .001, ++ p < .01, + p < .05.

~~~Test of statistical significance compares African American boys with African American girls. ~~~ p < .001, ~~ p < .01, ~ p < .05.

Tests of statistical significance calculated using adjusted sample weight to control for influence of large sample sizes.

Source: National Household Education Survey, 1993.

Figure 6. Percentage of 3- and 4-Year-Olds Enrolled in Preschool Programs: 1992

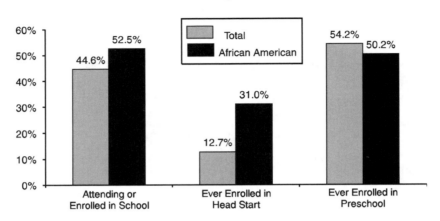

Source: National Household Education Survey, 1993.

- **Figure 9** shows that only 18.7% of African American 5-year-olds complained about school, 13.2% were reluctant to go to school, and 9.8% pretended to be sick to avoid going to school.

In response to questions about their activities during the week prior to the survey, about three-fourths (76.6%) of all parents reported they had told their 3- or 4-year-old a story; 86.3% reported having taught their child letters and words (see **Figure 10**).

- **Table 11** shows that, during the week prior to the survey, 63.9% of the parents of African American 3- and 4-year-old children reported that they taught their children letters and words three or more times, 72.8% had told their child stories, and 72.2% had taught their child music and songs.

About one-half (49.1%) of all parents of 3- and 4-year-olds reported having attended a religious event during the month prior to the survey. But smaller percentages reported visiting a zoo or aquarium (17.1%), visiting a library (37.8%), attending a play or a show (22.9%), or visiting a gallery or museum (18.0%).

- **Table 12** shows that a smaller percentage of African American preschoolers than all preschoolers had visited a library (28.9% versus 37.8%) during the month prior to the survey.

- But, a higher share of African Americans than of all preschoolers had attended a play or show (29.8% versus 22.9%).

- **Figure 10** shows that a relatively high percentage of African American parents reported talking with their children about ethnic heritage (55.0% compared with 42.2% overall).

Figure 11 presents parents' assessments of their 5-year-olds' reading level as yet another measure of their readiness for school.

- **Table 13** shows that a slightly higher percentage of African American parents than White parents reported that their children read books on their own (30.4% compared to 21.7%).

- African American 5-year-olds own fewer books than Whites, on average. Only 12.9% of African Americans, but 46.6% of Whites, owned more than 50 books.

Table 6. Enrollment in School Among 3- and 4-Year-Olds (as of 12/31/92) by Race and Sex
(weighted sample size in parentheses)

Enrollment Status	Total	Male	Female	White, Non-Hispanic			African American, Non-Hispanic			Hispanic			Other		
				Total	Male	Female	Total	Male	Female	Total	Male	Female	Total	Male	Female
Total Weighted Sample	100.0%	51.2%	48.8%	67.9%	34.1%	33.7%	15.3%	8.4%	6.9%	12.2%	6.3%	5.9%	4.6%	2.4%	2.3%
	(7,712,232)	(3,945,587)	(3,766,646)	(5,234,009)	(2,632,290)	(2,601,719)	(1,183,731)	(647,945)	(535,786)	(937,457)	(482,422)	(455,035)	(357,036)	(182,930)	(174,106)
Attending or Enrolled in School * +**	100.0%	100.0%	100.0%	100.0%	100.0%	100.0%	100.0%	100.0%	100.0%	100.0%	100.0%	100.0%	100.0%	100.0%	100.0%
	(7,712,232)	(3,945,587)	(3,766,646)	(5,234,009)	(2,632,290)	(2,601,719)	(1,183,730)	(647,945)	(535,786)	(937,456)	(482,422)	(455,035)	(357,037)	(182,930)	(174,106)
Yes	44.6%	43.0%	46.3%	43.5%	41.5%	45.6%	52.5%	51.3%	54.0%	38.5%	37.1%	40.0%	50.1%	50.9%	49.3%
	(3,439,285)	(1,696,494)	(1,742,791)	(2,277,308)	(1,091,853)	(1,185,455)	(621,971)	(332,647)	(289,324)	(361,045)	(178,907)	(182,138)	(178,961)	(93,087)	(85,874)
No	55.4%	57.0%	53.7%	56.5%	58.5%	54.4%	47.5%	48.7%	46.0%	61.5%	62.9%	60.0%	49.9%	49.1%	50.7%
	(4,272,947)	(2,249,093)	(2,023,854)	(2,956,701)	(1,540,437)	(1,416,264)	(561,759)	(315,298)	(246,461)	(576,411)	(303,514)	(272,897)	(178,076)	(89,844)	(88,232)
Grade Equivalent ***	100.0%	100.0%	100.0%	100.0%	100.0%	100.0%	100.0%	100.0%	100.0%	100.0%	100.0%	100.0%	100.0%	100.0%	100.0%
	(7,712,232)	(3,945,586)	(3,766,647)	(5,234,009)	(2,632,290)	(2,601,720)	(1,183,731)	(647,945)	(535,786)	(937,456)	(482,421)	(455,035)	(357,037)	(182,930)	(174,106)
Not Enrolled	55.4%	57.0%	53.7%	56.5%	58.5%	54.4%	47.5%	48.7%	46.0%	61.5%	62.9%	60.0%	49.9%	49.1%	50.7%
	(4,272,947)	(2,249,093)	(2,023,854)	(2,956,701)	(1,540,437)	(1,416,264)	(561,759)	(315,298)	(246,461)	(576,411)	(303,514)	(272,897)	(178,076)	(89,844)	(88,232)
First Grade or Equivalent	0.0%	0.0%	0.1%	0.0%	0.0%	0.0%	0.0%	0.0%	0.0%	0.0%	0.0%	0.0%	0.8%	0.0%	1.6%
	(2,749)	–	(2,749)	–	–	–	–	–	–	–	–	–	(2,749)	–	(2,749)
Kindergarten	0.7%	0.4%	1.1%	0.6%	0.3%	0.9%	1.4%	0.8%	2.2%	0.5%	0.3%	0.8%	0.6%	0.6%	0.5%
	(56,733)	(16,407)	(40,326)	(32,885)	(9,085)	(23,800)	(16,834)	(4,997)	(11,837)	(5,001)	(1,218)	(3,783)	(2,013)	(1,107)	(906)
Nursery School, Head Start, or Prekindergarten	43.2%	42.1%	44.3%	42.5%	40.8%	44.2%	49.2%	49.1%	49.2%	37.4%	36.4%	38.4%	48.1%	50.3%	45.8%
	(3,329,927)	(1,661,266)	(1,668,662)	(2,225,588)	(1,075,213)	(1,150,375)	(581,875)	(318,246)	(263,629)	(350,736)	(175,827)	(174,909)	(171,729)	(91,980)	(79,749)
Transitional Kindergarten	0.6%	0.5%	0.8%	0.4%	0.3%	0.4%	2.0%	1.5%	2.6%	0.6%	0.4%	0.8%	0.7%	0.0%	1.4%
	(49,876)	(18,821)	(31,056)	(18,836)	(7,555)	(11,281)	(23,263)	(9,404)	(13,859)	(5,308)	(1,862)	(3,446)	(2,470)	–	(2,470)

Notes:
"–" indicates sample size too small to estimate.
*** Test of statistical significance compares African Americans with Whites. *** $p < .001$, ** $p < .01$, * $p < .05$.
+++ Test of statistical significance compares White boys with White girls. +++ $p < .001$, ++ $p < .01$, + $p < .05$.
~~~ Test of statistical significance compares African American boys with African American girls. ~~~ $p < .001$, ~~ $p < .01$, ~ $p < .05$.
Tests of statistical significance calculated using adjusted sample weight to control for influence of large sample sizes.
Source: National Household Education Survey, 1993.

Test Performance

The National Longitudinal Survey of Youth began in 1979 as a study of 12,686 young people, aged 14 to 22. Virtually all of the youths in the original sample took the Armed Forces Qualifying Test (AFQT) the following year. A variety of other cognitive tests (the Wechsler Intelligence test among other IQ tests) were also taken by some of the participants. The data presented in this chapter are for young women who participated in the original 1979 sample and their children in 1986, 1988, 1990 and 1992. Included in the child data are several cognitive measures including the Peabody Picture Vocabulary Test (PPVT), the Verbal Memory Test and the Motor and Social Development Test. This section focuses upon the test performance of preschool children, defined as those 5 years of age or younger.

Sex differences on standardized test scores are evidenced among preschool-age children.

• **Table 14** shows that girls had average higher scores than boys on the Motor and Social De-

Table 7. Length of Time 3- and 4-Year-Olds Were Enrolled in Preschool Programs (as of 12/31/92) by Race and Sex
(weighted sample size in parentheses)

Enrollment Status	Total	Male	Female	White, Non-Hispanic			African American, Non-Hispanic			Hispanic			Other		
				Total	Male	Female	Total	Male	Female	Total	Male	Female	Total	Male	Female
Total Weighted Sample	100.0%	51.2%	48.8%	67.9%	34.1%	33.7%	15.3%	8.4%	6.9%	12.2%	6.3%	5.9%	4.6%	2.4%	2.3%
	(7,712,232)	(3,945,587)	(3,766,646)	(5,234,009)	(2,632,290)	(2,601,719)	(1,183,731)	(647,945)	(535,786)	(937,457)	(482,422)	(455,035)	(357,036)	(182,930)	(174,106)
Ever Enrolled in Head Start ***	100.0%	100.0%	100.0%	100.0%	100.0%	100.0%	100.0%	100.0%	100.0%	100.0%	100.0%	100.0%	100.0%	100.0%	100.0%
	(7,712,232)	(3,945,587)	(3,766,646)	(5,234,009)	(2,632,290)	(2,601,719)	(1,183,731)	(647,945)	(535,786)	(937,457)	(482,422)	(455,035)	(357,036)	(182,930)	(174,106)
Not Enrolled and Never Attended	87.3%	86.5%	88.1%	92.9%	93.3%	92.5%	69.0%	64.8%	74.2%	80.2%	80.5%	79.9%	84.0%	81.2%	86.8%
	(6,730,983)	(3,413,362)	(3,317,622)	(4,862,477)	(2,456,840)	(2,405,637)	(817,126)	(419,655)	(397,471)	(751,648)	(388,279)	(363,369)	(299,733)	(148,588)	(151,145)
Less Than One Year	8.7%	9.2%	8.1%	5.2%	4.9%	5.4%	18.7%	20.5%	16.4%	14.1%	14.0%	14.2%	12.2%	17.2%	6.9%
	(667,246)	(362,523)	(304,724)	(270,620)	(130,278)	(140,342)	(221,062)	(133,107)	(87,955)	(132,065)	(67,664)	(64,401)	(43,500)	(31,474)	(12,026)
One School Year	1.1%	1.0%	1.1%	0.3%	0.3%	0.3%	3.7%	3.6%	3.9%	1.6%	1.4%	1.9%	1.4%	0.9%	1.9%
	(81,375)	(39,374)	(42,001)	(16,488)	(7,760)	(8,728)	(44,361)	(23,268)	(21,093)	(15,429)	(6,625)	(8,804)	(5,097)	(1,721)	(3,376)
More Than One School Year	3.0%	3.3%	2.7%	1.6%	1.4%	1.8%	8.5%	11.1%	5.5%	4.1%	4.1%	4.1%	2.4%	0.6%	4.3%
	(232,629)	(130,330)	(102,299)	(84,426)	(37,414)	(47,012)	(101,182)	(71,915)	(29,267)	(38,314)	(19,853)	(18,461)	(8,707)	(1,148)	(7,559)
Ever Enrolled in Preschool Program ***	100.0%	100.0%	100.0%	100.0%	100.0%	100.0%	100.0%	100.0%	100.0%	100.0%	100.0%	100.0%	100.0%	100.0%	100.0%
	(7,712,232)	(3,945,587)	(3,766,646)	(5,234,009)	(2,632,290)	(2,601,719)	(1,183,731)	(647,945)	(535,786)	(937,457)	(482,422)	(455,035)	(357,036)	(182,930)	(174,106)
Not Enrolled and Never Attended	45.8%	46.5%	45.0%	41.8%	43.5%	40.0%	49.8%	48.0%	51.9%	61.5%	59.8%	63.2%	49.7%	47.9%	51.6%
	(3,529,975)	(1,833,860)	(1,696,116)	(2,186,620)	(1,146,330)	(1,040,290)	(589,410)	(311,155)	(278,255)	(576,420)	(288,662)	(287,758)	(177,526)	(87,713)	(89,813)
Less Than One Year	26.2%	24.9%	27.5%	28.1%	26.0%	30.3%	19.6%	19.8%	19.3%	24.2%	27.6%	20.6%	24.2%	20.2%	28.5%
	(2,017,639)	(982,855)	(1,034,784)	(1,471,951)	(684,239)	(787,712)	(232,057)	(128,514)	(103,543)	(227,101)	(133,191)	(93,910)	(86,530)	(36,911)	(49,619)
One School Year	15.3%	15.2%	15.5%	16.5%	16.5%	16.5%	14.3%	13.8%	14.9%	9.4%	7.1%	11.8%	17.0%	22.1%	11.7%
	(1,180,107)	(598,102)	(582,003)	(862,349)	(434,148)	(428,201)	(169,130)	(89,341)	(79,789)	(87,769)	(34,160)	(53,609)	(60,857)	(40,453)	(20,404)
Two or More School Years	12.8%	13.5%	12.0%	13.6%	14.0%	13.3%	16.3%	18.4%	13.8%	4.9%	5.5%	4.3%	9.0%	9.8%	8.2%
	(984,512)	(530,767)	(453,742)	(713,088)	(367,572)	(345,516)	(193,133)	(118,934)	(74,199)	(46,166)	(26,408)	(19,758)	(32,122)	(17,853)	(14,269)
Average Age in Months															
Started Head Start ***	42	42	42	43	43	43	40	40	39	42	42	42	42	44	41
	(981,249)	(532,226)	(449,023)	(371,533)	(175,451)	(196,082)	(366,605)	(228,290)	(138,315)	(185,809)	(94,143)	(91,666)	(57,303)	(34,342)	(22,961)
Started Preschool ***	31	31	31	31	31	32	28	28	29	33	33	32	33	32	33
	(4,182,258)	(2,111,728)	(2,070,530)	(3,047,389)	(1,485,960)	(1,561,429)	(594,321)	(336,790)	(257,531)	(361,037)	(193,760)	(167,277)	(179,510)	(95,218)	(84,292)

Notes:

*** Test of statistical significance compares African Americans with Whites. *** p < .001, ** p < .01, * p < .05.

+++ Test of statistical significance compares White boys with White girls. +++ p < .001, ++ p < .01, + p < .05.

~~~ Test of statistical significance compares African American boys with African American girls. ~~~ p < .001, ~~ p < .01, ~ p < .05.

Tests of statistical significance calculated using adjusted sample weight to control for influence of large sample sizes.

Source: National Household Education Survey, 1993.

Figure 7. Percentage of 3- and 4-Year-Olds Enrolled in School by Household Income: 1992

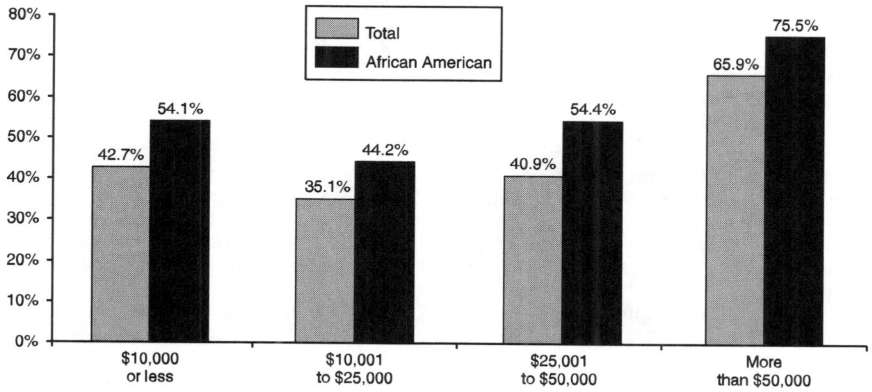

Source: National Household Education Survey, 1993.

velopment Test among both African Americans (101.7 versus 98.2) and Whites (100.5 versus 95.2).

- Test scores were higher on the Verbal Memory Test for girls than for boys among both African Americans (99.0 versus 93.3) and Whites (100.5 versus 95.2).

- Scores for African American girls and boys were similar on the PPVT (75.7 versus 73.3).

Figure 12 shows that African Americans and Whites had similar scores on the Verbal Memory Test (96.2 versus 97.7 overall).

- But on the Motor and Social Development measure, African Americans scored slightly lower than Whites (100.0 versus 102.6).

- Differences were largest on the PPVT, on which African Americans averaged a score of 74.6 compared with an average score of 98.2 for Whites.

Table 8. School Enrollment of 3- and 4-Year-Olds (as of 12/31/92) by Household Income, Mother's Employment Status, Race, and Sex

(weighted sample size in parentheses)

Household Income	Total	Male	Female	White, Non-Hispanic Total	Male	Female	African American, Non-Hispanic Total	Male	Female	Hispanic Total	Male	Female	Other Total	Male	Female
Total Weighted Sample	100.0% (7,712,232)	51.2% (3,945,587)	48.8% (3,766,646)	67.9% (5,234,009)	34.1% (2,632,290)	33.7% (2,601,719)	15.3% (1,183,731)	8.4% (647,945)	6.9% (535,786)	12.2% (937,457)	6.3% (482,422)	5.9% (455,035)	4.6% (357,036)	2.4% (182,930)	2.3% (174,106)
$10,000 or less	100.0% (1,406,788)	100.0% (791,968)	100.0% (614,820)	100.0% (498,655)	100.0% (269,934)	100.0% (228,721)	100.0% (518,947)	100.0% (300,655)	100.0% (218,292)	100.0% (309,758)	100.0% (165,535)	100.0% (144,223)	100.0% (79,428)	100.0% (55,844)	100.0% (23,584)
Attending or Enrolled in School ***	42.7% (600,597)	43.0% (340,658)	42.3% (259,939)	33.6% (167,469)	33.3% (89,777)	34.0% (77,692)	54.1% (280,515)	54.1% (162,556)	54.0% (117,959)	38.9% (120,642)	37.2% (61,634)	40.9% (59,008)	40.3% (31,971)	47.8% (26,691)	22.4% (5,280)
Mother Employed Full-Time, Full-Year	100.0% (118,526)	100.0% (69,352)	100.0% (49,174)	100.0% (33,945)	100.0% (22,980)	100.0% (10,965)	100.0% (54,525)	100.0% (31,471)	100.0% (23,054)	100.0% (30,056)	100.0% (14,901)	100.0% (15,155)	0.0% –	0.0% –	0.0% –
Attending or Enrolled in School	50.6% (59,958)	58.8% (40,792)	39.0% (19,166)	41.6% (14,108)	41.1% (9,434)	42.6% (4,674)	58.0% (31,636)	66.3% (20,875)	46.7% (10,761)	47.3% (14,214)	70.4% (10,483)	24.6% (3,731)	0.0% –	0.0% –	0.0% –
$10,001 to $25,000	100.0% (2,158,567)	100.0% (1,098,937)	100.0% (1,059,630)	100.0% (1,345,159)	100.0% (673,972)	100.0% (671,187)	100.0% (367,065)	100.0% (202,148)	100.0% (164,917)	100.0% (348,372)	100.0% (171,009)	100.0% (177,363)	100.0% (97,971)	100.0% (51,808)	100.0% (46,163)
Attending or Enrolled in School **	35.1% (757,388)	33.2% (364,624)	37.1% (392,766)	33.5% (450,023)	30.3% (204,129)	36.6% (245,894)	44.2% (162,220)	41.5% (83,896)	47.5% (78,324)	31.4% (109,477)	32.9% (56,218)	30.0% (53,259)	36.4% (35,670)	39.3% (20,381)	33.1% (15,289)
Mother Employed Full-Time, Full-Year	100.0% (457,020)	100.0% (231,635)	100.0% (225,385)	100.0% (255,053)	100.0% (108,463)	100.0% (146,590)	100.0% (131,143)	100.0% (82,527)	100.0% (48,616)	100.0% (49,772)	100.0% (27,853)	100.0% (21,919)	100.0% (21,052)	100.0% (12,792)	100.0% (8,260)
Attending or Enrolled in School	44.3% (202,502)	44.6% (103,412)	44.0% (99,090)	46.8% (119,382)	49.8% (54,067)	44.6% (65,315)	45.3% (59,434)	41.9% (34,579)	51.1% 24,855	34.1% (16,984)	29.0% (8,064)	40.7% (8,920)	31.8% (6,702)	52.4% (6,702)	0.0% (0)
$25,001 to $50,000	100.0% (2,612,659)	100.0% (1,324,472)	100.0% (1,288,186)	100.0% (2,088,296)	100.0% (1,066,538)	100.0% (1,021,758)	100.0% (215,619)	100.0% (105,095)	100.0% (110,524)	100.0% (196,697)	100.0% (103,217)	100.0% (93,480)	100.0% (112,046)	100.0% (49,622)	100.0% (62,424)
Attending or Enrolled in School **	40.9% (1,069,730)	38.3% (506,977)	43.7% (562,753)	39.0% (814,070)	36.4% (388,379)	41.7% (425,691)	54.4% (117,229)	53.5% (56,263)	55.2% (60,966)	41.0% (80,649)	35.3% (36,486)	47.2% (44,163)	51.6% (57,782)	52.1% (25,849)	51.2% (31,933)
Mother Employed Full-Time, Full-Year	100.0% (764,692)	100.0% (339,629)	100.0% (425,063)	100.0% (561,548)	100.0% (247,463)	100.0% (314,085)	100.0% (105,564)	100.0% (48,830)	100.0% (56,734)	100.0% (64,059)	100.0% (31,157)	100.0% (32,902)	100.0% (33,521)	100.0% (12,179)	100.0% (21,342)
Attending or Enrolled in School **	41.3% (315,492)	38.5% (130,876)	43.4% (184,616)	37.7% (211,448)	35.1% (86,928)	39.6% (124,520)	60.5% (63,826)	57.5% (28,077)	63.0% 35,749	36.9% (23,640)	29.9% (9,315)	43.5% (14,325)	49.5% (16,578)	53.8% (6,556)	47.0% (10,022)
More than $50,000	100.0% (1,534,217)	100.0% (730,209)	100.0% (804,008)	100.0% (1,301,898)	100.0% (621,845)	100.0% (680,053)	100.0% (82,099)	100.0% (40,047)	100.0% (42,052)	100.0% (82,630)	100.0% (42,661)	100.0% (39,969)	100.0% (67,590)	100.0% (25,656)	100.0% (41,934)
Attending or Enrolled in School	65.9% (1,011,571)	66.3% (484,235)	65.6% (527,336)	65.0% (845,747)	65.9% (409,568)	64.1% (436,179)	75.5% (62,007)	74.7% (29,931)	76.3% (32,076)	60.8% (50,279)	57.6% (24,570)	64.3% (25,709)	79.2% (53,538)	78.6% (20,166)	79.6% (33,372)
Mother Employed Full-Time, Full-Year	100.0% (521,762)	100.0% (244,493)	100.0% (277,269)	100.0% (402,861)	100.0% (180,684)	100.0% (222,177)	100.0% (54,645)	100.0% (25,501)	100.0% (29,144)	100.0% (40,243)	100.0% (23,039)	100.0% (17,204)	100.0% (24,013)	100.0% (15,269)	100.0% (8,744)
Attending or Enrolled in School *	65.9% (343,968)	67.6% (165,391)	64.4% (178,577)	63.5% (255,894)	65.2% (117,862)	62.1% (138,032)	83.2% (45,454)	85.9% (21,917)	80.8% 23,537	63.6% (25,598)	64.2% (14,789)	62.8% (10,809)	70.9% (17,022)	70.9% (10,823)	70.9% (6,199)

Notes:

"–" indicates sample size too small to estimate.

*** Test of statistical significance compares African Americans with Whites. *** p < .001, ** p < .01, * p < .05.

+++ Test of statistical significance compares White boys with White girls. +++ p < .001, ++ p < .01, + p < .05.

~~~Test of statistical significance compares African American boys with African American girls. ~~~ p < .001, ~~ p < .01, ~ p < .05.

Tests of statistical significance calculated using adjusted sample weight to control for influence of large sample sizes.

Source: National Household Education Survey, 1993.

Table 9. Readiness for School Among 3- and 4-Year-Olds (as of 12/31/92) by Race and Sex
(weighted sample size in parentheses)

Ability	Total	Male	Female	White, Non-Hispanic			African American, Non-Hispanic			Hispanic			Other		
				Total	Male	Female	Total	Male	Female	Total	Male	Female	Total	Male	Female
Total Weighted Sample	100.0%	51.2%	48.8%	67.9%	34.1%	33.7%	15.3%	8.4%	6.9%	12.2%	6.3%	5.9%	4.6%	2.4%	2.3%
	(7,712,232)	(3,945,587)	(3,766,646)	(5,234,009)	(2,632,290)	(2,601,719)	(1,183,731)	(647,945)	(535,786)	(937,457)	(482,422)	(455,035)	(357,036)	(182,930)	(174,106)
Total Respondents	100.0%	51.4%	48.6%	68.2%	34.4%	33.8%	15.0%	8.3%	6.7%	12.2%	6.3%	5.9%	4.6%	2.4%	2.2%
	(7,602,874)	(3,910,359)	(3,692,515)	(5,182,288)	(2,615,650)	(2,566,638)	(1,143,634)	(633,544)	(510,090)	(927,148)	(479,342)	(447,806)	(349,804)	(181,823)	(167,981)
Identifies All Colors *** +++	76.2%	73.3%	79.3%	83.7%	80.8%	86.6%	62.9%	64.4%	61.0%	54.9%	47.9%	62.4%	65.5%	62.2%	69.1%
	(5,793,809)	(2,864,643)	(2,929,167)	(4,336,280)	(2,114,009)	(2,222,271)	(719,064)	(407,740)	(311,324)	(509,234)	(229,734)	(279,500)	(229,232)	(113,160)	(116,072)
Recognizes All Letters of the Alphabet * +++	18.9%	16.8%	21.1%	21.0%	18.1%	23.9%	16.5%	17.1%	15.7%	8.9%	6.0%	12.1%	22.2%	24.7%	19.6%
	(1,434,946)	(655,953)	(778,992)	(1,085,956)	(473,760)	(612,196)	(188,433)	(108,546)	(79,887)	(82,827)	(28,790)	(54,037)	(77,729)	(44,857)	(32,872)
Counts up to 50 or Higher ++	12.3%	11.0%	13.7%	12.9%	11.1%	14.6%	13.9%	14.8%	12.8%	7.0%	5.4%	8.8%	12.7%	10.6%	14.9%
	(934,453)	(429,047)	(505,405)	(665,947)	(290,296)	(375,651)	(158,887)	(93,550)	(65,337)	(65,240)	(25,908)	(39,332)	(44,378)	(19,293)	(25,085)
Writes First Name * ++	45.5%	42.9%	48.3%	47.5%	44.7%	50.4%	42.2%	43.0%	41.3%	37.2%	31.5%	43.4%	48.4%	47.3%	49.6%
	(3,459,905)	(1,677,372)	(1,782,532)	(2,462,516)	(1,168,210)	(1,294,306)	(482,765)	(272,246)	(210,519)	(345,278)	(150,900)	(194,378)	(169,345)	(86,016)	(83,329)
Buttons Clothes *** +++	88.0%	83.4%	92.8%	86.4%	80.6%	92.2%	94.5%	92.9%	96.5%	89.1%	86.1%	92.4%	86.9%	83.5%	90.5%
	(6,687,766)	(3,262,401)	(3,425,365)	(4,476,344)	(2,109,084)	(2,367,260)	(1,081,070)	(588,691)	(492,379)	(826,371)	(412,732)	(413,639)	(303,981)	(151,894)	(152,087)
Holds Pencil Properly *** +++	90.2%	87.2%	93.4%	89.5%	85.5%	93.6%	94.2%	93.5%	95.1%	91.0%	90.5%	91.5%	86.0%	81.0%	91.3%
	(6,859,726)	(3,410,445)	(3,449,281)	(4,638,067)	(2,236,854)	(2,401,213)	(1,077,346)	(592,335)	(485,011)	(843,587)	(433,904)	(409,683)	(300,726)	(147,352)	(153,374)
Writes and Draws +++	63.8%	58.5%	69.4%	64.5%	57.9%	71.1%	66.6%	68.5%	64.3%	55.0%	47.8%	62.7%	67.8%	60.1%	76.2%
	(4,849,187)	(2,286,755)	(2,562,433)	(3,340,030)	(1,514,155)	(1,825,875)	(762,106)	(434,269)	(327,837)	(509,784)	(229,108)	(280,676)	(237,268)	(109,223)	(128,045)
Can Be Left With Sitter Easily ***	89.5%	88.9%	90.1%	92.9%	92.9%	92.9%	86.8%	86.3%	87.3%	75.1%	70.5%	79.9%	85.5%	88.7%	82.1%
	(6,802,082)	(3,475,357)	(3,326,725)	(4,814,652)	(2,429,107)	(2,385,545)	(992,268)	(547,038)	(445,230)	(695,934)	(337,914)	(358,020)	(299,228)	(161,298)	(137,930)
Trips, Stumbles, or Falls Easily ** +	12.8%	14.2%	11.3%	11.1%	12.3%	9.8%	16.4%	16.0%	17.0%	17.5%	20.8%	14.0%	14.4%	18.3%	10.1%
	(974,932)	(556,908)	(418,024)	(574,364)	(322,606)	(251,758)	(188,048)	(101,396)	(86,652)	(162,316)	(99,672)	(62,644)	(50,204)	(33,234)	(16,970)
Often Has Tantrums	25.9%	26.6%	25.2%	22.9%	23.9%	21.9%	25.6%	23.9%	27.6%	39.9%	41.8%	38.0%	33.6%	33.7%	33.5%
	(1,969,081)	(1,039,118)	(929,963)	(1,188,710)	(625,921)	(562,789)	(292,467)	(151,576)	(140,891)	(370,329)	(200,290)	(170,039)	(117,575)	(61,331)	(56,244)
Is Afraid to Talk to Strangers *** +++	43.5%	40.5%	46.6%	44.8%	40.9%	48.8%	34.6%	34.3%	35.0%	44.9%	46.1%	43.7%	49.1%	41.5%	57.2%
	(3,306,699)	(1,584,143)	(1,722,554)	(2,322,503)	(1,070,406)	(1,252,097)	(395,932)	(217,377)	(178,555)	(416,585)	(220,840)	(195,745)	(171,677)	(75,520)	(96,157)
Fidgets a Lot * +++ ~	27.8%	31.4%	23.9%	24.9%	28.6%	21.1%	30.1%	34.0%	25.2%	41.3%	43.3%	39.1%	26.4%	31.1%	21.3%
	(2,110,567)	(1,228,587)	(881,979)	(1,291,232)	(748,745)	(542,487)	(344,232)	(215,686)	(128,546)	(382,771)	(207,681)	(175,090)	(92,331)	(56,475)	(35,856)
Has Short Attention Span +++	23.9%	26.8%	20.9%	21.0%	24.4%	17.6%	24.8%	26.8%	22.3%	38.6%	38.9%	38.2%	25.4%	28.9%	21.7%
	(1,819,797)	(1,047,608)	(772,190)	(1,089,884)	(639,124)	(450,760)	(283,392)	(169,477)	(113,915)	(357,555)	(186,543)	(171,012)	(88,967)	(52,464)	(36,503)
Is Understandable to Strangers * +++	90.5%	88.8%	92.2%	92.2%	89.5%	95.0%	88.4%	90.1%	86.3%	84.5%	84.4%	84.6%	87.3%	86.4%	88.2%
	(6,879,085)	(3,473,674)	(3,405,414)	(4,778,939)	(2,341,107)	(2,437,832)	(1,011,329)	(570,875)	(440,454)	(783,615)	(404,614)	(379,001)	(305,205)	(157,078)	(148,127)
Began Speaking Late +++ ~~~	16.6%	21.0%	11.8%	16.1%	20.3%	11.7%	14.9%	19.7%	9.0%	18.2%	22.2%	13.9%	24.6%	32.0%	16.6%
	(1,258,431)	(821,396)	(437,036)	(833,682)	(532,175)	(301,507)	(170,308)	(124,642)	(45,666)	(168,406)	(106,363)	(62,043)	(86,036)	(58,216)	(27,820)
Stutters or Stammers *** +++ ~~	8.4%	10.8%	5.8%	6.2%	7.9%	4.3%	12.6%	16.1%	8.3%	14.8%	17.4%	12.1%	10.2%	15.4%	4.6%
	(636,728)	(421,184)	(215,544)	(319,246)	(207,765)	(111,481)	(144,329)	(101,965)	(42,364)	(137,504)	(83,538)	(53,966)	(35,649)	(27,916)	(7,733)

Notes:
*** Test of statistical significance compares African Americans with Whites. *** p < .001, ** p < .01, * p < .05.
+++ Test of statistical significance compares White boys with White girls. +++ p < .001, ++ p < .01, + p < .05.
~~~ Test of statistical significance compares African American boys with African American girls. ~~~ p < .001, ~~ p < .01, ~ p < .05.
Tests of statistical significance calculated using adjusted sample weight to control for influence of large sample sizes.
Source: National Household Education Survey, 1993.

Figure 8. Readiness for School Among 3- and 4-Year-Olds: 1992

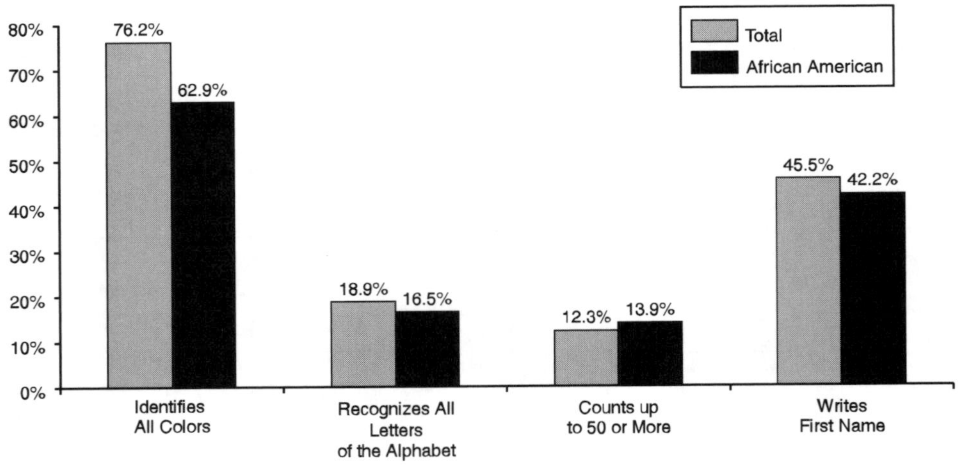

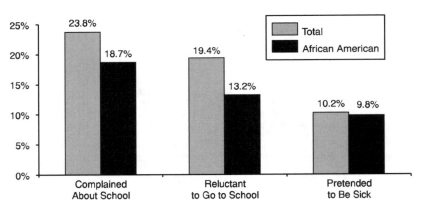

Source: National Household Education Survey, 1993.

Figure 9. Feelings About School (as Reported by Parents) of 5-Year-Olds Who Were Enrolled in Kindergarten: 1992

Source: National Household Education Survey, 1993.

Table 10. Feelings About School of 5-Year-Olds Who Were Enrolled in Kindergarten as Reported by Their Parents (as of 12/31/92) by Race and Sex

(weighted sample size in parentheses)

Child's Feelings About School	Total	Male	Female	White, Non-Hispanic Total	Male	Female	African American, Non-Hispanic Total	Male	Female	Hispanic Total	Male	Female	Other Total	Male	Female
Total Children Aged 5 Enrolled in Kindergarten	100.0% (2,717,022)	51.3% (1,394,963)	48.7% (1,322,059)	62.5% (1,697,798)	32.3% (876,348)	30.2% (821,450)	19.2% (520,588)	9.5% (256,797)	9.7% (263,791)	13.5% (367,208)	7.2% (195,731)	6.3% (171,477)	4.8% (131,428)	2.4% (66,087)	2.4% (65,341)
Total Respondents	100.0% (2,665,890)	51.2% (1,365,426)	48.8% (1,300,464)	62.3% (1,661,894)	32.0% (854,203)	30.3% (807,691)	19.4% (516,224)	9.6% (256,797)	9.7% (259,427)	13.5% (360,998)	7.1% (189,521)	6.4% (171,477)	4.8% (126,774)	2.4% (64,905)	2.3% (61,869)
Complained About School	23.8% (635,367)	23.5% (321,070)	24.2% (314,297)	23.9% (397,071)	25.3% (215,724)	22.5% (181,347)	18.7% (96,428)	15.0% (38,518)	22.3% (57,910)	26.5% (95,531)	23.7% (45,006)	29.5% (50,525)	36.6% (46,337)	33.6% (21,822)	39.6% (24,515)
Reluctant to Go to School	19.4% (518,068)	20.7% (282,143)	18.1% (235,925)	18.7% (310,726)	21.1% (179,816)	16.2% (130,910)	13.2% (67,975)	11.8% (30,282)	14.5% (37,693)	27.2% (98,228)	28.0% (53,036)	26.4% (45,192)	32.5% (41,139)	29.3% (19,009)	35.8% (22,130)
Pretended to Be Sick	10.2% (272,592)	11.5% (157,167)	8.9% (115,425)	8.7% (143,970)	10.2% (87,420)	7.0% (56,550)	9.8% (50,357)	9.9% (25,515)	9.6% (24,842)	16.7% (60,181)	19.0% (36,065)	14.1% (24,116)	14.3% (18,084)	12.6% (8,167)	16.0% (9,917)
Says Good Things About School	95.5% (2,546,864)	95.6% (1,305,400)	95.5% (1,241,464)	95.8% (1,592,028)	96.6% (825,080)	95.0% (766,948)	95.6% (493,393)	93.0% (238,871)	98.1% (254,522)	95.7% (345,549)	95.7% (181,412)	95.7% (164,137)	91.4% (115,894)	92.5% (60,037)	90.3% (55,857)
Said Liked Teacher *	95.5% (2,545,149)	95.1% (1,298,551)	95.9% (1,246,598)	96.4% (1,602,348)	95.6% (816,238)	97.3% (786,110)	93.1% (480,592)	93.2% (239,288)	93.0% (241,304)	96.9% (349,772)	96.9% (183,724)	96.8% (166,048)	88.7% (112,437)	91.4% (59,301)	85.9% (53,136)
Looked Forward to School	95.3% (2,539,865)	94.9% (1,295,122)	95.7% (1,244,743)	94.9% (1,577,719)	94.0% (802,898)	95.9% (774,821)	98.1% (506,252)	99.1% (254,510)	97.0% (251,742)	93.8% (338,499)	93.8% (177,789)	93.7% (160,710)	92.6% (117,395)	92.3% (59,925)	92.9% (57,470)
Teacher says that:															
Child Gets Along Well With Others	89.1% (2,375,306)	89.5% (1,222,047)	88.7% (1,153,259)	89.5% (1,488,054)	90.5% (772,729)	88.6% (715,325)	91.4% (471,897)	91.2% (234,267)	91.6% (237,630)	87.4% (315,336)	87.1% (165,040)	87.6% (150,296)	78.9% (100,019)	77.1% (50,011)	80.8% (50,008)
Child is Enthusiastic **	83.5% (2,225,292)	82.7% (1,129,280)	84.3% (1,096,011)	82.4% (1,369,201)	81.8% (698,816)	83.0% (670,385)	90.3% (466,369)	88.0% (225,866)	92.7% (240,503)	78.7% (284,044)	80.9% (153,403)	76.2% (130,641)	83.4% (105,677)	78.9% (51,195)	88.1% (54,482)
Child Lacks Confidence ~~	15.1% (403,839)	16.9% (230,714)	13.3% (173,125)	13.5% (224,162)	14.6% (124,953)	12.3% (99,209)	16.5% (85,379)	23.5% (60,333)	9.7% (25,046)	19.3% (69,808)	17.3% (32,788)	21.6% (37,020)	19.3% (24,490)	19.5% (12,640)	19.2% (11,850)
Child Hard to Understand	8.4% (223,760)	9.2% (125,590)	7.5% (98,170)	7.6% (125,836)	7.9% (67,703)	7.2% (58,133)	9.0% (46,661)	11.5% (29,427)	6.6% (17,234)	11.3% (40,659)	11.6% (22,053)	10.9% (18,606)	8.4% (10,604)	9.9% (6,407)	6.8% (4,197)
Child Sleepy in Class	3.3% (87,398)	3.0% (41,522)	3.5% (45,877)	2.8% (45,848)	1.9% (16,265)	3.7% (29,583)	4.0% (20,561)	4.9% (12,697)	3.0% (7,864)	4.3% (15,487)	4.4% (8,309)	4.2% (7,178)	4.3% (5,503)	6.5% (4,251)	2.0% (1,252)
Child Speaks Out in Class ~	60.6% (1,615,746)	60.7% (828,567)	60.5% (787,180)	60.3% (1,001,748)	61.8% (527,627)	58.7% (474,121)	63.6% (328,217)	56.9% (145,991)	70.2% (182,226)	58.8% (212,124)	61.7% (116,911)	55.5% (95,213)	58.1% (73,658)	58.6% (38,038)	57.6% (35,620)

Notes:

*** Test of statistical significance compares African Americans with Whites. *** p < .001, ** p < .01, * p < .05.

+++ Test of statistical significance compares White boys with White girls. +++ p < .001, ++ p < .01, + p < .05.

~~~ Test of statistical significance compares African American boys with African American girls. ~~~ p < .001, ~~ p < .01, ~ p < .05.

Tests of statistical significance calculated using adjusted sample weight to control for influence of large sample sizes.

Source: National Household Education Survey, 1993.

Table 11. Percentage of Parents Who Participated in Various Activities During the Last Week With Their 3- and 4-Year-Olds (as of 12/31/92) by Race and Sex

(weighted sample size in parentheses)

Activity in Last Week	Total	Male	Female	White, Non-Hispanic			African American, Non-Hispanic			Hispanic			Other		
				Total	Male	Female	Total	Male	Female	Total	Male	Female	Total	Male	Female
Total Weighted Sample	100.0%	51.2%	48.8%	67.9%	34.1%	33.7%	15.3%	8.4%	6.9%	12.2%	6.3%	5.9%	4.6%	2.4%	2.3%
	(7,712,232)	(3,945,587)	(3,766,646)	(5,234,009)	(2,632,290)	(2,601,719)	(1,183,731)	(647,945)	(535,786)	(937,457)	(482,422)	(455,035)	(357,036)	(182,930)	(174,106)
Total Respondents	100.0%	51.2%	48.8%	67.9%	34.1%	33.7%	15.4%	8.4%	6.9%	12.2%	6.3%	5.9%	4.6%	2.4%	2.2%
	(7,709,484)	(3,945,587)	(3,763,897)	(5,234,009)	(2,632,290)	(2,601,719)	(1,183,731)	(647,945)	(535,786)	(937,457)	(482,422)	(455,035)	(354,287)	(182,930)	(171,357)
Told Child a Story **	76.6%	76.0%	77.2%	77.9%	77.6%	78.2%	72.8%	71.0%	75.0%	73.3%	73.9%	72.6%	78.5%	76.3%	80.8%
	(5,903,688)	(2,997,164)	(2,906,524)	(4,077,358)	(2,041,553)	(2,035,805)	(861,535)	(459,723)	(401,812)	(686,814)	(356,378)	(330,436)	(277,981)	(139,510)	(138,471)
Told Child a Story 3 or More Times **	44.0%	43.9%	44.1%	45.6%	45.8%	45.4%	39.3%	39.4%	39.3%	38.8%	36.9%	40.9%	49.4%	50.4%	48.5%
	(3,390,965)	(1,730,943)	(1,660,023)	(2,385,925)	(1,205,817)	(1,180,108)	(465,678)	(255,074)	(210,604)	(364,169)	(177,942)	(186,227)	(175,194)	(92,110)	(83,084)
Taught Child Letters & Words	86.3%	85.5%	87.1%	86.3%	85.8%	86.8%	88.0%	87.0%	89.3%	83.7%	81.8%	85.8%	86.8%	85.5%	88.2%
	(6,650,263)	(3,372,456)	(3,277,806)	(4,515,813)	(2,257,906)	(2,257,907)	(1,041,885)	(563,676)	(478,209)	(785,029)	(394,514)	(390,515)	(307,535)	(156,360)	(151,175)
Taught Child Letters & Words 3 or More Times **	57.9%	57.9%	57.8%	57.2%	57.8%	56.6%	63.9%	65.7%	61.7%	54.1%	50.8%	57.7%	57.5%	51.4%	63.9%
	(4,461,332)	(2,286,329)	(2,175,001)	(2,994,254)	(1,521,799)	(1,472,455)	(755,915)	(425,489)	(330,426)	(507,551)	(244,946)	(262,605)	(203,610)	(94,095)	(109,515)
Taught Child Songs & Music ++	71.8%	69.6%	74.2%	72.8%	70.4%	75.1%	72.2%	70.7%	73.9%	69.2%	65.9%	72.7%	63.9%	63.8%	64.0%
	(5,537,618)	(2,746,257)	(2,791,361)	(3,808,550)	(1,853,729)	(1,954,821)	(854,180)	(457,981)	(396,199)	(648,466)	(317,782)	(330,684)	(226,422)	(116,765)	(109,657)
Taught Child Songs & Music 3 or More Times *** ++	42.0%	39.4%	44.8%	41.4%	38.2%	44.6%	48.8%	46.2%	52.0%	39.8%	36.8%	43.0%	33.9%	38.0%	29.5%
	(3,238,160)	(1,552,908)	(1,685,251)	(2,166,857)	(1,006,599)	(1,160,258)	(578,088)	(299,228)	(278,860)	(373,108)	(177,533)	(195,575)	(120,106)	(69,548)	(50,558)
Arts & Crafts with Child *** +	68.2%	65.5%	71.1%	73.9%	71.7%	76.0%	55.0%	51.8%	58.8%	53.7%	48.1%	59.5%	68.2%	70.1%	66.2%
	(5,261,089)	(2,584,496)	(2,676,593)	(3,865,522)	(1,888,462)	(1,977,060)	(650,935)	(335,756)	(315,179)	(502,967)	(232,104)	(270,863)	(241,665)	(128,174)	(113,491)
Arts & Crafts With Child 3 or More Times *** + ~	33.5%	30.9%	36.4%	36.3%	34.9%	37.7%	28.1%	22.8%	34.4%	25.4%	21.7%	29.3%	32.6%	25.3%	40.3%
	(2,586,140)	(1,217,784)	(1,368,356)	(1,900,868)	(919,161)	(981,707)	(332,105)	(147,772)	(184,333)	(237,843)	(104,546)	(133,297)	(115,324)	(46,305)	(69,019)
Played with Toys or Games Indoors * ++ ~	96.1%	96.5%	95.6%	97.0%	97.9%	96.1%	94.4%	92.7%	96.4%	93.1%	94.6%	91.5%	96.5%	95.3%	97.7%
	(7,406,393)	(3,806,829)	(3,599,564)	(5,075,141)	(2,575,980)	(2,499,161)	(1,117,102)	(600,429)	(516,673)	(872,396)	(456,160)	(416,236)	(341,754)	(174,260)	(167,494)
Played With Toys or Games Indoors 3 or More Times ** +	81.2%	83.2%	79.2%	83.0%	85.7%	80.4%	76.6%	76.7%	76.5%	78.4%	79.7%	76.9%	77.7%	79.9%	75.5%
	(6,263,395)	(3,282,425)	(2,980,969)	(4,346,471)	(2,254,762)	(2,091,709)	(906,841)	(496,961)	(409,880)	(734,624)	(384,576)	(350,048)	(275,458)	(146,126)	(129,332)
Played With Child Outside *** ++	62.8%	66.9%	58.5%	63.6%	67.8%	59.3%	55.0%	57.2%	52.4%	68.4%	74.9%	61.4%	62.5%	67.1%	57.5%
	(4,839,930)	(2,638,016)	(2,201,915)	(3,326,776)	(1,783,397)	(1,543,379)	(650,893)	(370,377)	(280,516)	(640,968)	(361,561)	(279,407)	(221,294)	(122,681)	(98,613)
Played With Child Outside 3 or More Times *** ++	32.0%	35.3%	28.4%	31.4%	36.1%	26.7%	30.0%	32.1%	27.5%	38.4%	40.2%	36.4%	29.2%	22.8%	36.0%
	(2,464,026)	(1,394,504)	(1,069,523)	(1,645,542)	(950,624)	(694,918)	(355,397)	(208,063)	(147,334)	(359,649)	(194,123)	(165,526)	(103,439)	(41,694)	(61,745)

Notes:

*** Test of statistical significance compares African Americans with Whites. *** p < .001, ** p < .01, * p < .05.

+++ Test of statistical significance compares White boys with White girls. +++ p < .001, ++ p < .01, + p < .05.

~~~Test of statistical significance compares African American boys with African American girls. ~~~ p < .001, ~~ p < .01, ~ p < .05.

Tests of statistical significance calculated using adjusted sample weight to control for influence of large sample sizes.

Source: National Household Education Survey, 1993.

Table 12. Percentage of Parents Who Participated in Various Activities During the Last Month With Their 3- and 4-Year-Olds (as of 12/31/92) by Race and Sex

(weighted sample size in parentheses)

Activity in Last Month	Total	Male	Female	White, Non-Hispanic Total	White, Non-Hispanic Male	White, Non-Hispanic Female	African American, Non-Hispanic Total	African American, Non-Hispanic Male	African American, Non-Hispanic Female	Hispanic Total	Hispanic Male	Hispanic Female	Other Total	Other Male	Other Female
Total Weighted Sample	100.0% (7,712,232)	51.2% (3,945,587)	48.8% (3,766,646)	67.9% (5,234,009)	34.1% (2,632,290)	33.7% (2,601,719)	15.3% (1,183,731)	8.4% (647,945)	6.9% (535,786)	12.2% (937,457)	6.3% (482,422)	5.9% (455,035)	4.6% (357,036)	2.4% (182,930)	2.3% (174,106)
Total Respondents	100.0% (7,712,232)	51.2% (3,945,587)	48.8% (3,766,646)	67.9% (5,234,009)	34.1% (2,632,290)	33.7% (2,601,719)	15.3% (1,183,731)	8.4% (647,945)	6.9% (535,786)	12.2% (937,457)	6.3% (482,422)	5.9% (455,035)	4.6% (357,036)	2.4% (182,930)	2.3% (174,106)
Visited Library ***	37.8% (2,916,995)	37.8% (1,490,678)	37.9% (1,426,317)	41.6% (2,178,628)	41.4% (1,090,802)	41.8% (1,087,826)	28.9% (341,970)	30.7% (198,869)	26.7% (143,101)	26.4% (247,597)	24.3% (117,143)	28.7% (130,454)	41.7% (148,800)	45.8% (83,864)	37.3% (64,936)
Went to Play, Concert, or Show ***	22.9% (1,768,634)	23.1% (910,274)	22.8% (858,361)	22.2% (1,159,573)	22.5% (592,993)	21.8% (566,580)	29.8% (352,200)	29.6% (191,730)	30.0% (160,470)	19.7% (184,342)	20.5% (98,820)	18.8% (85,522)	20.3% (72,520)	14.6% (26,731)	26.3% (45,789)
Visited Gallery or Museum ++ ~	18.0% (1,390,613)	19.6% (773,153)	16.4% (617,460)	18.5% (966,148)	20.4% (537,093)	16.5% (429,055)	16.3% (192,530)	19.6% (126,851)	12.3% (65,679)	15.7% (146,747)	12.2% (59,062)	19.3% (87,685)	23.9% (85,188)	27.4% (50,147)	20.1% (35,041)
Took Child to Zoo or Aquarium	17.1% (1,322,062)	18.3% (722,248)	15.9% (599,814)	15.4% (807,915)	16.7% (439,252)	14.2% (368,663)	17.0% (201,318)	18.6% (120,342)	15.1% (80,976)	22.8% (213,576)	23.4% (112,652)	22.2% (100,924)	27.8% (99,253)	27.3% (50,002)	28.3% (49,251)
Talked With Child About Ethnic Heritage ***	42.2% (3,252,380)	41.2% (1,626,817)	43.2% (1,625,563)	38.0% (1,991,291)	36.8% (968,406)	39.3% (1,022,885)	55.0% (651,381)	53.0% (343,556)	57.5% (307,825)	45.0% (421,977)	44.7% (215,822)	45.3% (206,155)	52.6% (187,731)	54.1% (99,033)	50.9% (88,698)
Attended Event by Religious Group +	49.1% (3,788,342)	46.9% (1,852,255)	51.4% (1,936,086)	50.7% (2,654,056)	48.6% (1,278,001)	52.9% (1,376,055)	49.1% (581,367)	46.2% (299,142)	52.7% (282,225)	40.9% (383,613)	39.1% (188,638)	42.8% (194,975)	47.4% (169,305)	47.3% (86,474)	47.6% (82,831)

Notes:

*** Test of statistical significance compares African Americans with Whites. *** p < .001, ** p < .01, * p < .05.

+++ Test of statistical significance compares White boys with White girls. +++ p < .001, ++ p < .01, + p < .05.

~~~ Test of statistical significance compares African American boys with African American girls. ~~~ p < .001, ~~ p < .01, ~ p < .05.

Tests of statistical significance calculated using adjusted sample weight to control for influence of large sample sizes.

Source: National Household Education Survey, 1993.

Figure 10. Percentage of Parents of 3- and 4-Year-Olds
Who Participated in Various Activities With Their Child: 1992

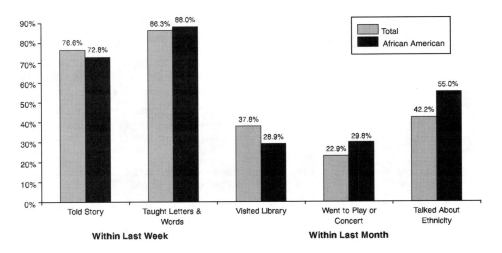

Source: National Household Education Survey, 1993.

Figure 11. Reading Levels of 5-Year-Olds
as Reported by Their Parents: 1992

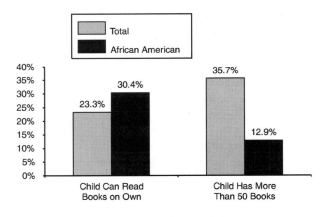

Source: National Household Education Survey, 1993.

Table 13. Reading Levels of 5-Year-Olds as Reported by Their Parents (as of 12/31/92) by Race and Sex
(weighted sample size in parentheses)

Characteristic	Total	Male	Female	White, Non-Hispanic			African American, Non-Hispanic			Hispanic			Other		
				Total	Male	Female	Total	Male	Female	Total	Male	Female	Total	Male	Female
Total Enrolled in Kindergarten	100.0%	100.0%	100.0%	100.0%	100.0%	100.0%	100.0%	100.0%	100.0%	100.0%	100.0%	100.0%	100.0%	100.0%	100.0%
	(2,717,022)	(1,394,963)	(1,322,059)	(1,697,798)	(876,348)	(821,450)	(520,588)	(256,797)	(263,791)	(367,208)	(195,731)	(171,477)	(131,428)	(66,087)	(65,341)
Can Read Books on Own *	100.0%	100.0%	100.0%	100.0%	100.0%	100.0%	100.0%	100.0%	100.0%	100.0%	100.0%	100.0%	100.0%	100.0%	100.0%
	(2,717,022)	(1,394,963)	(1,322,059)	(1,697,798)	(876,348)	(821,450)	(520,589)	(256,797)	(263,791)	(367,209)	(195,731)	(171,477)	(131,428)	(66,087)	(65,341)
Yes	23.3%	23.5%	23.2%	21.7%	19.8%	23.8%	30.4%	37.8%	23.2%	15.8%	16.6%	14.8%	37.0%	37.3%	36.7%
	(633,563)	(327,293)	(306,271)	(368,883)	(173,120)	(195,763)	(158,197)	(96,993)	(61,204)	(57,840)	(32,544)	(25,296)	(48,644)	(24,636)	(24,008)
No	76.7%	76.5%	76.8%	78.3%	80.2%	76.2%	69.6%	62.2%	76.8%	84.2%	83.4%	85.2%	63.0%	62.7%	63.3%
	(2,083,459)	(1,067,671)	(1,015,789)	(1,328,915)	(703,228)	(625,687)	(362,392)	(159,805)	(202,587)	(309,369)	(163,187)	(146,182)	(82,784)	(41,451)	(41,333)
Level of "Reading"	100.0%	100.0%	100.0%	100.0%	100.0%	100.0%	100.0%	100.0%	100.0%	100.0%	100.0%	100.0%	100.0%	100.0%	100.0%
	(2,717,022)	(1,394,963)	(1,322,059)	(1,697,798)	(876,348)	(821,450)	(520,589)	(256,797)	(263,791)	(367,209)	(195,731)	(171,477)	(131,427)	(66,087)	(65,341)
Does Not Read	76.7%	76.5%	76.8%	78.3%	80.2%	76.2%	69.6%	62.2%	76.8%	84.2%	83.4%	85.2%	63.0%	62.7%	63.3%
	(2,083,459)	(1,067,671)	(1,015,789)	(1,328,915)	(703,228)	(625,687)	(362,392)	(159,805)	(202,587)	(309,369)	(163,187)	(146,182)	(82,784)	(41,451)	(41,333)
Reads the Written Words	16.5%	17.7%	15.3%	15.4%	14.9%	15.9%	23.2%	32.0%	14.6%	8.8%	8.6%	9.1%	26.3%	26.5%	26.2%
	(449,083)	(246,891)	(202,193)	(261,267)	(130,328)	(130,939)	(120,760)	(82,263)	(38,497)	(32,426)	(16,801)	(15,625)	(34,631)	(17,499)	(17,132)
Pretends to Read	2.0%	1.8%	2.3%	1.4%	1.6%	1.2%	2.8%	1.7%	4.0%	3.5%	3.4%	3.6%	2.6%	0.0%	5.3%
	(54,789)	(24,837)	(29,952)	(23,704)	(13,774)	(9,930)	(14,826)	(4,370)	(10,456)	(12,785)	(6,693)	(6,092)	(3,474)	–	(3,474)
Does Both	4.8%	4.0%	5.6%	4.9%	3.3%	6.7%	4.3%	4.0%	4.6%	3.4%	4.6%	2.1%	8.0%	10.8%	5.2%
	(129,690)	(55,565)	(74,126)	(83,913)	(29,018)	(54,895)	(22,611)	(10,360)	(12,251)	(12,629)	(9,050)	(3,579)	(10,538)	(7,137)	(3,401)
Average Age in Months Started to Read * ~~**	63	63	63	64	64	65	60	61	57	65	65	65	61	58	64
	(578,774)	(302,456)	(276,318)	(345,180)	(159,346)	(185,833)	(143,371)	(92,623)	(50,748)	(45,055)	(25,851)	(19,204)	(45,169)	(24,636)	(20,533)
Number of Books Child Has *	100.0%	100.0%	100.0%	100.0%	100.0%	100.0%	100.0%	100.0%	100.0%	100.0%	100.0%	100.0%	100.0%	100.0%	100.0%
	(2,717,024)	(1,394,965)	(1,322,059)	(1,697,798)	(876,348)	(821,450)	(520,590)	(256,798)	(263,792)	(367,209)	(195,733)	(171,476)	(131,427)	(66,086)	(65,341)
None	0.4%	0.5%	0.3%	0.0%	0.0%	0.0%	0.5%	0.6%	0.3%	1.8%	1.8%	1.9%	0.9%	1.8%	0.0%
	(10,396)	(6,320)	(4,077)	–	–	–	(2,503)	(1,662)	(841)	(6,707)	(3,471)	(3,236)	(1,187)	(1,187)	–
1 or 2 Books	1.2%	0.7%	1.7%	0.0%	0.0%	0.0%	1.6%	0.0%	3.1%	6.2%	5.2%	7.2%	1.2%	0.0%	2.5%
	(32,304)	(10,194)	(22,110)	–	–	–	(8,075)	–	(8,075)	(22,591)	(10,194)	(12,397)	(1,638)	–	(1,638)
3 to 9 Books	11.0%	12.7%	9.1%	3.3%	4.1%	2.5%	25.2%	31.0%	19.4%	23.4%	24.9%	21.8%	18.3%	18.7%	17.9%
	(297,799)	(177,009)	(120,790)	(56,686)	(36,195)	(20,491)	(130,941)	(79,707)	(51,234)	(86,103)	(48,746)	(37,357)	(24,069)	(12,361)	(11,708)
10 to 25 Books	26.2%	26.1%	26.3%	19.7%	19.7%	19.6%	41.3%	44.1%	38.5%	33.2%	30.9%	35.7%	31.8%	26.6%	36.9%
	(712,018)	(364,128)	(347,890)	(333,721)	(172,748)	(160,973)	(214,781)	(113,233)	(101,548)	(121,784)	(60,547)	(61,237)	(41,732)	(17,600)	(24,132)
26 to 50 Books	25.6%	25.7%	25.4%	30.4%	31.0%	29.8%	18.7%	14.3%	22.9%	16.3%	18.0%	14.4%	15.6%	21.9%	9.2%
	(694,581)	(358,402)	(336,179)	(516,943)	(272,026)	(244,917)	(97,210)	(36,681)	(60,529)	(59,921)	(35,193)	(24,728)	(20,507)	(14,502)	(6,005)
More Than 50 Books	35.7%	34.3%	37.1%	46.6%	45.1%	48.1%	12.9%	9.9%	15.8%	19.1%	19.2%	19.0%	32.2%	30.9%	33.5%
	(969,925)	(478,912)	(491,013)	(790,448)	(395,379)	(395,069)	(67,080)	(25,515)	(41,565)	(70,103)	(37,582)	(32,521)	(42,294)	(20,436)	(21,858)

Notes:

"–" indicates sample size too small to estimate.

*** Test of statistical significance compares African Americans with Whites. *** p < .001, ** p < .01, * p < .05.

+++ Test of statistical significance compares White boys with White girls. +++ p < .001, ++ p < .01, + p < .05.

~~~ Test of statistical significance compares African American boys with African American girls. ~~~ p < .001, ~~ p < .01, ~ p < .05.

Tests of statistical significance calculated using adjusted sample weight to control for influence of large sample sizes.

Source: National Household Education Survey, 1993.

Table 14. Most Recent Motor/Social Development Score, Peabody Picture Vocabulary Test Score, and Verbal Memory Score for Preschoolers by Race and Sex
(weighted sample size in parentheses)

Test	Total	Male	Female	White, Non-Hispanic Total	White, Non-Hispanic Male	White, Non-Hispanic Female	African American, Non-Hispanic Total	African American, Non-Hispanic Male	African American, Non-Hispanic Female	Hispanic Total	Hispanic Male	Hispanic Female
Motor/Social * +++ ~~**												
Mean	101.3	98.9	103.9	102.6	99.8	105.5	100.0	98.2	101.7	95.7	94.3	97.1
Standard Deviation	14.0	14.2	14.0	13.5	13.2	13.2	14.4	14.2	14.3	14.7	13.8	15.5
	(15,569,341)	(8,004,713)	(7,564,628)	(10,035,817)	(5,195,092)	(4,840,725)	(2,288,266)	(1,115,335)	(1,172,931)	(1,037,343)	(540,909)	(496,434)
Peabody Picture * +**												
Mean	92.2	91.6	92.9	98.2	97.3	99.2	74.6	73.3	75.7	76.3	76.8	75.7
Standard Deviation	20.0	20.0	20.1	16.9	16.5	17.2	18.8	20.2	17.4	24.8	24.3	25.5
	(11,742,208)	(5,990,641)	(5,751,568)	(7,344,928)	(3,854,299)	(3,490,629)	(1,868,678)	(888,318)	(980,359)	(804,223)	(435,613)	(368,610)
Verbal Memory +++ ~~~												
Mean	96.6	94.1	99.2	97.7	95.2	100.5	96.2	93.3	99.0	90.2	89.6	91.0
Standard Deviation	15.1	14.8	15.1	15.4	15.0	15.5	13.9	13.7	13.5	14.9	15.3	14.4
	(10,745,483)	(5,453,498)	(5,291,985)	(6,605,443)	(3,439,228)	(3,166,216)	(1,769,127)	(856,841)	(912,286)	(760,379)	(407,289)	(353,090)

Notes:
*** Test of statistical significance compares African Americans with Whites. *** p < .001, ** p < .01, * p < .05.
+++ Test of statistical significance compares White boys with White girls. +++ p < .001, ++ p < .01, + p < .05.
~~~ Test of statistical significance compares African American boys with African American girls. ~~~ p < .001, ~~ p < .01, ~ p < .05.
Tests of statistical significance calculated using adjusted sample weight to control for influence of large sample sizes.
Source: The National Longitudinal Survey of Youth. Children 1986-1992, Females 1979-1992.

Figure 12. Test Scores of Preschoolers

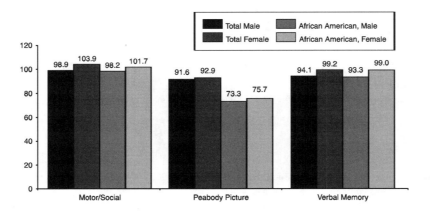

Source: The National Longitudinal Survey of Youth. Children 1986-1992, Females 1979-1992.

Asian/Pacific Islander			Other		
Total	Male	Female	Total	Male	Female
100.5	99.4	101.4	99.8	97.8	102.0
13.4	17.8	7.5	14.4	13.7	14.8
(99,954)	(46,178)	(53,776)	(2,107,961)	(1,107,199)	(1,000,762)
91.3	91.0	91.5	93.5	92.0	94.7
17.4	10.5	21.9	15.5	15.9	15.0
(98,327)	(47,031)	(51,296)	(1,626,053)	(765,380)	(860,673)
87.0	85.3	88.0	96.1	93.2	98.7
14.0	9.5	15.9	14.3	14.2	13.9
(83,544)	(29,189)	(54,356)	(1,526,989)	(720,951)	(806,038)

CHAPTER II.
Enrollment at America's Public and Private Elementary and Secondary Schools

---

How many African Americans attend America's public and private schools? How are African American public school students distributed among the 50 states? Does African American representation vary across schools of different levels, types, and locations?

Two databases provide data on public and private school enrollments. The U. S. Department of Education's Common Core of Data provides annual data on enrollment in America's public elementary and secondary schools. Each year data are collected from public elementary and secondary schools and school districts in each state. Private school enrollment data are obtained from the U.S. Department of Education's 1993/94 Schools and Staffing Survey. Conducted in 1987/88, 1990/91, and 1993/94, the Schools and Staffing Survey collects data from public school districts, public and private school administrators, and public and private school teachers on several topics including demographic characteristics of the student body.

CHAPTER ORGANIZATION

In this chapter, public school enrollment data are presented first. The private school enrollment data are then presented. Topics covered include:

1. Public school enrollment by state and grade level, high school completions by state, enrollment by region, enrollment by urbanicity, enrollment in America's largest high schools, and enrollment by school type; and

2. Private school enrollment by school level, school affiliation, school size, urbanicity, percentage of African American students, and tuition rate.

PART I — OVERVIEW

In 1993/94, approximately 43.5 million students were enrolled in America's public elementary and secondary schools, and nearly 5 million students were enrolled in America's private elementary and secondary schools. African Americans represented 16.5% of all public school enrollments. African Americans were underrepresented at America's private elementary and secondary schools, where they comprised only 9.3% of all enrollments.

The share of African American students enrolled in America's public schools declined as grade level increased, a finding that suggests African Americans may leave school at higher rates than their peers in other racial groups. Moreover, African Americans represented only 12.5% of those who received regular high school diplomas in 1993/94, but 15.3% of all students enrolled in grades 9 through 12, providing further evidence of the challenges African Americans face in their progression through America's public elementary and secondary schools. Similarly, African Americans represented a higher share of private school enrollments at the elementary school level than at the secondary school level.

About one-half (56.2%) of African American public school students attended schools located in the southern United States, compared with 33.1% of White students. African Americans also tended to attend public schools located in large central cities (cities with a population of 400,000 or more) rather than schools in small towns or rural areas.

Nearly all public elementary and secondary school students were enrolled in regular schools. But, African Americans were overrepresented among those attending special education, vocational, and alternative or other schools.

The characteristics of schools attended by private school students varied by race group. Compared with their White counterparts, a higher percentage of African Americans attended private schools affiliated with the Catholic church, schools with less than 300 students, schools located in urban areas, schools in which more than 60.0% of all students were African American, and schools with tuition rates less than $2,500.

PART II — DETAILED DESCRIPTIONS AND TABLES

PUBLIC SCHOOL ENROLLMENT

Enrollment by State

In 1993/94, approximately 43.5 million students were enrolled nationwide in America's public elementary and secondary schools. About 7.17 million or 16.5% of these students were African American.

Figure 1 shows that the representation of African Americans among public school enrollments varied by state.

- **Table 1** shows that in the District of Columbia, African Americans represented 88.5% of all public school enrollments in 1993/94 ($n = 80,678$).

- African Americans represented about one-half of all public school enrollments in Mississippi (50.9%) and Louisiana (45.4%).

- African Americans represented more than one-third of public school enrollments in South Carolina (41.4%), Georgia (37.0%), Alabama (35.4%), and Maryland (34.2%).

- African Americans represented more than one-fourth of public school enrollments in North Carolina (30.3%), Delaware (28.5%), and Virginia (25.8%).

- African Americans represented 1.0% or less of all public school enrollments in Wyoming (1.0%), North Dakota (0.8%), New Hampshire (0.8%), South Dakota (0.7%), Vermont (0.7%), Utah (0.6%), Idaho (0.5%), Montana (0.5%), and Maine.

- Nationwide, New York ($n = 550,455$), Texas ($n = 515,395$), Florida ($n = 504,913$), Georgia ($n = 457,192$), and California ($n = 455,954$) had the largest numbers of African American public school enrollments.

Preschool Enrollment

Nationwide, about 557,000 students were enrolled in preschools sponsored and administered by public schools in 1993/94.

- **Table 2** shows that, among the states with publicly sponsored preschools that reported the racial profile of students by grade level, African Americans represented 22.0% of all preschool enrollments.

Figure 1. Representation of African Americans
Among Public School Enrollments by State: 1993/94

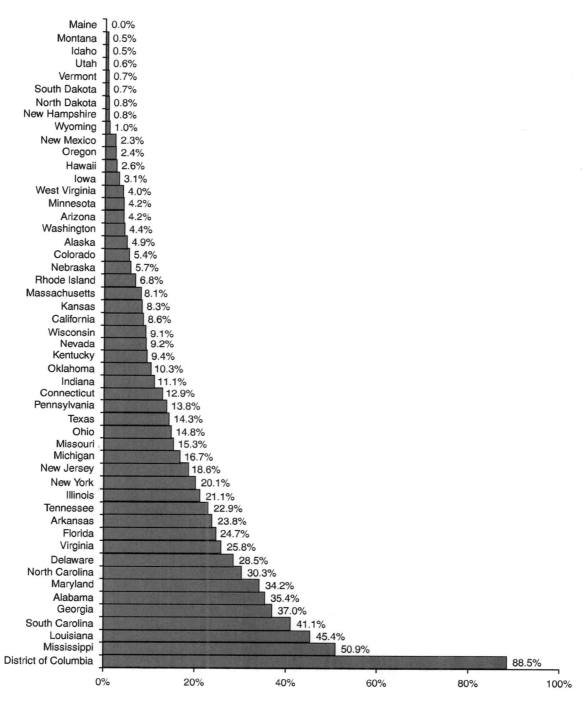

Source: Common Core of Data, 1994.

Table 1. Total Enrollment in Prekindergarten Through 12th Grade by State and Race: Fall 1993
(includes ungraded enrollment)

Rank	State	Total	White, Non-Hispanic			African American, Non-Hispanic			Hispanic		
			Number	% of Total	% of State	Number	% of Total	% of State	Number	% of Total	% of State
	Total (50 States+DC)	43,476,268	28,406,889	100.0%	65.3%	7,169,333	100.0%	16.5%	5,479,253	100.0%	12.6%
1	New York	2,733,813	1,591,444	5.6%	58.2%	550,455	7.7%	20.1%	452,091	8.3%	16.5%
2	Texas	3,608,262	1,721,788	6.1%	47.7%	515,395	7.2%	14.3%	1,282,531	23.4%	35.5%
3	Florida	2,040,763	1,215,592	4.3%	59.6%	504,913	7.0%	24.7%	282,189	5.2%	13.8%
4	Georgia	1,235,304	739,821	2.6%	59.9%	457,192	6.4%	37.0%	18,978	0.3%	1.5%
5	California	5,328,558	2,227,652	7.8%	41.8%	455,954	6.4%	8.6%	1,951,578	35.6%	36.6%
6	Illinois	1,893,078	1,224,014	4.3%	64.7%	400,188	5.6%	21.1%	211,113	3.9%	11.2%
7	Louisiana	800,560	414,052	1.5%	51.7%	363,473	5.1%	45.4%	9,151	0.2%	1.1%
8	North Carolina	1,133,231	744,557	2.6%	65.7%	343,538	4.8%	30.3%	14,680	0.3%	1.3%
9	Virginia	1,045,471	709,953	2.5%	67.9%	270,087	3.8%	25.8%	28,842	0.5%	2.8%
10	Ohio	1,807,319	1,496,674	5.3%	82.8%	267,117	3.7%	14.8%	24,200	0.4%	1.3%
11	Michigan	1,599,377	1,204,118	4.2%	75.3%	266,717	3.7%	16.7%	36,457	0.7%	2.3%
12	South Carolina	643,859	362,838	1.3%	56.4%	264,747	3.7%	41.1%	3,493	0.1%	0.5%
13	Maryland	772,638	454,751	1.6%	58.9%	264,444	3.7%	34.2%	22,479	0.4%	2.9%
14	Alabama	734,469	453,268	1.6%	61.7%	259,700	3.6%	35.4%	2,781	0.1%	0.4%
15	Mississippi	505,907	242,260	0.9%	47.9%	257,372	3.6%	50.9%	1,561	1.0%	0.3%
16	Pennsylvania	1,744,082	1,414,645	5.0%	81.1%	239,902	3.3%	13.8%	57,438	1.0%	3.3%
17	New Jersey	1,151,307	729,812	2.6%	63.4%	213,963	3.0%	18.6%	147,561	2.7%	12.8%
18	Tennessee	866,991	655,116	2.3%	75.6%	198,125	2.8%	22.9%	3,868	0.1%	0.4%
19	Missouri	875,639	701,571	2.5%	80.1%	133,599	1.9%	15.3%	7,254	0.1%	0.8%
20	Indiana	965,599	829,716	2.9%	85.9%	107,149	1.5%	11.1%	19,880	0.4%	2.1%
21	Arkansas	444,271	330,332	1.2%	74.4%	105,595	1.5%	23.8%	3,955	0.1%	0.9%
22	Wisconsin	844,001	711,736	2.5%	84.3%	76,446	1.1%	9.1%	24,603	0.4%	2.9%
23	District of Columbia	80,678	3,243	0.0%	4.0%	71,414	1.0%	88.5%	4,938	0.1%	6.1%
24	Massachusetts	877,726	695,687	2.4%	79.3%	71,023	1.0%	8.1%	77,015	1.4%	8.8%
25	Connecticut	496,298	360,690	1.3%	72.7%	64,047	0.9%	12.9%	54,539	1.0%	11.0%
26	Oklahoma	604,076	432,300	1.5%	71.6%	61,963	0.9%	10.3%	20,086	0.4%	3.3%
27	Kentucky	655,265	560,549	2.0%	85.5%	61,798	0.9%	9.4%	1,812	0.0%	0.3%
28	Washington	915,952	732,288	2.6%	79.9%	40,534	0.6%	4.4%	63,313	1.2%	6.9%
29	Kansas	457,614	382,394	1.3%	83.6%	38,169	0.5%	8.3%	24,129	0.4%	5.3%
30	Minnesota	810,233	719,781	2.5%	88.8%	33,870	0.5%	4.2%	13,443	0.2%	1.7%
31	Colorado	625,062	463,070	1.6%	74.1%	33,536	0.5%	5.4%	106,976	2.0%	17.1%
32	Delaware	105,547	69,905	0.2%	66.2%	30,038	0.4%	28.5%	3,598	0.1%	3.4%
33	Arizona	709,453	423,109	1.5%	59.6%	29,720	0.4%	4.2%	196,118	3.6%	27.6%
34	Nevada	235,800	166,201	0.6%	70.5%	21,702	0.3%	9.2%	33,755	0.6%	14.3%
35	Nebraska	285,097	251,750	0.9%	88.3%	16,253	0.2%	5.7%	10,129	0.2%	3.6%
36	Iowa	498,519	465,269	1.6%	93.3%	15,651	0.2%	3.1%	8,026	0.1%	1.6%
37	Oregon	516,611	447,781	1.6%	86.7%	12,630	0.2%	2.4%	30,244	0.6%	5.9%
38	West Virginia	314,383	299,829	1.1%	95.4%	12,423	0.2%	4.0%	643	0.0%	0.2%
39	Rhode Island	145,676	118,124	0.4%	81.1%	9,943	0.1%	6.8%	12,536	0.2%	8.6%
40	New Mexico	322,292	129,949	0.5%	40.3%	7,487	0.1%	2.3%	147,824	2.7%	45.9%
41	Alaska	125,948	82,127	0.3%	65.2%	6,153	0.1%	4.9%	3,069	0.1%	2.4%
42	Hawaii	180,430	42,700	0.2%	23.7%	4,732	0.1%	2.6%	9,082	0.2%	5.0%
43	Utah	471,365	429,506	1.5%	91.1%	2,913	0.0%	0.6%	21,069	0.4%	4.5%
44	New Hampshire	185,360	179,598	0.6%	96.9%	1,549	0.0%	0.8%	1,927	0.0%	1.0%
45	Idaho	236,774	212,198	0.7%	89.6%	1,278	0.0%	0.5%	17,663	0.3%	7.5%
46	South Dakota	142,825	121,253	0.4%	84.9%	1,008	0.0%	0.7%	906	0.0%	0.6%
47	Wyoming	100,899	90,202	0.3%	89.4%	1,008	0.0%	1.0%	6,242	0.1%	6.2%
48	North Dakota	119,127	108,420	0.4%	91.0%	905	0.0%	0.8%	913	0.0%	0.8%
49	Montana	163,009	143,072	0.5%	87.8%	791	0.0%	0.5%	2,251	0.0%	1.4%
50	Vermont	102,755	100,184	0.4%	97.5%	724	0.0%	0.7%	324	0.0%	0.3%
51	Maine	216,995	–	–	–	–	–	–	–	–	–
	Outlying Areas										
	Virgin Islands	14,484	–	–	–	–	–	–	–	–	–
	Puerto Rico	30,920	2,722	–	8.8%	560	–	1.8%	169	–	0.5%
	Guam	8,188	100	–	1.2%	–	–	–	0	–	–
	American Samoa	631,460	0	–	–	–	–	–	0	–	–
	Northern Marianas	22,752	197	–	0.9%	19,343	–	85.0%	3,008	–	13.2%

Note: "–" indicates numbers not reported.
Source: Common Core of Data, 1993-94.

| Asian American | | | American Indian | | | Unknown | | |
Number	% of Total	% of State	Number	% of Total	% of State	Number	% of Total	% of State
1,546,266	100.0%	3.6%	464,523	100.0%	1.1%	410,004	100.0%	0.9%
130,014	8.4%	4.8%	9,809	2.1%	0.4%	–	–	–
80,398	5.2%	2.2%	8,153	1.8%	0.2%	(3)	0.0%	0.0%
34,331	2.2%	1.7%	3,738	0.8%	0.2%	–	–	–
17,431	1.1%	1.4%	1,882	0.4%	0.2%	–	–	–
588,634	38.1%	11.0%	43,459	9.4%	0.8%	61,281	–	–
55,137	3.6%	2.9%	2,807	0.6%	0.1%	(181)	0.0%	0.0%
10,054	0.7%	1.3%	3,830	0.8%	0.5%	–	–	–
12,796	0.8%	1.1%	17,660	3.8%	1.6%	–	–	–
34,939	2.3%	3.3%	1,650	0.4%	0.2%	–	–	–
17,389	1.1%	1.0%	1,938	0.4%	0.1%	1	0.0%	0.0%
21,441	1.4%	1.3%	15,560	3.3%	1.0%	55,084	13.4%	3.4%
4,367	0.3%	0.7%	1,007	0.2%	0.2%	7,407	–	–
28,734	1.9%	3.7%	2,230	0.5%	0.3%	–	–	–
4,320	0.3%	0.6%	5,906	1.3%	0.8%	8,494	2.1%	1.2%
2,612	0.2%	0.5%	2,102	0.5%	0.4%	–	–	–
30,414	2.0%	1.7%	1,683	0.4%	0.1%	–	–	–
58,410	3.8%	5.1%	1,561	0.3%	0.1%	–	–	–
6,282	0.4%	0.7%	881	0.2%	0.1%	2,719	0.7%	0.3%
7,896	0.5%	0.9%	1,722	0.4%	0.2%	23,597	5.8%	2.7%
7,375	0.5%	0.8%	1,479	0.3%	0.2%	–	–	–
2,957	0.2%	0.7%	1,432	0.3%	0.3%	–	–	–
20,182	1.3%	2.4%	11,034	2.4%	1.3%	–	–	–
1,069	0.1%	1.3%	14	0.0%	0.0%	–	–	–
32,478	2.1%	3.7%	1,523	0.3%	0.2%	–	–	–
11,767	0.8%	2.4%	1,194	0.3%	0.2%	4,061	–	–
7,206	0.5%	1.2%	82,521	17.8%	13.7%	–	–	–
3,377	0.2%	0.5%	363	0.1%	0.1%	27,366	6.7%	4.2%
56,427	3.6%	6.2%	23,390	5.0%	2.6%	–	–	–
8,325	0.5%	1.8%	4,597	1.0%	1.0%	–	–	–
28,406	1.8%	3.5%	15,025	3.2%	1.9%	(292)	–0.1%	0.0%
15,243	1.0%	2.4%	6,237	1.3%	1.0%	–	–	–
1,777	0.1%	1.7%	229	0.0%	0.2%	–	–	–
11,373	0.7%	1.6%	49,133	10.6%	6.9%	–	–	–
9,490	0.6%	4.0%	4,652	1.0%	2.0%	–	–	–
3,355	0.2%	1.2%	3,610	0.8%	1.3%	–	–	–
7,617	0.5%	1.5%	1,956	0.4%	0.4%	–	–	–
16,137	1.0%	3.1%	9,819	2.1%	1.9%	–	–	–
1,237	0.1%	0.4%	251	0.1%	0.1%	–	–	–
4,514	0.3%	3.1%	559	0.1%	0.4%	–	–	–
3,048	0.2%	0.9%	32,855	7.1%	10.2%	1,129	0.3%	0.4%
5,144	0.3%	4.1%	29,455	6.3%	23.4%	–	–	–
123,327	8.0%	68.4%	589	0.1%	0.3%	–	–	–
9,559	0.6%	2.0%	6,587	1.4%	1.4%	1,731	0.4%	0.4%
1,847	0.1%	1.0%	439	0.1%	0.2%	–	–	–
2,628	0.2%	1.1%	3,007	0.6%	1.3%	–	–	–
1,020	0.1%	0.7%	18,638	4.0%	13.0%	–	–	–
736	0.0%	0.7%	2,711	0.6%	2.7%	–	–	–
876	0.1%	0.7%	7,398	1.6%	6.2%	615	0.1%	0.5%
1,281	0.1%	0.8%	15,614	3.4%	9.6%	–	–	–
889	0.1%	0.9%	634	0.1%	0.6%	–	–	–
–	–	–	–	–	–	216,995	52.9%	100.0%
14,484	–	100.0%	–	–	–	–	–	–
26,539	–	85.8%	26	–	0.1%	904	–	2.9%
7,630	–	93.2%	–	–	–	458	–	5.6%
–	–	–	–	–	–	631,460	–	100.0%
98	–	92.8%	22	–	–	84	–	0.4%

Table 2. Enrollment in Prekindergarten by State and Race: Fall 1993

Rank	State	Total	White, Non-Hispanic			African American, Non-Hispanic			Hispanic		
			Number	% of Total	% of State	Number	% of Total	% of State	Number	% of Total	% of State
	Total (50 States+DC)	556,918	197,484	100.0%	35.5%	122,734	100.0%	22.0%	93,913	100.0%	16.9%
1	Texas	120,446	30,853	15.6%	25.6%	23,122	18.8%	19.2%	63,020	67.1%	52.3%
2	Florida	34,793	14,552	7.4%	41.8%	15,944	13.0%	45.8%	3,944	4.2%	11.3%
3	Illinois	42,359	20,234	10.2%	47.8%	14,704	12.0%	34.7%	6,396	6.8%	15.1%
4	New York	31,687	14,090	7.1%	44.5%	9,461	7.7%	29.9%	6,695	7.1%	21.1%
5	Maryland	17,984	7,668	3.9%	42.6%	8,939	7.3%	49.7%	831	0.9%	4.6%
6	Louisiana	12,857	4,257	2.2%	33.1%	8,247	6.7%	64.1%	101	0.1%	0.8%
7	Michigan	11,704	7,553	3.8%	64.5%	7,489	6.1%	64.0%	484	0.5%	4.1%
8	District of Columbia	5,216	236	0.1%	4.5%	4,588	3.7%	88.0%	338	0.4%	6.5%
9	Ohio	17,210	12,433	6.3%	72.2%	4,421	3.6%	25.7%	160	0.2%	0.9%
10	Wisconsin	17,270	10,854	5.5%	62.8%	4,385	3.6%	25.4%	926	1.0%	5.4%
11	Georgia	5,534	2,522	1.3%	45.6%	2,897	2.4%	52.3%	80	0.1%	1.4%
12	New Jersey	9,225	4,371	2.2%	47.4%	2,635	2.1%	28.6%	1,799	1.9%	19.5%
13	North Carolina	8,469	5,480	2.8%	64.7%	2,616	2.1%	30.9%	154	0.2%	1.8%
14	Virginia	3,186	650	0.3%	20.4%	2,431	2.0%	76.3%	62	0.1%	1.9%
15	Connecticut	6,216	3,351	1.7%	53.9%	1,412	1.2%	22.7%	1,299	1.4%	20.9%
16	Mississippi	2,197	900	0.5%	41.0%	1,279	1.0%	58.2%	7	0.0%	0.3%
17	Indiana	3,971	2,657	1.3%	66.9%	1,231	1.0%	31.0%	63	0.1%	1.6%
18	Oklahoma	5,456	3,023	1.5%	55.4%	1,036	0.8%	19.0%	220	0.2%	4.0%
19	Pennsylvania	4,181	2,644	1.3%	63.2%	874	0.7%	20.9%	609	0.6%	14.6%
20	Massachusetts	13,178	10,652	5.4%	80.8%	747	0.6%	5.7%	1,336	1.4%	10.1%
21	Colorado	7,249	4,029	2.0%	55.6%	652	0.5%	9.0%	2,263	2.4%	31.2%
22	Arkansas	1,248	597	0.3%	47.8%	617	0.5%	49.4%	24	0.0%	1.9%
23	Minnesota	6,656	5,837	3.0%	87.7%	443	0.4%	6.7%	110	0.1%	1.7%
24	Iowa	5,430	4,764	2.4%	87.7%	380	0.3%	7.0%	161	0.2%	3.0%
25	Washington	5,087	3,778	1.9%	74.3%	379	0.3%	7.5%	534	0.6%	10.5%
26	Nebraska	3,577	2,983	1.5%	83.4%	352	0.3%	9.8%	115	0.1%	3.2%
27	Oregon	837	478	0.2%	57.1%	271	0.2%	32.4%	36	0.0%	4.3%
28	West Virginia	3,981	3,696	1.9%	92.8%	253	0.2%	6.4%	12	0.0%	0.3%
29	Delaware	565	328	0.2%	58.1%	213	0.2%	37.7%	21	0.0%	3.7%
30	Kansas	2,432	2,114	1.1%	86.9%	163	0.1%	6.7%	117	0.1%	4.8%
31	Nevada	1,237	896	0.5%	72.4%	139	0.1%	11.2%	135	0.1%	10.9%
32	Arizona	3,164	1,819	0.9%	57.5%	134	0.1%	4.2%	893	1.0%	28.2%
33	New Mexico	1,933	898	0.5%	46.5%	94	0.1%	4.9%	738	0.8%	38.2%
34	Alaska	2,787	896	0.5%	32.1%	64	0.1%	2.3%	29	0.0%	1.0%
35	Rhode Island	465	399	0.2%	85.8%	32	0.0%	6.9%	29	0.0%	6.2%
36	Hawaii	552	134	0.1%	24.3%	22	0.0%	4.0%	33	0.0%	6.0%
37	Vermont	2,024	1,979	1.0%	97.8%	20	0.0%	1.0%	4	0.0%	0.2%
38	South Dakota	612	475	0.2%	77.6%	17	0.0%	2.8%	11	0.0%	1.8%
39	New Hampshire	1,292	1,249	0.6%	96.7%	14	0.0%	1.1%	16	0.0%	1.2%
40	Utah	2,690	777	0.4%	28.9%	13	0.0%	0.5%	99	0.1%	3.7%
41	Montana	483	378	0.2%	78.3%	4	0.0%	0.8%	9	0.0%	1.9%
42	Alabama	8,445	–	–	–	–	–	–	–	–	–
43	California	61,281	–	–	–	–	–	–	–	–	–
44	Idaho	1,389	–	–	–	–	–	–	–	–	–
45	Kentucky	15,732	–	–	–	–	–	–	–	–	–
46	Maine	1,036	–	–	–	–	–	–	–	–	–
47	Missouri	23,597	–	–	–	–	–	–	–	–	–
48	North Dakota	615	–	–	–	–	–	–	–	–	–
49	South Carolina	7,407	–	–	–	–	–	–	–	–	–
50	Tennessee	9,976	–	–	–	–	–	–	–	–	–
51	Wyoming	–	–	–	–	–	–	–	–	–	–
	Outlying Areas										
	American Samoa	1,663	–	–	–	–	–	–	–	–	–
	Guam	486	–	–	–	–	–	–	–	–	–
	Northern Marianas	421	–	–	–	–	–	–	–	–	–
	Puerto Rico	281	–	–	–	–	–	–	–	–	–
	Virgin Islands	–	–	–	–	–	–	–	–	–	–

Note: "–" indicates numbers not reported.
Source: Common Core of Data, 1993-94.

Asian American			American Indian			Unknown		
Number	% of Total	% of State	Number	% of Total	% of State	Number	% of Total	% of State
10,133	100.0%	1.8%	5,546	100.0%	1.0%	127,108	100.0%	22.8%
3,180	31.4%	2.6%	271	4.9%	0.2%	–	–	–
283	2.8%	0.8%	70	1.3%	0.2%	–	–	–
985	9.7%	2.3%	40	0.7%	0.1%	–	–	–
1,241	12.2%	3.9%	200	3.6%	0.6%	–	–	–
472	4.7%	2.6%	74	1.3%	0.4%	–	–	–
176	1.7%	1.4%	76	1.4%	0.6%	–	–	–
207	2.0%	1.8%	72	1.3%	0.6%	–4,101	–3.2%	–35.0%
54	0.5%	1.0%	0			–	–	–
106	1.0%	0.6%	90	1.6%	0.5%	–	–	–
900	8.9%	5.2%	205	3.7%	1.2%	–	–	–
28	0.3%	0.5%	7	0.1%	0.1%	–	–	–
373	3.7%	4.0%	47	0.8%	0.5%	–	–	–
95	0.9%	1.1%	124	2.2%	1.5%	–	–	–
29	0.3%	0.9%	14	0.3%	0.4%	–	–	–
152	1.5%	2.4%	2	0.0%	0.0%	–	–	–
7	0.1%	0.3%	4	0.1%	0.2%	–	–	–
16	0.2%	0.4%	4	0.1%	0.1%	–	–	–
61	0.6%	1.1%	1,116	20.1%	20.5%	–	–	–
50	0.5%	1.2%	4	0.1%	0.1%	–	–	–
424	4.2%	3.2%	19	0.3%	0.1%	–	–	–
201	2.0%	2.8%	104	1.9%	1.4%	–	–	–
10	0.1%	0.8%	0			–	–	–
105	1.0%	1.6%	161	2.9%	2.4%	–	–	–
78	0.8%	1.4%	47	0.8%	0.9%	–	–	–
184	1.8%	3.6%	212	3.8%	4.2%	–	–	–
69	0.7%	1.9%	58	1.0%	1.6%	–	–	–
37	0.4%	4.4%	15	0.3%	1.8%	–	–	–
18	0.2%	0.5%	2	0.0%	0.1%	–	–	–
3	0.0%	0.5%	0			–	–	–
18	0.2%	0.7%	20	0.4%	0.8%	–	–	–
28	0.3%	2.3%	39	0.7%	3.2%	–	–	–
39	0.4%	1.2%	279	5.0%	8.8%	–	–	–
10	0.1%	0.5%	193	3.5%	10.0%	–	–	–
40	0.4%	1.4%	1,758	31.7%	63.1%	–	–	–
5	0.0%	1.1%	0			–	–	–
361	3.6%	65.4%	2	0.0%	0.4%	–	–	–
18	0.2%	0.9%	3	0.1%	0.1%	–	–	–
4	0.0%	0.7%	105	1.9%	17.2%	–	–	–
11	0.1%	0.9%	2	0.0%	0.2%	–	–	–
52	0.5%	1.9%	18	0.3%	0.7%	1,731	1.4%	64.3%
3	0.0%	0.6%	89	1.6%	18.4%	–	–	–
–	–	–	–	–	–	8,445	6.6%	100.0%
–	–	–	–	–	–	61,281	48.2%	100.0%
–	–	–	–	–	–	1,389	1.1%	100.0%
–	–	–	–	–	–	15,732	12.4%	100.0%
–	–	–	–	–	–	1,036	0.8%	100.0%
–	–	–	–	–	–	23,597	18.6%	100.0%
–	–	–	–	–	–	615	0.5%	100.0%
–	–	–	–	–	–	7,407	5.8%	100.0%
–	–	–	–	–	–	9,976	7.8%	100.0%
–	–	–	–	–	–	–	–	–
1,663	–	100.0%	–	–	–	–	–	–
–	–	–	–	–	–	486	–	100.0%
421	–	100.0%	–	–	–	–	–	–
–	–	–	–	–	–	281	–	100.0%
–	–	–	–	–	–	–	–	–

- The highest numbers of African Americans enrolled in preschools sponsored by public schools lived in Texas (*n* = 23,122), Florida (*n* = 15,944), Illinois (*n* = 14,704), and New York (*n* = 9,461).

- African Americans comprised more than one-half of preschool enrollments in the District of Columbia (88.0%), Virginia (76.3%), Louisiana (64.1%), Michigan (64.0%), Mississippi (58.2%), and Georgia (52.3%).

Elementary and Secondary School Enrollment

The share of African Americans among students enrolled in America's public schools declined as grade level increased. African Americans comprised 16.4% of students enrolled in kindergarten through the 5th grade (see **Table 3**); 16.1% of students enrolled in grades 6 through 8 (see **Table 4**); and 15.3% of students enrolled in grades 9 through 12 (see **Table 5**). This decline suggests that African Americans may leave school at higher rates than their peers in other racial groups.

Comparing the data presented in **Tables 3, 4,** and 5 also shows that the distribution of African Americans among the 50 states appeared to shift as grade level increased. This finding suggests that the state-by-state distribution of African Americans among the 50 states is shifting, or that African Americans progress through public schools at different rates in different states, or both.

- **Table 3** shows that the highest numbers of African Americans in kindergarten through the 5th grade attended schools in Florida (*n* = 250,006), Texas (*n* = 243,077), New York (*n* = 235,118), Georgia (*n* = 223,845), and California (*n* = 221,774).

- **Table 4** shows that the highest numbers of African Americans in grades 6 through 8 attended schools in Texas (*n* = 120,917), Florida (*n* = 114,835), Georgia (n = 112,369), New York (n = 108,829), and California (n = 100,299).

- **Table 5** shows that the highest numbers of African Americans in grades 9 through 12 attended schools in New York (n = 146,512), Texas (n = 128,279), Florida (*n* = 124,128), California (*n* = 118,799), and Georgia (*n* = 118,081).

- In New York, African Americans represented 19.0% of all students in kindergarten through 5th grade (see **Table 3**), 18.8% of students in grades 6 to 8 (see **Table 4**), and 19.7% of students in grades 9 through 12 (see **Table 5**).

- In Florida, African Americans comprised 24.8% of students in kindergarten through 5th grade, 24.4% of students in grades 6 to 8, and 23.6% of students in grades 9 through 12.

High School Completions by State

In 1993/94 African Americans represented 12.5% of those students who received regular high school diplomas (see **Table 6**) and 11.8% of those who received any type of high school completion credential, such as a regular high school diploma, nonregular diploma, high school equivalency certificate, or other certificate of completion (see **Table 7**).

- **Table 6** shows that the largest numbers of African Americans who received regular high school diplomas in 1993/94 lived in Texas (*n* = 19,068), Georgia (*n* = 18,938), Ohio (*n* = 18,920), New York (*n* = 18,374), and Florida (*n* = 18,259).

- African Americans represented 90.7% of all those who received regular high school diplomas in the District of Columbia and 45.8% of those who received regular high school diplomas in Mississippi.

Enrollments by Region

In 1993/94, one-third (35.3%) of all elementary and secondary students were enrolled in schools located in the southern part of the United States.

- **Figure 2** shows that a higher share of African Americans than of all public elementary and secondary school students attended schools located in the south (56.2% versus 35.3%).

- **Table 8** shows that 8.6% of all African American elementary and secondary school students nationwide were enrolled in the western United States, compared to 19.7% of White students.

- African Americans represented 25.9% of public school enrollments in the south, 15.0% in the northeast, 13.2% in the midwest, 6.2% in the west, and 2.8% in outlying areas such as Puerto Rico, Guam, American Samoa, and Northern Marianas.

Enrollment by Urbanicity

Overall, 9.7% of all public schools and 13.3% of all public school students were located in large central cities in 1993/94. In contrast, 26.3% of all public schools, but only 16.5% of all public school students, were located in rural areas. This only suggests that, on average, schools located in large central cities had larger student bodies than schools located in rural areas.

- **Figure 3** shows that a higher proportion of African American than of all public elementary and secondary school students were enrolled in schools located in large central cities (30.2% versus 13.3%).

- **Table 9** shows that a smaller percentage of African Americans than Whites attended schools located in small towns (12.8% versus 25.1%) and in rural areas (8.8% versus 20.6%).

Enrollment in the Largest High Schools

Table 10 shows the number of African American students enrolled in the nation's 75 largest public high schools in 1993/94. Two-thirds of these schools were located in large central cities (49 of 75). The average African American enrollment representation in the 75 largest high schools was 18.9%, higher than the average African American enroll-

ment representation in grades 9 through 12 nationwide (15.3%).

- The percentage of African American students enrolled in the nation's 75 largest high schools ranged from a high of 93.1% at Brooklyn's Boys and Girls High school to a low of 0.6% at James Garfield Senior High in Los Angeles.

- The median percentage of African Americans enrolled in the 75 largest high schools was higher in large central cities (23.6%) than in the urban fringe of large central cities (2.5%).

School Type

Nearly all (98.3%) public school students attended regular elementary and secondary schools. Only 0.5% of all students attended special education schools, 0.4% attended vocational education schools, and 0.8% attended alternative or other schools.

Figure 4 shows that, relative to their representation among all public school enrollments (16.5%), African Americans were overrepresented in the nation's public special education schools, vocational schools, and alternative or other schools.

- African Americans represented 16.1% of all regular public school students, but 28.7% of students attending special education schools, 29.8% of students attending vocational schools, and 23.0% of students attending alternative or other schools.

- **Table 11** shows that 0.8% of African Americans and 0.3% of Whites attended vocational education schools.

- Only 1.1% of African Americans and 0.5% of White school students attended alternative or other schools.

PRIVATE SCHOOL ENROLLMENT

School Enrollment

In 1993/94, nearly 5 million students or about 10.0% of all students enrolled in elementary and

Table 3. Enrollment in Kindergarten Through 5th Grade by State and Race: Fall 1993

Rank	State	Total	White, Non-Hispanic			African American, Non-Hispanic			Hispanic		
			Number	% of Total	% of State	Number	% of Total	% of State	Number	% of Total	% of State
	Total (50 States+DC)	20,483,474	12,739,695	100.0%	62.2%	3,355,617	100.0%	16.4%	2,688,950	100.0%	13.1%
1	Florida	1,009,994	604,386	4.7%	59.8%	250,006	7.5%	24.8%	138,563	5.2%	13.7%
2	Texas	1,714,437	814,476	6.4%	47.5%	243,077	7.2%	14.2%	617,735	23.0%	36.0%
3	New York	1,234,751	734,126	5.8%	59.5%	235,118	7.0%	19.0%	203,978	7.6%	16.5%
4	Georgia	607,312	363,707	2.9%	59.9%	223,845	6.7%	36.9%	10,657	0.4%	1.8%
5	California	2,588,539	1,073,520	8.4%	41.5%	221,774	6.6%	8.6%	1,001,321	37.2%	38.7%
6	Illinois	850,312	548,231	4.3%	64.5%	174,765	5.2%	20.6%	102,179	3.8%	12.0%
7	Louisiana	367,810	189,236	1.5%	51.4%	168,480	5.0%	45.8%	3,928	0.1%	1.1%
8	North Carolina	538,063	354,147	2.8%	65.8%	161,099	4.8%	29.9%	8,616	0.3%	1.6%
9	Virginia	494,845	336,032	2.6%	67.9%	129,273	3.9%	26.1%	13,786	0.5%	2.8%
10	Ohio	840,219	691,429	5.4%	82.3%	128,748	3.8%	15.3%	11,201	0.4%	1.3%
11	South Carolina	303,198	171,398	1.3%	56.5%	127,457	3.8%	42.0%	1,872	0.1%	0.6%
12	Michigan	751,298	569,117	4.5%	75.8%	124,836	3.7%	16.6%	17,968	0.7%	2.4%
13	Maryland	371,020	222,250	1.7%	59.9%	124,176	3.7%	33.5%	10,532	0.4%	2.8%
14	Alabama	345,825	216,714	1.7%	62.7%	123,590	3.7%	35.7%	1,452	0.1%	0.4%
15	Mississippi	234,302	112,731	0.9%	48.1%	118,603	3.5%	50.6%	578	0.0%	0.2%
16	Pennsylvania	813,521	654,348	5.1%	80.4%	116,041	3.5%	14.3%	28,658	1.1%	3.5%
17	New Jersey	531,843	337,136	2.6%	63.4%	98,488	2.9%	18.5%	68,455	2.5%	12.9%
18	Tennessee	404,665	307,989	2.4%	76.1%	97,654	2.9%	24.1%	1,970	0.1%	0.5%
19	Missouri	402,703	330,053	2.6%	82.0%	64,677	1.9%	16.1%	3,513	0.1%	0.9%
20	Arkansas	206,147	152,962	1.2%	74.2%	49,179	1.5%	23.9%	2,110	0.1%	1.0%
21	Indiana	436,547	375,199	2.9%	85.9%	48,568	1.4%	11.1%	8,884	0.3%	2.0%
22	Wisconsin	383,909	318,168	2.5%	82.9%	37,845	1.1%	9.9%	11,940	0.4%	3.1%
23	Massachusetts	431,958	340,842	2.7%	78.9%	35,269	1.1%	8.2%	38,770	1.4%	9.0%
24	District of Columbia	38,363	1,940	0.0%	5.1%	33,554	1.0%	87.5%	2,395	0.1%	6.2%
25	Connecticut	244,564	179,726	1.4%	73.5%	31,174	0.9%	12.7%	27,415	1.0%	11.2%
26	Oklahoma	291,254	205,586	1.6%	70.6%	30,957	0.9%	10.6%	10,955	0.4%	3.8%
27	Washington	437,471	346,590	2.7%	79.2%	20,135	0.6%	4.6%	33,472	1.2%	7.7%
28	Kansas	215,427	178,325	1.4%	82.8%	18,817	0.6%	8.7%	12,386	0.5%	5.7%
29	Minnesota	379,003	332,591	2.6%	87.8%	17,798	0.5%	4.7%	6,679	0.2%	1.8%
30	Colorado	304,017	223,232	1.8%	73.4%	16,701	0.5%	5.5%	53,683	2.0%	17.7%
31	Arizona	352,478	206,987	1.6%	58.7%	15,121	0.5%	4.3%	100,403	3.7%	28.5%
32	Delaware	50,747	33,326	0.3%	65.7%	14,662	0.4%	28.9%	1,809	0.1%	3.6%
33	Nevada	118,051	82,099	0.6%	69.5%	10,892	0.3%	9.2%	18,315	0.7%	15.5%
34	Nebraska	131,380	114,578	0.9%	87.2%	8,056	0.2%	6.1%	5,246	0.2%	4.0%
35	Iowa	218,590	203,055	1.6%	92.9%	7,124	0.2%	3.3%	3,869	0.1%	1.8%
36	Oregon	243,451	209,597	1.6%	86.1%	6,037	0.2%	2.5%	16,043	0.6%	6.6%
37	West Virginia	133,107	126,739	1.0%	95.2%	5,393	0.2%	4.1%	336	0.0%	0.3%
38	Rhode Island	70,717	56,831	0.4%	80.4%	4,764	0.1%	6.7%	6,513	0.2%	9.2%
39	New Mexico	148,196	59,618	0.5%	40.2%	3,381	0.1%	2.3%	69,423	2.6%	46.8%
40	Alaska	61,985	39,997	0.3%	64.5%	3,169	0.1%	5.1%	1,546	0.1%	2.5%
41	Hawaii	89,691	23,220	0.2%	25.9%	2,730	0.1%	3.0%	4,322	0.2%	4.8%
42	New Hampshire	89,869	87,145	0.7%	97.0%	759	0.0%	0.8%	932	0.0%	1.0%
43	South Dakota	65,538	54,623	0.4%	83.3%	535	0.0%	0.8%	439	0.0%	0.7%
44	Wyoming	46,614	41,512	0.3%	89.1%	518	0.0%	1.1%	2,868	0.1%	6.2%
45	Montana	76,278	65,863	0.5%	86.3%	390	0.0%	0.5%	1,095	0.0%	1.4%
46	Vermont	49,506	48,318	0.4%	97.6%	382	0.0%	0.8%	140	0.0%	0.3%
47	Kentucky	290,512	–	–	–	–	–	–	–	–	–
48	Utah	207,884	–	–	–	–	–	–	–	–	–
49	Idaho	106,843	–	–	–	–	–	–	–	–	–
50	Maine	103,937	–	–	–	–	–	–	–	–	–
51	North Dakota	54,783	–	–	–	–	–	–	–	–	–
	Outlying Areas										
	Virgin Islands	10,533	129	0.0%	1.2%	8,732	0.3%	82.9%	1,619	0.1%	15.4%
	Puerto Rico	296,757	–	–	–	–	–	–	–	–	–
	Guam	16,011	–	–	–	–	–	–	–	–	–
	American Samoa	6,575	–	–	–	–	–	–	–	–	–
	Northern Marianas	4,101	–	–	–	–	–	–	–	–	–

Note: "–" indicates numbers not reported.
Source: Common Core of Data, 1993-94.

Asian American			American Indian			Unknown		
Number	% of Total	% of State	Number	% of Total	% of State	Number	% of Total	% of State
706,235	100.0%	3.4%	213,714	100.0%	1.0%	779,263	100.0%	3.8%
15,178	2.1%	1.5%	1,861	0.9%	0.2%	–	–	–
35,107	5.0%	2.0%	4,042	1.9%	0.2%	–	–	–
57,108	8.1%	4.6%	4,421	2.1%	0.4%	–	–	–
8,175	1.2%	1.3%	928	0.4%	0.2%	–	–	–
272,362	38.6%	10.5%	19,562	9.2%	0.8%	–	–	–
24,086	3.4%	2.8%	1,050	0.5%	0.1%	1	0.0%	0.0%
4,423	0.6%	1.2%	1,743	0.8%	0.5%	–	–	–
5,937	0.8%	1.1%	8,264	3.9%	1.5%	–	–	–
14,955	2.1%	3.0%	799	0.4%	0.2%	–	–	–
8,000	1.1%	1.0%	840	0.4%	0.1%	1	0.0%	0.0%
1,951	0.3%	0.6%	520	0.2%	0.2%	–	–	–
10,697	1.5%	1.4%	6,922	3.2%	0.9%	21,758	2.8%	2.9%
12,895	1.8%	3.5%	1,167	0.5%	0.3%	–	–	–
2,026	0.3%	0.6%	2,043	1.0%	0.6%	–	–	–
1,277	0.2%	0.5%	1,113	0.5%	0.5%	–	–	–
13,808	2.0%	1.7%	666	0.3%	0.1%	–	–	–
27,203	3.9%	5.1%	561	0.3%	0.1%	–	–	–
3,020	0.4%	0.7%	422	0.2%	0.1%	–6,390	–0.8%	–1.6%
3,622	0.5%	0.9%	838	0.4%	0.2%	–	–	–
1,283	0.2%	0.6%	613	0.3%	0.3%	–	–	–
3,355	0.5%	0.8%	541	0.3%	0.1%	–	–	–
10,841	1.5%	2.8%	5,115	2.4%	1.3%	–	–	–
16,416	2.3%	3.8%	661	0.3%	0.2%	–	–	–
469	0.1%	1.2%	5	0.0%	0.0%	–	–	–
5,843	0.8%	2.4%	406	0.2%	0.2%	–	–	–
3,290	0.5%	1.1%	40,466	18.9%	13.9%	–	–	–
25,893	3.7%	5.9%	11,381	5.3%	2.6%	–	–	–
3,893	0.6%	1.8%	2,006	0.9%	0.9%	–	–	–
14,568	2.1%	3.8%	7,564	3.5%	2.0%	–197	0.0%	–0.1%
7,136	1.0%	2.3%	3,265	1.5%	1.1%	–	–	–
5,237	0.7%	1.5%	24,730	11.6%	7.0%	–	–	–
854	0.1%	1.7%	96	0.0%	0.2%	–	–	–
4,285	0.6%	3.6%	2,460	1.2%	2.1%	–	–	–
1,523	0.2%	1.2%	1,977	0.9%	1.5%	–	–	–
3,651	0.5%	1.7%	891	0.4%	0.4%	–	–	–
7,214	1.0%	3.0%	4,560	2.1%	1.9%	–	–	–
555	0.1%	0.4%	84	0.0%	0.1%	–	–	–
2,350	0.3%	3.3%	259	0.1%	0.4%	–	–	–
1,277	0.2%	0.9%	14,366	6.7%	9.7%	131	0.0%	0.1%
2,543	0.4%	4.1%	14,730	6.9%	23.8%	–	–	–
59,127	8.4%	65.9%	292	0.1%	0.3%	–	–	–
848	0.1%	0.9%	185	0.1%	0.2%	–	–	–
478	0.1%	0.7%	9,463	4.4%	14.4%	–	–	–
351	0.0%	0.8%	1,365	0.6%	2.9%	–	–	–
687	0.1%	0.9%	8,243	3.9%	10.8%	–	–	–
438	0.1%	0.9%	228	0.1%	0.5%	–	–	–
–	–	–	–	–	–	290,512	37.3%	100.0%
–	–	–	–	–	–	207,884	26.7%	100.0%
–	–	–	–	–	–	106,843	13.7%	100.0%
–	–	–	–	–	–	103,937	13.3%	100.0%
–	–	–	–	–	–	54,783	7.0%	100.0%
59	0.0%	0.6%	19	0.0%	0.2%	–25	0.0%	–0.2%
–	–	–	–	–	–	296,757	38.1%	100.0%
–	–	–	–	–	–	16,011	2.1%	100.0%
6,575	0.9%	100.0%	–	–	–	–	–	–
3,896	0.6%	95.0%	–	–	–	145	0.0%	3.5%

Table 4. Enrollment in Grades 6 Through 8 by State and Race: Fall 1993

Rank	State	Total	White, Non-Hispanic			African American, Non-Hispanic			Hispanic		
			Number	% of Total	% of State	Number	% of Total	% of State	Number	% of Total	% of State
	Total (50 States+DC)	9,960,435	6,304,189	100.0%	63.3%	1,598,995	100.0%	16.1%	1,200,479	100.0%	12.1%
1	Texas	846,170	411,799	6.5%	48.7%	120,917	7.6%	14.3%	293,437	24.4%	34.7%
2	Florida	470,407	282,837	4.5%	60.1%	114,835	7.2%	24.4%	64,024	5.3%	13.6%
3	Georgia	297,579	176,610	2.8%	59.3%	112,369	7.0%	37.8%	4,160	0.3%	1.4%
4	New York	578,976	349,976	5.6%	60.4%	108,829	6.8%	18.8%	90,655	7.6%	15.7%
5	California	1,184,192	511,188	8.1%	43.2%	100,299	6.3%	8.5%	425,250	35.4%	35.9%
6	Illinois	409,082	267,805	4.2%	65.5%	83,407	5.2%	20.4%	44,803	3.7%	11.0%
7	North Carolina	260,753	172,683	2.7%	66.2%	78,041	4.9%	29.9%	3,065	0.3%	1.2%
8	Louisiana	178,358	95,727	1.5%	53.7%	77,595	4.9%	43.5%	1,961	0.2%	1.1%
9	Alabama	181,548	111,926	1.8%	61.7%	66,093	4.1%	36.4%	683	0.1%	0.4%
10	South Carolina	156,509	88,906	1.4%	56.8%	65,649	4.1%	41.9%	759	0.1%	0.5%
11	Ohio	428,245	354,640	5.6%	82.8%	63,363	4.0%	14.8%	5,761	0.5%	1.3%
12	Mississippi	122,714	59,085	0.9%	48.1%	61,877	3.9%	50.4%	739	0.1%	0.6%
13	Virginia	239,828	164,053	2.6%	68.4%	61,386	3.8%	25.6%	6,006	0.5%	2.5%
14	Maryland	173,819	102,023	1.6%	58.7%	60,301	3.8%	34.7%	4,569	0.4%	2.6%
15	Michigan	355,116	277,700	4.4%	78.2%	56,661	3.5%	16.0%	7,992	0.7%	2.3%
16	Pennsylvania	397,592	328,609	5.2%	82.6%	49,561	3.1%	12.5%	12,162	1.0%	3.1%
17	Tennessee	198,376	151,602	2.4%	76.4%	46,349	2.9%	23.4%	847	0.1%	0.4%
18	New Jersey	244,116	156,036	2.5%	63.9%	43,235	2.7%	17.7%	31,256	2.6%	12.8%
19	Missouri	198,988	165,679	2.6%	83.3%	29,472	1.8%	14.8%	1,646	0.1%	0.8%
20	Indiana	233,450	200,603	3.2%	85.9%	25,996	1.6%	11.1%	4,857	0.4%	2.1%
21	Arkansas	108,470	80,571	1.3%	74.3%	25,957	1.6%	23.9%	897	0.1%	0.8%
22	Wisconsin	194,538	165,178	2.6%	84.9%	17,104	1.1%	8.8%	5,503	0.5%	2.8%
23	Massachusetts	193,386	154,063	2.4%	79.7%	14,809	0.9%	7.7%	16,976	1.4%	8.8%
24	Oklahoma	143,158	102,977	1.6%	71.9%	14,228	0.9%	9.9%	4,413	0.4%	3.1%
25	District of Columbia	15,540	518	0.0%	3.3%	13,914	0.9%	89.5%	901	0.1%	5.8%
26	Connecticut	107,796	79,835	1.3%	74.1%	13,441	0.8%	12.5%	11,708	1.0%	10.9%
27	Washington	217,866	175,152	2.8%	80.4%	9,493	0.6%	4.4%	14,197	1.2%	6.5%
28	Kansas	109,487	91,682	1.5%	83.7%	9,227	0.6%	8.4%	5,537	0.5%	5.1%
29	Colorado	147,452	109,912	1.7%	74.5%	7,778	0.5%	5.3%	24,900	2.1%	16.9%
30	Minnesota	191,321	170,711	2.7%	89.2%	7,638	0.5%	4.0%	3,158	0.3%	1.7%
31	Delaware	25,305	16,771	0.3%	66.3%	7,262	0.5%	28.7%	814	0.1%	3.2%
32	Arizona	166,576	100,745	1.6%	60.5%	6,815	0.4%	4.1%	45,337	3.8%	27.2%
33	Nevada	55,040	39,312	0.6%	71.4%	4,999	0.3%	9.1%	7,426	0.6%	13.5%
34	Nebraska	68,469	60,691	1.0%	88.6%	3,853	0.2%	5.6%	2,368	0.2%	3.5%
35	Iowa	115,153	108,263	1.7%	94.0%	3,271	0.2%	2.8%	1,656	0.1%	1.4%
36	West Virginia	75,983	72,662	1.2%	95.6%	2,881	0.2%	3.8%	96	0.0%	0.1%
37	Oregon	122,037	106,532	1.7%	87.3%	2,768	0.2%	2.3%	6,643	0.6%	5.4%
38	Rhode Island	32,886	26,940	0.4%	81.9%	2,041	0.1%	6.2%	2,666	0.2%	8.1%
39	New Mexico	76,158	30,950	0.5%	40.6%	1,706	0.1%	2.2%	35,028	2.9%	46.0%
40	Alaska	28,829	19,378	0.3%	67.2%	1,416	0.1%	4.9%	695	0.1%	2.4%
41	Hawaii	41,360	9,506	0.2%	23.0%	1,027	0.1%	2.5%	2,129	0.2%	5.1%
42	New Hampshire	44,498	43,218	0.7%	97.1%	333	0.0%	0.7%	409	0.0%	0.9%
43	Montana	39,231	34,539	0.5%	88.0%	227	0.0%	0.6%	518	0.0%	1.3%
44	Wyoming	24,788	22,088	0.4%	89.1%	227	0.0%	0.9%	1,631	0.1%	6.6%
45	South Dakota	34,516	29,754	0.5%	86.2%	192	0.0%	0.6%	185	0.0%	0.5%
46	Vermont	23,298	22,754	0.4%	97.7%	153	0.0%	0.7%	56	0.0%	0.2%
47	Kentucky	152,322	–	–	–	–	–	–	–	–	–
48	Utah	113,396	–	–	–	–	–	–	–	–	–
49	Idaho	57,985	–	–	–	–	–	–	–	–	–
50	Maine	49,044	–	–	–	–	–	–	–	–	–
51	North Dakota	28,729	–	–	–	–	–	–	–	–	–
	Outlying Areas										
	Virgin Islands	5,403	32	0.0%	0.6%	4,689	0.3%	86.8%	704	0.1%	13.0%
	Puerto Rico	158,315	–	–	–	–	–	–	–	–	–
	Guam	6,654	–	–	–	–	–	–	–	–	–
	American Samoa	2,736	–	–	–	–	–	–	–	–	–
	Northern Marianas	1,858	25	0.0%	1.3%	–	–	–	–	–	–

Note: " –" indicates numbers not reported.
Source: Common Core of Data, 1993-94.

Asian American			American Indian			Unknown		
Number	% of Total	% of State	Number	% of Total	% of State	Number	% of Total	% of State
348,624	100.0%	3.5%	104,369	100.0%	1.0%	403,779	100.0%	4.1%
18,218	5.2%	2.2%	1,799	1.7%	0.2%	–	–	–
7,919	2.3%	1.7%	792	0.8%	0.2%	–	–	–
4,066	1.2%	1.4%	374	0.4%	0.1%	–	–	–
27,457	7.9%	4.7%	2,059	2.0%	0.4%	–	–	–
137,395	39.4%	11.6%	10,060	9.6%	0.8%	–	–	–
12,416	3.6%	3.0%	651	0.6%	0.2%	–	–	–
2,923	0.8%	1.1%	4,041	3.9%	1.5%	–	–	–
2,251	0.6%	1.3%	824	0.8%	0.5%	–	–	–
1,006	0.3%	0.6%	1,840	1.8%	1.0%	–	–	–
971	0.3%	0.6%	224	0.2%	0.1%	–	–	–
4,053	1.2%	0.9%	428	0.4%	0.1%	–	–	–
561	0.2%	0.5%	452	0.4%	0.4%	–	–	–
8,022	2.3%	3.3%	361	0.3%	0.2%	–	–	–
6,436	1.8%	3.7%	490	0.5%	0.3%	–	–	–
4,588	1.3%	1.3%	3,860	3.7%	1.1%	4,315	1.1%	1.2%
6,803	2.0%	1.7%	457	0.4%	0.1%	–	–	–
1,422	0.4%	0.7%	192	0.2%	0.1%	–2,036	–0.5%	–1.0%
13,198	3.8%	5.4%	391	0.4%	0.2%	–	–	–
1,773	0.5%	0.9%	418	0.4%	0.2%	–	–	–
1,634	0.5%	0.7%	360	0.3%	0.2%	–	–	–
699	0.2%	0.6%	346	0.3%	0.3%	–	–	–
4,105	1.2%	2.1%	2,648	2.5%	1.4%	–	–	–
7,139	2.0%	3.7%	399	0.4%	0.2%	–	–	–
1,643	0.5%	1.1%	19,897	19.1%	13.9%	–	–	–
199	0.1%	1.3%	8	0.0%	0.1%	–	–	–
2,504	0.7%	2.3%	308	0.3%	0.3%	–	–	–
13,355	3.8%	6.1%	5,669	5.4%	2.6%	–	–	–
1,892	0.5%	1.7%	1,149	1.1%	1.0%	–	–	–
3,492	1.0%	2.4%	1,370	1.3%	0.9%	–	–	–
6,321	1.8%	3.3%	3,562	3.4%	1.9%	–69	0.0%	0.0%
419	0.1%	1.7%	39	0.0%	0.2%	–	–	–
2,563	0.7%	1.5%	11,116	10.7%	6.7%	–	–	–
2,236	0.6%	4.1%	1,067	1.0%	1.9%	–	–	–
723	0.2%	1.1%	834	0.8%	1.2%	–	–	–
1,553	0.4%	1.3%	410	0.4%	0.4%	–	–	–
268	0.1%	0.4%	76	0.1%	0.1%	–	–	–
3,715	1.1%	3.0%	2,379	2.3%	1.9%	–	–	–
1,111	0.3%	3.4%	128	0.1%	0.4%	–	–	–
664	0.2%	0.9%	7,717	7.4%	10.1%	93	0.0%	0.1%
1,126	0.3%	3.9%	6,214	6.0%	21.6%	–	–	–
28,557	8.2%	69.0%	141	0.1%	0.3%	–	–	–
424	0.1%	1.0%	114	0.1%	0.3%	–	–	–
262	0.1%	0.7%	3,685	3.5%	9.4%	–	–	–
157	0.0%	0.6%	685	0.7%	2.8%	–	–	–
223	0.1%	0.6%	4,162	4.0%	12.1%	–	–	–
162	0.0%	0.7%	173	0.2%	0.7%	–	–	–
–	–	–	–	–	–	152,322	37.7%	100.0%
–	–	–	–	–	–	113,396	28.1%	100.0%
–	–	–	–	–	–	57,985	14.4%	100.0%
–	–	–	–	–	–	49,044	12.1%	100.0%
–	–	–	–	–	–	28,729	7.1%	100.0%
26	0.0%	0.5%	2	0.0%	0.0%	–50	0.0%	–0.9%
–	–	–	–	–	–	158,315	39.2%	100.0%
–	–	–	–	–	–	6,654	1.6%	100.0%
2,736	0.8%	100.0%	–	–	–	–	–	–
1,645	0.5%	88.5%	–	–	–	188	0.0%	10.1%

Table 5. Enrollment in Grades 9 Through 12 by State and Race: Fall 1993

Rank	State	Total	White, Non-Hispanic			African American, Non-Hispanic			Hispanic		
			Number	% of Total	% of State	Number	% of Total	% of State	Number	% of Total	% of State
	Total (50 States+DC)	11,712,615	7,519,311	100.0%	64.2%	1,796,382	100.0%	15.3%	1,341,333	100.0%	11.5%
1	New York	743,933	437,351	5.8%	58.8%	146,512	8.2%	19.7%	115,509	8.6%	15.5%
2	Texas	927,209	464,660	6.2%	50.1%	128,279	7.1%	13.8%	308,339	23.0%	33.3%
3	Florida	525,569	313,817	4.2%	59.7%	124,128	6.9%	23.6%	75,658	5.6%	14.4%
4	California	1,393,530	603,296	8.0%	43.3%	118,799	6.6%	8.5%	485,593	36.2%	34.8%
5	Georgia	324,879	196,982	2.6%	60.6%	118,081	6.6%	36.3%	4,081	0.3%	1.3%
6	Illinois	503,024	340,120	4.5%	67.6%	96,252	5.4%	19.1%	48,965	3.7%	9.7%
7	North Carolina	305,060	202,451	2.7%	66.4%	91,246	5.1%	29.9%	2,661	0.2%	0.9%
8	Louisiana	202,283	110,703	1.5%	54.7%	84,674	4.7%	41.9%	2,891	0.2%	1.4%
9	South Carolina	176,745	102,534	1.4%	58.0%	71,641	4.0%	40.5%	862	0.1%	0.5%
10	Alabama	198,651	124,628	1.7%	62.7%	70,017	3.9%	35.2%	646	0.0%	0.3%
11	Ohio	517,122	435,408	5.8%	84.2%	68,878	3.8%	13.3%	7,056	0.5%	1.4%
12	Maryland	197,072	116,423	1.5%	59.1%	65,707	3.7%	33.3%	5,886	0.4%	3.0%
13	Michigan	423,081	337,047	4.5%	79.7%	65,304	3.6%	15.4%	9,194	0.7%	2.2%
14	Mississippi	131,112	64,794	0.9%	49.4%	64,860	3.6%	49.5%	227	0.0%	0.2%
15	Virginia	278,009	194,574	2.6%	70.0%	64,010	3.6%	23.0%	7,795	0.6%	2.8%
16	Pennsylvania	496,382	409,716	5.4%	82.5%	62,929	3.5%	12.7%	13,879	1.0%	2.8%
17	Tennessee	236,542	184,878	2.5%	78.2%	50,713	2.8%	21.4%	1,004	0.1%	0.4%
18	New Jersey	288,263	191,207	2.5%	66.3%	47,433	2.6%	16.5%	32,760	2.4%	11.4%
19	Missouri	241,874	201,822	2.7%	83.4%	35,055	2.0%	14.5%	2,067	0.2%	0.9%
20	Indiana	282,214	243,831	3.2%	86.4%	29,697	1.7%	10.5%	5,831	0.4%	2.1%
21	Arkansas	125,801	94,521	1.3%	75.1%	28,953	1.6%	23.0%	912	0.1%	0.7%
22	Massachusetts	232,208	185,479	2.5%	79.9%	19,221	1.1%	8.3%	18,706	1.4%	8.1%
23	Wisconsin	248,284	217,536	2.9%	87.6%	17,112	1.0%	6.9%	6,234	0.5%	2.5%
24	Connecticut	127,655	95,616	1.3%	74.9%	15,920	0.9%	12.5%	12,450	0.9%	9.8%
25	District of Columbia	17,854	444	0.0%	2.5%	15,876	0.9%	88.9%	1,216	0.1%	6.8%
26	Oklahoma	162,511	119,491	1.6%	73.5%	15,563	0.9%	9.6%	4,438	0.3%	2.7%
27	Washington	255,528	206,768	2.7%	80.9%	10,527	0.6%	4.1%	15,110	1.1%	5.9%
28	Kansas	127,081	107,829	1.4%	84.9%	9,486	0.5%	7.5%	5,910	0.4%	4.7%
29	Colorado	164,260	124,626	1.7%	75.9%	8,279	0.5%	5.0%	25,533	1.9%	15.5%
30	Minnesota	233,253	210,642	2.8%	90.3%	7,991	0.4%	3.4%	3,496	0.3%	1.5%
31	Delaware	28,930	19,480	0.3%	67.3%	7,901	0.4%	27.3%	954	0.1%	3.3%
32	Arizona	182,737	111,861	1.5%	61.2%	7,182	0.4%	3.9%	47,451	3.5%	26.0%
33	Nevada	60,727	43,412	0.6%	71.5%	5,556	0.3%	9.1%	7,771	0.6%	12.8%
34	Nebraska	81,671	73,498	1.0%	90.0%	3,992	0.2%	4.9%	2,400	0.2%	2.9%
35	Iowa	142,601	134,318	1.8%	94.2%	3,583	0.2%	2.5%	2,026	0.2%	1.4%
36	West Virginia	96,264	92,028	1.2%	95.6%	3,570	0.2%	3.7%	191	0.0%	0.2%
37	Oregon	147,819	129,275	1.7%	87.5%	3,235	0.2%	2.2%	7,408	0.6%	5.0%
38	Rhode Island	38,470	32,002	0.4%	83.2%	2,512	0.1%	6.5%	2,813	0.2%	7.3%
39	New Mexico	87,768	35,418	0.5%	40.4%	2,028	0.1%	2.3%	38,774	2.9%	44.2%
40	Alaska	32,347	21,856	0.3%	67.6%	1,504	0.1%	4.6%	799	0.1%	2.5%
41	Hawaii	48,728	9,817	0.1%	20.1%	949	0.1%	1.9%	2,590	0.2%	5.3%
42	New Hampshire	49,098	47,471	0.6%	96.7%	425	0.0%	0.9%	534	0.0%	1.1%
43	Wyoming	29,497	26,602	0.4%	90.2%	263	0.0%	0.9%	1,743	0.1%	5.9%
44	South Dakota	39,971	34,950	0.5%	87.4%	212	0.0%	0.5%	244	0.0%	0.6%
45	Montana	46,111	41,525	0.6%	90.1%	164	0.0%	0.4%	609	0.0%	1.3%
46	Vermont	27,377	26,604	0.4%	97.2%	163	0.0%	0.6%	117	0.0%	0.4%
47	Kentucky	184,356	–	–	–	–	–	–	–	–	–
48	Utah	137,235	–	–	–	–	–	–	–	–	–
49	Idaho	69,287	–	–	–	–	–	–	–	–	–
50	Maine	59,632	–	–	–	–	–	–	–	–	–
51	North Dakota	35,000	–	–	–	–	–	–	–	–	–
	Outlying Areas										
	Virgin Islands	5,508	21	0.0%	0.4%	5,128	0.3%	93.1%	481	0.0%	8.7%
	Puerto Rico	162,371	–	–	–	–	–	–	–	–	–
	Guam	7,752	–	–	–	–	–	–	–	–	–
	American Samoa	3,451	–	–	–	–	–	–	–	–	–
	Northern Marianas	1,808	15	0.0%	0.8%	–	–	–	–	–	–

Note: "–" indicates numbers not reported.
Source: Common Core of Data, 1993-94.

Asian American			American Indian			Unknown		
Number	% of Total	% of State	Number	% of Total	% of State	Number	% of Total	% of State
451,927	100.0%	3.9%	118,145	100.0%	1.0%	485,517	100.0%	4.1%
41,993	9.3%	5.6%	2,568	2.2%	0.3%	–	–	–
23,893	5.3%	2.6%	2,041	1.7%	0.2%	–3	0.0%	0.0%
10,951	2.4%	2.1%	1,015	0.9%	0.2%	–	–	–
173,013	38.3%	12.4%	12,829	10.9%	0.9%	–	–	–
5,162	1.1%	1.6%	573	0.5%	0.2%	–	–	–
16,778	3.7%	3.3%	909	0.8%	0.2%	–	–	–
3,750	0.8%	1.2%	4,952	4.2%	1.6%	–	–	–
3,084	0.7%	1.5%	931	0.8%	0.5%	–	–	–
1,445	0.3%	0.8%	263	0.2%	0.1%	–	–	–
1,288	0.3%	0.6%	2,023	1.7%	1.0%	49	0.0%	0.0%
5,205	1.2%	1.0%	575	0.5%	0.1%	–	–	–
8,608	1.9%	4.4%	448	0.4%	0.2%	–	–	–
5,748	1.3%	1.4%	4,466	3.8%	1.1%	1,322	0.3%	0.3%
743	0.2%	0.6%	488	0.4%	0.4%	–	–	–
11,199	2.5%	4.0%	431	0.4%	0.2%	–	–	–
9,332	2.1%	1.9%	526	0.4%	0.1%	–	–	–
1,798	0.4%	0.8%	255	0.2%	0.1%	–2,106	–0.4%	–0.9%
16,477	3.6%	5.7%	386	0.3%	0.1%	–	–	–
2,470	0.5%	1.0%	460	0.4%	0.2%	–	–	–
2,310	0.5%	0.8%	545	0.5%	0.2%	–	–	–
954	0.2%	0.8%	461	0.4%	0.4%	–	–	–
8,370	1.9%	3.6%	432	0.4%	0.2%	–	–	–
4,336	1.0%	1.7%	3,066	2.6%	1.2%	–	–	–
3,206	0.7%	2.5%	463	0.4%	0.4%	–	–	–
317	0.1%	1.8%	1	0.0%	0.0%	–	–	–
2,198	0.5%	1.4%	20,821	17.6%	12.8%	–	–	–
16,995	3.8%	6.7%	6,128	5.2%	2.4%	–	–	–
2,497	0.6%	2.0%	1,359	1.2%	1.1%	–	–	–
4,389	1.0%	2.7%	1,433	1.2%	0.9%	–	–	–
7,412	1.6%	3.2%	3,738	3.2%	1.6%	–26	0.0%	0.0%
501	0.1%	1.7%	94	0.1%	0.3%	–	–	–
3,506	0.8%	1.9%	12,737	10.8%	7.0%	–	–	–
2,915	0.6%	4.8%	1,073	0.9%	1.8%	–	–	–
1,040	0.2%	1.3%	741	0.6%	0.9%	–	–	–
2,200	0.5%	1.5%	474	0.4%	0.3%	–	–	–
390	0.1%	0.4%	85	0.1%	0.1%	–	–	–
5,114	1.1%	3.5%	2,787	2.4%	1.9%	–	–	–
990	0.2%	2.6%	153	0.1%	0.4%	–	–	–
1,051	0.2%	1.2%	9,726	8.2%	11.1%	771	0.2%	0.9%
1,435	0.3%	4.4%	6,753	5.7%	20.9%	–	–	–
35,218	7.8%	72.3%	154	0.1%	0.3%	–	–	–
532	0.1%	1.1%	136	0.1%	0.3%	–	–	–
228	0.1%	0.8%	661	0.6%	2.2%	–	–	–
295	0.1%	0.7%	4,270	3.6%	10.7%	–	–	–
326	0.1%	0.7%	3,487	3.0%	7.6%	–	–	–
265	0.1%	1.0%	228	0.2%	0.8%	–	–	–
–	–	–	–	–	–	184,356	38.0%	100.0%
–	–	–	–	–	–	137,235	28.3%	100.0%
–	–	–	–	–	–	69,287	14.3%	100.0%
–	–	–	–	–	–	59,632	12.3%	100.0%
–	–	–	–	–	–	35,000	7.2%	100.0%
7	0.0%	0.1%	1	0.0%	0.0%	–130	0.0%	–2.4%
–	–	–	–	–	–	162,371	33.4%	100.0%
–	–	–	–	–	–	7,752	1.6%	100.0%
3,451	0.8%	100.0%	–	–	–	–	–	–
1,668	0.4%	92.3%	–	–	–	125	0.0%	6.9%

Table 6. Number and Percentage of Individuals Who Received Regular High School Diplomas in Each State by Race in 1993/94

Rank	State	Total	White, Non-Hispanic			African American, Non-Hispanic			Hispanic		
			Number	% of Total	% of State	Number	% of Total	% of State	Number	% of Total	% of State
	Total (50 States+DC)	2,233,723	1,501,386	100.0%	67.2%	278,476	100.0%	12.5%	196,413	100.0%	8.8%
1	Texas	160,546	91,241	6.1%	56.8%	19,068	6.8%	11.9%	45,513	23.2%	28.3%
2	Georgia	57,602	37,078	2.5%	64.4%	18,938	6.8%	32.9%	541	0.3%	0.9%
3	Ohio	109,200	94,926	6.3%	86.9%	18,920	6.8%	17.3%	1,384	0.7%	1.3%
4	New York	132,963	94,378	6.3%	71.0%	18,374	6.6%	13.8%	12,108	6.2%	9.1%
5	Florida	89,428	56,934	3.8%	63.7%	18,259	6.6%	20.4%	11,812	6.0%	13.2%
6	California	249,320	120,853	8.0%	48.5%	18,219	6.5%	7.3%	71,466	36.4%	28.7%
7	North Carolina	60,460	41,543	2.8%	68.7%	16,960	6.1%	28.1%	391	0.2%	0.6%
8	Illinois	103,628	75,916	5.1%	73.3%	16,045	5.8%	15.5%	7,782	4.0%	7.5%
9	Louisiana	33,682	20,461	1.4%	60.7%	12,134	4.4%	36.0%	403	0.2%	1.2%
10	Virginia	56,948	41,142	2.7%	72.2%	11,874	4.3%	20.9%	1,224	0.6%	2.1%
11	Michigan	85,302	70,030	4.7%	82.1%	11,260	4.0%	13.2%	1,702	0.9%	2.0%
12	Maryland	39,523	25,380	1.7%	64.2%	10,997	3.9%	27.8%	1,002	0.5%	2.5%
13	Mississippi	23,597	12,546	0.8%	53.2%	10,816	3.9%	45.8%	47	0.0%	0.2%
14	Alabama	36,007	24,724	1.6%	68.7%	10,599	3.8%	29.4%	85	0.0%	0.2%
15	Pennsylvania	103,715	89,881	6.0%	86.7%	9,794	3.5%	9.4%	1,785	0.9%	1.7%
16	New Jersey	67,134	47,229	3.1%	70.4%	9,705	3.5%	14.5%	6,515	3.3%	9.7%
17	Tennessee	44,166	33,607	2.2%	76.1%	7,818	2.8%	17.7%	145	0.1%	0.3%
18	Arkansas	25,655	19,509	1.3%	76.0%	5,695	2.0%	22.2%	149	0.1%	0.6%
19	Missouri	46,864	40,459	2.7%	86.3%	5,308	1.9%	11.3%	411	0.2%	0.9%
20	Indiana	57,559	51,072	3.4%	88.7%	4,786	1.7%	8.3%	1,076	0.5%	1.9%
21	Connecticut	26,799	21,452	1.4%	80.0%	2,860	1.0%	10.7%	1,755	0.9%	6.5%
22	District of Columbia	3,136	75	0.0%	2.4%	2,845	1.0%	90.7%	170	0.1%	5.4%
23	Massachusetts	48,321	40,316	2.7%	83.4%	2,559	0.9%	5.3%	3,274	1.7%	6.8%
24	Oklahoma	30,542	23,253	1.5%	76.1%	2,468	0.9%	8.1%	761	0.4%	2.5%
25	Wisconsin	50,027	45,698	3.0%	91.3%	2,055	0.7%	4.1%	898	0.5%	1.8%
26	Kansas	24,720	21,697	1.4%	87.8%	1,368	0.5%	5.5%	931	0.5%	3.8%
27	Colorado	31,839	25,085	1.7%	78.8%	1,356	0.5%	4.3%	4,247	2.2%	13.3%
28	Delaware	5,492	4,050	0.3%	73.7%	1,181	0.4%	21.5%	135	0.1%	2.5%
29	Arizona	31,747	20,801	1.4%	65.5%	1,125	0.4%	3.5%	7,035	3.6%	22.2%
30	Minnesota	48,002	44,383	3.0%	92.5%	912	0.3%	1.9%	643	0.3%	1.3%
31	West Virginia	20,228	19,429	1.3%	96.1%	644	0.2%	3.2%	54	0.0%	0.3%
32	Nebraska	17,569	16,189	1.1%	92.1%	631	0.2%	3.6%	411	0.2%	2.3%
33	Nevada	9,042	6,998	0.5%	77.4%	629	0.2%	7.0%	833	0.4%	9.2%
34	Iowa	30,677	29,306	2.0%	95.5%	529	0.2%	1.7%	342	0.2%	1.1%
35	Oregon	26,301	23,577	1.6%	89.6%	448	0.2%	1.7%	915	0.5%	3.5%
36	Rhode Island	7,640	6,580	0.4%	86.1%	439	0.2%	5.7%	387	0.2%	5.1%
37	New Mexico	15,172	6,801	0.5%	44.8%	310	0.1%	2.0%	6,257	3.2%	41.2%
38	Alaska	5,535	3,921	0.3%	70.8%	204	0.1%	3.7%	119	0.1%	2.1%
39	Hawaii	8,854	1,718	0.1%	19.4%	122	0.0%	1.4%	484	0.2%	5.5%
40	Utah	24,197	22,677	1.5%	93.7%	86	0.0%	0.4%	685	0.3%	2.8%
41	North Dakota	7,310	6,901	0.5%	94.4%	39	0.0%	0.5%	41	0.0%	0.6%
42	Wyoming	6,174	5,653	0.4%	91.6%	38	0.0%	0.6%	335	0.2%	5.4%
43	South Dakota	7,952	7,280	0.5%	91.5%	35	0.0%	0.4%	38	0.0%	0.5%
44	Montana	9,389	8,637	0.6%	92.0%	24	0.0%	0.3%	122	0.1%	1.3%
45	Washington	45,262	–	–	–	–	–	–	–	–	–
46	Kentucky	36,361	–	–	–	–	–	–	–	–	–
47	South Carolina	31,297	–	–	–	–	–	–	–	–	–
48	Idaho	12,974	–	–	–	–	–	–	–	–	–
49	Maine	12,103	–	–	–	–	–	–	–	–	–
50	New Hampshire	10,065	–	–	–	–	–	–	–	–	–
51	Vermont	5,697	–	–	–	–	–	–	–	–	–
	Outlying Areas										
	Puerto Rico	29,064	–	–	–	–	–	–	–	–	–
	Virgin Islands	927	–	–	–	–	–	–	–	–	–
	Guam	912	–	–	–	–	–	–	–	–	–
	American Samoa	712	–	–	–	–	–	–	–	–	–
	Northern Marianas	245	–	–	–	–	–	–	–	–	–

Notes: Numbers do not include individuals who earned nonregular diplomas, high school equivalency certificates, or other certificates of completion.
"–" indicates numbers not reported.
Source: Common Core of Data, 1993-94.

Asian American			American Indian			Unknown		
Number	% of Total	% of State	Number	% of Total	% of State	Number	% of Total	% of State
90,531	100.0%	4.1%	18,475	100.0%	0.8%	148,442	100.0%	6.6%
4,401	4.9%	2.7%	323	1.7%	0.2%	–	–	–
962	1.1%	1.7%	83	0.4%	0.1%	–	–	–
1,301	1.4%	1.2%	112	0.6%	0.1%	–7,443	–5.0%	–6.8%
7,746	8.6%	5.8%	357	1.9%	0.3%	–	–	–
2,266	2.5%	2.5%	157	0.8%	0.2%	–	–	–
36,644	40.5%	14.7%	2,138	11.6%	0.9%	–	–	–
782	0.9%	1.3%	784	4.2%	1.3%	–	–	–
3,746	4.1%	3.6%	139	0.8%	0.1%	–	–	–
548	0.6%	1.6%	136	0.7%	0.4%	–	–	–
2,627	2.9%	4.6%	81	0.4%	0.1%	–	–	–
1,451	1.6%	1.7%	859	4.6%	1.0%	–	–	–
2,053	2.3%	5.2%	91	0.5%	0.2%	–	–	–
136	0.2%	0.6%	52	0.3%	0.2%	–	–	–
216	0.2%	0.6%	383	2.1%	1.1%	–	–	–
2,171	2.4%	2.1%	84	0.5%	0.1%	–	–	–
3,617	4.0%	5.4%	68	0.4%	0.1%	–	–	–
410	0.5%	0.9%	25	0.1%	0.1%	2,161	1.5%	4.9%
229	0.3%	0.9%	73	0.4%	0.3%	–	–	–
606	0.7%	1.3%	80	0.4%	0.2%	–	–	–
557	0.6%	1.0%	68	0.4%	0.1%	–	–	–
687	0.8%	2.6%	45	0.2%	0.2%	–	–	–
46	0.1%	1.5%	–	–	–	–	–	–
1,848	2.0%	3.8%	324	1.8%	0.7%	–	–	–
478	0.5%	1.6%	3,582	19.4%	11.7%	–	–	–
904	1.0%	1.8%	472	2.6%	0.9%	–	–	–
526	0.6%	2.1%	198	1.1%	0.8%	–	–	–
926	1.0%	2.9%	225	1.2%	0.7%	–	–	–
123	0.1%	2.2%	3	0.0%	0.1%	–	–	–
725	0.8%	2.3%	2,061	11.2%	6.5%	–	–	–
1,602	1.8%	3.3%	497	2.7%	1.0%	–35	0.0%	–0.1%
93	0.1%	0.5%	8	0.0%	0.0%	–	–	–
244	0.3%	1.4%	94	0.5%	0.5%	–	–	–
462	0.5%	5.1%	120	0.6%	1.3%	–	–	–
455	0.5%	1.5%	45	0.2%	0.1%	–	–	–
998	1.1%	3.8%	363	2.0%	1.4%	–	–	–
211	0.2%	2.8%	23	0.1%	0.3%	–	–	–
194	0.2%	1.3%	1,610	8.7%	10.6%	–	–	–
274	0.3%	5.0%	1,017	5.5%	18.4%	–	–	–
6,501	7.2%	73.4%	29	0.2%	0.3%	–	–	–
512	0.6%	2.1%	237	1.3%	1.0%	–	–	–
58	0.1%	0.8%	271	1.5%	3.7%	–	–	–
48	0.1%	0.8%	100	0.5%	1.6%	–	–	–
68	0.1%	0.9%	531	2.9%	6.7%	–	–	–
79	0.1%	0.8%	527	2.9%	5.6%	–	–	–
–	–	–	–	–	–	45,262	30.5%	100.0%
–	–	–	–	–	–	36,361	24.5%	100.0%
–	–	–	–	–	–	31,297	21.1%	100.0%
–	–	–	–	–	–	12,974	8.7%	100.0%
–	–	–	–	–	–	12,103	8.2%	100.0%
–	–	–	–	–	–	10,065	6.8%	100.0%
–	–	–	–	–	–	5,697	3.8%	100.0%
–	–	–	–	–	–	29,064	19.6%	100.0%
–	–	–	–	–	–	927	0.6%	100.0%
–	–	–	–	–	–	912	0.6%	100.0%
712	0.8%	100.0%	–	–	–	–	–	–
216	0.2%	88.2%	–	–	–	29	0.0%	11.8%

Table 7. Number and Percentage of Individuals Who Completed High School in Each State by Race in 1993/94

Rank	State	Total	White, Non-Hispanic			African American, Non-Hispanic			Hispanic		
			Number	% of Total	% of State	Number	% of Total	% of State	Number	% of Total	% of State
	Total (50 States+DC)	2,441,697	1,535,993	100.0%	62.9%	287,628	100.0%	11.8%	199,256	100.0%	8.2%
1	Georgia	59,520	37,825	2.5%	63.6%	20,019	7.0%	33.6%	563	0.3%	0.9%
2	Florida	102,404	58,356	3.8%	63.2%	19,401	6.7%	21.0%	12,147	6.1%	13.1%
3	Texas	160,546	91,241	5.9%	56.8%	19,068	6.6%	11.9%	45,513	22.8%	28.3%
4	Ohio	114,312	94,926	6.2%	86.9%	18,920	6.6%	17.3%	1,384	0.7%	1.3%
5	New York	147,150	94,378	6.1%	71.0%	18,374	6.4%	13.8%	12,108	6.1%	9.1%
6	California	292,009	120,853	7.9%	48.5%	18,219	6.3%	7.3%	71,466	35.9%	28.7%
7	North Carolina	66,504	41,557	2.7%	68.7%	16,968	5.9%	28.1%	391	0.2%	0.6%
8	Illinois	103,628	75,916	4.9%	73.3%	16,045	5.6%	15.5%	7,782	3.9%	7.5%
9	Virginia	58,263	41,903	2.7%	71.9%	12,381	4.3%	21.3%	1,250	0.6%	2.1%
10	Alabama	40,050	25,780	1.7%	66.7%	12,160	4.2%	31.5%	92	0.0%	0.2%
11	Louisiana	42,978	20,461	1.3%	60.7%	12,134	4.2%	36.0%	403	0.2%	1.2%
12	Mississippi	28,598	13,385	0.9%	52.0%	12,070	4.2%	46.9%	54	0.0%	0.2%
13	Michigan	90,860	74,935	4.9%	82.5%	11,561	4.0%	12.7%	1,952	1.0%	2.1%
14	Maryland	41,725	25,646	1.7%	64.0%	11,273	3.9%	28.1%	1,017	0.5%	2.5%
15	Pennsylvania	110,244	89,881	5.9%	86.7%	9,794	3.4%	9.4%	1,785	0.9%	1.7%
16	New Jersey	77,022	47,229	3.1%	70.4%	9,705	3.4%	14.5%	6,515	3.3%	9.7%
17	Tennessee	49,921	34,570	2.3%	75.6%	8,385	2.9%	18.3%	159	0.1%	0.3%
18	Arkansas	30,032	19,509	1.3%	76.0%	5,695	2.0%	22.2%	149	0.1%	0.6%
19	Indiana	63,371	55,456	3.6%	88.5%	5,337	1.9%	8.5%	1,179	0.6%	1.9%
20	Missouri	50,072	40,459	2.6%	86.3%	5,308	1.8%	11.3%	411	0.2%	0.9%
21	Oklahoma	37,206	28,022	1.8%	75.3%	3,152	1.1%	8.5%	983	0.5%	2.6%
22	Connecticut	28,188	22,395	1.5%	79.4%	3,047	1.1%	10.8%	1,981	1.0%	7.0%
23	District of Columbia	4,060	75	0.0%	2.4%	2,845	1.0%	90.7%	170	0.1%	5.4%
24	Massachusetts	48,321	40,316	2.6%	83.4%	2,559	0.9%	5.3%	3,274	1.6%	6.8%
25	Wisconsin	51,423	46,957	3.1%	91.3%	2,122	0.7%	4.1%	926	0.5%	1.8%
26	Colorado	35,108	25,340	1.6%	78.6%	1,389	0.5%	4.3%	4,342	2.2%	13.5%
27	Kansas	24,720	21,697	1.4%	87.8%	1,368	0.5%	5.5%	931	0.5%	3.8%
28	Delaware	6,132	4,459	0.3%	72.7%	1,368	0.5%	22.3%	173	0.1%	2.8%
29	Arizona	34,704	22,683	1.5%	65.4%	1,270	0.4%	3.7%	7,724	3.9%	22.3%
30	Minnesota	51,697	44,383	2.9%	92.5%	912	0.3%	1.9%	643	0.3%	1.3%
31	Nevada	11,342	7,517	0.5%	75.8%	762	0.3%	7.7%	975	0.5%	9.8%
32	Nebraska	18,115	16,603	1.1%	91.7%	705	0.2%	3.9%	449	0.2%	2.5%
33	Iowa	33,043	31,298	2.0%	94.7%	692	0.2%	2.1%	482	0.2%	1.5%
34	West Virginia	22,147	21,308	1.4%	96.2%	682	0.2%	3.1%	54	0.0%	0.2%
35	Oregon	36,940	25,810	1.7%	89.0%	571	0.2%	2.0%	1,069	0.5%	3.7%
36	Rhode Island	8,233	6,585	0.4%	86.0%	440	0.2%	5.7%	394	0.2%	5.1%
37	New Mexico	18,727	6,892	0.4%	44.5%	323	0.1%	2.1%	6,389	3.2%	41.3%
38	Alaska	6,331	3,938	0.3%	70.8%	204	0.1%	3.7%	122	0.1%	2.2%
39	Hawaii	9,311	1,787	0.1%	19.2%	134	0.0%	1.4%	518	0.3%	5.6%
40	Utah	25,972	24,027	1.6%	93.4%	111	0.0%	0.4%	749	0.4%	2.9%
41	South Dakota	8,587	7,757	0.5%	90.3%	46	0.0%	0.5%	47	0.0%	0.5%
42	North Dakota	7,618	6,901	0.4%	94.4%	39	0.0%	0.5%	41	0.0%	0.6%
43	Wyoming	6,257	5,717	0.4%	91.4%	39	0.0%	0.6%	347	0.2%	5.5%
44	Montana	10,209	9,260	0.6%	90.7%	31	0.0%	0.3%	153	0.1%	1.5%
45	Washington	50,249	–	–	–	–	–	–	–	–	–
46	South Carolina	36,699	–	–	–	–	–	–	–	–	–
47	Kentucky	36,361	–	–	–	–	–	–	–	–	–
48	Idaho	13,548	–	–	–	–	–	–	–	–	–
49	Maine	13,192	–	–	–	–	–	–	–	–	–
50	New Hampshire	12,111	–	–	–	–	–	–	–	–	–
51	Vermont	5,937	–	–	–	–	–	–	–	–	–
	Outlying Areas										
	Puerto Rico	45,995	–	–	–	–	–	–	–	–	–
	Virgin Islands	1,172	–	–	–	–	–	–	–	–	–
	Guam	912	–	–	–	–	–	–	–	–	–
	American Samoa	734	–	–	–	–	–	–	–	–	–
	Northern Marianas	245	–	–	–	–	–	–	–	–	–

Note: Numbers include individuals who earned regular diplomas, nonregular diplomas, high school equivalency certificates, or other certificates of completion.
"–" indicates numbers not reported.
Source: Common Core of Data, 1993-94.

Asian American			American Indian			Unknown		
Number	% of Total	% of State	Number	% of Total	% of State	Number	% of Total	% of State
91,582	100.0%	3.8%	20,308	100.0%	0.8%	306,930	100.0%	12.6%
1,022	1.1%	1.7%	91	0.4%	0.2%	–	–	–
2,335	2.5%	2.5%	161	0.8%	0.2%	10,004	–	–
4,401	4.8%	2.7%	323	1.6%	0.2%	–	–	–
1,301	1.4%	1.2%	112	0.6%	0.1%	–2,331	–5.0%	–6.8%
7,746	8.5%	5.8%	357	1.8%	0.3%	14,187	4.6%	9.6%
36,644	40.0%	14.7%	2,138	10.5%	0.9%	42,689	–	–
782	0.9%	1.3%	785	3.9%	1.3%	6,021	2.0%	9.1%
3,746	4.1%	3.6%	139	0.7%	0.1%	–	–	–
2,646	2.9%	4.5%	83	0.4%	0.1%	–	–	–
230	0.3%	0.6%	395	1.9%	1.0%	1,393	–	–
548	0.6%	1.6%	136	0.7%	0.4%	9,296	3.0%	21.6%
141	0.2%	0.5%	80	0.4%	0.3%	2,868	0.9%	10.0%
1,482	1.6%	1.6%	930	4.6%	1.0%	–	–	–
2,062	2.3%	5.1%	93	0.5%	0.2%	1,634	0.5%	3.9%
2,171	2.4%	2.1%	84	0.4%	0.1%	6,529	2.1%	5.9%
3,617	3.9%	5.4%	68	0.3%	0.1%	9,888	3.2%	12.8%
425	0.5%	0.9%	27	0.1%	0.1%	6,355	1.5%	4.7%
229	0.3%	0.9%	73	0.4%	0.3%	4,377	–	–
585	0.6%	0.9%	71	0.3%	0.1%	743	–	–
606	0.7%	1.3%	80	0.4%	0.2%	3,208	1.0%	6.4%
557	0.6%	1.5%	4,492	22.1%	12.1%	–	–	–
707	0.8%	2.5%	58	0.3%	0.2%	–	–	–
46	0.1%	1.5%	0	0.0%	0.0%	924	–	–
1,848	2.0%	3.8%	324	1.6%	0.7%	–	–	–
931	1.0%	1.8%	487	2.4%	0.9%	–	–	–
930	1.0%	2.9%	238	1.2%	0.7%	2,869	–	–
526	0.6%	2.1%	198	1.0%	0.8%	–	–	–
129	0.1%	2.1%	3	0.0%	0.0%	–	–	–
759	0.8%	2.2%	2,268	11.2%	6.5%	–	–	–
1,602	1.7%	3.3%	497	2.4%	1.0%	3,660	0.0%	–0.1%
515	0.6%	5.2%	150	0.7%	1.5%	1,423	0.5%	12.5%
254	0.3%	1.4%	104	0.5%	0.6%	–	–	–
491	0.5%	1.5%	80	0.4%	0.2%	–	–	–
95	0.1%	0.4%	8	0.0%	0.0%	–	–	–
1,114	1.2%	3.8%	428	2.1%	1.5%	7,948	2.6%	21.5%
213	0.2%	2.8%	23	0.1%	0.3%	578	0.2%	7.0%
196	0.2%	1.3%	1,680	8.3%	10.9%	3,247	1.1%	17.3%
276	0.3%	5.0%	1,023	5.0%	18.4%	768	–	–
6,841	7.5%	73.5%	31	0.2%	0.3%	–	–	–
567	0.6%	2.2%	271	1.3%	1.1%	247	0.1%	1.0%
74	0.1%	0.9%	663	3.3%	7.7%	–	–	–
58	0.1%	0.8%	271	1.3%	3.7%	308	0.1%	4.0%
51	0.1%	0.8%	103	0.5%	1.6%	–	–	–
83	0.1%	0.8%	682	3.4%	6.7%	–	–	–
–	–	–	–	–	–	50,249	30.5%	100.0%
–	–	–	–	–	–	36,699	21.1%	100.0%
–	–	–	–	–	–	36,361	24.5%	100.0%
–	–	–	–	–	–	13,548	8.7%	100.0%
–	–	–	–	–	–	13,192	8.2%	100.0%
–	–	–	–	–	–	12,111	6.8%	100.0%
–	–	–	–	–	–	5,937	3.8%	100.0%
–	–	–	–	–	–	45,995	19.6%	100.0%
–	–	–	–	–	–	1,172	0.6%	100.0%
–	–	–	–	–	–	912	0.6%	100.0%
734	0.8%	100.0%	–	–	–	–	0.0%	–
216	0.2%	88.2%	–	–	–	29	0.0%	11.8%

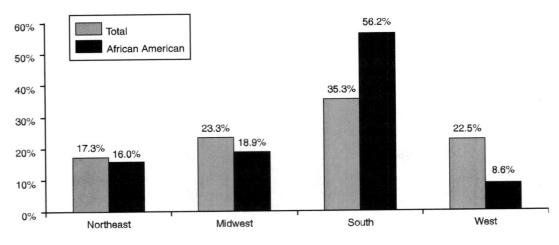

Figure 2. Distribution of Public Elementary and
Secondary School Enrollments by Region: 1993/94

Source: Common Core of Data, 1993-94.

Table 8. Enrollment in Public Elementary and Secondary Schools by Region and Race: 1993/94
(number of students in parentheses)

Region	Total	White, Non-Hispanic	African American	Hispanic	Asian/Pacific Islander	American Indian/ Alaska Native	Unknown
Total	100.0%	64.3%	16.3%	12.4%	3.6%	1.1%	2.4%
	100.0%	100.0%	100.0%	100.0%	100.0%	100.0%	100.0%
	(44,184,072)	(28,409,908)	(7,189,236)	(5,482,430)	(1,595,017)	(464,571)	(1,042,910)
Northeast	100.0%	67.8%	15.0%	10.5%	3.5%	0.2%	2.9%
	17.3%	18.3%	16.0%	14.7%	16.9%	3.7%	21.2%
	(7,654,012)	(5,190,184)	(1,151,606)	(803,431)	(270,333)	(17,402)	(221,056)
Midwest	100.0%	79.8%	13.2%	3.7%	1.7%	0.8%	0.8%
	23.3%	28.9%	18.9%	7.0%	11.2%	18.5%	7.6%
	(10,298,428)	(8,216,696)	(1,357,072)	(381,053)	(179,019)	(85,764)	(78,824)
South	100.0%	60.4%	25.9%	10.9%	1.6%	0.9%	0.3%
	35.3%	33.1%	56.2%	31.1%	15.9%	28.8%	4.4%
	(15,591,675)	(9,410,154)	(4,042,217)	(1,705,585)	(253,887)	(133,849)	(45,983)
West	100.0%	56.3%	6.2%	26.1%	8.5%	2.3%	0.6%
	22.5%	19.7%	8.6%	47.2%	52.9%	49.0%	6.2%
	(9,932,153)	(5,589,855)	(618,438)	(2,589,184)	(843,027)	(227,508)	(64,141)
Outlying Areas	100.0%	0.4%	2.8%	0.4%	6.9%	0.0%	89.4%
	1.6%	0.0%	0.3%	0.1%	3.1%	0.0%	60.7%
	(707,804)	(3,019)	(19,903)	(3,177)	(48,751)	(48)	(632,906)

Source: Common Core of Data, 1993-94.

Figure 3. Distribution of Public Elementary and Secondary Enrollments by School Urbanicity: 1993/94

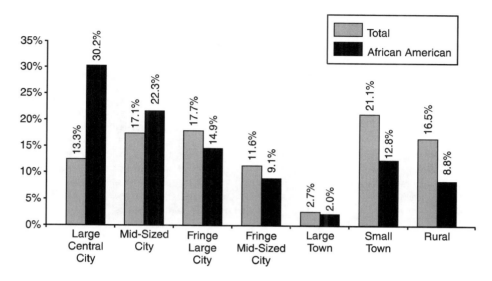

Source: Common Core of Data, 1993-94.

Table 9. Enrollment in Public Elementary and Secondary Schools by School Urbanicity and Race: 1993/94
(number of students in parentheses)

Urbanicity	Number of Schools	Total	White, Non-Hispanic	African American	Hispanic	Asian/Pacific Islander	American Indian/ Alaska Native	Unknown
Total	100.0%	100.0%	100.0%	100.0%	100.0%	100.0%	100.0%	100.0%
	83,624	(43,354,404)	(28,406,899)	(7,169,333)	(5,479,253)	(1,546,266)	(464,523)	(288,130)
Large Central City	9.7%	13.3%	5.1%	30.2%	31.9%	23.7%	6.4%	0.6%
	8,136	(5,773,653)	(1,459,941)	(2,167,227)	(1,748,857)	(366,145)	(29,658)	(1,825)
Mid-Sized City	14.5%	17.1%	15.3%	22.3%	19.4%	18.4%	12.8%	11.2%
	12,152	(7,402,776)	(4,359,098)	(1,602,107)	(1,065,351)	(284,440)	(59,391)	(32,389)
Urban Fringe of Large City	14.7%	17.7%	17.7%	14.9%	19.5%	31.2%	7.3%	0.3%
	12,310	(7,691,966)	(5,040,283)	(1,067,297)	(1,066,874)	(482,762)	(33,742)	(1,008)
Urban Fringe of Mid-Sized City	9.8%	11.6%	13.0%	9.1%	7.8%	13.0%	5.3%	9.5%
	8,193	(5,031,389)	(3,697,317)	(654,404)	(426,784)	(200,652)	(24,778)	(27,454)
Large Town	2.7%	2.7%	3.0%	2.0%	1.8%	1.8%	2.9%	14.4%
	2,227	(1,181,826)	(856,215)	(144,755)	(98,650)	(27,329)	(13,259)	(41,618)
Small Town	22.3%	21.1%	25.1%	12.8%	13.6%	7.5%	31.1%	30.8%
	18,642	(9,131,534)	(7,121,734)	(914,941)	(746,148)	(115,617)	(144,332)	(88,762)
Rural	26.3%	16.5%	20.6%	8.8%	5.7%	11.5%	34.2%	4.0%
	21,964	(7,141,260)	(5,852,157)	(629,395)	(311,553)	(177,900)	(158,813)	(11,442)

Source: Common Core of Data, 1993-94.

Table 10. 75 Largest Regular Public High Schools Nationwide by Percentage of African American Students Enrolled: Fall 1993

Size Rank	School Name	City	State	Low Grade	High Grade	Total Students	White Number	White %	African American Number	African American %	Hispanic Number	Hispanic %	Asian American Number	Asian American %	American Indian Number	American Indian %
9	Boys & Girls High School	Brooklyn	NY	9	12	4,363	2	0.0%	4,062	93.1%	291	6.7%	6	0.1%	2	0.0%
55	Martin Luther King High	New York	NY	9	12	3,402	41	1.2%	2,065	60.7%	1,103	32.4%	163	4.8%	30	0.9%
69	South Shore High School	Brooklyn	NY	9	12	3,255	998	30.7%	1,920	59.0%	243	7.5%	87	2.7%	7	0.2%
58	Evander Childs High School	Bronx	NY	9	12	3,332	32	1.0%	1,919	57.6%	1,295	38.9%	72	2.2%	14	0.4%
56	Hillcrest High School	Jamaica	NY	9	12	3,395	323	9.5%	1,713	50.5%	821	24.2%	523	15.4%	15	0.4%
37	Skyline High School	Dallas	TX	9	12	3,663	463	12.6%	1,782	48.6%	1,280	34.9%	124	3.4%	14	0.4%
6	Brooklyn Tech High School	Brooklyn	NY	9	12	4,582	677	14.8%	1,795	39.2%	623	13.6%	1,470	32.1%	17	0.4%
64	Sheepshead Bay High School	Brooklyn	NY	9	12	3,277	1,269	38.7%	1,270	38.8%	380	11.6%	355	10.8%	3	0.1%
36	De Witt Clinton High School	Bronx	NY	9	12	3,695	45	1.2%	1,386	37.5%	2,076	56.2%	183	5.0%	5	0.1%
12	Adlai E. Stevenson High	Bronx	NY	9	12	4,271	59	1.4%	1,600	37.5%	2,516	58.9%	90	2.1%	6	0.1%
19	John Jay High School	Brooklyn	NY	9	12	3,990	308	7.7%	1,444	36.2%	2,095	52.5%	138	3.5%	5	0.1%
75	Curie Metropolitan High	Chicago	IL	9	12	3,190	795	24.9%	1,140	35.7%	1,158	36.3%	83	2.6%	14	0.4%
10	William H. Taft High School	Bronx	NY	9	12	4,291	12	0.3%	1,528	35.6%	2,637	61.5%	100	2.3%	14	0.3%
54	John Dewey High School	Brooklyn	NY	9	12	3,408	1,016	29.8%	1,197	35.1%	714	21.0%	471	13.8%	10	0.3%
49	Murry Bergtraum High School	New York	NY	9	12	3,515	148	4.2%	1,229	35.0%	1,343	38.2%	783	22.3%	12	0.3%
70	Jordan High School	Long Beach	CA	9	12	3,247	423	13.0%	1,107	34.1%	1,126	34.7%	579	17.8%	12	0.4%
11	Elizabeth High School	Elizabeth	NJ	9	12	4,284	855	20.0%	1,252	29.2%	2,062	48.1%	114	2.7%	1	0.0%
16	Polytechnic High School	Long Beach	CA	9	12	4,022	890	22.1%	1,126	28.0%	565	14.0%	1,425	35.4%	16	0.4%
17	American Senior High School	Hialeah	FL	9	12	4,012	452	11.3%	1,121	27.9%	2,398	59.8%	40	1.0%	1	0.0%
23	Theodore Roosevelt High	Bronx	NY	9	12	3,961	20	0.5%	1,102	27.8%	2,609	65.9%	224	5.7%	6	0.2%
66	James Madison High School	Brooklyn	NY	9	12	3,260	1,698	52.1%	902	27.7%	340	10.4%	315	9.7%	5	0.2%
45	Christopher Columbus High	Bronx	NY	9	12	3,555	704	19.8%	933	26.2%	1,628	45.8%	284	8.0%	6	0.2%
5	Franklin K. Lane High School	Brooklyn	NY	9	12	4,597	512	11.1%	1,133	24.6%	2,474	53.8%	414	9.0%	64	1.4%
20	Elsik High School	Alief	TX	9	12	3,987	1,115	28.0%	960	24.1%	913	22.9%	995	25.0%	3	0.1%
57	South Mountain High School	Phoenix	AZ	9	12	3,367	553	16.4%	809	24.0%	1,962	58.3%	8	0.2%	35	1.0%
18	Hastings High School	Alief	TX	9	12	3,997	1,170	29.3%	945	23.6%	848	21.2%	1,032	25.8%	2	0.1%
27	Miami Killian Senior High	Miami	FL	9	12	3,905	1,605	41.1%	904	23.1%	1,276	32.7%	119	3.0%	1	0.0%
34	Edward R. Murrow High	Brooklyn	NY	9	12	3,765	1,822	48.4%	830	22.0%	558	14.8%	548	14.6%	7	0.2%
67	Green Valley High School	Henderson	NV	9	12	3,258	952	29.2%	714	21.9%	1,116	34.3%	461	14.1%	15	0.5%
59	Kingwood High School	Kingwood	TX	9	12	3,325	308	9.3%	681	20.5%	2,315	69.6%	21	0.6%	0	0.0%
1	John F. Kennedy High School	Bronx	NY	9	12	4,986	358	7.2%	985	19.8%	3,316	66.5%	314	6.3%	13	0.3%
38	Judson High School	Converse	TX	9	12	3,650	1,901	52.1%	703	19.3%	915	25.1%	124	3.4%	7	0.2%
15	Lane Technical High School	Chicago	IL	9	12	4,071	1,312	32.2%	766	18.8%	1,273	31.3%	703	17.3%	17	0.4%
62	New Bedford High School	New Bedford	MA	9	12	3,301	2,436	73.8%	465	14.1%	349	10.6%	40	1.2%	11	0.3%
61	Victor Valley High School	Victorville	CA	9	12	3,305	1,524	46.1%	449	13.6%	1,136	34.4%	169	5.1%	27	0.8%
63	Schurz High School	Chicago	IL	9	12	3,295	578	17.5%	440	13.4%	2,196	66.6%	72	2.2%	9	0.3%
29	James Logan High School	Union City	CA	9	12	3,836	885	23.1%	512	13.3%	886	23.1%	1,543	40.2%	10	0.3%
52	Coral Gables Senior High	Coral Gables	FL	9	12	3,448	688	20.0%	450	13.1%	2,262	65.6%	48	1.4%	0	0.0%
39	Millikan Senior High School	Long Beach	CA	9	12	3,590	961	26.8%	437	12.2%	1,589	44.3%	594	16.5%	9	0.3%
40	Benjamin Cardozo High	Bayside	NY	9	12	3,586	1,700	47.4%	425	11.9%	368	10.3%	1,084	30.2%	9	0.3%
31	Lakewood High School	Lakewood	CA	9	12	3,807	1,378	36.2%	433	11.4%	1,474	38.7%	509	13.4%	13	0.3%
48	Miami Senior High School	Miami	FL	9	12	3,520	101	2.9%	364	10.3%	3,029	86.1%	26	0.7%	0	0.0%
43	Jefferson (Thomas) Sr. High	Los Angeles	CA	9	12	3,563	2	0.1%	367	10.3%	3,180	89.3%	13	0.4%	1	0.0%
42	George Washington High	New York	NY	9	12	3,571	13	0.4%	320	9.0%	3,215	90.0%	16	0.4%	7	0.2%
50	William C. Bryant High School	Long Island City	NY	9	12	3,486	896	25.7%	310	8.9%	1,468	42.1%	803	23.0%	9	0.3%
46	Milby High School	Houston	TX	9	12	3,525	207	5.9%	302	8.6%	2,863	81.2%	152	4.3%	1	0.0%
64	Roosevelt High School	Fresno	CA	9	12	3,277	377	11.5%	278	8.5%	2,009	61.3%	598	18.2%	15	0.5%
52	Forest Hills High School	Forest Hills	NY	9	12	3,448	1,634	47.4%	288	8.4%	709	20.6%	812	23.5%	5	0.1%
30	Fontana High School	Fontana	CA	9	12	3,830	1,286	33.6%	319	8.3%	2,087	54.5%	131	3.4%	7	0.2%
74	Upland High School	Upland	CA	9	12	3,206	1,960	61.1%	266	8.3%	636	19.8%	341	10.6%	3	0.1%

—continued next page

Table 10. —continued from previous page

Size Rank	School Name	City	State	Low Grade	High Grade	Total Students	White Number	White %	African American Number	African American %	Hispanic Number	Hispanic %	Asian American Number	Asian American %	American Indian Number	American Indian %
35	Franklin D. Roosevelt High	Brooklyn	NY	9	12	3,754	1,609	42.9%	308	8.2%	1,145	30.5%	688	18.3%	4	0.1%
41	Miami Sunset Senior High	Miami	FL	9	12	3,576	1,028	28.7%	274	7.7%	2,161	60.4%	113	3.2%	0	0.0%
4	Newtown High School	Elmhurst	NY	9	12	4,639	402	8.7%	348	7.5%	2,753	59.3%	1,128	24.3%	8	0.2%
67	Wilson High School	Long Beach	CA	9	12	3,258	2,576	79.1%	230	7.1%	277	8.5%	167	5.1%	8	0.2%
7	Redlands Senior High School	Redlands	CA	9	12	4,544	2,577	56.7%	299	6.6%	1,076	23.7%	563	12.4%	29	0.6%
25	Tottenville High School	Staten Island	NY	9	12	3,927	3,092	78.7%	235	6.0%	306	7.8%	287	7.3%	7	0.2%
26	Independence High School	San Jose	CA	9	12	3,908	537	13.7%	224	5.7%	1,311	33.5%	1,786	45.7%	50	1.3%
2	G. Holmes Braddock Sr. High	Miami	FL	9	12	4,970	674	13.6%	264	5.3%	3,976	80.0%	50	1.0%	6	0.1%
33	Lake Braddock Secondary	Burke	VA	7	12	3,783	2,855	75.5%	190	5.0%	223	5.9%	506	13.4%	9	0.2%
32	Robinson Secondary School	Fairfax	VA	7	12	3,791	3,089	81.5%	188	5.0%	147	3.9%	356	9.4%	11	0.3%
22	Fort Hamilton High School	Brooklyn	NY	9	12	3,964	1,640	41.4%	176	4.4%	1,481	37.4%	656	16.5%	11	0.3%
51	Hesperia High School	Hesperia	CA	9	12	3,471	2,282	65.7%	146	4.2%	948	27.3%	57	1.6%	38	1.1%
72	Madera High School	Madera	CA	9	12	3,218	1,185	36.8%	131	4.1%	1,845	57.3%	54	1.7%	3	0.1%
44	Miami Coral Park Senior High	Miami	FL	9	12	3,560	205	5.8%	113	3.2%	3,215	90.3%	27	0.8%	0	0.0%
73	San Fernando Senior High	San Fernando	CA	10	12	3,208	40	1.2%	81	2.5%	3,045	94.9%	27	0.8%	15	0.5%
59	Hialeah-Miami Lakes Sr. High	Hialeah	FL	9	12	3,325	3,063	92.1%	45	1.4%	138	4.2%	75	2.3%	4	0.1%
8	Belmont Senior High School	Los Angeles	CA	9	12	4,458	40	0.9%	52	1.2%	3,854	86.5%	505	11.3%	7	0.2%
3	Sachem High School	Lake Ronkonkoma	NY	9	12	4,713	4,406	93.5%	50	1.1%	155	3.3%	98	2.1%	4	0.1%
71	East Detroit High School	Eastpointe	MI	7	12	3,232	3,110	96.2%	34	1.1%	10	0.3%	33	1.0%	45	1.4%
47	Alhambra High School	Alhambra	CA	9	12	3,521	330	9.4%	35	1.0%	1,307	37.1%	1,846	52.4%	3	0.1%
21	South Gate Senior High	SchoSouth Gate	CA	9	12	3,974	38	1.0%	20	0.5%	3,890	97.9%	22	0.6%	4	0.1%
14	Huntington Park Senior High	Huntington Park	CA	9	12	4,084	24	0.6%	17	0.4%	4,006	98.1%	29	0.7%	8	0.2%
24	Theodore Roosevelt Sr. High	Los Angeles	CA	10	12	3,945	20	0.5%	15	0.4%	3,879	98.3%	29	0.7%	2	0.1%
13	Bell Senior High School	Bell	CA	9	12	4,234	50	1.2%	11	0.3%	4,141	97.8%	16	0.4%	16	0.4%
28	James Garfield Senior High	Los Angeles	CA	10	12	3,872	25	0.6%	8	0.2%	3,806	98.3%	32	0.8%	1	0.0%

Summary

Location	Number of Schools	Median % African Americans
Large Central City	49	23.6%
Urban Fringe—Large City	15	2.5%
Mid-Size Central City	2	8.4%
Urban Fringe—Mid-Size City	3	6.6%
Large Town	1	14.1%
Small Town	3	4.2%
Rural	2	10.2%
Total	75	13.1%

Figure 4. Representation of African Americans at Different Types of Public Elementary and Secondary Schools: 1993/94

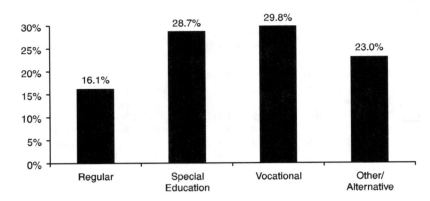

Source: Common Core of Data, 1993-94.

Table 11. Enrollment in Public Elementary and Secondary Schools by Type of School and Race: 1993/94

(number of students in parentheses)

School Type	Total	White, Non-Hispanic	African American	Hispanic	Asian/Pacific Islander	American Indian/ Alaska Native	Unknown
Total	100.0%	64.5%	16.3%	13.8%	3.6%	1.1%	0.7%
	100.0%	100.0%	100.0%	100.0%	100.0%	100.0%	100.0%
	(44,031,019)	(28,386,745)	(7,180,126)	(6,095,677)	(1,594,845)	(463,973)	(309,653)
Regular School	100.0%	64.8%	16.1%	13.7%	3.6%	1.0%	0.7%
	98.3%	98.8%	97.3%	97.4%	98.7%	97.9%	98.3%
	(43,292,489)	(28,035,816)	(6,986,033)	(5,938,519)	(1,573,537)	(454,123)	(304,461)
Special Education	100.0%	49.9%	28.7%	16.8%	2.5%	1.0%	1.2%
School	0.5%	0.4%	0.8%	0.6%	0.3%	0.4%	0.8%
	(208,029)	(103,704)	(59,662)	(35,010)	(5,185)	(2,053)	(2,415)
Vocational Education	100.0%	50.5%	29.8%	19.0%	1.8%	0.5%	−1.6%
School	0.4%	0.3%	0.8%	0.6%	0.2%	0.2%	−0.9%
	(181,750)	(91,716)	(54,235)	(34,461)	(3,347)	(864)	−(2,873)
Other/Alternative	100.0%	44.6%	23.0%	25.1%	3.7%	2.0%	1.6%
School	0.8%	0.5%	1.1%	1.4%	0.8%	1.5%	1.8%
	(348,751)	(155,509)	(80,196)	(87,687)	(12,776)	(6,933)	(5,650)

Notes: Data describes the 50 states and the District of Columbia as well as outlying areas.
Outlying areas include Puerto Rico, Virgin Islands, Northern Marianas, Guam, and American Samoa.
Source: Common Core of Data, 1993-94.

secondary schools nationwide were enrolled in private elementary and secondary schools. More than one-half (56.4%) of the students who were enrolled in private schools attended elementary schools. Only 16.3% attended secondary schools, and 27.3% attended combined elementary and secondary schools.

African Americans were underrepresented in America's private schools relative to their representation among school-age children in the U.S. population. In 1993/94, only 9.3% of students enrolled in private elementary and secondary schools nationwide were African American ($n = 462,105$).

- African American students represented a higher proportion of private elementary school students (10.5%) than of private secondary school students (7.2%) and of students at private combined elementary and secondary schools (8.1%).

- **Table 12** shows that, among private school students, a higher share of African Americans than of Whites attended elementary schools (63.7% versus 54.5%).

School Affiliation

About one-half (50.6%) of all private school students in 1993/94 attended Catholic schools. Regardless of school affiliation, African Americans were underrepresented among private school students nationwide.

- **Figure 5** shows that African Americans were somewhat better represented among Catholic school students (10.0% of all Catholic school students) than among nonsectarian school students (8.3%) and non-Catholic religious school students (8.7%).

- **Table 13** shows that, among private school students in 1993/94, a higher share of African Americans than of Whites attended Catholic schools (54.5% versus 48.3%).

School Size

About one-half (47.7%) of private school students in 1993/94 attended schools with fewer than 300 students. **Table 14** shows that a higher percentage of African American private school students than

Table 12. Enrollment in Private Elementary and Secondary Schools by School Level and Race: 1993/94

(total number of students enrolled in parentheses)

Level	Number of Schools	Total	White, Non-Hispanic	African American, Non-Hispanic	Hispanic	Asian American/ Pacific Islander	American Indian/ Alaskan Native
Representation by Race Group							
Total	26,093	100.0%	77.9%	9.3%	8.0%	4.1%	0.6%
		(4,970,548)	(3,873,996)	(462,105)	(399,706)	(203,749)	(30,992)
Elementary	15,537	100.0%	75.3%	10.5%	9.2%	4.2%	0.7%
		(2,803,152)	(2,111,734)	(294,544)	(258,985)	(119,114)	(18,775)
Secondary	2,551	100.0%	79.2%	7.2%	9.0%	4.2%	0.5%
		(811,087)	(642,419)	(58,018)	(72,611)	(33,817)	(4,222)
Combined Elementary & Secondary	8,006	100.0%	82.6%	8.1%	5.0%	3.7%	0.6%
		(1,356,308)	(1,119,843)	(109,542)	(68,110)	(50,818)	(7,995)
Distribution by Level							
Total		100.0%	100.0%	100.0%	100.0%	100.0%	100.0%
Elementary		56.4%	54.5%	63.7%	64.8%	58.5%	60.6%
Secondary		16.3%	16.6%	12.6%	18.2%	16.6%	13.6%
Combined		27.3%	28.9%	23.7%	17.0%	24.9%	25.8%

Source: Schools and Staffing Survey, 1993-94.

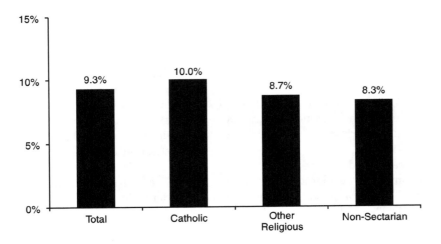

Figure 5. Representation of African Americans
Among Private Elementary and Secondary School
Enrollments by School Affiliation: 1993/94

Source: Schools and Staffing Survey, 1993-94.

Table 13. Enrollment in Private Elementary and Secondary Schools by School Affiliation and Race: 1993/94
(total number of students enrolled in parentheses)

Affiliation	Number of Schools	Total	White, Non-Hispanic	African American, Non-Hispanic	Hispanic	Asian American/ Pacific Islander	American Indian/ Alaskan Native
Representation by Race Group							
Total	26,093	100.0%	77.9%	9.3%	8.0%	4.1%	0.6%
		(4,970,548)	(3,873,996)	(462,105)	(399,706)	(203,749)	(30,992)
Catholic	8,351	100.0%	74.4%	10.0%	10.9%	4.1%	0.6%
		(2,516,028)	(1,871,000)	(252,033)	(275,051)	(102,071)	(15,873)
Other Religious	12,180	100.0%	81.9%	8.7%	4.9%	3.8%	0.7%
		(1,686,069)	(1,380,208)	(145,907)	(83,321)	(64,351)	(12,282)
Nonsectarian	5,563	100.0%	81.0%	8.3%	5.4%	4.9%	0.4%
		(768,450)	(622,788)	(64,165)	(41,335)	(37,326)	(2,836)
Distribution by School Affiliation							
Total		100.0%	100.0%	100.0%	100.0%	100.0%	100.0%
Catholic		50.6%	48.3%	54.5%	68.8%	50.1%	51.2%
Other Religious		33.9%	35.6%	31.6%	20.8%	31.6%	39.6%
Nonsectarian		15.5%	16.1%	13.9%	10.3%	18.3%	9.2%

Source: Schools and Staffing Survey, 1993-94.

Table 14. Enrollment in Private Elementary and Secondary Schools by Total School Enrollment and Race: 1993/94
(total number of students enrolled in parentheses)

School Enrollment	Number of Schools	Total	White, Non-Hispanic	African American, Non-Hispanic	Hispanic	Asian American/ Pacific Islander	American Indian/ Alaskan Native
Representation by Race Group							
Total	26,093	100.0%	77.9%	9.3%	8.0%	4.1%	0.6%
		(4,970,548)	(3,873,996)	(462,105)	(399,706)	(203,749)	(30,992)
0 to 149	14,154	100.0%	79.6%	10.3%	6.0%	2.7%	1.3%
		(890,241)	(708,769)	(91,938)	(53,258)	(24,394)	(11,882)
150 to 299	6,820	100.0%	74.6%	12.3%	9.0%	3.6%	0.5%
		(1,482,214)	(1,106,292)	(182,680)	(133,331)	(53,122)	(6,790)
300 to 499	3,271	100.0%	79.2%	7.0%	8.3%	5.0%	0.5%
		(1,243,578)	(984,588)	(87,298)	(102,995)	(62,028)	(6,669)
500 to 749	1,229	100.0%	77.1%	7.6%	9.6%	5.2%	0.6%
		(736,057)	(567,560)	(55,726)	(70,403)	(38,271)	(4,097)
750 or More	619	100.0%	81.9%	7.2%	6.4%	4.2%	0.3%
		(618,457)	(506,788)	(44,462)	(39,719)	(25,933)	(1,554)
Distribution by Total Enrollment							
Total		100.0%	100.0%	100.0%	100.0%	100.0%	100.0%
0 to 149		17.9%	18.3%	19.9%	13.3%	12.0%	38.3%
150 to 299		29.8%	28.6%	39.5%	33.4%	26.1%	21.9%
300 to 499		25.0%	25.4%	18.9%	25.8%	30.4%	21.5%
500 to 749		14.8%	14.7%	12.1%	17.6%	18.8%	13.2%
750 or more		12.4%	13.1%	9.6%	9.9%	12.7%	5.0%

Source: Schools and Staffing Survey, 1993-94.

of White private school students attended schools with fewer than 300 students (59.4% versus 46.9%).

- **Figure 6** shows that African Americans represented 10.3% of those who attended private schools with less than 150 students and 12.3% of those who attended schools with 150 to 299 students.

- African Americans represented only 7.0% of those who attended private schools with 300 to 499 students, 7.6% of those who attended schools with 500 to 749 students, and 7.2% of those who attended schools with 750 or more students.

Urbanicity

In 1993/94 nearly one-half (45.5%) of America's private school students attended schools located in urban areas. About one-third (36.4%) attended suburban schools and one-fifth (18.1%) attended rural schools. African American private school students were concentrated in urban schools.

- **Table 15** shows that 68.4% of African American private school students attended schools located in urban areas, compared with only 40.2% of their White counterparts.

- Only 27.3% of African American, but 38.4% of White private school students attended suburban schools.

- Just 4.3% of African American private school students attended rural schools, compared with 21.4% of their White counterparts.

- **Figure 7** shows that African Americans represented 14.0% of urban private school students, but only 7.0% of suburban private school students, and 2.2% of rural private school students.

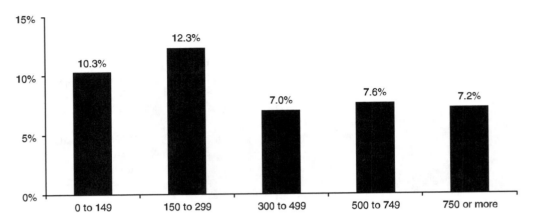

Figure 6. Representation of African Americans Among
Private Elementary and Secondary School Students
by Total School Enrollment: 1993/94

Source: Schools and Staffing Survey, 1993-94.

Table 15. Enrollment in Private Elementary and Secondary Schools by School Urbanicity and Race: 1993/94
(total number of students enrolled in parentheses)

Urbanicity	Number of Schools	Total	White, Non-Hispanic	African American, Non-Hispanic	Hispanic	Asian American/ Pacific Islander	American Indian/ Alaskan Native
Representation by Race Group							
Total	26,093	100.0%	77.9%	9.3%	8.0%	4.1%	0.6%
		(4,970,548)	(3,873,996)	(462,105)	(399,706)	(203,749)	(30,992)
Urban	9,707	100.0%	68.8%	14.0%	11.9%	5.0%	0.4%
		(2,261,125)	(1,555,860)	(316,015)	(268,500)	(112,187)	(8,563)
Suburban	8,583	100.0%	82.2%	7.0%	6.3%	4.0%	0.6%
		(1,810,230)	(1,487,662)	(126,010)	(113,496)	(72,110)	(10,952)
Rural	7,804	100.0%	92.4%	2.2%	2.0%	2.2%	1.3%
		(899,193)	(830,474)	(20,080)	(17,710)	(19,452)	(11,477)
Distribution by School Urbanicity							
Total		100.0%	100.0%	100.0%	100.0%	100.0%	100.0%
Urban		45.5%	40.2%	68.4%	67.2%	55.1%	27.6%
Suburban		36.4%	38.4%	27.3%	28.4%	35.4%	35.3%
Rural		18.1%	21.4%	4.3%	4.4%	9.5%	37.0%

Source: Schools and Staffing Survey, 1993-94.

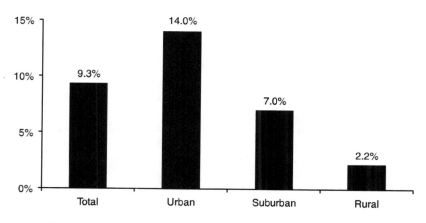

Figure 7. Representation of African Americans Among Private Elementary and Secondary School Students by School Urbanicity: 1993/94

Source: Schools and Staffing Survey, 1993-94.

Percentage of African American Students

In 1993/94, the majority (70.3%) of America's private school students attended schools in which African Americans comprised 5.0% or less of the student body. Only 4.9% attended schools in which African Americans comprised more than 60.0% of all students. In contrast, nearly one-half (48.7%) of all African American private school students attended schools in which African Americans comprised more than 60.0% of all enrolled students.

- **Table 16** shows that only 9.5% of African American private school students attended schools in which African Americans represented 5.0% or less of the student body.

- **Figure 8** shows that African Americans represented 93.1% of students attending schools in which African Americans comprised more than 60.0% of the student body.

- But African Americans represented only 1.3% of students attending schools where less than 6.0% of the student body was African American.

Tuition

About one-half (47.8%) of all private school students in 1993/94 attended schools with tuition levels between $1,000 and $2,500. Only 9.5% attended schools with tuition levels below $1,000. A smaller share of African Americans than Whites attended schools with tuition of $5,000 or more (9.1% versus 15.5%).

- **Table 17** shows that 63.1% of African American private school students attended schools with tuition under $2,500, compared with 56.9% of their White counterparts.

- **Figure 9** shows that African Americans represented only 5.8% of all students who were enrolled in schools that charged $5,000 or more per year in tuition.

Table 16. Enrollment in Private Elementary and Secondary Schools by Percentage of African American Students Enrolled and Race: 1993/94
(total number of students enrolled in parentheses)

% African American	Number of Schools	Total	White, Non-Hispanic	African American, Non-Hispanic	Hispanic	Asian American/ Pacific Islander	American Indian/ Alaskan Native
Representation by Race Group							
Total	26,093	100.0%	77.9%	9.3%	8.0%	4.1%	0.6%
		(4,970,548)	(3,873,996)	(462,105)	(399,706)	(203,749)	(30,992)
0% to 5%	17,502	100.0%	86.7%	1.3%	7.4%	3.9%	0.7%
		(3,493,442)	(3,029,210)	(44,117)	(258,674)	(135,789)	(25,652)
6% to 20%	4,162	100.0%	74.6%	10.6%	9.1%	5.2%	0.5%
		(788,688)	(588,744)	(83,956)	(71,480)	(40,672)	(3,836)
21% to 40%	1,266	100.0%	50.6%	29.4%	14.7%	5.0%	0.3%
		(178,905)	(90,592)	(52,586)	(26,214)	(8,897)	(616)
41% to 60%	611	100.0%	31.1%	49.9%	12.1%	6.9%	0.1%
		(82,826)	(25,722)	(41,306)	(9,994)	(5,744)	(60)
61% or more	1,427	100.0%	2.1%	93.1%	3.9%	0.9%	0.1%
		(241,828)	(4,984)	(225,058)	(9,451)	(2,076)	(259)
Distribution by % African American							
Total		100.0%	100.0%	100.0%	100.0%	100.0%	100.0%
0% to 5%		70.3%	78.2%	9.5%	64.7%	66.6%	82.8%
6% to 20%		15.9%	15.2%	18.2%	17.9%	20.0%	12.4%
21% to 40%		3.6%	2.3%	11.4%	6.6%	4.4%	2.0%
41% to 60%		1.7%	0.7%	8.9%	2.5%	2.8%	0.2%
61% or more		4.9%	0.1%	48.7%	2.4%	1.0%	0.8%

Source: Schools and Staffing Survey, 1993-94.

**Figure 8. Representation of African Americans
Among Private Elementary and Secondary School Students
by Percentage of African American Students Enrolled: 1993/94**

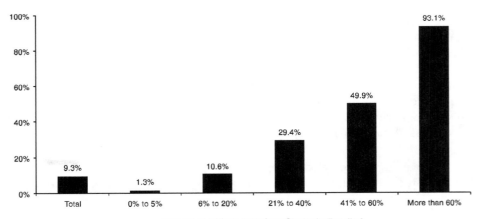

Percent of African American Students Enrolled

Source: Schools and Staffing Survey, 1993-94.

Table 17. Enrollment in Private Elementary and Secondary Schools by Amount of Tuition Charged and Race: 1993/94
(total number of students enrolled in parentheses)

Tuition	Number of Schools	Total	White, Non-Hispanic	African American, Non-Hispanic	Hispanic	Asian American/ Pacific Islander	American Indian/ Alaskan Native
Total	24,309	100.0%	78.0%	9.2%	8.1%	4.2%	0.5%
		(4,876,160)	(3,804,946)	(446,577)	(396,776)	(203,124)	(24,737)
Less than $1,000	3,350	100.0%	84.8%	7.8%	3.9%	2.0%	1.5%
		(462,022)	(391,619)	(36,184)	(17,982)	(9,166)	(7,071)
$1,000 to $2,499	12,259	100.0%	76.1%	10.5%	9.4%	3.5%	0.4%
		(2,329,363)	(1,773,169)	(245,635)	(219,032)	(82,276)	(9,251)
$2,500 to $4,999	5,541	100.0%	75.7%	8.9%	9.7%	5.2%	0.5%
		(1,390,235)	(1,052,133)	(124,324)	(135,525)	(71,704)	(6,549)
$5,000 or more	3,159	100.0%	84.7%	5.8%	3.5%	5.8%	0.3%
		(694,540)	(588,025)	(40,434)	(24,237)	(39,978)	(1,866)
Distribution by Tuition							
Total		100.0%	100.0%	100.0%	100.0%	100.0%	100.0%
Less than $1,000		9.5%	10.3%	8.1%	4.5%	4.5%	28.6%
$1,000 to $2,499		47.8%	46.6%	55.0%	55.2%	40.5%	37.4%
$2,500 to $4,999		28.5%	27.7%	27.8%	34.2%	35.3%	26.5%
$5,000 or more		14.2%	15.5%	9.1%	6.1%	19.7%	7.5%

Source: Schools and Staffing Survey, 1993-94.

Figure 9. Representation of African Americans Among Private Elementary and Secondary School Students by Amount of Tuition Charged: 1993/94

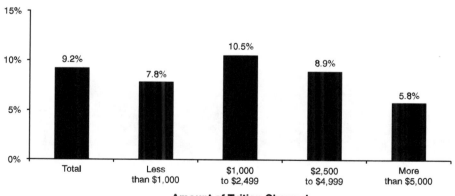

Source: Schools and Staffing Survey, 1993-94.

CHAPTER III.
Characteristics of Schools Attended by African American Students

To what extent are African Americans attending elementary and secondary schools in which they comprise the majority of students? How are the schools that are comprised primarily of African American students different from the schools with few African American students? Does the availability of various services and programs (e.g., remedial reading, gifted and talented programs, job placement for graduating seniors) vary based upon the concentration of African Americans in the student body?

Definitive answers on the effects of schooling and school climate remain elusive. Yet, data are available to explore many factors internal to schools that may affect educational outcomes for thousands of African American students. The national Schools and Staffing Survey (SASS), developed by the U.S. Department of Education, provides a vast range of data and information that allow comparisons between schools where the student body is predominantly African American and schools where virtually no African American students attend.

The most recent (1993/94) SASS data show the representation of African American students in elementary and secondary schools, both in the public and private sectors. The data offer a picture of the racial composition of the schools, as well as other characteristics, such as their admission requirements and programs. Such data provide a starting point for answering the question, "How equal is equal?"

CHAPTER ORGANIZATION

To allow the reader to compare and contrast African American schooling in the public and private sectors, the data have been arranged under common headings with the public sector information preceding the private. The chapter begins with an overview of the findings, followed by a detailed description of the tables and data.

PART I — OVERVIEW

While desegregation may have held out the hope of educational equality, essential differences appear to exist among America's schools. Not surprisingly,

many private and public schools have no African American students. About one-fifth of public elementary and secondary, one-third of private elementary, and one-fourth of private secondary schools have virtually no African American students enrolled. African Americans tended to be concentrated in schools that are academically inadequate, since those schools with a majority of African American students tended to be vocational or technical, special education, or alternative schools rather than regular schools.

Even in the public sector, schools with heavy African American concentrations pose more admission requirements. In contrast to schools with few

African Americans, however, schools where African Americans are the majority focus upon such factors as special needs and special aptitudes. Remediation programs are abundant in predominantly African American schools, where higher proportions of students participated in these programs. Head Start and Chapter One prekindergartens appear to be more common at schools where African American students represent the majority, although such programs were by no means widespread in 1993/94.

The quality of teachers at schools also appears to have varied depending on the concentration of African Americans in the student body. Moreover, in contrast to schools with few African American students, schools with a large percentage of African American students tended to rely upon long- and short-term substitutes to fill vacancies.

The challenges that face schools dominated by African Americans are further evidenced by lower graduation rates and lower college enrollment rates among their high school graduates. The greater availability of job placement services at such schools suggests one possible explanation for decreased college entry.

PART II — DETAILED DESCRIPTIONS AND TABLES

DEMOGRAPHIC CHARACTERISTICS

Public Schools

Figure 1 shows that, in 1993/94, one-fifth (20.3%) of America's 80,740 public elementary and secondary schools had virtually no African American students enrolled.

- **Table 1** shows that 40.3% of all public schools had student bodies in which African Americans comprised 1.0% to 5.0% of all students.

- African Americans represented between one-fifth and one-half of enrolled students at 13.5%

Figure 1. Distribution of America's Public Schools by Percentage of African American Students Enrolled: 1993/94

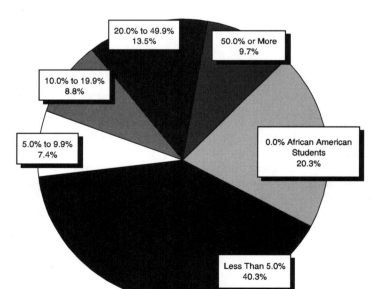

20.0% to 49.9%
13.5%

50.0% or More
9.7%

10.0% to 19.9%
8.8%

0.0% African American Students
20.3%

5.0% to 9.9%
7.4%

Less Than 5.0%
40.3%

Source: Schools and Staffing Survey, 1993-94.

Table 1. Distribution of Public Schools by Percentage of African American Students Enrolled: 1993/94
(weighted sample size in parentheses)

School Level	Total	0.0%	Less Than 5.0%	5.0% to 9.9%	10.0% to 19.9%	20.0% to 49.9%	50.0% or More
Total***	100.0%	20.3%	40.3%	7.4%	8.8%	13.5%	9.7%
	100.0%	100.0%	100.0%	100.0%	100.0%	100.0%	100.0%
	(80,740)	(16,426)	(32,564)	(5,986)	(7,069)	(10,893)	(7,802)
Elementary	100.0%	18.8%	41.2%	7.5%	9.0%	13.5%	10.1%
	71.9%	66.4%	73.3%	72.3%	73.5%	71.8%	75.4%
	(58,013)	(10,905)	(23,881)	(4,329)	(5,195)	(7,825)	(5,879)
Secondary	100.0%	23.8%	40.5%	7.5%	8.1%	12.2%	8.0%
	24.3%	28.5%	24.4%	24.5%	22.5%	22.0%	20.1%
	(19,648)	(4,677)	(7,955)	(1,464)	(1,594)	(2,391)	(1,566)
Combined Elementary and Secondary	100.0%	27.4%	23.7%	6.3%	9.1%	22.0%	11.6%
	3.8%	5.1%	2.2%	3.2%	4.0%	6.2%	4.6%
	(3,079)	(843)	(728)	(193)	(280)	(677)	(357)

Note:

***Test of statistical significance compares the six categories of schools by the percentage of African American students. *** p < .001, ** p < .01, * p < .05.
Source: Schools and Staffing Survey, 1993-94.

of public schools and at least one-half of enrolled students at 9.7% of public schools.

Private Schools

Figure 2 shows that, in 1993/94, virtually no African American students were enrolled in more than one-third (36.0%) of America's 26,093 private elementary and secondary schools.

- **Table 2** shows that, at an additional one-third (30.5%) of all private schools, 1.0% to 5.0% of enrolled students were African American. At only 6.5% of all private schools were more than one-half of enrolled students African American.

School Level

Public Schools

In 1993/94, 71.9% (*n* = 58,000) of America's public schools (*n* = 80,700) were elementary schools, 24.3% (*n* = 19,600) were secondary schools, and 3.8% (*n* = 3,000) were combined elementary and secondary schools.

Table 1 also shows that the distribution of elementary schools by the percentage of African Americans enrolled was comparable to the distribution of secondary schools. Although the number of combined elementary and secondary schools was small (*n* = 3,079), a higher percentage of combined elementary and secondary schools (27.4%) than of both stand-alone elementary schools (18.8%) and stand-alone secondary schools (23.8%) appeared to have no African American students enrolled.

Table 3 shows that public schools classified as vocational or technical, special education, or alternative had higher concentrations of African American students than regular elementary or secondary schools.

- African Americans represented more than one-half of total enrollments at 25.6% of vocational or technical schools, 16.8% of special education schools, and 14.3% of alternative schools.

- By comparison, African Americans represented 50.0% or more of total enrollments at only 8.6% of regular elementary and secondary schools.

Figure 2. Distribution of Private Schools by the Percentage of African American Students Enrolled: 1993/94

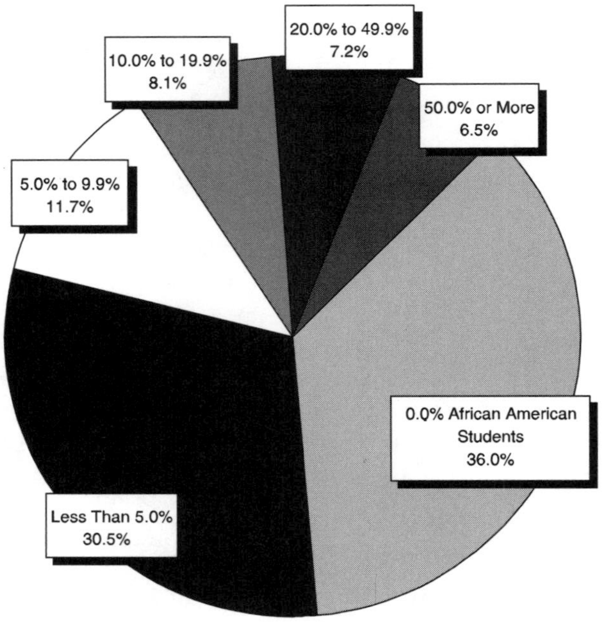

20.0% to 49.9%
7.2%

10.0% to 19.9%
8.1%

50.0% or More
6.5%

5.0% to 9.9%
11.7%

0.0% African American Students
36.0%

Less Than 5.0%
30.5%

Source: Schools and Staffing Survey, 1993-94.

Table 2. Distribution of Private Schools by Level of School and Percentage of African American Students Enrolled: 1993/94
(weighted sample size in parentheses)

School Level	Total	0.0%	Less Than 5.0%	5.0% to 9.9%	10.0% to 19.9%	20.0% to 49.9%	50.0% or More
Total***	100.0%	36.0%	30.5%	11.7%	8.1%	7.2%	6.5%
	100.0%	100.0%	100.0%	100.0%	100.0%	100.0%	100.0%
	(26,093)	(9,391)	(7,965)	(3,051)	(2,109)	(1,888)	(1,689)
Elementary	100.0%	37.8%	33.7%	8.5%	7.2%	5.6%	7.2%
	59.5%	62.5%	65.7%	43.2%	53.2%	46.1%	66.5%
	(15,537)	(5,873)	(5,231)	(1,317)	(1,121)	(871)	(1,123)
Secondary	100.0%	26.4%	38.9%	12.9%	10.0%	9.3%	2.5%
	9.8%	7.2%	12.5%	10.8%	12.1%	12.6%	3.7%
	(2,551)	(673)	(992)	(329)	(256)	(238)	(63)
Combined Elementary and Secondary	100.0%	35.5%	21.8%	17.6%	9.1%	9.7%	6.3%
	30.7%	30.3%	21.9%	46.1%	34.7%	41.2%	29.8%
	(8,006)	(2,845)	(1,742)	(1,405)	(732)	(778)	(503)

Note:
***Test of statistical significance compares the six categories of schools by the percentage of African American students. *** p < .001, ** p < .01, * p < .05.
Source: Schools and Staffing Survey, 1993-94

Table 3. Number and Percentage of Different Types of Public Elementary and Secondary Schools by Percentage of African American Students Enrolled: 1993/94
(weighted sample size in parentheses)

Type of School	Total	0.0%	Less Than 5.0%	5.0% to 9.9%	10.0% to 19.9%	2.0% to 49.9%	50.0% or More
Total***	100.0%	20.3%	40.3%	7.4%	8.8%	13.5%	9.7%
	100.0%	100.0%	100.0%	100.0%	100.0%	100.0%	100.0%
	(80,740)	(16,426)	(32,564)	(5,986)	(7,069)	(10,893)	(7,802)
Regular Elementary or Secondary	100.0%	21.1%	41.5%	7.6%	8.3%	12.8%	8.6%
	92.6%	95.9%	95.4%	94.8%	88.1%	88.1%	82.5%
	(74,751)	(15,753)	(31,058)	(5,674)	(6,229)	(9,598)	(6,439)
Special Education	100.0%	16.8%	8.1%	8.0%	22.5%	27.8%	16.8%
	1.5%	1.2%	0.3%	1.6%	3.8%	3.0%	2.5%
	(1,180)	(198)	(96)	(94)	(266)	(327)	(198)
Vocational/Technical	100.0%	10.8%	34.0%	5.0%	9.1%	15.5%	25.6%
	0.9%	0.5%	0.7%	0.6%	0.9%	1.0%	2.3%
	(687)	(74)	(234)	(34)	(62)	(106)	(176)
Alternative	100.0%	18.8%	27.5%	6.6%	14.4%	18.4%	14.3%
	2.1%	1.9%	1.4%	1.9%	3.4%	2.8%	3.1%
	(1,690)	(317)	(465)	(112)	(243)	(310)	(242)
Unknown	100.0%	3.4%	29.2%	3.0%	11.0%	22.7%	30.7%
	3.0%	0.5%	2.2%	1.2%	3.8%	5.1%	9.6%
	(2,433)	(83)	(712)	(73)	(268)	(552)	(746)
Total***	100.0%	100.0%	100.0%	100.0%	100.0%	100.0%	100.0%
	(80,740)	(16,426)	(32,564)	(5,986)	(7,069)	(10,893)	(7,802)
School Offers Magnet Program	6.5%	1.6%	4.9%	5.3%	8.9%	11.3%	15.8%
	(5,257)	(256)	(1,597)	(316)	(626)	(1,227)	(1,237)

Note:
***Test of statistical significance compares the six categories of schools by the percentage of African American students. *** p < .001, ** p < .01, * p < .05.
Source: Schools and Staffing Survey, 1993-94.

The share of public schools offering magnet programs increased with the representation of African Americans in the student body.

- Only 1.6% of schools with no African American students offered magnet programs, compared with 15.8% of schools with African American students represented the majority.

Private Schools

Table 2 shows that, in 1993/94, 59.5% of America's private schools were elementary schools, 9.8% were secondary schools, and 30.7% were combined elementary and secondary schools. At more than one-half of elementary, secondary, and combined schools less than 5.0% of enrolled students were African American.

- Schools in which African Americans comprised 50.0% or more of the student body represented 7.2% of all elementary schools, 2.5% of all secondary schools, and 6.3% of all combined elementary and secondary schools.

In 1993/94, 83.3% of all private schools were regular elementary or secondary schools. But, as the concentration of African American enrollments increased, the percentage of schools that were regular elementary or secondary schools declined, and the percentage that were special education or alternative schools appeared to increase.

- **Table 4** shows that 66.5% of schools in which African Americans comprised 50.0% or more of enrollments were regular elementary or secondary schools, compared with 88.6% of schools with no African American students.

- About 16.2% of schools in which African Americans represented the majority of students were alternative private schools, compared with 5.6% of schools with no African American students.

- About 10.3% of schools in which African Americans comprised the majority of students were special education schools, compared with 2.1% of schools with no African American students.

Affiliation

Private Schools Only

Catholic schools comprised 32.0% of all private schools, non-Catholic religious schools comprised 46.7%, and nonsectarian schools comprised 21.3%.

- **Table 5** shows that Catholic schools comprised more than one-third (35.6%) of private schools in which more than 50.0% of the student body was African American, but only one-fourth (23.1%) of private schools in which virtually no African Americans were enrolled.

- Non-Catholic religious schools comprised nearly two-thirds (59.9%) of private schools in which virtually no African Americans were enrolled, but only 39.6% of schools in which

Table 4. Number and Percentage of Different Types of Private Elementary and Secondary Schools by Percentage of African American Students Enrolled: 1993/94
(weighted sample size in parentheses)

Type of School	Total	0.0%	Less Than 5.0%	5.0% to 9.9%	10.0% to 19.9%	20.0% to 49.9%	50.0% or More
Total***	100.0%	36.0%	30.5%	11.7%	8.1%	7.2%	6.5%
	100.0%	100.0%	100.0%	100.0%	100.0%	100.0%	100.0%
	(26,093)	(9,391)	(7,965)	(3,050)	(2,109)	(1,888)	(1,690)
Regular Elementary or	100.0%	38.3%	33.6%	10.3%	6.9%	5.8%	5.2%
Secondary	83.3%	88.6%	91.6%	73.5%	71.3%	66.8%	66.5%
	(21,747)	(8,319)	(7,299)	(2,241)	(1,503)	(1,261)	(1,124)
Montessori	100.0%	25.2%	20.9%	26.6%	12.8%	8.8%	5.7%
	3.2%	2.3%	2.2%	7.4%	5.1%	3.9%	2.8%
	(845)	(213)	(177)	(225)	(108)	(74)	(48)
Elementary or Secondary	100.0%	24.7%	23.5%	24.0%	13.0%	2.6%	12.2%
With Special	2.2%	1.5%	1.7%	4.5%	3.6%	0.8%	4.1%
Program Emphasis	(575)	(142)	(135)	(138)	(75)	(15)	(70)
Special Education	100.0%	13.6%	7.8%	19.1%	18.9%	28.5%	12.2%
	5.5%	2.1%	1.4%	8.9%	12.8%	21.6%	10.3%
	(1,427)	(194)	(111)	(272)	(269)	(407)	(174)
Alternative	100.0%	35.1%	16.3%	11.7%	9.9%	8.8%	18.4%
	5.7%	5.6%	3.1%	5.7%	7.0%	6.9%	16.2%
	(1,492)	(523)	(243)	(174)	(147)	(131)	(274)

Note:
***Test of statistical significance compares the six categories of schools by the percentage of African American students. *** p < .001, ** p < .01, * p < .05.
Source: Schools and Staffing Survey, 1993-94.

Table 5. Affiliation of Private Elementary and Secondary Schools by Percentage of African American Students Enrolled: 1993/94
(weighted sample size in parentheses)

Affiliation	Total	0.0%	Less Than 5.0%	5.0% to 9.9%	10.0% to 19.9%	20.0% to 49.9%	50.0% or More
Total***	100.0%	36.0%	30.5%	11.7%	8.1%	7.2%	6.5%
	100.0%	100.0%	100.0%	100.0%	100.0%	100.0%	100.0%
	(26,093)	(9,391)	(7,965)	(3,051)	(2,109)	(1,888)	(1,690)
Catholic	100.0%	26.0%	49.0%	8.1%	4.8%	4.9%	7.2%
	32.0%	23.1%	51.4%	22.1%	19.2%	21.8%	35.6%
	(8,350)	(2,167)	(4,093)	(674)	(404)	(411)	(601)
Non-Catholic Religious	100.0%	46.2%	21.2%	10.8%	8.9%	7.4%	5.5%
	46.7%	59.9%	32.5%	43.2%	51.3%	47.7%	39.6%
	(12,181)	(5,627)	(2,585)	(1,317)	(1,081)	(901)	(670)
Nonsectarian	100.0%	28.7%	23.1%	19.1%	11.2%	10.4%	7.5%
	21.3%	17.0%	16.2%	34.7%	29.6%	30.5%	24.8%
	(5,563)	(1,597)	(1,287)	(1,060)	(624)	(576)	(419)

Note:
***Test of statistical significance compares the six categories of schools by the percentage of African American students. *** p < .001, ** p < .01, * p < .05.
Source: Schools and Staffing Survey, 1993-94.

African American students constituted the majority.

Enrollment

Public Schools

The concentration of African American students increased with the total number of enrolled students.

- **Table 6** shows that 74.5% of schools with fewer than 50 students had no African American students.

- At only 2.3% of schools with fewer than 50 students were more than one-half of all students African American.

- African Americans represented more than one-half of enrolled students at 11.5% of public schools with 750 or more students.

- Only 3.3% of schools with 750 or more students had no African American students.

The percentage of students absent on the most recent school day also seemed to increase with the concentration of African American students, ranging from 5.3% at schools at with no African American students to 7.4% at schools at which 50.0% or more of the students were African Americans.

Private Schools

The relationship between school size and the concentration of African American students is more difficult to determine at private schools because of both the smaller number of private schools and the smaller number of African American students enrolled at private schools.

- **Table 7** shows that African American students represented the majority of all students at 6.6% of all private schools, 7.3% of private schools

Table 6. Enrollment at Public Elementary and Secondary Schools by Percentage of African American Students Enrolled: 1993/94
(weighted sample size in parentheses)

Enrollment	Total	0.0%	Less Than 5.0%	5.0% to 9.9%	10.0% to 19.9%	20.0% to 49.9%	50.0% or More
Total***	100.0%	20.3%	40.3%	7.4%	8.8%	13.5%	9.7%
	100.0%	100.0%	100.0%	100.0%	100.0%	100.0%	100.0%
	(80,740)	(16,426)	(32,564)	(5,986)	(7,069)	(10,893)	(7,802)
0 to 49	100.0%	74.5%	4.1%	3.9%	8.0%	7.2%	2.3%
	3.0%	11.0%	0.3%	1.6%	2.8%	1.6%	0.7%
	(2,435)	(1,813)	(99)	(96)	(195)	(176)	(55)
50 to 99	100.0%	63.0%	16.2%	1.9%	4.5%	7.1%	7.3%
	3.8%	11.6%	1.5%	1.0%	1.9%	2.0%	2.8%
	(3,031)	(1,908)	(493)	(57)	(136)	(215)	(222)
100 to 199	100.0%	52.7%	25.4%	2.9%	3.6%	9.0%	6.4%
	10.1%	26.2%	6.4%	4.0%	4.2%	6.7%	6.7%
	(8,170)	(4,308)	(2,074)	(237)	(293)	(734)	(524)
200 to 299	100.0%	30.5%	40.3%	5.3%	5.7%	11.0%	7.2%
	12.1%	18.2%	12.1%	8.7%	7.9%	9.8%	9.1%
	(9,776)	(2,983)	(3,938)	(520)	(556)	(1,071)	(707)
300 to 399	100.0%	20.0%	41.5%	5.4%	9.8%	11.5%	11.8%
	14.2%	13.9%	14.6%	10.3%	15.9%	12.1%	17.3%
	(11,447)	(2,290)	(4,750)	(614)	(1,123)	(1,319)	(1,351)
400 to 499	100.0%	11.0%	48.4%	7.0%	8.9%	14.7%	10.0%
	14.4%	7.8%	17.3%	13.6%	14.6%	15.8%	15.0%
	(11,661)	(1,287)	(5,639)	(814)	(1,034)	(1,718)	(1,170)
500 to 749	100.0%	6.9%	47.9%	10.2%	8.5%	15.9%	10.6%
	24.5%	8.3%	29.1%	33.5%	23.7%	28.8%	27.0%
	(19,744)	(1,362)	(9,462)	(2,007)	(1,672)	(3,139)	(2,103)
750 or More	100.0%	3.3%	42.2%	11.3%	14.2%	17.4%	11.5%
	17.9%	2.9%	18.8%	27.4%	29.1%	23.1%	21.4%
	(14,476)	(474)	(6,110)	(1,642)	(2,060)	(2,521)	(1,671)
% Students Absent Most	5.9%	5.3%	5.6%	5.8%	6.5%	6.4%	7.4%
Recent School Day***	(80,740)	(16,426)	(32,564)	(5,986)	(7,069)	(10,893)	(7,802)

Note:
***Test of statistical significance compares the six categories of schools by the percentage of African American students. *** $p < .001$, ** $p < .01$, * $p < .05$.
Source: Schools and Staffing Survey, 1993-94.

Table 7. Enrollment at Private Elementary and Secondary Schools by Percentage of African American Students Enrolled: 1993/94
(weighted sample size in parentheses)

Enrollment	Total	0.0%	Less Than 5.0%	5.0% to 9.9%	10.0% to 19.9%	20.0% to 49.9%	50.0% or More
Total***	100.0%	36.6%	29.7%	11.9%	8.1%	7.3%	6.6%
	100.0%	100.0%	100.0%	100.0%	100.0%	100.0%	100.0%
	(25,690)	(9,391)	(7,623)	(3,051)	(2,069)	(1,866)	(1,689)
0 to 49	100.0%	61.4%	5.1%	10.8%	7.8%	7.6%	7.3%
	24.7%	41.5%	4.3%	22.5%	24.0%	25.8%	27.2%
	(6,342)	(3,894)	(324)	(686)	(497)	(481)	(460)
50 to 99	100.0%	39.4%	17.0%	14.7%	10.5%	12.6%	5.8%
	17.5%	18.8%	10.0%	21.7%	22.8%	30.3%	15.4%
	(4,490)	(1,767)	(764)	(662)	(472)	(565)	(260)
100 to 199	100.0%	30.6%	34.8%	10.4%	10.3%	6.6%	7.2%
	23.5%	19.7%	27.6%	20.5%	30.2%	21.4%	25.7%
	(6,035)	(1,849)	(2,103)	(625)	(624)	(400)	(434)
200 to 299	100.0%	21.5%	45.7%	11.8%	6.4%	6.9%	7.7%
	16.0%	9.4%	24.6%	15.9%	12.6%	15.2%	18.7%
	(4,109)	(885)	(1,879)	(484)	(261)	(284)	(316)
300 to 399	100.0%	22.6%	56.3%	10.4%	3.5%	2.6%	4.7%
	7.9%	4.9%	15.0%	6.9%	3.4%	2.8%	5.7%
	(2,035)	(459)	(1,146)	(211)	(71)	(52)	(96)
400 to 499	100.0%	17.3%	59.1%	11.4%	3.6%	4.9%	3.6%
	4.8%	2.3%	9.6%	4.6%	2.2%	3.3%	2.7%
	(1,236)	(214)	(730)	(141)	(45)	(61)	(45)
500 to 749	100.0%	19.3%	55.1%	10.7%	8.1%	1.9%	4.9%
	4.8%	2.5%	8.9%	4.3%	4.8%	1.3%	3.6%
	(1,229)	(237)	(677)	(132)	(99)	(23)	(60)
750 or More	100.0%	13.9%	55.2%	18.0%	6.4%	3.5%	3.0%
	2.4%	0.9%	4.5%	3.6%	1.9%	1.2%	1.1%
	(619)	(86)	(341)	(111)	(40)	(21)	(19)
% Students Absent Most	4.1%	3.9%	3.7%	4.5%	4.7%	5.6%	4.0%
Recent School Day***	(26,093)	(9,391)	(7,965)	(3,051)	(2,109)	(1,888)	(1,689)

Note:
***Test of statistical significance compares the six categories of schools by the percentage of African American students. *** p < .001, ** p < .01, * p < .05.
Source: Schools and Staffing Survey, 1993-94.

with fewer than 50 students, 5.8% of private schools with 50 to 99 students, and 7.2% of private schools with 100 to 199 students.

Location

Public Schools

Figure 3 shows that, on average, schools located in urban areas had higher concentrations of African American students than did schools located in rural and suburban areas.

- **Table 8** shows that schools where more than 50.0% of the student body was African American represented 21.9% of urban schools, but only 8.5% of suburban schools and 4.4% of rural schools.

- Schools in which no African Americans were enrolled comprised only 5.2% of urban schools and 8.6% of suburban schools, but 34.2% of rural schools.

- **Figure 3** shows that 53.8% of public schools in which African Americans represented more than one-half of enrollments were located in urban areas, 24.0% were located in suburban areas, and 22.2% in rural areas.

Private Schools

As with public schools, schools with a majority of African American students represented a larger share of urban private schools than of rural private schools.

- **Table 9** shows that schools with a majority of African American students represented 13.5% of urban private schools, but only 3.5% of suburban private schools and 1.1% of rural private schools.

- Schools with virtually no African American students comprised 16.9% of urban schools, but 28.8% of suburban schools and 67.7% of rural schools.

Figure 3. Distribution of Public Schools by Location and Percentage of African American Students Enrolled: 1993/94

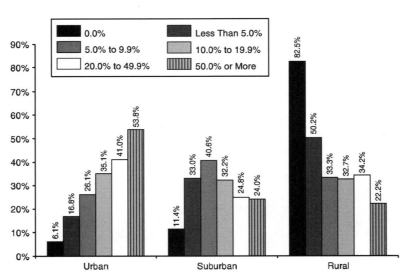

Source: Schools and Staffing Survey, 1993-94.

Table 8. Location of Public Elementary and Secondary Schools by Percentage of African American Students Enrolled: 1993/94
(weighted sample size in parentheses)

Location	Total	0.0%	Less Than 5.0%	5.0% to 9.9%	10.0% to 19.9%	20.0% to 49.9%	50.0% or More
Total***	100.0%	20.3%	40.3%	7.4%	8.8%	13.5%	9.7%
	100.0%	100.0%	100.0%	100.0%	100.0%	100.0%	100.0%
	(80,740)	(16,426)	(32,564)	(5,986)	(7,069)	(10,893)	(7,802)
Urban	100.0%	5.2%	28.5%	8.1%	12.9%	23.3%	21.9%
	23.8%	6.1%	16.8%	26.1%	35.1%	41.0%	53.8%
	(19,184)	(1,006)	(5,467)	(1,563)	(2,483)	(4,464)	(4,201)
Suburban	100.0%	8.6%	49.1%	11.1%	10.4%	12.3%	8.5%
	27.1%	11.4%	33.0%	40.6%	32.2%	24.8%	24.0%
	(21,912)	(1,876)	(10,752)	(2,431)	(2,275)	(2,706)	(1,872)
Rural	100.0%	34.2%	41.2%	5.0%	5.8%	9.4%	4.4%
	49.1%	82.5%	50.2%	33.3%	32.7%	34.2%	22.2%
	(39,644)	(13,543)	(16,345)	(1,992)	(2,311)	(3,723)	(1,729)

Note:
***Test of statistical significance compares the six categories of schools by the percentage of African American students. *** p < .001, ** p < .01, * p < .05.
Source: Schools and Staffing Survey, 1993-94.

Table 9. Location of Private Elementary and Secondary Schools by Percentage of African American Students Enrolled: 1993/94
(weighted sample size in parentheses)

Location	Total	0.0%	Less Than 5.0%	5.0% to 9.9%	10.0% to 19.9%	20.0% to 49.9%	50.0% or More
Total***	100.0%	36.0%	30.5%	11.7%	8.1%	7.2%	6.5%
	100.0%	100.0%	100.0%	100.0%	100.0%	100.0%	100.0%
	(26,092)	(9,391)	(7,965)	(3,050)	(2,109)	(1,888)	(1,689)
Urban	100.0%	16.9%	33.7%	13.5%	11.0%	11.4%	13.5%
	37.2%	17.5%	41.1%	42.9%	50.7%	58.8%	77.4%
	(9,707)	(1,639)	(3,275)	(1,307)	(1,069)	(1,110)	(1,307)
Suburban	100.0%	28.8%	38.0%	13.6%	8.3%	7.8%	3.5%
	32.9%	26.3%	41.0%	38.2%	33.6%	35.6%	17.8%
	(8,583)	(2,472)	(3,263)	(1,166)	(709)	(673)	(300)
Rural	100.0%	67.7%	18.3%	7.4%	4.2%	1.3%	1.1%
	29.9%	56.2%	17.9%	18.9%	15.7%	5.6%	4.9%
	(7,802)	(5,280)	(1,427)	(577)	(331)	(105)	(82)

Note:
***Test of statistical significance compares the six categories of schools by the percentage of African American students. *** p < .001, ** p < .01, * p < .05.
Source: Schools and Staffing Survey, 1993-94.

Minority Teachers and Students

Public Schools

Figure 4 shows that the percentage of minority teachers and students at America's public schools increased with the concentration of African American students.

- **Table 10** shows that, on average, only 5.1% (*n* = 1.3) of teachers were minorities at schools with no African American students.

- At schools in which African Americans represented a majority of the enrollments, 45.3% (*n* = 15.7) of teachers were minorities.

- At schools with no African American students, only 10.9% (*n* = 34.8) of all students were minorities.

- At schools in which more than one-half of all students were African American, 83.3% (*n* = 472.1) of all students were minorities.

Private Schools

Figure 4 also shows that, as at public schools, the percentage of minority teachers and students increased with the concentration of African American students.

- **Table 11** shows that 53.6% (*n* = 4.9) of teachers at schools in which African American students represented more than one-half of all students were minorities, compared with only 3.0% (*n* = 0.4) of teachers at schools with no African American students.

- The percentage of minority students ranged from a high of 94.5% (*n* = 156.9) at schools with

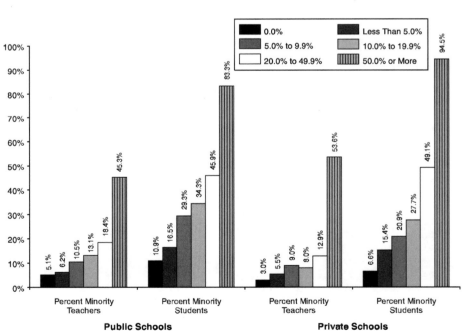

Figure 4. Percentage of Minority Students and Teachers at Public and Private Elementary and Secondary Schools by the Percentage of African American Students Enrolled: 1993/94

Source: Schools and Staffing Survey, 1993-94.

Table 10. Number and Percentage of Minority Students and Teachers at Public Elementary and Secondary Schools by Percentage of African American Students Enrolled: 1993/94
(weighted sample size in parentheses)

Minority Teachers and Students	Total	0.0%	Less Than 5.0%	5.0% to 9.9%	10.0% to 19.9%	20.0% to 49.9%	50.0% or More
Total	100.0% (80,740)	20.3% (16,426)	40.3% (32,564)	7.4% (5,986)	8.8% (7,069)	13.5% (10,893)	9.7% (7,802)
% Minority Teachers***	12.3% (80,740)	5.1% (16,426)	6.2% (32,564)	10.5% (5,986)	13.1% (7,069)	18.4% (10,893)	45.3% (7,802)
Number Minority Teachers***	4.4 (80,740)	1.3 (16,426)	2.3 (32,564)	3.9 (5,986)	4.9 (7,069)	7.0 (10,893)	15.7 (7,802)
% Minority Students***	28.3% (80,740)	10.9% (16,426)	16.5% (32,564)	29.3% (5,986)	34.3% (7,069)	45.9% (10,893)	83.3% (7,802)
Number Minority Students***	168.4 (80,740)	34.8 (16,426)	106.1 (32,564)	203.1 (5,986)	230.9 (7,069)	279.3 (10,893)	472.1 (7,802)

Note:

*** Test of statistical significance compares the six categories of schools by the percentage of African American students. *** p < .001, ** p < .01, * p < .05.
Source: Schools and Staffing Survey, 1993-94.

Table 11. Number and Percentage of Minority Students and Teachers at Private Elementary and Secondary Schools by Percentage of African American Students Enrolled: 1993/94
(weighted sample size in parentheses)

Minority Teachers and Students	Total	0.0%	Less Than 5.0%	5.0% to 9.9%	10.0% to 19.9%	20.0% to 49.9%	50.0% or More
Total	100.0% (25,690)	36.6% (9,391)	29.7% (7,623)	11.9% (3,051)	8.1% (2,069)	7.3% (1,866)	6.6% (1,689)
% Minority Teachers***	8.9% (26,093)	3.0% (9,391)	5.5% (7,965)	9.0% (3,051)	8.0% (2,109)	12.9% (1,888)	53.6% (1,689)
Number Minority Teachers***	1.1 (26,093)	0.4 (9,391)	1.1 (7,965)	1.2 (3,051)	1.1 (2,109)	1.5 (1,888)	4.9 (1,689)
% Minority Students***	21.4% (26,093)	6.6% (9,391)	15.4% (7,965)	20.9% (3,051)	27.7% (2,109)	49.1% (1,888)	94.5% (1,689)
Number Minority Students***	42.0 (26,093)	10.6 (9,391)	45.7 (7,965)	41.6 (3,051)	51.1 (2,109)	70.9 (1,888)	156.9 (1,689)

Note:

***Test of statistical significance compares the six categories of schools by the percentage of African American students. *** p < .001, ** p < .01, * p < .05.
Source: Schools and Staffing Survey, 1993-94.

a majority of African American students to a low of 6.6% ($n = 10.6$) at schools with no African American students.

TEACHER VACANCIES

Public Schools Only

Overall, about three-fourths (73.7%) of public schools had teacher vacancies during the 1993/94 school year. **Table 12** shows that a smaller percentage of schools with no African American students (64.7%) than of other schools had teacher vacancies.

- A smaller share of schools in which a majority of students were African American than of schools with no African American students reported that teachers hired to fill vacancies were fully qualified (87.2% versus 97.2%).

The use of long- or short-term substitutes to fill teacher vacancies generally increased with the concentration of African American students enrolled. The prevalence of other actions to cope with teacher vacancies (e.g., cancel courses, adding sections to teachers' normal loads, assigning administrators or counselors to teach classes) did not vary by the concentration of African American students enrolled.

- One-third (31.2%) of schools in which African American students were the majority used long- or short-term substitutes to fill teacher vacancies, compared with only 5.5% of schools with no African American students.

ADMISSIONS REQUIREMENTS

Public Schools

Only 9.1% of public elementary and secondary schools had special admission requirements (i.e., other than age, residency, or immunization). However, a higher percentage of schools in which 20.0% or more of the students were African Americans had special admissions requirements than of schools with smaller shares of African Americans.

- **Table 13** shows that 15.3% of schools in which African Americans represented 20.0% to 49.9% all students and 14.7% of schools in which African Americans comprised the majority had special admissions requirements, compared with only 6.8% of public schools with no African American students and 6.6% of schools with less than 5.0% African Americans.

Regardless of the percentage of African Americans enrolled, the most common admissions requirements were special student needs and academic record. Only 6.8% of schools with special admissions requirements used admissions tests.

- Overall, 38.5% of public schools with admissions requirements relied most on students' academic records and 31.2% relied most upon special student needs.

Private Schools

At private schools, the most common admissions requirement in 1993/94 was a personal interview (used by 43.8% of all private schools). Schools with a majority of African American students tended to use admissions tests, special student needs, recommendations, and special student aptitudes as admissions requirements rather than religious affiliation.

- **Table 14** shows that 31.5% of schools with a majority of African American students used admissions tests, compared with only 17.5% of schools with no African American students.

- Special student needs were used by 22.2% of schools with a majority of African American students, but only 9.7% of schools with no African American students.

- About 11.5% of schools with a majority of African American students used special student aptitudes, compared with only 3.2% of schools with no African American students.

- Only 6.4% of schools with a majority of African American students used religious affiliation as an admissions requirement, compared with

Table 12. Teacher Vacancies at Public Elementary and Secondary Schools by Percentage of African American Students Enrolled: 1993/94
(weighted sample size in parentheses)

Teacher Vacancies	Total	0.0%	Less Than 5.0%	5.0% to 9.9%	10.0% to 19.9%	20.0% to 49.9%	50.0% or More
Total***	100.0%	100.0%	100.0%	100.0%	100.0%	100.0%	100.0%
	(80,740)	(16,426)	(32,564)	(5,986)	(7,069)	(10,893)	(7,802)
Yes	73.7%	64.7%	76.4%	72.5%	75.3%	77.8%	74.8%
	(59,480)	(10,621)	(24,887)	(4,340)	(5,326)	(8,472)	(5,834)
No	26.3%	35.3%	23.6%	27.5%	24.7%	22.2%	25.2%
	(21,260)	(5,805)	(7,677)	(1,647)	(1,743)	(2,422)	(1,968)
Qualifications of Teachers Hired to Fill Vacancies							
Had Teacher Vacancies	100.0%	100.0%	100.0%	100.0%	100.0%	100.0%	100.0%
	(59,480)	(10,621)	(24,887)	(4,340)	(5,326)	(8,472)	(5,834)
Teachers Hired Fully Qualified***	94.6%	97.2%	95.8%	95.1%	92.2%	93.9%	87.2%
	(56,258)	(10,322)	(23,852)	(4,127)	(4,912)	(7,958)	(5,088)
Actions Because of Vacancies:							
Had Vacancies	100.0%	100.0%	100.0%	100.0%	100.0%	100.0%	100.0%
	(59,480)	(10,621)	(24,887)	(4,340)	(5,326)	(8,472)	(5,834)
Canceled Planned Courses*	1.4%	1.7%	1.0%	0.4%	0.8%	2.1%	2.3%
	(803)	(178)	(258)	(17)	(42)	(174)	(133)
Expanded Some Class Sizes**	5.6%	4.0%	5.5%	7.2%	4.4%	7.7%	5.8%
	(3,329)	(426)	(1,362)	(312)	(236)	(655)	(338)
Added Sections to Teachers' Normal Loads	4.0%	3.2%	3.8%	5.5%	5.7%	4.2%	3.1%
	(2,370)	(340)	(946)	(240)	(303)	(358)	(184)
Assigned Teachers of Other Subjects to Cover**	4.5%	3.2%	4.3%	5.3%	7.1%	5.4%	3.4%
	(2,671)	(341)	(1,062)	(231)	(378)	(459)	(200)
Assigned Administrator or Counselor to Teach Class	0.9%	1.1%	0.7%	0.7%	0.9%	1.5%	0.4%
	(517)	(116)	(177)	(30)	(46)	(125)	(23)
Used Long/Short-Term Substitutes***	14.9%	5.5%	13.1%	18.7%	16.8%	17.9%	31.2%
	(8,888)	(581)	(3,263)	(813)	(893)	(1,515)	(1,823)
Used Other Methods**	2.0%	1.4%	1.7%	1.6%	3.1%	2.2%	3.8%
	(1,216)	(145)	(428)	(68)	(167)	(185)	(224)

Note:
***Test of statistical significance compares the six categories of schools by the percentage of African American students. *** $p < .001$, ** $p < .01$, * $p < .05$.
Source: Schools and Staffing Survey, 1993-94.

Table 13. Admissions Requirements of Public Elementary and Secondary Schools by Percentage of African American Students Enrolled: 1993/94
(weighted sample size in parentheses)

Requirement	Total	0.0%	Less Than 5.0%	5.0% to 9.9%	10.0% to 19.9%	20.0% to 49.9%	50.0% or More
Total***	100.0% (80,740)	100.0% (16,426)	100.0% (32,564)	100.0% (5,986)	100.0% (7,069)	100.0% (10,893)	100.0% (7,802)
Yes	9.1% (7,386)	6.8% (1,112)	6.6% (2,143)	7.9% (476)	11.9% (840)	15.3% (1,665)	14.7% (1,150)
No	90.9% (73,355)	93.2% (15,314)	93.4% (30,421)	92.1% (5,511)	88.1% (6,229)	84.7% (9,228)	85.3% (6,652)
Type of Admissions Requirement							
Yes, Admissions Requirements	100.0% (7,386)	100.0% (1,112)	100.0% (2,143)	100.0% (476)	100.0% (840)	100.0% (1,665)	100.0% (1,150)
Admissions Test*	6.8% (500)	4.1% (46)	3.5% (75)	7.0% (33)	7.4% (62)	9.2% (153)	11.4% (131)
Standardized Achievement Test	11.9% (882)	12.3% (136)	8.3% (179)	16.9% (81)	7.0% (59)	14.9% (248)	15.5% (179)
Academic Record	38.9% (2,875)	36.2% (403)	42.3% (906)	42.7% (203)	33.5% (281)	43.0% (716)	31.8% (366)
Special Student Needs	38.8% (2,867)	38.4% (427)	35.3% (756)	43.2% (206)	46.3% (389)	38.7% (645)	38.6% (444)
Special Student Aptitudes*	11.6% (859)	6.0% (67)	11.2% (240)	22.6% (108)	10.7% (90)	10.7% (178)	15.3% (176)
Personal Interview**	22.0% (1,623)	18.0% (201)	19.9% (426)	30.7% (146)	36.2% (304)	19.7% (328)	19.0% (219)
Recommendations*	23.1% (1,706)	22.6% (251)	18.9% (405)	23.2% (110)	36.3% (305)	24.0% (400)	20.4% (235)
None of the Above	30.8% (2,272)	31.0% (344)	36.5% (781)	26.4% (125)	22.6% (189)	26.3% (438)	34.2% (393)
Most Important Requirement							
Total*	100.0% (5,114)	100.0% (768)	100.0% (1,362)	100.0% (350)	100.0% (650)	100.0% (1,227)	100.0% (756)
Admissions Test	4.1% (211)	3.2% (24)	4.6% (63)	7.6% (27)	0.3% (2)	3.9% (48)	6.3% (47)
Standardized Achievement Tests	3.9% (201)	7.4% (57)	2.1% (29)	2.5% (9)	3.9% (25)	4.1% (51)	4.0% (31)
Academic Record	38.5% (1,968)	36.7% (282)	49.0% (668)	38.1% (134)	27.1% (176)	41.2% (506)	26.7% (202)
Special Student Needs	31.2% (1,597)	36.9% (283)	21.4% (291)	22.8% (80)	39.4% (256)	30.4% (374)	41.4% (313)
Special Student Aptitudes	2.4% (125)	0.0% (0)	3.1% (43)	4.8% (17)	0.0% (0)	2.1% (26)	5.2% (39)
Personal Interview	12.2% (626)	11.9% (91)	12.9% (175)	18.1% (64)	20.2% (131)	8.2% (100)	8.5% (65)
Recommendations	7.5% (386)	4.0% (30)	6.8% (93)	6.0% (21)	9.3% (60)	10.0% (122)	7.8% (59)

Notes:

Special Admissions Requirements include those other than age, immunization, and residency.

***Test of statistical significance compares the six categories of schools by the percentage of African American students. *** $p < .001$, ** $p < .01$, * $p < .05$.

Source: Schools and Staffing Survey, 1993-94.

Table 14. Admissions Requirements at Private Elementary and Secondary Schools by Percentage of African American Students Enrolled: 1993/94
(weighted sample size in parentheses)

Requirement	Total	0.0%	Less Than 5.0%	5.0% to 9.9%	10.0% to 19.9%	20.0% to 49.9%	50.0% or More
Total	100.0% (25,690)	100.0% (9,391)	100.0% (7,623)	100.0% (3,051)	100.0% (2,069)	100.0% (1,866)	100.0% (1,689)
Admissions Test***	26.1% (6,704)	17.5% (1,640)	35.9% (2,735)	28.8% (878)	24.3% (503)	22.3% (416)	31.5% (532)
Standardized Achievement Tests***	18.6% (4,782)	10.5% (990)	25.6% (1,951)	25.4% (775)	21.0% (435)	19.0% (355)	16.3% (276)
Academic Record***	35.0% (9,002)	23.3% (2,189)	48.1% (3,670)	44.6% (1,360)	31.5% (651)	36.1% (674)	27.1% (458)
Special Student Needs***	13.3% (3,411)	9.7% (910)	11.9% (907)	12.7% (387)	17.2% (355)	25.6% (477)	22.2% (375)
Special Student Aptitudes***	4.9% (1,256)	3.2% (301)	5.2% (394)	6.6% (201)	4.2% (86)	4.3% (80)	11.5% (194)
Personal Interview***	43.8% (11,254)	36.9% (3,468)	48.9% (3,731)	54.1% (1,651)	35.2% (729)	51.4% (960)	42.3% (715)
Recommendations***	22.0% (5,662)	14.8% (1,393)	27.6% (2,101)	33.0% (1,007)	19.4% (402)	20.6% (384)	22.2% (375)
Religious Affiliation***	15.1% (3,872)	18.7% (1,758)	16.6% (1,267)	10.2% (312)	7.1% (147)	15.0% (280)	6.4% (108)
None of the Above***	1.9% (477)	3.6% (337)	0.4% (32)	3.1% (94)	0.0% –	0.0% –	0.0% –
Most Important Consideration for Admission*	100.0% (15,453)	100.0% (4,787)	100.0% (5,195)	100.0% (1,948)	100.0% (1,193)	100.0% (1,307)	100.0% (1,023)
Admissions Test	12.2% (1,880)	6.5% (310)	16.8% (872)	7.1% (138)	14.2% (170)	16.2% (212)	17.5% (179)
Standardized Achievement Tests	3.3% (512)	2.1% (101)	4.1% (211)	3.6% (70)	6.3% (75)	1.9% (25)	3.0% (31)
Academic Record	17.6% (2,719)	9.1% (438)	21.5% (1,118)	26.4% (514)	17.8% (212)	19.1% (249)	18.6% (190)
Special Student Needs	11.0% (1,695)	8.3% (399)	4.3% (222)	10.6% (206)	22.3% (266)	27.1% (354)	24.1% (247)
Special Student Aptitudes	0.4% (68)	0.0% –	0.0% –	0.0% –	0.0% –	0.0% –	3.7% (38)
Personal Interview	36.9% (5,709)	44.4% (2,124)	35.2% (1,828)	41.3% (805)	30.7% (366)	26.7% (349)	23.3% (238)
Recommendations	3.7% (572)	3.9% (185)	3.5% (182)	4.7% (92)	2.7% (32)	2.1% (28)	5.2% (53)
Religious Affiliation	14.9% (2,295)	25.3% (1,213)	14.5% (754)	6.2% (120)	6.0% (71)	6.9% (90)	4.6% (47)

Note:
***Test of statistical significance compares the six categories of schools by the percentage of African American students. *** p < .001, ** p < .01, * p < .05.
"–" indicates sample size too small to estimate.
Source: Schools and Staffing Survey, 1993-94.

18.7% of schools with no African American students.

- A smaller share of schools with a majority of African American students than of schools with no African American students relied most upon personal interviews (23.3% versus 44.4%).

TUITION POLICIES

Private Schools Only

Table 15 shows that about 93.2% of private elementary and secondary schools charged tuition and 90.1% had policies for discounting tuition.

- About 84.4% of schools with a majority of African American students had tuition discounting policies, compared with 88.6% of schools with

no African American students and 94.4% of schools with 1.0% to 5.0% of African American students.

- The relationship between tuition policies and the concentration of African American students at the school is difficult to discern because of the small numbers of private schools and African Americans attending private schools.

PROGRAMS OFFERED

Preschool Programs

Public Schools Only

Overall, Head Start programs were available at only 6.5% of public elementary and secondary schools in 1993/94. Schools with a majority of Afri-

Table 15. Tuition Policies at Private Elementary and Secondary Schools by Percentage of African American Students Enrolled: 1993/94
(weighted sample size in parentheses)

Tuition Policies	Total	0%	Less Than 5.0%	5.0% to 9.9%	10.0% to 19.9%	20.0% to 49.9%	50.0% or More
Tuition Charged*	100.0%	100.0%	100.0%	100.0%	100.0%	100.0%	100.0%
	(26,093)	(9,391)	(7,965)	(3,051)	(2,109)	(1,887)	(1,690)
Yes	93.2%	87.7%	99.5%	96.9%	94.0%	90.7%	89.6%
	(24,327)	(8,238)	(7,926)	(2,955)	(1,982)	(1,711)	(1,515)
No	6.8%	12.3%	0.5%	3.1%	6.0%	9.3%	10.4%
	(1,766)	(1,153)	(39)	(96)	(127)	(176)	(175)
Tuition Discounting*	100.0%	100.0%	100.0%	100.0%	100.0%	100.0%	100.0%
	(24,326)	(8,237)	(7,925)	(2,955)	(1,982)	(1,712)	(1,515)
Yes	90.1%	88.6%	94.4%	88.0%	92.4%	84.3%	84.4%
	(21,929)	(7,294)	(7,484)	(2,599)	(1,831)	(1,443)	(1,278)
No	9.9%	11.4%	5.6%	12.0%	7.6%	15.7%	15.6%
	(2,397)	(943)	(441)	(356)	(151)	(269)	(237)
Highest Annual Tuition Charged Full-Time Students*	$3,084	$2,355	$2,947	$4,256	$3,738	$4,581	$2,941
	(24,310)	(8,238)	(7,926)	(2,955)	(1,978)	(1,706)	(1,507)

Note:
***Test of statistical significance compares the six categories of schools by the percentage of African American students. *** $p < .001$, ** $p < .01$, * $p < .05$.
Source: Schools and Staffing Survey, 1993-94.

can American students were overrepresented among schools in which Head Start was administered by the school or district and underrepresented among schools in which Head Start was administered by outside agencies.

- **Table 16** shows that 5.9% of schools with a majority of African American students had Head Start programs administered by the school or district, compared with 2.3% of schools with no African American students.

- Only 3.0% of schools with a majority of African American students had Head Start programs administered by outside agencies, compared with 6.5% of schools with no African American students.

Schools in which the majority of students were African American were also overrepresented among schools with Chapter One prekindergarten programs and among schools with general prekindergarten programs administered by the school or district.

- Among schools in which the majority of students were African American, 12.8% had Chapter One prekindergarten programs and 15.7% had general prekindergarten programs administered by the school or district.

- By comparison, only 2.7% of schools with no African American students had Chapter One prekindergarten programs and 8.7% had general prekindergarten programs administered by the school or district.

National School Lunch Program

Public Schools

Overall, about 94.3% of public elementary and secondary schools participated in the National School Lunch Program and at least 93.0% had students eligible for the program.

- **Table 17** shows that 90.8% of schools with no African American students participated in the National School Lunch Program.

Private Schools

Table 18 shows that a higher percentage of schools with a majority of African American students than of all private schools participated in the National School Lunch Program (35.2% versus 22.8%).

Services Offered

Public Schools

About 80.9% of public schools had remedial reading programs, 60.9% had remedial math programs, 89.2% had programs for students with disabilities, and 70.7% had gifted and talented programs. **Figure 5** shows that the percentage of students participating in both remedial reading and remedial math seemed to increase with the concentration of African American students.

- Compared with schools with no African American students, a higher percentage of schools with a majority of African American students offered remedial reading programs (83.9% versus 78.2%) and remedial math programs (68.0% versus 59.7%).

- **Table 19** shows that at schools with a majority of African American students, 24.9% of all students participated in remedial reading and 22.1% participated in remedial math.

- By comparison, at schools with no African American students, 14.8% of all students participated in remedial reading and 11.8% participated in remedial math.

- A smaller share of schools with a majority of African American students than of schools with no African American students offered prescriptive services (73.6% versus 82.8%).

Private Schools

About one-half (53.6%) of all private schools offered remedial reading programs, and 41.0% offered remedial math programs. Additionally, 25.1% of all private schools had programs for students with disabilities, and 25.3% had gifted and talented programs.

Table 16. Preschool Programs Available at Public Elementary and Secondary Schools by Percentage of African American Students Enrolled: 1993/94
(weighted sample size in parentheses)

Preschool Programs	Total	0.0%	Less Than 5.0%	5.0% to 9.9%	10.0% to 19.9%	20.0% to 49.9%	50.0% or More
Total	100.0% (80,740)	100.0% (16,426)	100.0% (32,564)	100.0% (5,986)	100.0% (7,069)	100.0% (10,893)	100.0% (7,802)
Head Start Administered by School/District***	2.7% (2,166)	2.3% (375)	2.1% (696)	3.5% (208)	1.8% (126)	2.7% (298)	5.9% (462)
Head Start Administered by Outside Agency***	3.8% (3,055)	6.5% (1,063)	3.4% (1,091)	2.8% (165)	1.8% (128)	3.5% (376)	3.0% (232)
Day Care Program Administered by School/District**	2.6% (2,070)	1.7% (277)	2.2% (707)	3.6% (215)	4.0% (286)	2.9% (312)	3.5% (274)
Day Care Program Administered by Outside Agency	1.9% (1,554)	2.6% (426)	1.6% (535)	1.3% (77)	2.0% (140)	2.5% (268)	1.4% (108)
Chapter One Pre-K Program***	3.8% (3,079)	2.7% (443)	1.9% (611)	2.5% (151)	3.5% (245)	5.8% (629)	12.8% (1,000)
Pre-K Special Education Administered by School/District*	10.9% (8,780)	10.2% (1,682)	9.9% (3,213)	12.9% (772)	11.5% (811)	12.7% (1,387)	11.7% (916)
Pre-K Special Education Administered by Outside Agency***	2.1% (1,671)	4.7% (778)	1.9% (615)	0.3% (15)	0.9% (65)	1.3% (139)	0.8% (59)
General Pre-K Program Administered by School/District***	10.2% (8,257)	8.7% (1,433)	8.3% (2,711)	9.2% (552)	12.4% (873)	13.5% (1,466)	15.7% (1,223)
General Pre-K Program Administered by Outside Agency**	1.3% (1,047)	2.0% (327)	1.3% (426)	1.1% (65)	0.0% –	1.2% (129)	1.2% (94)

Note:
***Test of statistical significance compares the six categories of schools by the percentage of African American students. *** p < .001, ** p < .01, * p < .05.
"–" indicates sample size too small to estimate.
Source: Schools and Staffing Survey, 1993-94.

Schools with a majority of African American students were overrepresented among private schools with remedial reading programs and remedial math programs and underrepresented among private schools with library media centers.

- **Table 18** shows that 63.8% of schools with 50.0% or more African American students offered remedial reading programs, compared with 45.5% of schools with no African American students.

- About 61.6% of schools with a majority of African American students offered remedial math programs, compared with 33.5% of schools with no African American students.

Table 17. Participation in National School Lunch Program at Public Elementary and Secondary Schools by Percentage of African American Students Enrolled: 1993/94
(weighted sample size in parentheses)

National School Lunch Program	Total	0.0%	Less Than 5.0%	5.0% to 9.9%	10.0% to 19.9%	20.0% to 49.9%	50.0% or More
Participates in National School Lunch Program							
Total***	100.0%	100.0%	100.0%	100.0%	100.0%	100.0%	100.0%
	(80,740)	(16,426)	(32,564)	(5,986)	(7,069)	(10,893)	(7,802)
Yes	94.3%	90.8%	94.5%	96.1%	95.2%	96.4%	95.8%
	(76,143)	(14,909)	(30,775)	(5,753)	(6,732)	(10,498)	(7,477)
No	5.7%	9.2%	5.5%	3.9%	4.8%	3.6%	4.2%
	(4,597)	(1,517)	(1,789)	(233)	(337)	(396)	(326)
Regardless Whether Participates, Any Students Eligible							
Total***	100.0%	100.0%	100.0%	100.0%	100.0%	100.0%	100.0%
	(80,740)	(16,426)	(32,564)	(5,986)	(7,069)	(10,893)	(7,802)
Yes	93.0%	89.4%	92.7%	95.0%	95.4%	94.7%	95.3%
	(75,069)	(14,689)	(30,201)	(5,685)	(6,741)	(10,318)	(7,437)
No	1.9%	3.3%	1.8%	1.7%	1.4%	1.1%	1.5%
	(1,561)	(549)	(580)	(99)	(98)	(121)	(114)
Don't Know	5.1%	7.2%	5.5%	3.4%	3.3%	4.2%	3.2%
	(4,110)	(1,187)	(1,783)	(203)	(231)	(455)	(252)

Note:
***Test of statistical significance compares the six categories of schools by the percentage of African American students. *** $p < .001$, ** $p < .01$, * $p < .05$.
Source: Schools and Staffing Survey, 1993-94

- Only 68.6% of schools with a majority of African American students had library media centers, compared with 81.6% of all private schools.

Figure 6 shows that the percentages of students participating in remedial reading, remedial math, and programs for students with disabilities generally increased with the percentage of African American students enrolled.

- The percentage of students participating in remedial reading ranged from 17.9% at schools with no African American students to 25.6% at schools in which more than one-half of all students were African American.

- Only 17.7% of students at schools with no African American students participated in remedial math, compared with 28.1% of students at schools with a majority of African American students.

- The percentage of students participating in gifted and talented programs ranged from 17.9% at schools with no African American students to 32.7% at schools with a majority of African American students.

Table 18. Programs Available at Private Elementary and Secondary Schools by Percentage of African American Students Enrolled: 1993/94
(weighted sample size in parentheses)

Programs	Total	0.0%	Less Than 5.0%	5.0% to 9.9%	10.0% to 19.9%	20.0% to 49.9%	50.0% or More
Total	100.0%	100.0%	100.0%	100.0%	100.0%	100.0%	100.0%
	(25,690)	(9,391)	(7,623)	(3,051)	(2,069)	(1,866)	(1,689)
Remedial Reading, Even If No Funding***	53.6%	45.5%	61.0%	49.2%	50.3%	66.5%	63.8%
	(13,782)	(4,272)	(4,648)	(1,502)	(1,041)	(1,242)	(1,077)
% Students Participate in Remedial Reading***	18.0%	17.9%	10.0%	20.3%	20.3%	36.6%	25.6%
	(13,782)	(4,272)	(4,648)	(1,502)	(1,041)	(1,242)	(1,077)
Remedial Math, Even If No Funding***	41.0%	33.5%	44.2%	37.5%	40.7%	53.5%	61.6%
	(10,539)	(3,149)	(3,367)	(1,143)	(842)	(998)	(1,040)
% Students Participate in Remedial Math***	17.9%	17.7%	0.8%	21.6%	18.5%	36.1%	28.1%
	(10,539)	(3,149)	(3,367)	(1,143)	(842)	(998)	(1,040)
Programs for Students With Disabilities, Even If No Funding***	25.1%	20.1%	24.6%	31.5%	28.4%	36.9%	27.2%
	(6,460)	(1,887)	(1,876)	(961)	(587)	(689)	(460)
% Students Participate in Disabilities Programs***	28.7%	18.4%	9.3%	35.1%	48.3%	69.1%	50.7%
	(6,460)	(1,887)	(1,876)	(961)	(587)	(689)	(460)
Programs for Gifted and Talented, Even If No Funding	25.3%	22.7%	28.4%	29.0%	27.0%	20.1%	22.1%
	(6,488)	(2,129)	(2,168)	(884)	(559)	(375)	(373)
% Students Participate in Gifted and Talented Programs***	20.0%	17.9%	16.8%	29.3%	19.9%	15.2%	32.7%
	(6,488)	(2,129)	(2,168)	(884)	(559)	(375)	(373)
Prescriptive Services, Even If No Funding***	44.2%	38.6%	49.1%	41.1%	44.6%	48.2%	54.2%
	(11,354)	(3,623)	(3,740)	(1,255)	(922)	(899)	(915)
Medical Health Care Services, Even If No Funding***	31.5%	22.8%	38.9%	33.8%	30.7%	38.5%	35.1%
	(8,085)	(2,143)	(2,962)	(1,032)	(636)	(719)	(593)
Library Media Center***	81.6%	73.8%	95.0%	80.2%	77.8%	83.4%	68.6%
	(20,951)	(6,933)	(7,245)	(2,447)	(1,610)	(1,557)	(1,159)
National School Lunch Program Available***	22.8%	23.1%	24.2%	16.1%	17.2%	21.1%	35.2%
	(5,846)	(2,166)	(1,848)	(490)	(355)	(393)	(594)

Note:
***Test of statistical significance compares the six categories of schools by the percentage of African American students. *** $p < .001$, ** $p < .01$, * $p < .05$.
Source: Schools and Staffing Survey, 1993-94.

Figure 5. Percentage of Students Participating in Various Programs at Public Schools by Percentage of African American Students Enrolled: 1993/94

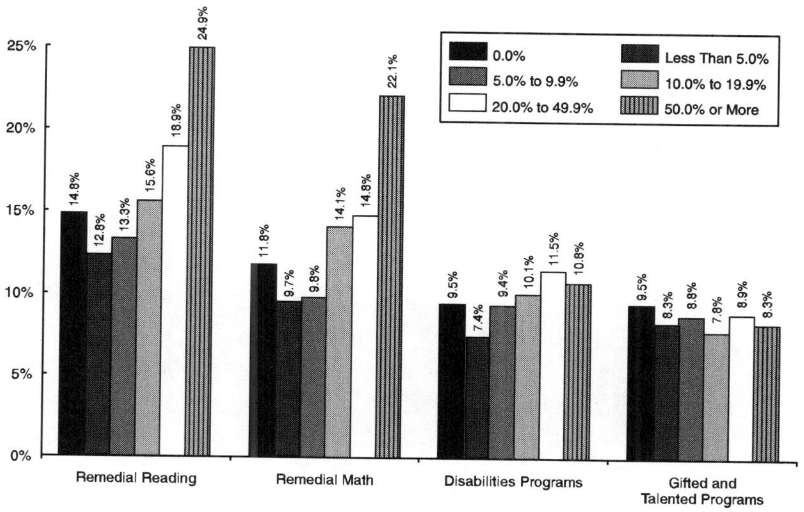

Source: Schools and Staffing Survey, 1993-94.

Programs for Graduating Seniors

Public Schools

Overall, 91.4% of 12th graders graduated from high school on time and 58.0% of high school graduates applied to college. But, **Figure 7** shows that both the percentage of seniors who graduated and the percentage of high school graduates who applied to college decreased as the percentage of African Americans in the student body increased.

- **Table 20** shows that 93.4% of seniors at high schools with no African American students graduated on time, compared with 87.0% of seniors at high schools in which African American students were in the majority.

- Only 51.6% of graduates from high schools in which 50.0% or more of the students were African American applied to college, compared with 60.1% of graduates from high schools with no African American students.

- The proportion of high schools with a majority of African American students that offered job placement to graduating seniors was more than twice as high as the proportion of high schools with no African American students (38.3% versus 15.7%).

Private Schools

About 92.9% of 12th graders graduated from private high schools on time. **Table 21** shows that more than three-fourths (78.4%) of private high school graduates applied to college.

Table 19. Programs Available at Public Elementary and Secondary Schools by Percentage of African American Students Enrolled: 1993-94
(weighted sample size in parentheses)

Programs	Total	0%	Less than 5%	5% to 9.9%	10% to 19.9%	20% to 49.9%	50% or more
Total	100.0% (80,740)	100.0% (16,426)	100.0% (32,564)	100.0% (5,986)	100.0% (7,069)	100.0% (10,893)	100.0% (7,802)
Remedial Reading Available Even If No Funding **	80.9% (65,321)	78.2% (12,849)	82.0% (26,697)	81.3% (4,866)	81.6% (5,768)	78.9% (8,591)	83.9% (6,550)
% Students Who Participate Remedial Reading ***	15.5% (65,321)	14.8% (12,849)	12.8% (26,697)	13.3% (4,866)	15.6% (5,768)	18.9% (8,591)	24.9% (6,550)
Remedial Math Available Even If No Funding ***	60.9% (49,208)	59.7% (9,801)	61.2% (19,934)	55.4% (3,314)	61.7% (4,362)	59.6% (6,490)	68.0% (5,308)
% Students Who Participate Remedial Math***	12.6% (49,208)	11.8% (9,801)	9.7% (19,934)	9.8% (3,314)	14.1% (4,362)	14.8% (6,490)	22.1% (5,308)
Programs for Students With Disabilities, Even If No Funding***	89.2% (71,982)	83.9% (13,781)	91.5% (29,786)	89.6% (5,366)	89.6% (6,337)	89.6% (9,761)	89.1% (6,952)
% Students Who Participate Disabilities Programs***	9.1% (71,982)	9.5% (13,781)	7.4% (29,786)	9.4% (5,366)	10.1% (6,337)	11.5% (9,761)	10.8% (6,952)
Programs for Gifted/ Talented Even If No Funding***	70.7% (57,111)	63.3% (10,405)	74.7% (24,319)	74.5% (4,458)	73.6% (5,201)	73.9% (8,047)	60.0% (4,681)
% Students Who Participate Gifted and Talented Programs*	8.6% (57,111)	9.5% (10,405)	8.3% (24,319)	8.8% (4,458)	7.8% (5,201)	8.9% (8,047)	8.3% (4,681)
Day, Before, After School Daycare, Even If No Funding***	23.9% (19,274)	10.4% (1,707)	24.6% (8,014)	30.8% (1,844)	32.1% (2,272)	28.5% (3,106)	29.9% (2,330)
English as Second Language Even If No Funding***	42.7% (34,466)	22.5% (3,698)	48.8% (15,888)	59.8% (3,579)	56.4% (3,985)	48.0% (5,230)	26.8% (2,087)
Prescriptive Services Available Even If No Funding***	82.6% (66,661)	82.8% (13,600)	85.3% (27,782)	82.2% (4,923)	81.8% (5,780)	81.1% (8,838)	73.6% (5,739)
Health Care Services Even If No Funding*	58.7% (47,422)	57.6% (9,461)	60.7% (19,755)	59.4% (3,556)	59.3% (4,194)	55.9% (6,085)	56.0% (4,370)
School has Library Media Center***	95.6% (77,218)	93.2% (15,300)	97.2% (31,638)	97.6% (5,845)	95.3% (6,737)	93.5% (10,185)	96.3% (7,513)

Note:
***Test of statistical significance compares the six categories of schools by the percentage of African American students. *** p < .001, ** p < .01, * p < .05.
Source: Schools and Staffing Survey, 1993-94.

Figure 6. Percentage of Students Participating in Various Programs at Private Schools by Percentage of African American Students Enrolled: 1993/94

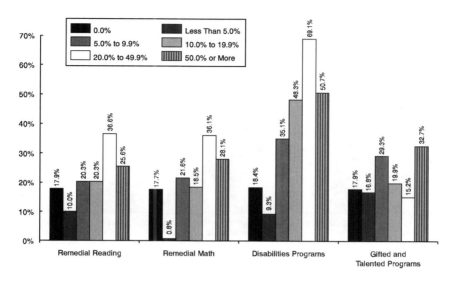

Source: Schools and Staffing Survey, 1993-94.

- **Figure 8** shows that the percentage of seniors who graduated from high school on time was lower at schools in which 20.0% to 49.9% of the student body was African American than at other schools (72.6% compared with 92.9% overall).

- The percentage of high school graduates who applied to college was lower at schools in which 20.0% to 49.9% of the student body was African American than at other schools (58.7% compared to 78.4% overall).

Figure 7. Characteristics of High School Seniors at Public Schools by Percentage of African American Students Enrolled: 1993/94

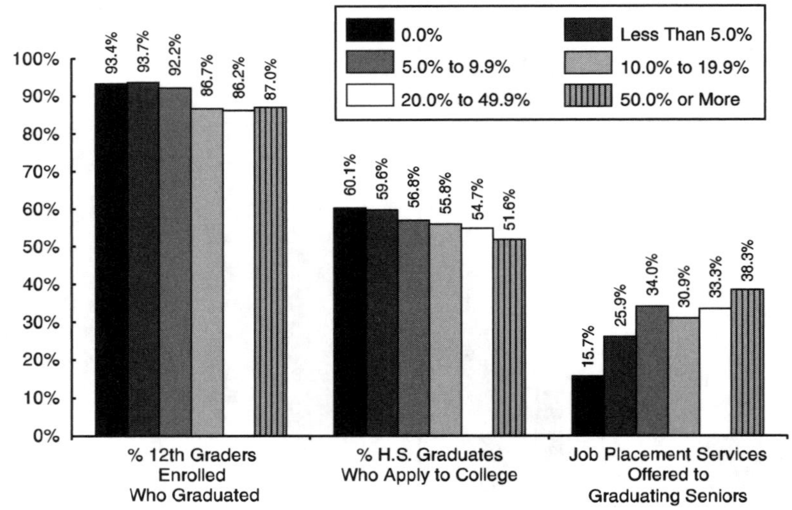

Source: Schools and Staffing Survey, 1993-94.

Table 20. Programs for Graduating Seniors at Public Schools by Percentage of African American Students Enrolled: 1993/94

(weighted sample size in parentheses)

Programs	Total	0.0%	Less Than 5.0%	5.0% to 9.9%	10.0% to 19.9%	20.0% to 49.9%	50.0% or More
School Provides Instruction to Students in Grade 12							
Total***	100.0%	100.0%	100.0%	100.0%	100.0%	100.0%	100.0%
	(80,740)	(16,426)	(32,564)	(5,986)	(7,069)	(10,893)	(7,802)
Yes	22.2%	28.8%	20.6%	20.0%	22.1%	21.3%	18.4%
	(17,958)	(4,734)	(6,713)	(1,197)	(1,565)	(2,316)	(1,433)
Total Provides Instruction to Students in Grade 12	100.0% (17,958)	100.0% (4,734)	100.0% (6,713)	100.0% (1,197)	100.0% (1,565)	100.0% (2,316)	100.0% (1,433)
% 12th Graders Enrolled Last Year Who Graduated***	91.4% (17,838)	93.4% (4,666)	93.7% (6,686)	92.2% (1,161)	86.7% (1,546)	86.2% (2,378)	87.0% (1,401)
Percent H. S. Graduates Who Apply to College***	58.0% (17,405)	60.1% (4,593)	59.6% (6,576)	56.8% (1,151)	55.8% (1,483)	54.7% (2,272)	51.6% (1,329)
Job Placement Services Offered to Graduating Seniors***	26.1% (4,692)	15.7% (744)	25.9% (1,738)	34.0% (407)	30.9% (484)	33.3% (771)	38.3% (548)
Has Tech-Prep Program	55.8% (10,016)	50.4% (2,384)	57.6% (3,864)	54.4% (652)	59.2% (926)	57.9% (1,342)	59.1% (847)

Note:

***Test of statistical significance compares the six categories of schools by the percentage of African American students. *** p < .001, ** p < .01, * p < .05.
Source: Schools and Staffing Survey, 1993-94.

Table 21. Programs for Graduating Seniors at Private Schools by Percentage of African American Students Enrolled: 1993/94
(weighted sample size in parentheses)

Programs	Total	0.0%	Less Than 5.0%	5.0% to 9.9%	10.0% to 19.9%	20.0% to 49.9%	50.0% or More
School Provides Instruction to Students in Grade 12							
Total***	100.0%	100.0%	100.0%	100.0%	100.0%	100.0%	100.0%
	(25,690)	(9,391)	(7,623)	(3,051)	(2,069)	(1,866)	(1,689)
Yes	32.0%	27.0%	31.7%	48.8%	37.2%	42.6%	12.0%
	(8,212)	(2,536)	(2,420)	(1,490)	(769)	(795)	(202)
Total Provides Instruction to Students in Grade 12	100.0% (8,212)	100.0% (2,536)	100.0% (2,420)	100.0% (1,490)	100.0% (769)	100.0% (795)	100.0% (202)
%12th Graders Enrolled Last Year Who Graduated***	92.9% (7,876)	93.5% (2,448)	97.9% (2,417)	91.9% (1,328)	94.8% (791)	72.6% (693)	95.4% (199)
% High School Graduates Who Apply to College***	78.4% (7,445)	73.0% (2,326)	88.4% (2,397)	79.2% (1,251)	75.2% (759)	58.7% (521)	79.7% (191)
Job Placement Services Offered to Graduating Seniors***	13.8% (1,131)	9.5% (242)	11.4% (276)	9.1% (136)	18.7% (144)	38.9% (309)	11.9% (24)
Regular High School Diploma Granted***	89.3% (7,335)	84.8% (2,151)	98.8% (2,392)	91.9% (1,369)	78.8% (606)	78.9% (627)	94.1% (190)

Note:

***Test of statistical significance compares the six categories of schools by the percentage of African American students. *** p < .001, ** p < .01, * p < .05.
Source: Schools and Staffing Survey, 1993-94.

Figure 8. Characteristics of High School Seniors at Private Schools by Percentage of African American Students Enrolled: 1993/94

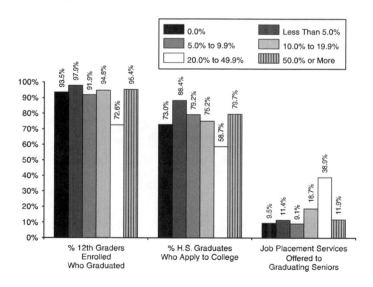

Source: Schools and Staffing Survey, 1993-94.

CHAPTER IV.
Attendance and Behavior Among 1988 8th Graders in 1988 and 1992

How frequently are African American students absent from and tardy to school? Do African American students come to class prepared to learn? How involved are African American youth in extracurricular activities at their schools? To what extent do their television viewing habits limit their ability to be involved with and prepared for school- and education-related activities?

While enrollment data document the representation of African Americans at elementary and secondary schools, these official counts do not answer questions regarding the extent to which African American students are actually present at school and ready to learn. One source of such data is the National Educational Longitudinal Study of 1988 8th graders (NELS:88). Sponsored by the U.S. Department of Education's National Center for Education Statistics, the NELS:88 tracks the educational experiences of students through their high school years and beyond. This chapter draws upon data collected from one group of students—1988 8th graders—in the base year (1988) and as part of the second follow-up in 1992.

CHAPTER ORGANIZATION

This chapter includes a description of several aspects of school attendance, including school absences and tardiness, preparation for class, and participation in extracurricular activities. The amount of time spent watching television is also described since this represents time that is not spent on school- and education-related activities. Changes in the indicators between 1988 (when students were in the 8th grade) and 1992 (when most students were high school seniors) are also examined.

PART I — OVERVIEW

On some measures, African American students appear to be as ready to learn as their White peers. Although preparation for class was generally higher for girls than for boys, class preparation rates did not vary for African Americans and Whites of the same sex. In both 1988 and 1992, similar percentages of African Americans and Whites consistently attended class with their books, their note-taking materials, and their completed homework.

Nonetheless, other indicators suggest that African American students are less ready to learn than White students. On average, African Americans had higher rates of unexcused absences and tardiness than White students. African Americans appeared to be disciplined for behavioral problems with greater frequency than White students since a higher percentage of African Americans than Whites were sent to the principal's office for misbehaving.

African American high school seniors also appear to be less involved with school-related activities than their White counterparts. Particularly troublesome is the decline between the 8th and 12th grades in the proportion of African Americans who participated in academic subject clubs, academic honor societies, and the school newspaper and yearbook.

Moreover, African American students seem to have less exposure to nonschool educational activities and opportunities. As 8th graders, a smaller percentage of African Americans than Whites participated in nonschool clubs, such as scouting, religious organizations, 4-H clubs, and other youth groups. On average, African Americans spent substantially greater amounts of time watching television than their White counterparts in both 1988 and 1992.

PART II — DETAILED DESCRIPTIONS AND TABLES

SCHOOL ATTENDANCE

Days Absent From School

One-half (55.1%) of 1988 8th graders reported that they had missed at least one day of school during the four-week period prior to the survey. Comparable shares of African Americans and Whites reported missing a day of school during this period (50.2% versus 55.9%).

Almost all (91.4%) students who were 8th graders in 1988 reported that they had missed at least one day of school during the previous term. But, **Figure 1** shows that a smaller share of African American boys than of other students had not missed one day of school during the last term.

- **Table 1** shows that, among 1988 8th graders in 1988, only 77.6% of African American boys reported missing at least one day of school during the previous term, compared with 88.6% of African American girls, 91.6% of White boys, and 94.3% of White girls.

Unexcused Absences

One-half (52.8%) of students who were 8th graders in 1988 reported at least one unexcused absence during the first half of the 1991/92 academic year. **Figure 2** shows that a higher share of girls than boys reported no unexcused absences among all students (51.9% versus 42.5%) and among African Americans (45.8% versus 35.9%).

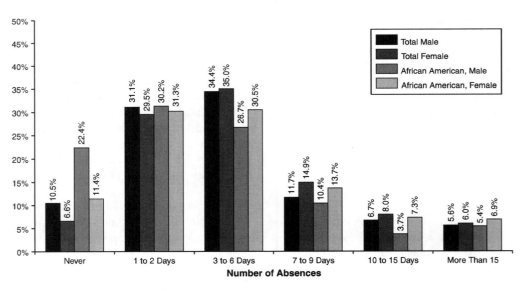

Figure 1. Attendance at School During the Last Term Among 1988 8th Graders in 1988

Source: National Educational Longitudinal Study of 1988 Eighth Graders, Base Year (1988).

Table 1. Attendance at School Among 1988 8th Graders in 1988 by Race and Sex
(weighted sample size in parentheses)

Attendance	Total	Male	Female	White, Non-Hispanic Total	Male	Female	African American, Non-Hispanic Total	Male	Female	Hispanic Total	Male	Female	Other Total	Male	Female
Number of Days Absent From School in Past 4 Weeks: 1988															
Total +++	100.0%	100.0%	100.0%	100.0%	100.0%	100.0%	100.0%	100.0%	100.0%	100.0%	100.0%	100.0%	100.0%	100.0%	100.0%
	(2,788,775)	(1,389,125)	(1,399,651)	(2,033,459)	(1,028,183)	(1,005,275)	(340,951)	(162,449)	(178,502)	(278,318)	(131,755)	(146,563)	(136,047)	(66,738)	(69,310)
None	44.9%	48.0%	41.8%	44.1%	47.5%	40.6%	49.8%	50.4%	49.4%	42.4%	45.6%	39.6%	50.0%	55.1%	45.0%
	(1,253,100)	(667,431)	(585,669)	(897,092)	(488,678)	(408,414)	(169,942)	(81,821)	(88,121)	(118,109)	(60,142)	(57,967)	(67,957)	(36,790)	(31,167)
At Least 1 Day *** ++ ~~	100.0%	100.0%	100.0%	100.0%	100.0%	100.0%	100.0%	100.0%	100.0%	100.0%	100.0%	100.0%	100.0%	100.0%	100.0%
	(1,535,676)	(721,694)	(813,982)	(1,136,367)	(539,506)	(596,861)	(171,009)	(80,628)	(90,382)	(160,209)	(71,613)	(88,596)	(68,090)	(29,947)	(38,143)
1 or 2 Days	61.8%	64.1%	59.7%	63.0%	64.9%	61.3%	58.3%	61.4%	55.5%	56.5%	61.4%	52.5%	62.0%	63.9%	60.5%
	(948,292)	(462,700)	(485,592)	(715,915)	(350,038)	(365,877)	(99,666)	(49,538)	(50,128)	(90,490)	(43,982)	(46,508)	(42,222)	(19,142)	(23,080)
3 or 4 Days	23.5%	22.2%	24.7%	23.3%	21.8%	24.6%	21.2%	20.7%	21.7%	28.0%	26.8%	28.9%	22.6%	22.4%	22.8%
	(361,095)	(160,107)	(200,988)	(264,530)	(117,497)	(147,033)	(36,333)	(16,692)	(19,640)	(44,840)	(19,220)	(25,619)	(15,393)	(6,697)	(8,696)
5 to 10 Days	10.5%	9.8%	11.0%	10.3%	9.8%	10.8%	11.7%	12.0%	11.5%	9.8%	7.3%	11.8%	11.6%	10.6%	12.4%
	(160,521)	(70,749)	(89,772)	(116,922)	(52,676)	(64,246)	(20,048)	(9,686)	(10,362)	(15,649)	(5,204)	(10,445)	(7,902)	(3,184)	(4,719)
More Than 10 Days	4.3%	3.9%	4.6%	3.4%	3.6%	3.3%	8.7%	5.8%	11.3%	5.8%	4.5%	6.8%	3.8%	3.1%	4.3%
	(65,767)	(28,137)	(37,630)	(39,001)	(19,294)	(19,706)	(14,962)	(4,711)	(10,251)	(9,231)	(3,208)	(6,023)	(2,573)	(924)	(1,649)
Number of Days Absent From School During Last Term															
Total *** +++ ~~~	100.0%	100.0%	100.0%	100.0%	100.0%	100.0%	100.0%	100.0%	100.0%	100.0%	100.0%	100.0%	100.0%	100.0%	100.0%
	(2,496,375)	(1,258,531)	(1,237,844)	(1,826,907)	(928,936)	(897,971)	(307,931)	(151,981)	(155,950)	(235,958)	(115,169)	(120,789)	(125,579)	(62,445)	(63,134)
Never	8.6%	10.5%	6.6%	7.1%	8.4%	5.7%	16.8%	22.4%	11.4%	7.9%	8.5%	7.3%	11.9%	16.5%	7.4%
	(214,509)	(132,245)	(82,265)	(129,097)	(78,071)	(51,026)	(51,835)	(34,071)	(17,765)	(18,642)	(9,818)	(8,824)	(14,934)	(10,284)	(4,650)
1 to 2 Days	30.3%	31.1%	29.5%	30.0%	30.5%	29.5%	30.8%	31.3%	30.2%	31.0%	35.9%	26.4%	31.9%	30.5%	33.3%
	(756,858)	(391,703)	(365,155)	(548,950)	(283,760)	(265,191)	(94,696)	(47,586)	(47,110)	(73,141)	(41,307)	(31,834)	(40,070)	(19,051)	(21,019)
3 to 6 Days	34.7%	34.4%	35.0%	36.1%	36.4%	35.8%	28.7%	26.7%	30.5%	35.8%	33.5%	37.9%	27.2%	24.5%	29.9%
	(866,312)	(432,872)	(433,440)	(659,422)	(338,333)	(321,089)	(88,253)	(40,634)	(47,619)	(84,446)	(38,618)	(45,828)	(34,191)	(15,286)	(18,905)
7 to 9 Days	13.2%	11.7%	14.9%	13.3%	11.6%	15.2%	12.1%	10.4%	13.7%	13.1%	11.7%	14.3%	15.1%	15.7%	14.5%
	(330,690)	(146,693)	(183,997)	(243,644)	(107,525)	(136,119)	(37,229)	(15,817)	(21,412)	(30,835)	(13,521)	(17,314)	(18,982)	(9,830)	(9,153)
10 to 15 Days	7.3%	6.7%	8.0%	7.8%	7.2%	8.3%	5.5%	3.7%	7.3%	6.1%	5.9%	6.4%	7.6%	7.3%	7.9%
	(183,075)	(84,181)	(98,894)	(142,034)	(67,190)	(74,844)	(16,971)	(5,648)	(11,323)	(14,507)	(6,769)	(7,738)	(9,563)	(4,573)	(4,990)
More Than 15 Days	5.8%	5.6%	6.0%	5.7%	5.8%	5.5%	6.2%	5.4%	6.9%	6.1%	4.5%	7.7%	6.2%	5.5%	7.0%
	(144,931)	(70,837)	(74,094)	(103,759)	(54,055)	(49,704)	(18,946)	(8,225)	(10,721)	(14,387)	(5,136)	(9,251)	(7,839)	(3,421)	(4,418)

Notes:

***Test of statistical significance compares African Americans with Whites. *** p < .001, ** p < .01, * p < .05.

+++Test of statistical significance compares White boys with White girls. +++ p < .001, ++ p < .01, + p < .05.

~~~Test of statistical significance compares African American boys with African American girls. ~~~ p < .001, ~~ p < .01, ~ p < .05.

Tests of statistical significance calculated using adjusted sample weight to control for influence of large sample sizes.

Source: National Educational Longitudinal Study of 1988 Eighth Graders, Base Year (1988) and Second Follow-Up (1992).

Figure 2. Time of Last Unexcused Absence From School Among 1988 8th Graders in 1992

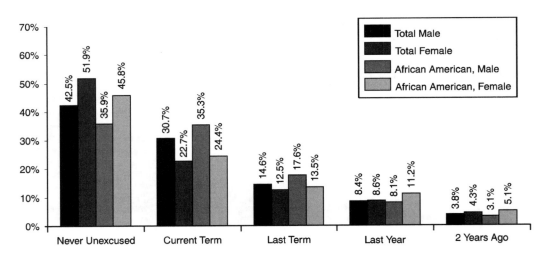

Source: National Educational Longitudinal Study of 1988 Eighth Graders, Base Year (1988) and Second Follow-Up (1992).

- **Table 2** shows that the proportion of African Americans who reported one or more unexcused absence was higher than the proportion of Whites (59.1% versus 50.8%).

Most (83.9%) students who reported at least one unexcused absence missed only one or two days during their last unexcused absence.

- But, among those with at least one unexcused absence in 1992, a higher share of African Americans than Whites missed more than two days during the last absence (24.6% versus 13.4%).

School Tardiness

More than one-third (36.9%) of 1988 8th graders reported that they were late for school at least once during the four-week period prior to the 1988 survey. **Figure 3** shows that, in both 1988 and 1992, school tardiness rates were higher for African Americans than for 8th graders overall in 1988.

- **Table 3** shows that, in 1988, a higher percentage of African American than of White 8th graders reported being late for school at least once during the four weeks prior to the survey (44.7% versus 34.4%).

- About 86.7% of African Americans, but 79.7% of Whites, reported being late for school at least once during the first term of the 1991/92 academic year, when most 1988 8th graders were high school seniors.

Parents Warned About Attendance

Overall, only 12.0% of 8th graders reported in 1988 that their parents had been warned about their school attendance.

- **Table 4** shows that a higher percentage of African Americans than Whites reported that their parents received attendance warnings (16.2% versus 10.7%).

Table 2. Number of Unexcused Absences From School Among 1988 8th Graders in 1992 by Race and Sex
(weighted sample size in parentheses)

Unexcused Absence	Total	Male	Female	White, Non-Hispanic Total	Male	Female	African American, Non-Hispanic Total	Male	Female	Hispanic Total	Male	Female	Other Total	Male	Female
Last Unexcused Absence															
Total *** +++ ~~~	100.0%	100.0%	100.0%	100.0%	100.0%	100.0%	100.0%	100.0%	100.0%	100.0%	100.0%	100.0%	100.0%	100.0%	100.0%
	(2,534,259)	(1,281,217)	(1,253,042)	(1,856,505)	(946,158)	(910,346)	(313,036)	(155,102)	(157,934)	(237,936)	(116,427)	(121,509)	(126,782)	(63,529)	(63,253)
Never Unexcused	47.2%	42.5%	51.9%	49.2%	44.5%	54.2%	40.9%	35.9%	45.8%	41.0%	36.3%	45.6%	43.8%	41.3%	46.4%
	(1,195,531)	(545,089)	(650,442)	(914,236)	(420,893)	(493,343)	(128,049)	(55,718)	(72,330)	(97,665)	(42,225)	(55,440)	(55,582)	(26,253)	(29,329)
At Least 1 Unexcused +++ ~~~	100.0%	100.0%	100.0%	100.0%	100.0%	100.0%	100.0%	100.0%	100.0%	100.0%	100.0%	100.0%	100.0%	100.0%	100.0%
	(1,338,728)	(736,128)	(602,600)	(942,269)	(525,266)	(417,003)	(184,988)	(99,384)	(85,604)	(140,271)	(74,202)	(66,069)	(71,200)	(37,276)	(33,924)
Current Term	50.6%	53.5%	47.2%	51.2%	54.4%	47.1%	50.4%	55.1%	45.0%	47.3%	45.2%	49.6%	50.7%	53.1%	48.0%
	(677,800)	(393,639)	(284,161)	(482,103)	(285,574)	(196,529)	(93,272)	(54,721)	(38,551)	(66,336)	(33,546)	(32,790)	(36,089)	(19,798)	(16,291)
Last Term	25.6%	25.3%	26.0%	25.0%	24.3%	25.9%	26.2%	27.4%	24.9%	29.1%	30.9%	27.0%	25.5%	23.0%	28.2%
	(343,227)	(186,523)	(156,703)	(235,775)	(127,801)	(107,974)	(48,557)	(27,221)	(21,335)	(40,775)	(22,942)	(17,832)	(18,120)	(8,559)	(9,561)
Last Year	16.1%	14.7%	18.0%	16.2%	14.7%	18.0%	16.4%	12.7%	20.6%	15.5%	15.3%	15.8%	16.3%	17.4%	15.1%
	(216,125)	(107,882)	(108,243)	(152,444)	(77,420)	(75,024)	(30,272)	(12,600)	(17,672)	(21,785)	(11,378)	(10,407)	(11,623)	(6,484)	(5,139)
Two Years Ago	7.6%	6.5%	8.9%	7.6%	6.6%	9.0%	7.0%	4.9%	9.4%	8.1%	8.5%	7.6%	7.5%	6.5%	8.6%
	(101,576)	(48,083)	(53,493)	(71,947)	(34,471)	(37,476)	(12,887)	(4,841)	(8,045)	(11,375)	(6,336)	(5,039)	(5,367)	(2,434)	(2,933)
Number of Days Missed During Last Unexcused Absence															
Total *** ++ ~~~	100.0%	100.0%	100.0%	100.0%	100.0%	100.0%	100.0%	100.0%	100.0%	100.0%	100.0%	100.0%	100.0%	100.0%	100.0%
	(1,324,362)	(727,312)	(597,050)	(932,451)	(518,016)	(414,435)	(182,490)	(98,297)	(84,193)	(138,951)	(74,001)	(64,950)	(70,470)	(36,998)	(33,472)
1 or 2 Days	83.9%	83.1%	84.9%	86.6%	85.4%	88.2%	75.4%	72.2%	79.3%	82.0%	84.3%	79.4%	73.9%	78.0%	69.3%
	(1,111,548)	(604,701)	(506,847)	(807,905)	(442,552)	(365,353)	(137,667)	(70,943)	(66,724)	(113,919)	(62,359)	(51,561)	(52,057)	(28,847)	(23,210)
3 or 4 Days	8.5%	9.1%	7.7%	6.6%	7.2%	5.7%	15.2%	18.3%	11.5%	10.1%	10.1%	10.1%	13.3%	8.8%	18.3%
	(112,259)	(66,232)	(46,027)	(61,135)	(37,464)	(23,671)	(27,710)	(18,029)	(9,681)	(14,038)	(7,498)	(6,540)	(9,376)	(3,241)	(6,135)
5 to 10 Days	4.7%	4.8%	4.5%	3.9%	4.4%	3.4%	6.8%	6.9%	6.7%	5.0%	2.9%	7.5%	8.4%	9.4%	7.2%
	(62,021)	(35,127)	(26,894)	(36,786)	(22,792)	(13,994)	(12,346)	(6,744)	(5,601)	(6,987)	(2,110)	(4,877)	(5,902)	(3,481)	(2,421)
11 to 15 Days	0.9%	1.0%	0.7%	0.8%	0.9%	0.7%	0.8%	1.4%	0.1%	0.9%	0.9%	1.0%	1.6%	2.6%	0.6%
	(11,553)	(7,531)	(4,022)	(7,563)	(4,493)	(3,070)	(1,523)	(1,410)	(112)	(1,313)	(668)	(645)	(1,155)	(960)	(195)
16 to 20 Days	0.6%	0.7%	0.5%	0.6%	0.7%	0.4%	0.9%	0.7%	1.0%	0.6%	0.7%	0.4%	0.1%	0.2%	0.0%
	(7,851)	(5,159)	(2,692)	(5,419)	(3,878)	(1,542)	(1,591)	(726)	(865)	(782)	(496)	(286)	(60)	(60)	
21 or More Days	1.4%	1.2%	1.8%	1.5%	1.3%	1.6%	0.9%	0.5%	1.4%	1.4%	1.2%	1.6%	2.7%	1.1%	4.5%
	(19,130)	(8,562)	(10,568)	(13,643)	(6,839)	(6,805)	(1,654)	(444)	(1,210)	(1,912)	(870)	(1,042)	(1,920)	(409)	(1,511)

Notes:

*** Test of statistical significance compares African Americans with Whites. *** p < .001, ** p < .01, * p < .05.

+++ Test of statistical significance compares White boys with White girls. +++ p < .001, ++ p < .01, + p < .05.

~~~ Test of statistical significance compares African American boys with African American girls. ~~~ p < .001, ~~ p < .01, ~ p < .05.

Tests of statistical significance calculated using adjusted sample weight to control for influence of large sample sizes.

Source: National Educational Longitudinal Study of 1988 Eighth Graders, Base Year (1988) and Second Follow-Up (1992).

Figure 3. Percentage of 1988 8th Graders Who Were Ever Late for School in 1988 and 1992

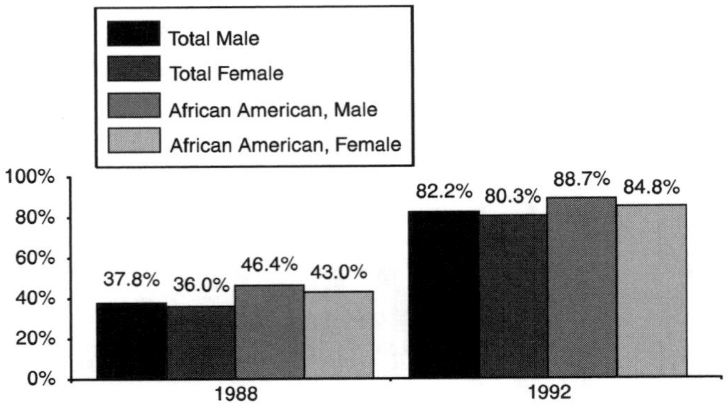

Source: National Educational Longitudinal Study of 1988 Eighth Graders, Base Year (1988) and Second Follow-Up (1992).

- **Figure 4** shows that a higher percentage of African American boys (20.2%) than of African American girls (12.4%), all boys (13.9%), and all girls (10.1%) reported that their parents were sent attendance warnings.

Parents Warned About Behavior

In 1988, 21.6% of 8th graders reported that their parents had been notified about their behavior in school. **Figure 4** shows that, overall and among African Americans, a higher percentage of boys than of girls reported parent notification (30.3% versus 13.0%, overall). A higher share of African Americans than of Whites reported parent notification about their behavior (33.0% versus 19.2%).

- **Table 4** also shows that 44.0% of African American boys and 22.6% of African American girls reported parent notification about their behavior in school, compared with only 27.5% of White boys and 10.7% of White girls.

Sent to the Office

On average, about one-third (32.4%) of 1988 8th graders reported that they had been sent to the school office for misbehaving. **Figure 4** shows that a higher share of boys than girls were sent to the office overall

(44.3% versus 20.4%) and among African Americans (54.1% versus 35.7%). A higher share of African Americans than Whites were sent to the office because of their behavior (44.7% versus 30.1%).

- **Table 4** also shows that one-half (54.1%) of African American boys, but only one-third (35.7%) of African American girls, were sent to the office for misbehaving.

PREPARATION FOR CLASS

Attend Class Without Homework Done

In 1988, about 26.7% of 8th graders reported that they never attended class without having done their homework. **Figure 5** shows that the percentage of students in this cohort who attended class without their homework remained stable between 1988 and 1992.

- **Table 5** shows that, in 1988, 11.0% of African American and 7.7% of White 8th graders reported that they usually attended class without having done their homework.

- In 1992, 7.6% of African Americans and 5.4% of Whites usually attended class without having completed their homework.

Table 3. Percentage of 1988 8th Graders Who Were Late for School in 1988 and 1992 by Race and Sex
(weighted sample size in parentheses)

Late for School	Total	Male	Female	White, Non-Hispanic Total	White Male	White Female	African American, Non-Hispanic Total	Af.Am. Male	Af.Am. Female	Hispanic Total	Hispanic Male	Hispanic Female	Other Total	Other Male	Other Female
Number of Days Late for School in Past 4 Weeks: 1988															
Total *** ~~	100.0%	100.0%	100.0%	100.0%	100.0%	100.0%	100.0%	100.0%	100.0%	100.0%	100.0%	100.0%	100.0%	100.0%	100.0%
	(2,813,480)	(1,404,022)	(1,409,458)	(2,046,315)	(1,035,774)	(1,010,540)	(344,624)	(165,369)	(179,255)	(284,608)	(134,567)	(150,042)	(137,932)	(68,312)	(69,620)
None	63.1%	62.2%	64.0%	65.6%	65.3%	66.1%	55.3%	53.6%	57.0%	55.0%	52.6%	57.1%	61.6%	55.4%	67.8%
	(1,775,650)	(873,088)	(902,562)	(1,343,405)	(675,870)	(667,535)	(190,701)	(88,600)	(102,102)	(156,517)	(70,771)	(85,746)	(85,026)	(37,847)	(47,179)
At Least 1 Day *** +++ ~~~	100.0%	100.0%	100.0%	100.0%	100.0%	100.0%	100.0%	100.0%	100.0%	100.0%	100.0%	100.0%	100.0%	100.0%	100.0%
	(1,037,830)	(530,934)	(506,896)	(702,909)	(359,904)	(343,005)	(153,923)	(76,769)	(77,154)	(128,091)	(63,796)	(64,296)	(52,906)	(30,465)	(22,441)
1 or 2 Days	68.0%	65.8%	70.4%	71.2%	69.1%	73.4%	58.1%	52.8%	63.4%	63.8%	65.2%	62.3%	64.6%	60.0%	70.8%
	(705,788)	(349,113)	(356,675)	(500,466)	(248,674)	(251,792)	(89,482)	(40,560)	(48,922)	(81,681)	(41,614)	(40,066)	(34,159)	(18,265)	(15,894)
3 or 4 Days	20.3%	21.8%	18.7%	18.6%	19.6%	17.5%	24.1%	28.1%	20.1%	24.3%	24.1%	24.6%	22.2%	26.5%	16.4%
	(210,474)	(115,564)	(94,911)	(130,435)	(70,517)	(59,918)	(37,124)	(21,604)	(15,520)	(31,158)	(15,371)	(15,787)	(11,757)	(8,071)	(3,686)
5 to 10 Days	7.2%	6.0%	8.4%	6.8%	6.2%	7.4%	9.3%	4.8%	13.6%	7.3%	6.1%	8.5%	6.4%	7.0%	5.6%
	(74,627)	(32,049)	(42,578)	(47,563)	(22,262)	(25,301)	(14,244)	(3,718)	(10,527)	(9,409)	(3,922)	(5,487)	(3,411)	(2,147)	(1,264)
More than 5 Days	4.5%	6.4%	2.5%	3.5%	5.1%	1.7%	8.5%	14.2%	2.8%	4.6%	4.5%	4.6%	6.8%	6.5%	7.1%
	(46,941)	(34,209)	(12,732)	(24,446)	(18,451)	(5,995)	(13,072)	(10,887)	(2,185)	(5,844)	(2,888)	(2,955)	(3,579)	(1,982)	(1,597)
Number of Times Late for School During Last Term: 1992															
Total *** + ~~	100.0%	100.0%	100.0%	100.0%	100.0%	100.0%	100.0%	100.0%	100.0%	100.0%	100.0%	100.0%	100.0%	100.0%	100.0%
	(2,514,479)	(1,269,306)	(1,245,174)	(1,840,863)	(937,026)	(903,837)	(309,978)	(153,235)	(156,743)	(237,502)	(116,140)	(121,363)	(126,136)	(62,905)	(63,231)
Never	18.7%	17.8%	19.7%	20.3%	19.6%	21.0%	13.3%	11.3%	15.2%	14.8%	13.5%	16.1%	16.5%	14.3%	18.7%
	(470,797)	(225,839)	(244,958)	(373,492)	(183,745)	(189,746)	(41,218)	(17,392)	(23,826)	(35,257)	(15,721)	(19,536)	(20,830)	(8,980)	(11,850)
At Least 1 Day *** +++ ~~~	100.0%	100.0%	100.0%	100.0%	100.0%	100.0%	100.0%	100.0%	100.0%	100.0%	100.0%	100.0%	100.0%	100.0%	100.0%
	(2,043,682)	(1,043,467)	(1,000,215)	(1,467,371)	(753,281)	(714,091)	(268,761)	(135,843)	(132,917)	(202,245)	(100,418)	(101,827)	(105,305)	(53,925)	(51,380)
1 to 2 Days	41.0%	39.3%	42.8%	42.8%	40.4%	45.3%	38.6%	41.2%	35.9%	34.0%	31.8%	36.2%	35.4%	32.8%	38.3%
	(837,939)	(409,970)	(427,969)	(628,011)	(304,342)	(323,669)	(103,743)	(55,991)	(47,751)	(68,861)	(31,966)	(36,894)	(37,325)	(17,670)	(19,655)
3 to 6 Days	30.8%	31.0%	30.6%	30.0%	30.4%	29.7%	34.3%	31.3%	37.4%	31.0%	35.1%	27.1%	32.2%	31.6%	32.9%
	(629,810)	(323,591)	(306,219)	(440,774)	(228,763)	(212,011)	(92,310)	(42,570)	(49,740)	(62,766)	(35,220)	(27,546)	(33,959)	(17,037)	(16,921)
7 to 9 Days	12.0%	12.1%	11.9%	11.4%	12.0%	10.6%	13.5%	10.8%	16.2%	14.3%	14.8%	13.9%	12.7%	11.7%	13.8%
	(245,331)	(126,599)	(118,731)	(166,690)	(90,731)	(75,959)	(36,254)	(14,659)	(21,595)	(29,004)	(14,897)	(14,108)	(13,382)	(6,313)	(7,070)
10 to 15 Days	6.7%	6.8%	6.6%	6.8%	7.0%	6.7%	5.3%	5.4%	5.2%	7.9%	6.6%	9.2%	6.8%	8.6%	4.8%
	(137,370)	(71,046)	(66,324)	(99,988)	(52,427)	(47,561)	(14,263)	(7,331)	(6,932)	(16,008)	(6,645)	(9,364)	(7,111)	(4,643)	(2,468)
More Than 15 Days	9.5%	10.8%	8.1%	9.0%	10.2%	7.7%	8.3%	11.3%	5.2%	12.7%	11.6%	13.7%	12.8%	15.3%	10.3%
	(193,233)	(112,260)	(80,972)	(131,908)	(77,017)	(54,891)	(22,191)	(15,291)	(6,899)	(25,605)	(11,690)	(13,915)	(13,528)	(8,262)	(5,267)

Notes:

***Test of statistical significance compares African Americans with Whites. *** p < .001, ** p < .01, * p < .05.

+++Test of statistical significance compares White boys with White girls. +++ p < .001, ++ p < .01, + p < .05.

~~~Test of statistical significance compares African American boys with African American girls. ~~~ p < .001, ~~ p < .01, ~ p < .05.

Tests of statistical significance calculated using adjusted sample weight to control for influence of large sample sizes.

Source: National Educational Longitudinal Study of 1988 Eighth Graders, Base Year (1988) and Second Follow-Up (1992).

Table 4. Percentage of 1988 8th Graders Who Were Warned About Their Behavior in 1988 by Race and Sex
(weighted sample size in parentheses)

Received Warning	Total	Male	Female	White, Non-Hispanic Total	Male	Female	African American, Non-Hispanic Total	Male	Female	Hispanic Total	Male	Female	Other Total	Male	Female
Parents Received Warning About Attendance															
Total *** +++ ~~~	100.0%	100.0%	100.0%	100.0%	100.0%	100.0%	100.0%	100.0%	100.0%	100.0%	100.0%	100.0%	100.0%	100.0%	100.0%
	(2,897,430)	(1,450,240)	(1,447,190)	(2,082,171)	(1,053,392)	(1,028,780)	(371,174)	(180,778)	(190,397)	(300,281)	(143,940)	(156,341)	(143,804)	(72,131)	(71,673)
Never	88.0%	86.1%	89.9%	89.3%	87.5%	91.0%	83.8%	79.8%	87.6%	84.8%	85.2%	84.5%	86.9%	83.2%	90.6%
	(2,549,327)	(1,248,992)	(1,300,335)	(1,858,679)	(922,074)	(936,605)	(310,980)	(144,233)	(166,747)	(254,771)	(122,690)	(132,081)	(124,896)	(59,994)	(64,902)
Once or Twice	9.1%	9.9%	8.3%	8.2%	8.9%	7.4%	12.0%	12.9%	11.1%	11.6%	11.5%	11.8%	9.8%	13.6%	6.0%
	(263,839)	(143,713)	(120,126)	(170,353)	(94,107)	(76,246)	(44,441)	(23,252)	(21,189)	(34,927)	(16,510)	(18,417)	(14,118)	(9,844)	(4,274)
More Than Twice	2.9%	4.0%	1.8%	2.6%	3.5%	1.5%	4.2%	7.4%	1.3%	3.5%	3.3%	3.7%	3.3%	3.2%	3.5%
	(84,264)	(57,535)	(26,729)	(53,139)	(37,211)	(15,929)	(15,753)	(13,292)	(2,461)	(10,582)	(4,740)	(5,842)	(4,790)	(2,293)	(2,497)
Parents Received Warning About Behavior															
Total *** +++ ~~~	100.0%	100.0%	100.0%	100.0%	100.0%	100.0%	100.0%	100.0%	100.0%	100.0%	100.0%	100.0%	100.0%	100.0%	100.0%
	(2,898,801)	(1,451,876)	(1,446,925)	(2,084,506)	(1,055,191)	(1,029,315)	(371,107)	(180,543)	(190,564)	(300,541)	(144,138)	(156,403)	(142,647)	(72,004)	(70,644)
Never	78.4%	69.7%	87.0%	80.8%	72.5%	89.3%	67.0%	56.0%	77.4%	74.8%	65.3%	83.5%	79.7%	72.5%	87.0%
	(2,271,701)	(1,012,484)	(1,259,217)	(1,684,651)	(764,963)	(919,688)	(248,573)	(101,118)	(147,455)	(224,837)	(94,190)	(130,647)	(113,639)	(52,213)	(61,427)
Once or Twice	15.5%	21.2%	9.9%	13.7%	19.1%	8.2%	24.4%	31.4%	17.7%	17.5%	24.4%	11.2%	15.0%	19.7%	10.1%
	(449,698)	(307,171)	(142,527)	(285,109)	(201,083)	(84,026)	(90,523)	(56,728)	(33,796)	(52,730)	(35,154)	(17,576)	(21,336)	(14,207)	(7,129)
More Than Twice	6.1%	9.1%	3.1%	5.5%	8.4%	2.5%	8.6%	12.6%	4.9%	7.6%	10.3%	5.2%	5.4%	7.8%	3.0%
	(177,402)	(132,220)	(45,182)	(114,746)	(89,145)	(25,600)	(32,010)	(22,697)	(9,313)	(22,975)	(14,794)	(8,181)	(7,672)	(5,584)	(2,088)
Sent to Office for Misbehaving															
Total *** +++ ~~~	100.0%	100.0%	100.0%	100.0%	100.0%	100.0%	100.0%	100.0%	100.0%	100.0%	100.0%	100.0%	100.0%	100.0%	100.0%
	(2,908,547)	(1,459,220)	(1,449,327)	(2,089,696)	(1,059,326)	(1,030,369)	(374,126)	(183,393)	(190,733)	(300,780)	(144,228)	(156,552)	(143,946)	(72,273)	(71,673)
Never	67.6%	55.7%	79.6%	69.9%	57.6%	82.6%	55.3%	45.9%	64.3%	64.5%	52.1%	75.9%	72.6%	60.4%	84.8%
	(1,966,035)	(812,740)	(1,153,296)	(1,460,715)	(609,833)	(850,883)	(206,866)	(84,130)	(122,736)	(194,001)	(75,107)	(118,894)	(104,453)	(43,670)	(60,783)
Once or Twice	22.6%	29.6%	15.7%	21.3%	28.6%	13.7%	30.5%	33.8%	27.4%	24.2%	33.2%	16.0%	18.7%	25.5%	11.7%
	(658,290)	(431,465)	(226,825)	(444,354)	(303,206)	(141,148)	(114,148)	(61,961)	(52,187)	(72,922)	(47,842)	(25,081)	(26,866)	(18,456)	(8,410)
More Than Twice	9.8%	14.7%	4.8%	8.8%	13.8%	3.7%	14.2%	20.3%	8.3%	11.3%	14.8%	8.0%	8.8%	14.0%	3.5%
	(284,222)	(215,016)	(69,206)	(184,627)	(146,288)	(38,339)	(53,112)	(37,302)	(15,809)	(33,857)	(21,280)	(12,577)	(12,627)	(10,146)	(2,481)

Notes:

*** Test of statistical significance compares African Americans with Whites. *** p < .001, ** p < .01, * p < .05.

+++ Test of statistical significance compares White boys with White girls. +++ p < .001, ++ p < .01, + p < .05.

~~~Test of statistical significance compares African American boys with African American girls. ~~~ p < .001, ~~ p < .01, ~ p < .05.

Tests of statistical significance calculated using adjusted sample weight to control for influence of large sample sizes.

Source: National Educational Longitudinal Study of 1988 Eighth Graders, Base Year (1988) and Second Follow-up (1992).

Figure 4. Percentage of 1988 8th Graders Who Were Warned About Their Behavior in 1988

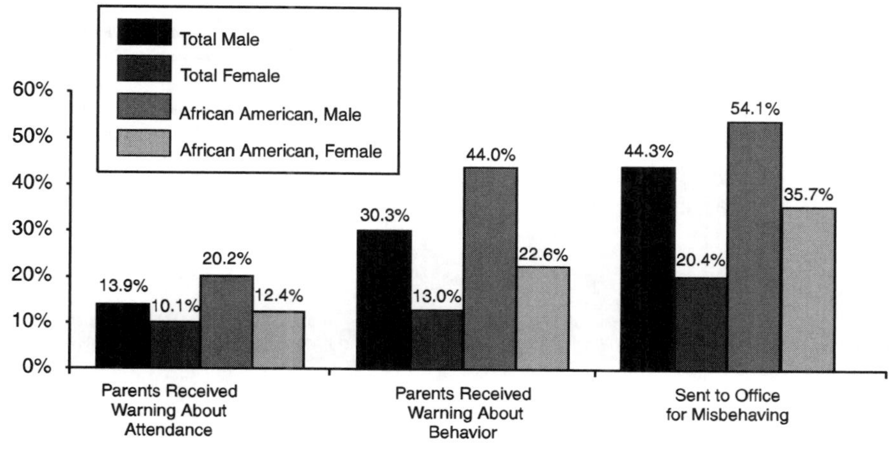

Legend:
- Total Male
- Total Female
- African American, Male
- African American, Female

Parents Received Warning About Attendance
- 13.9%
- 10.1%
- 20.2%
- 12.4%

Parents Received Warning About Behavior
- 30.3%
- 13.0%
- 44.0%
- 22.6%

Sent to Office for Misbehaving
- 44.3%
- 20.4%
- 54.1%
- 35.7%

Source: National Educational Longitudinal Study of 1988 Eighth Graders, Base Year (1988).

Figure 5. Percentage of 1988 8th Graders Who Attended Class Without Their Homework Done in 1988 and 1992

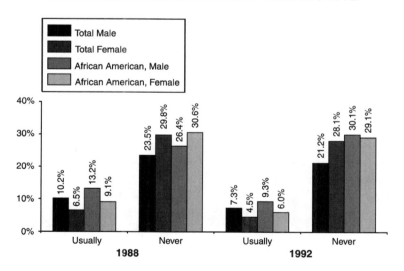

Legend:
- Total Male
- Total Female
- African American, Male
- African American, Female

1988

Usually
- 10.2%
- 6.5%
- 13.2%
- 9.1%

Never
- 23.5%
- 29.8%
- 26.4%
- 30.6%

1992

Usually
- 7.3%
- 4.5%
- 9.3%
- 6.0%

Never
- 21.2%
- 28.1%
- 30.1%
- 29.1%

Source: National Educational Longitudinal Study of 1988 Eighth Graders, Base Year (1988) and Second Follow-Up (1992).

Table 5. Percentage of 1988 8th Graders Who Attended Class Without Their Homework Done in 1988 and 1992 by Race and Sex
(weighted sample size in parentheses)

Attended Class Without Homework	Total	Male	Female	White, Non-Hispanic			African American, Non-Hispanic			Hispanic			Other		
				Total	Male	Female	Total	Male	Female	Total	Male	Female	Total	Male	Female
1988															
Total *** +++ ~~~	100.0%	100.0%	100.0%	100.0%	100.0%	100.0%	100.0%	100.0%	100.0%	100.0%	100.0%	100.0%	100.0%	100.0%	100.0%
	(2,776,732)	(1,379,239)	(1,397,493)	(2,026,750)	(1,022,344)	(1,004,406)	(333,118)	(157,858)	(175,260)	(280,665)	(132,012)	(148,653)	(136,199)	(67,025)	(69,174)
Usually	8.3%	10.2%	6.5%	7.7%	9.6%	5.8%	11.0%	13.2%	9.1%	9.4%	11.2%	7.8%	9.1%	10.4%	7.9%
	(231,627)	(140,688)	(90,939)	(155,911)	(98,061)	(57,850)	(36,800)	(20,810)	(15,990)	(26,463)	(14,824)	(11,638)	(12,453)	(6,994)	(5,460)
Often	13.9%	15.9%	11.8%	13.4%	15.2%	11.6%	13.2%	15.6%	10.9%	16.8%	19.0%	14.9%	16.0%	21.4%	10.6%
	(384,937)	(219,791)	(165,146)	(272,150)	(155,721)	(116,429)	(43,809)	(24,665)	(19,143)	(47,252)	(25,039)	(22,213)	(21,727)	(14,366)	(7,361)
Seldom	51.1%	50.4%	51.9%	53.4%	52.8%	53.9%	47.2%	44.8%	49.3%	44.6%	42.7%	46.3%	41.0%	41.2%	40.7%
	(1,419,560)	(694,447)	(725,114)	(1,081,364)	(539,703)	(541,661)	(157,198)	(70,743)	(86,455)	(125,177)	(56,364)	(68,813)	(55,821)	(27,637)	(28,184)
Never	26.7%	23.5%	29.8%	25.5%	22.4%	28.7%	28.6%	26.4%	30.6%	29.1%	27.1%	30.9%	33.9%	26.9%	40.7%
	(740,607)	(324,312)	(416,295)	(517,325)	(228,860)	(288,465)	(95,311)	(41,640)	(53,671)	(81,774)	(35,784)	(45,989)	(46,197)	(18,028)	(28,169)
1992															
Total *** +++ ~~~	100.0%	100.0%	100.0%	100.0%	100.0%	100.0%	100.0%	100.0%	100.0%	100.0%	100.0%	100.0%	100.0%	100.0%	100.0%
	(2,502,711)	(1,262,776)	(1,239,935)	(1,833,479)	(933,668)	(899,811)	(308,586)	(152,682)	(155,904)	(235,620)	(114,344)	(121,276)	(125,026)	(62,082)	(62,944)
Usually	5.9%	7.3%	4.5%	5.4%	6.6%	4.2%	7.6%	9.3%	6.0%	7.0%	9.4%	4.7%	7.0%	9.8%	4.3%
	(147,969)	(92,381)	(55,588)	(99,357)	(61,434)	(37,923)	(23,428)	(14,124)	(9,304)	(16,407)	(10,761)	(5,646)	(8,777)	(6,062)	(2,715)
Often	10.6%	14.1%	7.0%	10.8%	14.9%	6.5%	8.6%	10.3%	6.9%	10.7%	12.9%	8.6%	13.2%	14.9%	11.6%
	(265,621)	(178,625)	(86,996)	(197,425)	(138,860)	(58,565)	(26,543)	(15,794)	(10,749)	(25,128)	(14,728)	(10,400)	(16,524)	(9,243)	(7,281)
Seldom	58.9%	57.4%	60.4%	60.3%	58.8%	61.8%	54.2%	50.3%	58.0%	56.7%	55.4%	57.8%	54.0%	56.9%	51.1%
	(1,473,717)	(724,510)	(749,207)	(1,105,415)	(548,963)	(556,453)	(167,302)	(76,833)	(90,469)	(133,490)	(63,380)	(70,110)	(67,510)	(35,334)	(32,175)
Never	24.6%	21.2%	28.1%	23.5%	19.8%	27.4%	29.6%	30.1%	29.1%	25.7%	22.3%	29.0%	25.8%	18.4%	33.0%
	(615,404)	(267,260)	(348,144)	(431,281)	(184,410)	(246,871)	(91,313)	(45,932)	(45,381)	(60,595)	(25,475)	(35,120)	(32,215)	(11,443)	(20,772)

Notes:
***Test of statistical significance compares African Americans with Whites. *** p < .001, ** p < .01, * p < .05.
+++Test of statistical significance compares White boys with White girls. +++ p < .001, ++ p < .01, + p < .05.
~~~ Test of statistical significance compares African American boys with African American girls. ~~~ p < .001, ~~ p < .01, ~ p < .05.
Tests of statistical significance calculated using adjusted sample weight to control for influence of large sample sizes.
Source: National Educational Longitudinal Study of 1988 Eighth Graders, Base Year (1988) and Second Follow-up (1992).

Attend Class Without Books

Figure 6 shows that, in both 1988 and 1992, about one-half of 1988 8th graders always brought their books to class. Among both African Americans and Whites, a higher proportion of girls than boys consistently brought their books to class.

- In 1988, 53.6% of African American girls, 51.8% of White girls, 50.4% of African American boys, and 46.5% of White boys always brought their books to class.

- Table 6 shows that, in 1992, 63.9% of African American girls, 57.0% of White girls, 51.4% of African American boys, and 47.3% of White boys always brought their books to class.

Attend Class Without Pencil or Paper

The percentage of 1988 8th graders who always brought pencil and paper to class increased from 29.5% in 1988 to 51.7% in 1992. Figure 7 shows that, in both years, the percentage of girls who went to class with pencil and paper was higher than the

Figure 6. Percentage of 1988 8th Graders Who Attended Class Without Their Books in 1988 and 1992

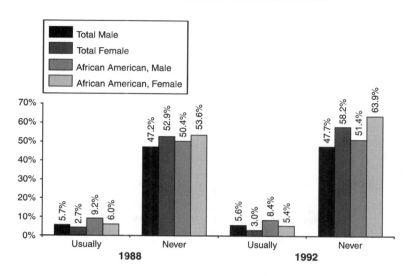

Source: National Educational Longitudinal Study of 1988 Eighth Graders, Base Year (1988) and Second Follow-up (1992).

percentage of boys overall and among African Americans.

- **Table 7** shows that, in 1988, 33.1% of African American girls, 33.9% of White girls, 21.1% of African American boys, and 24.5% of White boys always attended class with pencil and paper.

- In 1992, 62.5% of African American girls, 63.0% of White girls, 38.1% of African American boys, and 40.6% of White boys consistently attended class with pencil and paper.

PARTICIPATION IN SCHOOL CLUBS

Participation in School Clubs and Activities

In both 1988 and 1992 the most common extra-curricular activity among 1988 8th graders was varsity and intramural sports. But the percentage of 1988 8th graders who participated in sports declined from 59.9% in 1988 (**Table 8**) to 37.7% in 1992 (**Table 9**). A smaller percentage of girls than boys participated in sports in both 1988 (57.6% versus 62.1%) and 1992 (30.8% versus 44.6%).

- A smaller percentage of African Americans than Whites participated in sports in 1988 (56.8% versus 62.0%) and in 1992 (35.6% versus 39.3%).

Overall, about one-fifth (19.9%) of 1988 8th graders participated in academic subject clubs (e.g., foreign language, math, science) in 1988 and one-fourth (24.7%) in 1992. **Figure 8** shows that, in 1988, comparable shares of girls and boys were members of academic clubs (19.8% versus 20.1%). But, in 1992, participation in academic clubs was greater for girls than boys (27.1% versus 22.0%, overall).

- In 1988, a higher percentage of African American than of White 8th graders participated in academic subject clubs (28.4% versus 18.0%).

Table 6. Percentage of 1988 8th Graders Who Attended Class Without Their Books in 1988 and 1992 by Race and Sex
(weighted sample size in parentheses)

Attended Class Without Books	Total	Male	Female	White, Non-Hispanic Total	Male	Female	African American, Non-Hispanic Total	Male	Female	Hispanic Total	Male	Female	Other Total	Male	Female
1988															
Total *** +++ ~~	100.0%	100.0%	100.0%	100.0%	100.0%	100.0%	100.0%	100.0%	100.0%	100.0%	100.0%	100.0%	100.0%	100.0%	100.0%
	(2,772,959)	(1,377,120)	(1,395,839)	(2,024,143)	(1,020,134)	(1,004,009)	(332,278)	(157,908)	(174,370)	(280,298)	(132,028)	(148,270)	(136,241)	(67,051)	(69,190)
Usually	4.2%	5.7%	2.7%	3.3%	4.8%	1.8%	7.5%	9.2%	6.0%	5.6%	7.8%	3.6%	5.9%	8.1%	3.8%
	(116,143)	(79,069)	(37,074)	(67,502)	(48,941)	(18,561)	(24,932)	(14,451)	(10,481)	(15,671)	(10,279)	(5,392)	(8,038)	(5,398)	(2,640)
Often	5.8%	7.0%	4.6%	4.9%	5.9%	3.9%	6.6%	7.8%	5.4%	9.8%	10.7%	9.0%	8.5%	13.1%	4.2%
	(160,762)	(95,894)	(64,868)	(99,926)	(60,669)	(39,257)	(21,774)	(12,330)	(9,444)	(27,427)	(14,136)	(13,291)	(11,635)	(8,759)	(2,877)
Seldom	39.9%	40.1%	39.8%	42.6%	42.7%	42.5%	33.9%	32.6%	35.0%	31.2%	32.1%	30.3%	33.1%	33.2%	32.9%
	(1,107,269)	(552,251)	(555,018)	(862,385)	(435,973)	(426,412)	(112,509)	(51,547)	(60,962)	(87,331)	(42,442)	(44,889)	(45,045)	(22,290)	(22,755)
Never	50.1%	47.2%	52.9%	49.1%	46.5%	51.8%	52.1%	50.4%	53.6%	53.5%	49.4%	57.1%	52.5%	45.6%	59.1%
	(1,388,785)	(649,906)	(738,879)	(994,330)	(474,550)	(519,779)	(173,063)	(79,580)	(93,483)	(149,870)	(65,171)	(84,698)	(71,523)	(30,605)	(40,918)
1992															
Total *** +++ ~~~	100.0%	100.0%	100.0%	100.0%	100.0%	100.0%	100.0%	100.0%	100.0%	100.0%	100.0%	100.0%	100.0%	100.0%	100.0%
	(2,501,478)	(1,262,665)	(1,238,812)	(1,833,406)	(933,595)	(899,811)	(307,575)	(152,682)	(154,893)	(235,511)	(114,306)	(121,205)	(124,984)	(62,082)	(62,902)
Usually	4.3%	5.6%	3.0%	3.5%	4.7%	2.4%	6.9%	8.4%	5.4%	5.6%	7.4%	3.9%	5.8%	8.7%	3.0%
	(106,850)	(70,186)	(36,664)	(65,009)	(43,451)	(21,558)	(21,265)	(12,845)	(8,420)	(13,274)	(8,498)	(4,776)	(7,302)	(5,392)	(1,909)
Often	4.2%	5.7%	2.7%	4.1%	5.4%	2.8%	3.7%	6.1%	1.4%	5.9%	8.4%	3.6%	4.1%	5.1%	3.1%
	(106,149)	(72,550)	(33,599)	(75,652)	(50,524)	(25,128)	(11,432)	(9,261)	(2,171)	(13,951)	(9,607)	(4,344)	(5,114)	(3,159)	(1,955)
Seldom	38.6%	41.0%	36.2%	40.3%	42.6%	37.9%	31.7%	34.1%	29.3%	35.4%	37.9%	33.1%	37.1%	39.6%	34.6%
	(965,776)	(517,854)	(447,922)	(738,516)	(397,868)	(340,648)	(97,464)	(52,079)	(45,385)	(83,445)	(43,334)	(40,110)	(46,352)	(24,572)	(21,780)
Never	52.9%	47.7%	58.2%	52.0%	47.3%	57.0%	57.7%	51.4%	63.9%	53.0%	46.3%	59.4%	53.0%	46.6%	59.2%
	(1,322,703)	(602,076)	(720,627)	(954,229)	(441,752)	(512,478)	(177,415)	(78,498)	(98,917)	(124,841)	(52,867)	(71,974)	(66,217)	(28,959)	(37,258)

Notes:
***Test of statistical significance compares African Americans with Whites. *** p < .001, ** p < .01, * p < .05.
+++Test of statistical significance compares White boys with White girls. +++ p < .001, ++ p < .01, + p < .05.
~~~Test of statistical significance compares African American boys with African American gjrls. ~~~ p < .001, ~~ p < .01, ~ p < .05.
Tests of statistical significance calculated using adjusted sample weight to control for influence of large sample sizes.
Source: National Educational Longitudinal Study of 1988 Eighth Graders, Base Year (1988) and Second Follow-Up (1992).

- But, in 1992, a smaller proportion of African Americans than of Whites were members of academic subject clubs (20.3% versus 25.4%).

Overall, the percentage of 1988 8th graders who were members of an academic honors society increased from 13.1% in 1988 to 18.2% in 1992.

- In 1988, a higher percentage of African Americans than of Whites were members of academic honors societies (16.8% versus 12.1%).

- But, when most 1988 8th graders were high school seniors, only 13.6% of African Americans were members of academic honors societies, compared with 19.2% of Whites.

- In 1988, involvement with the school newspaper or yearbook was greater for African Americans than for Whites (23.1% versus 19.5%).

- But, in 1992, involvement with the school newspaper was lower for African Americans than for Whites (14.0% versus 19.3%).

Figure 7. Percentage of 1988 8th Graders Who Attended Class Without Paper and Pencil in 1988 and 1992

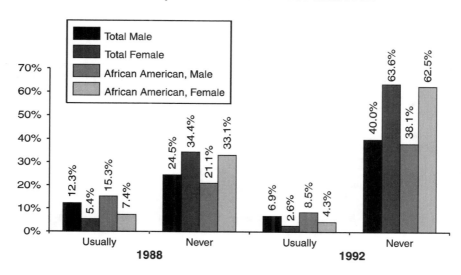

Source: National Educational Longitudinal Study of 1988 Eighth Graders, Base Year (1988) and Second Follow-up (1992).

Overall, nearly two-thirds (63.5%) of 1988 8th graders participated in nonschool activities, such as scouting, religious organizations, 4-H clubs, or other youth groups.

- **Table 8** shows that a smaller percentage of African Americans than of Whites participated in nonschool activities in 1988 (57.9% versus 67.2%).

Television Viewing Habits

In 1988, 13.2% of 8th graders watched more than 5 hours of television each weekday and 26.1% watched more than 5 hours per day on the weekends. **Figure 9** shows that African Americans watched more television than students overall, on average.

- **Table 10** shows that, in 1988, 80.0% of African American 8th graders, compared with 63.3% of Whites, watched more than 2 hours of television each weekday.

- Nearly one-third (30.1%) of African American students watched more than 5 hours of television each weekday, compared with only 10.5% of Whites.

- The proportion of African Americans who watched more than 5 hours of television each weekend day was more than twice as large as the proportion of Whites (49.0% versus 22.4%).

Table 7. Percentage of 1988 8th Graders Who Attended Class Without Paper or Pencil in 1988 and 1992 by Race and Sex
(weighted sample size in parentheses)

Attended Class Without Paper or Pencil	Total	Male	Female	White, Non-Hispanic Total	Male	Female	African American, Non-Hispanic Total	Male	Female	Hispanic Total	Male	Female	Other Total	Male	Female
1988															
Total *** +++ ~~~	100.0%	100.0%	100.0%	100.0%	100.0%	100.0%	100.0%	100.0%	100.0%	100.0%	100.0%	100.0%	100.0%	100.0%	100.0%
	(2,811,487)	(1,402,692)	(1,408,796)	(2,044,825)	(1,034,093)	(1,010,732)	(344,290)	(165,973)	(178,318)	(284,997)	(134,994)	(150,003)	(137,375)	(67,632)	(69,743)
Usually	8.9%	12.3%	5.4%	8.1%	11.6%	4.5%	11.2%	15.3%	7.4%	11.0%	13.3%	8.8%	10.0%	13.9%	6.3%
	(249,506)	(172,921)	(76,585)	(165,952)	(120,097)	(45,855)	(38,585)	(25,465)	(13,120)	(31,218)	(17,968)	(13,249)	(13,751)	(9,390)	(4,361)
Often	13.0%	16.0%	10.0%	12.5%	15.4%	9.5%	12.4%	14.8%	10.3%	17.7%	22.4%	13.6%	11.6%	14.2%	9.1%
	(364,851)	(223,827)	(141,025)	(255,590)	(159,583)	(96,008)	(42,796)	(24,489)	(18,307)	(50,524)	(30,180)	(20,344)	(15,941)	(9,575)	(6,366)
Seldom	48.6%	47.2%	50.1%	50.2%	48.4%	52.1%	49.1%	48.8%	49.3%	39.4%	37.5%	41.0%	43.0%	43.1%	42.9%
	(1,367,603)	(661,640)	(705,963)	(1,027,411)	(500,862)	(526,549)	(168,926)	(80,986)	(87,941)	(112,245)	(50,677)	(61,568)	(59,021)	(29,116)	(29,905)
Never	29.5%	24.5%	34.4%	29.1%	24.5%	33.9%	27.3%	21.1%	33.1%	31.9%	26.8%	36.6%	35.4%	28.9%	41.7%
	(829,527)	(344,304)	(485,223)	(595,872)	(253,552)	(342,320)	(93,983)	(35,033)	(58,950)	(91,010)	(36,168)	(54,841)	(48,662)	(19,550)	(29,112)
1992															
Total *** +++ ~~~	100.0%	100.0%	100.0%	100.0%	100.0%	100.0%	100.0%	100.0%	100.0%	100.0%	100.0%	100.0%	100.0%	100.0%	100.0%
	(2,503,302)	(1,263,904)	(1,239,398)	(1,834,486)	(934,124)	(900,362)	(308,022)	(153,129)	(154,893)	(235,632)	(114,434)	(121,198)	(125,162)	(62,218)	(62,944)
Usually	4.8%	6.9%	2.6%	4.4%	6.6%	2.1%	6.4%	8.5%	4.3%	4.8%	5.9%	3.8%	5.9%	8.7%	3.1%
	(119,069)	(86,833)	(32,236)	(80,850)	(61,725)	(19,125)	(19,571)	(12,976)	(6,595)	(11,271)	(6,698)	(4,572)	(7,377)	(5,435)	(1,943)
Often	5.9%	9.1%	2.6%	5.8%	9.1%	2.5%	4.8%	7.3%	2.4%	7.9%	12.4%	3.7%	4.7%	8.0%	1.4%
	(146,711)	(115,042)	(31,669)	(107,240)	(84,695)	(22,545)	(14,910)	(11,203)	(3,708)	(18,703)	(14,162)	(4,541)	(5,858)	(4,983)	(875)
Seldom	37.7%	44.1%	31.2%	38.1%	43.7%	32.4%	38.4%	46.1%	30.8%	35.6%	45.8%	25.9%	33.8%	41.6%	26.0%
	(944,249)	(557,055)	(387,194)	(699,834)	(408,153)	(291,680)	(118,319)	(70,588)	(47,731)	(83,847)	(52,405)	(31,441)	(42,249)	(25,909)	(16,341)
Never	51.7%	40.0%	63.6%	51.6%	40.6%	63.0%	50.4%	38.1%	62.5%	51.7%	36.0%	66.5%	55.7%	41.6%	69.6%
	(1,293,273)	(504,973)	(788,300)	(946,562)	(379,551)	(567,011)	(155,222)	(58,363)	(96,859)	(121,812)	(41,168)	(80,644)	(69,677)	(25,892)	(43,785)

Notes:
***Test of statistical significance compares African Americans with Whites. *** p < .001, ** p < .01, * p < .05
+++Test of statistical significance compares White boys with White girls. +++ p < .001, ++ p < .01, + p < .05
~~~Test of statistical significance compares African American boys with African American girls. ~~~ p < .001, ~~ p < .01, ~ p < .05
Tests of statistical significance calculated using adjusted sample weight to control for influence of large sample sizes.
Source: National Educational Longitudinal Study of 1988 Eighth Graders, Base Year (1988) and Second Follow-up (1992).

Regardless of race, the average number of hours of television watched by 1988 8th graders declined between 1988 and 1992. But, in 1992, when most 1988 8th graders were high school seniors, African Americans continued to watch more television than their White counterparts.

- **Table 11** shows that, in 1992, 69.7% of African Americans watched at least 2 hours of television each weekday, compared with 49.0% of Whites.

- More than one-fifth (22.3%) of African Americans, but only 6.4% of Whites, watched more than 5 hours of television each weekday.

- The proportion of African Americans who watched at least 5 hours of television each weekend day was nearly three times as large as the proportion of Whites (41.4% versus 14.7%).

Table 8. Participation of 1988 8th Graders in School Clubs and Activities in 1988 by Race and Sex
(weighted sample size in parentheses)

School Club or Activity	Total	Male	Female	White, Non-Hispanic			African American, Non-Hispanic			Hispanic			Other		
				Total	Male	Female	Total	Male	Female	Total	Male	Female	Total	Male	Female
Total	100.0%	100.0%	100.0%	100.0%	100.0%	100.0%	100.0%	100.0%	100.0%	100.0%	100.0%	100.0%	100.0%	100.0%	100.0%
	(2,946,419)	(1,482,828)	(1,463,591)	(2,106,252)	(1,068,296)	(1,037,956)	(387,402)	(192,794)	(194,607)	(306,576)	(147,845)	(158,731)	(146,191)	(73,894)	(72,297)
Science Fairs*** ~~~	27.5%	27.2%	28.0%	27.4%	27.3%	27.4%	32.0%	28.0%	35.9%	22.4%	24.7%	20.3%	29.5%	28.3%	30.7%
	(811,246)	(402,849)	(409,157)	(576,264)	(291,478)	(284,785)	(123,959)	(54,025)	(69,933)	(68,723)	(36,447)	(32,275)	(43,061)	(20,898)	(22,163)
Varsity/Intramural Sports or Cheerleading *** ++ ~~	59.9%	62.1%	57.6%	62.0%	63.3%	60.6%	56.8%	59.7%	53.9%	53.4%	59.8%	47.5%	51.3%	54.5%	47.9%
	(1,763,893)	(920,133)	(843,759)	(1,305,227)	(676,408)	(628,818)	(219,995)	(115,108)	(104,887)	(163,738)	(88,341)	(75,396)	(74,934)	(40,276)	(34,658)
Choir, Band, or Dance *** +++ ~~~	49.2%	40.5%	58.0%	52.1%	43.2%	61.2%	45.0%	35.4%	54.5%	38.1%	32.4%	43.5%	41.6%	31.1%	52.3%
	(1,448,604)	(600,398)	(848,206)	(1,096,631)	(461,216)	(635,415)	(174,266)	(68,282)	(105,984)	(116,938)	(47,942)	(68,996)	(60,769)	(22,958)	(37,811)
Academic Club ***	19.9%	20.1%	19.8%	18.0%	18.2%	17.8%	28.4%	29.6%	27.2%	20.5%	20.6%	20.5%	24.5%	22.6%	26.5%
	(587,381)	(298,081)	(289,300)	(378,739)	(193,946)	(184,793)	(109,866)	(57,003)	(52,863)	(62,945)	(30,427)	(32,517)	(35,831)	(16,705)	(19,126)
Debate, Speech, or Drama *** +++ ~~	11.0%	9.2%	12.7%	10.1%	7.6%	12.6%	14.0%	15.8%	12.3%	12.8%	11.8%	13.7%	11.5%	10.3%	12.8%
	(322,694)	(137,100)	(185,594)	(212,225)	(81,554)	(130,671)	(54,274)	(30,406)	(23,868)	(39,313)	(17,497)	(21,815)	(16,882)	(7,643)	(9,239)
Honors Society *** +++	13.1%	11.8%	14.4%	12.1%	10.8%	13.4%	16.8%	15.3%	18.3%	13.2%	11.5%	14.8%	18.1%	18.5%	17.8%
	(384,638)	(175,400)	(210,696)	(253,942)	(115,145)	(138,798)	(65,186)	(29,591)	(35,595)	(40,470)	(17,019)	(23,451)	(26,497)	(13,644)	(12,853)
School Newspaper or Yearbook*** +++ ~~~	19.7%	17.0%	22.4%	19.5%	16.9%	22.1%	23.1%	17.1%	29.1%	17.3%	17.6%	17.1%	18.2%	16.8%	19.6%
	(579,355)	(251,621)	(327,734)	(410,103)	(180,238)	(229,865)	(89,535)	(32,922)	(56,613)	(53,182)	(26,064)	(27,118)	(26,535)	(12,398)	(14,137)
Student Council*** +++ ~	12.0%	10.4%	13.6%	11.4%	9.7%	13.2%	14.3%	12.6%	16.1%	12.8%	12.7%	12.9%	12.4%	10.1%	14.7%
	(353,260)	(153,821)	(199,529)	(240,452)	(103,343)	(137,109)	(55,466)	(24,201)	(31,265)	(39,343)	(18,848)	(20,495)	(18,089)	(7,429)	(10,660)
Non-School Activities***	63.5%	64.3%	62.7%	67.2%	67.7%	66.7%	57.9%	57.5%	58.2%	49.8%	53.3%	46.7%	54.6%	56.0%	53.1%
	(1,872,043)	(953,698)	(918,344)	(1,415,330)	(722,746)	(692,584)	(224,125)	(110,815)	(113,311)	(152,801)	(78,747)	(74,054)	(79,786)	(41,390)	(38,396)

Notes:

***Test of statistical significance compares African Americans with Whites. *** $p < .001$, ** $p < .01$, * $p < .05$.

+++Test of statistical significance compares White boys with White girls. +++ $p < .001$, ++ $p < .01$, + $p < .05$.

~~~Test of statistical significance compares African American boys with African American girls. ~~~ $p < .001$, ~~ $p < .01$, ~ $p < .05$.

Tests of statistical significance calculated using adjusted sample weight to control for influence of large sample sizes.

Source: National Educational Longitudinal Study of 1988 Eighth Graders, Base Year (1988) and Second Follow-Up (1992).

Table 9. Participation of 1988 8th Graders in School Clubs and Activities in 1992 by Race and Sex
(weighted sample size in parentheses)

School Club or Activity	Total	Male	Female	White, Non-Hispanic Total	White, Non-Hispanic Male	White, Non-Hispanic Female	African American, Non-Hispanic Total	African American, Non-Hispanic Male	African American, Non-Hispanic Female	Hispanic Total	Hispanic Male	Hispanic Female	Other Total	Other Male	Other Female
Total	100.0%	100.0%	100.0%	100.0%	100.0%	100.0%	100.0%	100.0%	100.0%	100.0%	100.0%	100.0%	100.0%	100.0%	100.0%
	(2,946,419)	(1,482,828)	(1,463,591)	(2,106,252)	(1,068,296)	(1,037,956)	(387,402)	(192,794)	(194,607)	(306,576)	(147,845)	(158,731)	(146,191)	(73,894)	(72,297)
Team or Individual Sport*** +++ ~~~	37.7%	44.6%	30.8%	39.3%	46.1%	32.3%	35.6%	43.0%	28.2%	29.2%	36.9%	22.1%	38.2%	41.4%	34.9%
	(1,110,963)	(660,630)	(450,333)	(827,598)	(492,439)	(335,159)	(137,904)	(82,984)	(54,920)	(89,645)	(54,628)	(35,017)	(55,816)	(30,579)	(25,237)
School Play or Music** +++ ~~~	26.1%	21.4%	30.8%	26.2%	21.4%	31.1%	28.8%	23.0%	34.5%	22.1%	20.1%	23.9%	25.8%	19.1%	32.7%
	(768,003)	(317,095)	(451,202)	(551,296)	(228,909)	(322,387)	(111,596)	(44,398)	(67,197)	(67,667)	(29,678)	(37,988)	(37,738)	(14,109)	(23,629)
Academic Club*** +++ ~~~	24.7%	22.0%	27.1%	25.4%	23.1%	27.9%	20.3%	17.1%	23.5%	21.5%	20.0%	22.9%	29.2%	23.4%	35.0%
	(726,547)	(326,319)	(396,801)	(535,880)	(246,477)	(289,403)	(78,567)	(32,925)	(45,642)	(66,043)	(29,624)	(36,419)	(42,629)	(17,293)	(25,337)
Honor Society*** +++ ~~~	18.2%	14.1%	22.0%	19.2%	14.8%	23.8%	13.6%	10.5%	16.6%	11.4%	10.1%	12.6%	26.7%	22.2%	31.2%
	(536,899)	(209,587)	(322,394)	(405,295)	(157,894)	(247,401)	(52,611)	(20,276)	(32,335)	(35,053)	(14,985)	(20,069)	(39,022)	(16,433)	(22,590)
School Yearbook or Newspaper*** +++ ~~~	18.5%	13.7%	23.2%	19.3%	14.2%	24.5%	14.0%	10.2%	17.8%	16.0%	13.1%	18.7%	22.3%	16.8%	27.9%
	(545,642)	(203,284)	(339,039)	(406,316)	(151,849)	(254,466)	(54,358)	(19,707)	(34,651)	(49,084)	(19,339)	(29,745)	(32,566)	(12,390)	(20,177)
School Government +++ ~~~	15.0%	12.5%	17.5%	14.8%	12.4%	17.4%	16.1%	13.0%	19.2%	14.0%	12.5%	15.3%	16.2%	12.2%	20.2%
	(441,882)	(185,076)	(256,483)	(312,577)	(132,406)	(180,172)	(62,526)	(25,139)	(37,386)	(42,822)	(18,485)	(24,338)	(23,634)	(9,046)	(14,587)
Other School Club* +++ ~~~	26.6%	22.1%	31.2%	27.3%	23.2%	31.5%	25.4%	18.9%	31.8%	23.6%	19.5%	27.4%	27.2%	21.1%	33.4%
	(785,086)	(328,339)	(456,748)	(574,694)	(247,450)	(327,245)	(98,329)	(36,519)	(61,809)	(72,322)	(28,801)	(43,520)	(39,742)	(15,569)	(24,173)

Notes:
*** Test of statistical significance compares African Americans with Whites. *** p < .001, ** p < .01, * p < .05.
+++ Test of statistical significance compares White boys with White girls. +++ p < .001, ++ p < .01, + p < .05.
~~~ Test of statistical significance compares African American boys with African American girls. ~~~ p < .001, ~~ p < .01, ~ p < .05.
Tests of statistical significance calculated using adjusted sample weight to control for influence of large sample sizes.
Source: National Educational Longitudinal Study of 1988 Eighth Graders, Base Year (1988) and Second Follow-up (1992).

Figure 8. Participation of 1988 8th Graders in School Academic Activities in 1988 and 1992

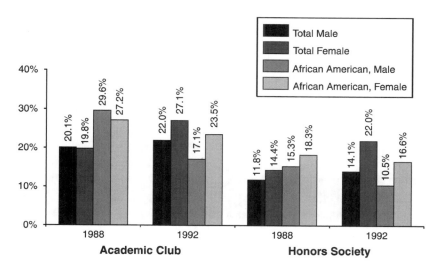

Source: National Educational Longitudinal Study of 1988 Eighth Graders, Base Year (1988) and Second Follow-Up (1992).

Figure 9. Percentage of 1988 8th Graders Who Spent More Than 5 Hours Per Day Watching Television in 1992

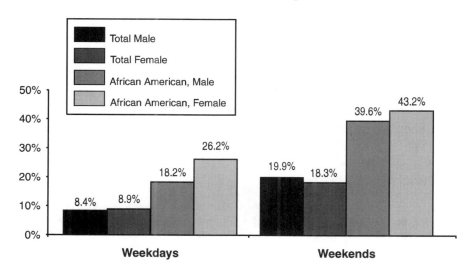

Source: National Educational Longitudinal Study of 1988 Eighth Graders, Base Year (1988) and Second Follow-Up (1992).

Table 10. Amount of Time 1988 8th Graders Spent Watching Television in 1988 by Race and Sex
(weighted sample size in parentheses)

Hours of Television	Total	Male	Female	White, Non-Hispanic Total	Male	Female	African American, Non-Hispanic Total	Male	Female	Hispanic Total	Male	Female	Other Total	Male	Female
Hours Watched on Weekdays															
Total*** ++ ~~~	100.0%	100.0%	100.0%	100.0%	100.0%	100.0%	100.0%	100.0%	100.0%	100.0%	100.0%	100.0%	100.0%	100.0%	100.0%
	(2,645,602)	(1,327,537)	(1,318,065)	(1,968,686)	(998,036)	(970,649)	(295,268)	(145,128)	(150,140)	(254,224)	(120,848)	(133,376)	(127,424)	(63,524)	(63,900)
Don't Watch TV	3.3%	3.2%	3.3%	3.1%	3.3%	2.9%	2.2%	1.6%	2.9%	4.1%	3.3%	4.8%	6.7%	5.8%	7.6%
	(86,506)	(42,900)	(43,607)	(60,980)	(33,045)	(27,935)	(6,630)	(2,253)	(4,377)	(10,358)	(3,946)	(6,412)	(8,539)	(3,656)	(4,883)
Less Than 1 Hour per Day	8.6%	8.3%	8.9%	9.2%	8.5%	10.0%	4.6%	4.8%	4.4%	7.7%	8.7%	6.8%	9.5%	11.7%	7.2%
	(226,632)	(109,821)	(116,811)	(181,576)	(84,947)	(96,629)	(13,518)	(6,941)	(6,576)	(19,491)	(10,481)	(9,010)	(12,048)	(7,452)	(4,596)
1 to 2 Hours per Day	22.4%	21.8%	23.0%	24.4%	24.2%	24.5%	13.2%	11.3%	15.1%	18.0%	16.5%	19.5%	21.1%	17.0%	25.2%
	(591,975)	(288,967)	(303,008)	(480,161)	(241,868)	(238,293)	(39,011)	(16,364)	(22,648)	(45,878)	(19,925)	(25,953)	(26,926)	(10,811)	(16,114)
2 to 3 Hours per Day	22.9%	23.9%	21.8%	24.1%	24.7%	23.5%	15.0%	18.0%	12.1%	22.6%	23.2%	22.0%	22.5%	26.2%	18.7%
	(605,241)	(317,469)	(287,771)	(474,896)	(246,657)	(228,239)	(44,340)	(26,126)	(18,214)	(57,393)	(28,027)	(29,366)	(28,611)	(16,659)	(11,953)
3 to 4 Hours per Day	18.2%	18.3%	18.2%	18.3%	18.1%	18.5%	15.8%	19.3%	12.4%	21.5%	20.4%	22.5%	15.9%	14.1%	17.7%
	(482,107)	(242,331)	(239,776)	(360,468)	(180,692)	(179,776)	(46,730)	(28,046)	(18,684)	(54,646)	(24,654)	(29,992)	(20,262)	(8,939)	(11,323)
4 to 5 Hours per Day	11.4%	11.0%	11.9%	10.4%	10.0%	10.7%	19.0%	16.6%	21.3%	11.0%	11.0%	11.0%	11.3%	13.0%	9.6%
	(302,745)	(145,865)	(156,880)	(204,365)	(100,193)	(104,172)	(56,067)	(24,105)	(31,962)	(27,929)	(13,319)	(14,610)	(14,384)	(8,248)	(6,136)
More Than 5 Hours per Day	13.2%	13.6%	12.9%	10.5%	11.1%	9.8%	30.1%	28.5%	31.8%	15.2%	17.0%	13.5%	13.1%	12.2%	13.9%
	(350,395)	(180,183)	(170,213)	(206,240)	(110,635)	(95,605)	(88,972)	(41,292)	(47,680)	(38,529)	(20,497)	(18,032)	(16,654)	(7,758)	(8,895)
Hours Watched on Weekends															
Total*** +++ ~~~	100.0%	100.0%	100.0%	100.0%	100.0%	100.0%	100.0%	100.0%	100.0%	100.0%	100.0%	100.0%	100.0%	100.0%	100.0%
	(2,576,356)	(1,294,227)	(1,282,129)	(1,939,524)	(983,266)	(956,257)	(276,066)	(137,207)	(138,858)	(240,630)	(113,448)	(127,182)	(120,137)	(60,306)	(59,831)
Don't Watch TV	4.0%	3.4%	4.7%	4.1%	3.6%	4.6%	2.6%	1.5%	3.7%	5.4%	4.0%	6.7%	3.7%	2.5%	4.8%
	(103,811)	(43,567)	(60,244)	(79,165)	(35,422)	(43,742)	(7,169)	(2,085)	(5,084)	(13,067)	(4,531)	(8,535)	(4,411)	(1,529)	(2,882)
Less than 1 Hour per Day	6.1%	5.6%	6.7%	6.6%	6.1%	7.2%	3.6%	3.9%	3.4%	5.9%	4.1%	7.6%	4.2%	3.4%	5.0%
	(158,297)	(71,876)	(86,421)	(128,943)	(59,820)	(69,123)	(10,072)	(5,394)	(4,678)	(14,236)	(4,598)	(9,637)	(5,046)	(2,064)	(2,983)
1 to 2 Hours per Day	12.6%	11.5%	13.6%	13.5%	12.8%	14.3%	6.5%	4.5%	8.5%	12.0%	9.2%	14.4%	12.3%	11.1%	13.4%
	(323,917)	(149,182)	(174,735)	(262,354)	(125,825)	(136,529)	(17,974)	(6,186)	(11,788)	(28,857)	(10,481)	(18,376)	(14,732)	(6,690)	(8,042)
2 to 3 Hours per Day	17.0%	15.8%	18.3%	18.5%	16.8%	20.3%	7.4%	7.2%	7.5%	16.4%	16.6%	16.1%	16.4%	17.6%	15.1%
	(439,068)	(205,008)	(234,060)	(359,670)	(165,606)	(194,065)	(20,386)	(9,902)	(10,484)	(39,345)	(18,859)	(20,485)	(19,668)	(10,641)	(9,026)
3 to 4 Hours per Day	17.3%	17.0%	17.7%	18.0%	17.6%	18.5%	13.6%	12.6%	14.6%	15.6%	15.8%	15.5%	17.9%	19.0%	16.8%
	(446,501)	(219,417)	(227,084)	(349,886)	(172,789)	(177,097)	(37,456)	(17,235)	(20,221)	(37,617)	(17,910)	(19,707)	(21,542)	(11,482)	(10,060)
4 to 5 Hours per Day	16.8%	17.6%	16.1%	16.8%	17.3%	16.2%	17.3%	20.5%	14.2%	15.1%	17.4%	13.0%	19.8%	14.8%	24.7%
	(433,186)	(227,370)	(205,816)	(325,243)	(170,514)	(154,730)	(47,835)	(28,120)	(19,715)	(36,359)	(19,788)	(16,571)	(23,749)	(8,948)	(14,801)
More Than 5 Hours per Day	26.1%	29.2%	22.9%	22.4%	25.8%	18.9%	49.0%	49.8%	48.2%	29.6%	32.9%	26.6%	25.8%	31.4%	20.1%
	(671,575)	(377,807)	(293,768)	(434,261)	(253,291)	(180,971)	(135,174)	(68,285)	(66,890)	(71,150)	(37,280)	(33,870)	(30,989)	(18,952)	(12,037)

Notes:

***Test of statistical significance compares African Americans with Whites. *** p < .001, ** p < .01, * p < .05.

+++Test of statistical significance compares White boys with White girls. +++ p < .001, ++ p < .01, + p < .05.

~~~Test of statistical significance compares African American boys with African American girls. ~~~ p < .001, ~~ p < .01, ~ p < .05.

Tests of statistical significance calculated using adjusted sample weight to control for influence of large sample sizes.

Source: National Educational Longitudinal Study of 1988 Eighth Graders, Base Year (1988) and Second Follow-Up (1992).

Table 11. Amount of Time 1988 8th Graders Spent Watching Television in 1992 by Race and Sex
(weighted sample size in parentheses)

Hours of Television	Total	Male	Female	White, Non-Hispanic Total	White, Non-Hispanic Male	White, Non-Hispanic Female	African American, Non-Hispanic Total	African American, Non-Hispanic Male	African American, Non-Hispanic Female	Hispanic Total	Hispanic Male	Hispanic Female	Other Total	Other Male	Other Female
Hours Watched on Weekdays															
Total*** +++ ~~~	100.0%	100.0%	100.0%	100.0%	100.0%	100.0%	100.0%	100.0%	100.0%	100.0%	100.0%	100.0%	100.0%	100.0%	100.0%
	(2,459,150)	(1,235,520)	(1,223,630)	(1,816,665)	(922,716)	(893,949)	(293,436)	(144,358)	(149,078)	(228,271)	(109,319)	(118,951)	(120,778)	(59,127)	(61,651)
Don't Watch TV	4.3%	4.3%	4.3%	4.4%	4.4%	4.4%	2.8%	3.9%	1.7%	4.2%	3.9%	4.5%	5.9%	4.3%	7.4%
	(105,398)	(53,344)	(52,054)	(80,635)	(40,993)	(39,642)	(8,119)	(5,620)	(2,500)	(9,537)	(4,215)	(5,322)	(7,106)	(2,516)	(4,590)
Less Than 1 Hour per Day	17.3%	16.4%	18.1%	18.7%	17.6%	19.9%	9.8%	11.3%	8.4%	15.3%	14.2%	16.2%	17.7%	15.3%	20.1%
	(424,754)	(203,048)	(221,706)	(339,558)	(162,091)	(177,467)	(28,898)	(16,378)	(12,520)	(34,864)	(15,538)	(19,326)	(21,434)	(9,041)	(12,393)
1 to 2 Hours per Day	26.1%	25.8%	26.5%	27.9%	27.1%	28.7%	17.7%	18.5%	16.9%	25.1%	24.8%	25.4%	22.4%	25.1%	19.9%
	(642,586)	(318,302)	(324,284)	(506,164)	(249,614)	(256,549)	(51,993)	(26,778)	(25,215)	(57,323)	(27,061)	(30,262)	(27,107)	(14,849)	(12,258)
2 to 3 Hours per Day	24.6%	24.9%	24.3%	24.9%	25.2%	24.6%	19.6%	18.1%	21.2%	27.8%	30.6%	25.2%	27.3%	27.9%	26.6%
	(605,673)	(308,239)	(297,434)	(451,639)	(232,145)	(219,494)	(57,644)	(26,070)	(31,574)	(63,437)	(33,501)	(29,937)	(32,953)	(16,523)	(16,430)
3 to 5 Hours per Day	19.1%	20.2%	17.9%	17.7%	19.1%	16.4%	27.8%	30.0%	25.6%	18.3%	17.0%	19.5%	18.9%	19.6%	18.2%
	(468,477)	(249,371)	(219,106)	(322,363)	(175,865)	(146,498)	(81,432)	(43,269)	(38,162)	(41,853)	(18,633)	(23,220)	(22,829)	(11,603)	(11,226)
More Than 5 Hours per Day	8.6%	8.4%	8.9%	6.4%	6.7%	6.1%	22.3%	18.2%	26.2%	9.3%	9.5%	9.2%	7.7%	7.8%	7.7%
	(212,262)	(103,216)	(109,046)	(116,307)	(62,008)	(54,299)	(65,351)	(26,243)	(39,108)	(21,256)	(10,371)	(10,885)	(9,349)	(4,594)	(4,755)
Hours Watched on Weekends															
Total *** ++ ~~~	100.0%	100.0%	100.0%	100.0%	100.0%	100.0%	100.0%	100.0%	100.0%	100.0%	100.0%	100.0%	100.0%	100.0%	100.0%
	(2,435,089)	(1,225,392)	(1,209,697)	(1,805,181)	(917,499)	(887,683)	(285,138)	(141,163)	(143,975)	(223,484)	(106,928)	(116,556)	(121,287)	(59,803)	(61,484)
Don't Watch TV	4.5%	3.9%	5.0%	4.5%	4.1%	4.9%	2.9%	2.9%	2.9%	5.7%	3.9%	7.4%	5.3%	4.1%	6.4%
	(108,706)	(48,177)	(60,529)	(81,239)	(37,492)	(43,747)	(8,329)	(4,106)	(4,223)	(12,735)	(4,118)	(8,617)	(6,403)	(2,462)	(3,942)
Less Than 1 Hour per Day	11.2%	11.0%	11.4%	12.3%	12.2%	12.3%	7.5%	5.3%	9.7%	8.4%	8.7%	8.1%	8.8%	9.5%	8.2%
	(272,020)	(134,597)	(137,423)	(221,264)	(112,230)	(109,033)	(21,339)	(7,417)	(13,921)	(18,716)	(9,261)	(9,455)	(10,702)	(5,688)	(5,014)
1 to 2 Hours per Day	18.5%	18.5%	18.4%	20.3%	20.3%	20.3%	9.0%	10.9%	7.1%	15.8%	15.4%	16.2%	18.9%	15.7%	22.0%
	(449,790)	(227,240)	(222,549)	(365,794)	(185,951)	(179,843)	(25,713)	(15,440)	(10,272)	(35,341)	(16,443)	(18,897)	(22,942)	(9,405)	(13,537)
2 to 3 Hours per Day	23.6%	23.5%	23.6%	25.1%	24.8%	25.3%	16.1%	17.4%	14.9%	20.9%	20.3%	21.5%	24.3%	24.4%	24.2%
	(574,571)	(288,520)	(286,051)	(452,377)	(227,709)	(224,668)	(45,913)	(24,516)	(21,398)	(46,814)	(21,706)	(25,107)	(29,467)	(14,589)	(14,878)
3 to 5 Hours per Day	23.2%	23.1%	23.3%	23.2%	22.8%	23.7%	23.0%	23.9%	22.2%	25.3%	26.6%	24.2%	18.9%	19.7%	18.1%
	(564,783)	(283,343)	(281,440)	(419,553)	(209,407)	(210,146)	(65,677)	(33,759)	(31,918)	(56,628)	(28,408)	(28,220)	(22,925)	(11,769)	(11,156)
More Than 5 Hours per Day	19.1%	19.9%	18.3%	14.7%	15.8%	13.5%	41.4%	39.6%	43.2%	23.8%	25.2%	22.5%	23.8%	26.6%	21.1%
	(465,220)	(243,516)	(221,703)	(264,954)	(144,709)	(120,245)	(118,168)	(55,925)	(62,242)	(53,251)	(26,991)	(26,259)	(28,847)	(15,890)	(12,957)

Notes:
***Test of statistical significance compares African Americans with Whites. *** p < .001, ** p < .01, * p < .05.
+++Test of statistical significance compares White boys with White girls. +++ p < .001, ++ p < .01, + p < .05.
~~~Test of statistical significance compares African American boys with African American girls. ~~~ p < .001, ~~ p < .01, ~ p < .05.
Tests of statistical significance calculated using adjusted sample weight to control for influence of large sample sizes.
Source: National Educational Longitudinal Study of 1988 Eighth Graders, Base Year (1988) and Second Follow-Up (1992).

CHAPTER V.
African American Student Performance on the National Assessment of Educational Progress

---

How well do African American students score on standardized tests in reading, history, geography, writing, and mathematics relative to their peers in other racial groups? Does their relative performance vary between the 4th, 8th, and 12th grades?

The National Assessment of Educational Progress (NAEP) has been reporting on the progress of American students at three grade levels for more than 25 years. For the NAEP, a sample of students is selected from among students nationwide in the 4th, 8th, and 12th grades. The selected students are administered assessments in the fields of reading, writing, mathematics, geography, and history. The sample is not selected randomly but according to a complex framework designed to obtain adequate representation of students and schools of various types. Consequently, the percentage of students by racial and ethnic group at each grade level may not necessarily represent the true national racial and ethnic representation. Both public and nonpublic (Catholic and other private) schools are included in the sample.

NAEP scores are provided in two ways: 1) on a proficiency scale ranging from 0 to 500, and 2) using the National Assessment Governing Board's (NAGB) achievement levels of Basic, Proficient, and Advanced. A student who achieves Basic has a partial mastery of the knowledge and skills necessary to function at grade level. According to the NAGB, a Proficient student has a full grasp of the subject matter for the grade level, and an Advanced student exhibits superior performance. The tables that follow were gathered from NAEP assessments in 1992 and 1994. All subject areas except science are reported since the science assessment data were not available at the time of this report.

PART I — OVERVIEW

NAEP scores are among the first indications of those subject-related challenges that African American students face throughout their educational experiences. The 1992 and 1994 NAEP data show that the majority of African Americans in the 4th, 8th, and 12th grades have not achieved a basic level of achievement in reading, history, geography, or mathematics. On the reading, history, geography, mathematics, and writing assessments, African Americans are concentrated in schools with the lowest average scores.

In all five subject areas and all three grade levels, the NAEP scores of African American students lag behind the scores of their White peers. Although mitigating factors such as school characteristics, socioeconomic status, and study habits are not considered here, these data illustrate one of the greatest educational challenges facing African Americans.

PART II — DETAILED DESCRIPTIONS AND TABLES

NATIONAL ASSESSMENT OF EDUCATIONAL PROGRESS (NAEP)

NAEP Reading Report Card

On average, reading scores for African Americans were lower than the scores achieved by White and Asian American examinees at each of the three grade levels.

- **Table 1** shows that, at the 4th-grade level, only 31% of African Americans achieved scores at or above the basic level, compared with 71% of Whites and 78% of Asian Americans.

- Among 12th graders, 52% of the African Americans, but 67% of Asian Americans and 81% of Whites, had achieved the basic level.

- **Figure 1** shows that only 1% of African American (but 9% of White) 4th graders and 1% of African American (but 5% of White) 12th graders achieved scores at the advanced level (denoting superior performance).

- About 69% African American 4th graders, 56% of African American 8th graders, and 48% of African American 12th graders scored below the basic level in reading.

When schools are ranked by the average score on the reading assessment, African Americans repre-

Table 1. Percentage of Students Scoring at Various Levels on the National Assessment of Educational Progress Reading Report Card: 1994

Representation	White	African American	Hispanic	Asian American	Pacific Islander	American Indian
Grade 4 Reading						
% Students in This Racial/Ethnic Group	69%	15%	12%	2%	1%	2%
Average Reading Proficiency	224	187	191	232	219	201
% Below Basic Level	29%	69%	64%	22%	33%	52%
% At or Above Basic Level	71%	31%	36%	78%	67%	48%
% At or Above Proficient	37%	9%	13%	48%	35%	18%
% At or Above Advanced Level	9%	1%	3%	16%	8%	2%
Grade 8 Reading						
% Students in This Racial/Ethnic Group	70%	15%	11%	2%	1%	1%
Average Reading Proficiency	268	237	251	273	259	240
% Below Basic Level	22%	56%	51%	19%	32%	37%
% At or Above Basic Level	78%	44%	49%	81%	68%	63%
% At or Above Proficient	36%	9%	14%	44%	26%	20%
% At or Above Advanced Level	4%	0%	1%	6%	3%	1%
Grade 12 Reading						
% Students in This Racial/Ethnic Group	73%	13%	8%	3%	1%	1%
Average Reading Proficiency	294	265	270	280	280	275
% Below Basic Level	19%	48%	42%	33%	29%	39%
% At or Above Basic Level	81%	52%	58%	67%	71%	61%
% At or Above Proficient	43%	13%	20%	33%	27%	20%
% At or Above Advanced Level	5%	1%	1%	3%	3%	2%

Source: NAEP 1994 Reading Report Card for the Nation and the States. January, 1996.
Office of Educational Research and Improvement, U.S. Department of Education.

Figure 1. Percentage of African Americans Scoring at Various Levels on the National Assessment of Educational Progress Reading Report Card: 1994

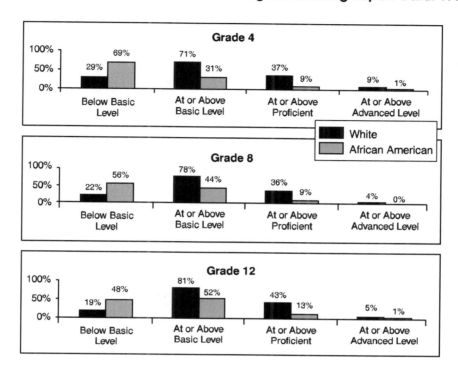

Source: NAEP 1994 Reading Report Card for the Nation and the States, January 1996.

sent a higher percentage of students in the bottom one-third than in the top one-third of all schools.

- **Table 2** shows that, among 4th graders, African Americans represented 30.1% of all students in the schools with the lowest reading scores but only 5.4% of all students in the schools with the top one-third of scores.

- For the 8th- and 12th-grade assessments, African Americans represented about one-fourth (25.7% in grade 8 and 25.8% in grade 12) of all students in the bottom one-third schools but only a fraction (2.8% in grade 8 and 3.6% in

grade 12) of all students in the top one-third schools.

NAEP History Report Card

The history assessment covers four themes over eight historical periods. In 1994, the test was administered to a sample of approximately 22,000 students at public and private elementary and secondary schools nationwide.

- **Table 3** shows that the percentage of African American 4th-grade students who had achieved at or above the basic level on the

Table 2. Percentage of Students at the Top- and Bottom-Performing Schools on the National Assessment of Educational Progress Reading Report Card: 1992

Rank of School	Attribute	White	African American	Hispanic	Asian American	Pacific Islander	American Indian
Grade 4 Reading							
Top Third	% Students	83.3%	5.4%	6.2%	2.8%	0.8%	1.1%
	Mean Score	238.4	215.9	225.9	249.0	236.7	227.9
Middle Third	% Students	80.6%	7.2%	8.0%	1.5%	0.6%	1.6%
	Mean Score	221.7	201.8	200.1	231.5	227.7	206.4
Lowest Third	% Students	45.7%	30.1%	19.3%	1.4%	0.7%	1.9%
	Mean Score	204.6	179.5	177.4	203.1	198.5	184.2
Grade 8 Reading							
Top Third	% Students	89.7%	2.8%	3.9%	1.9%	0.9%	0.7%
	Mean Score	282.3	269.6	267.2	295.1	282.4	276.4
Middle Third	% Students	78.9%	9.5%	6.7%	2.0%	1.1%	1.3%
	Mean Score	267.9	247.5	250.9	277.0	264.2	255.0
Lowest Third	% Students	52.0%	25.7%	17.1%	1.8%	1.6%	1.6%
	Mean Score	255.4	231.3	233.7	259.7	250.1	243.0
Grade 12 Reading							
Top Third	% Students	88.9%	3.6%	4.2%	2.1%	0.7%	0.3%
	Mean Score	280.6	270.0	270.3	292.6	272.4	266.2
Middle Third	% Students	76.9%	11.0%	7.2%	1.8%	1.1%	1.6%
	Mean Score	265.7	248.5	251.3	268.7	264.4	254.5
Lowest Third	% Students	50.5%	25.8%	17.9%	2.0%	1.5%	1.9%
	Mean Score	253.6	232.1	236.2	256.0	237.9	237.8

Source: NAEP 1994 National Reading Assessment, Grades 4, 8 and 12, Student Data From NAEP 1994 Trends in Academic Progress.

history assessment was one-half as large as the percentage of White students (36% versus 74%).

- **Figure 2** shows that the gap in the performance of African American and White students persisted at higher grade levels since 67% of African American 8th graders (but 29% of Whites) and 83% of African American 12th graders (but 50% of Whites) scored below the basic level.

- Only 4% of African American 4th graders (compared with 22% of Whites), 4% of African American 8th graders (compared with 17% of Whites), and 2% of African American 12th graders (compared with 13% of Whites) scored at or above the proficient level.

African Americans are concentrated in schools with the lowest average scores on the history assessment.

- **Table 4** shows that, on the 4th-grade assessment, African Americans represented 30.5% of all students in the schools with the lowest history scores but only 3.8% of all students in the schools with the highest scores.

Table 3. Percentage of Students Scoring at Various Levels on the National Assessment of Educational Progress History Report Card: 1994

Representation	White	African American	Hispanic	Asian American	Pacific Islander	American Indian
Grade 4 History						
% Students in This Racial/Ethnic Group	69%	15%	11%	2%	1%	2%
Average History Scale Score	215	177	180	209	200	190
% Below Basic Level	26%	64%	59%	36%	41%	49%
% At or Above Basic Level	74%	36%	41%	64%	59%	51%
% At or Above Proficient	22%	4%	6%	22%	16%	9%
% At or Above Advanced Level	3%	0%	1%	4%	3%	0%
Grade 8 History						
% Students in This Racial/Ethnic Group	69%	15%	11%	2%	1%	1%
Average History Scale Score	267	239	243	270	252	246
% Below Basic Level	29%	67%	59%	28%	48%	
% At or Above Basic Level	71%	4%	5%	23%	11%	42%
% At or Above Proficient	17%	4%	5%	23%	11%	5%
% At or Above Advanced Level	1%	0%	0%	2%	1%	0%
Grade 12 History						
% Students in This Racial/Ethnic Group	74%	12%	9%	3%	1%	1%
Average History Scale Score	292	265	267	287	280	279
% Below Basic Level	50%	83%	78%	54%	67%	70%
% At or Above Basic Level	50%	17%	22%	46%	33%	30%
% At or Above Proficient	13%	2%	4%	16%	7%	5%
% At or Above Advanced Level	1%	0%	0%	2%	0%	0%

Source: NAEP 1994 History Report Card for the Nation and the States. April, 1996.
Office of Educational Research and Improvement, U.S. Department of Education.

- For the 8th- and 12th-grade assessments, African Americans represented about one-fourth (25.8% in grade 8 and 24.8% in grade 12) of all students in the bottom one-third schools but only a fraction (3.6% in grade 8 and 5.8% in grade 12) of all students in the top one-third schools.

NAEP Geography Report Card

The 1994 geography assessment included a content dimension (Space and Place; Environment and Society; and Spatial Dynamics and Connection) and a cognitive dimension (Knowing, Understanding, and Applying).

- **Figure 3** shows that approximately one-third of African American students, but more than three-fourths of White students, had achieved at or above the basic level of achievement in geography in the 4th (34% versus 81%), 8th (34% versus 82%), and 12th grades (32% versus 78%).

- **Table 5** shows that no more than 5% of African Americans scored at or above the proficient level, compared with about one-third of Whites, in the 4th (3% versus 29%), 8th (5% versus 36%), and 12th grades (5% versus 33%).

Figure 2. Percentage of African Americans Scoring at Various Levels on the National Assessment of Educational Progress History Report Card: 1994

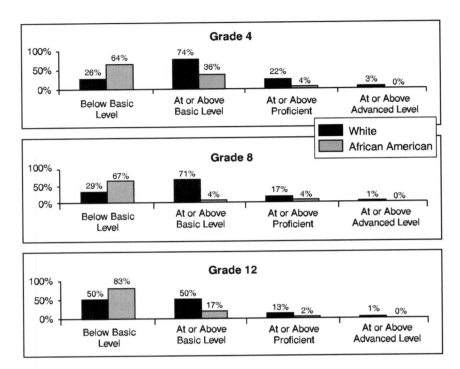

Source: NAEP 1994 History Report Card for the Nation and the States, April 1996.

- Average geography proficiency scores were lower for African Americans than for Whites in the 4th grade (168 versus 218), 8th grade (229 versus 270), and 12th grade (258 versus 291).

African Americans were also concentrated in schools with the lowest average scores on the geography assessment.

- **Table 6** shows that African Americans represented about one-third of students in the bottom one-third of all schools on the 4th-grade (31.7%) and 8th-grade (34.1%) geography assessments.

- On the grade 12 assessment, African Americans comprised 24.1% of students in schools

Table 4. Percentage of Students at the Top- and Bottom-Performing Schools on the National Assessment of Educational Progress History Report Card: 1992

Rank of School	Attribute	White	African American	Hispanic	Asian American	Pacific Islander	American Indian
Grade 4 History							
Top Third	% Students	85.9%	3.8%	6.4%	1.8%	0.6%	1.2%
	Mean Score	230.4	210.9	217.9	228.8	239.1	217.7
Middle Third	% Students	76.6%	9.9%	9.0%	1.5%	0.9%	1.7%
	Mean Score	211.3	193.4	193.6	209.6	207.9	201.0
Lowest Third	% Students	45.4%	30.5%	18.6%	1.7%	1.3%	1.9%
	Mean Score	194.8	167.8	161.3	188.5	178.2	164.2
Grade 8 History							
Top Third	% Students	88.9%	3.6%	4.2%	2.1%	0.7%	0.3%
	Mean Score	280.6	270.0	270.3	292.6	272.4	266.2
Middle Third	% Students	76.9%	11.0%	7.2%	1.8%	1.1%	1.6%
	Mean Score	265.7	248.5	251.3	268.7	264.4	254.5
Lowest Third	% Students	50.5%	25.8%	17.9%	2.0%	1.5%	1.9%
	Mean Score	253.6	232.1	236.2	256.0	237.9	237.8
Grade 12 History							
Top Third	% Students	84.5%	5.8%	4.1%	3.9%	0.9%	0.5%
	Mean Score	303.1	287.0	283.8	303.1	301.6	293.5
Middle Third	% Students	80.8%	8.4%	6.7%	2.1%	0.8%	0.7%
	Mean Score	289.2	268.5	274.8	283.3	285.3	282.5
Lowest Third	% Students	52.9%	24.8%	16.5%	2.7%	1.5%	1.3%
	Mean Score	278.7	257.8	257.7	265.3	262.2	270.8

Source: NAEP 1994 National History Assessment, Grades 4, 8 and 12: Student Data From NAEP 1994 Trends in Academic Progress.

with the lowest scores, but only 3.8% of students in schools with the highest scores.

NAEP Writing Report Card

The 1992 writing assessment did not provide the percentage of students achieving basic, proficient or advanced levels, but did provide information on the top performing and bottom performing schools participating in the assessment. For this section, schools were sorted based upon their average writing proficiency scores and divided into thirds.

Figure 4 shows that African American students were concentrated in the bottom one-third of schools in the 4th, 8th, and 12th grades.

Figure 3. Percentage of African Americans Scoring at Various Levels on the National Assessment of Educational Progress Geography Report Card: 1994

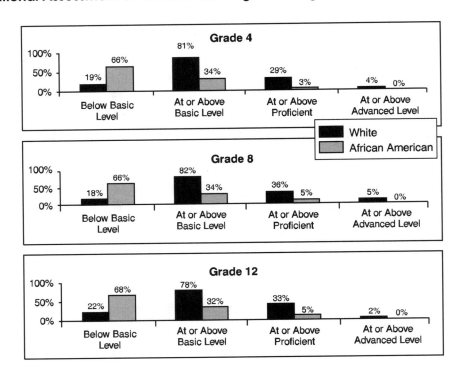

Source: NAEP 1994 Geography Report Card for the Nation and the States, May 1996.

- **Table 7** shows that, in the 4th grade, only 3% of the students in the top performing schools were African American, while 88% of the students were White.

- In the 8th grade, only 4% of students in the top performing schools were African American and 85% were White.

- In the 12th grade, only 7% of the students in the top performing schools were African American and 81% were White.

- In contrast, 38% of the 4th-grade students in the bottom performing schools were African American, and only 42% were White.

- In the 12th grade, 30% of the students in the bottom performing schools were African American, and 55% were White.

- Average writing proficiency scores were lower for African Americans than for Whites in the 4th grade (195 versus 229), 8th grade (242 versus 268), and 12th grade (268 versus 291).

Table 5. Percentage of Students Scoring at Various Levels on the National Assessment of Educational Progress Geography Report Card: 1994

Representation	White	African American	Hispanic	Asian American	Pacific Islander	American Indian
Grade 4 Geography						
% Students in This Racial/Ethnic Group	69%	15%	12%	2%	1%	1%
Average Geography Scale Score	218	168	183	218	205	193
% Below Basic Level	19%	66%	51%	21%	30%	38%
% At or Above Basic Level	81%	34%	49%	79%	70%	62%
% At or Above Proficient	29%	3%	10%	32%	17%	9%
% At or Above Advanced Level	4%	0%	1%	5%	1%	0%
Grade 8 Geography						
% Students in This Racial/Ethnic Group	69%	15%	11%	2%	1%	1%
Average Geography Scale Score	270	229	239	271	252	248
% Below Basic Level	18%	66%	50%	21%	37%	41%
% At or Above Basic Level	82%	34%	50%	79%	63%	59%
% At or Above Proficient	36%	5%	10%	40%	15%	15%
% At or Above Advanced Level	5%	0%	1%	8%	3%	2%
Grade 12 Geography						
% Students in This Racial/Ethnic Group	74%	12%	8%	3%	1%	1%
Average Geography Scale Score	291	258	268	287	282	–
% Below Basic Level	22%	68%	52%	31%	31%	–
% At or Above Basic Level	78%	32%	48%	69%	69%	–
% At or Above Proficient	33%	5%	10%	32%	19%	–
% At or Above Advanced Level	2%	0%	0%	3%	1%	–

"–" indicates sample too small to estimate.
Source: NAEP 1994 Geography Report Card for the Nation and the States. May, 1996.
Office of Educational Research and Improvement, U.S. Department of Education.

NAEP Mathematics Report Card

Mathematics test scores were lower for African American students than for their White counterparts at each grade level.

- Average mathematics scores were lower for African Americans than Whites in the 4th grade (192 versus 227), 8th grade (237 versus 277), and 12th grade (275 versus 305).

- **Table 8** shows that, in 4th grade, only one-fourth (24%) of African American students had achieved at or above basic, compared with three-fourths (72%) of White students.

- In the 8th grade, 27% of African American students had achieved at or above basic, compared to 74% of Whites.

- One-third (34%) of African American 12th graders scored at or above the basic level, compared to 72% of Whites and 81% of Asian/Pacific Islanders.

- **Figure 5** shows that the percentage of African Americans who scored at or above proficient was substantially smaller than the percentage of Whites in the 4th (3% versus 23%), 8th (3% versus 32%), and 12th grades (3% versus 19%).

Table 6. Percentage of Students at the Top- and Bottom-Performing Schools on the National Assessment of Educational Progress Geography Report Card: 1992

Rank of School	Attribute	White	African American	Hispanic	Asian American	Pacific Islander	American Indian
Grade 4 Geography							
Top Third	% of Students	84.7%	4.0%	7.1%	2.2%	1.0%	0.8%
	Mean Score	234.7	207.1	222.2	242.0	231.0	215.6
Middle Third	% Students	78.9%	7.9%	9.3%	1.2%	0.6%	1.7%
	Mean Score	215.5	184.6	192.3	225.5	204.2	204.6
Lowest Third	% Students	44.8%	31.7%	17.7%	1.8%	1.2%	2.0%
	Mean Score	192.8	159.3	164.5	186.8	186.7	175.6
Grade 8 Geography							
Top Third	% Students	89.7%	2.5%	4.0%	1.8%	0.4%	1.3%
	Mean Score	283.0	259.7	270.0	291.9	266.2	265.1
Middle Third	% Students	80.8%	7.1%	6.9%	2.1%	0.9%	1.6%
	Mean Score	266.7	243.7	248.9	271.8	258.7	251.7
Lowest Third	% Students	40.5%	34.1%	20.2%	1.3%	1.8%	1.7%
	Mean Score	255.5	224.2	230.4	248.9	245.6	235.3
Grade 12 Geography							
Top Third	% Students	88.1%	3.8%	3.9%	2.7%	0.7%	0.6%
	Mean Score	302.5	281.4	290.5	303.4	303.1	287.8
Middle Third	% Students	84.6%	5.8%	4.4%	2.2%	1.1%	1.4%
	Mean Score	289.9	265.3	275.3	285.6	279.9	280.9
Lowest Third	% Students	54.9%	24.1%	15.7%	2.8%	1.6%	0.6%
	Mean Score	277.7	253.9	261.4	275.4	275.5	274.8

Source: NAEP 1994 National Geography Assessment, Grades 4, 8 and 12: Student Data From NAEP 1994 Trends in Academic Progress.

Figure 4. Percentage of African Americans at the Top- and Bottom-Performing Schools on the National Assessment of Educational Progress Writing Report Card: 1992

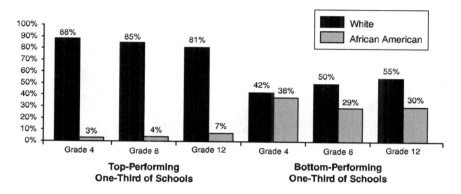

Source: NAEP 1992 Writing Report Card for the Nation and the States, June 1994.

Table 7. Percentage of Students at the Top- and Bottom-Performing Schools on the National Assessment of Educational Progress Writing Report Card: 1992

Rank of School	White	African American	Hispanic	Asian American	American Indian
Grade 4 Writing					
Average Writing Proficiency	229	195	208	233	215
Racial/Ethnic Composition of Top-Performing One-Third of Schools	88%	3%	5%	3%	1%
Racial/Ethnic Composition of Bottom-Performing One-Third of Schools	42%	38%	16%	2%	2%
Grade 8 Writing					
Average Writing Proficiency	268	242	242	267	248
Racial/Ethnic Composition of Top-Performing One-Third of Schools	85%	4%	7%	3%	1%
Racial/Ethnic Composition of Bottom-Performing One-Third of Schools	50%	29%	16%	2%	2%
Grade 12 Writing					
Average Writing Proficiency	291	268	277	277	270
Racial/Ethnic Composition of Top-Performing One-Third of Schools	81%	7%	7%	4%	0%
Racial/Ethnic Composition of Bottom-Performing One-Third of Schools	55%	30%	12%	2%	1%

Source: NAEP 1992 Writing Report Card for the Nation and the States. June, 1994
Office of Educational Research and Improvement, U.S. Department of Education.

Table 8. Percentage of Students Scoring at Various Levels on the National Assessment of Educational Progress Mathematics Report Card: 1994

Representation	White	African American	Hispanic	Asian American	American Indian
Grade 4 Mathematics					
% Students in This Racial/Ethnic Group	70%	16%	10%	2%	1%
Average Mathematics Proficiency	227	192	201	231	209
% Below Basic Level	28%	76%	63%	24%	54%
% At or Above Basic Level	72%	24%	37%	76%	46%
% At or Above Proficient	23%	3%	6%	30%	10%
% At or Above Advanced Level	3%	0%	0%	5%	2%
Grade 8 Mathematics					
% Students in This Racial/Ethnic Group	70%	16%	10%	2%	1%
Average Mathematics Proficiency	277	237	246	288	254
% Below Basic Level	26%	73%	61%	20%	53%
% At or Above Basic Level	74%	27%	39%	80%	47%
% At or Above Proficient	32%	3%	8%	44%	9%
% At or Above Advanced Level	4%	0%	1%	14%	0%
Grade 12 Mathematics					
% Students in This Racial/Ethnic Group	71%	15%	10%	4%	1%
Average Mathematics Proficiency	305	275	283	315	281
% Below Basic Level	28%	66%	55%	19%	54%
% At or Above Basic Level	72%	34%	45%	81%	46%
% At or Above Proficient	19%	3%	6%	31%	4%
% At or Above Advanced Level	2%	0%	1%	6%	0%

Source: NAEP 1992 Mathematics Report Card for the Nation and the States. May, 1994.
Office of Educational Research and Improvement, U.S. Department of Education.

Figure 5. Percentage of African Americans Scoring at Various Levels on the National Assessment of Educational Progress Mathematics Report Card: 1994

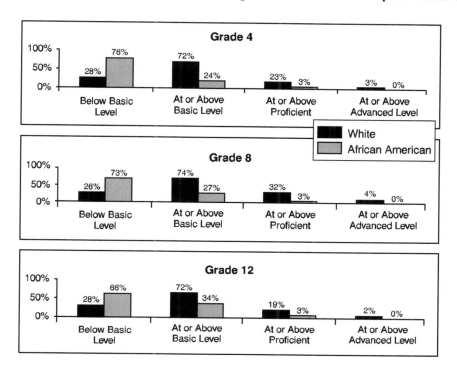

Source: NAEP 1994 Mathematics Report Card for the Nation and the States, May 1994.

CHAPTER VI.
School Safety and Alcohol and Drug Use in America's Schools

How safe do African American students feel at the schools they attend? How do their fears of harm vary based upon the characteristics of their schools? How common are weapons, fighting, gangs, and drug dealers in the schools attended by African Americans? What types of measures (e.g., security guards, metal detectors, and locked doors) limit African American students' movement within their schools? How available are alcohol and drugs to African American school children? How does the use of alcohol and drugs among African American high school seniors compare with usage among their White counterparts?

Educators have long recognized the need for a secure and orderly environment for learning. Hopes for peaceful, safe schools found their most determined expression in Goal Seven of the National Education Goals, established in 1990 by President Bush and the nation's governors. Goal Seven of the National Education Goals states: "By the year 2000, every school in America will be free of drugs, violence, and the unauthorized presence of firearms and alcohol and will offer a disciplined environment conducive to learning."

In an effort to monitor progress toward this goal, the 1993 National Household Education Survey (NHES) included a school safety and discipline component. The safety and discipline questions focused upon four topics: school environment, school safety, school discipline policy, and alcohol/other drug use and education. The NHES differs from other data collection initiatives sponsored by the U. S. Department of Education's National Center for Education Statistics in that data are collected from households rather than from schools or students. For the 1993 school safety and discipline component, interviews were conducted with the parents of 12,680 children in grades 3 through 12 and with 6,504 students in grades 6 through 12.

A number of other surveys include questions to measure alcohol and drug use among America's school children. For example, in addition to providing longitudinal data describing 1988 8th graders, the second follow-up to the National Education Longitudinal Study of 1988 8th graders (NELS:88) provides cross-sectional data describing the use of alcohol and drugs among 1992 high school seniors. Conducted in the spring of 1992, the second follow-up includes data from students and dropouts who participated in the 1988 and 1990 waves of the study, as well as a "freshened" sample of students. Consequently, when appropriate weights are applied, the NELS:88 second follow-up is representative of 1992 high school seniors nationwide.

CHAPTER ORGANIZATION

This chapter is divided into six subsections:

1. Characteristics of schools attended by students in grades 6 to 12, including level, type, size, urbanicity, and region;

2. Students' perceived safety, as evidenced by their fears of harm at school and traveling to and from school, their avoidance of places at school, on school grounds, and at school events, and their use of special routes to school;

3. Aspects of school safety, including the presence of weapons, fighting gangs, and drug dealers in America's schools;

4. School safety measures, such as teacher supervision of hallways, limits on restroom access, security guards, metal detectors, locked doors, and locker checks;

5. Availability of alcohol and drugs at schools attended by students in grades 6 through 12; and

6. The use of alcohol and drugs among high school seniors.

PART I — OVERVIEW

In terms of fears and perceived threats, African Americans appear to be more handicapped than Whites in their school environments, and possibly, as a result, in their prospects for learning. A greater proportion of African American students than Whites confront a variety of problems including: worries about their personal security at and around their schools; greater exposure to weapons, fighting gangs, and drug dealers in their schools; and more restricted school environments as evidenced by the greater presence of teacher-supervised hallways, limits on restroom access, security guards, metal detectors, and locked doors in their schools.

Some consolation derives from reports that a higher share of African American students than White students talked with their parents about their perceptions of the threats and dangers at school. The data also show that African American boys and girls talk more to their parents about alcohol and drugs than White boys and with the same frequency as White girls.

African Americans are underrepresented at private schools, schools in which both African American and White students report fewer personal security concerns. School location presents some anomalies since African American students expressed greater concerns and fears in suburban rather than in urban schools.

Some small differences are observed between African American girls and African American boys in their reporting on these topics. For example, African American boys tended to avoid areas on school grounds more than African American girls. Overall, however, perceptions of threats and fears are similar for African American girls and boys, although higher than the perceived fears of Whites in most instances.

A higher share of African American than White students in grades 6 through 12 reported that obtaining marijuana at school was easy. Nonetheless, a smaller share of African American high school seniors than of their White peers reported using marijuana, smoking cigarettes, and consuming alcohol regardless of region, urbanicity, poverty of the student body, school type, socioeconomic status, and test score.

PART II — DETAILED DESCRIPTIONS AND TABLES

CHARACTERISTICS OF SCHOOLS ATTENDED BY STUDENTS IN GRADES 6 TO 12

Relative to their representation among all students in grades 6 to 12 in 1993 (15.9%), African Americans were overrepresented among students attending public schools of their choice but underrepresented among those attending private schools.

- **Figure 1** shows that African Americans comprised 32.2% of all students attending public schools of their choice but only 8.6% of students attending private religious schools and 8.8% of

Figure 1. Representation of African Americans in Grades 6 to 12 at Schools With Various Characteristics: 1993

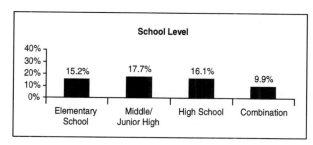

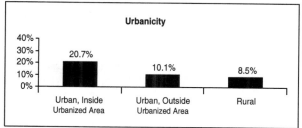

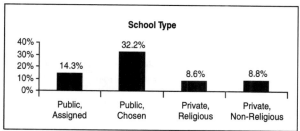

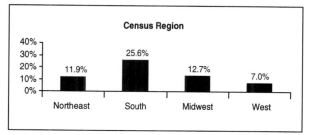

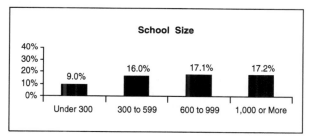

Source: National Household Education Survey, 1993 School Safety & Discipline Component.

students attending private nonreligious schools.

- **Table 1** shows that African Americans represented 9.0% of students at schools with less than 300 students, 16.0% of students at schools with 300 to 599 students, and 17.1% of students at schools with 600 or more students.

- African American students also typically attended schools located inside urbanized areas rather than schools outside urbanized areas and schools in rural areas. African Americans represented 20.7% of all students at schools inside urbanized areas but only 10.1% of students at schools outside urbanized areas and 8.5% of students at schools in rural areas.

- African Americans represented a higher share of students in the south (25.6% of all students) than of students in the west (7.0%), northeast (11.9%), or midwest (12.7%).

Table 1. Characteristics of Schools Attended by Students in Grades 6 to 12 by Race and Sex: 1993
(weighted sample size in parentheses)

Characteristic	Total	Male	Female	White, Non-Hispanic Total	Male	Female	African American, Non-Hispanic Total	Male	Female	Hispanic Total	Male	Female	Other Total	Male	Female
School Level															
Total *	100.0% (24,011,221)	50.0% (11,997,231)	50.0% (12,013,990)	70.0% (16,807,986)	34.9% (8,378,872)	35.1% (8,429,114)	15.9% (3,813,119)	7.8% (1,882,053)	8.0% (1,931,066)	11.0% (2,636,416)	5.7% (1,374,597)	5.3% (1,261,819)	3.1% (753,700)	1.5% (361,709)	1.6% (391,991)
Elementary School	100.0% (2,644,433)	51.2% (1,353,746)	48.8% (1,290,687)	66.6% (1,760,063)	34.6% (915,810)	31.9% (844,253)	15.2% (402,325)	7.9% (209,452)	7.3% (192,873)	14.2% (375,782)	7.3% (192,899)	6.9% (182,882)	4.0% (106,263)	1.3% (35,585)	2.7% (70,678)
Middle/Junior High	100.0% (7,418,272)	51.9% (3,851,505)	48.1% (3,566,767)	67.7% (5,023,776)	34.3% (2,544,044)	33.4% (2,479,732)	17.7% (1,314,846)	9.7% (716,798)	8.1% (598,048)	11.7% (866,049)	6.6% (492,784)	5.0% (373,266)	2.9% (213,601)	1.3% (97,880)	1.6% (115,721)
High School	100.0% (11,513,631)	48.0% (5,524,789)	52.0% (5,988,842)	70.4% (8,103,014)	34.0% (3,920,100)	36.3% (4,182,915)	16.1% (1,855,022)	7.3% (838,789)	8.8% (1,016,234)	10.6% (1,219,076)	5.2% (596,237)	5.4% (622,839)	2.9% (336,518)	1.5% (169,664)	1.4% (166,854)
Combination	100.0% (2,434,886)	52.0% (1,267,191)	48.0% (1,167,695)	78.9% (1,921,134)	41.0% (998,918)	37.9% (922,215)	9.9% (240,926)	4.8% (117,015)	5.1% (123,911)	7.2% (175,509)	3.8% (92,677)	3.4% (82,832)	4.0% (97,318)	2.4% (58,581)	1.6% (38,736)
School Type															
Total *** ~	100.0% (24,011,221)	50.0% (11,997,231)	50.0% (12,013,990)	70.0% (16,807,986)	34.9% (8,378,872)	35.1% (8,429,114)	15.9% (3,813,119)	7.8% (1,882,053)	8.0% (1,931,066)	11.0% (2,636,416)	5.7% (1,374,597)	5.3% (1,261,819)	3.1% (753,700)	1.5% (361,709)	1.6% (391,991)
Public, Assigned	100.0% (19,477,239)	50.2% (9,787,247)	49.8% (9,689,992)	72.2% (14,069,435)	36.0% (7,010,589)	36.2% (7,058,846)	14.3% (2,792,946)	7.3% (1,423,308)	7.0% (1,369,638)	10.7% (2,088,472)	5.7% (1,107,263)	5.0% (981,209)	2.7% (526,386)	1.3% (246,087)	1.4% (280,299)
Public, Chosen	100.0% (2,666,302)	48.5% (1,293,227)	51.5% (1,373,076)	47.8% (1,275,392)	23.6% (629,190)	24.2% (646,202)	32.2% (859,371)	14.8% (395,442)	17.4% (463,929)	14.7% (392,998)	7.5% (201,266)	7.2% (191,732)	5.2% (138,542)	2.5% (67,329)	2.7% (71,213)
Private, Religious	100.0% (1,547,655)	47.6% (736,452)	52.4% (811,203)	77.6% (1,201,288)	38.7% (599,410)	38.9% (601,878)	8.6% (132,557)	2.7% (41,653)	5.9% (90,903)	9.6% (148,001)	3.9% (60,013)	5.7% (87,988)	4.3% (65,808)	2.3% (35,375)	2.0% (30,433)
Private, Non-Religious	100.0% (320,025)	56.3% (180,306)	43.7% (139,720)	81.8% (261,871)	43.6% (139,683)	38.2% (122,188)	8.8% (28,246)	6.8% (21,650)	2.1% (6,596)	2.2% (6,945)	1.9% (6,055)	0.3% (891)	7.2% (22,963)	4.0% (12,918)	3.1% (10,045)
Number of Students															
Total	100.0% (24,011,221)	50.0% (11,997,231)	50.0% (12,013,990)	70.0% (16,807,986)	34.9% (8,378,872)	35.1% (8,429,114)	15.9% (3,813,119)	7.8% (1,882,053)	8.0% (1,931,066)	11.0% (2,636,416)	5.7% (1,374,597)	5.3% (1,261,819)	3.1% (753,700)	1.5% (361,709)	1.6% (391,991)
Under 300	100.0% (2,626,910)	49.4% (1,296,603)	50.6% (1,330,307)	77.1% (2,024,099)	37.5% (985,214)	39.5% (1,038,885)	9.0% (235,660)	4.9% (128,903)	4.1% (106,757)	10.8% (284,015)	5.4% (142,971)	5.4% (141,044)	3.2% (83,136)	1.5% (39,516)	1.7% (43,621)
300 to 599	100.0% (7,806,380)	50.9% (3,972,122)	49.1% (3,834,258)	71.0% (5,540,297)	36.0% (2,811,169)	35.0% (2,729,129)	16.0% (1,247,563)	8.5% (660,095)	7.5% (587,469)	10.1% (786,192)	4.9% (379,925)	5.2% (406,267)	3.0% (232,327)	1.5% (120,934)	1.4% (111,393)
600 to 999	100.0% (6,166,110)	49.2% (3,034,472)	50.8% (3,131,639)	71.0% (4,377,425)	35.0% (2,157,405)	36.0% (2,220,020)	17.1% (1,054,435)	8.0% (495,732)	9.1% (558,703)	9.2% (568,590)	5.2% (322,452)	4.0% (246,139)	2.7% (165,660)	1.0% (58,883)	1.7% (106,777)
1,000 or More	100.0% (7,411,821)	49.8% (3,694,034)	50.2% (3,717,787)	65.7% (4,866,165)	32.7% (2,425,084)	32.9% (2,441,081)	17.2% (1,275,461)	8.1% (597,324)	9.1% (678,137)	13.5% (997,619)	7.1% (529,249)	6.3% (468,370)	3.7% (272,576)	1.9% (142,377)	1.8% (130,199)
Urbanicity															
Total * ~	100.0% (24,011,221)	50.0% (11,997,231)	50.0% (12,013,990)	70.0% (16,807,986)	34.9% (8,378,872)	35.1% (8,429,114)	15.9% (3,813,119)	7.8% (1,882,053)	8.0% (1,931,066)	11.0% (2,636,416)	5.7% (1,374,597)	5.3% (1,261,819)	3.1% (753,700)	1.5% (361,709)	1.6% (391,991)
Urban, Inside Urbanized Area	100.0% (14,087,492)	49.5% (6,979,473)	50.5% (7,108,019)	60.8% (8,565,091)	30.4% (4,277,864)	30.4% (4,287,227)	20.7% (2,911,787)	10.0% (1,404,946)	10.7% (1,506,841)	14.7% (1,049,655)	7.5% (2,069,896)	7.2% (1,020,242)	3.8% (540,718)	1.8% (247,009)	2.1% (293,709)
Urban, Outside Urbanized Area	100.0% (3,578,904)	52.0% (1,861,677)	48.0% (1,717,227)	77.2% (2,761,185)	40.6% (1,451,417)	36.6% (1,309,767)	10.1% (362,339)	4.3% (153,913)	5.8% (208,426)	9.7% (346,899)	5.7% (204,901)	4.0% (141,998)	3.0% (108,481)	1.4% (51,446)	1.6% (57,035)
Rural	100.0% (6,344,826)	49.7% (3,156,082)	50.3% (3,188,744)	86.4% (5,481,711)	41.8% (2,649,591)	44.6% (2,832,120)	8.5% (538,993)	5.1% (323,194)	3.4% (215,798)	3.5% (219,621)	1.9% (120,041)	1.6% (99,580)	1.6% (104,501)	1.0% (63,255)	0.7% (41,246)
Census Region															
Total ***	100.0% (24,011,221)	50.0% (11,997,231)	50.0% (12,013,990)	70.0% (16,807,986)	34.9% (8,378,872)	35.1% (8,429,114)	15.9% (3,813,119)	7.8% (1,882,053)	8.0% (1,931,066)	11.0% (2,636,416)	5.7% (1,374,597)	5.3% (1,261,819)	3.1% (753,700)	1.5% (361,709)	1.6% (391,991)
Northeast	100.0% (4,387,344)	51.7% (2,268,653)	48.3% (2,118,692)	76.7% (3,363,320)	41.1% (1,802,305)	35.6% (1,561,016)	11.9% (521,058)	4.7% (204,526)	7.2% (316,532)	7.8% (343,215)	4.0% (177,048)	3.8% (166,167)	3.6% (159,752)	1.9% (84,775)	1.7% (74,977)
South	100.0% (8,493,859)	49.4% (4,197,261)	50.6% (4,296,598)	63.2% (5,371,377)	31.2% (2,654,040)	32.0% (2,717,337)	25.6% (2,177,806)	13.1% (1,110,041)	12.6% (1,067,765)	9.2% (779,394)	4.2% (357,266)	5.0% (422,128)	1.9% (165,282)	0.9% (75,914)	1.1% (89,368)
Midwest	100.0% (5,919,174)	48.7% (2,880,159)	51.3% (3,039,016)	81.8% (4,840,672)	39.3% (2,327,674)	42.5% (2,512,998)	12.7% (751,759)	6.6% (390,207)	6.1% (361,552)	3.6% (212,729)	1.7% (100,912)	1.9% (111,817)	1.9% (114,014)	1.0% (61,365)	0.9% (52,649)
West	100.0% (5,210,844)	50.9% (2,651,158)	49.1% (2,559,686)	62.0% (3,232,617)	30.6% (1,594,853)	31.4% (1,637,764)	7.0% (362,496)	3.4% (177,279)	3.6% (185,217)	25.0% (1,301,078)	14.2% (739,371)	10.8% (561,707)	6.0% (314,653)	2.7% (139,655)	3.4% (174,998)

Notes:
*** Test of statistical significance compares African Americans with Whites. *** p <.001, ** p <.01, * p <.05.
+++ Test of statistical significance compares White boys with White girls. +++ p <.001, ++ p <.01, + p <.05.
~~~ Test of statistical significance compares African American boys with African American girls. ~~~ p <.001, ~~ p <.01, ~ p <.05.
Tests of statistical significance calculated using adjusted sample weight to control for influence of large sample sizes.
Students' residence determined by ZIP code. An Urbanized Area (UA) comprises a place (e.g., city, village) and adjacent densely settled surrounding territory that together have a population of at least 50,000. "Urban, outside Urbanized Area" includes incorporated and unincorporated places outside of UA with population of at least 2,500. "Rural" represents all other places.
Source: National Household Education Survey, 1993 School Safety & Discipline Component.

STUDENTS' PERCEIVED SAFETY

Fears of Harm in the Classroom or on School Grounds

In 1993, about one in five (19.0%) students in grades 6 to 12 reported that they were worried about harm in their classrooms or on school grounds regardless of school size. Comparable percentages of girls and boys worried about harm at school (20.0% versus 18.0%).

- **Table 2** shows that the percentage of African American students who were worried about harm at school was higher than the percentage of White students (22.9% versus 16.5%).

Figure 2 shows that smaller percentages of high school students (14.9%) and combination school students (14.2%) than of middle and junior high school students (25.9%) and elementary school students (21.5%) worried about harm at school.

- About 24.7% of African Americans at assigned public schools worried about harm at school, compared with 17.2% of Whites.

- At the smallest and the largest schools, a higher share of African Americans than Whites worried about harm at school. For example, at schools with more than 1,000 students, 23.5% of African American students, but only 16.1% of White students, worried.

Among Whites, comparable percentages of urban school students and suburban school students worried about harm at school (17.5% versus 17.7%). Only 14.3% of White rural school students worried about harm at school. At both suburban and urban schools, a higher percentage of African American students than of White students worried about harm at school.

- Among African American students, a higher share of suburban school students (33.0%) than of urban (22.6%) and rural (18.3%) school students appeared to be worried about harm at school.

- In the midwest and the south, a higher proportion of African American students than of White students worried about harm in the classroom or on school grounds: 22.3% versus 14.4% in the midwest and 23.4% versus 19.1% in the south.

Fears of Harm Traveling To and From School

About one in ten (10.1%) students in grades 6 to 12 were worried about harm during trips to and from school. Fears of harm traveling to and from school were unrelated to sex among both African Americans and Whites.

- **Table 3** shows that the proportion of African Americans who worried about harm during their travels to and from school was more than twice the proportion of Whites (16.3% versus 7.0%).

Figure 3 shows that high school students were less worried about harm going to and from school than were elementary and middle or junior high school students (7.4%, 13.2%, and 13.7%, respectively). Regardless of school level, a higher percentage of African Americans than Whites worried about harm going to and from school.

- At the elementary school level, 23.9% of African Americans and 7.9% of Whites worried about traveling to and from school.

- Regardless of school type, a higher percentage of African Americans than Whites worried about harm going to and from school. For example, among private religious school students, 18.9% of African Americans and 5.4% of Whites had these concerns.

Regardless of school size, a higher proportion of African Americans than Whites were fearful about their school trips.

- About 20.2% of African Americans, but only 7.4% of Whites at schools with less than 300 students were fearful about their school trips.

Table 2. Percentage of Students in Grades 6 to 12 Who Were Worried About Harm in the Classroom or on School Grounds by School Characteristics, Race, and Sex: 1993
(weighted sample size in parentheses)

Characteristic	Total	Male	Female	White, Non-Hispanic Total	Male	Female	African American, Non-Hispanic Total	Male	Female	Hispanic Total	Male	Female	Other Total	Male	Female
Total ***	100.0%	100.0%	100.0%	100.0%	100.0%	100.0%	100.0%	100.0%	100.0%	100.0%	100.0%	100.0%	100.0%	100.0%	100.0%
	(23,810,309)	(11,926,918)	(11,883,391)	(16,721,186)	(8,353,179)	(8,368,007)	(3,745,525)	(1,860,254)	(1,885,271)	(2,598,884)	(1,359,295)	(1,239,589)	(744,714)	(354,190)	(390,524)
Worried About Harm at School	19.0%	18.0%	20.0%	16.5%	15.7%	17.3%	22.9%	21.2%	24.6%	26.8%	23.8%	30.1%	27.8%	34.3%	21.9%
	(4,522,233)	(2,149,538)	(2,372,695)	(2,758,588)	(1,309,373)	1,449,215()	(859,505)	(395,149)	(464,356)	(697,195)	(323,595)	(373,600)	(206,945)	(121,421)	(85,524)
School Level															
Elementary School +	21.5%	24.6%	18.2%	19.2%	23.0%	15.1%	23.0%	27.2%	18.4%	29.4%	30.6%	28.1%	25.0%	16.6%	29.3%
	(411,657)	(246,062)	(165,595)	(250,569)	(162,726)	(87,843)	(66,729)	(31,192)	(35,537)	(82,648)	(49,624)	(33,024)	(11,710)	(2,520)	(9,191)
Middle/Junior High *	25.9%	26.7%	25.0%	22.5%	24.0%	21.0%	32.0%	28.8%	35.8%	33.3%	33.4%	33.2%	38.6%	50.1%	28.9%
	(1,497,407)	(776,252)	(721,155)	(916,492)	(478,019)	(438,472)	(306,250)	(147,962)	(158,288)	(197,419)	(104,202)	(93,217)	(77,246)	(46,069)	(31,177)
High School ++	14.9%	12.0%	17.6%	13.5%	11.2%	15.7%	16.2%	13.0%	19.0%	20.9%	12.5%	29.3%	20.6%	25.9%	15.4%
	(1,222,414)	(461,987)	(760,427)	(707,831)	(286,510)	(421,320)	(249,958)	(80,948)	(169,010)	(204,823)	(52,518)	(152,305)	(59,802)	(42,010)	(17,791)
Combination ** +++	14.2%	10.4%	18.3%	10.8%	5.4%	16.7%	23.5%	22.2%	24.9%	29.9%	32.4%	27.4%	31.3%	41.8%	15.4%
	(242,706)	(84,358)	(158,348)	(154,443)	(45,707)	(108,736)	(29,558)	(3,922)	(25,636)	(32,971)	(14,967)	(18,004)	(25,733)	(19,762)	(5,971)
School Type															
Public, Assigned ***	19.7%	18.6%	20.8%	17.2%	15.9%	18.4%	24.7%	23.4%	26.1%	28.7%	27.2%	30.4%	25.6%	28.8%	22.8%
	(2,810,862)	(1,296,069)	(1,514,793)	(1,780,910)	(832,283)	(948,627)	(492,687)	(204,430)	(288,257)	(427,937)	(200,296)	(227,642)	(109,328)	(59,060)	(50,268)
Public, Chosen	19.8%	17.7%	21.8%	17.6%	18.8%	16.3%	18.4%	13.6%	22.6%	22.5%	10.3%	34.9%	41.7%	53.3%	30.8%
	(417,715)	(186,011)	(231,703)	(154,799)	(84,335)	(70,464)	(135,625)	(48,813)	(86,812)	(78,768)	(18,204)	(60,565)	(48,522)	(34,659)	(13,863)
Private, Religious	10.8%	11.5%	10.1%	9.2%	9.2%	9.1%	16.3%	23.6%	12.9%	12.2%	4.0%	17.8%	26.3%	50.5%	0.0%
	(118,978)	(61,737)	(57,241)	(73,288)	(36,006)	(37,281)	(19,880)	(8,264)	(11,616)	(9,168)	(825)	(8,344)	(16,642)	(16,642)	–
Private, Non-Relig.	9.7%	15.7%	2.2%	9.5%	17.1%	1.1%	15.2%	11.6%	27.1%	28.6%	32.8%	0.0%	0.0%	0.0%	0.0%
	(26,629)	(24,843)	(1,787)	(20,338)	(20,338)	–	(4,304)	(2,517)	(1,787)	(1,987)	(1,987)	–	–	–	–
Number of Students															
Under 300 *	18.9%	19.8%	18.1%	16.5%	18.2%	14.9%	26.9%	25.1%	29.0%	25.2%	19.3%	30.9%	34.7%	45.4%	25.1%
	(369,993)	(184,211)	(185,782)	(250,453)	(138,512)	(111,940)	(45,265)	(17,269)	(27,996)	(50,117)	(15,213)	(34,904)	(24,158)	(13,217)	(10,941)
300 to 599 ***	19.3%	19.2%	19.4%	16.3%	15.9%	16.6%	25.8%	25.7%	25.8%	28.6%	29.0%	28.2%	25.4%	28.6%	21.8%
	(1,203,619)	(613,923)	(589,696)	(715,745)	(373,175)	(342,569)	(252,799)	(122,944)	(129,855)	(184,891)	(86,543)	(98,348)	(50,185)	(31,261)	(18,924)
600 to 999	18.6%	17.5%	19.5%	17.2%	15.5%	19.0%	18.0%	16.2%	19.7%	25.8%	29.4%	20.9%	31.9%	39.8%	27.5%
	(776,152)	(327,345)	(448,807)	(512,999)	(211,020)	(301,979)	(133,752)	(49,691)	(84,061)	(88,282)	(46,135)	(42,147)	(41,120)	(20,500)	(20,620)
1,000 or More **	19.1%	16.5%	21.6%	16.1%	14.5%	17.7%	23.5%	19.6%	26.9%	26.5%	17.8%	36.5%	25.2%	33.7%	16.4%
	(1,024,420)	(443,181)	(581,239)	(550,139)	(250,255)	(299,884)	(220,680)	(74,121)	(146,559)	(194,572)	(73,421)	(121,151)	(59,029)	(45,384)	(13,645)
Urbanicity															
Urban, Inside ** Urbanized Area	20.5%	20.1%	20.8%	17.5%	17.8%	17.3%	22.6%	21.7%	23.4%	27.8%	24.2%	31.5%	28.0%	34.8%	22.4%
	(2,064,820)	(983,551)	(1,081,270)	(1,027,328)	(540,288)	(487,039)	(486,963)	(196,501)	(290,463)	(418,071)	(171,558)	(246,512)	(132,459)	(75,203)	(57,256)
Urban, Outside *** Urbanized Area	20.7%	17.9%	23.8%	17.7%	15.7%	19.9%	33.0%	22.8%	40.2%	28.0%	24.4%	33.3%	34.2%	40.0%	28.9%
	(575,528)	(261,246)	(314,281)	(389,521)	(181,064)	(208,456)	(92,567)	(29,394)	(63,173)	(72,361)	(33,142)	(39,219)	(21,079)	(17,646)	(3,433)
Rural +	14.7%	13.5%	16.0%	14.3%	12.3%	16.1%	18.3%	18.6%	18.0%	15.4%	19.0%	11.3%	20.1%	27.7%	8.3%
	(733,836)	(323,863)	(409,973)	(612,487)	(251,610)	(360,877)	(72,966)	(38,130)	(34,835)	(27,430)	(16,611)	(10,819)	(20,954)	(17,512)	(3,442)
Census Region															
Northeast	17.5%	16.1%	18.9%	14.7%	13.5%	16.2%	20.9%	14.1%	25.5%	29.6%	29.6%	29.6%	38.6%	50.8%	25.2%
	(758,972)	(363,893)	(395,079)	(493,739)	(242,650)	(251,089)	(105,154)	(28,094)	(77,061)	(100,816)	(52,435)	(48,381)	(59,262)	(40,714)	(18,549)
South * +	20.9%	18.7%	23.0%	19.1%	17.0%	21.1%	23.4%	20.9%	25.9%	25.0%	23.3%	26.5%	27.9%	26.5%	29.1%
	(1,756,966)	(779,122)	(977,844)	(1,017,812)	(447,980)	(569,832)	(503,705)	(230,841)	(272,864)	(189,312)	(80,206)	(109,106)	(46,136)	(20,094)	(26,043)
Midwest **	16.1%	16.1%	16.0%	14.4%	14.1%	14.6%	22.3%	25.0%	19.3%	26.0%	20.7%	30.7%	28.7%	29.6%	27.6%
	(943,583)	(463,316)	(480,267)	(692,575)	(327,946)	(364,629)	(163,086)	(96,306)	(66,780)	(55,233)	(20,894)	(34,339)	(32,689)	(18,170)	(14,519)
West	20.5%	20.6%	20.4%	17.2%	18.2%	16.2%	24.5%	23.1%	25.7%	27.3%	23.1%	32.9%	22.1%	31.0%	15.1%
	(1,062,711)	(543,207)	(519,504)	(554,461)	(290,796)	(263,666)	(87,559)	(39,909)	(47,651)	(351,833)	(170,059)	(181,774)	(68,857)	(42,443)	(26,414)

Notes:
"–" indicates sample size too small to estimate.
*** Test of statistical significance compares African Americans with Whites. *** p <.001, ** p <.01, * p <.05.
+++ Test of statistical significance compares White boys with White girls. +++ p <.001, ++ p <.01, + p <.05.
~~~Test of statistical significance compares African American boys with African American girls. ~~~ p <.001, ~~ p <.01, ~ p <.05.
Tests of statistical significance calculated using adjusted sample weight to control for influence of large sample sizes.
Student's residence determined by ZIP code. An Urbanized Area (UA) comprises a place (e.g., city, village) and adjacent densely settled surrounding territory that together have a population of at least 50,000. "Urban, outside Urbanized Area" includes incorporated and unincorporated places outside of UA with population of at least 2,500. "Rural" represents all other places.
Source: National Household Education Survey, 1993 School Safety & Discipline Component.

Figure 2. Percentage of Students in Grades 6 to 12 Who Were Worried About Harm In the Classroom or on School Grounds by School Characteristics: 1993

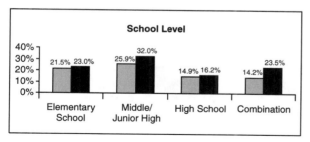

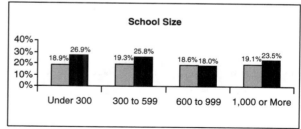

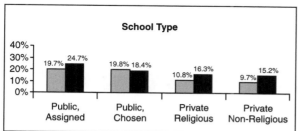

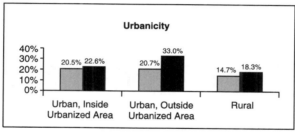

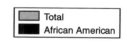

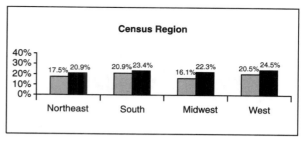

Source: National Household Education Survey, 1993 School Safety & Discipline Component.

At both urban and suburban schools, African Americans generally had greater fear of harm while traveling to and from school than Whites.

- Among African Americans, a higher share of students at suburban schools (27.3%) than of students at urban (16.2%) and rural (9.4%) schools worried about harm traveling to and from school.

- In all four census regions, a higher proportion of African American students than of White students worried about harm traveling to and from school: 17.5% versus 6.0% in the northeast, 15.1% versus 7.4% in the south, 17.8% versus 6.2% in the midwest, and 18.5% versus 8.3% in the west.

Avoidance of Places in Their Schools

About one-fifth (19.8%) of students in grades 6 to 12 reported that they avoided certain places in their schools because they worried that someone might hurt or bother them. Comparable percentages of

Table 3. Percentage of Students in Grades 6 to 12 Who Were Worried About Harm To and From School by School Characteristics, Race, and Sex: 1993
(weighted sample size in parentheses)

Characteristic	Total	Male	Female	White, Non-Hispanic Total	Male	Female	African American, Non-Hispanic Total	Male	Female	Hispanic Total	Male	Female	Other Total	Male	Female
Total ***	100.0%	100.0%	100.0%	100.0%	100.0%	100.0%	100.0%	100.0%	100.0%	100.0%	100.0%	100.0%	100.0%	100.0%	100.0%
	(23,810,309)	(11,926,918)	(11,883,391)	(16,721,186)	(8,353,179)	(8,368,007)	(3,745,525)	(1,860,254)	(1,885,271)	(2,598,884)	(1,359,295)	(1,239,589)	(744,714)	(354,190)	(390,524)
Worried about Harm to and from School	10.1%	9.9%	10.3%	7.0%	6.9%	7.0%	16.3%	15.2%	17.4%	19.0%	17.3%	20.9%	18.3%	25.4%	11.8%
	(2,403,204)	(1,183,587)	(1,219,616)	(1,162,206)	(574,966)	(587,240)	(610,767)	(283,666)	(327,101)	(493,999)	(234,881)	(259,118)	(136,232)	(90,075)	(46,157)
School Level															
Elementary School **	13.2%	15.2%	11.1%	7.9%	9.3%	6.3%	23.9%	29.9%	17.4%	25.4%	27.0%	23.8%	16.9%	13.8%	18.4%
	(348,201)	(205,279)	(142,922)	(138,559)	(85,596)	(52,963)	(96,093)	(62,604)	(33,489)	(95,601)	(52,156)	(43,445)	(17,948)	(4,924)	(13,024)
Middle/Junior High *	13.7%	14.6%	12.8%	10.6%	11.4%	9.7%	17.3%	17.6%	17.0%	22.9%	23.1%	22.7%	29.2%	33.4%	25.7%
	(1,019,852)	(562,755)	(457,097)	(531,043)	(289,707)	(241,336)	(227,861)	(126,469)	(101,392)	(198,591)	(113,912)	(84,678)	(62,358)	(32,667)	(29,691)
High School *** ~	7.4%	6.3%	8.4%	4.8%	4.4%	5.1%	13.5%	9.7%	16.7%	14.8%	10.0%	19.6%	10.8%	19.7%	2.1%
	(839,538)	(344,220)	(495,318)	(385,066)	(173,596)	(211,470)	(241,907)	(79,168)	(162,739)	(177,109)	(59,444)	(117,666)	(35,455)	(32,013)	(3,442)
Combination *** ++	8.1%	5.7%	10.7%	5.6%	2.6%	8.9%	18.9%	13.2%	24.4%	14.0%	11.7%	16.1%	21.0%	34.9%	0.0%
	(195,613)	(71,333)	(124,280)	(107,538)	(26,067)	(81,471)	(44,906)	(15,425)	(29,481)	(22,698)	(9,369)	(13,329)	(20,471)	(20,471)	–
School Type															
Public, Assigned ***	10.2%	10.2%	10.2%	7.2%	7.2%	7.2%	16.5%	16.3%	16.7%	20.3%	19.1%	21.6%	17.3%	20.8%	14.3%
	(1,979,270)	(996,607)	(982,663)	(1,013,832)	(506,255)	(507,577)	(455,283)	(229,157)	(226,126)	(419,397)	(210,615)	(208,782)	(90,758)	(50,580)	(40,179)
Public, Chosen ***	11.3%	9.5%	13.1%	5.7%	4.3%	7.1%	15.6%	12.0%	18.8%	16.4%	11.5%	21.5%	23.5%	39.5%	8.6%
	(293,407)	(121,156)	(172,252)	(71,097)	(26,921)	(44,176)	(128,862)	(46,680)	(82,181)	(61,774)	(21,858)	(39,916)	(31,675)	(25,697)	(5,978)
Private, Religious *	7.5%	7.0%	8.1%	5.4%	4.8%	6.0%	18.9%	14.6%	20.9%	8.7%	4.0%	11.8%	21.8%	41.9%	0.0%
	(115,738)	(51,036)	(64,702)	(64,242)	(28,755)	(35,487)	(24,868)	(6,075)	(18,794)	(12,829)	(2,408)	(10,421)	(13,799)	(13,799)	–
Private, Non-Religious	4.7%	8.4%	0.0%	5.1%	9.6%	0.0%	6.2%	8.1%	0.0%	0.0%	0.0%	0.0%	0.0%	0.0%	0.0%
	(14,788)	(14,788)	–	(13,035)	(13,035)	–	(1,754)	(1,754)	–	–	–	–	–	–	–
Number of Students															
Under 300 **	10.1%	9.5%	10.7%	7.4%	8.0%	6.9%	20.2%	14.0%	27.6%	13.5%	5.9%	20.6%	35.7%	45.4%	27.0%
	(262,579)	(121,487)	(141,092)	(148,864)	(77,996)	(70,868)	(47,161)	(17,713)	(29,448)	(36,844)	(7,834)	(29,010)	(29,710)	(17,944)	(11,766)
300 to 599 ***	10.7%	10.7%	10.7%	7.3%	7.1%	7.4%	18.8%	19.3%	18.3%	21.0%	21.7%	20.4%	15.9%	13.1%	19.0%
	(834,080)	(426,389)	(407,690)	(401,380)	(200,762)	(200,618)	(232,530)	(127,470)	(105,060)	(163,272)	(82,374)	(80,898)	(36,897)	(15,783)	(21,114)
600 to 999 **	9.8%	10.8%	8.8%	7.6%	8.0%	7.3%	13.4%	12.7%	14.0%	17.8%	22.5%	11.7%	16.8%	32.6%	8.0%
	(601,376)	(326,509)	(274,867)	(333,769)	(172,251)	(161,518)	(139,164)	(62,858)	(76,306)	(100,789)	(72,218)	(28,571)	(27,654)	(19,182)	(8,471)
1,000 or More ***	9.6%	8.5%	10.8%	5.8%	5.1%	6.4%	15.5%	13.0%	17.6%	19.6%	13.8%	26.4%	15.8%	27.6%	3.7%
	(705,169)	(309,202)	(395,967)	(278,192)	(123,956)	(154,236)	(191,912)	(75,625)	(116,286)	(193,094)	(72,454)	(120,639)	(41,971)	(37,166)	(4,805)
Urbanicity															
Urban, Inside *** Urbanized Area	11.6%	11.5%	11.8%	7.6%	7.5%	7.6%	16.2%	16.1%	16.4%	20.7%	18.6%	22.8%	17.0%	24.9%	10.6%
	(1,618,875)	(795,684)	(823,192)	(641,941)	(317,994)	(323,946)	(463,038)	(223,248)	(239,790)	(423,261)	(194,776)	(228,485)	(90,635)	(59,665)	(30,970)
Urban, Outside *** Urbanized Area	10.8%	9.9%	11.8%	7.1%	6.4%	7.8%	27.3%	24.6%	29.2%	18.7%	17.5%	20.3%	27.0%	34.1%	20.6%
	(385,765)	(183,116)	(202,648)	(194,472)	(93,238)	(101,235)	(97,569)	(36,744)	(60,825)	(64,451)	(35,607)	(28,844)	(29,273)	(17,528)	(11,745)
Rural	6.3%	6.5%	6.1%	6.0%	6.2%	5.7%	9.4%	7.3%	12.5%	3.1%	4.1%	1.9%	15.6%	20.4%	8.3%
	(398,564)	(204,787)	(193,776)	(325,793)	(163,733)	(162,059)	(50,160)	(23,674)	(26,485)	(6,288)	(4,498)	(1,790)	(16,324)	(12,882)	(3,442)
Census Region															
Northeast ***	9.3%	8.4%	10.2%	6.0%	6.3%	5.6%	17.5%	8.3%	23.6%	19.1%	15.8%	22.7%	33.1%	41.6%	23.9%
	(404,225)	(190,746)	(213,479)	(200,241)	(112,910)	(87,331)	(87,986)	(16,529)	(71,457)	(65,087)	(27,961)	(37,125)	(50,912)	(33,346)	(17,566)
South ***	10.4%	9.7%	11.0%	7.4%	7.3%	7.6%	15.1%	14.7%	15.6%	17.0%	11.0%	22.1%	12.4%	13.1%	11.9%
	(871,186)	(401,442)	(469,744)	(395,614)	(191,360)	(204,254)	(326,205)	(162,241)	(163,964)	(128,793)	(37,860)	(90,933)	(20,574)	(9,981)	(10,593)
Midwest ***	8.3%	10.0%	6.8%	6.2%	7.2%	5.3%	17.8%	22.1%	13.0%	19.8%	23.6%	16.3%	15.4%	17.4%	12.9%
	(489,145)	(286,129)	(203,015)	(299,367)	(166,407)	(132,960)	(130,227)	(85,209)	(45,018)	(42,041)	(23,817)	(18,224)	(17,510)	(10,697)	(6,813)
West **	12.3%	11.6%	13.1%	8.3%	6.5%	10.0%	18.5%	11.4%	25.2%	20.0%	19.7%	20.4%	15.1%	26.3%	6.4%
	(638,647)	(305,269)	(333,378)	(266,984)	(104,289)	(162,695)	(66,349)	(19,687)	(46,662)	(258,079)	(145,242)	(112,837)	(47,236)	(36,051)	(11,185)

Notes:
"–" indicates sample size too small to estimate.
*** Test of statistical significance compares African Americans with Whites.*** p <.001, ** p <.01, * p <.05.
+++ Test of statistical significance compares White boys with White girls. +++ p <.001, ++ p <.01, + p <.05.
~~~ Test of statistical significance compares African American boys with African American girls. ~~~ p <.001, ~~ p <.01, ~ p <.05.
Tests of statistical significance calculated using adjusted sample weight to control for influence of large sample sizes.
Student's residence determined by ZIP code. An Urbanized Area (UA) comprises a place (e.g., city, village) and adjacent densely settled surrounding territory that together have a population of at least 50,000. "Urban, outside Urbanized Area" includes incorporated and unincorporated places outside of UA with population of at least 2,500. "Rural" represents all other places.
Source: National Household Education Survey, 1993 School Safety & Discipline Component.

Figure 3. Percentage of Students in Grades 6 to 12 Who Were Worried About Harm To and From School by School Characteristics: 1993

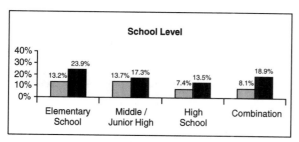

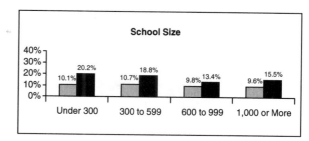

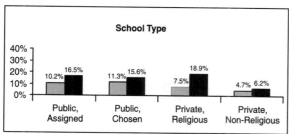

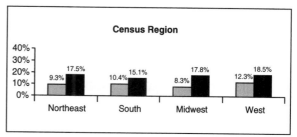

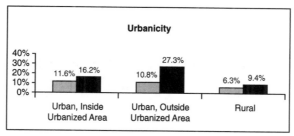

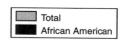

Source: National Household Education Survey, 1993 School Safety & Discipline Component.

boys and girls (18.9% versus 20.6%) avoided certain places in their schools because they worried about harm.

- **Table 4** shows that the proportion of African American students who avoided places at their schools was nearly twice the proportion of White students (29.5% versus 16.1%).

Figure 4 shows that, regardless of school level, a higher percentage of African Americans than of all students avoided places in their schools.

- For example, **Table 4** shows that at middle schools, 37.0% of African Americans, but only 20.6% of Whites, avoided places in their schools.

Overall, a higher share of public school students (24.2% at chosen public schools) than of private school students (4.4% at private religious schools) avoided places in their schools.

- A higher percentage of African Americans than Whites avoided places in their schools among

Table 4. Percentage of Students in Grades 6 to 12 Who Avoided Places in Their Schools by School Characteristics, Race, and Sex: 1993
(weighted sample size in parentheses)

Characteristic	Total	Male	Female	White, Non-Hispanic Total	Male	Female	African American, Non-Hispanic Total	Male	Female	Hispanic Total	Male	Female	Other Total	Male	Female
Total *** + +	100.0% (24,011,221)	100.0% (11,997,231)	100.0% (12,013,990)	100.0% (16,807,986)	100.0% (8,378,872)	100.0% (8,429,114)	100.0% (3,813,119)	100.0% (1,882,053)	100.0% (1,931,066)	100.0% (2,636,416)	100.0% (1,374,597)	100.0% (1,261,819)	100.0% (753,700)	100.0% (361,709)	100.0% (391,991)
Avoided Places in School	19.8% (4,748,066)	18.9% (2,273,192)	20.6% (2,474,874)	16.1% (2,699,847)	14.3% (1,200,080)	17.8% (1,499,767)	29.5% (1,125,378)	31.1% (586,221)	27.9% (539,157)	27.7% (729,472)	27.0% (371,160)	28.4% (358,312)	25.7% (193,369)	32.0% (115,732)	19.8% (77,638)
School Level Elementary **	20.9% (552,917)	20.1% (271,608)	21.8% (281,308)	16.2% (285,183)	14.5% (133,011)	18.0% (152,172)	29.6% (118,921)	25.9% (54,276)	33.5% (64,644)	31.6% (118,902)	36.0% (69,439)	27.0% (49,463)	28.1% (29,912)	41.8% (14,882)	21.3% (15,029)
Middle/Junior High ***	25.5% (1,891,487)	26.3% (1,014,648)	24.6% (876,839)	20.6% (1,036,141)	19.8% (504,229)	21.5% (531,913)	37.0% (485,927)	41.8% (299,351)	31.2% (186,576)	32.9% (285,359)	31.8% (156,793)	34.4% (128,567)	39.4% (84,059)	55.5% (54,275)	25.7% (29,784)
High School *** + +	16.7% (1,927,281)	14.5% (798,604)	18.8% (1,128,677)	14.0% (1,134,702)	11.6% (453,787)	16.3% (680,915)	23.3% (433,053)	21.9% (183,493)	24.6% (249,559)	23.7% (288,329)	20.6% (122,951)	26.6% (165,378)	21.2% (71,197)	22.6% (38,373)	19.7% (32,824)
Combination ***	15.5% (376,381)	14.9% (188,332)	16.1% (188,049)	12.7% (243,821)	10.9% (109,053)	14.6% (134,768)	36.3% (87,477)	42.0% (49,100)	31.0% (38,378)	21.0% (36,882)	23.7% (21,978)	18.0% (14,904)	8.4% (8,201)	14.0% (8,201)	0.0% –
School Type Public, Assigned *** +	20.6% (4,013,662)	19.7% (1,924,794)	21.6% (2,088,867)	16.9% (2,382,278)	14.8% (1,040,475)	19.0% (1,341,803)	31.6% (882,202)	34.1% (485,169)	29.0% (397,033)	29.1% (607,403)	28.1% (311,189)	30.2% (296,214)	26.9% (141,780)	35.7% (87,961)	19.2% (53,818)
Public, Chosen	24.2% (645,689)	23.2% (300,624)	25.1% (345,064)	21.9% (279,309)	21.9% (137,998)	21.9% (141,311)	25.8% (221,625)	24.4% (96,574)	27.0% (125,050)	25.8% (101,393)	22.3% (44,903)	29.5% (56,489)	31.3% (43,362)	31.4% (21,149)	31.2% (22,213)
Private, Religious ***	4.4% (68,433)	5.6% (40,943)	3.4% (27,490)	1.9% (23,197)	2.5% (14,776)	1.4% (8,422)	12.3% (16,331)	10.7% (4,477)	13.0% (11,854)	14.0% (20,677)	25.1% (15,068)	6.4% (5,609)	12.5% (8,228)	18.7% (6,622)	5.3% (1,606)
Private, Non-Religious	6.3% (20,283)	3.8% (6,831)	9.6% (13,452)	5.8% (15,062)	4.9% (6,831)	6.7% (8,232)	18.5% (5,221)	0.0% –	79.1% (5,221)	0.0% –	0.0% –	0.0% –	0.0% –	0.0% –	0.0% –
Number of Students Under 300 ***	15.1% (397,835)	13.1% (169,661)	17.2% (228,174)	12.4% (250,053)	11.4% (112,129)	13.3% (137,925)	33.0% (77,812)	22.7% (29,321)	45.4% (48,491)	18.9% (53,550)	15.1% (21,588)	22.7% (31,961)	19.7% (16,419)	16.8% (6,622)	22.5% (9,797)
300 to 599 *** ~~	19.8% (1,541,935)	20.9% (829,887)	18.6% (712,049)	15.0% (832,766)	14.9% (418,037)	15.2% (414,729)	31.7% (396,044)	38.9% (256,711)	23.7% (139,333)	29.5% (232,214)	27.5% (104,556)	31.4% (127,658)	34.8% (80,911)	41.8% (50,582)	27.2% (30,329)
600 to 999 *** + +	20.8% (1,282,815)	19.1% (580,077)	22.4% (702,737)	17.8% (779,943)	14.6% (314,202)	21.0% (465,741)	30.3% (319,787)	29.4% (145,686)	31.2% (174,101)	26.2% (148,834)	29.9% (96,388)	21.3% (52,446)	20.7% (34,251)	40.4% (23,801)	9.8% (10,450)
More than 1,000 *** +	20.6% (1,525,482)	18.8% (693,568)	22.4% (831,914)	17.2% (837,084)	14.7% (355,712)	19.7% (481,372)	26.0% (331,734)	25.9% (154,502)	26.1% (177,232)	29.6% (294,875)	28.1% (148,627)	31.2% (146,248)	22.7% (61,789)	24.4% (34,727)	20.8% (27,062)
Urbanicity Urban, Inside *** + + Urbanized Area	20.8% (2,933,316)	19.3% (1,348,591)	22.3% (1,584,724)	16.3% (1,397,795)	14.3% (610,106)	18.4% (787,689)	27.5% (801,729)	26.9% (377,761)	28.1% (423,968)	29.3% (607,379)	27.8% (292,119)	30.9% (315,259)	23.4% (126,413)	27.8% (68,605)	19.7% (57,808)
Urban, Outside *** ~~ Urbanized Area	21.7% (778,137)	22.1% (410,619)	21.4% (367,518)	17.5% (484,556)	16.1% (233,344)	19.2% (251,212)	42.4% (153,594)	57.6% (88,677)	31.1% (64,917)	25.7% (89,304)	26.5% (54,302)	24.6% (35,001)	46.7% (50,683)	66.7% (34,295)	28.7% (16,388)
Rural ***	16.3% (1,036,614)	16.3% (513,982)	16.4% (522,632)	14.9% (817,495)	13.5% (356,630)	16.3% (460,866)	31.6% (170,055)	37.1% (119,783)	23.3% (50,273)	14.9% (32,790)	20.6% (24,738)	8.1% (8,052)	15.6% (16,273)	20.3% (12,831)	8.3% (3,442)
Census Region Northeast ***	16.9% (740,000)	15.5% (351,492)	18.3% (388,508)	13.2% (445,338)	12.2% (220,052)	14.4% (225,286)	27.1% (141,388)	19.4% (39,724)	32.1% (101,664)	29.4% (100,959)	32.6% (57,634)	26.1% (43,324)	32.7% (52,315)	40.2% (34,082)	24.3% (18,234)
South *** + ~	23.0% (1,952,745)	22.5% (946,084)	23.4% (1,006,661)	19.1% (1,027,014)	16.9% (447,713)	21.3% (579,301)	30.1% (655,545)	34.4% (382,035)	25.6% (273,511)	30.2% (235,424)	26.1% (93,210)	33.7% (142,214)	21.0% (34,763)	30.5% (23,127)	13.0% (11,636)
Midwest ***	17.7% (919,846)	15.3% (404,508)	20.1% (515,338)	18.8% (608,828)	16.6% (264,506)	21.0% (344,322)	63.8% (231,132)	59.0% (104,667)	68.3% (126,464)	4.4% (57,080)	4.2% (30,705)	4.7% (26,375)	7.2% (22,806)	3.3% (4,630)	10.4% (18,176)
West	19.2% (1,135,475)	19.8% (571,108)	18.6% (564,366)	12.8% (618,667)	11.5% (267,809)	14.0% (350,858)	12.9% (97,313)	15.3% (59,795)	10.4% (37,518)	158.0% (336,009)	187.9% (189,611)	130.9% (146,399)	73.2% (83,485)	87.8% (53,894)	56.2% (29,592)

Notes:
"–" indicates sample size too small to estimate.
*** Test of statistical significance compares African Americans with Whites. *** p < .001, ** p < .01, * p < .05.
+++ Test of statistical significance compares White boys with White girls. +++ p < .001, ++ p < .01, + p < .05.
~~~Test of statistical significance compares African American boys with African American girls. ~~~ p < .001, ~~ p < .01, ~ p < .05.
Tests of statistical significance calculated using adjusted sample weight to control for influence of large sample sizes.
Student's residence determined by ZIP code. An Urbanized Area (UA) comprises a place (e.g., city, village) and adjacent densely settled surrounding territory that together have a population of at least 50,000. "Urban, outside Urbanized Area" includes incorporated and unincorporated places outside of UA with population of at least 2,500. "Rural" represents all other places.
Source: National Household Education Survey, 1993 School Safety & Discipline Component.

Figure 4. Percentage of Students in Grades 6 to 12 Who Avoided Places In Their Schools by School Characteristics: 1993

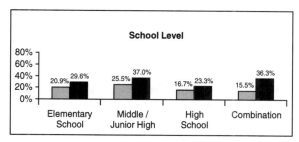

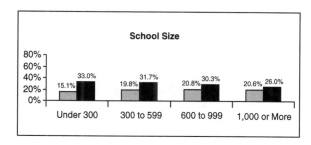

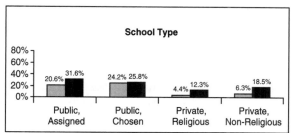

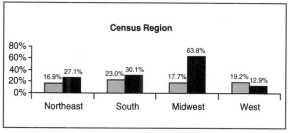

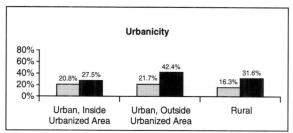

Source: National Household Education Survey, 1993 School Safety & Discipline Component.

those attending assigned public schools (31.6% versus 16.9%) and among those attending private religious schools (12.3% versus 1.9%).

- Regardless of school location, a higher share of African Americans than Whites avoided places in their schools (urban, 27.5% versus 16.3%; suburban, 42.4% versus 17.5%; and rural, 31.6% versus 14.9%).

- In the midwest, the percentage of African Americans who avoided places in their schools was more than three times as large as the share of their White counterparts (63.8% versus 18.8%).

- The proportion of African American students who avoided places in their schools was also larger than the proportion of Whites in the northeast (27.1% versus 13.2%) and in the south (30.1% versus 19.1%).

- Comparable shares of African Americans and Whites in the west avoided places in their schools (12.9% versus 12.8%).

Avoidance of Places on School Grounds

About one in eight (13.7%) students in grades 6 to 12 avoided school parking lots or other places on their school grounds because they worried that someone might hurt or bother them.

- **Table 5** shows that the share of African Americans who reported avoiding places on school grounds was more than twice the share of Whites (23.3% versus 9.5%).

Figure 5 shows that avoidance of places on school grounds declined from 21.4% of elementary school students and 17.9% of middle and junior high school students to 9.9% of high school students.

Regardless of school level, the percentage of African Americans who avoided places on school grounds was larger than the percentage of Whites.

- For example, among middle and junior high school students, 31.9% of African Americans, but only 11.8% of Whites, avoided places on school grounds.

- Avoidance of places on school grounds ranged from a high of 17.7% of students at chosen public schools to a low of 4.1% of students at private religious schools.

- The share of African Americans who avoided places on school grounds was more than twice the share of Whites among students attending their assigned public schools (23.6% versus 10.0%) and the public schools of their choice (24.6% versus 10.5%).

Regardless of school size or location, a higher share of African Americans than Whites avoided places on school grounds.

- For example, 19.4% of African Americans at schools with more than 1,000 students avoided places on school grounds, compared with only 9.2% of Whites.

- Among African Americans, a higher share of suburban school students than of urban and

rural school students avoided places on school grounds (40.6% versus 22.6% and 15.1%).

- A higher share of African American boys than of African American girls attending suburban schools avoided places on school grounds (74.6% versus 15.5%).

- In all four census regions, a higher proportion of African American students than of White students avoided places on school grounds: 27.0% versus 7.2% in the northeast, 22.7% versus 11.3% in the south, 24.6% versus 8.0% in the midwest, and 18.6% versus 10.8% in the west.

Avoidance of School Events

About 7.6% of students in grades 6 to 12 reported that they avoided school events, such as dances or sports events, because they worried that someone might hurt or bother them.

- The percentage of African American students who avoided school events was about twice as large as the percentage of White students (10.7% versus 5.9%).

Figure 6 shows that, overall, the percentage of students who avoided school events was not related to school level.

- **Table 6** shows that a higher share of African Americans than Whites avoided school events among high school students (12.0% versus 5.2%) and combination school students (19.7% versus 6.4%).

- Similar proportions of African Americans and Whites avoided school events among those at elementary (7.9% versus 6.1%) and middle (8.0% versus 6.9%) schools.

- A higher percentage of African Americans than of Whites avoided school events at both public assigned schools (10.2% versus 6.1%) and private religious schools (11.6% versus 2.0%).

- The percentage of African Americans who avoided school events was higher than the per-

Table 5. Percentage of Students in Grades 6 to 12 Who Avoided Places on School Grounds by School Characteristics, Race, and Sex: 1993
(weighted sample size in parentheses)

Characteristic	Total	Male	Female	White, Non-Hispanic Total	Male	Female	African American, Non-Hispanic Total	Male	Female	Hispanic Total	Male	Female	Other Total	Male	Female
Total ***	100.0% (24,011,221)	100.0% (11,997,231)	100.0% (12,013,990)	100.0% (16,807,986)	100.0% (8,378,872)	100.0% (8,429,114)	100.0% (3,813,119)	100.0% (1,882,053)	100.0% (1,931,066)	100.0% (2,636,416)	100.0% (1,374,597)	100.0% (1,261,819)	100.0% (753,700)	100.0% (361,709)	100.0% (391,991)
Avoided Places on School Grounds	13.7% (3,285,097)	14.0% (1,675,717)	13.4% (1,609,380)	9.5% (1,590,814)	9.4% (791,034)	9.5% (799,780)	23.3% (887,820)	24.4% (459,358)	22.2% (428,462)	24.6% (649,093)	25.0% (343,513)	24.2% (305,580)	20.9% (157,370)	22.6% (81,813)	19.3% (75,557)
School Level															
Elementary School ** +	21.4% (566,641)	24.9% (337,721)	17.7% (228,920)	16.2% (284,404)	20.2% (184,728)	11.8% (99,676)	27.2% (109,289)	24.9% (52,171)	29.6% (57,118)	39.8% (149,621)	45.7% (88,217)	33.6% (61,404)	22.0% (23,327)	35.4% (12,605)	15.2% (10,722)
Middle/Junior High ***	17.9% (1,324,756)	19.1% (734,177)	16.6% (590,579)	11.8% (592,328)	11.8% (301,021)	11.7% (291,307)	31.9% (419,750)	36.0% (257,761)	27.1% (161,989)	28.1% (243,052)	28.9% (142,481)	26.9% (100,571)	32.6% (69,627)	33.6% (32,914)	31.7% (36,713)
High School ***	9.9% (1,143,812)	8.8% (488,741)	10.9% (655,071)	6.8% (553,369)	5.9% (232,999)	7.7% (320,370)	16.6% (308,356)	15.6% (130,480)	17.5% (177,876)	18.2% (222,398)	15.7% (93,697)	20.7% (128,701)	17.7% (59,689)	18.6% (31,566)	16.9% (28,123)
Combination **	10.3% (249,888)	9.1% (115,078)	11.5% (134,810)	8.4% (160,713)	7.2% (72,285)	9.6% (88,427)	20.9% (50,425)	16.2% (18,946)	25.4% (31,479)	19.4% (34,022)	20.6% (19,118)	18.0% (14,904)	4.9% (4,728)	8.1% (4,728)	0.0% –
School Type															
Public, Assigned ***	14.0% (2,731,120)	14.2% (1,390,793)	13.8% (1,340,327)	10.0% (1,400,493)	9.5% (667,929)	10.4% (732,564)	23.6% (659,793)	25.9% (368,460)	21.3% (291,333)	26.1% (545,512)	25.1% (278,198)	27.2% (267,313)	23.8% (125,322)	31.0% (76,206)	17.5% (49,116)
Public, Chosen ***	17.7% (470,872)	18.2% (235,693)	17.1% (235,178)	10.5% (134,431)	13.7% (86,037)	7.5% (48,394)	24.6% (211,166)	21.5% (85,049)	27.2% (126,116)	23.7% (93,226)	29.3% (59,000)	17.9% (34,226)	23.1% (32,048)	8.3% (5,607)	37.1% (26,441)
Private, Religious	4.1% (64,214)	4.4% (32,126)	4.0% (32,088)	3.5% (42,423)	3.9% (23,601)	3.1% (18,822)	9.5% (12,557)	8.0% (3,332)	10.1% (9,225)	6.2% (9,234)	8.7% (5,193)	4.6% (4,040)	0.0% –	0.0% –	0.0% –
Private, Non-Religious	5.9% (18,892)	9.5% (17,105)	1.3% (1,787)	5.1% (13,467)	9.6% (13,467)	0.0% –	15.2% (4,304)	11.6% (2,517)	27.1% (1,787)	16.2% (1,122)	18.5% (1,122)	0.0% –	0.0% –	0.0% –	0.0% –
Number of Students															
Under 300 ***	11.7% (306,654)	13.0% (167,912)	10.4% (138,742)	9.2% (187,143)	10.0% (98,838)	8.5% (88,304)	24.5% (57,821)	25.4% (32,687)	23.5% (25,135)	17.4% (49,286)	22.1% (31,659)	12.5% (17,627)	14.9% (12,404)	12.0% (4,728)	17.6% (7,676)
300 to 599 ***	15.4% (1,199,595)	16.3% (646,445)	14.4% (553,151)	10.0% (551,499)	10.6% (297,799)	9.3% (253,700)	30.8% (383,860)	34.3% (226,651)	26.8% (157,209)	26.6% (208,941)	23.2% (88,273)	29.7% (120,669)	23.8% (55,295)	27.9% (33,723)	19.4% (21,573)
600 to 999 ***	13.1% (810,649)	13.2% (401,184)	13.1% (409,465)	9.3% (405,339)	8.7% (188,624)	9.8% (216,715)	18.8% (198,578)	17.6% (87,063)	20.0% (111,515)	28.7% (163,174)	31.5% (101,696)	25.0% (61,478)	26.3% (43,559)	40.4% (23,801)	18.5% (19,758)
More than 1,000 ***	13.1% (968,199)	12.5% (460,177)	13.7% (508,022)	9.2% (446,834)	8.5% (205,773)	9.9% (241,062)	19.4% (247,560)	18.9% (112,957)	19.8% (134,603)	22.8% (227,693)	23.0% (121,886)	22.6% (105,807)	16.9% (46,112)	13.7% (19,561)	20.4% (26,551)
Urbanicity															
Urban, Inside *** Urbanized Area	15.1% (2,128,898)	14.9% (1,040,130)	15.3% (1,088,768)	9.8% (835,309)	10.1% (430,666)	9.4% (404,642)	22.6% (659,457)	21.5% (301,384)	23.8% (358,073)	25.3% (523,502)	24.6% (258,576)	26.0% (264,926)	20.5% (110,630)	20.0% (49,503)	20.8% (61,127)
Urban, Outside *** ~~~ Urbanized Area	15.3% (546,856)	18.1% (336,546)	12.2% (210,310)	9.4% (259,415)	8.9% (129,831)	9.9% (129,584)	40.6% (147,225)	74.6% (114,891)	15.5% (32,335)	29.3% (101,547)	31.3% (64,145)	26.3% (37,402)	35.6% (38,668)	53.8% (27,679)	19.3% (10,989)
Rural *	9.6% (609,343)	9.5% (299,041)	9.7% (310,302)	9.0% (496,090)	8.7% (230,536)	9.4% (265,554)	15.1% (81,137)	13.3% (43,083)	17.6% (38,054)	10.9% (24,044)	17.3% (20,792)	3.3% (3,252)	7.7% (8,072)	7.3% (4,630)	8.3% (3,442)
Census Region															
Northeast ***	11.2% (492,231)	10.2% (231,615)	12.3% (260,616)	7.2% (243,777)	6.9% (124,469)	7.6% (119,307)	27.0% (140,591)	23.8% (48,696)	29.0% (91,895)	20.5% (70,419)	18.5% (32,676)	22.7% (37,742)	23.4% (37,445)	30.4% (25,774)	15.6% (11,671)
South ***	15.3% (1,301,493)	15.2% (636,294)	15.5% (665,198)	11.3% (608,169)	10.8% (285,425)	11.9% (322,744)	22.7% (494,607)	25.3% (280,515)	20.1% (214,092)	23.0% (179,115)	18.1% (64,808)	27.1% (114,307)	11.9% (19,602)	7.3% (5,546)	15.7% (14,055)
Midwest ***	10.7% (632,731)	10.8% (310,988)	10.6% (321,743)	8.0% (389,532)	8.3% (194,278)	7.8% (195,254)	24.6% (185,237)	22.9% (89,469)	26.5% (95,769)	22.2% (47,165)	22.4% (22,611)	22.0% (24,553)	9.5% (10,797)	7.5% (4,630)	11.7% (6,167)
West *	16.5% (858,642)	18.7% (496,820)	14.1% (361,822)	10.8% (349,337)	11.7% (186,862)	9.9% (162,475)	18.6% (67,384)	22.9% (40,678)	14.4% (26,706)	27.1% (352,395)	30.2% (223,418)	23.0% (128,977)	28.5% (89,526)	32.8% (45,862)	25.0% (43,664)

Notes:

"–" indicates sample size too small to estimate.

*** Test of statistical significance compares African Americans with Whites. *** p < .001, ** p < .01, * p < .05.

+++ Test of statistical significance compares White boys with White girls. +++ p < .001, ++ p < .01, + p < .05.

~~~ Test of statistical significance compares African American boys with African American girls. ~~~ p < .001, ~~ p < .01, ~ p <.05.

Tests of statistical significance calculated using adjusted sample weight to control for influence of large sample sizes.

Student's residence determined by ZIP code. An Urbanized Area (UA) comprises a place (e.g., city, village) and adjacent densely settled surrounding territory that together have a population of at least 50,000. "Urban, outside Urbanized Area" includes incorporated and unincorporated places outside of UA with population of at least 2,500. "Rural" represents all other places.

Source: National Household Education Survey, 1993 School Safety & Discipline Component.

Figure 5. Percentage of Students in Grades 6 to 12 Who Avoided Places on School Grounds by School Characteristics: 1993

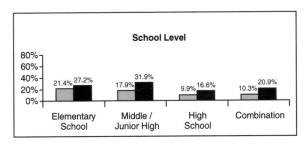

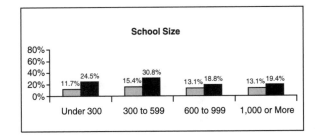

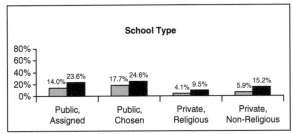

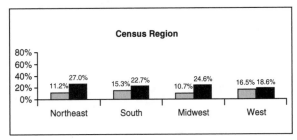

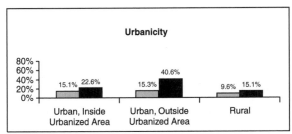

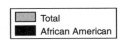

Source: National Household Education Survey, 1993 School Safety & Discipline Component.

centage of Whites at schools with 600 to 999 students (13.7% versus 5.3%) and at schools with more than 1,000 students (10.8% versus 6.2%).

- The proportion of African Americans who avoided school events was higher than the proportion of Whites at suburban schools (14.9% versus 6.5%), urban schools (9.9% versus 5.6%), and rural schools (11.9% versus 6.1%).

- A higher percentage of African Americans than Whites in the south (12.5% versus 6.3%) and in

the midwest (10.5% versus 5.1%) avoided school events.

- Comparable proportions of African American and White students avoided school events in the northeast (5.9% versus 4.9%) and west (6.9% versus 7.6%).

Special Route to School

About 4.6% of students in grades 6 to 12 took special routes to their schools because they were worried that someone might hurt or bother them.

Figure 6. Percentage of Students in Grades 6 to 12 Who Avoided School Events by School Characteristics: 1993

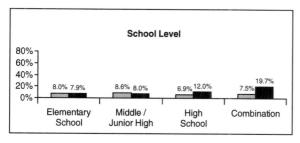

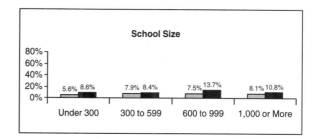

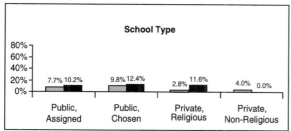

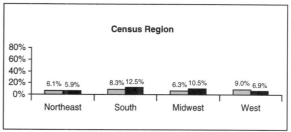

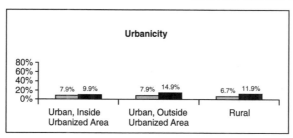

Source: National Household Education Survey, 1993 School Safety & Discipline Component.

- **Table 7** shows that a higher percentage of African American students than of White students took special routes to their schools (8.4% versus 3.0%).

- **Figure 7** shows that the percentage of African Americans who took a special route to school was higher than the share of all students among middle schools students (12.7% versus 6.7%) and high school students (4.7% versus 2.9%).

Regardless of school type, size, location, and region, a higher percentage of African American students than of White students took special routes to their schools.

Table 6. Percentage of Students in Grades 6 to 12 Who Avoided School Events by School Characteristics, Race, and Sex: 1993
(weighted sample size in parentheses)

Characteristic	Total	Male	Female	White, Non-Hispanic Total	Male	Female	African American, Non-Hispanic Total	Male	Female	Hispanic Total	Male	Female	Other Total	Male	Female
Total ***	100.0%	100.0%	100.0%	100.0%	100.0%	100.0%	100.0%	100.0%	100.0%	100.0%	100.0%	100.0%	100.0%	100.0%	100.0%
	(24,011,221)	(11,997,231)	(12,013,990)	(16,807,986)	(8,378,872)	(8,429,114)	(3,813,119)	(1,882,053)	(1,931,066)	(2,636,416)	(1,374,597)	(1,261,819)	(753,700)	(361,709)	(391,991)
Avoided School Events	7.6%	7.9%	7.3%	5.9%	6.2%	5.7%	10.7%	10.7%	10.7%	12.5%	13.0%	12.0%	11.5%	13.2%	10.0%
	(1,822,251)	(947,186)	(875,065)	(997,364)	(519,730)	(477,634)	(407,622)	(201,141)	(206,480)	(330,296)	(178,650)	(151,646)	(86,969)	(47,664)	(39,305)
School Level															
Elementary School +	8.0%	10.4%	5.5%	6.1%	8.4%	3.6%	7.9%	6.1%	9.9%	17.2%	25.1%	9.0%	7.8%	6.8%	8.4%
	(211,660)	(140,300)	(71,360)	(106,790)	(76,738)	(30,052)	(31,738)	(12,728)	(19,010)	(64,802)	(48,429)	(16,373)	(8,330)	(2,405)	(5,925)
Middle/Junior High ~	8.6%	9.1%	8.0%	6.9%	6.5%	7.3%	8.0%	10.9%	4.6%	14.8%	15.7%	13.8%	25.8%	30.4%	21.9%
	(635,930)	(350,898)	(285,032)	(346,795)	(166,042)	(180,754)	(105,396)	(77,966)	(27,429)	(128,597)	(77,133)	(51,464)	(55,142)	(29,758)	(25,385)
High School *** ~	6.9%	6.3%	7.4%	5.2%	5.4%	5.0%	12.0%	8.6%	14.8%	10.2%	8.4%	11.9%	7.0%	9.1%	4.8%
	(792,079)	(350,255)	(441,824)	(421,498)	(212,050)	(209,448)	(223,035)	(72,465)	(150,570)	(124,049)	(50,239)	(73,810)	(23,497)	(15,502)	(7,996)
Combination *** ~	7.5%	8.3%	6.6%	6.4%	6.5%	6.2%	19.7%	32.5%	7.6%	7.3%	3.1%	12.1%	0.0%	0.0%	0.0%
	(182,582)	(105,733)	(76,849)	(122,281)	(64,901)	(57,380)	(47,453)	(37,982)	(9,471)	(12,848)	(2,850)	(9,999)	–	–	–
School Type															
Public, Assigned ***	7.7%	7.9%	7.6%	6.1%	6.0%	6.3%	10.2%	10.9%	9.5%	13.8%	14.3%	13.4%	12.5%	16.0%	9.4%
	(1,504,603)	(771,367)	(733,236)	(863,593)	(418,273)	(445,320)	(285,981)	(155,509)	(130,472)	(289,190)	(158,123)	(131,067)	(65,839)	(39,462)	(26,377)
Public, Chosen +	9.8%	10.4%	9.2%	7.6%	10.9%	4.4%	12.4%	9.9%	14.5%	9.8%	10.2%	9.4%	13.8%	9.2%	18.2%
	(260,991)	(134,439)	(126,552)	(97,106)	(68,585)	(28,522)	(106,301)	(39,144)	(67,157)	(38,472)	(20,526)	(17,945)	(19,112)	(6,184)	(12,928)
Private, Religious **	2.8%	3.9%	1.9%	2.0%	3.3%	0.6%	11.6%	15.6%	9.7%	1.8%	0.0%	3.0%	3.1%	5.7%	0.0%
	(43,725)	(28,447)	(15,277)	(23,732)	(19,940)	(3,792)	(15,340)	(6,489)	(8,851)	(2,634)	–	(2,634)	(2,019)	(2,019)	–
Private, Non-Religious	4.0%	7.2%	0.0%	4.9%	9.3%	0.0%	0.0%	0.0%	0.0%	0.0%	0.0%	0.0%	0.0%	0.0%	0.0%
	(12,932)	(12,932)	–	(12,932)	(12,932)	–	–	–	–	–	–	–	–	–	–
Number of Students															
Under 300 ~	5.6%	7.4%	3.8%	5.0%	6.2%	3.8%	8.6%	15.7%	0.0%	4.3%	3.4%	5.3%	15.3%	23.5%	7.9%
	(145,969)	(95,368)	(50,601)	(100,769)	(61,026)	(39,743)	(20,182)	(20,182)		(12,314)	(4,889)	(7,426)	(12,704)	(9,271)	(3,433)
300 to 599 ~~	7.9%	8.3%	7.4%	6.5%	6.3%	6.7%	8.4%	12.8%	3.6%	16.0%	16.0%	16.0%	9.9%	6.0%	14.1%
	(613,541)	(329,519)	(284,022)	(359,440)	(177,256)	(182,185)	(105,392)	(84,353)	(21,038)	(125,777)	(60,638)	(65,140)	(22,931)	(7,273)	(15,659)
600 to 999 ***	7.5%	7.3%	7.6%	5.3%	5.3%	5.4%	13.7%	11.5%	15.7%	10.3%	10.3%	10.3%	14.7%	30.0%	6.3%
	(461,568)	(222,018)	(239,550)	(233,747)	(113,932)	(119,815)	(144,807)	(57,132)	(87,675)	(58,611)	(33,316)	(25,295)	(24,403)	(17,637)	(6,766)
More than 1,000 ** ~	8.1%	8.1%	8.1%	6.2%	6.9%	5.6%	10.8%	6.6%	14.4%	13.4%	15.1%	11.5%	9.9%	9.5%	10.3%
	(601,173)	(300,281)	(300,892)	(303,408)	(167,517)	(135,891)	(137,241)	(39,474)	(97,768)	(133,593)	(79,807)	(53,786)	(26,931)	(13,483)	(13,448)
Urbanicity															
Urban, Inside *** Urbanized Area	7.9%	7.9%	8.0%	5.6%	5.8%	5.5%	9.9%	8.7%	11.0%	13.5%	14.3%	12.7%	12.4%	12.6%	12.2%
	(1,115,548)	(550,204)	(565,343)	(479,844)	(245,985)	(233,859)	(289,202)	(122,775)	(166,427)	(279,601)	(150,416)	(129,185)	(66,900)	(31,028)	(35,872)
Urban, Outside ** Urbanized Area	7.9%	8.4%	7.3%	6.5%	6.8%	6.3%	14.9%	22.9%	9.0%	11.7%	9.2%	15.2%	5.9%	5.7%	6.0%
	(281,467)	(155,520)	(125,947)	(180,485)	(98,398)	(82,087)	(54,161)	(35,313)	(18,848)	(40,438)	(18,859)	(21,579)	(6,383)	(2,951)	(3,433)
Rural **	6.7%	7.7%	5.8%	6.1%	6.6%	5.7%	11.9%	13.3%	9.8%	4.7%	7.8%	0.9%	13.1%	21.6%	0.0%
	(425,237)	(241,461)	(183,775)	(337,035)	(175,347)	(161,688)	(64,260)	(43,054)	(21,206)	(10,257)	(9,375)	(881)	(13,686)	(13,686)	–
Census Region															
Northeast	6.1%	6.9%	5.3%	4.9%	5.2%	4.5%	5.9%	6.4%	5.6%	12.1%	18.1%	5.7%	20.9%	21.7%	20.0%
	(268,802)	(156,720)	(112,083)	(163,134)	(93,155)	(69,979)	(30,777)	(13,095)	(17,682)	(41,481)	(32,090)	(9,391)	(33,410)	(18,379)	(15,031)
South ***	8.3%	8.2%	8.5%	6.3%	6.1%	6.6%	12.5%	13.1%	11.9%	10.1%	8.7%	11.3%	10.1%	6.4%	13.3%
	(707,979)	(343,291)	(364,688)	(339,935)	(161,936)	(177,998)	(272,756)	(145,547)	(127,210)	(78,516)	(30,940)	(47,576)	(16,772)	(4,868)	(11,904)
Midwest **	6.3%	7.0%	5.7%	5.1%	5.6%	4.7%	10.5%	8.2%	13.0%	14.2%	23.9%	5.4%	14.8%	25.2%	2.7%
	(374,509)	(201,338)	(173,170)	(248,451)	(129,826)	(118,625)	(79,030)	(31,921)	(47,109)	(30,159)	(24,136)	(6,023)	(16,868)	(15,455)	(1,414)
West	9.0%	9.3%	8.8%	7.6%	8.5%	6.8%	6.9%	6.0%	7.8%	13.8%	12.4%	15.8%	6.3%	6.4%	6.3%
	(470,962)	(245,837)	(225,124)	(245,844)	(134,812)	(111,032)	(25,059)	(10,579)	(14,480)	(180,139)	(91,483)	(88,656)	(19,919)	(8,963)	(10,957)

Notes:

"–" indicates sample size too small to estimate.

*** Test of statistical significance compares African Americans with Whites. *** p <.001, ** p < .01, * p < .05.

+++ Test of statistical significance compares White boys with White girls. +++ p <.001, ++ p <.01, + p < .05.

~~~Test of statistical significance compares African American boys with African American girls. ~~~ p <.001, ~~ p < .01, ~ p .05.

Tests of statistical significance calculated using adjusted sample weight to control for influence of large sample sizes.

Student's residence determined by ZIP code. An Urbanized Area (UA) comprises a place (e.g., city, village) and adjacent densely settled surrounding territory that together have a population of at least 50,000."Urban, outside Urbanized Area" includes incorporated and unincorporated places outside of UA with population of at least 2,500. "Rural" represents all other places.

Source: National Household Education Survey, 1993 School Safety & Discipline Component.

Table 7. Percentage of Students in Grades 6 to 12 Who Took a Special Route to School by School Characteristics, Race, and Sex: 1993
(weighted sample size in parentheses)

Characteristic	Total	Male	Female	White, Non-Hispanic Total	Male	Female	African American, Non-Hispanic Total	Male	Female	Hispanic Total	Male	Female	Other Total	Male	Female
Total *** +	100.0%	100.0%	100.0%	100.0%	100.0%	100.0%	100.0%	100.0%	100.0%	100.0%	100.0%	100.0%	100.0%	100.0%	100.0%
	(24,011,221)	(11,997,231)	(12,013,990)	(16,807,986)	(8,378,872)	(8,429,114)	(3,813,119)	(1,882,053)	(1,931,066)	(2,636,416)	(1,374,597)	(1,261,819)	(753,700)	(361,709)	(391,991)
Took Special Route	4.6%	5.0%	4.2%	3.0%	3.6%	2.4%	8.4%	8.0%	8.8%	9.6%	10.0%	9.1%	4.6%	5.0%	4.3%
to School	(1,109,706)	(605,660)	(504,046)	(502,015)	(299,571)	(202,444)	(320,503)	(151,053)	(169,451)	(252,167)	(136,884)	(115,282)	(35,021)	(18,152)	(16,869)
School Level															
Elementary School	6.7%	7.7%	5.7%	4.3%	4.5%	4.2%	8.6%	6.2%	11.2%	17.3%	24.9%	9.4%	2.4%	7.1%	0.0%
	(178,195)	(104,381)	(73,814)	(75,941)	(40,857)	(35,084)	(34,545)	(12,996)	(21,549)	(65,189)	(48,008)	(17,181)	(2,520)	(2,520)	–
Middle/Junior High ***	6.7%	8.1%	5.0%	4.6%	6.2%	2.9%	12.7%	13.7%	11.5%	10.3%	11.5%	8.7%	3.3%	0.0%	6.1%
	(493,330)	(313,435)	(179,895)	(230,132)	(158,479)	(71,652)	(167,021)	(98,396)	(68,625)	(89,118)	(56,559)	(32,558)	(7,060)	–	(7,060)
High School ***	2.9%	2.6%	3.1%	1.7%	2.0%	1.4%	4.7%	2.7%	6.4%	7.1%	5.1%	9.0%	6.7%	7.5%	5.9%
	(332,101)	(144,288)	(187,814)	(135,326)	(78,138)	(57,188)	(87,768)	(22,774)	(64,994)	(86,428)	(30,606)	(55,822)	(22,580)	(12,770)	(9,810)
Combination ***	4.4%	3.4%	5.4%	3.2%	2.2%	4.2%	12.9%	14.4%	11.5%	6.5%	1.8%	11.7%	2.9%	4.9%	0.0%
	(106,079)	(43,556)	(62,523)	(60,616)	(22,097)	(38,519)	(31,169)	(16,886)	(14,283)	(11,432)	(1,711)	(9,721)	(2,862)	(2,862)	–
School Type															
Public, Assigned *** +	4.7%	5.4%	4.0%	3.3%	3.9%	2.6%	8.2%	8.8%	7.6%	10.1%	11.0%	9.1%	3.7%	5.2%	2.3%
	(917,660)	(531,393)	(386,267)	(457,938)	(271,269)	(186,668)	(229,140)	(125,094)	(104,046)	(211,345)	(122,259)	(89,085)	(19,237)	(12,770)	(6,467)
Public, Chosen ***	5.8%	4.8%	6.8%	2.4%	3.5%	1.4%	9.3%	5.7%	12.3%	7.9%	7.3%	8.6%	9.6%	4.3%	14.6%
	(155,438)	(62,440)	(92,998)	(31,036)	(22,305)	(8,731)	(79,934)	(22,648)	(57,285)	(31,205)	(14,625)	(16,580)	(13,264)	(2,862)	(10,402)
Private, Religious ***	1.8%	0.9%	2.7%	0.5%	0.5%	0.6%	7.3%	3.7%	8.9%	6.5%	0.0%	10.9%	3.8%	7.1%	0.0%
	(28,367)	(6,796)	(21,570)	(6,554)	(2,721)	(3,834)	(9,676)	(1,556)	(8,120)	(9,617)	–	(9,617)	(2,520)	(2,520)	–
Private, Non-Religious	2.6%	2.8%	2.3%	2.5%	2.3%	2.6%	6.2%	8.1%	0.0%	0.0%	0.0%	0.0%	0.0%	0.0%	0.0%
	(8,241)	(5,030)	(3,211)	(6,487)	(3,277)	(3,211)	(1,754)	(1,754)	–	–	–	–	–	–	–
Number of Students															
Under 300 ***	2.7%	1.4%	4.0%	1.6%	0.9%	2.3%	9.5%	3.7%	16.5%	3.9%	1.7%	6.0%	5.6%	6.4%	4.9%
	(71,343)	(18,769)	(52,574)	(33,274)	(8,999)	(24,275)	(22,455)	(4,807)	(17,648)	(10,974)	(2,443)	(8,530)	(4,640)	(2,520)	(2,121)
300 to 599 ***	5.3%	6.4%	4.2%	3.0%	3.6%	2.4%	10.7%	13.2%	7.9%	14.0%	15.9%	12.2%	2.1%	4.0%	0.0%
	(416,032)	(254,140)	(161,892)	(167,504)	(101,723)	(65,781)	(133,435)	(87,001)	(46,434)	(110,258)	(60,581)	(49,677)	(4,835)	(4,835)	–
600 to 999 **	4.8%	5.4%	4.2%	3.8%	4.8%	2.8%	7.9%	5.8%	9.7%	7.3%	9.0%	5.2%	2.9%	4.3%	2.1%
	(296,842)	(164,365)	(132,478)	(166,948)	(103,943)	(63,005)	(83,373)	(28,999)	(54,375)	(41,727)	(28,883)	(12,843)	(4,795)	(2,540)	(2,255)
More than 1,000 **	4.4%	4.6%	4.2%	2.8%	3.5%	2.0%	6.4%	5.1%	7.5%	8.9%	8.5%	9.4%	7.6%	5.8%	9.6%
	(325,488)	(168,386)	(157,102)	(134,289)	(84,907)	(49,382)	(81,240)	(30,245)	(50,994)	(89,208)	(44,976)	(44,232)	(20,751)	(8,257)	(12,494)
Urbanicity															
Urban, Inside *** +	5.1%	5.4%	4.8%	3.0%	3.8%	2.2%	7.7%	6.2%	9.1%	10.1%	11.2%	9.1%	5.6%	5.4%	5.7%
Urbanized Area	(720,323)	(379,661)	(340,661)	(255,953)	(161,813)	(94,140)	(224,555)	(87,428)	(137,126)	(209,629)	(117,103)	(92,526)	(30,186)	(13,317)	(16,869)
Urban, Outside ***	5.7%	6.7%	4.7%	3.9%	4.6%	3.2%	16.8%	25.1%	10.7%	8.8%	7.2%	11.2%	4.5%	9.4%	0.0%
Urbanized Area	(205,289)	(125,236)	(80,053)	(108,783)	(67,071)	(41,712)	(61,031)	(38,642)	(22,389)	(30,640)	(14,688)	(15,952)	(4,835)	(4,835)	–
Rural **	2.9%	3.2%	2.6%	2.5%	2.7%	2.4%	6.5%	7.7%	4.6%	5.4%	4.2%	6.8%	0.0%	0.0%	0.0%
	(184,094)	(100,763)	(83,332)	(137,279)	(70,687)	(66,592)	(34,918)	(24,982)	(9,935)	(11,898)	(5,094)	(6,804)	–	–	–
Census Region															
Northeast *** +	3.8%	4.3%	3.3%	2.1%	3.0%	1.1%	14.5%	12.7%	15.7%	5.3%	8.1%	2.3%	1.6%	3.0%	0.0%
	(167,835)	(96,982)	(70,853)	(71,460)	(54,086)	(17,374)	(75,600)	(25,975)	(49,625)	(18,235)	(14,381)	(3,854)	(2,540)	(2,540)	–
South ***	4.7%	5.2%	4.2%	3.0%	3.5%	2.4%	7.2%	8.7%	5.7%	10.0%	7.8%	11.8%	1.3%	0.0%	2.3%
	(396,699)	(217,177)	(179,523)	(158,840)	(92,811)	(66,030)	(157,792)	(96,409)	(61,383)	(77,975)	(27,957)	(50,018)	(2,092)	–	(2,092)
Midwest *	3.7%	3.7%	3.6%	2.9%	3.3%	2.6%	6.3%	3.6%	9.1%	12.9%	15.3%	10.7%	0.0%	0.0%	0.0%
	(216,891)	(107,115)	(109,776)	(142,246)	(77,475)	(64,772)	(47,295)	(14,242)	(33,053)	(27,350)	(15,398)	(11,952)	–	–	–
West **	6.3%	7.0%	5.6%	4.0%	4.7%	3.3%	11.0%	8.1%	13.7%	9.9%	10.7%	8.8%	9.7%	11.2%	8.4%
	(328,280)	(184,387)	(143,893)	(129,468)	(75,200)	(54,268)	(39,816)	(14,426)	(25,390)	(128,607)	(79,149)	(49,458)	(30,389)	(15,612)	(14,778)

Notes:
"–" indicates sample size too small to estimate.
*** Test of statistical significance compares African Americans with Whites. *** p <.001, ** p <.01, * p <.05.
+++ Test of statistical significance compares White boys with White girls. +++ p <.001, ++ p <.01, + p <.05.
~~~ Test of statistical significance compares African American boys with African American girls. ~~~ p <.001, ~~ p <.01, ~ p <.05.
Tests of statistical significance calculated using adjusted sample weight to control for influence of large sample sizes.
Student's residence determined by ZIP code. An Urbanized Area (UA) comprises a place (e.g., city, village) and adjacent densely settled surrounding territory that together have a population of at least 50,000. "Urban, outside Urbanized Area" includes incorporated and unincorporated places outside of UA with population of at least 2,500. "Rural" represents all other places.
Source: National Household Education Survey, 1993 School Safety & Discipline Component.

Figure 7. Percentage of Students in Grades 6 to 12 Who Took a Special Route to School by School Characteristics: 1993

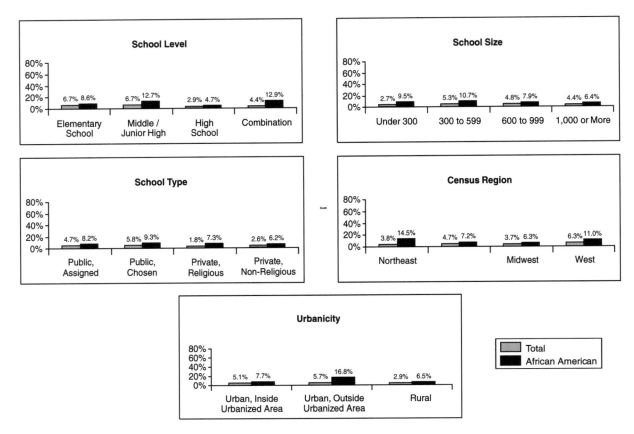

Source: National Household Education Survey, 1993 School Safety & Discipline Component.

- About 8.2% of African Americans but only 3.3% of Whites attending their assigned public schools took special routes to school.

- At schools with less than 300 students, 9.5% of African Americans, but only 1.6% of Whites, took special routes to school.

- At suburban schools, 16.8% of African Americans, but 3.9% of Whites, took special routes to school.

- A higher share of African Americans than Whites took special routes to school among students in the northeast (14.5% versus 2.1%), south (7.2% versus 3.0%), midwest (6.3% versus 2.9%), and west (11.0% versus 4.0%).

Communication Between Parents and Their Children About Threats or Danger

Overall, about 44.3% of students in grades 6 to 12 talked with their parents about threats or danger at school. The share of White girls who talked to their parents about threats or danger was higher than the share of White boys (46.9% versus 35.0%). But, among African Americans, the percentages of girls and boys who talked to their parents about threats or danger were comparable (55.1% versus 52.0%). **Figure 8** shows that, generally, a higher share of African American students than of all students talked with their parents about threats or danger.

- **Table 8** shows that a higher percentage of African Americans than Whites talked to their parents about threats or danger at middle and

junior high schools (58.5% versus 48.4%), high schools (46.8% versus 35.9%), and combination schools (61.9% versus 32.3%).

- About 54.3% of African Americans at assigned public schools talked to their parents about threats or danger, compared with only 41.0% of Whites.

- Among those at schools with more than 300 students, a higher share of African Americans than Whites talked to their parents about threats or danger.

Figure 8. Percentage of Students in Grades 6 to 12 Who Reported Talking With Their Parents About Threats or Danger at School by School Characteristics: 1993

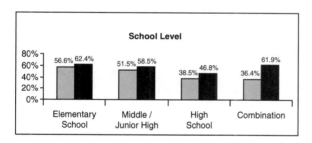

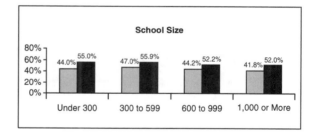

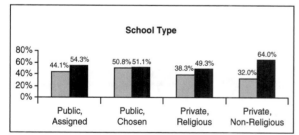

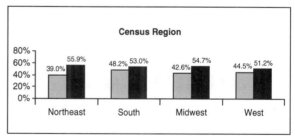

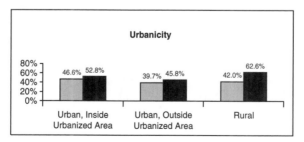

Source: National Household Education Survey, 1993 School Safety & Discipline Component.

Table 8. Percentage of Students in Grades 6 to 12 Who Reported Talking With Their Parents About Threats or Danger at School by School Characteristics, Race, and Sex: 1993

(weighted sample size in parentheses)

Characteristic	Total	Male	Female	White, Non-Hispanic Total	Male	Female	African American, Non-Hispanic Total	Male	Female	Hispanic Total	Male	Female	Other Total	Male	Female
Total *** +++	100.0%	100.0%	100.0%	100.0%	100.0%	100.0%	100.0%	100.0%	100.0%	100.0%	100.0%	100.0%	100.0%	100.0%	100.0%
	(23,810,309)	(11,926,918)	(11,883,391)	(16,721,186)	(8,353,179)	(8,368,007)	(3,745,525)	(1,860,254)	(1,885,271)	(2,598,884)	(1,359,295)	(1,239,589)	(744,714)	(354,190)	(390,524)
Talk to Parents about	44.3%	39.1%	49.6%	40.9%	35.0%	46.9%	53.5%	52.0%	55.1%	52.4%	44.7%	60.8%	46.2%	45.3%	47.0%
Threats or Danger	(10,554,696)	(4,658,030)	(5,896,666)	(6,843,806)	(2,922,690)	(3,921,116)	(2,005,058)	(967,013)	(1,038,045)	(1,361,961)	(607,837)	(754,124)	(343,871)	(160,490)	(183,381)
School Level															
Elementary +	56.6%	53.7%	59.6%	52.0%	47.2%	57.3%	62.4%	70.0%	54.3%	69.6%	66.0%	73.5%	63.4%	57.3%	66.4%
	(1,496,200)	(726,913)	(769,287)	(916,052)	(432,675)	(483,377)	(251,220)	(146,572)	(104,648)	(261,607)	(127,273)	(134,334)	(67,321)	(20,392)	(46,929)
Middle/Junior High ** ++	51.5%	47.5%	55.8%	48.4%	44.9%	52.0%	58.5%	54.0%	63.8%	59.6%	53.0%	68.2%	47.5%	37.8%	55.8%
	(3,819,053)	(1,827,911)	(1,991,142)	(2,432,687)	(1,142,572)	(1,290,115)	(769,031)	(387,216)	(381,816)	(515,799)	(261,130)	(254,669)	(101,536)	(36,993)	(64,543)
High School *** +++	38.5%	31.3%	45.2%	35.9%	28.3%	43.0%	46.8%	43.5%	49.5%	43.7%	31.2%	56.1%	38.0%	41.5%	34.6%
	(4,364,738)	(1,713,155)	(2,651,582)	(2,880,721)	(1,105,211)	(1,775,510)	(837,361)	(355,634)	(481,727)	(522,210)	(185,096)	(337,114)	(124,447)	(67,215)	(57,231)
Combination *** +++	36.4%	31.3%	41.9%	32.3%	24.4%	40.7%	61.9%	66.3%	57.7%	38.3%	43.0%	33.8%	52.0%	61.3%	37.9%
	(874,706)	(390,051)	(484,654)	(614,347)	(242,233)	(372,114)	(147,445)	(77,591)	(69,854)	(62,346)	(34,339)	(28,007)	(50,568)	(35,889)	(14,679)
School Type															
Public, Assigned *** +++	44.1%	38.6%	49.7%	41.0%	34.6%	47.3%	54.3%	53.1%	55.6%	52.0%	44.7%	60.4%	44.4%	43.0%	45.6%
	(8,552,139)	(3,765,543)	(4,786,596)	(5,744,538)	(2,420,113)	(3,324,425)	(1,499,469)	(748,049)	(751,420)	(1,075,837)	(492,784)	(583,054)	(232,294)	(104,597)	(127,697)
Public, Chosen	50.8%	46.2%	55.2%	47.5%	43.9%	51.1%	51.1%	45.8%	55.9%	61.0%	53.6%	68.6%	50.5%	49.8%	51.3%
	(1,312,768)	(587,898)	(724,869)	(592,490)	(275,626)	(316,864)	(422,741)	(178,104)	(244,637)	(229,408)	(101,803)	(127,605)	(68,129)	(32,365)	(35,764)
Private, Religious	38.3%	35.1%	41.3%	36.3%	33.6%	39.1%	49.3%	62.3%	43.3%	37.0%	20.2%	48.4%	56.7%	55.2%	58.3%
	(588,850)	(257,408)	(331,443)	(433,463)	(201,159)	(232,304)	(64,766)	(25,940)	(38,826)	(54,703)	(12,128)	(42,575)	(35,919)	(18,181)	(17,738)
Private, Non-Religious *	32.0%	26.8%	38.5%	28.5%	19.1%	38.9%	64.0%	68.9%	47.9%	29.0%	18.5%	100.0%	32.8%	41.4%	21.7%
	(100,939)	(47,181)	(53,758)	(73,316)	(25,793)	(47,523)	(18,082)	(14,920)	(3,162)	(2,013)	(1,122)	(891)	(7,529)	(5,347)	(2,182)
Number of Students															
Under 300	44.0%	42.5%	45.5%	42.5%	41.5%	43.4%	55.0%	53.0%	57.4%	49.4%	37.2%	61.0%	31.6%	49.5%	15.4%
	(1,141,920)	(541,854)	(600,066)	(852,006)	(405,945)	(446,061)	(128,221)	(66,891)	(61,330)	(135,442)	(49,465)	(85,977)	(26,251)	(19,554)	(6,698)
300 to 599 *** +++	47.0%	41.5%	52.6%	43.3%	36.5%	50.4%	55.9%	57.2%	54.5%	59.1%	50.2%	67.6%	45.6%	45.9%	45.2%
	(3,646,799)	(1,649,508)	(1,997,291)	(2,391,254)	(1,025,830)	(1,365,425)	(690,837)	(377,509)	(313,328)	(458,772)	(190,639)	(268,134)	(105,936)	(55,531)	(50,405)
600 to 999 *** +++	44.2%	38.2%	50.0%	39.9%	33.1%	46.5%	52.2%	48.7%	55.5%	58.2%	53.4%	64.4%	58.4%	52.3%	61.8%
	(2,708,155)	(1,154,903)	(1,553,252)	(1,742,015)	(712,461)	(1,029,554)	(541,463)	(240,063)	(301,400)	(328,747)	(171,556)	(157,191)	(95,931)	(30,823)	(65,108)
1,000 or More *** +++	41.8%	35.9%	47.7%	38.5%	32.2%	44.7%	52.0%	48.7%	54.9%	44.6%	37.3%	53.0%	43.7%	40.5%	47.0%
	(3,057,822)	(1,311,765)	(1,746,057)	(1,858,531)	(778,455)	(1,080,076)	(644,537)	(282,550)	(361,987)	(439,001)	(196,178)	(242,823)	(115,753)	(54,582)	(61,171)
Urbanicity															
Urban, Inside *** +++ Urbanized Area	46.6%	40.6%	52.4%	42.4%	35.9%	48.9%	52.8%	49.9%	55.5%	54.4%	45.8%	63.4%	48.9%	47.1%	50.4%
	(6,486,665)	(2,816,812)	(3,669,853)	(3,605,876)	(1,531,643)	(2,074,233)	(1,505,854)	(693,193)	(812,661)	(1,114,781)	(479,200)	(635,581)	(260,154)	(112,776)	(147,379)
Urban, Outside ++ Urbanized Area	39.7%	35.1%	44.7%	37.5%	32.7%	42.8%	45.8%	45.8%	45.8%	50.0%	40.4%	63.7%	42.4%	50.7%	34.9%
	(1,414,251)	(649,491)	(764,760)	(1,031,897)	(472,863)	(559,033)	(163,775)	(68,367)	(95,408)	(172,564)	(82,157)	(90,407)	(46,015)	(26,104)	(19,912)
Rural *** +++	42.0%	37.9%	46.1%	40.3%	34.7%	45.6%	62.6%	63.6%	61.2%	36.3%	42.3%	29.4%	36.1%	34.2%	39.0%
	(2,653,780)	(1,191,727)	(1,462,053)	(2,206,034)	(918,184)	(1,287,850)	(335,428)	(205,452)	(129,976)	(74,616)	(46,480)	(28,136)	(37,702)	(21,611)	(16,091)
Census Region															
Northeast *** +++	39.0%	31.9%	46.7%	35.5%	29.7%	42.2%	55.9%	48.0%	61.1%	41.5%	30.9%	53.0%	55.4%	43.1%	68.8%
	(1,695,866)	(719,918)	(975,948)	(1,188,947)	(534,763)	(654,184)	(280,675)	(95,930)	(184,746)	(141,099)	(54,681)	(86,417)	(85,145)	(34,544)	(50,601)
South ** +++	48.2%	42.9%	53.3%	45.4%	37.7%	52.8%	53.0%	54.0%	51.9%	54.6%	46.2%	61.6%	46.4%	48.3%	44.7%
	(4,051,494)	(1,784,272)	(2,267,222)	(2,420,138)	(993,070)	(1,427,068)	(1,141,474)	(595,341)	(546,133)	(413,248)	(159,199)	(254,049)	(76,634)	(36,661)	(39,973)
Midwest *** +	42.6%	39.2%	45.8%	40.2%	36.8%	43.4%	54.7%	50.8%	59.0%	52.6%	50.1%	54.9%	46.2%	41.8%	51.3%
	(2,499,494)	(1,125,815)	(1,373,679)	(1,935,162)	(853,903)	(1,081,259)	(399,742)	(195,733)	(204,009)	(111,962)	(50,543)	(61,418)	(52,629)	(25,636)	(26,993)
West * +++	44.5%	38.9%	50.4%	40.3%	33.9%	46.6%	51.2%	46.4%	55.7%	54.0%	46.6%	63.8%	41.5%	46.5%	37.6%
	(2,307,841)	(1,028,025)	(1,279,816)	(1,299,559)	(540,954)	(758,605)	(183,166)	(80,009)	(103,157)	(695,653)	(343,413)	(352,239)	(129,463)	(63,649)	(65,815)

Notes:
*** Test of statistical significance compares African Americans with Whites. *** p <.001, ** p <.01, * p <.05.
+++ Test of statistical significance compares White boys with White girls. +++ p <.001, ++ p <.01, + p <.05.
~~~ Test of statistical significance compares African American boys with African American girls. ~~~ p <.001, ~~ p <.01, ~ p <.05.
Tests of statistical significance calculated using adjusted sample weight to control for influence of large sample sizes.
Student's residence determined by ZIP code. An Urbanized Area (UA) comprises a place (e.g., city, village) and adjacent densely settled surrounding territory that together have a population of at least 50,000. "Urban, outside Urbanized Area" includes incorporated and unincorporated places outside of UA with population of at least 2,500. "Rural" represents all other places.
Source: National Household Education Survey, 1993 School Safety & Discipline Component.

- At urban (52.8% versus 42.4%) and rural (62.6% versus 40.3%) schools, but not at suburban schools (45.8% versus 37.5%), a higher share of African Americans than Whites talked with their parents about threats or danger.

- Regardless of region, a higher share of African Americans than Whites discussed threats or danger at school with their parents.

ASPECTS OF SCHOOL SAFETY

Weapons in School

Overall, 41.8% students in grades 6 to 12 reported that they had heard of or knew of other students who brought weapons to school.

- A higher percentage of African American students than White students reported that other students brought weapons to school (48.2% versus 40.8%).

- **Figure 9** shows that among high school students, the percentage of African Americans who reported that others brought weapons to school was comparable to the percentage of all students (51.0% versus 48.8%).

- **Table 9** shows that a higher percentage of African Americans than Whites reported that other students had weapons at elementary schools (35.6% versus 22.5%) and middle and junior high schools (47.3% versus 39.8%).

Figure 9. Percentage of Students in Grades 6 to 12 Who Reported That Other Students Bring Weapons to School: 1993

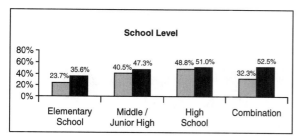

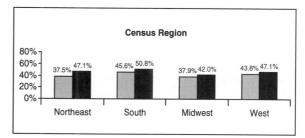

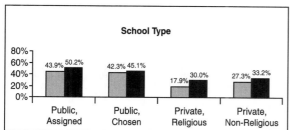

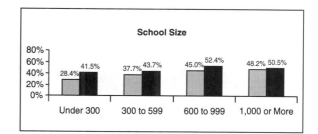

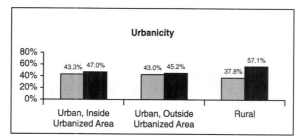

Source: National Household Education Survey, 1993 School Safety & Discipline Component.

Table 9. Percentage of Students in Grades 6 to 12 Who Reported That Other Students Bring Weapons to School by Race and Sex: 1993
(weighted sample size in parentheses)

Characteristic	Total	Male	Female	White, Non-Hispanic Total	Male	Female	African American, Non-Hispanic Total	Male	Female	Hispanic Total	Male	Female	Other Total	Male	Female
Total *** +++	100.0% (24,011,221)	100.0% (11,997,231)	100.0% (12,013,990)	100.0% (16,807,986)	100.0% (8,378,872)	100.0% (8,429,114)	100.0% (3,813,119)	100.0% (1,882,053)	100.0% (1,931,066)	100.0% (2,636,416)	100.0% (1,374,597)	100.0% (1,261,819)	100.0% (753,700)	100.0% (361,709)	100.0% (391,991)
Other Students Bring Weapons to School	41.8% (10,037,381)	45.2% (5,422,077)	38.4% (4,615,304)	40.8% (6,862,580)	45.1% (3,780,877)	36.6% (3,081,702)	48.2% (1,838,694)	48.9% (919,996)	47.6% (918,698)	41.3% (1,089,716)	43.3% (594,744)	39.2% (494,973)	32.7% (246,391)	35.0% (126,460)	30.6% (119,931)
Level of School															
Elementary ** +++	23.7% (627,818)	27.6% (373,206)	19.7% (254,612)	22.5% (396,282)	27.5% (252,230)	17.1% (144,052)	35.6% (143,255)	36.3% (76,019)	34.9% (67,236)	20.7% (77,879)	21.1% (40,652)	20.4% (37,226)	9.8% (10,403)	12.1% (4,305)	8.6% (6,098)
Middle/Junior High *	40.5% (3,006,407)	45.5% (1,753,183)	35.1% (1,253,224)	39.8% (1,999,184)	46.1% (1,172,393)	33.3% (826,792)	47.3% (622,168)	48.1% (344,735)	46.4% (277,433)	38.5% (333,473)	41.6% (205,028)	34.4% (128,445)	24.1% (51,581)	31.7% (31,027)	17.8% (20,554)
High School +++	48.8% (5,616,149)	52.0% (2,872,055)	45.8% (2,744,094)	48.2% (3,904,945)	52.2% (2,046,203)	44.4% (1,858,742)	51.0% (946,828)	52.8% (442,700)	49.6% (504,128)	50.0% (609,447)	52.9% (315,472)	47.2% (293,975)	46.0% (154,930)	39.9% (67,680)	52.3% (87,250)
Combination ***	32.3% (787,007)	33.4% (423,632)	31.1% (363,374)	29.3% (562,169)	31.0% (310,052)	27.3% (252,117)	52.5% (126,443)	48.3% (56,541)	56.4% (69,902)	39.3% (68,918)	36.2% (33,591)	42.6% (35,327)	30.3% (29,477)	40.0% (23,448)	15.6% (6,029)
Type of School															
Public, Assigned ***	43.9% (8,544,268)	47.8% (4,679,710)	39.9% (3,864,559)	42.9% (6,042,367)	47.6% (3,339,987)	38.3% (2,702,380)	50.2% (1,401,621)	50.9% (723,883)	49.5% (677,739)	43.5% (908,572)	46.4% (513,531)	40.3% (395,041)	36.4% (191,708)	41.6% (102,309)	31.9% (89,399)
Public, Chosen	42.3% (1,128,999)	41.7% (539,598)	42.9% (589,401)	43.6% (555,549)	46.8% (294,585)	40.4% (260,964)	45.1% (387,908)	44.9% (177,522)	45.3% (210,386)	37.5% (147,565)	28.3% (57,025)	47.2% (90,540)	27.4% (37,976)	15.5% (10,466)	38.6% (27,510)
Private, Religious	17.9% (276,844)	19.1% (140,932)	16.8% (135,913)	16.9% (202,670)	17.7% (106,286)	16.0% (96,384)	30.0% (39,794)	26.4% (11,007)	31.7% (28,787)	19.4% (28,668)	32.1% (19,276)	10.7% (9,392)	8.7% (5,714)	12.3% (4,363)	4.4% (1,350)
Private, Non-Religious	27.3% (87,270)	34.3% (61,838)	18.2% (25,432)	23.7% (61,994)	28.7% (40,020)	18.0% (21,974)	33.2% (9,371)	35.0% (7,585)	27.1% (1,787)	70.7% (4,912)	81.1% (4,912)	0.0% –	47.9% (10,994)	72.2% (9,323)	16.6% (1,671)
Number of Students at the School															
Under 300 * ~	28.4% (747,227)	29.5% (382,249)	27.4% (364,977)	26.8% (542,960)	29.7% (292,342)	24.1% (250,618)	41.5% (97,783)	29.9% (38,592)	55.4% (59,191)	30.4% (86,283)	32.6% (46,587)	28.1% (39,696)	24.3% (20,200)	12.0% (4,728)	35.5% (15,473)
300 to 599 * +++	37.7% (2,941,345)	42.4% (1,682,989)	32.8% (1,258,355)	36.3% (2,010,271)	41.3% (1,161,968)	31.1% (848,304)	43.7% (545,123)	46.7% (308,495)	40.3% (236,627)	39.4% (309,862)	41.3% (156,838)	37.7% (153,024)	32.8% (76,089)	46.0% (55,689)	18.3% (20,401)
600 to 999 *	45.0% (2,776,611)	47.4% (1,437,098)	42.8% (1,339,513)	43.9% (1,921,257)	46.2% (996,506)	41.7% (924,751)	52.4% (552,148)	54.4% (269,672)	50.6% (282,476)	43.3% (246,315)	47.3% (152,642)	38.1% (93,672)	34.3% (56,891)	31.0% (18,277)	36.2% (38,613)
1,000 or More +++	48.2% (3,572,199)	52.0% (1,919,741)	44.4% (1,652,458)	49.1% (2,388,091)	54.8% (1,330,062)	43.3% (1,058,029)	50.5% (643,640)	50.8% (303,236)	50.2% (340,404)	44.8% (447,257)	45.1% (238,676)	44.5% (208,581)	34.2% (93,211)	33.5% (47,767)	34.9% (45,444)
Urbanicity															
Urban, Inside Urbanized Area	43.3% (6,102,227)	43.9% (3,064,071)	42.7% (3,038,156)	43.3% (3,710,594)	44.6% (1,906,358)	42.1% (1,804,236)	47.0% (1,367,353)	44.7% (627,742)	49.1% (739,611)	40.9% (846,792)	41.8% (439,243)	39.9% (407,548)	32.8% (177,488)	36.7% (90,728)	29.5% (86,760)
Urban, Outside +++ Urbanized Area	43.0% (1,537,634)	49.3% (918,145)	36.1% (619,489)	42.6% (1,175,540)	50.6% (734,459)	33.7% (441,081)	45.2% (163,625)	50.1% (77,095)	41.5% (86,530)	44.0% (152,679)	44.4% (90,964)	43.5% (61,715)	42.2% (45,790)	30.4% (15,627)	52.9% (30,163)
Rural *** +++ ~~	37.8% (2,397,520)	45.6% (1,439,861)	30.0% (957,659)	36.1% (1,976,446)	43.0% (1,140,060)	29.5% (836,385)	57.1% (307,716)	66.6% (215,158)	42.9% (92,557)	41.1% (90,246)	53.8% (64,537)	25.8% (25,709)	22.1% (23,113)	31.8% (20,105)	7.3% (3,007)
Census Region															
Northeast * +++	37.5% (1,643,728)	42.5% (963,225)	32.1% (680,503)	36.3% (1,220,331)	42.4% (764,266)	29.2% (456,065)	47.1% (245,615)	49.9% (101,957)	45.4% (143,659)	39.6% (135,898)	39.2% (69,486)	40.0% (66,413)	26.2% (41,883)	32.5% (27,516)	19.2% (14,366)
South **	45.6% (3,871,924)	47.3% (1,985,450)	43.9% (1,886,475)	44.2% (2,374,382)	46.4% (1,232,725)	42.0% (1,141,657)	50.8% (1,106,976)	51.3% (569,501)	50.3% (537,476)	43.1% (336,179)	44.4% (158,804)	42.0% (177,374)	32.9% (54,387)	32.2% (24,419)	33.5% (29,968)
Midwest +++	37.9% (2,240,951)	42.1% (1,213,610)	33.8% (1,027,341)	36.9% (1,785,370)	42.3% (985,439)	31.8% (799,931)	42.0% (315,452)	41.6% (162,240)	42.4% (153,212)	53.1% (113,033)	53.1% (53,607)	53.1% (59,426)	23.8% (27,095)	20.1% (12,324)	28.1% (14,772)
West +	43.8% (2,280,778)	47.5% (1,259,793)	39.9% (1,020,985)	45.9% (1,482,495)	50.1% (798,447)	41.8% (684,048)	47.1% (170,650)	48.7% (86,298)	45.5% (84,352)	38.8% (504,606)	42.3% (312,846)	34.1% (191,760)	39.1% (123,026)	44.5% (62,201)	34.8% (60,825)

Notes:

"–" indicates sample size too small to estimate.

*** Test of statistical significance compares African Americans with Whites. *** p <.001, ** p <.01, * p <.05.

+++ Test of statistical significance compares White boys with White girls. +++ p <.001, ++ p <.01, + p <.05.

~~~ Test of statistical significance compares African American boys with African American girls. ~~~ p <.001, ~~ p <.01, ~ p <.05.

Tests of statistical significance calculated using adjusted sample weight to control for influence of large sample sizes.

Student's residence determined by ZIP code. An Urbanized Area (UA) comprises a place (e.g., city, village) and adjacent densely settled surrounding territory that together have a population of at least 50,000. "Urban, outside Urbanized Area" includes incorporated and unincorporated places outside of UA with population of at least 2,500. "Rural" represents all other places.

Source: National Household Education Survey, 1993 School Safety & Discipline Component.

The share of public school students (42.3% to 43.9%, depending on school type) who reported that other students brought weapons to school was higher than the share of private school students (17.9% to 27.3%, depending on type).

- Comparable percentages of African Americans and Whites at public chosen schools reported that other students brought weapons to school (45.1% versus 43.6%).

- The percentage of African Americans who reported that others brought weapons to school was higher than the percentage of Whites among those attending public assigned schools (50.2% versus 42.9%).

The share of students who reported that other students brought weapons to school appeared to increase with school size from 28.4% at schools with fewer than 300 students to 48.2% of students at schools with 1,000 or more students.

- At schools with 1,000 or more students, the percentage of African Americans who reported that other students had weapons was comparable to the percentage of Whites (50.5% versus 49.1%).

- Among rural school students, the percentage of African Americans who reported that students had weapons was higher than the percentage of Whites (57.1% versus 36.1%).

- Comparable percentages of African Americans and Whites at urban schools (47.0% versus 43.3%) and suburban schools (45.2% versus 42.6%) reported that other students in their schools had weapons.

- A higher proportion of African Americans than Whites reported that other students brought weapons to school in the northeast (47.1% versus 36.3%) and in the south (50.8% versus 44.2%).

Fighting Gangs

In 1993, about one-third (35.2%) of students in grades 6 to 12 reported that other students in their schools belonged to fighting gangs. The percentage who reported that other students belonged to fighting gangs was not related to students' sex among African Americans or Whites.

- **Table 10** shows that a higher share of African Americans than of Whites reported that others in their schools belonged to fighting gangs (41.5% versus 31.0%).

- A higher share of African Americans than Whites reported that others belonged to fighting gangs at elementary schools (27.5% versus 12.9%), middle and junior high schools (45.1% versus 34.1%), and combination schools (38.7% versus 11.4%).

Figure 10 shows that a higher percentage of public school students (36.6% to 41.0%, depending on type) than of private school students (10.3% to 16.3%, depending on type) had fighting gangs in their schools.

- The percentages of African Americans and Whites who reported fighting gangs were comparable among those at private religious schools (10.8% versus 9.7%) and at chosen public schools (42.8% versus 36.0%).

At schools with less than 1,000 students, a higher share of African Americans than Whites reported that others belonged to fighting gangs.

- Comparable percentages of African Americans and Whites attending schools with at least 1,000 students reported fighting gangs in their schools (44.0% versus 44.4%).

- Among urban school students, comparable shares of African Americans and Whites reported fighting gangs in their schools (42.8% versus 40.2%).

- The percentage of African Americans who reported fighting gangs in their schools was higher than the percentage of Whites at suburban schools (46.2% versus 28.9%) and rural schools (31.4% versus 17.7%).

Table 10. Percentage of Students in Grades 6 to 12 Who Reported That Other Students in Their School Belong to Fighting Gangs by Race and Sex: 1993
(weighted sample size in parentheses)

Characteristic	Total	Male	Female	White, Non-Hispanic Total	Male	Female	African American, Non-Hispanic Total	Male	Female	Hispanic Total	Male	Female	Other Total	Male	Female
Total ***	100.0% (24,011,221)	100.0% (11,997,231)	100.0% (12,013,990)	100.0% (16,807,986)	100.0% (8,378,872)	100.0% (8,429,114)	100.0% (3,813,119)	100.0% (1,882,053)	100.0% (1,931,066)	100.0% (2,636,416)	100.0% (1,374,597)	100.0% (1,261,819)	100.0% (753,700)	100.0% (361,709)	100.0% (391,991)
Other Students Belong to Fighting Gangs	35.2% (8,441,379)	35.9% (4,310,173)	34.4% (4,131,206)	31.0% (5,209,077)	31.3% (2,620,517)	30.7% (2,588,560)	41.5% (1,581,598)	42.7% (803,720)	40.3% (777,877)	51.3% (1,353,245)	53.4% (734,259)	49.1% (618,985)	39.5% (297,460)	41.9% (151,676)	37.2% (145,783)
School Level															
Elementary ***	17.3% (456,890)	19.4% (262,443)	15.1% (194,446)	12.9% (227,465)	14.5% (133,241)	11.2% (94,224)	27.5% (110,610)	31.2% (65,266)	23.5% (45,344)	26.5% (99,726)	28.4% (54,757)	24.6% (44,969)	18.0% (19,089)	25.8% (9,179)	14.0% (9,910)
Middle/Junior High *** ++	38.2% (2,834,398)	40.3% (1,553,147)	35.9% (1,281,252)	34.1% (1,713,642)	37.6% (955,322)	30.6% (758,320)	45.1% (593,588)	42.2% (302,726)	48.6% (290,862)	53.0% (459,424)	55.9% (275,481)	49.3% (183,943)	31.7% (67,744)	20.0% (19,617)	41.6% (48,127)
Senior High School	41.2% (4,745,168)	41.8% (2,308,824)	40.7% (2,436,343)	37.6% (3,048,081)	37.0% (1,451,972)	38.2% (1,596,109)	42.3% (784,244)	45.6% (382,249)	39.6% (401,996)	60.6% (738,454)	63.7% (379,785)	57.6% (358,668)	51.8% (174,389)	55.9% (94,818)	47.7% (79,570)
Combination *** +	16.6% (404,923)	14.7% (185,759)	18.8% (219,164)	11.4% (219,889)	8.0% (79,982)	15.2% (139,907)	38.7% (93,155)	45.7% (53,478)	32.0% (39,676)	31.7% (55,641)	26.2% (24,236)	37.9% (31,405)	37.2% (36,238)	47.9% (28,062)	21.1% (8,176)
Type of School															
Public, Assigned ***	36.6% (7,137,457)	37.6% (3,681,662)	35.7% (3,455,795)	32.7% (4,599,722)	33.0% (2,315,829)	32.4% (2,283,894)	42.5% (1,187,630)	42.8% (608,506)	42.3% (579,124)	54.5% (1,138,634)	58.0% (642,483)	50.6% (496,151)	40.2% (211,471)	46.7% (114,844)	34.5% (96,627)
Public, Chosen	41.0% (1,091,917)	40.3% (521,099)	41.6% (570,818)	36.0% (459,717)	36.1% (227,407)	36.0% (232,310)	42.8% (368,040)	44.9% (177,573)	41.1% (190,467)	47.7% (187,273)	41.2% (82,936)	54.4% (104,337)	55.5% (76,887)	49.3% (33,183)	61.4% (43,704)
Private, Religious	10.3% (159,685)	9.6% (70,612)	11.0% (89,074)	9.7% (115,991)	9.3% (55,699)	10.0% (60,292)	10.8% (14,358)	14.6% (6,072)	9.1% (8,287)	18.5% (27,338)	14.7% (8,841)	21.0% (18,497)	3.0% (1,997)	0.0% –	6.6% (1,997)
Private, Non-Religious *	16.3% (52,320)	20.4% (36,801)	11.1% (15,519)	12.8% (33,646)	15.5% (21,582)	9.9% (12,064)	41.0% (11,570)	53.4% (11,570)	0.0% –	0.0% –	0.0% –	0.0% –	30.9% (7,104)	28.2% (3,649)	34.4% (3,455)
Number of Students															
Under 300 ***	19.0% (499,893)	19.2% (249,541)	18.8% (250,352)	14.3% (288,542)	14.3% (141,110)	14.2% (147,432)	37.0% (87,275)	35.2% (45,414)	39.2% (41,860)	34.8% (98,854)	33.3% (47,592)	36.3% (51,262)	30.3% (25,222)	39.0% (15,425)	22.5% (9,797)
300 to 599 ***	28.7% (2,242,226)	31.6% (1,254,414)	25.8% (987,812)	23.7% (1,313,366)	25.4% (714,571)	21.9% (598,795)	38.3% (477,257)	41.2% (272,263)	34.9% (204,994)	47.3% (372,255)	59.2% (224,949)	36.3% (147,305)	34.2% (79,348)	35.3% (42,631)	33.0% (36,718)
600 to 999 **	36.3% (2,238,876)	36.4% (1,105,251)	36.2% (1,133,625)	33.0% (1,445,584)	32.3% (696,059)	33.8% (749,525)	43.2% (455,337)	48.2% (238,826)	38.8% (216,512)	47.4% (269,498)	44.6% (143,665)	51.1% (125,833)	41.3% (68,457)	45.3% (26,701)	39.1% (41,756)
1,000 or More	46.7% (3,460,383)	46.0% (1,700,966)	47.3% (1,759,417)	44.4% (2,161,585)	44.1% (1,068,777)	44.8% (1,092,808)	44.0% (561,729)	41.4% (247,217)	46.4% (314,512)	61.4% (612,638)	60.1% (318,053)	62.9% (294,585)	45.7% (124,432)	47.0% (66,919)	44.2% (57,513)
Urbanicity															
Urban, Inside Urbanized Area	42.9% (6,038,305)	44.2% (3,086,636)	41.5% (2,951,670)	40.2% (3,441,955)	41.1% (1,759,657)	39.2% (1,682,298)	42.8% (1,244,940)	44.7% (627,977)	40.9% (616,963)	54.5% (1,128,031)	56.4% (592,015)	52.5% (536,017)	41.3% (223,380)	43.3% (106,987)	39.6% (116,392)
Urban, Outside Urbanized Area ***	32.3% (1,155,399)	30.9% (575,396)	33.8% (580,003)	28.9% (796,903)	28.1% (408,260)	29.7% (388,643)	46.2% (167,528)	39.2% (60,330)	51.4% (107,198)	44.5% (154,374)	44.6% (91,440)	44.3% (62,934)	33.7% (36,594)	29.9% (15,365)	37.2% (21,229)
Rural ***	19.7% (1,247,674)	20.5% (648,141)	18.8% (599,533)	17.7% (970,220)	17.1% (452,601)	18.3% (517,619)	31.4% (169,129)	35.7% (115,413)	24.9% (53,716)	32.3% (70,839)	42.3% (50,804)	20.1% (20,035)	35.9% (37,486)	46.4% (29,324)	19.8% (8,163)
Census Region															
Northeast **	25.4% (1,115,009)	25.1% (570,358)	25.7% (544,652)	22.1% (744,250)	21.7% (391,512)	22.6% (352,738)	34.6% (180,210)	38.5% (78,678)	32.1% (101,532)	38.4% (131,876)	41.7% (73,856)	34.9% (58,021)	36.7% (58,673)	31.0% (26,312)	43.2% (32,361)
South **	32.3% (2,741,539)	31.1% (1,304,379)	33.4% (1,437,160)	29.4% (1,579,848)	28.6% (759,825)	30.2% (820,023)	36.3% (790,534)	34.9% (387,061)	37.8% (403,473)	41.2% (321,223)	36.0% (128,652)	45.6% (192,571)	30.2% (49,934)	38.0% (28,841)	23.6% (21,093)
Midwest ***	33.4% (1,979,386)	35.4% (1,020,026)	31.6% (959,361)	29.9% (1,448,198)	31.3% (729,421)	28.6% (718,777)	51.2% (384,808)	53.8% (209,839)	48.4% (174,968)	45.7% (97,248)	50.7% (51,131)	41.2% (46,117)	43.1% (49,132)	48.3% (29,634)	37.0% (19,498)
West ** ~	50.0% (2,605,444)	53.4% (1,415,411)	46.5% (1,190,033)	44.4% (1,436,781)	46.4% (739,759)	42.6% (697,021)	62.4% (226,046)	72.3% (128,142)	52.9% (97,905)	61.7% (802,897)	65.0% (480,621)	57.4% (322,276)	44.4% (139,720)	47.9% (66,889)	41.6% (72,831)

Notes:

"–" indicates sample size too small to estimate.

*** Test of statistical significance compares African Americans with Whites. *** p <.001, ** p <.01, * p <.05.

+++ Test of statistical significance compares White boys with White girls +++ p <.001, ++ p <.01, + p <.05.

~~~Test of statistical significance compares African American boys with African American girls. ~~~ p <.001, ~~ p <.01, ~ p <.05.

Tests of statistical significance calculated using adjusted sample weight to control for influence of large sample sizes.

Student's residence determined by ZIP code. An Urbanized Area (UA) comprises a place (e.g., city, village) and adjacent densely settled surrounding territory that together have a population of at least 50,000. "Urban, outside Urbanized Area" includes incorporated and unincorporated places outside of UA with population of at least 2,500. "Rural" represents all other places.

Source: National Household Education Survey, 1993 School Safety & Discipline Component.

Figure 10. Percentage of Students in Grades 6 to 12 Who Reported That Other Students in Their School Belong to Fighting Gangs: 1993

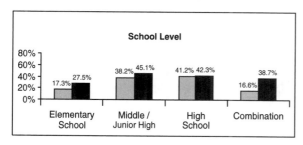

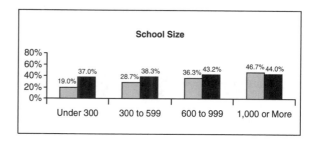

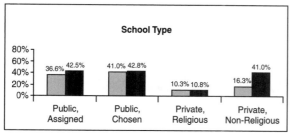

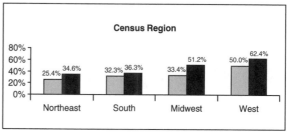

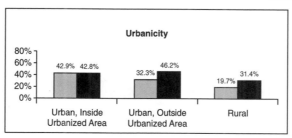

Source: National Household Education Survey, 1993 School Safety & Discipline Component.

- Regardless of region, a higher proportion of African Americans than Whites reported that other students in their schools belonged to fighting gangs: 62.4% versus 44.4% in the west; 51.2% versus 29.9% in the midwest; 36.3% versus 29.4% in the south; and 34.6% versus 22.1% in the northeast.

Drug Dealers

About one of every six (16.7%) students in grades 6 to 12 reported that they had seen or heard of others dealing drugs at school or within sight of school property within the past year. Girls and boys were equally likely to report the presence of drug dealers at their schools (15.8% versus 17.6%, overall).

- **Table 11** shows that a higher percentage of African American students than of White students reported the presence of drug dealers (20.9% versus 15.6%).

- A higher percentage of African Americans than of Whites reported drug dealers at elementary schools (12.7% versus 5.0%), middle and junior high schools (15.8% versus 10.0%), and combination schools (29.7% versus 7.9%).

Table 11. Percentage of Students in Grades 6 to 12 Who Reported Drug Dealers at School by Race and Sex: 1993

(weighted sample size in parentheses)

Characteristic	Total	Male	Female	White, Non-Hispanic Total	Male	Female	African American, Non-Hispanic Total	Male	Female	Hispanic Total	Male	Female	Other Total	Male	Female
Total ***	100.0%	100.0%	100.0%	100.0%	100.0%	100.0%	100.0%	100.0%	100.0%	100.0%	100.0%	100.0%	100.0%	100.0%	100.0%
	(24,011,221)	(11,997,231)	(12,013,990)	(16,807,986)	(8,378,872)	(8,429,114)	(3,813,119)	(1,882,053)	(1,931,066)	(2,636,416)	(1,374,597)	(1,261,819)	(753,700)	(361,709)	(391,991)
Drug Dealers at School	16.7%	17.6%	15.8%	15.6%	16.5%	14.8%	20.9%	21.4%	20.5%	18.9%	20.1%	17.6%	11.7%	14.1%	9.5%
	(4,010,606)	(2,109,373)	(1,901,233)	(2,624,787)	(1,378,738)	(1,246,049)	(798,252)	(402,810)	(395,442)	(499,140)	(276,687)	(222,453)	(88,428)	(51,138)	(37,290)
Level of School															
Elementary **	6.2%	7.5%	5.0%	5.0%	5.7%	4.1%	12.7%	16.6%	8.5%	5.4%	5.3%	5.5%	6.5%	10.2%	4.6%
	(165,222)	(101,076)	(64,146)	(87,128)	(52,585)	(34,543)	(51,019)	(34,694)	(16,325)	(20,185)	(10,172)	(10,012)	(6,890)	(3,624)	(3,266)
Middle/Junior High ** +	10.8%	11.9%	9.6%	10.0%	11.7%	8.2%	15.8%	14.2%	17.6%	10.8%	12.0%	9.1%	0.0%	0.0%	0.0%
	(803,607)	(460,180)	(343,426)	(503,087)	(298,876)	(204,211)	(207,303)	(102,133)	(105,170)	(93,217)	(59,172)	(34,045)	–	–	–
High School	24.3%	25.8%	22.9%	23.2%	24.5%	22.1%	25.3%	26.5%	24.3%	30.4%	33.2%	27.7%	22.7%	26.7%	18.6%
	(2,797,367)	(1,423,821)	(1,373,547)	(1,882,343)	(958,836)	(923,506)	(468,465)	(221,917)	(246,548)	(370,227)	(197,738)	(172,489)	(76,332)	(45,329)	(31,003)
Combination ***	10.0%	9.8%	10.3%	7.9%	6.9%	9.1%	29.7%	37.7%	22.1%	8.8%	10.4%	7.1%	5.3%	3.7%	7.8%
	(244,410)	(124,297)	(120,114)	(152,229)	(68,441)	(83,788)	(71,465)	(44,067)	(27,398)	(15,510)	(9,605)	(5,906)	(5,206)	(2,185)	(3,021)
Type of School															
Public, Assigned ***	17.6%	18.7%	16.5%	16.6%	17.7%	15.4%	22.1%	22.0%	22.3%	19.7%	21.1%	18.1%	13.5%	17.1%	10.3%
	(3,431,784)	(1,831,670)	(1,600,114)	(2,330,745)	(1,242,173)	(1,088,572)	(618,590)	(313,300)	(305,291)	(411,484)	(234,086)	(177,399)	(70,964)	(42,111)	(28,853)
Public, Chosen	17.1%	16.4%	17.7%	15.9%	14.2%	17.5%	18.5%	20.1%	17.1%	20.7%	18.1%	23.5%	8.4%	9.2%	7.6%
	(454,696)	(211,774)	(242,923)	(202,535)	(89,477)	(113,058)	(159,051)	(79,656)	(79,395)	(81,511)	(36,457)	(45,054)	(11,599)	(6,184)	(5,415)
Private, Religious	6.7%	7.8%	5.6%	6.5%	7.3%	5.6%	11.5%	10.8%	11.8%	4.2%	10.2%	0.0%	6.4%	8.0%	4.4%
	(103,111)	(57,317)	(45,795)	(77,499)	(43,811)	(33,688)	(15,275)	(4,518)	(10,756)	(6,144)	(6,144)	–	(4,193)	(2,843)	(1,350)
Private, Non-Religious	6.6%	4.8%	8.9%	5.3%	2.3%	8.8%	18.9%	24.6%	0.0%	0.0%	0.0%	0.0%	7.3%	0.0%	16.6%
	(21,015)	(8,613)	(12,402)	(14,007)	(3,277)	(10,731)	(5,336)	(5,336)	–	–	–	–	(1,671)	–	(1,671)
Number of Students															
Under 300	9.0%	8.1%	9.9%	8.7%	7.5%	9.8%	14.4%	10.4%	19.3%	9.0%	12.1%	5.9%	0.0%	0.0%	0.0%
	(235,584)	(104,511)	(131,073)	(175,958)	(73,849)	(102,109)	(34,045)	(13,406)	(20,639)	(25,582)	(17,256)	(8,325)	–	–	–
300 to 599 **	14.0%	14.3%	13.7%	12.5%	12.7%	12.2%	19.5%	20.2%	18.6%	16.5%	15.9%	17.1%	12.1%	14.3%	9.6%
	(1,092,560)	(569,136)	(523,424)	(691,935)	(358,176)	(333,759)	(242,804)	(133,306)	(109,498)	(129,805)	(60,384)	(69,421)	(28,016)	(17,270)	(10,746)
600 to 999 *	17.4%	18.8%	16.0%	16.3%	17.6%	15.0%	22.5%	25.6%	19.7%	18.0%	18.6%	17.2%	12.1%	10.5%	12.9%
	(1,072,195)	(571,861)	(500,334)	(713,054)	(378,942)	(334,112)	(236,848)	(126,835)	(110,013)	(102,330)	(59,919)	(42,411)	(19,962)	(6,164)	(13,798)
1,000 or More	21.7%	23.4%	20.1%	21.5%	23.4%	19.5%	22.3%	21.6%	22.9%	24.2%	26.3%	21.8%	14.8%	19.5%	9.8%
	(1,610,267)	(863,866)	(746,401)	(1,043,839)	(567,770)	(476,069)	(284,555)	(129,264)	(155,292)	(241,423)	(139,128)	(102,295)	(40,450)	(27,704)	(12,746)
Urbanicity															
Urban, Inside Urbanized Area *	18.9%	20.1%	17.7%	18.1%	19.2%	17.0%	21.9%	22.7%	21.3%	19.9%	21.5%	18.3%	11.1%	14.7%	8.0%
	(2,662,980)	(1,401,357)	(1,261,623)	(1,551,989)	(821,254)	(730,735)	(639,031)	(318,248)	(320,783)	(412,106)	(225,493)	(186,613)	(59,853)	(36,362)	(23,492)
Urban, Outside Urbanized Area	14.7%	13.2%	16.4%	14.4%	13.6%	15.3%	14.3%	8.0%	19.0%	17.2%	14.2%	21.5%	16.9%	15.5%	18.2%
	(527,209)	(246,344)	(280,866)	(397,338)	(196,992)	(200,346)	(51,970)	(12,268)	(39,702)	(59,584)	(29,122)	(30,461)	(18,318)	(7,962)	(10,356)
Rural **	12.9%	14.6%	11.3%	12.3%	13.6%	11.1%	19.9%	22.4%	16.2%	12.5%	18.4%	5.4%	9.8%	10.8%	8.3%
	(820,417)	(461,672)	(358,745)	(675,460)	(360,492)	(314,968)	(107,251)	(72,294)	(34,956)	(27,450)	(22,072)	(5,378)	(10,257)	(6,815)	(3,442)
Census Region															
Northeast ~~	17.1%	18.9%	15.2%	16.9%	17.4%	16.2%	19.5%	31.8%	11.5%	16.9%	18.8%	14.8%	15.2%	19.9%	9.8%
	(750,763)	(429,455)	(321,309)	(567,269)	(314,326)	(252,943)	(101,358)	(64,995)	(36,363)	(57,926)	(33,254)	(24,672)	(24,210)	(16,879)	(7,331)
South * ++	15.8%	16.7%	15.0%	15.0%	17.7%	12.3%	18.8%	16.1%	21.6%	15.9%	13.1%	18.2%	4.5%	5.5%	3.6%
	(1,346,212)	(700,472)	(645,740)	(805,667)	(470,375)	(335,292)	(409,319)	(179,019)	(230,300)	(123,798)	(46,868)	(76,931)	(7,428)	(4,210)	(3,218)
Midwest ***	14.3%	15.2%	13.5%	13.3%	13.4%	13.2%	22.8%	26.8%	18.5%	5.8%	7.5%	4.2%	19.0%	22.3%	15.2%
	(847,156)	(436,997)	(410,159)	(641,785)	(311,037)	(330,747)	(171,420)	(104,694)	(66,727)	(12,276)	(7,609)	(4,667)	(21,675)	(13,657)	(8,019)
West **	20.5%	20.5%	20.5%	18.9%	17.7%	20.0%	32.0%	30.5%	33.5%	23.5%	25.6%	20.7%	11.2%	11.7%	10.7%
	(1,066,475)	(542,450)	(524,025)	(610,066)	(282,999)	(327,067)	(116,155)	(54,102)	(62,052)	(305,139)	(188,957)	(116,183)	(35,114)	(16,392)	(18,722)

Notes:

"–" indicates sample size too small to estimate.

*** Test of statistical significance compares African Americans with Whites. *** p <.001, ** p <.01, * p <.05.

+++ Test of statistical significance compares White boys with White girls. +++ p <.001, ++ p <.01, + p <.05.

~~~Test of statistical significance compares African American boys with African American girls. ~~~ p <.001, ~~ p <.01, ~ p <.05.

Tests of statistical significance calculated using adjusted sample weight to control for influence of large sample sizes.

Student's residence determined by ZIP code. An Urbanized Area (UA) comprises a place (e.g., city, village) and adjacent densely settled surrounding territory that together have a population of at least 50,000. "Urban, outside Urbanized Area" includes incorporated and unincorporated places outside of UA with population of at least 2,500. "Rural" represents all other places.

Source: National Household Education Survey, 1993 School Safety & Discipline Component.

Figure 11 shows that, on average, the percentage who reported drug dealers at their schools increased with the school's enrollment, from 9.0% at schools with fewer than 300 students to 14.0% at schools with 300 to 599 students, 17.4% at schools with 600 to 999 students, and 21.7% at schools with 1,000 or more students.

- A higher percentage of African Americans than Whites reported drug dealers among students at schools with 300 to 599 students (19.5% versus 12.5%) and 600 to 999 students (22.5% versus 16.3%).

- The proportion of African Americans who reported drug dealers in their schools was higher than the proportion of Whites at urban schools (21.9% versus 18.1%) and rural schools (19.9% versus 12.3%), but comparable to the proportion of Whites at suburban schools (14.3% versus 14.4%).

- Comparable shares of African Americans and Whites reported drug dealers in their schools in the northeast (19.5% versus 16.9%).

- But, a higher share of African Americans than of Whites reported drug dealers in the south

Figure 11. Percentage of Students in Grades 6 to 12
Who Reported Drug Dealers at School: 1993

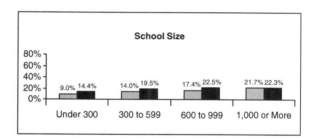

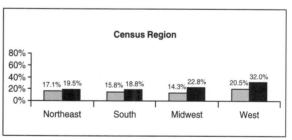

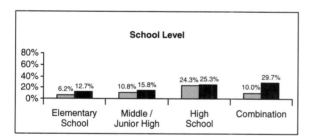

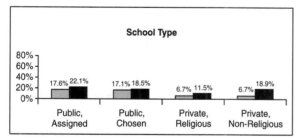

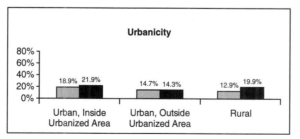

Source: National Household Education Survey, 1993 School Safety & Discipline Component.

(18.8% versus 15.0%), midwest (22.8% versus 13.3%), and the west (32.0% versus 18.9%).

SCHOOL MEASURES TO ENSURE STUDENT SAFETY

Teacher Supervision of Hallways

About two-thirds (66.8%) of students in grades 6 to 12 reported that their teachers supervise school hallways to ensure their safety.

- **Table 12** shows that a higher percentage of African American students than of White students reported teacher supervision of hallways (74.6% versus 65.5%).

- A higher share of African Americans than Whites reported teacher supervision of hallways at elementary schools (64.9% versus 46.2%), middle and junior high schools (78.7% versus 71.4%), high schools (73.4% versus 68.4%), and combination schools (78.5% versus 55.2%).

- **Figure 12** shows that comparable percentages of African Americans and all students reported teacher supervision of school hallways at private religious schools (40.7% versus 42.7%).

- The percentage of African Americans who reported teacher supervision of hallways was higher than the percentage of Whites for those attending assigned public schools (76.5% versus 68.2%) and chosen public schools (73.7% versus 62.6%).

- A higher share of African Americans than of Whites reported teacher supervision of hallways at suburban schools (84.2% versus 63.8%), urban schools (73.3% versus 68.8%), and rural schools (75.6% versus 64.3%).

- Comparable shares of African American students than of White students reported teacher supervision of hallways in the northeast (67.7% versus 65.2%) and the west (62.0% versus 54.7%).

- Higher shares of African Americans than Whites reported teacher supervision of hallways in the midwest (76.0% versus 64.3%) and the south (77.9% versus 73.2%).

Limits on Restroom Access

About one-third (35.9%) of students in grades 6 to 12 reported that access to school restrooms was limited to ensure the safety of students.

- **Table 13** shows that a higher percentage of African American students than of White students reported that access to school restrooms was limited (43.0% versus 32.3%).

Regardless of race, a higher percentage of elementary (44.8%) and middle (44.9%) school students than of high school (29.8%) and combination school (27.6%) students reported that restroom access was limited. At all school levels, a higher share of African Americans than Whites reported limited restroom access.

- Among students attending assigned public schools, 44.5% of African Americans, and 33.4% of Whites, had limited restroom access.

Figure 13 shows that school size was not related to restroom access. At schools with more than 300 students, a higher percentage of African Americans than Whites reported limited restroom access.

- **Table 13** shows that differences varied from 44.3% of African Americans and 33.3% of Whites at schools with 300 to 599 students to 47.1% of African Americans and 31.6% of Whites at schools with 600 to 999 students.

- The percentage of African American students who reported limited restroom access was higher than the percentage of White students at both urban schools (45.6% versus 34.5%) and suburban schools (39.1% versus 30.6%) and comparable to the percentage of White students at rural schools (31.9% versus 29.9%).

- The proportion of African American students who reported limits on restroom access was

Table 12. Percentage of Students in Grades 6 to 12 Who Report Teacher Supervision of School Hallways by School Characteristics, Race, and Sex: 1993

(weighted sample size in parentheses)

Characteristic	Total	Male	Female	White, Non-Hispanic Total	Male	Female	African American, Non-Hispanic Total	Male	Female	Hispanic Total	Male	Female	Other Total	Male	Female
Total ***	100.0% (24,011,221)	100.0% (11,997,231)	100.0% (12,013,990)	100.0% (16,807,986)	100.0% (8,378,872)	100.0% (8,429,114)	100.0% (3,813,119)	100.0% (1,882,053)	100.0% (1,931,066)	100.0% (2,636,416)	100.0% (1,374,597)	100.0% (1,261,819)	100.0% (753,700)	100.0% (361,709)	100.0% (391,991)
Teacher Supervision of Hallways	66.8% (16,050,066)	67.1% (8,049,134)	66.6% (8,000,932)	65.5% (11,004,485)	65.6% (5,496,857)	65.3% (5,507,627)	74.6% (2,845,947)	75.5% (1,420,263)	73.8% (1,425,684)	63.8% (1,681,072)	63.1% (866,796)	64.5% (814,276)	68.8% (518,562)	73.3% (265,217)	64.6% (253,345)
School Level															
Elementary ***	49.4% (1,306,697)	50.6% (684,446)	48.2% (622,251)	46.2% (812,698)	47.4% (434,209)	44.8% (378,489)	64.9% (261,275)	62.7% (131,386)	67.3% (129,889)	50.7% (190,482)	53.9% (103,957)	47.3% (86,525)	39.8% (42,243)	41.9% (14,895)	38.7% (27,348)
Middle/Junior High **	72.8% (5,399,671)	71.2% (2,741,752)	74.5% (2,657,919)	71.4% (3,587,716)	69.6% (1,771,888)	73.2% (1,815,828)	78.7% (1,034,282)	79.6% (570,422)	77.6% (463,859)	70.5% (610,357)	63.9% (314,998)	79.1% (295,359)	78.3% (167,316)	86.3% (84,443)	71.6% (82,873)
High School *	68.8% (7,920,406)	70.0% (3,865,168)	67.7% (4,055,239)	68.4% (5,542,997)	69.9% (2,740,824)	67.0% (2,802,174)	73.4% (1,361,290)	74.6% (625,896)	72.4% (735,394)	62.2% (758,694)	62.6% (373,101)	61.9% (385,592)	76.5% (257,425)	73.9% (125,347)	79.2% (132,079)
Combination ***	58.5% (1,423,292)	59.8% (757,768)	57.0% (665,524)	55.2% (1,061,074)	55.1% (549,937)	55.4% (511,137)	78.5% (189,101)	79.1% (92,559)	77.9% (96,542)	69.2% (121,539)	80.6% (74,740)	56.5% (46,799)	53.0% (51,579)	69.2% (40,532)	28.5% (11,047)
School Type															
Public, Assigned ***	69.3% (13,490,497)	69.2% (6,776,538)	69.3% (6,713,959)	68.2% (9,598,927)	68.5% (4,803,281)	67.9% (4,795,646)	76.5% (2,137,732)	75.0% (1,067,232)	78.2% (1,070,501)	66.7% (1,393,626)	66.3% (734,147)	67.2% (659,478)	68.4% (360,212)	69.8% (171,878)	67.2% (188,334)
Public, Chosen ** ~	66.4% (1,771,265)	66.8% (863,629)	66.1% (907,636)	62.6% (797,945)	60.3% (379,378)	64.8% (418,566)	73.7% (633,513)	80.2% (317,279)	68.2% (316,234)	58.0% (227,768)	52.8% (106,258)	63.4% (121,510)	80.9% (112,039)	90.2% (60,713)	72.1% (51,326)
Private, Religious	42.7% (661,345)	43.5% (320,129)	42.1% (341,216)	42.1% (506,038)	41.0% (245,524)	43.3% (260,515)	40.7% (53,905)	48.4% (20,176)	37.1% (33,729)	38.3% (56,754)	39.1% (23,467)	37.8% (33,287)	67.8% (44,648)	87.5% (30,963)	45.0% (13,686)
Private, Non-Religious	39.7% (126,959)	49.3% (88,838)	27.3% (38,121)	38.8% (101,575)	49.2% (68,675)	26.9% (32,900)	73.6% (20,797)	71.9% (15,577)	79.1% (5,221)	42.1% (2,924)	48.3% (2,924)	0.0% –	7.2% (1,663)	12.9% (1,663)	0.0% –
Number of Students															
Under 300	56.6% (1,486,326)	58.9% (763,742)	54.3% (722,584)	53.9% (1,091,176)	56.9% (560,954)	51.0% (530,222)	59.5% (140,277)	56.3% (72,564)	63.4% (67,713)	65.6% (186,352)	69.3% (99,032)	61.9% (87,319)	82.4% (68,522)	78.9% (31,192)	85.6% (37,330)
300 to 599 ***	62.6% (4,883,861)	63.8% (2,533,063)	61.3% (2,350,799)	60.2% (3,332,629)	61.4% (1,725,294)	58.9% (1,607,336)	74.2% (925,673)	75.7% (499,948)	72.5% (425,726)	62.8% (493,748)	61.2% (232,559)	64.3% (261,189)	56.7% (131,811)	62.2% (75,263)	50.8% (56,549)
600 to 999 **	69.6% (4,289,157)	72.9% (2,211,623)	66.3% (2,077,534)	69.1% (3,022,818)	71.2% (1,536,613)	66.9% (1,486,206)	77.7% (818,895)	81.7% (404,796)	74.1% (414,099)	61.0% (346,957)	67.7% (218,280)	52.3% (128,677)	60.7% (100,487)	88.2% (51,935)	45.5% (48,552)
1,000 or More ++	72.7% (5,390,721)	68.8% (2,540,706)	76.7% (2,850,016)	73.1% (3,557,861)	69.0% (1,673,997)	77.2% (1,883,863)	75.4% (961,103)	74.2% (442,956)	76.4% (518,147)	65.6% (654,016)	59.9% (316,925)	72.0% (337,090)	79.9% (217,742)	75.0% (106,827)	85.2% (110,915)
Urbanicity															
Urban, Inside Urbanized Area ** +	68.0% (9,586,434)	66.7% (4,652,062)	69.4% (4,934,372)	66.8% (5,718,357)	64.7% (2,766,281)	68.9% (2,952,076)	73.3% (2,133,368)	73.5% (1,032,762)	73.0% (1,100,605)	64.7% (1,339,185)	63.7% (668,443)	65.7% (670,742)	73.1% (395,524)	74.7% (184,575)	71.8% (210,949)
Urban, Outside Urbanized Area ***	64.9% (2,323,232)	65.7% (1,223,112)	64.1% (1,100,120)	63.8% (1,760,404)	65.0% (943,692)	62.4% (816,712)	84.2% (305,002)	88.6% (136,349)	80.9% (168,653)	53.9% (187,058)	53.7% (110,110)	54.2% (76,948)	65.2% (70,769)	64.1% (32,962)	66.3% (37,807)
Rural ** +	65.3% (4,140,399)	68.9% (2,173,959)	61.7% (1,966,440)	64.3% (3,525,723)	67.4% (1,786,885)	61.4% (1,738,838)	75.6% (407,578)	77.7% (251,152)	72.5% (156,426)	70.5% (154,829)	73.5% (88,243)	66.9% (66,586)	50.0% (52,270)	75.4% (47,679)	11.1% (4,590)
Census Region															
Northeast	66.2% (2,903,019)	65.3% (1,480,322)	67.1% (1,422,698)	65.2% (2,191,216)	64.2% (1,156,531)	66.3% (1,034,685)	67.7% (352,933)	72.2% (147,640)	64.9% (205,293)	65.6% (225,071)	59.2% (104,897)	72.3% (120,173)	83.8% (133,799)	84.0% (71,253)	83.4% (62,546)
South *	74.3% (6,309,384)	74.8% (3,140,852)	73.7% (3,168,532)	73.2% (3,931,879)	73.1% (1,941,228)	73.3% (1,990,651)	77.9% (1,696,929)	78.3% (869,571)	77.5% (827,358)	71.2% (554,708)	72.9% (260,625)	69.7% (294,083)	76.2% (125,867)	91.5% (69,428)	63.2% (56,440)
Midwest ** +	65.7% (3,890,849)	68.3% (1,968,377)	63.3% (1,922,472)	64.3% (3,111,569)	67.1% (1,561,289)	61.7% (1,550,280)	76.0% (571,216)	76.3% (297,864)	75.6% (273,352)	61.8% (131,513)	56.7% (57,189)	66.5% (74,324)	67.1% (76,551)	84.8% (52,035)	46.6% (24,516)
West	56.6% (2,946,814)	55.1% (1,459,583)	58.1% (1,487,231)	54.7% (1,769,821)	52.5% (837,809)	56.9% (932,012)	62.0% (224,869)	59.3% (105,188)	64.6% (119,681)	59.2% (769,780)	60.1% (444,085)	58.0% (325,695)	58.0% (182,345)	51.9% (72,501)	62.8% (109,843)

Notes:

"–" indicates sample size too small to estimate.

*** Test of statistical significance compares African Americans with Whites. *** p < .001, ** p < .01, * p < .05.

+++ Test of statistical significance compares White boys with White girls. +++ p < .001, ++ p < .01, + p < .05.

~~~ Test of statistical significance compares African American boys with African American girls. ~~~ p < .001, ~~ p < .01, ~ p < .05.

Tests of statistical significance calculated using adjusted sample weight to control for influence of large sample sizes.

Student's residence determined by ZIP code. An Urbanized Area (UA) comprises a place (e.g., city, village) and adjacent densely settled surrounding territory that together have a population of at least 50,000. "Urban, outside Urbanized Area" includes incorporated and unincorporated places outside of UA with population of at least 2,500. "Rural" represents all other places.

Source: National Household Education Survey, 1993 School Safety & Discipline Component.

Figure 12. Percentage of Students in Grades 6 to 12 Who Report Teacher Supervision of School Hallways by School Characteristic: 1993

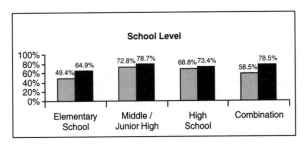

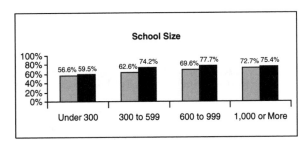

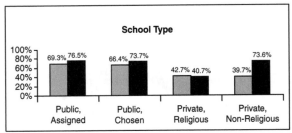

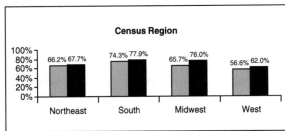

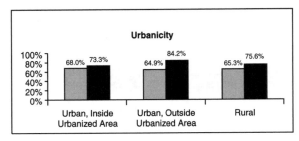

Source: , National Household Education Survey, 1993 School Safety & Discipline Component.

more than twice as high as the proportion of White students in the west (54.4% versus 25.0%).

- Higher shares of African American than White students in the northeast (47.9% versus 36.5%) and midwest (46.0% versus 31.6%) reported limited restroom access.

Security Guards

Overall, one-third (32.1%) of students in grades 6 to 12 reported that their schools had security guards to ensure the safety of students.

- **Table 14** shows that the percentage of African Americans with security guards in their schools was more than twice the percentage of Whites (53.3% versus 23.5%).

- Regardless of school level, the percentage of African Americans with security guards in their schools was more than twice the percentage of Whites. For example, 63.2% of African American high school students had security guards in their schools, compared with only 34.2% of their White counterparts.

Table 13. Percentage of Students in Grades 6 to 12 Who Report Their School Limits Restroom Access by School Characteristics, Race, and Sex: 1993

(weighted sample size in parentheses)

Characteristic	Total	Male	Female	White, Non-Hispanic			African American, Non-Hispanic			Hispanic			Other		
				Total	Male	Female	Total	Male	Female	Total	Male	Female	Total	Male	Female
Total ***++	100.0%	100.0%	100.0%	100.0%	100.0%	100.0%	100.0%	100.0%	100.0%	100.0%	100.0%	100.0%	100.0%	100.0%	100.0%
	(24,011,221)	(11,997,231)	(12,013,990)	(16,807,986)	(8,378,872)	(8,429,114)	(3,813,119)	(1,882,053)	(1,931,066)	(2,636,416)	(1,374,597)	(1,261,819)	(753,700)	(361,709)	(391,991)
Limits on Restroom Access	35.9%	37.5%	34.2%	32.3%	34.2%	30.5%	43.0%	42.0%	44.0%	46.1%	50.4%	41.3%	43.1%	43.0%	43.1%
	(8,613,844)	(4,504,958)	(4,108,885)	(5,434,181)	(2,865,945)	(2,568,235)	(1,640,731)	(790,569)	(850,163)	(1,214,430)	(692,732)	(521,698)	(324,500)	(155,712)	(168,789)
School Level															
Elementary * ++	44.8%	51.4%	37.8%	40.1%	47.2%	32.4%	53.6%	57.8%	49.0%	55.6%	66.4%	44.2%	49.9%	37.7%	56.1%
	(1,183,496)	(695,256)	(488,239)	(705,971)	(432,631)	(273,340)	(215,621)	(121,164)	(94,457)	(208,874)	(128,051)	(80,823)	(53,029)	(13,410)	(39,619)
Middle/Junior High *	44.9%	44.5%	45.2%	41.2%	41.3%	41.1%	48.4%	44.0%	53.6%	57.1%	58.8%	54.8%	59.8%	60.1%	59.6%
	(3,328,290)	(1,714,827)	(1,613,463)	(2,070,123)	(1,050,475)	(1,019,648)	(636,004)	(315,712)	(320,292)	(494,372)	(289,838)	(204,534)	(127,791)	(58,802)	(68,989)
High School ***	29.8%	30.6%	29.1%	26.9%	27.6%	26.2%	37.5%	37.6%	37.5%	36.7%	39.1%	34.4%	32.6%	33.5%	31.7%
	(3,430,284)	(1,688,153)	(1,742,131)	(2,177,019)	(1,082,867)	(1,094,152)	(696,302)	(315,470)	(380,832)	(447,265)	(233,001)	(214,264)	(109,698)	(56,815)	(52,883)
Combination * ++	27.6%	32.1%	22.7%	25.0%	30.0%	19.6%	38.5%	32.7%	44.0%	36.4%	45.1%	26.7%	34.9%	45.6%	18.8%
	(671,774)	(406,722)	(265,052)	(481,069)	(299,973)	(181,096)	(92,804)	(38,223)	(54,581)	(63,919)	(41,841)	(22,078)	(33,982)	(26,685)	(7,297)
School Type															
Public, Assigned *** +	36.7%	38.5%	34.9%	33.4%	35.0%	31.7%	44.5%	44.4%	44.5%	47.1%	51.8%	41.8%	42.6%	41.8%	43.3%
	(7,142,744)	(3,763,881)	(3,378,863)	(4,693,069)	(2,455,910)	(2,237,159)	(1,241,466)	(631,297)	(610,168)	(983,928)	(573,802)	(410,126)	(224,281)	(102,871)	(121,409)
Public, Chosen *	37.4%	37.4%	37.4%	31.3%	35.0%	27.8%	39.5%	33.0%	45.1%	48.4%	48.9%	47.8%	49.1%	52.1%	46.3%
	(997,236)	(483,885)	(513,351)	(399,668)	(220,007)	(179,661)	(339,441)	(130,427)	(209,014)	(190,102)	(98,400)	(91,702)	(68,024)	(35,051)	(32,974)
Private, Religious	27.1%	30.2%	24.3%	25.8%	28.5%	23.0%	33.7%	45.3%	28.3%	27.3%	34.2%	22.6%	37.4%	34.1%	41.2%
	(418,986)	(222,133)	(196,852)	(309,361)	(170,667)	(138,694)	(44,630)	(18,870)	(25,760)	(40,400)	(20,530)	(19,870)	(24,595)	(12,066)	(12,529)
Private, Non-Religious	17.1%	19.4%	14.2%	12.3%	13.9%	10.4%	53.8%	46.1%	79.1%	0.0%	0.0%	0.0%	33.1%	44.3%	18.7%
	(54,878)	(35,059)	(19,819)	(32,083)	(19,362)	(12,721)	(15,194)	(9,974)	(5,221)	–	–	–	(7,601)	(5,724)	(1,877)
Number of Students															
Under 300 +	33.2%	37.7%	28.8%	30.0%	34.9%	25.4%	38.0%	34.9%	41.8%	49.4%	53.9%	44.8%	39.9%	56.9%	24.5%
	(871,153)	(488,412)	(382,741)	(608,205)	(344,006)	(264,198)	(89,565)	(44,934)	(44,631)	(140,206)	(76,991)	(63,216)	(33,177)	(22,481)	(10,696)
300 to 599 *** +	37.1%	39.2%	35.0%	33.3%	36.3%	30.2%	44.3%	43.9%	44.8%	48.7%	49.1%	48.4%	51.5%	50.6%	52.5%
	(2,898,258)	(1,556,680)	(1,341,578)	(1,842,429)	(1,019,422)	(823,007)	(553,017)	(289,659)	(263,358)	(383,104)	(186,410)	(196,695)	(119,708)	(61,190)	(58,518)
600 to 999 ***	36.1%	37.1%	35.1%	31.6%	31.7%	31.6%	47.1%	46.2%	47.9%	47.2%	56.0%	35.6%	45.3%	56.7%	39.0%
	(2,224,193)	(1,125,920)	(1,098,273)	(1,384,076)	(682,867)	(701,209)	(496,997)	(229,210)	(267,787)	(268,120)	(180,446)	(87,674)	(74,999)	(33,397)	(41,602)
1,000 or More *	35.4%	36.1%	34.6%	32.9%	33.8%	31.9%	39.3%	38.0%	40.5%	42.4%	47.0%	37.2%	35.4%	27.1%	44.5%
	(2,620,239)	(1,333,946)	(1,286,294)	(1,599,471)	(819,650)	(779,821)	(501,152)	(226,765)	(274,386)	(423,000)	(248,886)	(174,114)	(96,617)	(38,644)	(57,973)
Urbanicity															
Urban, Inside Urbanized Area ***	39.0%	40.2%	38.0%	34.5%	35.3%	33.7%	45.6%	45.7%	45.5%	48.0%	52.0%	43.9%	42.2%	43.4%	41.2%
	(5,501,001)	(2,803,249)	(2,697,752)	(2,952,547)	(1,509,445)	(1,443,102)	(1,326,799)	(641,363)	(685,435)	(993,425)	(545,361)	(448,065)	(228,230)	(107,081)	(121,150)
Urban, Outside Urbanized Area	33.0%	32.6%	33.3%	30.6%	31.1%	30.0%	39.1%	32.2%	44.3%	41.7%	43.5%	39.1%	44.7%	33.5%	54.8%
	(1,179,971)	(607,543)	(572,428)	(845,154)	(451,716)	(393,439)	(141,730)	(49,487)	(92,243)	(144,643)	(89,124)	(55,519)	(48,443)	(17,216)	(31,227)
Rural +++	30.5%	34.7%	26.3%	29.9%	34.1%	25.8%	31.9%	30.9%	33.6%	34.8%	48.5%	18.2%	45.8%	49.7%	39.8%
	(1,932,872)	(1,094,166)	(838,706)	(1,636,480)	(904,785)	(731,695)	(172,202)	(99,718)	(72,484)	(76,363)	(58,248)	(18,115)	(47,827)	(31,415)	(16,412)
Census Region															
Northeast *	39.2%	39.1%	39.3%	36.5%	36.2%	36.9%	47.9%	46.3%	49.0%	49.3%	54.9%	43.4%	43.9%	49.2%	38.0%
	(1,718,501)	(886,595)	(831,906)	(1,229,270)	(652,905)	(576,365)	(249,757)	(94,730)	(155,027)	(169,324)	(97,287)	(72,036)	(70,151)	(41,673)	(28,478)
South +	37.6%	39.4%	35.8%	34.8%	37.3%	32.3%	39.0%	36.3%	41.7%	47.6%	57.6%	39.1%	62.5%	70.3%	56.0%
	(3,191,159)	(1,653,372)	(1,537,786)	(1,868,517)	(990,865)	(877,652)	(848,463)	(403,493)	(444,970)	(370,808)	(205,655)	(165,152)	(103,371)	(53,359)	(50,012)
Midwest ***	34.1%	35.0%	33.4%	31.6%	33.0%	30.3%	46.0%	44.4%	47.6%	48.7%	52.0%	45.7%	37.1%	20.8%	56.1%
	(2,020,841)	(1,006,720)	(1,014,121)	(1,529,444)	(768,290)	(761,154)	(345,452)	(173,183)	(172,268)	(103,609)	(52,469)	(51,140)	(42,336)	(12,777)	(29,558)
West *** + ~	32.3%	36.1%	28.3%	25.0%	28.5%	21.6%	54.4%	67.2%	42.1%	43.9%	45.6%	41.5%	34.5%	34.3%	34.7%
	(1,683,343)	(958,272)	(725,072)	(806,950)	(453,886)	(353,065)	(197,060)	(119,162)	(77,897)	(570,690)	(337,321)	(233,370)	(108,643)	(47,903)	(60,740)

Notes:

"–" indicates sample size too small to estimate.

*** Test of statistical significance compares African Americans with Whites. *** p < .001, ** p < .01, * p < .05.

+++ Test of statistical significance compares White boys with White girls. +++ p < .001, ++ p < .01, + p < .05.

~~~ Test of statistical significance compares African American boys with African American girls. ~~~ p < .001, ~~ p < .01, ~ p < .05.

Tests of statistical significance calculated using adjusted sample weight to control for influence of large sample sizes.

Student's residence determined by ZIP code. An Urbanized Area (UA) comprises a place (e.g., city, village) and adjacent densely settled surrounding territory that together have a population of at least 50,000. "Urban, outside Urbanized Area" includes incorporated and unincorporated places outside of UA with population of at least 2,500 "Rural" represents all other places.

Source: National Household Education Survey, 1993 School Safety & Discipline Component.

Figure 13. Percentage of Students in Grades 6 to 12 Who Report Their School Limits Restroom Access by School Characteristic: 1993

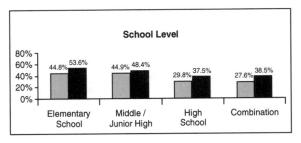

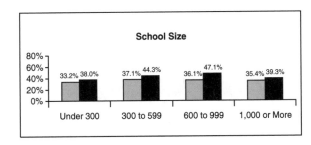

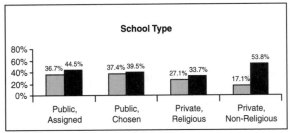

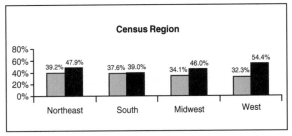

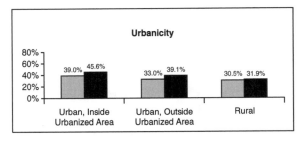

Source: National Household Education Survey, 1993 School Safety & Discipline Component.

- The percentage of African Americans with security guards in their schools was more than twice the percentage of Whites among students attending assigned public schools (49.8% versus 23.6%), the public schools of their choice (69.9% versus 34.8%), and private religious schools (24.1% versus 11.7%).

- Regardless of school size, the percentage of African Americans with security guards in their schools was higher than the percentage of Whites—39.5% of African Americans versus 7.7% of Whites at schools with fewer than 300 students and 60.3% of African Americans versus 44.2% of Whites at schools with 1,000 or more students.

Figure 14 shows that, overall, 46.5% of urban school students reported security guards, compared with 17.1% of suburban school students and 8.8% of rural school students.

- At rural schools the percentages of African Americans and Whites with security guards in their schools were comparable (7.2% versus 8.6%).

Table 14. Percentage of Students in Grades 6 to 12 Who Report School Has Security Guards by School Characteristics, Race, and Sex: 1993
(weighted sample size in parentheses)

Characteristic	Total	Male	Female	White, Non-Hispanic Total	White Male	White Female	African American, Non-Hispanic Total	AA Male	AA Female	Hispanic Total	Hispanic Male	Hispanic Female	Other Total	Other Male	Other Female
Total	100.0% (24,011,221)	100.0% (11,997,231)	100.0% (12,013,990)	100.0% (16,807,986)	100.0% (8,378,872)	100.0% (8,429,114)	100.0% (3,813,119)	100.0% (1,882,053)	100.0% (1,931,066)	100.0% (2,636,416)	100.0% (1,374,597)	100.0% (1,261,819)	100.0% (753,700)	100.0% (361,709)	100.0% (391,991)
Security Guards at School *** ~	32.1% (7,715,037)	31.6% (3,792,352)	32.7% (3,922,685)	23.5% (3,945,955)	23.7% (1,988,858)	23.2% (1,957,097)	53.3% (2,031,294)	50.0% (940,907)	56.5% (1,090,387)	54.7% (1,441,041)	52.6% (723,180)	56.9% (717,861)	39.4% (296,747)	38.5% (139,407)	40.1% (157,340)
School Level															
Elementary *** +	16.0% (423,425)	18.5% (250,108)	13.4% (173,317)	8.4% (148,641)	11.1% (101,900)	5.5% (46,741)	32.8% (131,950)	38.2% (80,034)	26.9% (51,915)	30.4% (114,418)	32.2% (62,031)	28.6% (52,387)	26.7% (28,417)	17.3% (6,144)	31.5% (22,273)
Middle/Junior High ***	28.1% (2,083,793)	28.7% (1,104,107)	27.5% (979,687)	17.9% (899,827)	18.2% (463,697)	17.6% (436,130)	47.6% (626,494)	47.6% (340,939)	47.7% (285,555)	51.8% (448,641)	50.4% (248,373)	53.7% (200,268)	51.0% (108,832)	52.2% (51,098)	49.9% (57,733)
High School *** ~	42.6% (4,910,103)	41.8% (2,307,955)	43.4% (2,602,148)	34.2% (2,769,910)	34.5% (1,353,801)	33.9% (1,416,109)	63.2% (1,171,901)	57.9% (485,337)	67.6% (686,563)	68.2% (831,136)	66.7% (397,593)	69.6% (433,543)	40.8% (137,155)	42.0% (71,224)	39.5% (65,932)
Combination ***	12.2% (297,717)	10.3% (130,182)	14.3% (167,534)	6.6% (127,577)	7.0% (69,461)	6.3% (58,116)	41.9% (100,950)	29.6% (34,597)	53.5% (66,353)	26.7% (46,847)	16.4% (15,183)	38.2% (31,664)	23.0% (22,343)	18.7% (10,942)	29.4% (11,402)
School Type															
Public, Assigned *** ~	31.5% (6,126,063)	31.3% (3,067,571)	31.6% (3,058,492)	23.6% (3,317,995)	24.2% (1,694,453)	23.0% (1,623,542)	49.8% (1,389,721)	46.1% (656,624)	53.5% (733,097)	58.2% (1,214,876)	56.2% (622,809)	60.3% (592,067)	38.7% (203,471)	38.1% (93,685)	39.2% (109,786)
Public, Chosen ***	49.5% (1,320,619)	46.9% (606,029)	52.0% (714,591)	34.8% (443,871)	33.2% (208,731)	36.4% (235,140)	69.9% (601,090)	67.8% (267,971)	71.8% (333,119)	52.2% (205,337)	46.4% (93,367)	58.4% (111,970)	50.8% (70,321)	53.4% (35,959)	48.3% (34,362)
Private, Religious *	13.4% (206,795)	12.9% (94,752)	13.8% (112,044)	11.7% (140,183)	12.4% (74,086)	11.0% (66,098)	24.1% (32,007)	23.1% (9,622)	24.6% (22,385)	14.1% (20,829)	11.7% (7,004)	15.7% (13,825)	20.9% (13,776)	11.4% (4,040)	32.0% (9,736)
Private, Non-Religious +	19.2% (61,560)	13.3% (24,001)	26.9% (37,559)	16.8% (43,905)	8.3% (11,588)	26.4% (32,317)	30.0% (8,476)	30.9% (6,689)	27.1% (1,787)	0.0% –	0.0% –	0.0% –	40.0% (9,179)	44.3% (5,724)	34.4% (3,455)
Number of Students															
Under 300 ***	14.7% (386,050)	14.8% (192,302)	14.6% (193,748)	7.7% (156,769)	9.8% (96,733)	5.8% (60,036)	39.5% (93,115)	35.4% (45,588)	44.5% (47,527)	40.7% (115,515)	33.2% (47,462)	48.3% (68,054)	24.8% (20,650)	6.4% (2,520)	41.6% (18,130)
300 to 599 ***	22.4% (1,746,892)	22.9% (908,402)	21.9% (838,490)	12.5% (691,959)	13.5% (378,392)	11.5% (313,567)	52.5% (655,471)	50.2% (331,395)	55.2% (324,076)	42.4% (333,690)	41.7% (158,540)	43.1% (175,150)	28.3% (65,772)	33.1% (40,075)	23.1% (25,697)
600 to 999***	29.6% (1,824,141)	29.1% (884,218)	30.0% (939,923)	21.6% (946,190)	21.3% (459,704)	21.9% (486,486)	48.7% (513,699)	46.4% (230,115)	50.8% (283,584)	53.3% (303,212)	50.8% (163,829)	56.6% (139,382)	36.8% (61,040)	51.9% (30,570)	28.5% (30,471)
1,000 or More ***	50.7% (3,757,954)	48.9% (1,807,430)	52.5% (1,950,524)	44.2% (2,151,037)	43.5% (1,054,029)	44.9% (1,097,008)	60.3% (769,008)	55.9% (333,808)	64.2% (435,200)	69.0% (688,625)	66.8% (353,350)	71.6% (335,275)	54.8% (149,285)	46.5% (66,243)	63.8% (83,042)
Urbanicity															
Urban, Inside Urbanized Area ***	46.5% (6,545,688)	45.4% (3,171,801)	47.5% (3,373,887)	36.2% (3,104,320)	36.2% (1,550,407)	36.2% (1,553,912)	65.1% (1,894,955)	62.3% (874,598)	67.7% (1,020,357)	62.5% (1,293,096)	60.7% (636,933)	64.3% (656,162)	46.8% (253,318)	44.5% (109,862)	48.8% (143,455)
Urban, Outside Urbanized Area ***	17.1% (610,909)	18.3% (339,892)	15.8% (271,018)	13.4% (371,290)	14.7% (212,948)	12.1% (158,341)	27.0% (97,661)	30.8% (47,385)	24.1% (50,276)	29.4% (101,971)	24.4% (50,014)	36.6% (51,957)	36.9% (39,987)	57.4% (29,545)	18.3% (10,443)
Rural	8.8% (558,440)	8.9% (280,660)	8.7% (277,780)	8.6% (470,346)	8.5% (225,502)	8.6% (244,843)	7.2% (38,678)	5.9% (18,924)	9.2% (19,753)	20.9% (45,975)	30.2% (36,233)	9.8% (9,742)	3.3% (3,442)	0.0% –	8.3% (3,442)
Census Region															
Northeast ***	27.9% (1,224,999)	24.9% (565,338)	31.1% (659,660)	16.6% (559,087)	16.0% (288,758)	17.3% (270,329)	74.4% (387,883)	69.9% (143,032)	77.4% (244,851)	61.6% (211,406)	57.4% (101,664)	66.0% (109,742)	41.7% (66,624)	37.6% (31,884)	46.3% (34,739)
South *** ~	33.8% (2,871,046)	31.0% (1,299,373)	36.6% (1,571,673)	25.7% (1,381,031)	24.0% (636,189)	27.4% (744,841)	43.6% (949,493)	39.2% (435,409)	48.1% (514,085)	60.0% (467,480)	56.0% (199,974)	63.4% (267,505)	44.2% (73,042)	36.6% (27,801)	50.6% (45,242)
Midwest *** +	25.3% (1,500,302)	28.4% (818,916)	22.4% (681,387)	18.8% (908,474)	21.4% (497,112)	16.4% (411,362)	61.3% (460,766)	65.3% (254,728)	57.0% (206,038)	46.5% (98,828)	50.6% (51,029)	42.7% (47,799)	28.3% (32,234)	26.1% (16,046)	30.7% (16,188)
West ***	40.7% (2,118,690)	41.8% (1,108,725)	39.5% (1,009,965)	33.9% (1,097,364)	35.5% (566,799)	32.4% (530,565)	64.3% (233,152)	60.8% (107,738)	67.7% (125,414)	51.0% (663,328)	50.1% (370,513)	52.1% (292,815)	39.7% (124,847)	45.6% (63,676)	35.0% (61,171)

Notes:

"–" indicates sample size too small to estimate.

*** Test of statistical significance compares African Americans with Whites. *** p <.001, ** p <.01, * p <.05.

+++ Test of statistical significance compares White boys with White girls. +++ p <.001, ++ p <.01, + p <.05.

~~~ Test of statistical significance compares African American boys with African American girls. ~~~ p <.001, ~~ p <.01, ~ p <.05.

Tests of statistical significance calculated using adjusted sample weight to control for influence of large sample sizes.

Student's residence determined by ZIP code. An Urbanized Area (UA) comprises a place (e.g., city, village) and adjacent densely settled surrounding territory that together have a population of at least 50,000. "Urban, outside Urbanized Area" includes incorporated and unincorporated places outside of UA with population of at least 2,500. "Rural" represents all other places.

Source: National Household Education Survey, 1993 School Safety & Discipline Component.

Figure 14. Percentage of Students in Grades 6 to 12 Who Report School Has Security Guards by School Characteristic: 1993

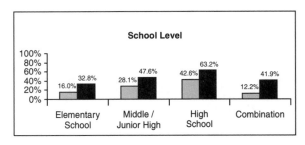

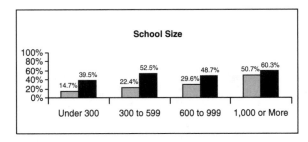

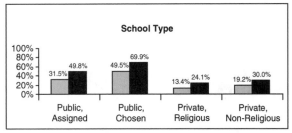

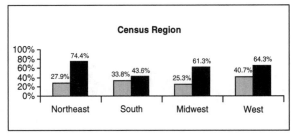

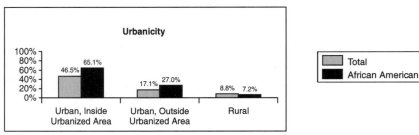

Source: National Household Education Survey, 1993 School Safety & Discipline Component.

- But, a higher share of African Americans than Whites reported security guards at their schools in urban (65.1% versus 36.2%) and sub-urban (27.0% versus 13.4%) areas.

- Regardless of census region, the proportion of African Americans who reported security guards in their schools was higher than the proportion of Whites. The gap appeared to be greatest among students in the northeast, where nearly three-fourths (74.4%) of African Americans reported security guards, compared with only 16.6% of Whites.

Metal Detectors

Overall, 5.6% of students in grades 6 to 12 reported metal detectors in their schools.

- **Table 15** shows that the percentage of African Americans who reported metal detectors in their schools was more than six times as large (15.7%) as the percentage of Whites (2.6%).

Figure 15 shows that metal detectors were virtually nonexistent in America's private schools, since only 0.8% of all private religious school students and

Table 15. Percentage of Students in Grades 6 to 12 Who Report School Has Metal Detectors by School Characteristics, Race, and Sex: 1993
(weighted sample size in parentheses)

Characteristic	Total	Male	Female	White, Non-Hispanic Total	White, Non-Hispanic Male	White, Non-Hispanic Female	African American, Non-Hispanic Total	African American, Non-Hispanic Male	African American, Non-Hispanic Female	Hispanic Total	Hispanic Male	Hispanic Female	Other Total	Other Male	Other Female
Total	100.0% (24,011,221)	100.0% (11,997,231)	100.0% (12,013,990)	100.0% (16,807,986)	100.0% (8,378,872)	100.0% (8,429,114)	100.0% (3,813,119)	100.0% (1,882,053)	100.0% (1,931,066)	100.0% (2,636,416)	100.0% (1,374,597)	100.0% (1,261,819)	100.0% (753,700)	100.0% (361,709)	100.0% (391,991)
Metal Detectors at School ***	5.6% (1,350,757)	5.5% (656,959)	5.8% (693,798)	2.6% (431,476)	2.9% (241,574)	2.3% (189,902)	15.7% (598,019)	14.2% (267,379)	17.1% (330,640)	10.6% (278,953)	9.7% (133,326)	11.5% (145,627)	5.6% (42,309)	4.1% (14,679)	7.0% (27,630)
School Level															
Elementary ***	2.7% (70,774)	3.4% (46,617)	1.9% (24,156)	0.9% (15,062)	0.7% (6,677)	1.0% (8,386)	9.2% (36,947)	13.6% (28,583)	4.3% (8,364)	3.8% (14,253)	5.9% (11,358)	1.6% (2,895)	4.2% (4,511)	0.0% –	6.4% (4,511)
Middle/Junior High ***	5.1% (378,889)	5.3% (202,874)	4.9% (176,015)	2.4% (118,498)	2.2% (55,621)	2.5% (62,877)	10.7% (141,322)	11.7% (83,508)	9.7% (57,814)	11.0% (94,933)	11.4% (56,189)	10.4% (38,744)	11.3% (24,136)	7.7% (7,557)	14.3% (16,580)
High School *** + ~	7.4% (846,440)	6.9% (383,341)	7.7% (463,100)	3.5% (285,168)	4.4% (170,998)	2.7% (114,170)	21.5% (398,016)	17.5% (146,638)	24.7% (251,378)	12.3% (149,595)	9.8% (58,582)	14.6% (91,012)	4.1% (13,661)	4.2% (7,122)	3.9% (6,539)
Combination***	2.2% (54,653)	1.9% (24,126)	2.6% (30,527)	0.7% (12,748)	0.8% (8,279)	0.5% (4,469)	9.0% (21,733)	7.4% (8,650)	10.6% (13,083)	11.5% (20,172)	7.8% (7,197)	15.7% (12,975)	0.0% –	0.0% –	0.0% –
School Type															
Public, Assigned ***	5.1% (996,399)	4.9% (480,641)	5.3% (515,757)	2.5% (352,771)	2.9% (200,245)	2.2% (152,526)	14.3% (399,982)	12.6% (178,921)	16.1% (221,061)	10.4% (216,929)	8.7% (96,641)	12.3% (120,288)	5.1% (26,717)	2.0% (4,835)	7.8% (21,882)
Public, Chosen ***	12.8% (340,326)	13.1% (169,315)	12.5% (171,011)	5.5% (69,515)	5.8% (36,274)	5.1% (33,241)	23.0% (198,037)	22.4% (88,458)	23.6% (109,579)	14.6% (57,182)	17.3% (34,739)	11.7% (22,444)	11.3% (15,592)	14.6% (9,844)	8.1% (5,748)
Private, Religious	0.8% (12,911)	0.8% (5,880)	0.9% (7,030)	0.8% (9,191)	0.8% (5,056)	0.7% (4,135)	0.0% –	0.0% –	0.0% –	2.5% (3,720)	1.4% (825)	3.3% (2,895)	0.0% –	0.0% –	0.0% –
Private, Non-Religious	0.4% (1,122)	0.6% (5,880)	0.0% –	0.8% –	0.0% –	0.0% –	0.0% –	0.0% –	0.0% –	16.2% (1,122)	0.0% –	0.0% –	0.0% –	0.0% –	0.0% –
Number of Students															
Under 300 ***	3.6% (93,870)	4.3% (55,814)	2.9% (38,056)	1.0% (20,178)	1.5% (14,876)	0.5% (5,303)	18.1% (42,608)	25.8% (33,241)	8.8% (9,367)	10.9% (31,084)	5.4% (7,698)	16.6% (23,386)	0.0% –	0.0% –	0.0% –
300 to 599 *** ~	4.5% (354,224)	4.0% (158,054)	5.1% (196,170)	1.2% (65,369)	1.4% (39,321)	1.0% (26,049)	16.9% (210,305)	13.0% (86,049)	21.2% (124,256)	7.4% (58,205)	5.3% (20,293)	9.3% (37,913)	8.8% (20,344)	10.2% (12,391)	7.1% (7,952)
600 to 999 ***	4.9% (300,135)	5.4% (163,218)	4.4% (136,917)	2.3% (101,133)	2.4% (51,298)	2.2% (49,836)	12.8% (135,486)	14.9% (73,829)	11.0% (61,657)	9.7% (55,283)	11.8% (38,091)	7.0% (17,192)	5.0% (8,232)	0.0% –	7.7% (8,232)
1,000 or More ***	8.1% (602,527)	7.6% (279,872)	8.7% (322,655)	5.0% (244,795)	5.6% (136,080)	4.5% (108,715)	16.4% (209,619)	12.4% (74,260)	20.0% (135,359)	13.5% (134,380)	12.7% (67,245)	14.3% (67,136)	5.0% (13,733)	1.6% (2,287)	8.8% (11,446)
Urbanicity															
Urban, Inside Urbanized Area ***	8.0% (1,129,462)	7.5% (525,985)	8.5% (603,477)	3.9% (334,261)	4.2% (178,932)	3.6% (155,329)	17.0% (495,586)	15.1% (211,908)	18.8% (283,679)	12.7% (262,140)	11.9% (125,301)	13.4% (136,839)	6.9% (37,474)	4.0% (9,844)	9.4% (27,630)
Urban, Outside Urbanized Area ***	3.3% (119,035)	3.6% (67,038)	3.0% (51,998)	1.8% (49,130)	2.3% (33,848)	1.2% (15,282)	15.5% (56,100)	16.3% (25,094)	14.9% (31,006)	2.6% (8,970)	1.6% (3,260)	4.0% (5,710)	4.5% (4,835)	9.4% (4,835)	0.0% –
Rural ***	1.6% (102,259)	2.0% (63,936)	1.2% (38,323)	0.9% (48,085)	1.1% (28,794)	0.7% (19,290)	8.6% (46,332)	9.4% (30,377)	7.4% (15,955)	3.6% (7,842)	4.0% (4,765)	3.1% (3,078)	0.0% –	0.0% –	0.0% –
Census Region															
Northeast ***	5.7% (252,025)	4.8% (108,431)	6.8% (143,595)	1.8% (61,556)	2.3% (41,184)	1.3% (20,372)	29.1% (151,535)	26.3% (53,730)	30.9% (97,805)	7.9% (27,229)	6.3% (11,229)	9.6% (16,000)	7.3% (11,706)	2.7% (2,287)	12.6% (9,418)
South ***	7.1% (600,653)	7.0% (293,550)	7.1% (307,103)	4.1% (219,025)	5.0% (132,737)	3.2% (86,288)	13.7% (298,817)	11.9% (131,871)	15.6% (166,946)	7.9% (61,660)	6.0% (21,385)	9.5% (40,275)	12.8% (21,151)	10.0% (7,557)	15.2% (13,594)
Midwest ***	4.3% (255,049)	4.4% (127,329)	4.2% (127,720)	1.7% (81,385)	1.9% (43,495)	1.5% (37,891)	16.2% (121,534)	16.1% (62,971)	16.2% (58,563)	23.4% (49,766)	20.7% (20,863)	25.8% (28,903)	2.1% (2,363)	0.0% –	4.5% (2,363)
West **	4.7% (243,030)	4.8% (127,649)	4.5% (115,380)	2.2% (69,510)	1.5% (24,159)	2.8% (45,351)	7.2% (26,133)	10.6% (18,807)	4.0% (7,326)	10.8% (140,298)	10.8% (79,849)	10.8% (60,449)	2.3% (7,089)	3.5% (4,835)	1.3% (2,255)

Notes:

"–" indicates sample size too small to estimate.

*** Test of statistical significance compares African Americans with Whites. *** p <.001, ** p <.01, * p <.05.

+++ Test of statistical significance compares White boys with White girls. +++ p <.001, ++ p <.01, + p <.05.

~~~Test of statistical significance compares African American boys with African American girls. ~~~ p <.001, ~~ p <.01, ~ p <.05.

Tests of statistical significance calculated using adjusted sample weight to control for influence of large sample sizes.

Student's residence determined by ZIP code. An Urbanized Area (UA) comprises a place (e.g., city, village) and adjacent densely settled surrounding territory that together have a population of at least 50,000. "Urban, outside Urbanized Area" includes incorporated and unincorporated places outside of UA with population of at least 2,500. "Rural" represents all other places.

Source: National Household Education Survey, 1993 School Safety & Discipline Component.

Figure 15. Percentage of Students in Grades 6 to 12 Who Report School Has Metal Detectors by School Characteristic: 1993

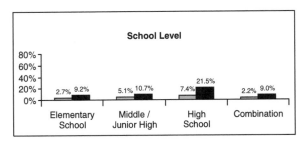

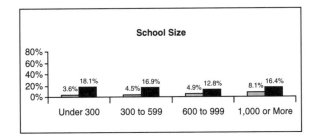

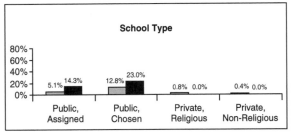

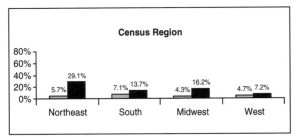

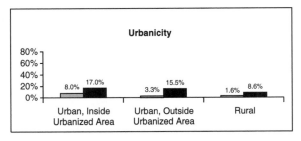

Source: National Household Education Survey, 1993 School Safety & Discipline Component.

0.4% of all private nonreligious school students reported metal detectors.

- A higher percentage of African Americans than Whites at chosen public schools (23.0% versus 5.5%) and at assigned public schools (14.3% versus 2.5%) reported metal detectors.

Regardless of school level, size, location, and region, a higher percentage of African Americans than Whites reported metal detectors in their schools.

- For example, more than one-fourth (29.1%) of African American students in the northeast reported metal detectors at school, compared with only 1.8% of White students.

Locked Doors

More than one-fourth (29.1%) of students in grades 6 to 12 reported that their school locked its doors during the school day.

- **Table 16** shows that more than one-third (35.4%) of African Americans reported that

Table 16. Percentage of Students in Grades 6 to 12 Who Report School Has Locked Doors by School Characteristics, Race, and Sex: 1993

(weighted sample size in parentheses)

Characteristic	Total	Male	Female	White, Non-Hispanic Total	Male	Female	African American, Non-Hispanic Total	Male	Female	Hispanic Total	Male	Female	Other Total	Male	Female
Total ***	100.0% (24,011,221)	100.0% (11,997,231)	100.0% (12,013,990)	100.0% (16,807,986)	100.0% (8,378,872)	100.0% (8,429,114)	100.0% (3,813,119)	100.0% (1,882,053)	100.0% (1,931,066)	100.0% (2,636,416)	100.0% (1,374,597)	100.0% (1,261,819)	100.0% (753,700)	100.0% (361,709)	100.0% (391,991)
Locked Doors at School	29.1% (6,975,520)	30.0% (3,595,005)	28.1% (3,380,515)	25.9% (4,350,184)	27.0% (2,258,237)	24.8% (2,091,946)	35.4% (1,348,687)	35.1% (661,163)	35.6% (687,524)	38.5% (1,015,433)	40.6% (558,433)	36.2% (457,000)	34.7% (261,216)	32.4% (117,172)	36.7% (144,045)
School Level															
Elementary	37.6% (995,559)	39.4% (533,865)	35.8% (461,694)	34.1% (600,104)	38.2% (349,387)	29.7% (250,717)	39.4% (158,411)	31.5% (65,998)	47.9% (92,413)	51.4% (193,191)	54.2% (104,563)	48.5% (88,627)	41.3% (43,853)	39.1% (13,916)	42.4% (29,937)
Middle/Junior High +	34.1% (2,527,485)	35.8% (1,378,036)	32.2% (1,149,449)	31.7% (1,591,755)	34.6% (881,394)	28.6% (710,360)	35.4% (466,040)	35.8% (256,913)	35.0% (209,126)	43.0% (372,020)	40.9% (201,664)	45.6% (170,356)	45.7% (97,671)	38.9% (38,064)	51.5% (59,606)
High School ***	25.5% (2,939,283)	25.2% (1,391,358)	25.8% (1,547,925)	22.2% (1,797,170)	20.6% (807,224)	23.7% (989,946)	34.1% (632,477)	35.0% (293,565)	33.3% (338,913)	33.3% (405,388)	39.3% (234,244)	27.5% (171,144)	31.0% (104,247)	33.2% (56,325)	28.7% (47,923)
Combination *** +	21.1% (513,193)	23.0% (291,746)	19.0% (221,447)	18.8% (361,154)	22.0% (220,231)	15.3% (140,923)	38.1% (91,759)	38.2% (44,687)	38.0% (47,072)	25.5% (44,835)	19.4% (17,961)	32.4% (26,874)	15.9% (15,445)	15.1% (8,867)	17.0% (6,578)
School Type															
Public, Assigned *** +	27.8% (5,407,178)	29.4% (2,874,551)	26.1% (2,532,627)	24.8% (3,491,227)	26.4% (1,848,778)	23.3% (1,642,449)	34.2% (954,732)	35.3% (501,882)	33.1% (452,850)	37.6% (784,630)	40.1% (444,175)	34.7% (340,455)	33.5% (176,589)	32.4% (79,716)	34.6% (96,872)
Public, Chosen	35.0% (933,418)	33.3% (430,911)	36.6% (502,507)	30.9% (394,365)	30.7% (193,420)	31.1% (200,946)	37.6% (322,983)	33.3% (131,657)	41.2% (191,326)	43.1% (169,427)	44.2% (88,993)	42.0% (80,434)	33.7% (46,642)	25.0% (16,841)	41.8% (29,801)
Private, Religious	36.3% (562,421)	35.1% (258,339)	37.5% (304,082)	34.7% (416,485)	33.2% (198,786)	36.2% (217,700)	43.7% (57,987)	46.7% (19,449)	42.4% (38,538)	40.3% (59,573)	39.1% (23,463)	41.0% (36,111)	43.1% (28,375)	47.0% (16,642)	38.6% (11,734)
Private, Non-Religious	22.7% (72,502)	17.3% (31,204)	29.6% (41,298)	18.4% (48,106)	12.4% (17,254)	25.2% (30,852)	46.0% (12,985)	37.8% (8,176)	72.9% (4,809)	26.0% (1,802)	29.8% (1,802)	0.0% –	41.8% (9,610)	30.8% (3,972)	56.1% (5,637)
Number of Students															
Under 300 **	26.6% (698,500)	30.1% (389,957)	23.2% (308,543)	23.4% (473,998)	26.8% (263,748)	20.2% (210,250)	43.1% (101,581)	46.7% (60,161)	38.8% (41,421)	41.7% (118,415)	43.0% (61,542)	40.3% (56,872)	5.4% (4,506)	11.4% (4,506)	0.0% –
300 to 599 *** ++	28.4% (2,217,022)	29.9% (1,188,248)	26.8% (1,028,774)	24.2% (1,342,164)	27.5% (772,756)	20.9% (569,408)	36.7% (458,367)	33.8% (223,365)	40.0% (235,002)	41.9% (329,627)	40.7% (154,593)	43.1% (175,034)	37.4% (86,864)	31.0% (37,535)	44.3% (49,330)
600 to 999 ***	31.1% (1,916,602)	31.5% (954,914)	30.7% (961,688)	27.6% (1,206,704)	26.7% (576,914)	28.4% (629,790)	41.9% (441,732)	45.4% (225,302)	38.7% (216,430)	36.7% (208,751)	39.3% (126,724)	33.3% (82,027)	35.9% (59,415)	44.1% (25,974)	31.3% (33,441)
1,000 or More	28.9% (2,143,396)	28.7% (1,061,886)	29.1% (1,081,510)	27.3% (1,327,318)	26.6% (644,820)	28.0% (682,498)	27.2% (347,007)	25.5% (152,336)	28.7% (194,671)	35.9% (358,641)	40.7% (215,573)	30.5% (143,067)	40.5% (110,431)	34.5% (49,157)	47.1% (61,274)
Urbanicity															
Urban, Inside Urbanized Area ***	35.5% (5,006,060)	35.8% (2,499,142)	35.3% (2,506,917)	32.2% (2,760,234)	31.7% (1,356,674)	32.7% (1,403,561)	39.1% (1,139,917)	38.7% (543,313)	39.6% (596,605)	43.0% (889,930)	46.6% (489,267)	39.3% (400,663)	39.9% (215,977)	44.5% (109,888)	36.1% (106,089)
Urban, Outside Urbanized Area ++	19.5% (697,843)	21.3% (396,222)	17.6% (301,621)	18.6% (514,143)	22.2% (321,739)	14.7% (192,403)	19.8% (71,705)	18.6% (28,597)	20.7% (43,109)	22.1% (76,769)	19.3% (39,540)	26.2% (37,229)	32.5% (35,226)	12.3% (6,346)	50.6% (28,880)
Rural +	20.0% (1,271,618)	22.2% (699,641)	17.9% (571,976)	19.6% (1,075,806)	21.9% (579,824)	17.5% (495,982)	25.4% (137,064)	27.6% (89,254)	22.2% (47,810)	22.2% (48,734)	24.7% (29,626)	19.2% (19,109)	9.6% (10,013)	1.5% (937)	22.0% (9,075)
Census Region															
Northeast ***	31.6% (1,387,059)	31.6% (717,637)	31.6% (669,422)	26.0% (873,303)	27.2% (489,431)	24.6% (383,872)	58.2% (303,391)	60.6% (123,956)	56.7% (179,435)	42.0% (144,214)	40.4% (71,606)	43.7% (72,607)	41.4% (66,151)	38.5% (32,644)	44.7% (33,507)
South	26.7% (2,269,851)	27.0% (1,131,802)	26.5% (1,138,049)	25.8% (1,386,784)	25.3% (670,169)	26.4% (716,615)	28.7% (625,279)	29.6% (328,280)	27.8% (297,000)	26.4% (205,504)	29.5% (105,545)	23.7% (99,959)	31.6% (52,283)	36.6% (27,808)	27.4% (24,475)
Midwest *** +	27.3% (1,616,824)	29.6% (853,295)	25.1% (763,529)	24.4% (1,181,543)	27.3% (634,397)	21.8% (547,147)	40.8% (306,378)	40.8% (159,370)	40.7% (147,007)	41.0% (87,321)	48.1% (48,568)	34.7% (38,753)	36.5% (41,582)	17.9% (10,961)	58.2% (30,622)
West	32.7% (1,701,786)	33.7% (892,271)	31.6% (809,515)	28.1% (908,552)	29.1% (464,240)	27.1% (444,312)	31.3% (113,639)	28.0% (49,557)	34.6% (64,082)	44.5% (578,395)	45.0% (332,714)	43.7% (245,681)	32.2% (101,200)	32.8% (45,759)	31.7% (55,440)

Notes:

"–" indicates sample size too small to estimate.

*** Test of statistical significance compares African Americans with Whites. *** p < .001, ** p < .01, * p < .05.

+++ Test of statistical significance compares White boys with White girls. +++ p < .001, ++ p < .01, + p <.05.

~~~Test of statistical significance compares African American boys with African American girls. ~~~ p < .001, ~~ p < .01, ~ p < .05.

Tests of statistical significance calculated using adjusted sample weight to control for influence of large sample sizes.

Student's residence determined by ZIP code. An Urbanized Area (UA) comprises a place (e.g., city, village) and adjacent densely settled surrounding territory that together have a population of at least 50,000. "Urban, outside Urbanized Area" includes incorporated and unincorporated places outside of UA with population of at least 2,500. "Rural" represents all other places.

Source: National Household Education Survey, 1993 School Safety & Discipline Component.

their schools had locked doors, compared with only one-fourth (25.9%) of Whites.

- The percentages of African American and White students who reported locked school doors were comparable for elementary school students (39.4% versus 34.1%) and middle and junior high school students (35.4% versus 31.7%).

- But, among high school students, a higher percentage of African American students than

White students reported locked school doors (34.1% versus 22.2%).

- At public assigned schools, a higher percentage of African Americans than Whites attended schools with locked doors (34.2% versus 24.8%).

Figure 16 shows that, overall, the share of students who reported locked school doors was not related to school size.

Figure 16. Percentage of Students in Grades 6 to 12 Who Report School Has Locked Doors by School Characteristic: 1993

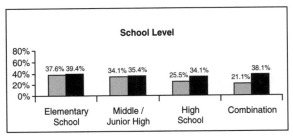

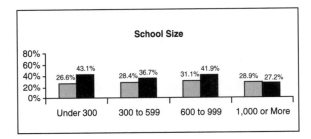

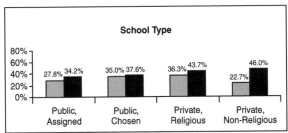

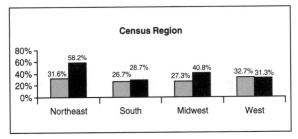

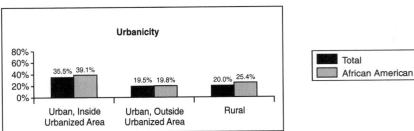

Source: National Household Education Survey, 1993 School Safety & Discipline Component.

- Among students who attended schools with 1,000 or more students, the percentages of African Americans and Whites who reported locked school doors were comparable (27.2% versus 27.3%).

- But, at schools with fewer than 1,000 students, the share of African Americans reporting locked doors was higher than the share of Whites.

The majority of students who reported locked school doors attended urban (35.5%) rather than suburban (19.5%) or rural (20.0%) schools.

- The percentages of African American and White students with locked school doors were comparable at both suburban (19.8% versus 18.6%) and rural (25.4% versus 19.6%) schools.

- But, a higher percentage of African Americans than Whites had locked school doors at urban (39.1% versus 32.2%) schools.

- The share of African American students who reported locked school doors was twice the proportion of White students in the northeast (58.2% versus 26.0%) and in the midwest (40.8% versus 24.4%).

- Comparable shares of African Americans and Whites reported locked school doors in the south (28.7% versus 25.8%) and west (31.3% versus 28.1%).

Locker Checks

About 29.5% of all students in grades 6 to 12 reported regular locker checks at their schools.

- **Table 17** shows that 31.3% of African American students and 28.9% of White students reported regular locker checks.

- **Figure 17** shows that the percentages of African American students and of all students who reported regular locker checks were similar, regardless of school level, type, size, location, or region.

AVAILABILITY OF ALCOHOL AND DRUGS AT SCHOOL

Availability of Beer or Wine, Liquor, Marijuana, and Other Drugs at School

Figure 18 shows that more than one-fourth of students in grades 6 to 12 reported that obtaining beer or wine (29.2%), liquor (26.0%), and marijuana (29.0%) at school or on school grounds was "very easy" or "fairly easy."

- **Table 18** shows that comparable percentages of African American and White students reported that obtaining beer or wine (30.0% versus 29.6%) and liquor (26.7% versus 26.0%) at school or on school grounds was easy.

- But, a higher percentage of African Americans than Whites reported that obtaining marijuana (36.9% versus 27.1%) and other drugs (25.2% versus 20.6%) was easy.

Availability of Alcohol and Drugs by School Level

The percentage of students who reported that obtaining beer or wine at school or on school grounds was easy generally increased with school level from 7.6% of elementary school students to 42.3% of high school students.

Table 19 shows that, among those attending elementary, middle and junior high, and high schools, similar percentages of African American and White students reported that obtaining beer or wine, liquor, and other drugs was very or fairly easy.

- **Figure 19** shows that a higher share of African American students than of all students reported that obtaining marijuana at school or on school grounds was easy among middle and junior high school students (22.2% versus 15.8%), high school students (51.4% versus 44.8%), and combination school students (51.3% versus 20.2%).

Table 17. Percentage of Students in Grades 6 to 12 Who Report Regular Locker Checks by School Characteristics, Race, and Sex: 1993
(weighted sample size in parentheses)

Characteristic	Total	Male	Female	White, Non-Hispanic Total	White, Non-Hispanic Male	White, Non-Hispanic Female	African American, Non-Hispanic Total	African American, Non-Hispanic Male	African American, Non-Hispanic Female	Hispanic Total	Hispanic Male	Hispanic Female	Other Total	Other Male	Other Female
Total ++	100.0% (24,011,221)	100.0% (11,997,231)	100.0% (12,013,990)	100.0% (16,807,986)	100.0% (8,378,872)	100.0% (8,429,114)	100.0% (3,813,119)	100.0% (1,882,053)	100.0% (1,931,066)	100.0% (2,636,416)	100.0% (1,374,597)	100.0% (1,261,819)	100.0% (753,700)	100.0% (361,709)	100.0% (391,991)
Regular Locker Checks	29.5% (7,092,779)	28.1% (3,373,326)	31.0% (3,719,454)	28.9% (4,864,207)	27.1% (2,266,769)	30.8% (2,597,438)	31.3% (1,192,120)	31.1% (584,840)	31.4% (607,280)	31.0% (817,463)	29.1% (400,157)	33.1% (417,306)	29.1% (218,989)	33.6% (121,560)	24.9% (97,429)
School Level															
Elementary	16.6% (439,249)	17.6% (238,415)	15.6% (200,834)	15.7% (277,150)	15.5% (142,023)	16.0% (135,127)	17.3% (69,660)	22.4% (46,850)	11.8% (22,810)	18.9% (71,057)	21.0% (40,540)	16.7% (30,517)	20.1% (21,383)	25.3% (9,003)	17.5% (12,380)
Middle/Junior High ++	41.6% (3,084,484)	38.4% (1,479,012)	45.0% (1,605,473)	41.8% (2,099,715)	38.2% (971,906)	45.5% (1,127,809)	41.1% (540,075)	40.7% (291,762)	41.5% (248,314)	42.2% (365,312)	34.5% (170,201)	52.3% (195,110)	37.2% (79,382)	46.1% (45,143)	29.6% (34,240)
High School * +	25.2% (2,900,143)	23.6% (1,304,163)	26.6% (1,595,981)	23.7% (1,918,706)	21.3% (834,245)	25.9% (1,084,461)	29.1% (540,252)	27.9% (233,894)	30.1% (306,358)	27.1% (330,891)	28.3% (168,610)	26.1% (162,282)	32.8% (110,294)	39.7% (67,414)	25.7% (42,880)
Combination *	27.5% (668,903)	27.8% (351,736)	27.2% (317,167)	29.6% (568,637)	31.9% (318,595)	27.1% (250,042)	17.5% (42,133)	10.5% (12,335)	24.0% (29,798)	28.6% (50,203)	22.4% (20,806)	35.5% (29,397)	8.1% (7,930)	0.0% –	20.5% (7,930)
School Type															
Public, Assigned ++	31.5% (6,129,234)	29.3% (2,871,181)	33.6% (3,258,052)	30.8% (4,335,107)	28.3% (1,982,475)	33.3% (2,352,633)	33.2% (927,251)	32.4% (461,727)	34.0% (465,525)	34.3% (716,689)	31.6% (349,850)	37.4% (366,840)	28.5% (150,186)	31.3% (77,131)	26.1% (73,055)
Public, Chosen	24.9% (663,821)	26.0% (336,006)	23.9% (327,815)	23.6% (300,445)	24.9% (156,762)	22.2% (143,684)	28.6% (245,558)	29.7% (117,437)	27.6% (128,121)	19.3% (75,811)	20.9% (41,965)	17.7% (33,846)	30.3% (42,007)	29.5% (19,842)	31.1% (22,165)
Private, Religious	15.7% (242,806)	16.0% (117,711)	15.4% (125,095)	14.7% (175,992)	13.5% (80,716)	15.8% (95,276)	13.2% (17,524)	13.6% (5,676)	13.0% (11,848)	16.9% (24,963)	13.9% (8,343)	18.9% (16,621)	37.0% (24,327)	65.0% (22,977)	4.4% (1,350)
Private, Non-Religious	17.8% (56,919)	26.9% (48,427)	6.1% (8,492)	20.1% (52,663)	33.5% (46,817)	4.8% (5,846)	6.3% (1,787)	0.0% –	27.1% (1,787)	0.0% –	0.0% –	0.0% –	10.8% (2,469)	12.5% (1,610)	8.6% (859)
Number of Students															
Under 300	25.6% (671,203)	24.7% (319,648)	26.4% (351,556)	24.1% (487,838)	22.8% (224,241)	25.4% (263,598)	22.4% (52,747)	28.6% (36,818)	14.9% (15,928)	32.6% (92,681)	30.3% (43,283)	35.0% (49,398)	45.6% (37,938)	38.7% (15,305)	51.9% (22,632)
300 to 599 *	29.7% (2,317,116)	28.4% (1,128,211)	31.0% (1,188,905)	28.1% (1,555,071)	25.8% (726,129)	30.4% (828,942)	34.2% (426,695)	35.4% (233,742)	32.8% (192,953)	34.3% (269,651)	32.7% (124,184)	35.8% (145,467)	28.3% (65,698)	36.5% (44,156)	19.3% (21,543)
600 to 999 +	32.0% (1,973,030)	29.0% (879,826)	34.9% (1,093,205)	31.9% (1,395,695)	28.7% (618,888)	35.0% (776,806)	33.3% (351,217)	28.8% (142,827)	37.3% (208,389)	31.5% (178,932)	30.7% (99,052)	32.5% (79,881)	28.5% (47,187)	32.4% (19,059)	26.3% (28,128)
1,000 or More	28.8% (2,131,430)	28.3% (1,045,641)	29.2% (1,085,789)	29.3% (1,425,603)	28.8% (697,511)	29.8% (728,092)	28.3% (361,462)	28.7% (171,453)	28.0% (190,010)	27.7% (276,199)	25.3% (133,638)	30.4% (142,561)	25.0% (68,166)	30.2% (43,040)	19.3% (25,126)
Urbanicity															
Urban, Inside Urbanized Area ++	28.8% (4,054,044)	27.4% (1,913,857)	30.1% (2,140,187)	27.7% (2,371,910)	24.7% (1,058,685)	30.6% (1,313,225)	30.0% (872,875)	31.4% (440,474)	28.7% (432,401)	30.7% (635,834)	30.2% (317,379)	31.2% (318,455)	32.1% (173,425)	39.4% (97,319)	25.9% (76,106)
Urban, Outside Urbanized Area	32.3% (1,157,559)	30.1% (561,063)	34.7% (596,496)	32.5% (898,106)	32.0% (464,514)	33.1% (433,591)	37.8% (136,904)	31.3% (48,179)	42.6% (88,726)	29.4% (102,125)	20.8% (42,689)	41.9% (59,436)	18.8% (20,424)	11.0% (5,681)	25.8% (14,744)
Rural	29.6% (1,881,176)	28.5% (898,405)	30.8% (982,771)	29.1% (1,594,191)	28.1% (743,570)	30.0% (850,622)	33.8% (182,341)	29.8% (96,187)	39.9% (86,154)	36.2% (79,505)	33.4% (40,089)	39.6% (39,416)	24.1% (25,139)	29.3% (18,559)	16.0% (6,580)
Census Region															
Northeast +++	24.8% (1,088,143)	20.9% (473,209)	29.0% (614,934)	24.5% (823,976)	18.5% (332,857)	31.5% (491,119)	24.9% (129,738)	28.8% (58,955)	22.4% (70,782)	24.5% (84,087)	30.6% (54,170)	18.0% (29,917)	31.5% (50,342)	32.1% (27,227)	30.8% (23,115)
South	36.1% (3,065,341)	36.1% (1,513,423)	36.1% (1,551,918)	35.1% (1,888,003)	35.5% (942,014)	34.8% (945,989)	36.1% (785,369)	35.1% (389,242)	37.1% (396,127)	42.6% (331,691)	40.2% (143,581)	44.6% (188,110)	36.5% (60,278)	50.8% (38,586)	24.3% (21,692)
Midwest	29.2% (1,728,325)	28.9% (831,630)	29.5% (896,695)	29.4% (1,422,832)	29.6% (688,582)	29.2% (734,251)	28.2% (211,970)	27.4% (106,723)	29.1% (105,247)	29.6% (63,031)	14.1% (14,273)	43.6% (48,757)	26.7% (30,492)	35.9% (22,052)	16.0% (8,440)
West +	23.2% (1,210,971)	20.9% (555,063)	25.6% (655,908)	22.6% (729,397)	19.0% (303,317)	26.0% (426,080)	17.9% (65,043)	16.9% (29,920)	19.0% (35,123)	26.0% (338,654)	25.4% (188,133)	26.8% (150,522)	24.8% (77,877)	24.1% (33,694)	25.2% (44,183)

Notes:

"–" indicates sample size too small to estimate.

*** Test of statistical significance compares African Americans with Whites. *** p <.001, ** p <.01, * p <.05.

+++ Test of statistical significance compares White boys with White girls. +++ p <.001, ++ p <.01, + p <.05.

~~~Test of statistical significance compares African American boys with African American girls. ~~~ p <.001, ~~ p <.01, ~ p <.05.

Tests of statistical significance calculated using adjusted sample weight to control for influence of large sample sizes.

Student's residence determined by ZIP code. An Urbanized Area (UA) comprises a place (e.g., city, village) and adjacent densely settled surrounding territory that together have a population of at least 50,000. "Urban, outside Urbanized Area" includes incorporated and unincorporated places outside of UA with population of at least 2,500. "Rural" represents all other places.

Source: National Household Education Survey, 1993 School Safety & Discipline Component.

Figure 17. Percentage of Students in Grades 6 to 12 Who Report Regular Locker Checks by School Characteristic: 1993

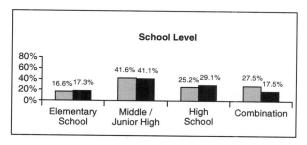

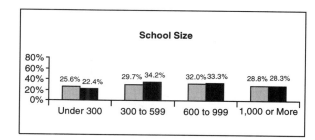

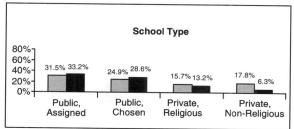

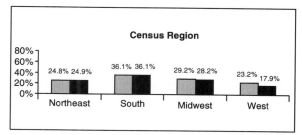

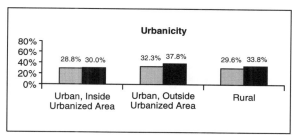

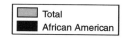

Source: National Household Education Survey, 1993 School Safety & Discipline Component.

Availability of Alcohol and Drugs by School Type

In general, the percentage of public school students who reported that obtaining beer or wine, liquor, marijuana, and other drugs was easy was higher than the percentage of private school students.

- **Table 20** shows that among students attending public schools of their choice, higher percentages of African Americans than Whites reported that obtaining beer or wine (40.3%

versus 25.8%), liquor (35.5% versus 24.5%), and marijuana (44.9% versus 29.7%) was easy.

- Higher percentages of African Americans than Whites attending their assigned public schools reported that obtaining marijuana (35.2% versus 28.3%) and other drugs (24.8% versus 21.5%) was easy.

- **Figure 20** shows that, among students attending private religious schools, comparable percentages of African Americans and all students

Figure 18. Percentage of Students in Grades 6 to 12 Who Reported That It Was Very or Fairly Easy to Obtain Beer or Wine, Liquor, Marijuana, and Other Drugs at School or on School Grounds: 1993

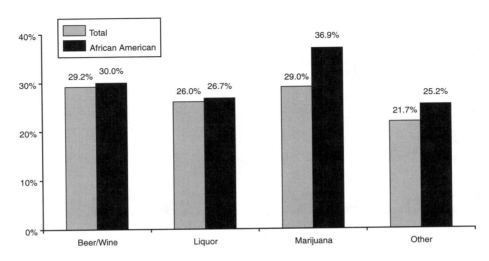

Source: National Household Education Survey, 1993 School Safety & Discipline Component.

reported that obtaining beer or wine (14.9% versus 15.8%) and liquor (13.6% versus 14.4%) was easy.

- The percentage of African Americans at private religious schools who reported that obtaining marijuana was easy was greater than the percentage of Whites (24.2% versus 11.7%).

Availability of Alcohol and Drugs by School Size

Regardless of race, the availability of alcohol and drugs at school or on school grounds increased with school size. For example, **Figure 21** shows that 19.1% of students at schools with fewer than 300 students reported that obtaining beer or wine at school was easy, compared with 36.8% of students at schools with 1,000 or more students.

- **Table 21** shows that, among students at schools with more than 1,000 students, a smaller percentage of African Americans than of Whites reported that it was easy to obtain beer or wine (33.0% versus 39.1%).

- At schools with more than 1,000 students, comparable shares of African Americans and Whites reported that obtaining liquor (30.0% versus 35.4%), marijuana (43.0% versus 40.4%), and other drugs (27.7% versus 29.1%) was easy.

- A higher share of African Americans than Whites reported that obtaining marijuana was easy among those attending schools with under 300 students (29.3% versus 12.5%), 300 to 599 students (30.8% versus 20.8%), and 600 to 999 students (38.3% versus 27.0%).

Availability of Alcohol and Drugs by School Location

Figure 22 shows that the percentage of students who reported that obtaining beer or wine at school was easy did not vary by school location—29.3% of urban school students, 30.7% of suburban school students, and 28.0% of rural school students.

- **Table 22** shows that comparable percentages of African American and White urban students

Table 18. Percentage of Students in Grades 6 to 12 Who Reported That It Was Very or Fairly Easy to Obtain Beer/Wine, Liquor, Marijuana, and Other Drugs at School or on School Grounds by Race and Sex: 1993
(weighted sample size in parentheses)

Alcohol or Drugs	Total	Male	Female	White, Non-Hispanic			African American, Non-Hispanic			Hispanic			Other		
				Total	Male	Female	Total	Male	Female	Total	Male	Female	Total	Male	Female
Beer or Wine ++	100.0%	100.0%	100.0%	100.0%	100.0%	100.0%	100.0%	100.0%	100.0%	100.0%	100.0%	100.0%	100.0%	100.0%	100.0%
	(24,011,221)	(11,997,231)	(12,013,990)	(16,807,986)	(8,378,872)	(8,429,114)	(3,813,119)	(1,882,053)	(1,931,066)	(2,636,416)	(1,374,597)	(1,261,819)	(753,700)	(361,709)	(391,991)
Very/Fairly Easy to Obtain at School	29.2%	27.0%	31.3%	29.6%	27.2%	31.9%	30.0%	28.5%	31.4%	26.6%	24.7%	28.7%	25.0%	23.9%	26.1%
	(7,001,445)	(3,245,192)	(3,756,253)	(4,966,871)	(2,282,111)	(2,684,760)	(1,143,747)	(536,568)	(607,179)	(702,124)	(340,199)	(361,924)	(188,703)	(86,313)	(102,389)
Liquor ++	100.0%	100.0%	100.0%	100.0%	100.0%	100.0%	100.0%	100.0%	100.0%	100.0%	100.0%	100.0%	100.0%	100.0%	100.0%
	(24,011,221)	(11,997,231)	(12,013,990)	(16,807,986)	(8,378,872)	(8,429,114)	(3,813,119)	(1,882,053)	(1,931,066)	(2,636,416)	(1,374,597)	(1,261,819)	(753,700)	(361,709)	(391,991)
Very/Fairly Easy to Obtain at School	26.0%	23.7%	28.2%	26.0%	23.8%	28.2%	26.7%	25.1%	28.4%	24.6%	21.9%	27.5%	25.9%	20.1%	31.2%
	(6,233,132)	(2,841,348)	(3,391,784)	(4,371,085)	(1,996,384)	(2,374,701)	(1,019,384)	(471,870)	(547,514)	(647,499)	(300,381)	(347,119)	(195,164)	(72,712)	(122,451)
Marijuana ***	100.0%	100.0%	100.0%	100.0%	100.0%	100.0%	100.0%	100.0%	100.0%	100.0%	100.0%	100.0%	100.0%	100.0%	100.0%
	(24,011,221)	11,997,231	(12,013,990)	(16,807,986)	(8,378,872)	(8,429,114)	(3,813,119)	(1,882,053)	(1,931,066)	(2,636,416)	(1,374,597)	(1,261,819)	(753,700)	(361,709)	(391,991)
Very/Fairly Easy to Obtain at School	29.0%	29.8%	28.3%	27.1%	27.1%	27.1%	36.9%	39.8%	34.0%	30.9%	32.9%	28.8%	26.6%	27.8%	25.6%
	(6,971,141)	(3,570,259)	(3,400,882)	(4,548,906)	(2,268,133)	(2,280,773)	(1,405,450)	(749,093)	(656,357)	(815,930)	(452,634)	(363,296)	(200,854)	(100,399)	(100,455)
Other Drugs ** +	100.0%	100.0%	100.0%	100.0%	100.0%	100.0%	100.0%	100.0%	100.0%	100.0%	100.0%	100.0%	100.0%	100.0%	100.0%
	(24,011,221)	(11,997,231)	(12,013,990)	(16,807,986)	(8,378,872)	(8,429,114)	(3,813,119)	(1,882,053)	(1,931,066)	(2,636,416)	(1,374,597)	(1,261,819)	(753,700)	(361,709)	(391,991)
Very/Fairly Easy to Obtain at School	21.7%	20.7%	22.6%	20.6%	19.2%	22.1%	25.2%	26.4%	24.1%	23.8%	22.8%	25.0%	18.9%	18.7%	19.1%
	(5,199,321)	(2,484,814)	(2,714,507)	(3,466,584)	(1,606,934)	(1,859,650)	(961,987)	(497,220)	(464,767)	(628,024)	(312,994)	(315,030)	(142,727)	(67,666)	(75,060)

Notes:
*** Test of statistical significance compares African Americans with Whites. *** p <.001, ** p <.01, * p <.05.
+++ Test of statistical significance compares White boys with White girls. +++ p <.001, ++ p <.01, + p <.05.

(29.1% versus 30.2%) and African American and White suburban students (27.7% versus 31.2%) reported that obtaining beer or wine was easy.

- A higher percentage of African American urban school students than of their White counterparts reported that obtaining marijuana was easy (37.7% versus 30.5%).

- Among suburban school students, comparable percentages of African Americans and Whites reported that obtaining marijuana at school or on school grounds was easy (28.6% versus 26.1%).

- Among rural school students, a higher percentage of African Americans than Whites reported that it was easy to obtain beer or wine (36.1%

versus 27.7%), liquor (32.1% versus 23.8%), marijuana (37.6% versus 22.2%), and other drugs (34.1% versus 16.9%).

Availability of Alcohol and Drugs by School Census Region

About one-fourth of students in the northeast (26.4%) and south (26.0%) reported that it was easy to obtain beer or wine on school grounds, compared with one-third of students in the midwest (31.6%) and west (33.8%).

- **Table 23** shows that, among students in the south, a higher share of African Americans than Whites reported that it was easy to obtain beer or wine (29.4% versus 24.9%), liquor (27.5% versus 22.1%), marijuana (33.5% versus 27.7%), and other drugs (26.4% versus 21.5%).

Table 19. Percentage of Students in Grades 6 to 12 Who Reported That It Was Very or Fairly Easy to Obtain Alcohol or Marijuana at School or on School Grounds by School Level, Race, and Sex: 1993

(weighted sample size in parentheses)

School Level	Total	Male	Female	White, Non-Hispanic Total	Male	Female	African American, Non-Hispanic Total	Male	Female	Hispanic Total	Male	Female	Other Total	Male	Female
Beer or Wine															
Elementary School	7.6%	8.7%	6.4%	6.7%	7.3%	6.1%	8.9%	10.7%	7.0%	11.0%	12.0%	9.8%	4.1%	12.1%	0.0%
	(199,888)	(117,284)	(82,603)	(118,461)	(67,275)	(51,186)	(35,930)	(22,485)	(13,445)	(41,192)	(23,219)	(17,973)	(4,305)	(4,305)	–
Middle/Junior High School	18.7%	17.7%	19.9%	17.8%	16.7%	19.0%	21.5%	21.0%	22.2%	19.3%	17.9%	21.3%	20.2%	18.3%	21.8%
	(1,390,048)	(680,553)	(709,495)	(896,176)	(423,859)	(472,317)	(283,299)	(150,620)	(132,679)	(167,493)	(88,169)	(79,325)	(43,080)	(17,906)	(25,174)
High School +	42.3%	40.2%	44.3%	43.8%	41.5%	46.0%	39.9%	38.3%	41.3%	37.8%	36.8%	38.8%	35.8%	29.8%	41.8%
	(4,873,667)	(2,218,465)	(2,655,202)	(3,551,772)	(1,627,516)	(1,924,256)	(740,181)	(320,926)	(419,256)	(461,291)	(219,380)	(241,910)	(120,424)	(50,643)	(69,780)
Combination School * ++	22.1%	18.1%	26.5%	20.8%	16.4%	25.7%	35.0%	36.4%	33.7%	18.3%	10.2%	27.4%	21.5%	23.0%	19.2%
	(537,842)	(228,889)	(308,953)	(400,463)	(163,462)	(237,001)	(84,338)	(42,537)	(41,800)	(32,147)	(9,431)	(22,716)	(20,894)	(13,459)	(7,435)
Liquor															
Elementary School	6.6%	5.1%	8.2%	6.1%	4.6%	7.7%	7.0%	7.1%	7.0%	9.5%	4.1%	15.2%	4.1%	12.1%	0.0%
	(175,610)	(69,295)	(106,315)	(107,244)	(42,255)	(64,990)	(28,312)	(14,868)	(13,445)	(35,748)	(7,868)	(27,881)	(4,305)	(4,305)	–
Middle/Junior High School	15.1%	15.2%	14.9%	13.8%	14.1%	13.6%	17.9%	17.7%	18.0%	17.0%	16.5%	17.8%	18.6%	18.3%	18.8%
	(1,117,191)	(584,290)	(532,901)	(694,827)	(357,863)	(336,964)	(235,012)	(127,162)	(107,850)	(147,632)	(81,358)	(66,274)	(39,720)	(17,906)	(21,813)
High School +	38.6%	35.7%	41.3%	39.3%	36.6%	41.9%	36.8%	34.3%	38.9%	35.6%	34.2%	37.0%	41.0%	26.5%	55.9%
	(4,441,846)	(1,970,242)	(2,471,605)	(3,187,372)	(1,434,312)	(1,753,061)	(682,397)	(287,303)	(395,094)	(433,959)	(203,711)	(230,248)	(138,118)	(44,916)	(93,202)
Combination School * +	20.5%	17.2%	24.1%	19.9%	16.2%	23.8%	30.6%	36.4%	25.1%	17.2%	8.0%	27.4%	13.4%	9.5%	19.2%
	(498,485)	(217,521)	(280,964)	(381,641)	(161,955)	(219,687)	(73,663)	(42,537)	(31,125)	(30,160)	(7,444)	(22,716)	(13,021)	(5,585)	(7,435)
Marijuana															
Elementary School	6.0%	7.4%	4.5%	4.5%	6.3%	2.7%	8.9%	7.4%	10.6%	9.2%	10.2%	8.1%	7.2%	21.6%	0.0%
	(158,229)	(100,617)	(57,612)	(80,045)	(57,606)	(22,439)	(36,001)	(15,573)	(20,428)	(34,497)	(19,751)	(14,745)	(7,687)	(7,687)	–
Middle/Junior High School *** ~	15.6%	18.3%	12.7%	13.2%	14.9%	11.3%	22.2%	26.6%	17.0%	20.8%	25.2%	15.1%	10.8%	10.4%	11.1%
	(1,156,565)	(704,365)	(452,200)	(661,069)	(379,790)	(281,279)	(292,049)	(190,411)	(101,638)	(180,438)	(124,007)	(56,431)	(23,009)	(10,156)	(12,853)
High School ** ~	44.8%	46.3%	43.5%	43.0%	43.5%	42.5%	51.4%	57.0%	46.8%	47.4%	49.6%	45.4%	43.6%	45.4%	41.8%
	(5,163,421)	(2,557,596)	(2,605,826)	(3,484,608)	(1,706,895)	(1,777,713)	(953,870)	(478,191)	(475,679)	(578,287)	(295,539)	(282,748)	(146,656)	(76,971)	(69,686)
Combination School *** ++	20.2%	16.4%	24.4%	16.8%	12.4%	21.6%	51.3%	55.5%	47.3%	12.9%	14.4%	11.3%	24.1%	9.5%	46.3%
	(492,925)	(207,681)	(285,244)	(323,185)	(123,842)	(199,343)	(123,530)	(64,917)	(58,613)	(22,708)	(13,337)	(9,372)	(23,502)	(5,585)	(17,917)
Other Drugs															
Elementary School	5.6%	6.1%	5.2%	4.9%	5.6%	4.2%	7.5%	8.3%	6.6%	7.7%	7.1%	8.3%	3.1%	0.0%	4.6%
	(149,238)	(82,306)	(66,932)	(86,972)	(51,209)	(35,763)	(30,054)	(17,356)	(12,698)	(28,947)	(13,741)	(15,206)	(3,266)	–	(3,266)
Middle/Junior High School	15.0%	16.2%	13.8%	14.3%	15.0%	13.5%	17.0%	19.7%	13.8%	17.7%	17.8%	17.4%	10.3%	11.0%	9.7%
	(1,116,290)	(622,473)	(493,816)	(717,595)	(382,435)	(335,160)	(223,773)	(141,340)	(82,433)	(152,901)	(87,894)	(65,007)	(22,021)	(10,804)	(11,217)
High School +	31.2%	29.6%	32.6%	30.0%	28.0%	32.0%	33.5%	33.9%	33.1%	34.6%	33.7%	35.4%	33.5%	31.6%	35.5%
	(3,588,620)	(1,635,347)	(1,953,273)	(2,433,171)	(1,095,991)	(1,337,181)	(620,829)	(284,703)	(336,127)	(421,720)	(200,981)	(220,738)	(112,899)	(53,672)	(59,228)
Combination School *** ++	14.2%	11.4%	17.2%	11.9%	7.7%	16.4%	36.2%	46.0%	27.0%	13.9%	11.2%	17.0%	4.7%	5.4%	3.5%
	(345,173)	(144,688)	(200,485)	(228,846)	(77,299)	(151,547)	(87,330)	(53,821)	(33,510)	(24,456)	(10,378)	(14,078)	(4,541)	(3,191)	(1,350)

Notes:

"–" indicates sample size too small to estimate.

*** Test of statistical significance compares African Americans with Whites. *** $p < .001$, ** $p < .01$, * $p < .05$.

+++ Test of statistical significance compares White boys with White girls. +++ $p < .001$, ++ $p < .01$, + $p < .05$.

~~~ Test of statistical significance compares African American boys with African American girls. ~~~ $p < .001$, ~~ $p < .01$, ~ $p < .05$.

Tests of statistical significance calculated using adjusted sample weight to control for influence of large sample sizes.

Source: National Household Education Survey, 1993 School Safety & Discipline Component.

Figure 19. Percentage of Students In Grades 6 to 12 Who Reported That It Was Very or Fairly Easy to Obtain Alcohol or Marijuana at School or on School Grounds by School Level: 1993

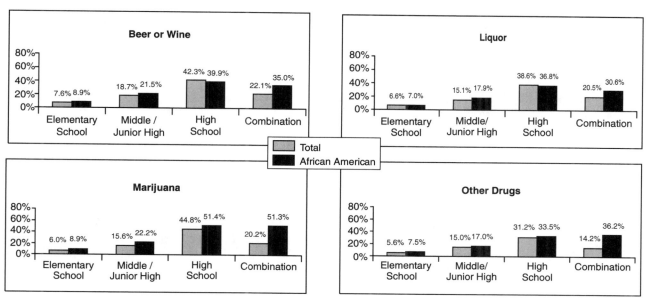

Source: National Household Education Survey, 1993 School Safety & Discipline Component.

- **Figure 23** shows that comparable shares of African Americans and all students reported that it was easy to obtain beer or wine in the northeast (27.1% versus 26.4%), midwest (30.6% versus 31.6%), and west (36.6% versus 33.8%).

- A higher share of African Americans than Whites reported that it was easy to obtain marijuana in the northeast (42.4% versus 26.0%), south (33.5% versus 27.7%), midwest (38.2% versus 23.8%), and west (46.1% versus 32.0%).

Communication Between Parents and Their Children About Drugs

One-third (35.0%) of students in grades 6 to 12 reported that they talked with their parents about drugs.

- **Table 24** shows that a smaller percentage of White boys (29.4%) than of White girls (36.5%), African American girls (36.1%), and African American boys (37.5%) talked with their parents about drugs.

Table 20. Percentage of Students in Grades 6 to 12 Who Reported That It Was Very or Fairly Easy to Obtain Alcohol or Marijuana at School or on School Grounds by School Type, Race, and Sex: 1993

(weighted sample size in parentheses)

School Type	Total	Male	Female	White, Non-Hispanic Total	Male	Female	African American, Non-Hispanic Total	Male	Female	Hispanic Total	Male	Female	Other Total	Male	Female
Beer or Wine															
Public, Assigned School ++	30.3%	28.2%	32.3%	31.2%	29.1%	33.2%	27.6%	24.5%	30.9%	28.3%	27.2%	29.5%	53.8%	27.7%	26.1%
	(5,893,480)	(2,761,384)	(3,132,096)	(4,389,867)	(2,043,521)	(2,346,345)	(772,206)	(348,708)	(423,498)	(590,086)	(300,993)	(289,093)	(141,322)	(68,162)	(73,160)
Public, Chosen School ***	29.7%	26.0%	33.2%	25.8%	21.6%	29.9%	40.3%	43.1%	37.9%	22.1%	12.7%	32.0%	21.9%	6.1%	36.8%
	(792,116)	(335,709)	(456,407)	(328,940)	(135,766)	(193,174)	(345,918)	(170,313)	(175,605)	(86,910)	(25,490)	(61,420)	(30,348)	(4,140)	(26,208)
Private, Religious	15.8%	15.6%	16.1%	16.0%	13.8%	18.2%	14.9%	27.9%	8.9%	15.6%	19.5%	13.0%	14.9%	23.8%	4.4%
	(244,988)	(114,521)	(130,467)	(192,368)	(82,739)	(109,629)	(19,703)	(11,627)	(8,077)	(23,141)	(11,729)	(11,412)	(9,776)	(8,426)	(1,350)
Private, Non-Religious	22.1%	18.6%	26.7%	21.3%	14.4%	29.1%	21.0%	27.3%	0.0%	28.6%	32.8%	0.0%	31.6%	43.2%	16.6%
	(70,861)	(33,578)	(37,283)	(55,697)	(20,085)	(35,612)	(5,921)	(5,921)	–	(1,987)	(1,987)	–	(7,256)	(5,585)	(1,671)
Liquor															
Public, Assigned School + ~	26.8%	24.6%	29.0%	27.3%	25.4%	29.1%	24.7%	20.7%	28.9%	25.5%	24.1%	27.1%	29.7%	25.0%	33.8%
	(5,214,780)	(2,404,147)	(2,810,633)	(3,835,880)	(1,781,998)	(2,053,882)	(690,298)	(294,102)	(396,196)	(532,408)	(266,541)	(265,867)	(156,194)	(61,507)	(94,688)
Public, Chosen School ** +	27.6%	23.6%	31.4%	24.5%	19.2%	29.6%	35.5%	40.5%	31.2%	23.0%	9.8%	36.9%	20.8%	6.1%	34.7%
	(736,847)	(305,157)	(431,691)	(312,423)	(121,073)	(191,350)	(305,099)	(160,221)	(144,877)	(90,443)	(19,722)	(70,721)	(28,882)	(4,140)	(24,742)
Private, Religious	14.4%	14.6%	14.2%	14.7%	13.4%	16.0%	13.6%	27.9%	7.1%	16.7%	23.5%	12.0%	4.3%	4.2%	4.4%
	(222,573)	(107,661)	(114,912)	(177,028)	(80,436)	(96,591)	(18,067)	(11,627)	(6,441)	(24,648)	(14,118)	(10,530)	(2,830)	(1,480)	(1,350)
Private, Non-Religious	18.4%	13.5%	24.7%	17.5%	9.2%	26.9%	21.0%	27.3%	0.0%	0.0%	0.0%	0.0%	31.6%	43.2%	16.6%
	(58,931)	(24,383)	(34,548)	(45,754)	(12,877)	(32,877)	(5,921)	(5,921)	–	–	–	–	(7,256)	(5,585)	(1,671)
Marijuana															
Public, Assigned School ***	29.7%	30.8%	28.6%	28.3%	28.8%	27.7%	35.2%	37.3%	33.0%	31.9%	34.3%	29.2%	29.9%	33.0%	27.2%
	(5,782,855)	(3,010,699)	(2,772,156)	(3,975,719)	(2,018,663)	(1,957,056)	(982,700)	(530,649)	(452,051)	(667,137)	(380,231)	(286,907)	(157,299)	(81,156)	(76,143)
Public, Chosen School ***	34.2%	33.2%	35.2%	29.7%	25.7%	33.5%	44.9%	51.5%	39.4%	31.1%	27.4%	34.9%	19.2%	13.1%	25.0%
	(913,189)	(429,405)	(483,784)	(378,275)	(161,879)	(216,396)	(386,244)	(203,600)	(182,644)	(122,038)	(55,130)	(66,908)	(26,631)	(8,796)	(17,835)
Private, Religious *	13.2%	14.7%	11.8%	11.7%	13.0%	10.5%	24.2%	24.9%	23.8%	16.7%	25.5%	10.8%	9.4%	13.7%	4.4%
	(204,120)	(108,514)	(95,606)	(141,108)	(77,995)	(63,112)	(32,033)	(10,371)	(21,662)	(24,767)	(15,286)	(9,481)	(6,212)	(4,862)	(1,350)
Private, Non-Religious ++	22.2%	12.0%	35.3%	20.5%	6.9%	36.2%	15.8%	20.7%	0.0%	28.6%	32.8%	0.0%	46.6%	43.2%	51.0%
	(70,977)	(21,641)	(49,336)	(53,805)	(9,596)	(44,209)	(4,473)	(4,473)	–	(1,987)	(1,987)	–	(10,712)	(5,585)	(5,127)
Other Drugs															
Public, Assigned School *	22.3%	21.2%	23.5%	21.5%	20.3%	22.7%	24.8%	23.5%	26.2%	24.7%	23.1%	26.5%	20.9%	22.1%	19.9%
	(4,346,904)	(2,070,819)	(2,276,084)	(3,027,147)	(1,425,508)	(1,601,639)	(693,843)	(335,053)	(358,790)	(515,674)	(255,894)	(259,780)	(110,240)	(54,365)	(55,875)
Public, Chosen School ~	25.1%	25.3%	24.9%	23.2%	19.4%	26.9%	29.9%	38.2%	22.8%	22.6%	22.0%	23.2%	19.2%	13.1%	25.0%
	(668,999)	(326,554)	(342,445)	(296,425)	(122,362)	(174,063)	(257,183)	(151,206)	(105,977)	(88,760)	(44,190)	(44,570)	(26,631)	(8,796)	(17,835)
Private, Religious ~	9.4%	10.5%	8.5%	9.3%	9.1%	9.4%	4.9%	15.6%	0.0%	15.9%	21.5%	12.1%	6.4%	8.0%	4.4%
	(145,823)	(76,962)	(68,861)	(111,551)	(54,720)	(56,831)	(6,489)	(6,489)	–	(23,590)	(12,910)	(10,680)	(4,193)	(2,843)	(1,350)
Private, Non-Religious +	11.7%	5.8%	19.4%	12.0%	3.1%	22.2%	15.8%	20.7%	0.0%	0.0%	0.0%	0.0%	7.2%	12.9%	0.0%
	(37,596)	(10,479)	(27,117)	(31,460)	(4,344)	(27,117)	(4,473)	(4,473)	–	–	–	–	(1,663)	(1,663)	–

Notes:

"–" indicates sample size too small to estimate.

*** Test of statistical significance compares African Americans with Whites. *** p <.001, ** p <.01, * p <.05.

+++ Test of statistical significance compares White boys with White girls. +++ p <.001, ++ p <.01, + p <.05.

~~~ Test of statistical significance compares African American boys with African American girls. ~~~ p <.001, ~~ p <.01, ~ p <.05.

Tests of statistical significance calculated using adjusted sample weight to control for influence of large sample sizes.

Source: National Household Education Survey, 1993 School Safety & Discipline Component.

Figure 20. Percentage of Students in Grades 6 to 12 Who Reported That It Was Very or Fairly Easy to Obtain Alcohol or Marijuana at School or on School Grounds by School Type: 1993

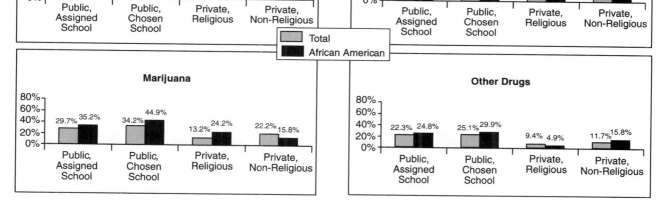

Source: National Household Education Survey, 1993 School Safety & Discipline Component.

- A higher percentage of African American elementary school students than of their White counterparts talked to their parents about drugs (53.1% versus 41.9%).

- Comparable percentages of African Americans and Whites talked with their parents among those at combination schools (35.5% versus 30.1%), middle schools (41.7% versus 39.6%), and high schools (29.7% versus 27.6%).

- **Figure 24** shows that the percentage of African Americans who talked with their parents about drugs was higher than the percentage of all students at rural schools (45.1% versus 34.0%), but comparable to the percentage of all students at urban (36.7% versus 36.3%) and suburban (25.3% versus 31.9%) schools.

- The percentages of African Americans and Whites who talked with their parents about drugs were comparable among students in the south (35.8% versus 36.8%) and west (32.9% versus 32.5%).

- A higher proportion of African Americans than Whites in the northeast (37.1% versus 28.5%) and in the midwest (41.5% versus 32.2%) talked with their parents about drugs.

USE OF ALCOHOL AND DRUGS AMONG 1992 HIGH SCHOOL SENIORS

Prevalence of Cigarette Smoking

About one in five (20.5%) 1992 high school seniors smoked cigarettes. The proportion of girls who

Figure 21. Percentage of Students in Grades 6 to 12 Who Reported That It Was Very or Fairly Easy to Obtain Alcohol or Marijuana at School or on School Grounds by School Size: 1993

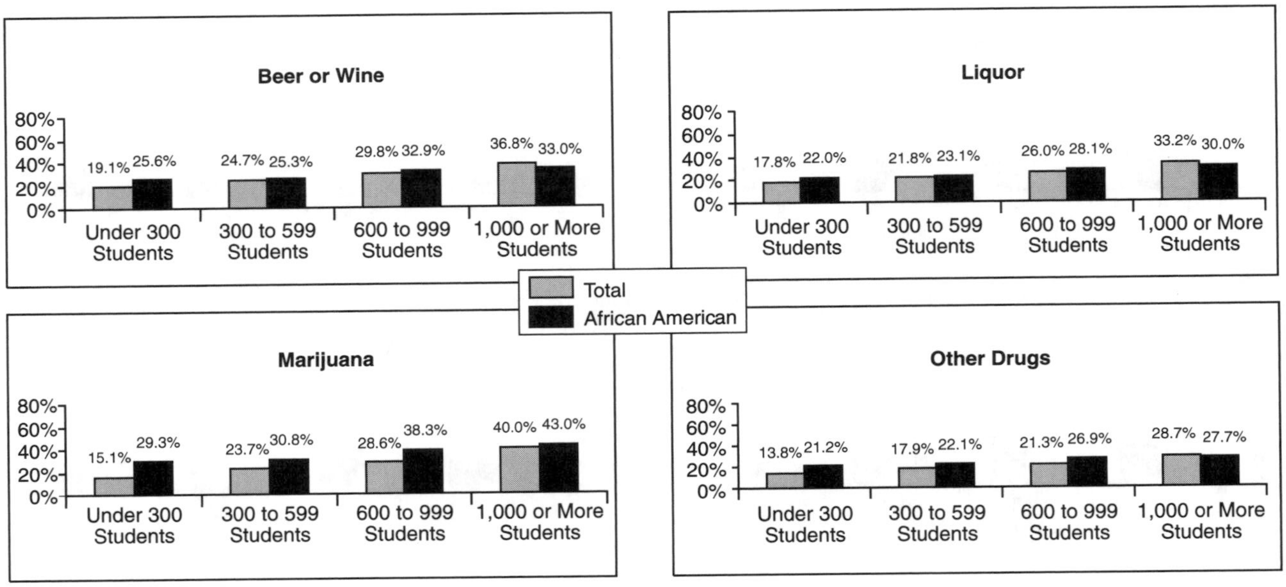

Beer or Wine

	Under 300 Students	300 to 599 Students	600 to 999 Students	1,000 or More Students
Total	19.1%	24.7%	29.8%	36.8%
African American	25.6%	25.3%	32.9%	33.0%

Liquor

	Under 300 Students	300 to 599 Students	600 to 999 Students	1,000 or More Students
Total	17.8%	21.8%	26.0%	33.2%
African American	22.0%	23.1%	28.1%	30.0%

Marijuana

	Under 300 Students	300 to 599 Students	600 to 999 Students	1,000 or More Students
Total	15.1%	23.7%	28.6%	40.0%
African American	29.3%	30.8%	38.3%	43.0%

Other Drugs

	Under 300 Students	300 to 599 Students	600 to 999 Students	1,000 or More Students
Total	13.8%	17.9%	21.3%	28.7%
African American	21.2%	22.1%	26.9%	27.7%

Source: National Household Education Survey, 1993 School Safety & Discipline Component.

smoked cigarettes was comparable to the proportion of boys among African Americans (4.5% versus 5.0%) and Whites (23.6% versus 23.7%).

- **Table 25** shows that the proportion of African American high school seniors who smoked cigarettes was substantially smaller than the proportion of White seniors (4.7% versus 23.6%).

Use of Alcohol

The majority (88.6%) of 1992 high school seniors consumed alcohol at some point in their lives and about one-half (50.7%) consumed alcohol in the past month. The proportion of African Americans who drank alcohol was smaller than the proportion of their White counterparts.

- **Table 26** shows that 80.5% of African Americans and 90.2% of Whites had ever used alcohol.

- Only 36.4% of African Americans had used alcohol in the past month, compared with 53.9% of Whites.

Figure 25 shows that more than one in every four high school seniors (28.5%) indicated that they had ever consumed at least five drinks in a row. A smaller proportion of girls than boys reported binge drinking among both African Americans (9.9% versus 20.8%) and Whites (22.9% versus 38.9%).

- The percentage of African American high school seniors who ever drank at least five

Table 21. Percentage of Students in Grades 6 to 12 Who Reported That It Was Very or Fairly Easy to Obtain Alcohol or Marijuana at School or on School Grounds by School Size, Race, and Sex: 1993
(weighted sample size in parentheses)

School Size	Total	Male	Female	White, Non-Hispanic Total	Male	Female	African American, Non-Hispanic Total	Male	Female	Hispanic Total	Male	Female	Other Total	Male	Female
Beer or Wine															
Under 300 Students ~	19.1%	16.1%	22.1%	18.0%	16.9%	19.1%	25.6%	14.6%	38.8%	19.8%	13.6%	26.1%	26.0%	10.4%	40.1%
	(502,647)	(208,665)	(293,982)	(364,410)	(166,211)	(198,199)	(60,334)	(18,870)	(41,463)	(56,325)	(19,481)	(36,844)	(21,578)	(4,102)	(17,476)
300 to 599 Students ++	24.7%	22.3%	27.2%	24.7%	21.3%	28.2%	25.3%	23.6%	27.2%	26.1%	29.3%	23.1%	18.3%	18.8%	17.7%
	(1,930,738)	(887,476)	(1,043,262)	(1,367,571)	(597,644)	(769,927)	(315,419)	(155,723)	(159,696)	(205,288)	(111,382)	(93,906)	(42,460)	(22,727)	(19,733)
600 to 999 Students	29.8%	30.8%	28.9%	30.4%	31.2%	29.6%	32.9%	37.9%	28.4%	21.9%	15.4%	30.3%	23.1%	38.1%	14.9%
	(1,840,162)	(933,641)	(906,520)	(1,330,774)	(673,758)	(657,016)	(346,653)	(187,745)	(158,908)	(124,407)	(49,716)	(74,692)	(38,327)	(22,422)	(15,905)
1,000 or More Students * ++	36.8%	32.9%	40.7%	39.1%	34.8%	43.4%	33.0%	29.2%	36.4%	31.7%	30.2%	33.4%	31.7%	26.0%	37.8%
	(2,727,899)	(1,215,410)	(1,512,489)	(1,904,116)	(844,498)	(1,059,618)	(421,341)	(174,229)	(247,112)	(316,104)	(159,621)	(156,483)	(86,338)	(37,062)	(49,276)
Liquor															
Under 300 Students	17.8%	13.8%	21.7%	16.1%	14.4%	17.8%	22.0%	13.5%	32.3%	20.7%	13.6%	27.8%	37.3%	0.0%	71.1%
	(468,138)	(178,973)	(289,165)	(326,544)	(142,070)	(184,473)	(51,928)	(17,422)	(34,507)	(58,666)	(19,481)	(39,185)	(31,000)	–	(31,000)
300 to 599 Students	21.8%	20.1%	23.6%	21.4%	19.5%	23.4%	23.1%	21.3%	25.2%	23.7%	24.3%	23.3%	17.6%	15.7%	19.8%
	(1,702,956)	(799,222)	(903,733)	(1,186,688)	(547,323)	(639,365)	(288,559)	(140,722)	(147,838)	(186,711)	(92,222)	(94,488)	(40,998)	(18,956)	(22,042)
600 to 999 Students ~	26.0%	26.6%	25.4%	26.0%	26.0%	26.0%	28.1%	34.0%	22.8%	21.6%	17.2%	27.4%	27.7%	38.1%	22.0%
	(1,601,877)	(806,637)	(795,240)	(1,136,940)	(560,051)	(576,889)	(296,255)	(168,727)	(127,528)	(122,765)	(55,436)	(67,329)	(45,917)	(22,422)	(23,494)
1,000 or More Students ++ ~	33.2%	28.6%	37.8%	35.4%	30.8%	39.9%	30.0%	24.3%	35.0%	28.0%	25.2%	31.2%	28.3%	22.0%	35.3%
	(2,460,162)	(1,056,515)	(1,403,647)	(1,720,913)	(746,940)	(973,973)	(382,642)	(145,000)	(237,642)	(279,358)	(133,242)	(146,116)	(77,250)	(31,334)	(45,915)
Marijuana															
Under 300 Students ***	15.1%	13.9%	16.2%	12.5%	11.4%	13.5%	29.3%	21.3%	39.0%	21.7%	27.7%	15.7%	14.3%	0.0%	27.3%
	(395,566)	(179,724)	(215,842)	(252,805)	(112,591)	(140,215)	(69,118)	(27,509)	(41,609)	(61,721)	(39,625)	(22,096)	(11,922)	–	(11,922)
300 to 599 Students ***	23.7%	23.3%	24.0%	20.8%	20.3%	21.2%	30.8%	29.0%	32.7%	31.7%	32.7%	30.7%	27.6%	32.5%	22.2%
	(1,847,510)	(927,400)	(920,111)	(1,150,775)	(571,962)	(578,814)	(383,713)	(191,714)	(191,999)	(248,913)	(124,382)	(124,531)	(64,109)	(39,342)	(24,767)
600 to 999 Students *** ~~~	28.6%	31.3%	25.9%	27.0%	27.9%	26.1%	38.3%	50.5%	27.5%	25.9%	27.0%	24.4%	18.3%	18.1%	18.5%
	(1,761,680)	(949,728)	(811,951)	(1,180,301)	(601,528)	(578,773)	(403,930)	(250,401)	(153,529)	(147,058)	(87,113)	(59,945)	(30,391)	(10,686)	(19,705)
1,000 or More Students	40.0%	41.0%	39.1%	40.4%	40.5%	40.3%	43.0%	46.8%	39.7%	35.9%	38.1%	33.5%	34.6%	35.4%	33.8%
	(2,966,384)	(1,513,407)	(1,452,978)	(1,965,024)	(982,053)	(982,972)	(548,689)	(279,469)	(269,220)	(358,238)	(201,514)	(156,724)	(94,432)	(50,371)	(44,061)
Other Drugs															
Under 300 Students *	13.8%	12.0%	15.5%	12.3%	10.3%	14.2%	21.2%	14.9%	28.7%	18.8%	24.3%	13.3%	11.6%	0.0%	22.1%
	(362,594)	(155,829)	(206,765)	(249,550)	(101,765)	(147,786)	(49,910)	(19,260)	(30,650)	(53,505)	(34,804)	(18,700)	(9,629)	–	(9,629)
300 to 599 Students *	17.9%	17.2%	18.6%	16.3%	15.6%	17.0%	22.1%	22.2%	21.9%	22.4%	19.3%	25.3%	18.1%	20.7%	15.3%
	(1,396,080)	(683,683)	(712,397)	(902,654)	(438,859)	(463,796)	(275,388)	(146,603)	(128,785)	(175,993)	(73,204)	(102,790)	(42,044)	(25,018)	(17,026)
600 to 999 Students * ~~~	21.3%	22.1%	20.6%	20.6%	19.2%	21.9%	26.9%	37.6%	17.3%	18.6%	19.2%	17.8%	15.5%	13.1%	16.7%
	(1,314,985)	(670,863)	(644,122)	(900,297)	(414,882)	(485,415)	(283,311)	(186,400)	(96,911)	(105,776)	(61,846)	(43,931)	(25,601)	(7,735)	(17,866)
1,000 or More Students	28.7%	26.4%	31.0%	29.1%	26.9%	31.2%	27.7%	24.3%	30.7%	29.3%	27.0%	31.9%	24.0%	24.5%	23.5%
	(2,125,661)	(974,438)	(1,151,223)	(1,414,082)	(651,429)	(762,653)	(353,378)	(144,957)	(208,421)	(292,749)	(143,140)	(149,609)	(65,452)	(34,913)	(30,539)

Notes:

"–" indicates sample size too small to estimate.

*** Test of statistical significance compares African Americans with Whites. *** p <.001, ** p <.01, * p <.05.

+++ Test of statistical significance compares White boys with White girls. +++ p <.001, ++ p <.01, + p <.05.

~~~ Test of statistical significance compares African American boys with African American girls. ~~~ p <.001, ~~ p <.01, ~ p <.05.

Tests of statistical significance calculated using adjusted sample weight to control for influence of large sample sizes.

Source: National Household Education Survey, 1993 School Safety & Discipline Component.

Figure 22. Percentage of Students in Grades 6 to 12 Who Reported That It Was Very or Fairly Easy to Obtain Alcohol or Marijuana at School or on School Grounds by Urbanicity: 1993

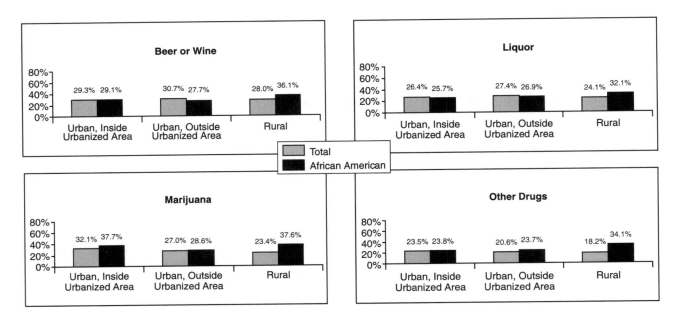

Source: National Household Education Survey, 1993 School Safety & Discipline Component.

drinks in a row was about one-half that of White high school seniors (15.0% versus 30.9%).

Use of Marijuana

Figure 26 shows that about one in every four (26.9%) 1992 high school seniors had smoked marijuana at some point in their lives and one in ten (9.6%) had smoked marijuana in the last month. A smaller percentage of girls than boys had ever used marijuana among both African Americans (10.8% versus 27.9%) and Whites (25.3% versus 31.2%).

- **Table 27** shows that 18.8% of African Americans, but 28.3% of Whites, had ever used marijuana

and 4.5% of African Americans, but 10.7% of Whites, had used marijuana in the past month.

Use of Cocaine

About 4.3% of 1992 high school seniors had ever used cocaine and 1.0% had used cocaine in the past month.

- **Table 28** shows that only 1.3% of African American high school seniors had ever used cocaine, compared with 4.5% of their White counterparts.

Table 22. Percentage of Students in Grades 6 to 12 Who Reported That It Was Very or Fairly Easy to Obtain Alcohol or Marijuana at School or on School Grounds by Urbanicity, Race, and Sex: 1993
(weighted sample size in parentheses)

Urbanicity	Total	Male	Female	White, Non-Hispanic			African American, Non-Hispanic			Hispanic			Other		
				Total	Male	Female	Total	Male	Female	Total	Male	Female	Total	Male	Female
Beer or Wine															
Urban Inside Urbanized Area	29.3%	27.4%	31.2%	30.2%	27.9%	32.5%	29.1%	27.8%	30.4%	27.0%	25.1%	28.9%	25.0%	25.1%	25.0%
	(4,129,208)	(1,910,670)	(2,218,537)	(2,586,141)	(1,194,215)	(1,391,927)	(848,501)	(390,665)	(457,837)	(559,182)	(263,823)	(295,358)	(135,383)	(61,968)	(73,416)
Urban Outside Urbanized Area ~	30.7%	28.2%	33.4%	31.2%	29.5%	33.2%	27.7%	16.3%	36.2%	27.1%	27.1%	27.1%	37.8%	32.0%	43.1%
	(1,097,576)	(524,803)	(572,773)	(862,020)	(427,771)	(434,250)	(100,505)	(25,019)	(75,486)	(94,018)	(55,542)	(38,477)	(41,032)	(16,472)	(24,560)
Rural * +	28.0%	25.7%	30.3%	27.7%	24.9%	30.3%	36.1%	37.4%	34.2%	22.3%	17.4%	28.2%	11.8%	12.4%	10.7%
	(1,774,662)	(809,718)	(964,944)	(1,518,710)	(660,126)	(858,584)	(194,741)	(120,884)	(73,856)	(48,924)	(20,834)	(28,089)	(12,287)	(7,873)	(4,414)
Liquor															
Urban Inside Urbanized Area +	26.4%	24.1%	28.8%	27.1%	24.4%	29.8%	25.7%	25.1%	26.3%	24.5%	21.4%	27.7%	27.0%	22.8%	30.5%
	(3,724,559)	(1,679,092)	(2,045,467)	(2,322,990)	(1,044,966)	(1,278,024)	(748,698)	(353,072)	(395,627)	(506,917)	(224,814)	(282,103)	(145,954)	(56,240)	(89,713)
Urban Outside Urbanized Area ~	27.4%	24.4%	30.6%	26.8%	25.0%	28.9%	26.9%	13.2%	37.1%	29.0%	26.7%	32.4%	37.8%	32.0%	43.1%
	(980,133)	(454,330)	(525,803)	(740,774)	(362,772)	(378,002)	(97,642)	(20,354)	(77,288)	(100,685)	(54,732)	(45,953)	(41,032)	(16,472)	(24,560)
Rural *	24.1%	22.4%	25.7%	23.8%	22.2%	25.4%	32.1%	30.5%	34.6%	18.2%	17.4%	19.1%	7.8%	0.0%	19.8%
	(1,528,440)	(707,926)	(820,515)	(1,307,321)	(588,646)	(718,675)	(173,044)	(98,445)	(74,599)	(39,897)	(20,834)	(19,063)	(8,178)	–	(8,178)
Marijuana															
Urban Inside Urbanized Area *	32.1%	33.3%	30.9%	30.5%	30.4%	30.5%	37.7%	41.0%	34.7%	32.0%	35.3%	28.7%	26.8%	29.9%	24.1%
	(4,518,370)	(2,322,647)	(2,195,723)	(2,611,854)	(1,302,498)	(1,309,357)	(1,098,863)	(575,710)	(523,153)	(662,916)	(370,490)	(292,426)	(144,737)	(73,949)	(70,788)
Urban Outside Urbanized Area	27.0%	27.5%	26.5%	26.1%	26.9%	25.3%	28.6%	29.4%	28.1%	30.3%	27.0%	35.0%	33.9%	42.8%	25.9%
	(967,124)	(512,506)	(454,618)	(721,502)	(390,016)	(331,486)	(103,783)	(45,177)	(58,606)	(105,018)	(55,278)	(49,740)	(36,821)	(22,035)	(14,785)
Rural ***	23.4%	23.3%	23.5%	22.2%	21.7%	22.6%	37.6%	39.7%	34.6%	21.9%	22.4%	21.2%	18.5%	7.0%	36.1%
	(1,485,647)	(735,106)	(750,541)	(1,215,550)	(575,619)	(639,931)	(202,804)	(128,206)	(74,598)	(47,996)	(26,866)	(21,130)	(19,297)	(4,415)	(14,882)
Other Drugs															
Urban Inside Urbanized Area	23.5%	22.8%	24.2%	23.0%	21.8%	24.3%	23.8%	24.8%	22.9%	25.7%	24.5%	26.9%	20.7%	21.6%	20.0%
	(4,518,370)	(2,322,647)	(2,195,723)	(2,611,854)	(1,302,498)	(1,309,357)	(1,098,863)	(575,710)	(523,153)	(662,916)	(370,490)	(292,426)	(144,737)	(73,949)	(70,788)
Urban Outside Urbanized Area	20.6%	20.0%	21.3%	20.6%	20.1%	21.2%	23.7%	21.6%	25.2%	18.1%	17.8%	18.6%	18.7%	21.6%	16.1%
	(967,124)	(512,506)	(454,618)	(721,502)	(390,016)	(331,486)	(103,783)	(45,177)	(58,606)	(105,018)	(55,278)	(49,740)	(36,821)	(22,035)	(14,785)
Rural *** +	18.2%	16.5%	19.8%	16.9%	14.5%	19.1%	34.1%	35.8%	31.5%	15.3%	16.3%	14.1%	9.9%	5.0%	17.5%
	(1,485,647)	(735,106)	(750,541)	(1,215,550)	(575,619)	(639,931)	(202,804)	(128,206)	(74,598)	(47,996)	(26,866)	(21,130)	(19,297)	(4,415)	(14,882)

Notes:
"–" indicates sample size too small to estimate.
*** Test of statistical significance compares African Americans with Whites. *** p <.001, ** p <.01, * p <.05.
+++ Test of statistical significance compares White boys with White girls. +++ p <.001, ++ p <.01, + p <.05.
~~~Test of statistical significance compares African American boys with African American girls. ~~~ p <.001, ~~ p <.01, ~ p <.05.
Tests of statistical significance calculated using adjusted sample weight to control for influence of large sample sizes.
Student's residence determined by ZIP code. An Urbanized Area (UA) comprises a place (e.g., city, village) and adjacent densely settled surrounding territory that together have a population of at least 50,000. "Urban, outside Urbanized Area" includes incorporated and unincorporated places outside of UA with population of at least 2,500. "Rural" represents all other places.
Source: National Household Education Survey, 1993 School Safety & Discipline Component.

- About 0.3% of African Americans and 0.9% of Whites had used cocaine within the past month.

Use of Alcohol and Drugs at School

About 12.8% of 1992 high school seniors reported that they had ever been under the influence of alcohol while at school, 6.6% had ever been under the influence of marijuana, and 1.0% had ever been under the influence of cocaine. The proportion of girls who had ever been under the influence of alcohol, marijuana, or cocaine at school was smaller than the proportion of boys among both African Americans and Whites.

Figure 27 shows that a smaller percentage of African American high school seniors than of all high school seniors had ever been under the influence of alcohol or marijuana at school.

- **Table 29** shows that 9.7% of African Americans, but 13.6% of Whites, had ever been under the influence of alcohol while at school.

Table 23. Percentage of Students in Grades 6 to 12 Who Reported That It Was Very or Fairly Easy to Obtain Alcohol or Marijuana at School or on School Grounds by Census Region, Race, and Sex: 1993

(weighted sample size in parentheses)

Region	Total	Male	Female	White, Non-Hispanic			African American, Non-Hispanic			Hispanic			Other		
				Total	Male	Female	Total	Male	Female	Total	Male	Female	Total	Male	Female
Beer or Wine															
Northeast	26.4% (1,158,166)	25.6% (581,767)	27.2% (576,399)	26.8% (900,454)	26.1% (469,881)	27.6% (430,574)	27.1% (141,149)	30.1% (61,596)	25.1% (79,552)	20.3% (69,572)	17.3% (30,566)	23.5% (39,006)	29.4% (46,991)	23.3% (19,724)	36.4% (27,268)
South * +	26.0% (2,211,886)	23.6% (991,272)	28.4% (1,220,614)	24.9% (1,336,056)	22.5% (597,208)	27.2% (738,848)	29.4% (639,590)	26.8% (297,849)	32.0% (341,741)	24.2% (188,737)	21.0% (75,152)	26.9% (113,585)	28.7% (47,503)	27.7% (21,062)	29.6% (26,440)
Midwest	31.6% (1,871,248)	30.6% (882,603)	32.5% (988,644)	32.5% (1,575,142)	31.0% (721,438)	34.0% (853,705)	30.6% (230,338)	32.6% (127,063)	28.6% (103,274)	23.7% (50,481)	27.8% (28,009)	20.1% (22,472)	13.4% (15,287)	9.9% (6,093)	17.5% (9,194)
West ++	33.8% (1,760,146)	29.8% (789,550)	37.9% (970,595)	35.7% (1,155,219)	30.9% (493,585)	40.4% (661,634)	36.6% (132,671)	28.2% (50,059)	44.6% (82,612)	30.2% (393,334)	27.9% (206,473)	33.3% (186,862)	25.1% (78,922)	28.2% (39,434)	22.6% (39,488)
Liquor															
Northeast	21.9% (961,056)	20.9% (475,148)	22.9% (485,908)	23.1% (778,264)	21.4% (385,067)	25.2% (393,197)	17.1% (89,211)	24.2% (49,496)	12.5% (39,715)	15.8% (54,301)	13.4% (23,746)	18.4% (30,555)	24.6% (39,280)	19.9% (16,839)	29.9% (22,441)
South ** + ~~	23.7% (2,010,774)	20.4% (856,378)	26.9% (1,154,396)	22.1% (1,189,549)	19.8% (525,086)	24.5% (664,463)	27.5% (599,959)	22.8% (252,599)	32.5% (347,360)	22.1% (172,581)	18.3% (65,504)	25.4% (107,077)	29.5% (48,685)	17.4% (13,189)	39.7% (35,496)
Midwest	28.2% (1,669,954)	27.8% (801,097)	28.6% (868,856)	28.6% (1,382,655)	28.2% (656,348)	28.9% (726,306)	29.4% (221,089)	30.7% (119,716)	28.0% (101,372)	24.2% (51,458)	21.6% (21,783)	26.5% (29,675)	12.9% (14,752)	5.3% (3,250)	21.8% (11,502)
West ++	30.5% (1,591,348)	26.7% (708,724)	34.5% (882,624)	31.6% (1,020,617)	27.0% (429,883)	36.1% (590,733)	30.1% (109,126)	28.2% (50,059)	31.9% (59,067)	28.4% (369,160)	25.6% (189,348)	32.0% (179,812)	29.4% (92,446)	28.2% (39,434)	30.3% (53,012)
Marijuana															
Northeast ***	28.2% (1,236,515)	28.2% (640,396)	28.1% (596,120)	26.0% (873,077)	25.8% (464,963)	26.1% (408,113)	42.4% (221,105)	48.6% (99,309)	38.5% (121,796)	29.7% (101,894)	31.5% (55,697)	27.8% (46,197)	25.3% (40,440)	24.1% (20,427)	26.7% (20,014)
South **	28.9% (2,455,174)	30.4% (1,275,142)	27.5% (1,180,032)	27.7% (1,489,468)	29.3% (776,863)	26.2% (712,604)	33.5% (730,100)	35.4% (392,942)	31.6% (337,158)	24.7% (192,534)	23.7% (84,787)	25.5% (107,747)	26.1% (43,073)	27.1% (20,550)	25.2% (22,522)
Midwest ***	25.5% (1,509,539)	25.0% (721,276)	25.9% (788,263)	23.8% (1,151,030)	22.5% (524,109)	24.9% (626,921)	38.2% (287,044)	41.3% (161,276)	34.8% (125,768)	23.2% (49,301)	26.6% (26,865)	20.1% (22,436)	19.4% (22,165)	14.7% (9,027)	25.0% (13,138)
West **	34.0% (1,769,912)	35.2% (933,445)	32.7% (836,466)	32.0% (1,035,332)	31.5% (502,197)	32.6% (533,135)	46.1% (167,202)	53.9% (95,567)	38.7% (71,635)	36.3% (472,201)	38.6% (285,286)	33.3% (186,915)	30.2% (95,176)	36.1% (50,395)	25.6% (44,781)
Other Drugs															
Northeast	20.1% (881,711)	19.0% (430,026)	21.3% (451,684)	19.0% (638,848)	17.1% (308,661)	21.2% (330,186)	23.5% (122,445)	28.5% (58,347)	20.3% (64,098)	24.5% (84,175)	26.4% (46,789)	22.5% (37,386)	22.7% (36,242)	19.1% (16,229)	26.7% (20,014)
South *	22.9% (1,942,914)	21.9% (919,829)	23.8% (1,023,085)	21.5% (1,154,991)	21.2% (563,140)	21.8% (591,851)	26.4% (575,954)	25.7% (285,524)	27.2% (290,430)	22.9% (178,387)	15.9% (56,844)	28.8% (121,542)	20.3% (33,582)	18.9% (14,321)	21.6% (19,260)
Midwest	18.2% (1,077,488)	18.2% (523,477)	18.2% (554,011)	17.5% (849,291)	16.4% (382,013)	18.6% (467,278)	23.1% (173,490)	27.7% (107,956)	18.1% (65,533)	15.6% (33,222)	24.3% (24,481)	7.8% (8,740)	18.8% (21,486)	14.7% (9,027)	23.7% (12,459)
West +	24.9% (1,297,208)	23.1% (611,481)	26.8% (685,727)	25.5% (823,454)	22.1% (353,120)	28.7% (470,334)	24.9% (90,098)	25.6% (45,393)	24.1% (44,705)	25.5% (332,240)	25.0% (184,879)	26.2% (147,361)	16.3% (51,416)	20.1% (28,090)	13.3% (23,327)

Notes:

*** Test of statistical significance compares African Americans with Whites. *** p < .001, ** p < .01, * p < .05.

+++ Test of statistical significance compares White boys with White girls. +++ p < .001, ++ p < .01, + p < .05.

~~~ Test of statistical significance compares African American boys with African American girls. ~~~ p < .001, ~~ p < .01, ~ p < .05.

Tests of statistical significance calculated using adjusted sample weight to control for influence of large sample sizes.

Source: National Household Education Survey, 1993 School Safety & Discipline Component.

Figure 23. Percentage of Students in Grades 6 to 12 Who Reported That It Was Very or Fairly Easy to Obtain Alcohol or Marijuana at School or on School Grounds by Census Region: 1993

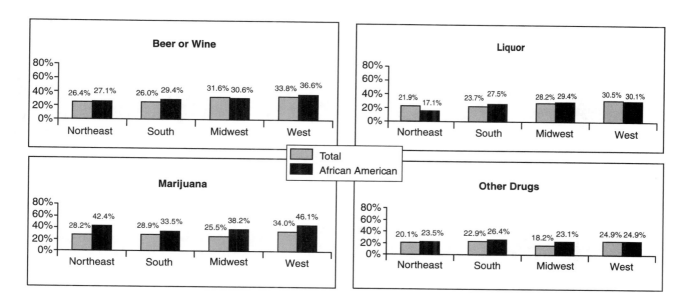

Source: National Household Education Survey, 1993 School Safety & Discipline Component.

- About 3.8% of African Americans, compared with 7.1% of Whites, had ever been under the influence of marijuana at school.

- Comparable percentages of African Americans and Whites had ever been under the influence of cocaine at school (0.7% versus 0.9%).

Use of Alcohol by Region

Figure 28 shows that the share of African Americans who consumed alcohol in the past month did not vary by region (about 36.4%). Regardless of region, a smaller percentage of African Americans than Whites had used alcohol in the past month.

- For example, **Table 30** shows that 37.5% of African American high school seniors in the midwest had used alcohol in the past

month, compared with 56.6% of their White counterparts.

Use of Alcohol by School Urbanicity

Regardless of school urbanicity, a higher share of boys than girls used alcohol in the past month among both African Americans and Whites. About shows that 30.0% of African American girls and 39.3% of African American boys at urban schools had used alcohol in the past month.

Figure 29 shows that the percentage of African Americans who had used alcohol in the past month was smaller than the percentage of all students, regardless of school location.

- **Table 31** shows that 34.1% of African Americans at urban high schools had used alcohol in

Table 24. Percentage of Students in Grades 6 to 12 who Reported Talking With Their Parents About Drugs by School Characteristics, Race, and Sex: 1993
(weighted sample size in parentheses)

Characteristic	Total	Male	Female	White, Non-Hispanic Total	Male	Female	African American, Non-Hispanic Total	Male	Female	Hispanic Total	Male	Female	Other Total	Male	Female
Total * + + +	100.0% (23,810,309)	100.0% (11,926,918)	100.0% (11,883,391)	100.0% (16,721,186)	100.0% (8,353,179)	100.0% (8,368,007)	100.0% (3,745,525)	100.0% (1,860,254)	100.0% (1,885,271)	100.0% (2,598,884)	100.0% (1,359,295)	100.0% (1,239,589)	100.0% (744,714)	100.0% (354,190)	100.0% (390,524)
Talk to Parents about Drugs	35.0% (8,344,518)	32.5% (3,877,566)	37.6% (4,466,952)	33.0% (5,514,492)	29.4% (2,459,925)	36.5% (3,054,567)	36.8% (1,377,976)	37.5% (697,563)	36.1% (680,413)	44.9% (1,166,691)	44.3% (601,498)	45.6% (565,193)	38.3% (285,359)	33.5% (118,580)	42.7% (166,779)
School Level															
Elementary * +	46.8% (1,237,726)	42.1% (570,095)	51.7% (667,631)	41.9% (737,096)	36.7% (335,814)	47.5% (401,282)	53.1% (213,652)	52.1% (109,056)	54.2% (104,596)	64.3% (241,603)	60.4% (116,562)	68.4% (125,041)	42.7% (45,374)	24.3% (8,663)	51.9% (36,712)
Middle/Junior High +	41.4% (3,069,567)	39.1% (1,504,913)	43.9% (1,564,654)	39.6% (1,990,753)	36.6% (930,298)	42.8% (1,060,455)	41.7% (547,758)	42.4% (303,964)	40.8% (243,794)	50.1% (434,036)	49.9% (245,952)	50.4% (188,084)	45.4% (97,020)	25.2% (24,700)	62.5% (72,320)
High School + +	28.9% (3,277,404)	26.4% (1,445,345)	31.2% (1,832,059)	27.6% (2,213,776)	24.4% (953,728)	30.5% (1,260,048)	29.7% (531,949)	28.8% (235,529)	30.5% (296,420)	36.3% (434,161)	34.5% (204,646)	38.2% (229,516)	29.8% (97,518)	31.7% (51,442)	27.9% (46,076)
Combination + +	31.6% (759,822)	28.7% (357,214)	34.8% (402,608)	30.1% (572,867)	24.2% (240,085)	36.4% (332,782)	35.5% (84,618)	41.9% (49,015)	29.4% (35,603)	35.0% (56,890)	43.0% (34,338)	27.2% (22,552)	46.7% (45,447)	57.7% (33,776)	30.1% (11,671)
School Type															
Public, Assigned * + + +	35.1% (6,795,945)	32.7% (3,190,888)	37.4% (3,605,057)	33.1% (4,647,909)	29.8% (2,080,567)	36.5% (2,567,342)	37.2% (1,025,685)	38.1% (536,937)	36.2% (488,748)	45.6% (943,257)	46.3% (510,749)	44.8% (432,508)	34.2% (179,094)	25.7% (62,635)	41.5% (116,459)
Public, Chosen +	37.2% (960,570)	32.7% (416,009)	41.5% (544,561)	33.3% (415,546)	27.1% (170,137)	39.6% (245,409)	36.4% (301,031)	35.7% (139,063)	37.0% (161,968)	45.8% (172,275)	39.2% (74,359)	52.6% (97,916)	53.2% (71,718)	49.9% (32,450)	56.3% (39,268)
Private, Religious	32.1% (492,552)	29.0% (212,687)	34.9% (279,865)	32.1% (382,398)	28.4% (170,169)	35.8% (212,229)	28.2% (37,119)	29.4% (12,231)	27.7% (24,888)	32.4% (48,003)	23.5% (14,125)	38.5% (33,878)	39.5% (25,032)	49.0% (16,162)	29.1% (8,870)
Private, Non-Religious	30.2% (95,452)	33.0% (57,983)	26.8% (37,469)	26.7% (68,639)	28.9% (39,052)	24.2% (29,587)	50.1% (14,142)	43.1% (9,333)	72.9% (4,809)	45.4% (3,156)	37.4% (2,265)	100.0% (891)	41.4% (9,515)	56.8% (7,333)	21.7% (2,182)
Number of Students															
Under than 300 ~ ~	36.6% (949,523)	35.8% (457,234)	37.3% (492,289)	35.2% (706,436)	33.3% (325,723)	37.0% (380,713)	40.0% (93,118)	54.7% (69,049)	22.5% (24,068)	40.8% (111,709)	30.3% (40,211)	50.7% (71,497)	46.0% (38,260)	56.3% (22,251)	36.7% (16,009)
300 to 599 * + + +	37.6% (2,922,224)	33.6% (1,335,606)	41.8% (1,586,619)	35.1% (1,936,419)	29.8% (836,566)	40.6% (1,099,854)	40.9% (505,515)	42.8% (282,311)	38.8% (223,203)	52.1% (404,362)	48.3% (183,413)	55.7% (220,950)	32.7% (75,928)	27.5% (33,316)	38.3% (42,612)
600 to 999 + +	34.6% (2,122,201)	33.3% (1,006,659)	35.9% (1,115,542)	33.0% (1,440,668)	29.2% (628,650)	36.7% (812,018)	35.7% (370,279)	39.5% (195,056)	32.2% (175,222)	44.1% (248,980)	51.3% (164,678)	34.5% (84,301)	37.9% (62,275)	31.0% (18,275)	41.8% (44,000)
1,000 or More ~	32.1% (2,350,570)	29.5% (1,078,067)	34.7% (1,272,503)	29.6% (1,430,969)	27.7% (668,987)	31.6% (761,982)	33.0% (409,066)	26.0% (151,146)	39.1% (257,919)	40.8% (401,640)	40.6% (213,195)	41.2% (188,444)	41.1% (108,896)	33.2% (44,739)	49.3% (64,157)
Urbanicity															
Urban, Inside Urbanized Area + +	36.3% (5,064,394)	34.0% (2,354,213)	38.7% (2,710,181)	33.8% (2,873,875)	30.7% (1,309,154)	36.9% (1,564,721)	36.7% (1,045,845)	35.8% (497,106)	37.5% (548,739)	45.2% (926,302)	44.9% (470,092)	45.5% (456,210)	41.1% (218,372)	32.5% (77,861)	48.1% (140,511)
Urban, Outside Urbanized Area	31.9% (1,136,460)	30.5% (564,955)	33.4% (571,505)	30.2% (830,302)	27.9% (402,978)	32.7% (427,324)	25.3% (90,506)	32.5% (48,451)	20.2% (42,055)	49.5% (171,082)	42.6% (86,625)	59.5% (84,456)	41.1% (44,570)	52.3% (26,900)	31.0% (17,670)
Rural ** + + +	34.0% (2,143,664)	30.5% (958,398)	37.4% (1,185,266)	33.1% (1,810,315)	28.3% (747,793)	37.7% (1,062,521)	45.1% (241,625)	47.0% (152,006)	42.2% (89,619)	33.7% (69,307)	40.7% (44,780)	25.6% (24,527)	21.5% (22,417)	21.8% (13,819)	20.8% (8,598)
Census Region															
Northeast * + + +	30.7% (1,335,329)	25.9% (584,489)	35.9% (750,839)	28.5% (955,376)	23.3% (420,123)	34.5% (535,253)	37.1% (186,195)	32.3% (64,459)	40.3% (121,735)	37.4% (127,246)	45.1% (79,796)	29.1% (47,450)	43.3% (66,511)	25.1% (20,111)	63.1% (46,400)
South + +	37.3% (3,137,178)	35.6% (1,479,213)	39.0% (1,657,965)	36.8% (1,962,648)	33.1% (871,684)	40.4% (1,090,964)	35.8% (771,051)	39.1% (431,137)	32.3% (339,914)	46.5% (351,752)	46.1% (158,661)	46.8% (193,091)	31.3% (51,727)	23.4% (17,731)	38.0% (33,996)
Midwest *	33.6% (1,974,377)	33.1% (948,263)	34.2% (1,026,114)	32.2% (1,550,200)	31.5% (731,380)	32.9% (818,820)	41.5% (303,089)	40.3% (155,095)	42.8% (147,994)	42.3% (89,909)	46.5% (46,913)	38.5% (42,996)	27.3% (31,179)	24.2% (14,875)	31.0% (16,304)
West + +	36.6% (1,897,635)	32.8% (865,601)	40.6% (1,032,034)	32.5% (1,046,268)	27.4% (436,738)	37.4% (609,530)	32.9% (117,642)	27.2% (46,872)	38.2% (70,770)	46.4% (597,783)	42.9% (316,127)	51.0% (281,656)	43.6% (135,942)	48.1% (65,863)	40.0% (70,079)

Notes:

*** Test of statistical significance compares African Americans with Whites. *** p < .001, ** p < .01, * p < .05.

+++ Test of statistical significance compares White boys with White girls. +++ p < .001, ++ p < .01, + p < .05.

~~~Test of statistical significance compares African American boys with African American girls. ~~~ p < .001, ~~ p < .01, ~ p < .05.

Tests of statistical significance calculated using adjusted sample weight to control for influence of large sample sizes.

Student's residence determined by ZIP code. An Urbanized Area (UA) comprises a place (e.g., city, village) and adjacent densely settled surrounding territory that together have a population of at least 50,000. "Urban, outside Urbanized Area" includes incorporated and unincorporated places outside of UA with population of at least 2,500. "Rural" represents all other places.

Source: National Household Education Survey, 1993 School Safety & Discipline Component.

Figure 24. Percentage of Students in Grades 6 to 12 Who Reported Talking With Their Parents About Drugs by School Characteristics: 1993

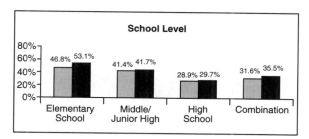

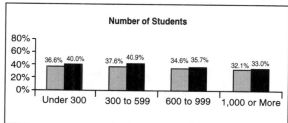

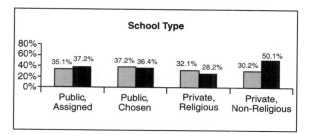

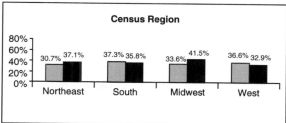

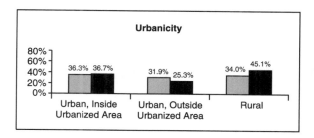

Source: National Household Education Survey, 1993 School Safety & Discipline Component.

the past month, compared with 50.8% of their White peers.

- At suburban high schools, 36.2% of African American seniors, but 56.2% of White seniors, had used alcohol in the past month.

- At rural schools, 40.1% of African Americans and 52.7% of Whites had used alcohol in the past month.

Use of Alcohol by School Poverty

Overall, the use of alcohol within the past month appeared to increase as the level of school poverty declined. **Figure 30** shows that at schools in which more than 40% of students received free or reduced lunch, 45.3% of high school seniors had used alcohol in the past month. But, at schools in which 5% or less of the students received free or reduced lunch, 55.2% of high school seniors had used alcohol in the past month.

Table 25. Percentage of 1992 High School Seniors Who Smoke Cigarettes by Race and Sex
(weighted sample size in parenthesis)

Smoke Cigarettes	Total	Male	Female	White, Non-Hispanic Total	Male	Female	African American, Non-Hispanic Total	Male	Female	Hispanic Total	Male	Female	Other Total	Male	Female
Total ***	100.0%	100.0%	100.0%	100.0%	100.0%	100.0%	100.0%	100.0%	100.0%	100.0%	100.0%	100.0%	100.0%	100.0%	100.0%
	(1,979,128)	(987,869)	(991,258)	(1,486,747)	(749,933)	(736,814)	(206,045)	(98,848)	(107,197)	(181,156)	(88,975)	(92,181)	(105,180)	(50,114)	(55,066)
Don't Smoke	79.5%	79.1%	79.9%	76.4%	76.3%	76.4%	95.3%	95.0%	95.5%	83.7%	82.2%	85.1%	86.3%	84.9%	87.7%
	(1,573,877)	(781,751)	(792,125)	(1,135,155)	(572,145)	(563,011)	(196,334)	(93,950)	(102,385)	(151,577)	(73,118)	(78,459)	(90,810)	(42,539)	(48,271)
Smoke	20.5%	20.9%	20.1%	23.6%	23.7%	23.6%	4.7%	5.0%	4.5%	16.3%	17.8%	14.9%	13.7%	15.1%	12.3%
	(405,251)	(206,118)	(199,133)	(351,592)	(177,788)	(173,803)	(9,710)	(4,898)	(4,812)	(29,579)	(15,857)	(13,722)	(14,370)	(7,575)	(6,795)
Amount Smoked * +++**															
Less Than 1 Cigarette per Day	5.2%	5.3%	5.1%	5.6%	5.7%	5.6%	2.1%	2.6%	1.7%	5.9%	6.1%	5.7%	4.2%	4.3%	4.2%
	(103,314)	(52,823)	(50,491)	(83,792)	(42,693)	(41,099)	(4,410)	(2,605)	(1,805)	(10,644)	(5,395)	(5,249)	(4,469)	(2,131)	(2,338)
1 to 5 Cigarettes per Day	5.8%	5.3%	6.3%	6.5%	5.8%	7.2%	1.4%	1.0%	1.8%	6.7%	7.3%	6.1%	4.0%	4.1%	3.9%
	(115,501)	(52,710)	(62,791)	(96,351)	(43,180)	(53,171)	(2,892)	(1,010)	(1,882)	(12,091)	(6,478)	(5,613)	(4,168)	(2,042)	(2,126)
1/2 Pack per Day	4.7%	4.6%	4.8%	5.6%	5.3%	5.9%	0.8%	1.0%	0.6%	2.5%	2.5%	2.4%	3.7%	4.9%	2.7%
	(93,303)	(45,643)	(47,660)	(83,280)	(39,936)	(43,344)	(1,616)	(1,009)	(607)	(4,500)	(2,258)	(2,242)	(3,908)	(2,440)	(1,467)
1/2 to 2 Packs per Day	4.2%	4.7%	3.7%	5.4%	6.1%	4.8%	0.4%	0.3%	0.5%	0.6%	0.5%	0.6%	1.4%	1.1%	1.6%
	(83,992)	(46,923)	(37,070)	(80,725)	(45,599)	(35,125)	(793)	(274)	(518)	(1,050)	(488)	(562)	(1,426)	(562)	(864)
2 or More Packs per Day	0.5%	0.8%	0.1%	0.5%	0.9%	0.1%	0.0%	0.0%	0.0%	0.7%	1.4%	0.1%	0.4%	0.8%	0.0%
	(9,140)	(8,020)	(1,120)	(7,445)	(6,381)	(1,064)	–	–	–	(1,296)	(1,239)	(56)	(400)	(400)	–

Notes:
"–" indicates sample size too small to estimate.
*** Test of statistical significance compares African Americans with Whites. *** p <.001, ** p <.01, * p <.05.
+++ Test of statistical significance compares White boys with White girls. +++ p <.001, ++ p <.01, + p <.05.
~~~ Test of statistical significance compares African American boys with African American girls. ~~~ p <.001, ~~ p <.01, ~ p <.05.
Tests of statistical significance calculated using adjusted sample weight to control for influence of large sample sizes.
Source: National Education Longitudinal Study of 1988 Eighth Graders, Second Follow-Up (1992).

The percentage of African American high school seniors who used alcohol in the past month was smaller than the percentage of White high school seniors regardless of the level of school poverty.

- For example, **Table 32** shows that at schools with the highest levels of poverty, 34.6% of African Americans, but 52.2% of Whites, had consumed alcohol in the past month.

- At schools with the lowest levels of poverty, 31.0% of African Americans had used alcohol in the last month, compared with 57.5% of Whites.

Use of Alcohol by School Type

Figure 31 shows that nearly two-thirds (61.3%) of high school seniors at Catholic schools had used alcohol in the past month, compared with one-half (50.3%) of their counterparts at public schools and 44.0% of those at non-Catholic private schools.

- **Table 33** shows that a smaller share of African Americans than Whites had used alcohol in the past month among those at public (37.0% versus 53.4%) and Catholic (24.5% versus 65.4%) schools.

- At public schools, a smaller percentage of girls than boys had used alcohol in the past month among both African Americans (28.6% versus 45.4%) and Whites (49.0% versus 58.0%).

Use of Alcohol by Socioeconomic Status

Figure 32 shows that 45.6% of seniors in the lowest socioeconomic status quartile consumed alcohol in the past month, compared with 52.4% of those

Table 26. Use of Alcohol Among 1992 High School Seniors by Race and Sex
(weighted sample size in parenthesis)

Use of Alcohol	Total	Male	Female	White, Non-Hispanic Total	White Male	White Female	African American, Non-Hispanic Total	AA Male	AA Female	Hispanic Total	Hispanic Male	Hispanic Female	Other Total	Other Male	Other Female
Number Times in Lifetime Had Alcohol to Drink															
Total *** +++ ~~~	100.0%	100.0%	100.0%	100.0%	100.0%	100.0%	100.0%	100.0%	100.0%	100.0%	100.0%	100.0%	100.0%	100.0%	100.0%
	(1,899,450)	(944,154)	(955,297)	(1,436,906)	(722,925)	(713,981)	(191,903)	(90,417)	(101,486)	(169,613)	(83,503)	(86,110)	(101,028)	(47,309)	(53,719)
No Occasions	11.4%	10.5%	12.4%	9.8%	9.6%	10.1%	19.5%	16.3%	22.4%	10.4%	7.5%	13.2%	20.4%	17.9%	22.5%
	(217,082)	(98,986)	(118,097)	(141,357)	(69,487)	(71,870)	(37,443)	(14,716)	(22,727)	(17,705)	(6,296)	(11,409)	(20,578)	(8,487)	(12,091)
Any Occasions	88.6%	89.5%	87.6%	90.2%	90.4%	89.9%	80.5%	83.7%	77.6%	89.6%	92.5%	86.8%	79.6%	82.1%	77.5%
	(1,682,368)	(845,168)	(837,200)	(1,295,550)	(653,439)	(642,111)	(154,461)	(75,701)	(78,759)	(151,908)	(77,207)	(74,701)	(80,450)	(38,822)	(41,628)
1 to 2 Occasions	15.9%	13.9%	17.8%	13.8%	12.8%	14.8%	25.4%	20.4%	29.9%	19.1%	14.2%	23.9%	21.3%	17.7%	24.4%
	(301,065)	(131,215)	(169,851)	(198,392)	(92,514)	(105,879)	(48,779)	(18,464)	(30,315)	(32,422)	(11,851)	(20,571)	(21,472)	(8,386)	(13,086)
3 to 19 Occasions	32.1%	28.0%	36.2%	31.1%	26.0%	36.3%	38.1%	39.8%	36.5%	33.9%	31.0%	36.7%	31.9%	30.3%	33.4%
	(610,389)	(264,481)	(345,908)	(447,587)	(188,275)	(259,312)	(73,079)	(35,995)	(37,085)	(57,488)	(25,894)	(31,594)	(32,235)	(14,317)	(17,918)
20 or More Occasions	40.6%	47.6%	33.6%	45.2%	51.5%	38.8%	17.0%	23.5%	11.2%	36.6%	47.3%	26.2%	26.5%	34.1%	19.8%
	(770,914)	(449,473)	(321,441)	(649,570)	(372,650)	(276,921)	(32,602)	(21,243)	(11,359)	(61,998)	(39,462)	(22,536)	(26,743)	(16,119)	(10,625)
Number Times in Last 30 Days Had Alcohol to Drink															
Total *** +++ ~~~	100.0%	100.0%	100.0%	100.0%	100.0%	100.0%	100.0%	100.0%	100.0%	100.0%	100.0%	100.0%	100.0%	100.0%	100.0%
	(1,842,714)	(920,095)	(922,619)	(1,409,548)	(707,519)	(702,028)	(175,399)	(85,099)	(90,300)	(162,188)	(81,179)	(81,009)	(95,580)	(46,298)	(49,282)
No Occasions	49.3%	44.1%	54.5%	46.1%	41.6%	50.7%	63.6%	55.0%	71.7%	52.3%	46.8%	57.9%	65.5%	59.2%	71.5%
	(909,029)	(406,202)	(502,827)	(649,973)	(294,056)	(355,918)	(111,561)	(46,798)	(64,763)	(84,850)	(37,957)	(46,894)	(62,645)	(27,393)	(35,252)
Any Occasions	50.7%	55.9%	45.5%	53.9%	58.4%	49.3%	36.4%	45.0%	28.3%	47.7%	53.2%	42.1%	34.5%	40.8%	28.5%
	(933,685)	(513,893)	(419,792)	(759,574)	(413,464)	(346,110)	(63,839)	(38,302)	(25,537)	(77,338)	(43,222)	(34,115)	(32,935)	(18,905)	(14,029)
1 to 2 Occasions	28.0%	26.8%	29.3%	28.7%	26.7%	30.7%	26.7%	30.4%	23.1%	27.2%	24.2%	30.2%	22.3%	25.1%	19.7%
	(516,685)	(246,325)	(270,360)	(404,470)	(189,215)	(215,255)	(46,765)	(25,867)	(20,897)	(44,100)	(19,611)	(24,489)	(21,350)	(11,632)	(9,719)
3 to 19 Occasions	19.7%	24.3%	15.0%	21.9%	26.5%	17.3%	8.3%	12.2%	4.6%	17.6%	24.4%	10.8%	10.5%	13.2%	7.9%
	(362,223)	(223,684)	(138,539)	(309,014)	(187,306)	(121,708)	(14,565)	(10,421)	(4,144)	(28,597)	(19,825)	(8,773)	(10,047)	(6,133)	(3,914)
20 or More Occasions	3.0%	4.8%	1.2%	3.3%	5.2%	1.3%	1.4%	2.4%	0.5%	2.9%	4.7%	1.1%	1.6%	2.5%	0.8%
	(54,777)	(43,884)	(10,893)	(46,091)	(36,943)	(9,148)	(2,509)	(2,013)	(496)	(4,640)	(3,787)	(853)	(1,537)	(1,141)	(397)
Number Times Had 5 or More Drinks in a Row															
Total *** +++ ~~~	100.0%	100.0%	100.0%	100.0%	100.0%	100.0%	100.0%	100.0%	100.0%	100.0%	100.0%	100.0%	100.0%	100.0%	100.0%
	(1,924,726)	(957,133)	(967,593)	(1,457,797)	(733,454)	(724,344)	(193,890)	(90,939)	(102,951)	(170,701)	(84,397)	(86,303)	(102,337)	(48,343)	(53,994)
None	71.5%	63.8%	79.2%	69.1%	61.1%	77.1%	85.0%	79.2%	90.1%	70.3%	61.2%	79.1%	83.3%	79.7%	86.6%
	(1,376,999)	(610,674)	(766,325)	(1,006,986)	(448,447)	(558,539)	(164,789)	(72,000)	(92,789)	(119,932)	(51,682)	(68,250)	(85,292)	(38,546)	(46,746)
Any Occasions	28.5%	36.2%	20.8%	30.9%	38.9%	22.9%	15.0%	20.8%	9.9%	29.7%	38.8%	20.9%	16.7%	20.3%	13.4%
	(547,727)	(346,459)	(201,268)	(450,811)	(285,007)	(165,804)	(29,102)	(18,940)	(10,162)	(50,769)	(32,715)	(18,053)	(17,046)	(9,797)	(7,248)
Once	10.9%	12.6%	9.3%	11.6%	13.3%	9.9%	6.5%	8.6%	4.7%	12.6%	13.4%	11.7%	7.4%	8.8%	6.2%
	(210,671)	(120,732)	(89,939)	(169,036)	(97,367)	(71,669)	(12,639)	(7,825)	(4,814)	(21,426)	(11,302)	(10,124)	(7,570)	(4,238)	(3,332)
2 Times	7.1%	9.0%	5.3%	7.7%	9.6%	5.9%	4.5%	5.9%	3.3%	6.8%	8.8%	4.9%	3.7%	5.5%	2.1%
	(137,203)	(85,728)	(51,475)	(112,942)	(70,240)	(42,702)	(8,777)	(5,363)	(3,415)	(11,663)	(7,462)	(4,201)	(3,820)	(2,663)	(1,157)
3 to 5 Times	6.2%	8.3%	4.2%	7.1%	9.4%	4.8%	2.2%	3.2%	1.3%	5.6%	7.7%	3.5%	2.8%	2.7%	3.0%
	(119,964)	(79,544)	(40,419)	(103,234)	(68,819)	(34,415)	(4,328)	(2,942)	(1,386)	(9,485)	(6,463)	(3,022)	(2,916)	(1,320)	(1,596)
6 to 9 Times	2.1%	3.1%	1.1%	2.4%	3.5%	1.3%	0.6%	1.2%	0.1%	1.5%	2.8%	0.3%	0.5%	0.8%	0.3%
	(39,493)	(29,313)	(10,180)	(35,161)	(25,509)	(9,652)	(1,176)	(1,068)	(108)	(2,634)	(2,372)	(262)	(521)	(364)	(157)
10 or More Times	2.1%	3.3%	1.0%	2.1%	3.1%	1.0%	1.1%	1.9%	0.4%	3.3%	6.1%	0.5%	2.2%	2.5%	1.9%
	(40,397)	(31,143)	(9,255)	(30,438)	(23,072)	(7,366)	(2,181)	(1,742)	(439)	(5,561)	(5,117)	(443)	(2,217)	(1,211)	(1,006)

Notes:

*** Test of statistical significance compares African Americans with Whites. *** p < .001, ** p < .01, * p < .05.

+++ Test of statistical significance compares White boys with White girls. +++ p <.001, ++ p < .01, + p < .05.

~~~Test of statistical significance compares African American boys with African American girls. ~~~ p < .001, ~~ p < .01, ~ p < .05.

Tests of statistical significance calculated using adjusted sample weight to control for influence of large sample sizes.

Source: National Education Longitudinal Study of 1988 Eighth Graders, Second Follow-Up (1992).

Figure 25. Use of Alcohol Among 1992 High School Seniors

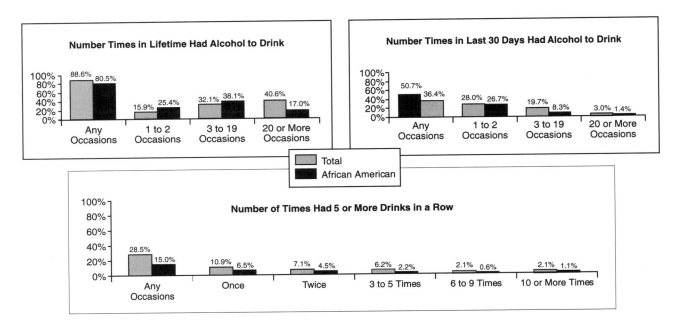

Source: National Education Longitudinal Study of 1988 Eighth Graders, Second Follow-Up (1992).

in the second quartile, 52.2% of those in the third quartile, and 52.2% of those in the highest quartile.

The proportion of girls who had consumed alcohol in the past month was smaller than the proportion of boys among both African Americans and Whites in the lowest two quartiles of socioeconomic status.

- For example, **Table 34** shows that 28.1% of African Americans girls in the lowest socioeconomic status quartile had consumed alcohol in the past month, compared with 46.2% of African American boys.

A smaller percentage of African Americans than Whites had consumed alcohol within the past month, regardless of socioeconomic status.

- **Table 34** shows that, among high school seniors in the lowest socioeconomic status quartile,

35.8% of African Americans and 49.9% of Whites drank alcohol in the past month.

- About 36.2% of African Americans in the highest socioeconomic status quartile had consumed alcohol in the past month, compared with 54.2% of their White peers.

Use of Alcohol by Test Score

Figure 33 shows that 46.3% of seniors with the highest test scores drank alcohol in the past month, compared with 52.7% of those in the lowest quartile, 54.4% of those in the second quartile, and 53.0% of those in the third quartile.

A smaller percentage of African Americans than Whites consumed alcohol in the past month, regardless of test score.

Figure 26. Use of Marijuana Among 1992 High School Seniors

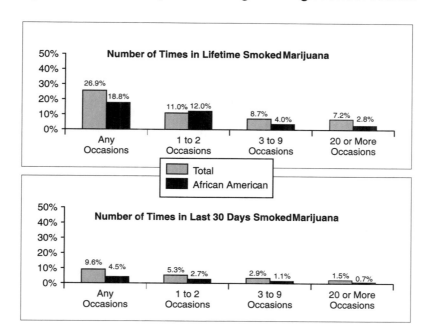

Source: National Education Longitudinal Study of 1988 Eighth Graders, Second Follow-Up (1992).

- For example, **Table 35** shows that, among high school seniors with test scores in the highest quartile, 30.4% of African Americans but 48.5% of Whites drank alcohol in the past month.

- Among those with test scores in the lowest quartile, 37.8% of African Americans but 60.8% of Whites drank alcohol in the past month.

Table 27. Use of Marijuana Among 1992 High School Seniors by Race and Sex
(weighted sample size in parenthesis)

Use of Marijuana	Total	Male	Female	White, Non-Hispanic			African American, Non-Hispanic			Hispanic			Other		
				Total	Male	Female	Total	Male	Female	Total	Male	Female	Total	Male	Female
Number Times in Lifetime Smoked Marijuana															
Total *** +++ ~~~	100.0%	100.0%	100.0%	100.0%	100.0%	100.0%	100.0%	100.0%	100.0%	100.0%	100.0%	100.0%	100.0%	100.0%	100.0%
	(1,860,627)	(921,715)	(938,912)	(1,408,505)	(705,167)	(703,339)	(186,602)	(87,690)	(98,912)	(164,825)	(81,401)	(83,424)	(100,694)	(47,457)	(53,238)
No Occasions	73.1%	69.4%	76.8%	71.7%	68.8%	74.7%	81.2%	72.1%	89.2%	72.1%	67.7%	76.4%	79.4%	77.1%	81.5%
	(1,360,522)	(639,891)	(720,632)	(1,010,289)	(484,946)	(525,343)	(151,439)	(63,231)	(88,208)	(118,847)	(55,146)	(63,701)	(79,947)	(36,568)	(43,379)
Any Occasions	26.9%	30.6%	23.2%	28.3%	31.2%	25.3%	18.8%	27.9%	10.8%	27.9%	32.3%	23.6%	20.6%	22.9%	18.5%
	(500,105)	(281,824)	(218,281)	(398,216)	(220,221)	(177,995)	(35,163)	(24,459)	(10,703)	(45,978)	(26,255)	(19,723)	(20,747)	(10,889)	(9,859)
1 to 2 Occasions	11.0%	12.4%	9.5%	10.8%	11.6%	10.0%	12.0%	18.6%	6.2%	13.5%	16.5%	10.5%	7.4%	6.8%	7.8%
	(204,020)	(114,723)	(89,297)	(151,974)	(81,721)	(70,253)	(22,451)	(16,297)	(6,154)	(22,187)	(13,460)	(8,727)	(7,408)	(3,245)	(4,163)
3 to 19 Occasions	8.7%	9.1%	8.3%	9.1%	9.3%	8.8%	4.0%	5.0%	3.2%	10.2%	9.9%	10.5%	9.9%	11.8%	8.2%
	(161,827)	(83,585)	(78,242)	(127,496)	(65,485)	(62,011)	(7,527)	(4,403)	(3,124)	(16,848)	(8,085)	(8,763)	(9,956)	(5,611)	(4,344)
20 or More Occasions	7.2%	9.1%	5.4%	8.4%	10.4%	6.5%	2.8%	4.3%	1.4%	4.2%	5.8%	2.7%	3.4%	4.3%	2.5%
	(134,257)	(83,516)	(50,741)	(118,746)	(73,015)	(45,731)	(5,184)	(3,759)	(1,425)	(6,943)	(4,710)	(2,234)	(3,383)	(2,032)	(1,351)
Number Times in Last 30 Days Smoked Marijuana															
Total *** +++ ~	100.0%	100.0%	100.0%	100.0%	100.0%	100.0%	100.0%	100.0%	100.0%	100.0%	100.0%	100.0%	100.0%	100.0%	100.0%
	(1,761,550)	(867,472)	(894,078)	(1,346,490)	(667,324)	(679,166)	(166,758)	(78,560)	(88,198)	(152,657)	(76,454)	(76,203)	(95,645)	(45,135)	(50,511)
No Occasions	90.4%	88.3%	92.4%	89.3%	87.1%	91.5%	95.5%	93.6%	97.1%	92.0%	90.6%	93.4%	93.2%	92.1%	94.2%
	(1,591,599)	(765,892)	(825,708)	(1,202,715)	(581,456)	(621,259)	(159,208)	(73,570)	(85,638)	(140,507)	(69,302)	(71,205)	(89,170)	(41,564)	(47,606)
Any Occasions	9.6%	11.7%	7.6%	10.7%	12.9%	8.5%	4.5%	6.4%	2.9%	8.0%	9.4%	6.6%	6.8%	7.9%	5.8%
	(169,951)	(101,581)	(68,370)	(143,776)	(85,869)	(57,907)	(7,550)	(4,990)	(2,560)	(12,150)	(7,151)	(4,998)	(6,476)	(3,571)	(2,905)
1 to 2 Occasions	5.3%	5.6%	4.9%	5.6%	5.8%	5.4%	2.7%	3.4%	2.0%	5.4%	6.5%	4.2%	4.2%	5.3%	3.3%
	(92,501)	(48,897)	(43,604)	(75,840)	(38,885)	(36,954)	(4,432)	(2,654)	(1,778)	(8,206)	(4,986)	(3,221)	(4,023)	(2,372)	(1,651)
3 to 19 Occasions	2.9%	3.6%	2.1%	3.3%	4.2%	2.4%	1.1%	1.6%	0.7%	1.6%	1.4%	1.7%	2.1%	1.9%	2.2%
	(50,407)	(31,297)	(19,110)	(44,155)	(28,131)	(16,025)	(1,903)	(1,247)	(656)	(2,366)	(1,062)	(1,304)	(1,983)	(857)	(1,126)
20 or More Occasions	1.5%	2.5%	0.6%	1.8%	2.8%	0.7%	0.7%	1.4%	0.1%	1.0%	1.4%	0.6%	0.5%	0.8%	0.3%
	(27,043)	(21,386)	(5,656)	(23,781)	(18,853)	(4,928)	(1,215)	(1,088)	(127)	(1,577)	(1,104)	(473)	(470)	(342)	(129)

Notes:

*** Test of statistical significance compares African Americans with Whites. *** p <.001, ** p <.01, * p <.05.

+++ Test of statistical significance compares White boys with White girls. +++ p <.001, ++ p <.01, + p <.05.

~~~ Test of statistical significance compares African American boys with African American girls. ~~~ p <.001, ~~ p <.01, ~ p <.05.

Tests of statistical significance calculated using adjusted sample weight to control for influence of large sample sizes.

Source: National Education Longitudinal Study of 1988 Eighth Graders, Second Follow-Up (1992).

Table 28. Use of Cocaine Among 1992 High School Seniors by Race and Sex
(weighted sample size in parenthesis)

Use of Cocaine	Total	Male	Female	White, Non-Hispanic Total	Male	Female	African American, Non-Hispanic Total	Male	Female	Hispanic Total	Male	Female	Other Total	Male	Female
Number Times in Lifetime Used Cocaine															
Total *** +++ ~	100.0%	100.0%	100.0%	100.0%	100.0%	100.0%	100.0%	100.0%	100.0%	100.0%	100.0%	100.0%	100.0%	100.0%	100.0%
	(1,867,918)	(925,967)	(941,950)	(1,414,414)	(708,765)	(705,648)	(187,367)	(88,322)	(99,045)	(165,027)	(81,176)	(83,851)	(101,110)	(47,704)	(53,406)
No Occasions	95.7%	94.3%	97.1%	95.5%	94.3%	96.7%	98.7%	97.9%	99.5%	93.0%	89.3%	96.6%	96.9%	95.7%	98.0%
	(1,787,480)	(873,016)	(914,464)	(1,351,132)	(668,483)	(682,649)	(184,970)	(86,441)	(98,529)	(153,418)	(72,452)	(80,966)	(97,960)	(45,640)	(52,320)
Any Occasions	4.3%	5.7%	2.9%	4.5%	5.7%	3.3%	1.3%	2.1%	0.5%	7.0%	10.7%	3.4%	3.1%	4.3%	2.0%
	(80,438)	(52,951)	(27,486)	(63,281)	(40,282)	(22,999)	(2,397)	(1,881)	(516)	(11,609)	(8,724)	(2,885)	(3,150)	(2,064)	(1,086)
1 to 2 Occasions	2.5%	3.3%	1.7%	2.6%	3.3%	1.9%	0.9%	1.6%	0.2%	3.8%	5.7%	2.0%	2.0%	2.5%	1.5%
	(47,083)	(30,789)	(16,294)	(37,052)	(23,470)	(13,582)	(1,675)	(1,447)	(228)	(6,341)	(4,664)	(1,677)	(2,016)	(1,208)	(808)
3 to 19 Occasions	1.0%	1.1%	0.9%	1.1%	1.0%	1.1%	0.3%	0.5%	0.2%	1.7%	2.6%	0.8%	0.7%	1.3%	0.2%
	(19,070)	(10,632)	(8,438)	(14,898)	(7,432)	(7,466)	(612)	(434)	(178)	(2,812)	(2,126)	(685)	(748)	(639)	(109)
20 or More Occasions	0.8%	1.2%	0.3%	0.8%	1.3%	0.3%	0.1%	0.0%	0.1%	1.5%	2.4%	0.6%	0.4%	0.5%	0.3%
	(14,284)	(11,530)	(2,754)	(11,331)	(9,380)	(1,951)	(111)	–	(111)	(2,456)	(1,933)	(523)	(386)	(217)	(169)
Number Times in Last 30 Days Used Cocaine															
Total +++	100.0%	100.0%	100.0%	100.0%	100.0%	100.0%	100.0%	100.0%	100.0%	100.0%	100.0%	100.0%	100.0%	100.0%	100.0%
	(1,761,218)	(866,770)	(894,448)	(1,346,814)	(667,072)	(679,742)	(166,545)	(78,275)	(88,270)	(152,168)	(76,026)	(76,142)	(95,691)	(45,397)	(50,294)
No Occasions	99.0%	98.5%	99.6%	99.1%	98.5%	99.6%	99.7%	99.4%	99.9%	98.3%	97.6%	98.9%	99.1%	98.4%	99.7%
	(1,744,386)	(853,802)	(890,584)	(1,334,060)	(657,083)	(676,977)	(166,003)	(77,841)	(88,162)	(149,508)	(74,229)	(75,279)	(94,815)	(44,649)	(50,166)
Any Occasions	1.0%	1.5%	0.4%	0.9%	1.5%	0.4%	0.3%	0.6%	0.1%	1.7%	2.4%	1.1%	0.9%	1.6%	0.3%
	(16,832)	(12,968)	(3,864)	(12,754)	(9,989)	(2,765)	(542)	(434)	(108)	(2,660)	(1,797)	(863)	(875)	(747)	(128)
1 to 2 Occasions	0.4%	0.6%	0.3%	0.4%	0.6%	0.2%	0.1%	0.0%	0.1%	0.8%	1.0%	0.6%	0.1%	0.0%	0.2%
	(7,078)	(4,797)	(2,281)	(5,648)	(4,043)	(1,605)	(108)	–	(108)	(1,239)	(753)	(485)	(82)	–	(82)
3 to 19 Occasions	0.3%	0.4%	0.1%	0.2%	0.3%	0.1%	0.1%	0.2%	0.0%	0.6%	1.1%	0.1%	0.5%	1.0%	0.1%
	(4,758)	(3,603)	(1,155)	(3,206)	(2,187)	(1,019)	(145)	(145)	–	(911)	(821)	(91)	(496)	(451)	(46)
20 or More Occasions	0.3%	0.5%	0.0%	0.3%	0.6%	0.0%	0.2%	0.4%	0.0%	0.3%	0.3%	0.4%	0.3%	0.7%	0.0%
	(4,997)	(4,569)	(428)	(3,901)	(3,759)	(141)	(289)	(289)	–	(511)	(224)	(287)	(297)	(297)	–

Notes:

"–" indicates sample size too small to estimate.

*** Test of statistical significance compares African Americans with Whites. *** p <.001, ** p <.01, * p <.05.

+++ Test of statistical significance compares White boys with White girls.

~~~Test of statistical significance compares African American boys with African American girls. ~~~ p <.001, ~~ p <.01, ~ p <.05.

Tests of statistical significance calculated using adjusted sample weight to control for influence of large sample sizes.

Source: National Education Longitudinal Study of 1988 Eighth Graders, Second Follow-Up (1992).

Figure 27. Percentage of 1992 High School Seniors Ever Under the Influence of Alcohol and Drugs At School

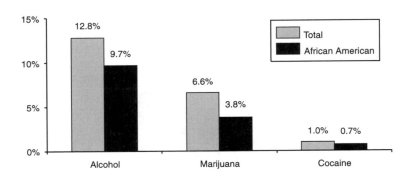

Source: National Education Longitudinal Study of 1988 Eighth Graders, Second Follow-up (1992).

Table 29. Percentage of 1992 High School Seniors Ever Under the Influence of Alcohol and Drugs at School by Race and Sex
(weighted sample size in parenthesis)

Under Influence at School	Total	Male	Female	White, Non-Hispanic Total	Male	Female	African American, Non-Hispanic Total	Male	Female	Hispanic Total	Male	Female	Other Total	Male	Female
Ever Under Influence of Alcohol															
Total *** +++ ~~~	100.0%	100.0%	100.0%	100.0%	100.0%	100.0%	100.0%	100.0%	100.0%	100.0%	100.0%	100.0%	100.0%	100.0%	100.0%
	(1,907,464)	(946,810)	(960,654)	(1,449,360)	(728,063)	(721,297)	(189,338)	(88,836)	(100,501)	(167,129)	(82,295)	(84,834)	(101,638)	(47,616)	(54,022)
Yes	12.8%	16.4%	9.2%	13.6%	17.0%	10.1%	9.7%	13.7%	6.1%	12.8%	17.7%	8.1%	7.2%	10.0%	4.8%
	(243,789)	(155,387)	(88,402)	(196,715)	(123,882)	(72,833)	(18,294)	(12,171)	(6,123)	(21,416)	(14,557)	(6,859)	(7,364)	(4,776)	(2,588)
Ever Under Influence of Marijuana															
Total *** +++ ~~~	100.0%	100.0%	100.0%	100.0%	100.0%	100.0%	100.0%	100.0%	100.0%	100.0%	100.0%	100.0%	100.0%	100.0%	100.0%
	(1,837,156)	(909,839)	(927,317)	(1,398,679)	(698,809)	(699,871)	(179,434)	(84,561)	(94,872)	(159,568)	(79,639)	(79,929)	(99,475)	(46,830)	(52,645)
Yes	6.6%	8.7%	4.6%	7.1%	9.2%	5.0%	3.8%	6.0%	1.9%	5.8%	7.4%	4.2%	6.2%	7.5%	4.9%
	(121,616)	(78,704)	(42,913)	(99,382)	(64,239)	(35,143)	(6,858)	(5,034)	(1,824)	(9,259)	(5,912)	(3,347)	(6,118)	(3,519)	(2,600)
Ever Under Influence of Cocaine															
Total +++ ~	100.0%	100.0%	100.0%	100.0%	100.0%	100.0%	100.0%	100.0%	100.0%	100.0%	100.0%	100.0%	100.0%	100.0%	100.0%
	(1,832,784)	(907,690)	(925,094)	(1,396,402)	(697,117)	(699,285)	(178,086)	(84,561)	(93,524)	(159,305)	(79,457)	(79,848)	(98,991)	(46,555)	(52,436)
Yes	1.0%	1.5%	0.5%	0.9%	1.3%	0.5%	0.7%	1.3%	0.2%	2.5%	3.5%	1.4%	1.4%	2.6%	0.4%
	(18,905)	(13,839)	(5,066)	(12,289)	(8,719)	(3,570)	(1,286)	(1,111)	(175)	(3,905)	(2,790)	(1,115)	(1,425)	(1,218)	(207)

Notes:

*** Test of statistical significance compares African Americans with Whites. *** p <.001, ** p <.01, * p <.05.

+++ Test of statistical significance compares White boys with White girls. +++ p <.001, ++ p <.01, + p <.05.

~~~Test of statistical significance compares African American boys with African American girls. ~~~ p <.001, ~~ p <.01, ~ p <.05.

Tests of statistical significance calculated using adjusted sample weight to control for influence of large sample sizes.

Source: National Education Longitudinal Study of 1988 Eighth Graders, Second Follow-Up (1992).

Figure 28. Percentage of 1992 High School Seniors Who Used Alcohol In the Last 30 Days by Region

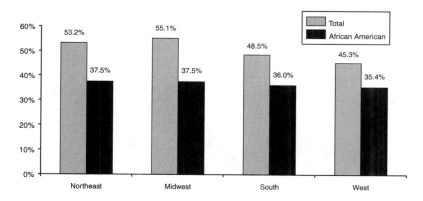

Source: National Education Longitudinal Study of 1988 Eighth Graders, Second Follow-Up (1992).

Figure 29. Percentage of 1992 High School Seniors Who Used Alcohol In the Last 30 Days by School Urbanicity

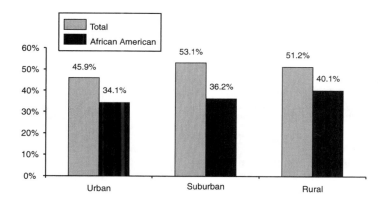

Source: National Education Longitudinal Study of 1988 Eighth Graders, Second Follow-Up (1992).

Table 30. Use of Alcohol in the Last 30 Days Among 1992 High School Seniors by Region, Race, and Sex
(weighted sample size in parenthesis)

Region	Total	Male	Female	White, Non-Hispanic Total	White, Non-Hispanic Male	White, Non-Hispanic Female	African American, Non-Hispanic Total	African American, Non-Hispanic Male	African American, Non-Hispanic Female	Hispanic Total	Hispanic Male	Hispanic Female	Other Total	Other Male	Other Female
Northeast *+++**	100.0% (365,131)	100.0% (177,707)	100.0% (187,424)	100.0% (307,324)	100.0% (151,791)	100.0% (155,533)	100.0% (21,074)	100.0% (10,004)	100.0% (11,070)	100.0% (19,412)	100.0% (8,253)	100.0% (11,159)	100.0% (17,321)	100.0% (7,659)	100.0% (9,662)
No Occasions	46.8% (170,882)	42.4% (75,378)	51.0% (95,504)	44.5% (136,900)	40.8% (61,941)	48.2% (74,959)	62.5% (13,167)	52.8% (5,285)	71.2% (7,882)	48.3% (9,375)	43.2% (3,567)	52.0% (5,808)	66.0% (11,440)	59.9% (4,585)	71.0% (6,856)
Any Occasions	53.2% (194,249)	57.6% (102,329)	49.0% (91,920)	55.5% (170,425)	59.2% (89,850)	51.8% (80,575)	37.5% (7,907)	47.2% (4,719)	28.8% (3,188)	51.7% (10,037)	56.8% (4,685)	48.0% (5,351)	34.0% (5,881)	40.1% (3,074)	29.0% (2,806)
1 to 2 Occasions	28.5% (104,163)	24.5% (43,542)	32.3% (60,621)	28.5% (87,625)	23.9% (36,233)	33.0% (51,392)	26.2% (5,529)	34.2% (3,425)	19.0% (2,104)	39.9% (7,739)	32.0% (2,644)	45.7% (5,095)	18.9% (3,270)	16.2% (1,240)	21.0% (2,030)
3 to 19 Occasions	21.6% (78,840)	27.9% (49,654)	15.6% (29,186)	23.7% (72,885)	30.1% (45,713)	17.5% (27,172)	10.1% (2,134)	11.5% (1,153)	8.9% (981)	7.5% (1,458)	14.6% (1,202)	2.3% (257)	13.6% (2,363)	20.7% (1,587)	8.0% (776)
20 or More Occasions	3.1% (11,246)	5.1% (9,133)	1.1% (2,113)	3.2% (9,915)	5.2% (7,905)	1.3% (2,010)	1.2% (244)	1.4% (141)	0.9% (103)	4.3% (840)	10.2% (840)	0.0% –	1.4% (247)	3.2% (247)	0.0% –
Midwest *+++~**	100.0% (519,989)	100.0% (262,089)	100.0% (257,900)	100.0% (463,660)	100.0% (233,663)	100.0% (229,997)	100.0% (24,312)	100.0% (11,692)	100.0% (12,620)	100.0% (16,701)	100.0% (9,100)	100.0% (7,601)	100.0% (15,317)	100.0% (7,634)	100.0% (7,682)
No Occasions	44.9% (233,507)	40.8% (106,994)	49.1% (126,513)	43.4% (201,457)	40.0% (93,397)	47.0% (108,060)	62.5% (15,199)	52.1% (6,092)	72.2% (9,107)	50.8% (8,483)	48.5% (4,416)	53.5% (4,067)	54.6% (8,367)	40.5% (3,089)	68.7% (5,278)
Any Occasions	55.1% (286,482)	59.2% (155,095)	50.9% (131,387)	56.6% (262,203)	60.0% (140,266)	53.0% (121,937)	37.5% (9,113)	47.9% (5,600)	27.8% (3,513)	49.2% (8,217)	51.5% (4,683)	46.5% (3,534)	45.4% (6,949)	59.5% (4,545)	31.3% (2,404)
1 to 2 Occasions	30.1% (156,506)	29.3% (76,885)	30.9% (79,621)	30.4% (141,009)	28.9% (67,479)	32.0% (73,530)	26.7% (6,499)	33.6% (3,926)	20.4% (2,573)	25.2% (4,203)	25.2% (2,291)	25.2% (1,912)	31.3% (4,795)	41.8% (3,189)	20.9% (1,606)
3 to 19 Occasions	21.8% (113,334)	24.7% (64,720)	18.9% (48,614)	22.7% (105,333)	25.7% (60,078)	19.7% (45,255)	10.8% (2,614)	14.3% (1,674)	7.4% (940)	19.8% (3,301)	18.5% (1,679)	21.3% (1,622)	13.6% (2,087)	16.9% (1,289)	10.4% (798)
20 or More Occasions	3.2% (16,642)	5.1% (13,490)	1.2% (3,152)	3.4% (15,861)	5.4% (12,709)	1.4% (3,152)	0.0% –	0.0% –	0.0% –	4.3% (713)	7.8% (713)	0.0% –	0.4% (67)	0.9% (67)	0.0% –
South *+++~~~**	100.0% (594,725)	100.0% (296,378)	100.0% (298,347)	100.0% (407,816)	100.0% (203,066)	100.0% (204,751)	100.0% (118,430)	100.0% (59,561)	100.0% (58,869)	100.0% (49,388)	100.0% (25,557)	100.0% (23,831)	100.0% (19,091)	100.0% (8,194)	100.0% (10,897)
No Occasions	51.5% (306,455)	44.4% (131,450)	58.7% (175,004)	47.3% (193,071)	40.0% (81,310)	54.6% (111,761)	64.0% (75,748)	56.2% (33,496)	71.8% (42,252)	50.6% (24,987)	48.2% (12,327)	53.1% (12,660)	66.3% (12,650)	52.7% (4,319)	76.5% (8,331)
Any Occasions	48.5% (288,271)	55.6% (164,928)	41.3% (123,343)	52.7% (214,746)	60.0% (121,756)	45.4% (92,990)	36.0% (42,682)	43.8% (26,066)	28.2% (16,616)	49.4% (24,402)	51.8% (13,231)	46.9% (11,171)	33.7% (6,441)	47.3% (3,875)	23.5% (2,566)
1 to 2 Occasions	27.4% (163,108)	26.9% (79,653)	28.0% (83,455)	27.6% (112,376)	25.9% (52,650)	29.2% (59,726)	27.3% (32,313)	30.1% (17,944)	24.4% (14,369)	29.6% (14,622)	26.9% (6,864)	32.6% (7,758)	19.9% (3,797)	26.8% (2,195)	14.7% (1,601)
3 to 19 Occasions	18.2% (108,298)	24.4% (72,278)	12.1% (36,020)	21.8% (88,782)	28.8% (58,539)	14.8% (30,244)	7.7% (9,145)	11.8% (7,058)	3.5% (2,087)	17.0% (8,412)	21.2% (5,407)	12.6% (3,004)	10.3% (1,959)	15.5% (1,274)	6.3% (685)
20 or More Occasions	2.8% (16,865)	4.4% (12,997)	1.3% (3,868)	3.3% (13,588)	5.2% (10,568)	1.5% (3,020)	1.0% (1,224)	1.8% (1,064)	0.3% (160)	2.8% (1,368)	3.8% (959)	1.7% (409)	3.6% (685)	5.0% (406)	2.6% (279)
West *+++~~**	100.0% (362,353)	100.0% (183,730)	100.0% (178,623)	100.0% (230,569)	100.0% (119,001)	100.0% (111,568)	100.0% (11,524)	100.0% (3,783)	100.0% (7,741)	100.0% (76,541)	100.0% (38,269)	100.0% (38,272)	100.0% (43,719)	100.0% (22,678)	100.0% (21,041)
No Occasions	54.7% (198,053)	50.2% (92,247)	59.2% (105,805)	51.4% (118,546)	48.2% (57,409)	54.8% (61,138)	64.6% (7,446)	50.9% (1,925)	71.3% (5,521)	54.9% (42,005)	46.1% (17,646)	63.6% (24,359)	68.7% (30,055)	67.3% (15,267)	70.3% (14,788)
Any Occasions	45.3% (164,300)	49.8% (91,483)	40.8% (72,817)	48.6% (112,022)	51.8% (61,592)	45.2% (50,430)	35.4% (4,078)	49.1% (1,858)	28.7% (2,220)	45.1% (34,536)	53.9% (20,623)	36.4% (13,913)	31.3% (13,664)	32.7% (7,410)	29.7% (6,253)
1 to 2 Occasions	25.6% (92,704)	25.1% (46,186)	26.0% (46,517)	27.5% (63,460)	27.6% (32,854)	27.4% (30,607)	20.5% (2,365)	13.6% (513)	23.9% (1,852)	22.7% (17,390)	20.4% (7,812)	25.0% (9,578)	21.7% (9,488)	22.1% (5,007)	21.3% (4,481)
3 to 19 Occasions	17.0% (61,572)	20.2% (37,032)	13.7% (24,539)	18.1% (41,835)	19.3% (22,977)	16.9% (18,858)	5.8% (672)	14.2% (536)	1.8% (136)	20.2% (15,427)	30.1% (11,537)	10.2% (3,890)	8.3% (3,638)	8.7% (1,983)	7.9% (1,655)
20 or More Occasions	2.8% (10,025)	4.5% (8,264)	1.0% (1,761)	2.9% (6,727)	4.8% (5,761)	0.9% (966)	9.0% (1,041)	21.4% (809)	3.0% (232)	2.2% (1,719)	3.3% (1,274)	1.2% (445)	1.2% (537)	1.9% (420)	0.6% (117)

Notes:

"–" indicates sample size too small to estimate.

*** Test of statistical significance compares African Americans with Whites. *** p < .001, ** p < .01, * p < .05.

+++ Test of statistical significance compares White boys with White girls. +++ p < .001, ++ p < .01, + p < .05.

~~~Test of statistical significance compares African American boys with African American girls. ~~~ p < .001, ~~ p < .01, ~ p < .05.

Tests of statistical significance calculated using adjusted sample weight to control for influence of large sample sizes.

Source: National Education Longitudinal Study of 1988 Eighth Graders, Second Follow-Up (1992).

Table 31. Use of Alcohol in the Last 30 Days Among 1992 High School Seniors by Urbanicity, Race, and Sex
(weighted sample size in parenthesis)

Urbanicity	Total	Male	Female	White, Non-Hispanic Total	Male	Female	African American, Non-Hispanic Total	Male	Female	Hispanic Total	Male	Female	Other Total	Male	Female
Urban	100.0% (457,935)	100.0% (223,928)	100.0% (234,007)	100.0% (273,107)	100.0% (138,261)	100.0% (134,845)	100.0% (73,958)	100.0% (33,009)	100.0% (40,949)	100.0% (71,776)	100.0% (34,428)	100.0% (37,348)	100.0% (39,094)	100.0% (18,230)	100.0% (20,864)
No Occasions *** +++~	54.1% (247,910)	49.4% (110,677)	58.6% (137,233)	49.2% (134,350)	45.5% (62,953)	52.9% (71,397)	65.9% (48,714)	60.7% (20,035)	70.0% (28,679)	54.3% (38,955)	50.8% (17,487)	57.5% (21,467)	66.2% (25,891)	56.0% (10,201)	75.2% (15,690)
Any Occasions	45.9% (210,025)	50.6% (113,251)	41.4% (96,774)	50.8% (138,757)	54.5% (75,308)	47.1% (63,449)	34.1% (25,244)	39.3% (12,973)	30.0% (12,271)	45.7% (32,821)	49.2% (16,940)	42.5% (15,881)	33.8% (13,203)	44.0% (8,029)	24.8% (5,174)
1 to 2 Occasions	26.7% (122,394)	25.1% (56,140)	28.3% (66,254)	27.5% (75,021)	24.4% (33,718)	30.6% (41,303)	25.0% (18,471)	26.5% (8,761)	23.7% (9,710)	27.8% (19,935)	23.5% (8,079)	31.7% (11,856)	22.9% (8,967)	30.6% (5,582)	16.2% (3,385)
3 to 19 Occasions	16.3% (74,635)	21.0% (47,080)	11.8% (27,555)	20.1% (54,771)	25.1% (34,742)	14.9% (20,029)	7.3% (5,400)	9.8% (3,233)	5.3% (2,168)	15.0% (10,792)	20.6% (7,082)	9.9% (3,710)	9.4% (3,671)	11.1% (2,023)	7.9% (1,648)
20 or More Occasions	2.8% (12,995)	4.5% (10,031)	1.3% (2,964)	3.3% (8,965)	5.0% (6,849)	1.6% (2,117)	1.9% (1,373)	3.0% (980)	1.0% (393)	2.9% (2,094)	5.2% (1,779)	0.8% (314)	1.4% (564)	2.3% (423)	0.7% (141)
Suburban	100.0% (775,270)	100.0% (398,020)	100.0% (377,250)	100.0% (630,575)	100.0% (323,644)	100.0% (306,931)	100.0% (53,639)	100.0% (30,505)	100.0% (23,134)	100.0% (52,240)	100.0% (25,018)	100.0% (27,222)	100.0% (38,816)	100.0% (18,854)	100.0% (19,962)
No Occasions *** +++ ~~	46.9% (363,512)	43.2% (171,969)	50.8% (191,543)	43.8% (276,356)	40.1% (129,917)	47.7% (146,440)	63.8% (34,208)	57.0% (17,383)	72.7% (16,825)	53.3% (27,828)	53.2% (13,298)	53.4% (14,531)	64.7% (25,119)	60.3% (11,371)	68.9% (13,748)
Any Occasions	53.1% (411,759)	56.8% (226,052)	49.2% (185,707)	56.2% (354,219)	59.9% (193,727)	52.3% (160,492)	36.2% (19,431)	43.0% (13,121)	27.3% (6,310)	46.7% (24,412)	46.8% (11,720)	46.6% (12,692)	35.3% (13,697)	39.7% (7,483)	31.1% (6,214)
1 to 2 Occasions	29.6% (229,303)	27.7% (110,194)	31.6% (119,109)	30.2% (190,669)	27.9% (90,391)	32.7% (100,277)	30.3% (16,238)	34.4% (10,491)	24.8% (5,747)	27.8% (14,538)	23.2% (5,800)	32.1% (8,738)	20.2% (7,859)	18.6% (3,513)	21.8% (4,346)
3 to 19 Occasions	20.8% (161,206)	24.7% (98,202)	16.7% (63,004)	23.0% (144,999)	27.2% (88,020)	18.6% (56,979)	5.5% (2,943)	7.8% (2,380)	2.4% (563)	15.3% (8,000)	17.0% (4,250)	13.8% (3,751)	13.6% (5,263)	18.8% (3,552)	8.6% (1,711)
20 or More Occasions	2.7% (21,250)	4.4% (17,655)	1.0% (3,595)	2.9% (18,551)	4.7% (15,316)	1.1% (3,235)	0.5% (251)	0.8% (251)	0.0% –	3.6% (1,874)	6.7% (1,671)	0.7% (203)	1.5% (575)	2.2% (418)	0.8% (157)
Rural	100.0% (609,509)	100.0% (298,147)	100.0% (311,362)	100.0% (505,866)	100.0% (245,614)	100.0% (260,251)	100.0% (47,802)	100.0% (21,586)	100.0% (26,216)	100.0% (38,172)	100.0% (21,733)	100.0% (16,438)	100.0% (17,670)	100.0% (9,214)	100.0% (8,456)
No Occasions ***+++~~~	48.8% (297,608)	41.4% (123,557)	55.9% (174,051)	47.3% (239,267)	41.2% (101,186)	53.1% (138,081)	59.9% (28,639)	43.4% (9,379)	73.5% (19,260)	47.3% (18,067)	33.0% (7,171)	66.3% (10,896)	65.8% (11,634)	63.2% (5,820)	68.8% (5,814)
Any Occasions	51.2% (311,902)	58.6% (174,590)	44.1% (137,311)	52.7% (266,598)	58.8% (144,428)	46.9% (122,170)	40.1% (19,163)	56.6% (12,207)	26.5% (6,957)	52.7% (20,104)	67.0% (14,562)	33.7% (5,543)	34.2% (6,035)	36.8% (3,394)	31.2% (2,642)
1 to 2 Occasions	27.1% (164,988)	26.8% (79,991)	27.3% (84,997)	27.4% (138,781)	26.5% (65,106)	28.3% (73,675)	25.2% (12,056)	30.6% (6,616)	20.8% (5,440)	25.2% (9,627)	26.4% (5,732)	23.7% (3,895)	25.6% (4,524)	27.5% (2,537)	23.5% (1,987)
3 to 19 Occasions	20.7% (126,382)	26.3% (78,402)	15.4% (47,980)	21.6% (109,243)	26.3% (64,544)	17.2% (44,699)	13.0% (6,221)	22.3% (4,808)	5.4% (1,413)	25.7% (9,805)	39.1% (8,493)	8.0% (1,312)	6.3% (1,113)	6.0% (557)	6.6% (556)
20 or More Occasions	3.4% (20,532)	5.4% (16,198)	1.4% (4,334)	3.7% (18,574)	6.0% (14,778)	1.5% (3,796)	1.9% (886)	3.6% (783)	0.4% (103)	1.8% (673)	1.5% (337)	2.0% (336)	2.3% (398)	3.2% (299)	1.2% (99)

Notes:

"–" indicates sample size too small to estimate.

*** Test of statistical significance compares African Americans with Whites. *** p <.001, ** p <.01, * p <.05.

+++ Test of statistical significance compares White boys with White girls. +++ p <.001, ++ p <.01, + p <.05.

~~~Test of statistical significance compares African American boys with African American girls. ~~~ p <.001, ~~ p <.01, ~ p <.05.

Tests of statistical significance calculated using adjusted sample weight to control for influence of large sample sizes.

Source: National Education Longitudinal Study of 1988 Eighth Graders, Second Follow-Up (1992).

Figure 30. Percentage of 1992 High School Seniors Who Used Alcohol In the Last 30 Days by School Poverty

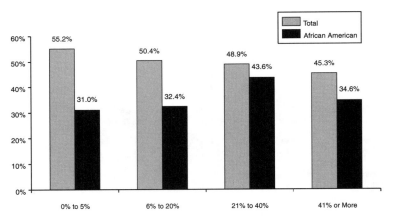

Percentage of Students at School Who Receive Free Lunch

Source: National Education Longitudinal Study of 1988 Eighth Graders, Second Follow-Up (1992).

Figure 31. Percentage of 1992 High School Seniors Who Used Alcohol In the Last 30 Days by School Type

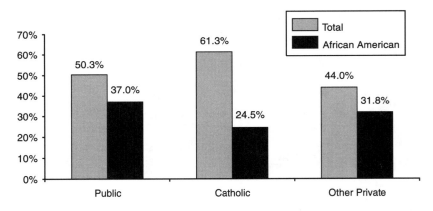

Source: National Education Longitudinal Study of 1988 Eighth Graders, Second Follow-Up (1992).

Table 32. Use of Alcohol in the Last 30 Days Among 1992 High School Seniors by Percentage Students at School Who Receive Free Lunch, Race, and Sex
(weighted sample size in parenthesis)

Percent Students Receive Free or Reduced Lunch	Total	Male	Female	White, Non-Hispanic Total	Male	Female	African American, Non-Hispanic Total	Male	Female	Hispanic Total	Male	Female	Other Total	Male	Female
0% to 5% *+++**	100.0%	100.0%	100.0%	100.0%	100.0%	100.0%	100.0%	100.0%	100.0%	100.0%	100.0%	100.0%	100.0%	100.0%	100.0%
	(546,101)	(284,529)	(261,572)	(465,613)	(244,356)	(221,257)	(20,803)	(11,176)	(9,627)	(24,123)	(13,468)	(10,655)	(35,562)	(15,529)	(20,033)
No Occasions	44.8%	40.3%	49.6%	42.5%	38.6%	46.7%	69.0%	65.4%	73.2%	42.4%	36.0%	50.5%	62.5%	53.4%	69.6%
	(244,536)	(114,760)	(129,775)	(197,700)	(94,308)	(103,392)	(14,359)	(7,309)	(7,050)	(10,233)	(4,848)	(5,385)	(22,243)	(8,295)	(13,948)
Any Occasions	55.2%	59.7%	50.4%	57.5%	61.4%	53.3%	31.0%	34.6%	26.8%	57.6%	64.0%	49.5%	37.5%	46.6%	30.4%
	(301,566)	(169,768)	(131,797)	(267,913)	(150,048)	(117,865)	(6,444)	(3,868)	(2,576)	(13,890)	(8,619)	(5,270)	(13,319)	(7,234)	(6,085)
1 to 2 Occasions	29.0%	26.3%	32.1%	29.8%	26.4%	33.6%	19.3%	21.8%	16.4%	30.8%	27.6%	34.8%	23.0%	25.6%	21.0%
	(158,553)	(74,717)	(83,836)	(138,918)	(64,590)	(74,328)	(4,014)	(2,432)	(1,583)	(7,427)	(3,714)	(3,713)	(8,195)	(3,982)	(4,213)
3 to 19 Occasions	23.1%	28.4%	17.4%	24.6%	29.9%	18.7%	7.3%	5.6%	9.3%	21.9%	27.6%	14.6%	14.0%	20.9%	8.6%
	(126,233)	(80,683)	(45,551)	(114,451)	(73,080)	(41,371)	(1,518)	(627)	(890)	(5,280)	(3,723)	(1,558)	(4,984)	(3,252)	(1,732)
20 or More Occasions	3.1%	5.0%	0.9%	3.1%	5.1%	1.0%	4.4%	7.2%	1.1%	4.9%	8.8%	0.0%	0.4%	0.0%	0.7%
	(16,779)	(14,369)	(2,410)	(14,544)	(12,377)	(2,167)	(912)	(809)	(103)	(1,182)	(1,182)	–	(141)	–	(141)
6% to 20% *+++**	100.0%	100.0%	100.0%	100.0%	100.0%	100.0%	100.0%	100.0%	100.0%	100.0%	100.0%	100.0%	100.0%	100.0%	100.0%
	(562,704)	(281,405)	(281,299)	(454,465)	(226,935)	(227,529)	(44,693)	(23,179)	(21,514)	(38,791)	(19,350)	(19,441)	(24,755)	(11,941)	(12,814)
No Occasions	49.6%	45.3%	53.9%	47.2%	42.5%	51.9%	67.6%	68.0%	67.1%	46.0%	41.7%	50.4%	66.8%	60.2%	73.0%
	(279,281)	(127,544)	(151,737)	(214,681)	(96,530)	(118,151)	(30,202)	(15,762)	(14,440)	(17,855)	(8,062)	(9,793)	(16,544)	(7,191)	(9,353)
Any Occasions	50.4%	54.7%	46.1%	52.8%	57.5%	48.1%	32.4%	32.0%	32.9%	54.0%	58.3%	49.6%	33.2%	39.8%	27.0%
	(283,423)	(153,861)	(129,562)	(239,784)	(130,405)	(109,378)	(14,491)	(7,417)	(7,075)	(20,937)	(11,289)	(9,648)	(8,211)	(4,750)	(3,461)
1 to 2 Occasions	28.4%	27.6%	29.3%	28.9%	27.9%	29.8%	23.3%	21.2%	25.5%	32.2%	31.1%	33.2%	24.3%	28.6%	20.2%
	(160,043)	(77,668)	(82,375)	(131,150)	(63,315)	(67,835)	(10,393)	(4,909)	(5,484)	(12,485)	(6,024)	(6,461)	(6,015)	(3,420)	(2,595)
3 to 19 Occasions	18.9%	22.3%	15.4%	20.5%	24.1%	16.8%	8.3%	10.2%	6.3%	19.5%	23.4%	15.6%	7.5%	9.7%	5.5%
	(106,215)	(62,821)	(43,394)	(93,054)	(54,768)	(38,286)	(3,724)	(2,367)	(1,358)	(7,571)	(4,530)	(3,041)	(1,865)	(1,156)	(709)
20 or More Occasions	3.1%	4.8%	1.3%	3.4%	5.4%	1.4%	0.8%	0.6%	1.1%	2.3%	3.8%	0.8%	1.3%	1.5%	1.2%
	(17,165)	(13,372)	(3,792)	(15,580)	(12,323)	(3,257)	(373)	(141)	(232)	(881)	(735)	(146)	(331)	(174)	(157)
21% to 40% *+++ ~~~**	100.0%	100.0%	100.0%	100.0%	100.0%	100.0%	100.0%	100.0%	100.0%	100.0%	100.0%	100.0%	100.0%	100.0%	100.0%
	(465,317)	(217,395)	(247,922)	(350,472)	(164,770)	(185,702)	(60,776)	(28,394)	(32,382)	(37,281)	(16,605)	(20,676)	(16,788)	(7,626)	(9,162)
No Occasions	51.1%	45.2%	56.3%	48.9%	44.5%	52.7%	56.4%	39.1%	71.5%	57.7%	54.9%	60.0%	63.9%	59.9%	67.1%
	(237,855)	(98,193)	(139,662)	(171,343)	(73,401)	(97,941)	(34,265)	(11,104)	(23,160)	(21,528)	(9,118)	(12,410)	(10,719)	(4,570)	(6,150)
Any Occasions	48.9%	54.8%	43.7%	51.1%	55.5%	47.3%	43.6%	60.9%	28.5%	42.3%	45.1%	40.0%	36.1%	40.1%	32.9%
	(227,462)	(119,202)	(108,261)	(179,129)	(91,368)	(87,761)	(26,512)	(17,290)	(9,222)	(15,753)	(7,487)	(8,265)	(6,069)	(3,056)	(3,012)
1 to 2 Occasions	28.1%	28.1%	28.2%	27.9%	26.7%	29.0%	33.5%	43.2%	24.9%	25.6%	20.1%	30.0%	19.0%	19.5%	18.7%
	(130,894)	(61,029)	(69,865)	(97,807)	(43,935)	(53,872)	(20,336)	(12,266)	(8,069)	(9,555)	(3,343)	(6,212)	(3,196)	(1,484)	(1,712)
3 to 19 Occasions	18.4%	23.0%	14.4%	20.7%	25.0%	16.8%	9.4%	16.1%	3.6%	12.9%	17.3%	9.4%	15.1%	17.4%	13.1%
	(85,594)	(50,011)	(35,583)	(72,528)	(41,243)	(31,284)	(5,712)	(4,560)	(1,153)	(4,825)	(2,880)	(1,945)	(2,529)	(1,328)	(1,202)
20 or More Occasions	2.4%	3.8%	1.1%	2.5%	3.8%	1.4%	0.8%	1.6%	0.0%	3.7%	7.6%	0.5%	2.0%	3.2%	1.1%
	(10,974)	(8,162)	(2,812)	(8,794)	(6,190)	(2,605)	(464)	(464)	–	(1,373)	(1,265)	(109)	(343)	(244)	(99)
41% or More *+++ ~~**	100.0%	100.0%	100.0%	100.0%	100.0%	100.0%	100.0%	100.0%	100.0%	100.0%	100.0%	100.0%	100.0%	100.0%	100.0%
	(245,190)	(124,668)	(120,521)	(122,802)	(61,336)	(61,466)	(46,064)	(21,612)	(24,451)	(59,488)	(31,418)	(28,070)	(16,836)	(10,302)	(6,534)
No Occasions	54.7%	48.5%	61.0%	47.8%	41.8%	53.7%	65.4%	56.9%	72.9%	55.9%	49.8%	62.7%	71.2%	67.3%	77.5%
	(134,056)	(60,525)	(73,531)	(58,676)	(25,649)	(33,027)	(30,132)	(12,300)	(17,832)	(33,254)	(15,646)	(17,608)	(11,994)	(6,930)	(5,064)
Any Occasions	45.3%	51.5%	39.0%	52.2%	58.2%	46.3%	34.6%	43.1%	27.1%	44.1%	50.2%	37.3%	28.8%	32.7%	22.5%
	(111,133)	(64,144)	(46,990)	(64,126)	(35,688)	(28,438)	(15,932)	(9,312)	(6,619)	(26,233)	(15,772)	(10,462)	(4,843)	(3,372)	(1,471)
1 to 2 Occasions	25.6%	24.1%	27.1%	27.0%	24.9%	29.0%	25.3%	27.5%	23.4%	24.2%	20.6%	28.1%	20.9%	22.5%	18.4%
	(62,689)	(30,031)	(32,658)	(33,129)	(15,285)	(17,844)	(11,669)	(5,953)	(5,716)	(14,373)	(6,475)	(7,898)	(3,518)	(2,319)	(1,199)
3 to 19 Occasions	16.1%	21.6%	10.3%	20.1%	24.7%	15.4%	7.6%	12.8%	3.0%	17.9%	27.7%	7.0%	3.6%	3.2%	4.2%
	(39,398)	(26,944)	(12,454)	(24,637)	(15,162)	(9,474)	(3,502)	(2,759)	(743)	(10,657)	(8,692)	(1,965)	(602)	(330)	(272)
20 or More Occasions	3.7%	5.8%	1.6%	5.2%	8.5%	1.8%	1.7%	2.8%	0.7%	2.0%	1.9%	2.1%	4.3%	7.0%	0.0%
	(9,047)	(7,169)	(1,878)	(6,360)	(5,241)	(1,119)	(760)	(600)	(160)	(1,204)	(605)	(599)	(723)	(723)	–

Notes:

"–" indicates sample size too small to estimate.

*** Test of statistical significance compares African Americans with Whites. *** p <.001, ** p <.01, * p <.05.

+++ Test of statistical significance compares White boys with White girls. +++ p <.001, ++ p <.01, + p <.05.

~~~Test of statistical significance compares African American boys with African American girls. ~~~ p <.001, ~~ p <.01, ~ p <.05.

Tests of statistical significance calculated using adjusted sample weight to control for influence of large sample sizes.

Source: National Education Longitudinal Study of 1988 Eighth Graders, Second Follow-Up (1992).

Table 33. Use of Alcohol in the Last 30 Days Among 1992 High School Seniors by School Type, Race, and Sex
(weighted sample size in parenthesis)

School Type	Total	Male	Female	White, Non-Hispanic Total	Male	Female	African American, Non-Hispanic Total	Male	Female	Hispanic Total	Male	Female	Other Total	Male	Female
Public * +++ ~~~**	100.0%	100.0%	100.0%	100.0%	100.0%	100.0%	100.0%	100.0%	100.0%	100.0%	100.0%	100.0%	100.0%	100.0%	100.0%
	(1,679,564)	(829,191)	(850,373)	(1,279,983)	(631,062)	(648,922)	(166,154)	(82,797)	(83,356)	(150,641)	(74,823)	(75,818)	(82,786)	(40,509)	(42,277)
No Occasions	49.7%	44.7%	54.7%	46.6%	42.0%	51.0%	63.0%	54.6%	71.4%	53.6%	47.9%	59.2%	64.9%	60.0%	69.5%
	(835,392)	(370,320)	(465,072)	(596,258)	(264,997)	(331,261)	(104,705)	(45,197)	(59,507)	(80,739)	(35,835)	(44,904)	(53,690)	(24,291)	(29,399)
Any Occasions	50.3%	55.3%	45.3%	53.4%	58.0%	49.0%	37.0%	45.4%	28.6%	46.4%	52.1%	40.8%	35.1%	40.0%	30.5%
	(844,172)	(458,871)	(385,301)	(683,725)	(366,065)	(317,661)	(61,449)	(37,600)	(23,849)	(69,901)	(38,987)	(30,914)	(29,096)	(16,219)	(12,878)
1 to 2 Occasions	28.3%	26.9%	29.6%	28.9%	26.9%	30.9%	27.3%	30.7%	24.1%	26.6%	23.9%	29.2%	22.9%	24.9%	20.9%
	(474,774)	(223,103)	(251,671)	(370,390)	(169,731)	(200,659)	(45,433)	(25,385)	(20,047)	(40,009)	(17,885)	(22,125)	(18,943)	(10,102)	(8,840)
3 to 19 Occasions	19.2%	23.9%	14.6%	21.4%	26.1%	16.8%	8.1%	12.3%	4.0%	17.1%	23.7%	10.5%	10.4%	12.3%	8.7%
	(321,675)	(197,839)	(123,837)	(273,823)	(164,892)	(108,931)	(13,507)	(10,202)	(3,306)	(25,705)	(17,770)	(7,936)	(8,639)	(4,976)	(3,664)
20 or More Occasions	2.8%	4.6%	1.2%	3.1%	5.0%	1.2%	1.5%	2.4%	0.6%	2.8%	4.5%	1.1%	1.8%	2.8%	0.9%
	(47,723)	(37,929)	(9,793)	(39,513)	(31,442)	(8,071)	(2,509)	(2,013)	(496)	(4,187)	(3,333)	(853)	(1,514)	(1,141)	(373)
Catholic * ++**	100.0%	100.0%	100.0%	100.0%	100.0%	100.0%	100.0%	100.0%	100.0%	100.0%	100.0%	100.0%	100.0%	100.0%	100.0%
	(101,575)	(55,339)	(46,237)	(77,504)	(44,738)	(32,766)	(8,036)	(1,974)	(6,062)	(10,483)	(5,842)	(4,641)	(5,551)	(2,783)	(2,768)
No Occasions	38.7%	31.0%	47.9%	34.5%	29.8%	40.8%	75.5%	75.2%	75.7%	34.5%	32.9%	36.5%	52.2%	14.4%	90.2%
	(39,306)	(17,154)	(22,152)	(26,725)	(13,350)	(13,375)	(6,071)	(1,484)	(4,586)	(3,612)	(1,919)	(1,693)	(2,898)	(400)	(2,498)
Any Occasions	61.3%	69.0%	52.1%	65.5%	70.2%	59.2%	24.5%	24.8%	24.3%	65.5%	67.1%	63.5%	47.8%	85.6%	9.8%
	(62,270)	(38,185)	(24,085)	(50,779)	(31,388)	(19,391)	(1,966)	(490)	(1,476)	(6,871)	(3,923)	(2,948)	(2,653)	(2,383)	(270)
1 to 2 Occasions	28.8%	29.2%	28.3%	29.6%	28.8%	30.6%	13.3%	17.4%	12.0%	35.6%	26.7%	46.8%	28.0%	50.3%	5.6%
	(29,264)	(16,176)	(13,087)	(22,903)	(12,870)	(10,033)	(1,071)	(343)	(727)	(3,734)	(1,562)	(2,172)	(1,556)	(1,401)	(155)
3 to 19 Occasions	27.6%	32.7%	21.6%	30.2%	33.7%	25.5%	11.1%	7.4%	12.3%	25.6%	32.6%	16.7%	19.8%	35.3%	4.2%
	(28,080)	(18,094)	(9,986)	(23,404)	(15,057)	(8,346)	(895)	(147)	(748)	(2,683)	(1,907)	(776)	(1,098)	(983)	(115)
20 or More Occasions	4.8%	7.1%	2.2%	5.8%	7.7%	3.1%	0.0%	0.0%	0.0%	4.3%	7.8%	0.0%	0.0%	0.0%	0.0%
	(4,926)	(3,914)	(1,012)	(4,473)	(3,461)	(1,012)	–	–	–	(454)	(454)	–	–	–	–
Other Private +	100.0%	100.0%	100.0%	100.0%	100.0%	100.0%	100.0%	100.0%	100.0%	100.0%	100.0%	100.0%	100.0%	100.0%	100.0%
	(61,059)	(35,374)	(25,685)	(51,881)	(31,720)	(20,162)	(1,151)	(269)	(882)	(917)	(513)	(404)	(7,109)	(2,872)	(4,237)
No Occasions	56.0%	52.6%	60.7%	52.0%	49.5%	56.0%	68.2%	43.1%	75.9%	54.3%	39.3%	73.4%	83.3%	89.4%	79.2%
	(34,198)	(18,595)	(15,603)	(26,991)	(15,709)	(11,282)	(785)	(116)	(669)	(498)	(202)	(297)	(5,924)	(2,569)	(3,355)
Any Occasions	44.0%	47.4%	39.3%	48.0%	50.5%	44.0%	31.8%	56.9%	24.1%	45.7%	60.7%	26.6%	16.7%	10.6%	20.8%
	(26,861)	(16,779)	(10,081)	(24,891)	(16,011)	(8,880)	(366)	(153)	(212)	(419)	(312)	(107)	(1,185)	(304)	(882)
1 to 2 Occasions	20.4%	19.8%	21.2%	21.5%	20.9%	22.6%	17.7%	30.1%	13.9%	22.9%	31.9%	11.6%	12.0%	4.5%	17.1%
	(12,443)	(6,988)	(5,456)	(11,178)	(6,614)	(4,563)	(204)	(81)	(123)	(210)	(164)	(47)	(852)	(129)	(723)
3 to 19 Occasions	20.1%	21.9%	17.7%	22.4%	23.2%	21.1%	14.1%	26.8%	10.2%	22.7%	28.9%	15.0%	4.4%	6.1%	3.2%
	(12,289)	(7,752)	(4,537)	(11,608)	(7,356)	(4,252)	(162)	(72)	(90)	(209)	(148)	(60)	(310)	(175)	(135)
20 or More Occasions	3.5%	5.8%	0.3%	4.1%	6.4%	0.3%	0.0%	0.0%	0.0%	0.0%	0.0%	0.0%	0.0%	0.0%	0.0%
	(2,128)	(2,040)	(65)	(2,105)	(2,040)	(65)	–	–	–	–	–	–	–	–	–

Notes:

"–" indicates sample size too small to estimate.

*** Test of statistical significance compares African Americans with Whites. *** p <.001, ** p <.01, * p <.05.

+++ Test of statistical significance compares White boys with White girls. +++ p <.001, ++ p <.01, + p <.05.

~~~Test of statistical significance compares African American boys with African American girls. ~~~ p <.001, ~~ p <.01, ~ p <.05.

Tests of statistical significance calculated using adjusted sample weight to control for influence of large sample sizes.

Source: National Education Longitudinal Study of 1988 Eighth Graders, Second Follow-Up (1992).

Figure 32. Percentage of 1992 High School Seniors Who Used Alcohol In the Last 30 Days by Socioeconomic Status

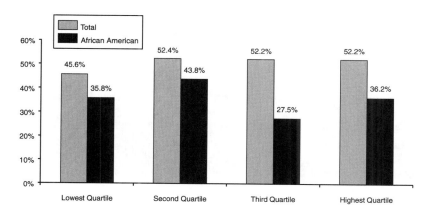

Source: National Education Longitudinal Study of 1988 Eighth Graders, Second Follow-Up (1992).

Figure 33. Percentage of 1992 High School Seniors Who Used Alcohol In the Last 30 Days by Test Score

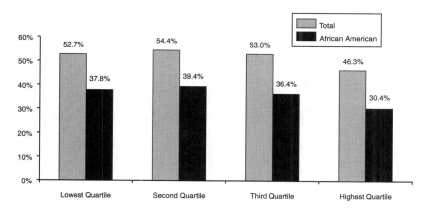

Source: National Education Longitudinal Study of 1988 Eighth Graders, Second Follow-Up (1992).

Table 34. Use of Alcohol in the Last 30 Days Among 1992 High School Seniors by Socioeconomic Status, Race, and Sex
(weighted sample size in parenthesis)

Socioeconomic Status	Total	Male	Female	White, Non-Hispanic Total	Male	Female	African American, Non-Hispanic Total	Male	Female	Hispanic Total	Male	Female	Other Total	Male	Female
Lowest Quartile * +++ ~~~**	100.0% (436,527)	100.0% (202,278)	100.0% (234,248)	100.0% (261,139)	100.0% (125,670)	100.0% (135,470)	100.0% (75,728)	100.0% (32,391)	100.0% (43,337)	100.0% (77,557)	100.0% (33,900)	100.0% (43,657)	100.0% (22,102)	100.0% (10,318)	100.0% (11,784)
No Occasions	54.4% (237,528)	48.8% (98,767)	59.2% (138,761)	50.1% (130,798)	45.4% (57,109)	54.4% (73,689)	64.2% (48,602)	53.8% (17,432)	71.9% (31,170)	56.4% (43,764)	53.9% (18,282)	58.4% (25,482)	65.0% (14,364)	57.6% (5,944)	71.5% (8,421)
Any Occasions	45.6% (198,998)	51.2% (103,511)	40.8% (95,487)	49.9% (130,341)	54.6% (68,561)	45.6% (61,781)	35.8% (27,126)	46.2% (14,959)	28.1% (12,168)	43.6% (33,793)	46.1% (15,617)	41.6% (18,176)	35.0% (7,738)	42.4% (4,375)	28.5% (3,363)
1 to 2 Occasions	26.6% (116,093)	24.3% (49,066)	28.6% (67,027)	27.6% (71,969)	25.9% (32,509)	29.1% (39,459)	25.5% (19,339)	27.0% (8,753)	24.4% (10,586)	25.0% (19,411)	15.5% (5,248)	32.4% (14,163)	24.3% (5,374)	24.8% (2,555)	23.9% (2,820)
3 to 19 Occasions	15.6% (68,074)	21.1% (42,601)	10.9% (25,473)	17.9% (46,781)	21.5% (27,038)	14.6% (19,742)	9.4% (7,138)	17.2% (5,556)	3.6% (1,582)	16.0% (12,418)	26.0% (8,813)	8.3% (3,605)	7.9% (1,737)	11.6% (1,194)	4.6% (544)
20 or More Occasions	3.4% (14,831)	5.9% (11,844)	1.3% (2,987)	4.4% (11,592)	7.2% (9,013)	1.9% (2,579)	0.9% (649)	2.0% (649)	0.0% –	2.5% (1,964)	4.6% (1,556)	0.9% (408)	2.8% (626)	6.1% (626)	0.0% –
Second Quartile * +++~~**	100.0% (457,879)	100.0% (228,125)	100.0% (229,754)	100.0% (355,816)	100.0% (174,092)	100.0% (181,724)	100.0% (47,507)	100.0% (27,027)	100.0% (20,480)	100.0% (35,975)	100.0% (18,889)	100.0% (17,086)	100.0% (18,581)	100.0% (8,117)	100.0% (10,464)
No Occasions	47.6% (218,040)	40.3% (91,928)	54.9% (126,112)	44.9% (159,611)	37.7% (65,574)	51.7% (94,037)	56.2% (26,720)	48.2% (13,021)	66.9% (13,699)	53.8% (19,339)	42.3% (7,988)	66.4% (11,351)	66.6% (12,371)	65.9% (5,346)	67.1% (7,025)
Any Occasions	52.4% (239,839)	59.7% (136,196)	45.1% (103,642)	55.1% (196,205)	62.3% (108,518)	48.3% (87,687)	43.8% (20,787)	51.8% (14,006)	33.1% (6,781)	46.2% (16,636)	57.7% (10,901)	33.6% (5,735)	33.4% (6,210)	34.1% (2,771)	32.9% (3,439)
1 to 2 Occasions	29.6% (135,620)	31.1% (70,860)	28.2% (64,760)	30.0% (106,581)	30.4% (52,884)	29.5% (53,697)	34.4% (16,334)	41.0% (11,086)	25.6% (5,248)	24.7% (8,902)	26.2% (4,944)	23.2% (3,958)	20.5% (3,803)	24.0% (1,946)	17.7% (1,857)
3 to 19 Occasions	19.8% (90,494)	23.6% (53,820)	16.0% (36,673)	22.0% (78,230)	26.3% (45,838)	17.8% (32,392)	7.1% (3,374)	7.4% (2,002)	6.7% (1,372)	19.2% (6,916)	28.4% (5,373)	9.0% (1,543)	10.6% (1,974)	7.5% (608)	13.1% (1,366)
20 or More Occasions	3.0% (13,725)	5.0% (11,517)	1.0% (2,209)	3.2% (11,394)	5.6% (9,797)	0.9% (1,598)	2.3% (1,079)	3.4% (919)	0.8% (160)	2.3% (819)	3.1% (585)	1.4% (234)	2.3% (433)	2.7% (217)	2.1% (216)
Third Quartile * +++**	100.0% (459,286)	100.0% (234,322)	100.0% (224,964)	100.0% (373,632)	100.0% (188,968)	100.0% (184,664)	100.0% (33,927)	100.0% (16,654)	100.0% (17,273)	100.0% (26,520)	100.0% (15,608)	100.0% (10,911)	100.0% (25,207)	100.0% (13,092)	100.0% (12,116)
No Occasions	47.8% (219,734)	43.6% (102,154)	52.3% (117,580)	44.9% (167,785)	40.9% (77,277)	49.0% (90,508)	72.5% (24,603)	69.6% (11,597)	75.3% (13,006)	42.0% (11,150)	37.9% (5,921)	47.9% (5,228)	64.2% (16,195)	56.2% (7,358)	72.9% (8,837)
Any Occasions	52.2% (239,552)	56.4% (132,168)	47.7% (107,384)	55.1% (205,847)	59.1% (111,691)	51.0% (94,156)	27.5% (9,324)	30.4% (5,057)	24.7% (4,267)	58.0% (15,370)	62.1% (9,687)	52.1% (5,683)	35.8% (9,012)	43.8% (5,734)	27.1% (3,278)
1 to 2 Occasions	28.2% (129,390)	26.3% (61,738)	30.1% (67,652)	28.8% (107,628)	26.2% (49,572)	31.4% (58,056)	20.5% (6,944)	20.4% (3,390)	20.6% (3,554)	31.9% (8,450)	30.9% (4,818)	33.3% (3,632)	25.3% (6,368)	30.2% (3,958)	19.9% (2,410)
3 to 19 Occasions	20.8% (95,335)	25.0% (58,588)	16.3% (36,747)	22.9% (85,478)	27.6% (52,113)	18.1% (33,365)	5.8% (1,965)	8.1% (1,355)	3.5% (610)	20.2% (5,368)	22.2% (3,464)	17.4% (1,904)	10.0% (2,523)	12.6% (1,655)	7.2% (868)
20 or More Occasions	3.2% (14,827)	5.1% (11,843)	1.3% (2,984)	3.4% (12,740)	5.3% (10,005)	1.5% (2,735)	1.2% (415)	1.9% (312)	0.6% (103)	5.8% (1,551)	9.0% (1,405)	1.3% (146)	0.5% (121)	0.9% (121)	0.0% –
Highest Quartile ** +++	100.0% (489,022)	100.0% (255,370)	100.0% (233,652)	100.0% (418,960)	100.0% (218,790)	100.0% (200,171)	100.0% (18,237)	100.0% (9,027)	100.0% (9,209)	100.0% (22,136)	100.0% (12,781)	100.0% (9,354)	100.0% (29,689)	100.0% (14,772)	100.0% (14,917)
No Occasions	47.8% (233,727)	44.4% (113,353)	51.5% (120,373)	45.8% (191,779)	43.0% (94,095)	48.8% (97,684)	63.8% (11,635)	52.6% (4,748)	74.8% (6,888)	47.9% (10,597)	45.1% (5,765)	51.7% (4,833)	66.4% (19,715)	59.2% (8,745)	73.5% (10,969)
Any Occasions	52.2% (255,296)	55.6% (142,017)	48.5% (113,278)	54.2% (227,181)	57.0% (124,694)	51.2% (102,487)	36.2% (6,601)	47.4% (4,280)	25.2% (2,322)	52.1% (11,539)	54.9% (7,017)	48.3% (4,522)	33.6% (9,975)	40.8% (6,027)	26.5% (3,948)
1 to 2 Occasions	27.7% (135,582)	25.3% (64,662)	30.4% (70,920)	28.2% (118,293)	24.8% (54,250)	32.0% (64,043)	22.7% (4,147)	29.2% (2,638)	16.4% (1,509)	33.1% (7,337)	36.0% (4,601)	29.3% (2,736)	19.6% (5,805)	21.5% (3,173)	17.6% (2,632)
3 to 19 Occasions	22.2% (108,320)	26.9% (68,675)	17.0% (39,645)	23.5% (98,525)	28.5% (62,316)	18.1% (36,208)	11.4% (2,087)	16.7% (1,508)	6.3% (580)	17.6% (3,895)	17.0% (2,175)	18.4% (1,721)	12.8% (3,812)	18.1% (2,676)	7.6% (1,136)
20 or More Occasions	2.3% (11,393)	3.4% (8,680)	1.2% (2,713)	2.5% (10,364)	3.7% (8,128)	1.1% (2,236)	2.0% (366)	1.5% (134)	2.5% (232)	1.4% (306)	1.9% (242)	0.7% (65)	1.2% (357)	1.2% (177)	1.2% (180)

Notes:

"–" indicates sample size too small to estimate.

*** Test of statistical significance compares African Americans with Whites. *** p .001, ** p .01, * p .05.

+++ Test of statistical significance compares White boys with White girls. +++ p .001, ++ p .01, + p .05.

~~~Test of statistical significance compares African American boys with African American girls. ~~~ p .001, ~~ p .01, ~ p .05.

Tests of statistical significance calculated using adjusted sample weight to control for influence of large sample sizes.

Source: National Education Longitudinal Study of 1988 Eighth Graders, Second Follow-Up (1992).

Table 35. Use of Alcohol in the Last 30 Days Among 1992 High School Seniors by Test Score, Race, and Sex
(weighted sample size in parenthesis)

Test Score	Total	Male	Female	White, Non-Hispanic Total	Male	Female	African American, Non-Hispanic Total	Male	Female	Hispanic Total	Male	Female	Other Total	Male	Female
Lowest Quartile *+++ ~**	100.0% (350,633)	100.0% (194,387)	100.0% (156,246)	100.0% (213,594)	100.0% (122,748)	100.0% (90,846)	100.0% (73,033)	100.0% (40,814)	100.0% (32,219)	100.0% (47,366)	100.0% (22,870)	100.0% (24,496)	100.0% (16,640)	100.0% (7,955)	100.0% (8,685)
No Occasions	47.3% (165,728)	39.7% (77,108)	56.7% (88,620)	39.2% (83,708)	30.9% (37,871)	50.5% (45,838)	62.2% (45,397)	57.3% (23,401)	68.3% (21,996)	55.3% (26,191)	48.5% (11,098)	61.6% (15,093)	62.7% (10,431)	59.6% (4,738)	65.5% (5,693)
Any Occasions	52.7% (184,905)	60.3% (117,279)	43.3% (67,626)	60.8% (129,886)	69.1% (84,877)	49.5% (45,009)	37.8% (27,635)	42.7% (17,413)	31.7% (10,222)	44.7% (21,175)	51.5% (11,772)	38.4% (9,403)	37.3% (6,209)	40.4% (3,217)	34.5% (2,992)
1 to 2 Occasions	25.3% (88,634)	23.8% (46,229)	27.1% (42,405)	25.4% (54,260)	23.8% (29,200)	27.6% (25,060)	28.1% (20,492)	29.5% (12,040)	26.2% (8,452)	21.4% (10,156)	13.7% (3,133)	28.7% (7,023)	22.4% (3,726)	23.3% (1,855)	21.5% (1,871)
3 to 19 Occasions	21.3% (74,620)	27.0% (52,420)	14.2% (22,200)	27.0% (57,609)	32.6% (40,067)	19.3% (17,542)	8.7% (6,389)	11.3% (4,618)	5.5% (1,771)	18.0% (8,544)	28.9% (6,620)	7.9% (1,924)	12.5% (2,078)	14.0% (1,114)	11.1% (964)
20 or More Occasions	6.2% (21,651)	9.6% (18,631)	1.9% (3,021)	8.4% (18,017)	12.7% (15,610)	2.6% (2,407)	1.0% (755)	1.8% (755)	0.0% –	5.2% (2,475)	8.8% (2,019)	1.9% (457)	2.4% (404)	3.1% (247)	1.8% (157)
Second Quartile *+++~~~**	100.0% (383,614)	100.0% (191,024)	100.0% (192,590)	100.0% (284,058)	100.0% (144,169)	100.0% (139,888)	100.0% (39,592)	100.0% (17,927)	100.0% (21,665)	100.0% (41,547)	100.0% (19,783)	100.0% (21,764)	100.0% (18,418)	100.0% (9,146)	100.0% (9,272)
No Occasions	45.6% (174,783)	42.0% (80,276)	49.1% (94,507)	41.6% (118,047)	39.5% (57,012)	43.6% (61,035)	60.6% (24,004)	47.2% (8,459)	71.8% (15,545)	48.5% (20,151)	43.7% (8,641)	52.9% (11,510)	68.3% (12,581)	67.4% (6,164)	69.2% (6,417)
Any Occasions	54.4% (208,831)	58.0% (110,748)	50.9% (98,083)	58.4% (166,010)	60.5% (87,157)	56.4% (78,853)	39.4% (15,588)	52.8% (9,468)	28.2% (6,120)	51.5% (21,396)	56.3% (11,142)	47.1% (10,254)	31.7% (5,837)	32.6% (2,982)	30.8% (2,856)
1 to 2 Occasions	30.2% (115,879)	28.3% (54,114)	32.1% (61,765)	31.1% (88,445)	28.8% (41,590)	33.5% (46,855)	29.8% (11,790)	37.7% (6,755)	23.2% (5,035)	28.0% (11,614)	19.8% (3,913)	35.4% (7,701)	21.9% (4,030)	20.3% (1,856)	23.4% (2,173)
3 to 19 Occasions	21.7% (83,120)	25.8% (49,278)	17.6% (33,841)	24.3% (69,115)	27.3% (39,375)	21.3% (29,740)	9.6% (3,798)	15.1% (2,713)	5.0% (1,085)	20.9% (8,686)	31.6% (6,253)	11.2% (2,433)	8.3% (1,521)	10.3% (938)	6.3% (583)
20 or More Occasions	2.6% (9,833)	3.9% (7,356)	1.3% (2,477)	3.0% (8,450)	4.3% (6,193)	1.6% (2,258)	0.0% –	0.0% –	0.0% –	2.6% (1,095)	4.9% (975)	0.6% (120)	1.6% (287)	2.1% (188)	1.1% (99)
Third Quartile *+++~~~**	100.0% (403,962)	100.0% (191,041)	100.0% (212,921)	100.0% (333,453)	100.0% (155,594)	100.0% (177,859)	100.0% (25,141)	100.0% (10,505)	100.0% (14,636)	100.0% (26,989)	100.0% (15,647)	100.0% (11,342)	100.0% (18,379)	100.0% (9,296)	100.0% (9,084)
No Occasions	47.0% (189,999)	41.0% (78,323)	52.4% (111,676)	45.0% (150,140)	39.5% (61,507)	49.8% (88,633)	63.6% (15,985)	43.3% (4,548)	78.1% (11,437)	39.3% (10,597)	38.3% (5,985)	40.7% (4,612)	72.2% (13,277)	67.6% (6,283)	77.0% (6,994)
Any Occasions	53.0% (213,963)	59.0% (112,718)	47.6% (101,245)	55.0% (183,313)	60.5% (94,087)	50.2% (89,226)	36.4% (9,156)	56.7% (5,957)	21.9% (3,199)	60.7% (16,392)	61.7% (9,662)	59.3% (6,730)	27.8% (5,102)	32.4% (3,013)	23.0% (2,090)
1 to 2 Occasions	30.1% (121,576)	29.0% (55,405)	31.1% (66,170)	30.4% (101,380)	28.0% (43,491)	32.5% (57,889)	26.1% (6,555)	37.6% (3,953)	17.8% (2,601)	38.2% (10,296)	38.9% (6,081)	37.2% (4,215)	18.2% (3,344)	20.2% (1,880)	16.1% (1,465)
3 to 19 Occasions	20.8% (84,125)	26.5% (50,549)	15.8% (33,576)	22.5% (75,067)	28.9% (45,037)	16.9% (30,029)	6.7% (1,690)	11.4% (1,195)	3.4% (495)	21.7% (5,863)	21.8% (3,414)	21.6% (2,450)	8.2% (1,505)	9.7% (903)	6.6% (602)
20 or More Occasions	2.0% (8,263)	3.5% (6,764)	0.7% (1,499)	2.1% (6,866)	3.6% (5,558)	0.7% (1,308)	3.6% (912)	7.7% (809)	0.7% (103)	0.9% (232)	1.1% (167)	0.6% (65)	1.4% (253)	2.5% (230)	0.3% (23)
Highest Quartile *+++**	100.0% (704,505)	100.0% (343,643)	100.0% (360,862)	100.0% (578,443)	100.0% (285,009)	100.0% (293,434)	100.0% (37,633)	100.0% (15,853)	100.0% (21,780)	100.0% (46,286)	100.0% (22,878)	100.0% (23,408)	100.0% (42,142)	100.0% (19,902)	100.0% (22,241)
No Occasions	53.7% (378,519)	49.6% (170,495)	57.6% (208,024)	51.5% (298,078)	48.3% (137,666)	54.7% (160,412)	69.6% (26,174)	65.5% (10,389)	72.5% (15,785)	60.3% (27,911)	53.5% (12,232)	67.0% (15,679)	62.5% (26,356)	51.3% (10,207)	72.6% (16,149)
Any Occasions	46.3% (325,986)	50.4% (173,147)	42.4% (152,838)	48.5% (280,365)	51.7% (147,343)	45.3% (133,022)	30.4% (11,459)	34.5% (5,464)	27.5% (5,995)	39.7% (18,375)	46.5% (10,646)	33.0% (7,729)	37.5% (15,786)	48.7% (9,694)	27.4% (6,092)
1 to 2 Occasions	27.1% (190,597)	26.4% (90,577)	27.7% (100,020)	27.7% (160,384)	26.3% (74,934)	29.1% (85,451)	21.1% (7,929)	19.7% (3,119)	22.1% (4,810)	26.0% (12,034)	28.3% (6,483)	23.7% (5,551)	24.3% (10,250)	30.4% (6,041)	18.9% (4,209)
3 to 19 Occasions	17.1% (120,358)	20.8% (71,437)	13.6% (48,921)	18.5% (107,223)	22.0% (62,827)	15.1% (44,397)	7.1% (2,688)	12.0% (1,895)	3.6% (793)	11.9% (5,503)	15.5% (3,537)	8.4% (1,966)	11.7% (4,943)	16.0% (3,178)	7.9% (1,765)
20 or More Occasions	2.1% (15,030)	3.2% (11,133)	1.1% (3,897)	2.2% (12,758)	3.4% (9,583)	1.1% (3,175)	2.2% (842)	2.8% (450)	1.8% (393)	1.8% (838)	2.7% (626)	0.9% (212)	1.4% (593)	2.4% (475)	0.5% (117)

Notes:

"–" indicates sample size too small to estimate.

*** Test of statistical significance compares African Americans with Whites. *** p <.001, ** p <.01, * p <.05.

+++ Test of statistical significance compares White boys with White girls. +++ p <.001, ++ p < .01, + p <.05.

~~~ Test of statistical significance compares African American boys with African American girls. ~~~ p <.001, ~~ p <.01, ~ p < .05.

Tests of statistical significance calculated using adjusted sample weight to control for influence of large sample sizes.

Source: National Education Longitudinal Study of 1988 Eighth Graders, Second Follow-Up (1992).

CHAPTER VII.
Participation in Community Service by 1992 High School Seniors

What percentage of African American students participate in community service? To what extent is their participation voluntary, rather than required for a class or other reasons? How do participation rates vary by students' characteristics (e.g., test scores and socioeconomic status) and characteristics of the schools they attend (e.g., school urbanicity, poverty, and type)?

Community service experiences are believed to shape the lives of participants and enable students to contribute to their home environment. The second followup to the National Education Longitudinal Study of 1988 Eighth Graders (NELS:88) provides national data regarding participation in community service among high school seniors.

NELS:88 provides not only longitudinal data describing 1988 8th graders, but also cross-sectional data describing 1992 high school seniors. The second follow-up to the NELS:88, conducted in the spring of 1992, included surveys of students and dropouts who had participated in the 1988 and 1990 waves of the study, as well as a "freshened" sample of students. Consequently, when appropriate weights are applied, the second follow-up is representative of 1992 high school seniors nationwide.

CHAPTER ORGANIZATION

The purpose of this chapter is to describe 1992 high school seniors who participated in community service. This chapter includes descriptions of:

1. Participation in community service by race and sex; and

2. Factors related to participation in community service, such as test scores, socioeconomic status, school urbanicity, school poverty, and school type.

PART I — OVERVIEW

Overall, about 44% of 1992 seniors participated in community service during their last two years of high school. Girls of all races participated at higher rates than boys, and African Americans generally participated at lower rates than their White counterparts. While community service was voluntary for most of the seniors surveyed, this was the case for a smaller share of African Americans than Whites.

Test scores appeared to influence the likelihood of community service, since students with lower scores participated at less than half the rate of higher scoring seniors. Among students in the three lowest test quartiles, participation rates were comparable for African Americans and Whites. But, among those with the highest test scores, a smaller percentage of African Americans than Whites engaged in community service.

More than one-half of high school seniors with the highest socioeconomic status participated in community service, compared with only one-third of those with the lowest socioeconomic status. Participation rates were comparable for African Americans and Whites with the lowest socioeconomic status. At higher levels of socioeconomic status, African American high school seniors appeared to participate at lower rates than their White counterparts.

A higher share of girls than boys engaged in community service among both Whites and African Americans at urban, suburban, and rural high schools. Regardless of school location, a smaller percentage of African Americans than Whites took part.

Overall, about one-half of students attending schools with the lowest levels of poverty (as measured by the percentage of students who receive free or reduced lunch) participated in community serv-

ice, compared with about 38% of students attending schools with the greatest poverty. Rates of participation were comparable for African Americans and Whites attending schools with the least poverty. But, at schools in which at least 6% of students received free or reduced lunch, a smaller share of African Americans than Whites participated.

About two-thirds of high school seniors attending Catholic high schools participated in community service, compared with less than one-half (42.4%) of seniors at public high schools. At public schools, African Americans' participation in community service lagged behind that of Whites. But, at Catholic and other private schools, participation rates for African Americans and Whites were comparable.

PART II — DETAILED DESCRIPTIONS AND TABLES

PARTICIPATION IN COMMUNITY SERVICE

About 44.1% of 1992 high school seniors participated in community service during their last 2 years of high school. **Figure 1** shows that a higher percentage of girls than boys engaged in community service overall (50.0% versus 38.2%) and among African Americans (43.8% versus 24.2%). Participation rates were lower for African Americans than for Whites.

Figure 1. Percentage of 1992 High School Seniors Who Participated in Community Service During the Past 2 Years

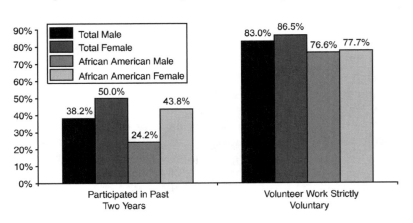

Source: National Educational Longitudinal Study of 1988 Eighth Graders, Second (1992) Follow-Up.

- **Table 1** shows that only 34.3% of African Americans participated in community service, compared with 45.9% of Whites.

The majority (84.9%) of 1992 high school seniors who participated in community service activities indicated that their participation was strictly voluntary.

- A smaller share of African American high school seniors than of their White counterparts indicated that community service was strictly voluntary (77.3% versus 87.1%).

- Comparable shares of African Americans and Whites indicated that their community service was required by court order (4.1% versus 3.0%) or for a class (17.9% versus 15.8%).

- A higher share of African American high school seniors than White seniors were required to perform their community service for some other reason (26.9% versus 18.6%).

FACTORS RELATED TO COMMUNITY SERVICE

Test Score

Rates of community service participation generally increased with students' test scores. Only 24.1% of 1992 high school seniors with the lowest test scores performed community service, compared with 57.5% of seniors with the highest test scores.

Regardless of test score, a higher share of girls than boys participated in community service. For example, **Figure 2** shows that 29.5% of girls with test scores in the

---

Table 1. Percentage of 1992 High School Seniors Who Participated in Community Service in the Past 2 Years by Race and Sex
(weighted sample size in parentheses)

Community Service	Total	Male	Female	White, Non-Hispanic			African American, Non-Hispanic			Hispanic			Other		
				Total	Male	Female	Total	Male	Female	Total	Male	Female	Total	Male	Female
Total ***+++~~~	100.0%	100.0%	100.0%	100.0%	100.0%	100.0%	100.0%	100.0%	100.0%	100.0%	100.0%	100.0%	100.0%	100.0%	100.0%
	(2,072,535)	(1,044,361)	(1,028,174)	(1,538,843)	(782,098)	(756,745)	(225,194)	(108,601)	(116,593)	(196,100)	(98,103)	(97,997)	(112,398)	(55,559)	(56,839)
Participated in Past 2 Years	44.1%	38.2%	50.0%	45.9%	40.2%	51.7%	34.3%	24.2%	43.8%	40.6%	38.1%	43.2%	45.1%	38.1%	51.9%
	(913,311)	(398,913)	(514,398)	(705,692)	(314,148)	(391,544)	(77,311)	(26,282)	(51,028)	(79,645)	(37,333)	(42,312)	(50,663)	(21,150)	(29,513)
Participated in Past 2 Years	100.0%	100.0%	100.0%	100.0%	100.0%	100.0%	100.0%	100.0%	100.0%	100.0%	100.0%	100.0%	100.0%	100.0%	100.0%
	(913,311)	(398,913)	(514,398)	(705,692)	(314,148)	(391,544)	(77,311)	(26,282)	(51,028)	(79,645)	(37,333)	(42,312)	(50,663)	(21,150)	(29,513)
Volunteer Work Strictly Voluntary ***+++	84.9%	83.0%	86.5%	87.1%	84.4%	89.3%	77.3%	76.6%	77.7%	74.9%	77.7%	72.4%	82.1%	79.1%	84.2%
	(775,641)	(330,940)	(444,701)	(614,625)	(265,082)	(349,544)	(59,794)	(20,124)	(39,669)	(59,639)	(29,006)	(30,633)	(41,584)	(16,728)	(24,856)
Volunteer Work Court Ordered +++	3.3%	5.5%	1.5%	3.0%	5.0%	1.4%	4.1%	5.9%	3.2%	4.3%	8.3%	0.8%	3.9%	6.7%	1.9%
	(29,832)	(21,880)	(7,952)	(21,235)	(15,793)	(5,443)	(3,166)	(1,553)	(1,614)	(3,452)	(3,113)	(338)	(1,979)	(1,421)	(558)
Volunteer Work Required for Class	16.6%	16.3%	16.8%	15.8%	16.1%	15.6%	17.9%	14.7%	19.6%	21.1%	18.6%	23.2%	18.4%	18.6%	18.2%
	(151,606)	(65,216)	(86,390)	(111,660)	(50,462)	(61,198)	(13,863)	(3,865)	(9,998)	(16,780)	(6,957)	(9,824)	(9,303)	(3,932)	(5,370)
Volunteer Work Required Other Reason ***	20.3%	20.0%	20.5%	18.6%	18.5%	18.7%	26.9%	26.3%	27.2%	27.3%	26.9%	27.8%	22.8%	22.7%	22.9%
	(185,442)	(79,953)	(105,489)	(131,301)	(58,218)	(73,084)	(20,804)	(6,914)	(13,890)	(21,772)	(10,029)	(11,744)	(11,565)	(4,794)	(6,771)
Volunteer Work Encouraged by Other	38.2%	38.7%	37.9%	38.0%	38.0%	37.9%	39.2%	38.7%	39.5%	39.3%	41.5%	37.4%	38.9%	43.3%	35.7%
	(349,314)	(154,256)	(195,057)	(267,995)	(119,441)	(148,554)	(30,312)	(10,161)	(20,150)	(31,314)	(15,489)	(15,825)	(19,692)	(9,165)	(10,528)

Notes:
*** Test of statistical significance compares African Americans with Whites. *** p < .001, ** p < .01, * p < .05.
+++ Test of statistical significance compares White boys with White girls. +++ p < .001, ++ p < .01, + p < .05.
~~~Test of statistical significance compares African American boys with African American girls. ~~~ p < .001, ~~ p < .01, ~ p < .05.
Tests of statistical significance calculated using adjusted sample weight to control for influence of large sample sizes.
Source: National Education Longitudinal Study of 1988 Eighth Graders, Second Follow-Up (1992).

Figure 2. Percentage of 1992 High School Seniors Who Participated in Community Service During the Past 2 Years by Test Score

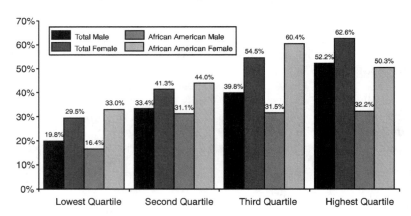

Source: National Educational Longitudinal Study of 1988 Eighth Graders, Second (1992) Follow-Up.

lowest quartile performed community service, compared with only 19.8% of boys. Among those with test scores in the highest quartile, 62.6% of girls, but 52.2% of boys, engaged in community service.

- **Table 2** shows that the percentage of African Americans who participated in community service was comparable to the percentage of Whites for those with test scores in the bottom three quartiles.

- Only 42.7% of African Americans with the highest test scores engaged in community service, compared with 59.3% of their White counterparts

- **Table 2** also shows that only 72.2% of African Americans with the highest test scores participated in their community service activities on a strictly voluntary basis, compared with 89.1% of Whites.

Socioeconomic Status

The percentage of 1992 high school seniors who performed community service increased with socioeconomic status. Only 31.3% of high school seniors

with the lowest socioeconomic status performed community service, compared with 58.8% of those with the highest socioeconomic status.

Figure 3 shows that, among African Americans and Whites, a smaller percentage of boys than girls participated in community service during the past 2 years regardless of socioeconomic status.

- Among high school seniors with the lowest socioeconomic status, 22.0% of African American boys and 25.6% of White boys participated in community service, compared with 35.6% of African American girls and 35.3% of White girls.

- Participation rates were comparable for African Americans and Whites with the lowest socioeconomic status (29.5% versus 30.5%).

But, the percentage of African Americans who participated in community service appears to be smaller than the percentage of Whites among students with higher socioeconomic status.

- For example, **Table 3** shows that, among high school seniors with the second lowest socioeconomic status, 32.8% of African Americans par-

Table 2. Percentage of 1992 High School Seniors Who Participated in Community Service in the Past 2 Years by Test Score, Race, and Sex
(weighted sample size in parentheses)

Community Service	Total	Male	Female	White, Non-Hispanic			African American, Non-Hispanic			Hispanic			Other		
				Total	Male	Female	Total	Male	Female	Total	Male	Female	Total	Male	Female
Lowest Quartile	100.0%	100.0%	100.0%	100.0%	100.0%	100.0%	100.0%	100.0%	100.0%	100.0%	100.0%	100.0%	100.0%	100.0%	100.0%
	(434,619)	(242,996)	(191,623)	(250,699)	(146,665)	(104,034)	(97,468)	(52,576)	(44,892)	(63,895)	(31,766)	(32,128)	(22,557)	(11,989)	(10,568)
Participated in Past 2 Years +++~~	24.1%	19.8%	29.5%	22.7%	18.3%	28.9%	24.0%	16.4%	33.0%	31.2%	34.8%	27.6%	19.2%	13.7%	25.6%
	(104,596)	(48,126)	(56,470)	(56,914)	(26,851)	(30,063)	(23,429)	(8,598)	(14,831)	(19,912)	(11,039)	(8,873)	(4,341)	(1,639)	(2,702)
If Participated, Strictly Voluntary *	69.3%	68.7%	69.8%	76.8%	75.7%	77.8%	67.9%	72.2%	65.4%	50.1%	52.8%	46.8%	66.6%	42.9%	81.0%
	(72,492)	(33,057)	(39,435)	(43,724)	(20,321)	(23,403)	(15,902)	(6,209)	(9,693)	(9,973)	(5,824)	(4,149)	(2,893)	(703)	(2,190)
Second Quartile	100.0%	100.0%	100.0%	100.0%	100.0%	100.0%	100.0%	100.0%	100.0%	100.0%	100.0%	100.0%	100.0%	100.0%	100.0%
	(440,058)	(219,218)	(220,840)	(315,602)	(160,401)	(155,202)	(52,388)	(24,036)	(28,353)	(48,503)	(23,171)	(25,333)	(23,564)	(11,611)	(11,953)
Participated in Past 2 Years ++~	37.4%	33.4%	41.3%	37.1%	34.0%	40.4%	38.1%	31.1%	44.0%	39.0%	31.9%	45.6%	35.1%	32.9%	37.2%
	(164,384)	(73,153)	(91,231)	(117,228)	(54,464)	(62,765)	(19,954)	(7,478)	(12,476)	(18,937)	(7,394)	(11,543)	(8,264)	(3,817)	(4,447)
If Participated, Strictly Voluntary	85.7%	84.5%	86.7%	86.8%	85.5%	87.9%	82.6%	76.8%	86.1%	84.2%	86.0%	83.0%	81.8%	83.4%	80.5%
	(140,920)	(61,847)	(79,073)	(101,722)	(46,561)	(55,161)	(16,489)	(5,742)	(10,748)	(15,945)	(6,362)	(9,583)	(6,763)	(3,182)	(3,581)
Third Quartile	100.0%	100.0%	100.0%	100.0%	100.0%	100.0%	100.0%	100.0%	100.0%	100.0%	100.0%	100.0%	100.0%	100.0%	100.0%
	(445,247)	(212,842)	(232,405)	(358,286)	(170,296)	(187,990)	(33,109)	(14,181)	(18,927)	(31,664)	(17,660)	(14,004)	(22,188)	(10,705)	(11,483)
Participated in Past 2 Years +++~~	47.5%	39.8%	54.5%	46.6%	39.3%	53.2%	48.0%	31.5%	60.4%	51.8%	47.9%	56.8%	54.3%	45.0%	63.0%
	(211,400)	(84,742)	(126,658)	(167,040)	(66,993)	(100,046)	(15,901)	(4,470)	(11,431)	(16,413)	(8,465)	(7,948)	(12,046)	(4,814)	(7,232)
If Participated, Strictly Voluntary ++++~~	86.5%	81.8%	89.6%	86.5%	81.6%	89.8%	90.5%	76.0%	96.1%	86.3%	88.9%	83.5%	82.1%	78.8%	84.2%
(182,870)	(69,359)	(113,512)	(144,434)	(54,638)	(89,797)	(14,386)	(3,399)	(10,988)	(14,166)	(7,530)	(6,636)	(9,884)	(3,793)	(6,092)
Highest Quartile	100.0%	100.0%	100.0%	100.0%	100.0%	100.0%	100.0%	100.0%	100.0%	100.0%	100.0%	100.0%	100.0%	100.0%	100.0%
	(752,611)	(369,305)	(383,306)	(614,256)	(304,736)	(309,520)	(42,229)	(17,808)	(24,420)	(52,038)	(25,506)	(26,532)	(44,088)	(21,254)	(22,834)
Participated in Past 2 Years ***+++~~	57.5%	52.2%	62.6%	59.3%	54.4%	64.2%	42.7%	32.2%	50.3%	46.9%	40.9%	52.6%	59.0%	51.2%	66.3%
	(432,932)	(192,892)	(240,040)	(364,510)	(165,840)	(198,671)	(18,026)	(5,736)	(12,290)	(24,383)	(10,434)	(13,948)	(26,012)	(10,881)	(15,131)
If Participated, Strictly Voluntary ***+++	87.6%	86.4%	88.6%	89.1%	86.6%	91.2%	72.2%	83.2%	67.1%	80.2%	89.0%	73.6%	84.7%	83.2%	85.9%
(379,359)	(166,678)	(212,681)	(324,745)	(143,562)	(181,183)	(13,016)	(4,775)	(8,241)	(19,555)	(9,290)	(10,264)	(22,043)	(9,050)	(12,993)

Notes:
*** Test of statistical significance compares African Americans with Whites. *** p < .001, ** p < .01, * p < .05.
+++ Test of statistical significance compares White boys with White girls. +++ p < .001, ++ p < .01, + p < .05.
~~~Test of statistical significance compares African American boys with African American girls. ~~~ p < .001, ~~ p < .01, ~ p < .05.
Tests of statistical significance calculated using adjusted sample weight to control for influence of large sample sizes.
Source: National Education Longitudinal Study of 1988 Eighth Graders, Second Follow-Up (1992).

ticipated in community service, compared with 41.3% of Whites.

Of those who participated, a smaller share of African Americans than Whites with the lowest and the highest socioeconomic status participated in community service on a strictly voluntary basis.

- Among those in the lowest socioeconomic status quartile, 72.4% of African Americans vol-

untarily participated in community service, compared with 82.8% of Whites.

School Urbanicity

About 48.9% of seniors at urban high schools, 43.7% of seniors at suburban high schools, and 40.8% of seniors at rural high schools participated in community service. Among both African Americans and Whites, a higher share of girls than boys engaged in

Figure 3. Percentage of 1992 High School Seniors Who Participated in Community Service During the Past 2 Years by Socioeconomic Status

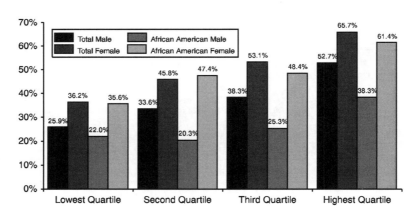

Source: National Educational Longitudinal Study of 1988 Eighth Graders, Second (1992) Follow-Up.

community service regardless of school location. **Figure 4** shows that 54.4% of girls and only 43.1% of boys at urban schools performed community service, compared with 50.0% of girls and 37.9% of boys at suburban schools and 46.5% of girls and 34.9% of boys at rural schools.

The share of African American high school seniors who performed community service was smaller than the share of their White counterparts, regardless of school location.

- **Table 4** shows that 39.4% of African Americans and 54.0% of Whites at urban high schools participated in community service.

- At suburban high schools, 29.5% of African Americans and 45.4% of Whites s participated.

- About one-third (31.9%) of African Americans at rural high schools engaged in community service, compared with 42.1% of Whites.

At suburban high schools, a smaller share of African Americans than Whites performed their community service on a strictly voluntary basis.

- At suburban schools, 72.6% of African Americans and 86.9% of Whites voluntarily performed community service.

- At urban schools, 79.4% of African American and 85.8% of White high school seniors voluntarily performed community service.

- At rural schools, 78.5% of African Americans and 88.2% of Whites performed community service on a strictly voluntary basis.

School Poverty

About one-half (50.4%) of seniors who attended schools with the lowest levels of poverty (as measured by the percentage of students who received free or reduced lunch) participated in community service, compared with 37.7% of seniors who attended schools with the highest levels of poverty.

Regardless of the extent of school poverty, a higher proportion of White girls than White boys engaged in community service. **Figure 5** shows that, overall, about 56.7% of girls and 44.6% of boys at schools with the least poverty engaged in commu-

Table 3. Percentage of 1992 High School Seniors Who Participated in Community Service in the Past 2 Years by Socioeconomic Status, Race, and Sex
(weighted sample size in parentheses)

Community Service	Total	Male	Female	White, Non-Hispanic			African American, Non-Hispanic			Hispanic			Other		
				Total	Male	Female	Total	Male	Female	Total	Male	Female	Total	Male	Female
Lowest Quartile	100.0%	100.0%	100.0%	100.0%	100.0%	100.0%	100.0%	100.0%	100.0%	100.0%	100.0%	100.0%	100.0%	100.0%	100.0%
	(508,683)	(241,927)	(266,756)	(288,090)	(142,678)	(145,411)	(96,409)	(43,204)	(53,205)	(97,747)	(43,468)	(54,279)	(26,437)	(12,576)	(13,861)
Participated in Past 2 Years +++~~~	31.3%	25.9%	36.2%	30.5%	25.6%	35.3%	29.5%	22.0%	35.6%	34.5%	30.1%	37.9%	35.5%	28.8%	41.7%
	(159,326)	(62,762)	(96,564)	(87,802)	(36,539)	(51,263)	(28,450)	(9,512)	(18,938)	(33,677)	(13,092)	(20,584)	(9,397)	(3,619)	(5,778)
If Participated, Strictly Voluntary **~	77.5%	77.4%	77.5%	82.8%	84.6%	81.6%	72.4%	63.8%	76.7%	68.5%	70.8%	67.0%	75.1%	64.9%	81.4%
	(123,440)	(48,582)	(74,858)	(72,742)	(30,896)	(41,846)	(20,585)	(6,064)	(14,521)	(23,059)	(9,272)	(13,788)	(7,053)	(2,350)	(4,703)
Second Quartile	100.0%	100.0%	100.0%	100.0%	100.0%	100.0%	100.0%	100.0%	100.0%	100.0%	100.0%	100.0%	100.0%	100.0%	100.0%
	(512,674)	(255,791)	(256,883)	(389,504)	(191,410)	(198,094)	(58,881)	(31,807)	(27,075)	(41,730)	(21,635)	(20,095)	(22,559)	(10,939)	(11,620)
Participated in Past 2 Years **+++~~~	39.7%	33.6%	45.8%	41.3%	35.9%	46.5%	32.8%	20.3%	47.4%	39.9%	37.0%	43.1%	30.5%	25.4%	35.4%
	(203,693)	(85,932)	(117,760)	(160,835)	(68,694)	(92,141)	(19,314)	(6,468)	(12,846)	(16,653)	(7,997)	(8,657)	(6,890)	(2,773)	(4,117)
If Participated, Strictly Voluntary ++	85.1%	82.6%	86.8%	86.5%	83.4%	88.9%	83.9%	92.4%	79.7%	73.7%	69.3%	77.8%	80.7%	80.0%	81.1%
	(173,248)	(71,001)	(102,247)	(139,203)	(57,268)	(81,935)	(16,208)	(5,974)	(10,234)	(12,279)	(5,540)	(6,739)	(5,559)	(2,219)	(3,340)
Third Quartile	100.0%	100.0%	100.0%	100.0%	100.0%	100.0%	100.0%	100.0%	100.0%	100.0%	100.0%	100.0%	100.0%	100.0%	100.0%
	(512,288)	(262,853)	(249,435)	(408,919)	(210,217)	(198,702)	(43,025)	(19,641)	(23,384)	(30,904)	(17,757)	(13,147)	(29,440)	(15,238)	(14,202)
Participated in Past 2 Years **+++~~~	45.5%	38.3%	53.1%	46.6%	39.1%	54.6%	37.8%	25.3%	48.4%	47.5%	48.3%	46.4%	39.3%	31.9%	47.3%
	(233,239)	(100,679)	(132,559)	(190,715)	(82,278)	(108,437)	(16,276)	(4,964)	(11,312)	(14,666)	(8,571)	(6,095)	(11,582)	(4,867)	(6,715)
If Participated, Strictly Voluntary *+++	86.5%	83.3%	88.9%	87.5%	82.7%	91.2%	77.2%	81.0%	75.5%	81.9%	85.4%	77.0%	89.5%	93.8%	86.5%
	(201,822)	(83,913)	(117,909)	(166,879)	(68,008)	(98,870)	(12,559)	(4,023)	(8,535)	(12,014)	(7,318)	(4,696)	(10,370)	(4,563)	(5,807)
Highest Quartile	100.0%	100.0%	100.0%	100.0%	100.0%	100.0%	100.0%	100.0%	100.0%	100.0%	100.0%	100.0%	100.0%	100.0%	100.0%
	(538,891)	(283,791)	(255,100)	(452,331)	(237,793)	(214,538)	(26,878)	(13,949)	(12,929)	(25,719)	(15,243)	(10,476)	(33,963)	(16,806)	(17,157)
Participated in Past 2 Years *+++~~	58.8%	52.7%	65.7%	58.9%	53.3%	65.1%	49.4%	38.3%	61.4%	57.0%	50.3%	66.6%	67.1%	58.9%	75.2%
	(317,054)	(149,539)	(167,515)	(266,340)	(126,637)	(139,703)	(13,270)	(5,338)	(7,932)	(14,650)	(7,674)	(6,976)	(22,794)	(9,891)	(12,903)
If Participated, Strictly Voluntary **++	87.4%	85.2%	89.4%	88.5%	86.0%	90.8%	78.7%	76.1%	80.4%	83.9%	89.6%	77.5%	81.6%	76.8%	85.3%
	(277,132)	(127,444)	(149,687)	(235,802)	(108,909)	(126,893)	(10,442)	(4,063)	(6,379)	(12,286)	(6,877)	(5,410)	(18,601)	(7,595)	(11,006)

Notes:
*** Test of statistical significance compares African Americans with Whites. *** p < .001, ** p < .01, * p < .05.
+++ Test of statistical significance compares White boys with White girls. +++ p < .001, ++ p < .01, + p < .05.
~~~Test of statistical significance compares African American boys with African American girls. ~~~ p < .001, ~~ p < .01, ~ p < .05.
Tests of statistical significance calculated using adjusted sample weight to control for influence of large sample sizes.
Source: National Education Longitudinal Study of 1988 Eighth Graders, Second Follow-Up (1992).

nity service, compared with 41.8% of girls and 33.5% of boys at schools with the most poverty.

- **Table 5** shows that, at schools with the least poverty, the share of African Americans who performed community service was comparable to the share of Whites (50.6% versus 49.9%).

At schools in which more than 5% of the student body received free or reduced lunches, a smaller share of African American than White high school seniors performed community service.

- **Table 5** shows that at schools with the highest levels of school poverty, only 27.4% of African

Figure 4. Percentage of 1992 High School Seniors Who Participated in Community Service During the Past 2 Years by Urbanicity

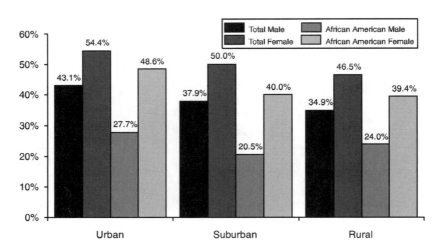

Source: National Educational Longitudinal Study of 1988 Eighth Graders, Second (1992) Follow-Up.

Americans engaged in community service, compared with 41.9% of Whites.

At schools in which at least 20% of students received free or reduced lunch, a smaller share of African Americans than Whites performed community service on a strictly voluntary basis.

- Only 71.8% of African Americans attending schools with the highest level of poverty performed community service on a strictly voluntary basis, compared with 88.2% of their White counterparts.

School Type

About two-thirds (65.2%) of 1992 high school seniors attending Catholic schools engaged in community service, compared with 57.3% of seniors attending other private schools and 42.4% of seniors attending public high schools. **Figure 6** shows that,

among 1992 high school seniors at public schools, 48.8% of girls participated in community service, compared with only 35.9% of boys.

The percentage of African American high school seniors who participated in community service was smaller than the percentage of Whites at public schools, but comparable to the percentage of Whites at Catholic and other private schools.

- **Table 6** shows that 33.1% of African Americans but 44.2% of Whites at public schools engaged in community service.

- At Catholic schools, 60.6% of African Americans and 65.3% of Whites s participated in community service.

- At non-Catholic private schools, 47.1% of African Americans and 59.7% of Whites performed community service.

Table 4. Percentage of 1992 High School Seniors Who Participated in Community Service in the Past 2 Years by Urbanicity, Race, and Sex
(weighted sample size in parentheses)

Community Service	Total	Male	Female	White, Non-Hispanic			African American, Non-Hispanic			Hispanic			Other		
				Total	Male	Female	Total	Male	Female	Total	Male	Female	Total	Male	Female
Urban	100.0%	100.0%	100.0%	100.0%	100.0%	100.0%	100.0%	100.0%	100.0%	100.0%	100.0%	100.0%	100.0%	100.0%	100.0%
	(521,029)	(253,413)	(267,616)	(295,640)	(149,656)	(145,984)	(95,466)	(42,060)	(53,406)	(84,761)	(40,307)	(44,455)	(45,161)	(21,390)	(23,771)
Participated in Past 2 Years ***+++~~~	48.9%	43.1%	54.4%	54.0%	48.3%	59.7%	39.4%	27.7%	48.6%	44.3%	43.6%	45.0%	45.1%	36.4%	52.8%
	(255,042)	(109,346)	(145,696)	(159,498)	(72,319)	(87,180)	(37,610)	(11,642)	(25,968)	(37,578)	(17,591)	(19,987)	(20,356)	(7,794)	(12,562)
If Participated, Strictly Voluntary *+++	82.4%	80.4%	83.9%	85.8%	82.0%	89.0%	79.4%	81.6%	78.4%	72.4%	78.0%	67.5%	79.5%	69.3%	85.8%
	(210,146)	(87,894)	(122,252)	(136,894)	(59,270)	(77,624)	(29,847)	(9,496)	(20,351)	(27,220)	(13,724)	(13,496)	(16,184)	(5,404)	(10,781)
Suburban	100.0%	100.0%	100.0%	100.0%	100.0%	100.0%	100.0%	100.0%	100.0%	100.0%	100.0%	100.0%	100.0%	100.0%	100.0%
	(871,599)	(451,437)	(420,162)	(689,850)	(357,204)	(332,646)	(69,665)	(37,471)	(32,194)	(66,017)	(33,049)	(32,969)	(46,067)	(23,714)	(22,353)
Participated in Past 2 Years ***+++~~~	43.7%	37.9%	50.0%	45.4%	40.0%	51.3%	29.5%	20.5%	40.0%	37.8%	31.9%	43.6%	48.5%	41.8%	55.7%
	(381,194)	(170,908)	(210,285)	(313,364)	(142,772)	(170,591)	(20,534)	(7,671)	(12,863)	(24,932)	(10,544)	(14,389)	(22,364)	(9,921)	(12,443)
If Participated, Strictly Voluntary ***+	85.1%	83.3%	86.5%	86.9%	84.9%	88.7%	72.6%	74.0%	71.8%	73.8%	68.7%	77.5%	83.1%	83.5%	82.8%
	(324,301)	(142,382)	(181,919)	(272,415)	(121,185)	(151,230)	(14,908)	(5,676)	(9,232)	(18,396)	(7,240)	(11,156)	(18,582)	(8,281)	(10,302)
Rural	100.0%	100.0%	100.0%	100.0%	100.0%	100.0%	100.0%	100.0%	100.0%	100.0%	100.0%	100.0%	100.0%	100.0%	100.0%
	(679,907)	(339,511)	(340,396)	(553,352)	(275,238)	(278,115)	(60,063)	(29,070)	(30,993)	(45,321)	(24,748)	(20,573)	(21,171)	(10,456)	(10,715)
Participated in Past 2 Years ***+++~~	40.8%	34.9%	46.5%	42.1%	36.0%	48.1%	31.9%	24.0%	39.4%	37.8%	37.2%	38.6%	37.5%	32.9%	42.1%
	(277,075)	(118,659)	(158,416)	(232,830)	(99,057)	(133,773)	(19,167)	(6,969)	(12,198)	(17,135)	(9,198)	(7,937)	(7,943)	(3,435)	(4,508)
If Participated, Strictly Voluntary *++~	87.1%	84.8%	88.7%	88.2%	85.4%	90.2%	78.5%	71.1%	82.7%	81.8%	87.4%	75.4%	85.8%	88.6%	83.7%
	(241,195)	(100,665)	(140,530)	(205,317)	(84,627)	(120,689)	(15,038)	(4,952)	(10,087)	(14,023)	(8,042)	(5,981)	(6,817)	(3,044)	(3,774)

Notes:
*** Test of statistical significance compares African Americans with Whites. *** p < .001, ** p < .01, * p < .05,
+++ Test of statistical significance compares White boys with White girls. +++ p < .001, ++ p < .01, + p < .05.
~~~Test of statistical significance compares African American boys with African American girls. ~~~ p < .001, ~~ p < .01, ~ p < .05.
Tests of statistical significance calculated using adjusted sample weight to control for influence of large sample sizes.
Source: National Education Longitudinal Study of 1988 Eighth Graders, Second Follow-Up (1992).

- Among 1992 high school seniors who participated in community service and who attended public schools, a smaller percentage of African Americans than Whites indicated that their service was strictly voluntary (77.6% versus 88.1%).

- The percentage of African Americans who voluntarily performed community service was comparable to the percentage of Whites at both Catholic schools (72.4% versus 74.6%) and non-Catholic private schools (87.9% versus 88.8%).

Figure 5. Percentage of 1992 High School Seniors Who Participated in Community Service During the Past 2 Years by Percentage of Students at School Who Received Free or Reduced Lunch

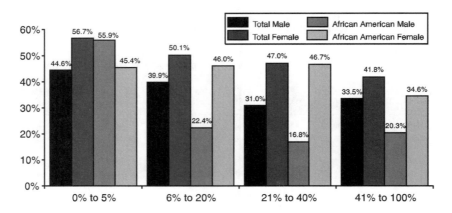

Source: National Educational Longitudinal Study of 1988 Eighth Graders, Second (1992) Follow-Up.

Table 5. Percentage of 1992 High School Seniors Who Participated in Community Service in the Past 2 Years by Percentage of Students at School Who Received Free or Reduced Lunch, Race, and Sex
(weighted sample size in parentheses)

Community Service	Total	Male	Female	White, Non-Hispanic Total	Male	Female	African American, Non-Hispanic Total	Male	Female	Hispanic Total	Male	Female	Other Total	Male	Female
0% to 5%	100.0% (593,394)	100.0% (309,917)	100.0% (283,478)	100.0% (498,994)	100.0% (262,255)	100.0% (236,740)	100.0% (27,398)	100.0% (13,383)	100.0% (14,015)	100.0% (27,260)	100.0% (15,602)	100.0% (11,658)	100.0% (39,741)	100.0% (18,677)	100.0% (21,065)
Participated in Past 2 Years +++	50.4% (298,903)	44.6% (138,101)	56.7% (160,802)	49.9% (249,217)	43.9% (115,239)	56.6% (133,979)	50.6% (13,853)	55.9% (7,487)	45.4% (6,366)	56.4% (15,375)	49.5% (7,730)	65.6% (7,645)	51.5% (20,457)	40.9% (7,645)	60.8% (12,811)
If Participated, Strictly Voluntary ++	86.6% (258,993)	84.5% (116,747)	88.5% (142,245)	87.0% (216,870)	84.2% (96,982)	89.5% (119,887)	82.8% (11,477)	86.0% (6,441)	79.1% (5,036)	89.1% (13,697)	90.5% (6,997)	87.6% (6,700)	82.9% (16,949)	82.8% (6,327)	82.9% (10,622)
6% to 20%	100.0% (636,101)	100.0% (320,477)	100.0% (315,625)	100.0% (501,970)	100.0% (252,261)	100.0% (249,709)	100.0% (57,863)	100.0% (28,676)	100.0% (29,186)	100.0% (47,089)	100.0% (24,473)	100.0% (22,616)	100.0% (29,179)	100.0% (15,066)	100.0% (14,113)
Participated in Past 2 Years ***+++~~	45.0% (286,082)	39.9% (127,881)	50.1% (158,201)	47.1% (236,284)	42.8% (108,017)	51.4% (128,267)	34.3% (19,845)	22.4% (6,432)	46.0% (13,413)	36.1% (17,013)	30.0% (7,341)	42.8% (9,672)	44.3% (12,941)	40.4% (6,091)	48.5% (6,850)
If Participated, Strictly Voluntary +	86.0% (245,946)	84.5% (108,007)	87.2% (137,939)	87.0% (205,581)	84.6% (91,348)	89.1% (114,233)	80.2% (15,914)	89.1% (5,734)	75.9% (10,179)	80.2% (13,642)	83.3% (6,115)	77.8% (7,527)	83.5% (10,809)	79.0% (4,810)	87.6% (6,000)
21% to 40%	100.0% (527,872)	100.0% (255,182)	100.0% (272,690)	100.0% (385,467)	100.0% (189,617)	100.0% (195,850)	100.0% (77,424)	100.0% (35,906)	100.0% (41,517)	100.0% (44,441)	100.0% (20,646)	100.0% (23,794)	100.0% (20,541)	100.0% (9,013)	100.0% (11,528)
Participated in Past 2 Years **+++~~	39.3% (207,378)	31.0% (79,197)	47.0% (128,180)	40.6% (156,644)	33.1% (62,819)	47.9% (93,825)	32.8% (25,390)	16.8% (6,022)	46.7% (19,368)	37.0% (16,430)	34.4% (7,102)	39.2% (9,328)	43.4% (8,913)	36.1% (3,255)	49.1% (5,659)
If Participated, Strictly Voluntary ***++~~	84.6% (175,539)	78.9% (62,490)	88.2% (113,048)	87.1% (136,446)	83.3% (52,334)	89.6% (84,113)	76.0% (19,305)	50.3% (3,031)	84.0% (16,274)	72.9% (11,985)	61.9% (4,393)	81.4% (7,592)	87.5% (7,803)	84.0% (2,733)	89.6% (5,070)
41% to 100%	100.0% (291,549)	100.0% (146,801)	100.0% (144,749)	100.0% (136,564)	100.0% (68,305)	100.0% (68,259)	100.0% (58,982)	100.0% (29,648)	100.0% (29,333)	100.0% (74,705)	100.0% (36,944)	100.0% (37,761)	100.0% (21,299)	100.0% (11,903)	100.0% (9,396)
Participated in Past 2 Years ***+++~~	37.7% (109,769)	33.5% (49,244)	41.8% (60,526)	41.9% (57,190)	35.9% (24,503)	47.9% (32,687)	27.4% (16,174)	20.3% (6,019)	34.6% (10,155)	39.1% (29,182)	40.5% (14,954)	37.7% (14,228)	33.9% (7,224)	31.7% (3,769)	36.8% (3,455)
If Participated, Strictly Voluntary ***	79.2% (86,936)	80.1% (39,440)	78.5% (47,496)	88.2% (50,447)	86.0% (21,082)	89.8% (29,365)	71.8% (11,610)	76.4% (4,596)	69.1% (7,014)	68.5% (19,985)	75.5% (11,295)	61.1% (8,690)	67.8% (4,894)	65.5% (2,468)	70.2% (2,426)

Notes:
*** Test of statistical significance compares African Americans with Whites. *** p < .001, ** p < .01, * p < .05.
+++ Test of statistical significance compares White boys with White girls. +++ p < .001, ++ p < .01, + p < .05.
~~~Test of statistical significance compares African American boys with African American girls. ~~~ p < .001, ~~ p < .01, ~ p < .05.
Tests of statistical significance calculated using adjusted sample weight to control for influence of large sample sizes.
Source: National Education Longitudinal Study of 1988 Eighth Graders, Second Follow-Up (1992).

Figure 6. Percentage of 1992 High School Seniors Who Participated in Community Service by School Type

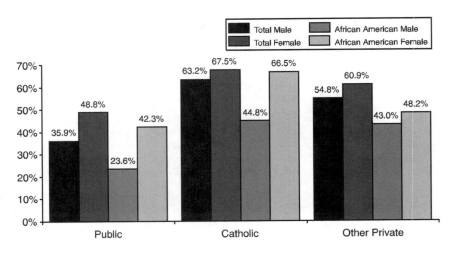

Source: National Educational Longitudinal Study of 1988 Eighth Graders, Second (1992) Follow-Up.

Table 6. Percentage of 1992 High School Seniors Who Participated in Community Service in the Past 2 Years by School Type, Race, and Sex
(weighted sample size in parentheses)

Community Service	Total	Male	Female	White, Non-Hispanic			African American, Non-Hispanic			Hispanic			Other		
				Total	Male	Female	Total	Male	Female	Total	Male	Female	Total	Male	Female
Public	100.0%	100.0%	100.0%	100.0%	100.0%	100.0%	100.0%	100.0%	100.0%	100.0%	100.0%	100.0%	100.0%	100.0%	100.0%
	(1,897,099)	(945,991)	(951,108)	(1,402,271)	(701,345)	(700,926)	(213,783)	(105,545)	(108,238)	(183,390)	(91,058)	(92,332)	(97,655)	(48,044)	(49,611)
Participated in Past 2 Years ***+++~~~	42.4%	35.9%	48.8%	44.2%	37.7%	50.7%	33.1%	23.6%	42.3%	39.1%	36.3%	41.9%	43.2%	36.1%	50.0%
	(804,334)	(340,034)	(464,301)	(619,716)	(264,644)	(355,072)	(70,677)	(24,945)	(45,732)	(71,751)	(33,078)	(38,673)	(42,191)	(17,367)	(24,824)
If Participated, Strictly Voluntary ***+++	85.7%	83.5%	87.4%	88.1%	85.2%	90.2%	77.6%	76.7%	78.1%	74.7%	76.5%	73.1%	83.6%	80.2%	86.0%
	(689,495)	(283,882)	(405,612)	(545,796)	(225,516)	(320,280)	(54,858)	(19,141)	(35,718)	(53,564)	(25,299)	(28,265)	(35,276)	(13,926)	(21,350)
Catholic	100.0%	100.0%	100.0%	100.0%	100.0%	100.0%	100.0%	100.0%	100.0%	100.0%	100.0%	100.0%	100.0%	100.0%	100.0%
	(107,454)	(58,821)	(48,633)	(81,050)	(47,048)	(34,003)	(9,554)	(2,602)	(6,951)	(11,105)	(6,273)	(4,832)	(5,745)	(2,898)	(2,847)
Participated in Past 2 Years	65.2%	63.2%	67.5%	65.3%	64.3%	66.8%	60.6%	44.8%	66.5%	64.7%	61.5%	68.9%	71.0%	66.4%	75.6%
	(70,008)	(37,177)	(32,831)	(52,955)	(30,229)	(22,726)	(5,787)	(1,167)	(4,621)	(7,188)	(3,857)	(3,331)	(4,077)	(1,924)	(2,154)
If Participated, Strictly Voluntary	74.1%	76.5%	71.4%	74.6%	75.8%	72.9%	72.4%	71.9%	72.6%	78.9%	87.9%	68.5%	61.4%	66.2%	57.2%
	(51,862)	(28,426)	(23,436)	(39,492)	(22,922)	(16,571)	(4,191)	(839)	(3,352)	(5,674)	(3,392)	(2,282)	(2,505)	(1,273)	(1,232)
Other Private	100.0%	100.0%	100.0%	100.0%	100.0%	100.0%	100.0%	100.0%	100.0%	100.0%	100.0%	100.0%	100.0%	100.0%	100.0%
	(67,467)	(39,358)	(28,108)	(55,343)	(33,705)	(21,638)	(1,799)	(396)	(1,403)	(1,459)	(772)	(687)	(8,866)	(4,485)	(4,381)
Participated in Past 2 Years	57.3%	54.8%	60.9%	59.7%	57.2%	63.5%	47.1%	43.0%	48.2%	38.4%	51.5%	23.6%	48.1%	38.5%	57.9%
	(38,690)	(21,569)	(17,120)	(33,021)	(19,274)	(13,746)	(847)	(170)	(676)	(560)	(398)	(162)	(4,262)	(1,727)	(2,535)
If Participated, Strictly Voluntary	88.3%	85.8%	91.4%	88.8%	86.4%	92.3%	87.9%	85.0%	88.6%	71.6%	79.2%	53.1%	86.1%	80.8%	89.7%
	(34,152)	(18,499)	(15,652)	(29,337)	(16,644)	(12,693)	(744)	(145)	(599)	(401)	(315)	(86)	(3,669)	(1,396)	(2,274)

Notes:
*** Test of statistical significance compares African Americans with Whites. *** p < .001, ** p < .01, * p < .05.
+++ Test of statistical significance compares White boys with White girls. +++ p < .001, ++ p < .01, + p < .05.
~~~Test of statistical significance compares African American boys with African American girls. ~~~ p < .001, ~~ p < .01, ~ p < .05.
Tests of statistical significance calculated using adjusted sample weight to control for influence of large sample sizes.
Source: National Education Longitudinal Study of 1988 Eighth Graders, Second Follow-Up (1992).

CHAPTER VIII.
Characteristics of Public and Private School Teachers

What percentage of America's public and private school teachers are African American? How does the representation of African Americans among public and private school teachers vary by school level and other school characteristics such as urbanicity, region, and racial composition of the student body? How does the education and experience of African American teachers compare with that of their White counterparts? What subjects do African American public school teachers teach and how do they organize their classes? In what types of professional development activities do African American teachers participate? How do the salaries earned by African American teachers compare with those of their majority counterparts?

Two components of the Schools and Staffing Survey (SASS) provide data on the background characteristics and employment experiences of the nation's public and private school teachers: the Teacher Demand and Shortage Survey and the Teacher Survey. The most recent (1993/94) SASS data are used for the analyses that follow.

CHAPTER ORGANIZATION

To facilitate comparisons between public and private school teachers, the data are arranged under common headings with the public sector information preceding the private. The data are organized into five sections:

1. Representation of African Americans among public and private school teachers overall and by school level, affiliation, urbanicity, region, racial composition of student body, and other school characteristics;

2. Education and experience of African American teachers including their highest level of education attained, certification, previous experience, and age;

3. The duties and responsibilities, including main assignment, subject taught, organization of classes, and professional development activities;

4. Salaries overall and by age, urbanicity, and region; and

5. Aspects of school life teachers perceive to be problematic.

PART I — OVERVIEW

At 7.4%, African Americans are underrepresented among America's public school teachers relative to both their representation in the U.S. population (12.5%) and their representation among the nation's public school students (16.4%). African Americans are even more severely under-

---

represented in America's private schools, where they comprise only 3.1% of all private school teachers. The older average age of African American public school teachers suggests that the current underrepresentation of African Americans will not be corrected soon.

The majority of African American public and private school teachers work in schools located in urban areas. While African American public school teachers are concentrated in the south (63.7%), African American private school teachers are more evenly distributed by geographic region. African American teachers are also most heavily concentrated in schools where African American students comprise at least 60% of the student body in both the public and private sectors. African Americans tend to teach in public and private schools with higher percentages of minority students and teachers than their White counterparts.

Overall, the salaries of African American public and private school teachers appear to be comparable to those of their White counterparts. Some differences are observed for public school teachers age 40 and older, with African Americans receiving lower salaries than Whites. School location also played a role in salaries since African Americans earned lower salaries than Whites at urban, suburban, and rural public schools.

Other important differences appear in the distribution of African Americans by subject area. For example, African American women teachers are concentrated in general elementary and secondary special education, while African American men tend to teach social studies. Moreover, African Americans are more likely than their White counterparts to be Chapter One teachers. Interestingly, African American public school teachers generally participate in several curriculum-related activities, such as committees to integrate academic skills into vocational curriculum, education technology programs, student assessment programs, and in-depth study in their subject areas, at a higher rate than do Whites.

Educational attainment levels are generally similar for African American and White public school teachers. But, among African American elementary

school teachers, only 37.3% of men have earned at least a master's degree, compared with 52.2% of women. A higher share of African American women than of other public school teachers have earned advanced professional certificates.

At private schools, African Americans appear to be handicapped by a lack of teaching certificates. Only 43.3% of African American, but 64.9% of White, private school teachers had teaching certificates in their main assignment field. Perhaps compensating for these problems, African American men were taking college courses in their subject areas at a higher rate than were other private school teachers.

Career paths into teaching appear to be different for African Americans and Whites. Only two-thirds of African Americans, but three-fourths of Whites, were college students in the year prior to teaching. About one-fourth of African American male public school teachers and 38.9% of African American male private school teachers worked in occupations outside of the field of education prior to becoming teachers, compared with only 9.3% of all public school teachers and 12.8% of all private school teachers. African American men also had fewer years of teaching experience, on average, in both the public and private sectors.

PART II — DETAILED DESCRIPTIONS AND TABLES

REPRESENTATION OF AFRICAN AMERICANS AMONG PUBLIC AND PRIVATE SCHOOL TEACHERS

Representation of African Americans

In 1993/94, there were 2,561,294 teachers working in America's public schools and 378,365 teachers working in America's private schools.

Public Schools

Relative to their share of the U.S. population (12.5%) and their share of America's public school children (16.4%), African Americans were underrepresented among America's public school teachers (7.4%) in 1993/94.

Women comprised the majority of public school teachers overall (72.9% women versus 27.1% men). This was true to an even greater extent among African Americans (80.2% women versus 19.8% men).

- **Table 1** shows that African American women represented 5.9% and African American men represented 1.5% of public school teachers nationwide.

- The number of African American women working as public school teachers was more than four times as large as the number of African American men (151,138 versus 37,233).

Private Schools

At 3.1%, African Americans were also underrepresented among America's private school teachers relative to their share of private school enrollments (9.3%). Women comprised the majority of private school teachers overall (75.4%).

- **Table 2** shows that African American women represented 2.2% and African American men represented 0.9% of private school teachers.

Representation by School Level

Public Schools

In 1993/94, about one-half (52.0%) of the nation's public school teachers taught at the elementary school level and one-half (48.0%) at the secondary school level. **Table 1** shows that women represented a higher percentage of elementary school teachers (88.4%) than of secondary school teachers (56.2%).

- **Figure 1** shows that 63.1% of African American women and 63.0% of all women taught in elementary schools.

- Only 23.7% of African American men and 22.3% of all men worked at elementary schools.

Table 1. Representation of Public School Teachers by School Level, Race, and Sex: 1993/94
(weighted sample size in parentheses)

School Level	Total	Male	Female	White, Non-Hispanic			African American, Non-Hispanic			Hispanic			Other		
				Total	Male	Female	Total	Male	Female	Total	Male	Female	Total	Male	Female
Total *** +++ ~~~	100.0%	27.1%	72.9%	86.5%	23.9%	62.6%	7.4%	1.5%	5.9%	4.2%	1.2%	3.0%	1.9%	0.5%	1.4%
	100.0%	100.0%	100.0%	100.0%	100.0%	100.0%	100.0%	100.0%	100.0%	100.0%	100.0%	100.0%	100.0%	100.0%	100.0%
	(2,561,294)	(694,098)	(1,867,195)	(2,216,604)	(613,178)	(1,603,426)	(188,371)	(37,233)	(151,138)	(108,744)	(30,696)	(78,048)	(47,574)	(12,991)	(34,583)
Elementary	100.0%	11.6%	88.4%	85.6%	10.0%	75.6%	7.8%	0.7%	7.2%	4.6%	0.7%	3.9%	2.0%	0.2%	1.7%
	52.0%	22.3%	63.0%	51.4%	21.7%	62.7%	55.3%	23.7%	63.1%	56.7%	31.8%	66.5%	54.9%	23.2%	66.8%
	(1,331,281)	(154,788)	(1,176,493)	(1,139,263)	(133,204)	(1,006,059)	(104,246)	(8,821)	(95,425)	(61,648)	(9,752)	(51,896)	(26,124)	(3,011)	(23,113)
Secondary	100.0%	43.8%	56.2%	87.6%	39.0%	48.6%	6.8%	2.3%	4.5%	3.8%	1.7%	2.1%	1.7%	0.8%	0.9%
	48.0%	77.7%	37.0%	48.6%	78.3%	37.3%	44.7%	76.3%	36.9%	43.3%	68.2%	33.5%	45.1%	76.8%	33.2%
	(1,230,013)	(539,310)	(690,702)	(1,077,342)	(479,974)	(597,368)	(84,125)	(28,412)	(55,713)	(47,095)	(20,944)	(26,151)	(21,450)	(9,980)	(11,470)

Notes:

*** Test of statistical significance compares African Americans with Whites. *** p. < .001, ** p < .01, * p < .05.

+++ Test of statistical significance compares White men with White women. +++ p < .001, ++ p < .01, + p < .05.

~~~Test of statistical significance compares African American men with African American women. ~~~ p < .001, ~~ p < .01, ~ p < .05.

Tests of statistical significance calculated using adjusted sample weight to control for influence of large sample sizes.

Source: Schools and Staffing Survey, 1993-94.

Table 2. Representation of Private School Teachers by School Level, Race, and Sex: 1993/94
(weighted sample size in parentheses)

School Level	Total	Male	Female	White, Non-Hispanic Total	Male	Female	African American, Non-Hispanic Total	Male	Female	Hispanic Total	Male	Female	Other Total	Male	Female
Total *** +++ ~~~	100.0%	24.6%	75.4%	91.9%	22.4%	69.5%	3.1%	0.9%	2.2%	3.2%	0.8%	2.4%	1.8%	0.5%	1.3%
	100.0%	100.0%	100.0%	100.0%	100.0%	100.0%	100.0%	100.0%	100.0%	100.0%	100.0%	100.0%	100.0%	100.0%	100.0%
	(378,365)	(93,130)	(285,235)	(347,812)	(84,873)	(262,939)	(11,664)	(3,413)	(8,251)	(12,221)	(3,088)	(9,133)	(6,670)	(1,757)	(4,913)
Elementary	100.0%	11.1%	88.9%	91.9%	10.1%	81.9%	3.7%	0.6%	3.1%	2.8%	0.3%	2.5%	1.6%	0.2%	1.4%
	58.4%	26.4%	68.9%	58.4%	26.3%	68.8%	69.9%	39.8%	82.4%	50.1%	19.0%	60.6%	52.7%	21.1%	64.0%
	(221,036)	(24,602)	(196,434)	(203,242)	(22,286)	(180,956)	(8,158)	(1,360)	(6,798)	(6,124)	(586)	(5,538)	(3,512)	(370)	(3,142)
Secondary	100.0%	43.6%	56.4%	91.9%	39.8%	52.1%	2.2%	1.3%	0.9%	3.9%	1.6%	2.3%	2.0%	0.9%	1.1%
	41.6%	73.6%	31.1%	41.6%	73.7%	31.2%	30.1%	60.2%	17.6%	49.9%	81.0%	39.4%	47.3%	78.9%	36.0%
	(157,329)	(68,528)	(88,802)	(144,570)	(62,587)	(81,983)	(3,506)	(2,053)	(1,453)	(6,096)	(2,501)	(3,595)	(3,158)	(1,387)	(1,771)

Notes:
*** Test of statistical significance compares African Americans with Whites. *** p < .001, ** p < .01, * p < .05.
+++ Test of statistical significance compares White men with White women. +++ p < .001, ++ p < .01, + p < .05.
~~~Test of statistical significance compares African American men with African American women. ~~~ p < .001, ~~ p < .01, ~ p < .05.
Tests of statistical significance calculated using adjusted sample weight to control for influence of large sample sizes.
Source: Schools and Staffing Survey, 1993-94.

Figure 1. Distribution of Public School Teachers by School Level: 1993/94

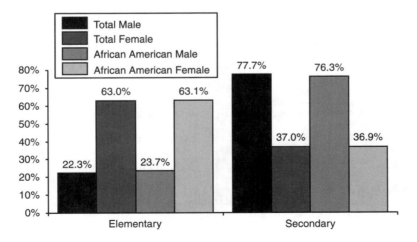

Source: Schools and Staffing Survey, 1993-94.

Private Schools

About 58.4% of all private school teachers taught at the elementary school level and 41.6% at the secondary school level.

- **Table 2** shows that 82.4% of African American women and 68.9% of all women taught in elementary schools.

- Only 39.8% of African American men and 26.4% of all men worked at elementary schools.

Representation by School Affiliation

Private Schools

About 39.6% of all private school teachers worked in Catholic schools, 37.1% in non-Catholic religious schools, and 23.3% in nonsectarian schools. Women represented about three-fourths of teachers at Catholic, non-Catholic religious, and nonsectarian schools (78.8%, 72.5%, and 74.3%, respectively).

- **Table 3** shows that African Americans represented 2.8% of Catholic school teachers, 3.5% of non-Catholic religious school teachers, and 2.9% of nonsectarian school teachers.

Representation by Urbanicity

Public Schools

Figure 2 shows that, in 1993/94, 28.0% of the nation's public school teachers taught in urban schools, 31.1% in suburban schools, and 40.9% in rural schools. By comparison, African Americans tended to work in urban schools rather than in suburban and rural schools.

- **Table 4** shows that about 55.6% of African American public school teachers taught in ur-

---

Table 3. Representation of Private School Teachers by School Affliation, Race, and Sex: 1993/94
(weighted sample size in parentheses)

School Affliation	Total	Male	Female	White, Non-Hispanic Total	Male	Female	African American, Non-Hispanic Total	Male	Female	Hispanic Total	Male	Female	Other Total	Male	Female
Total															
Total +++	100.0%	24.6%	75.4%	91.9%	22.4%	69.5%	3.1%	0.9%	2.2%	3.2%	0.8%	2.4%	1.8%	0.5%	1.3%
	100.0%	100.0%	100.0%	100.0%	100.0%	100.0%	100.0%	100.0%	100.0%	100.0%	100.0%	100.0%	100.0%	100.0%	100.0%
	(378,365)	(93,128)	(285,234)	(347,812)	(84,873)	(262,939)	(11,664)	(3,413)	(8,251)	(12,221)	(3,088)	(9,133)	(6,670)	(1,757)	(4,913)
Catholic	100.0%	21.2%	78.8%	92.2%	18.8%	73.4%	2.8%	1.0%	1.8%	3.6%	1.1%	2.5%	1.4%	0.3%	1.1%
	39.6%	34.2%	41.4%	39.7%	33.2%	41.8%	36.0%	44.6%	32.4%	43.9%	52.9%	40.9%	31.7%	29.4%	32.5%
	(149,840)	(31,833)	(118,006)	(138,160)	(28,161)	(109,999)	(4,195)	(1,522)	(2,673)	(5,370)	(1,633)	(3,737)	(2,114)	(517)	(1,597)
Other Religious	100.0%	27.5%	72.5%	92.3%	25.5%	66.7%	3.5%	0.9%	2.6%	2.5%	0.5%	2.0%	1.8%	0.5%	1.3%
	37.1%	41.4%	35.7%	37.2%	42.2%	35.6%	42.2%	38.1%	43.9%	28.2%	22.9%	30.1%	37.5%	42.4%	35.7%
	(140,279)	(38,575)	(101,704)	(129,409)	(35,824)	(93,585)	(4,919)	(1,300)	(3,619)	(3,452)	(706)	(2,746)	(2,499)	(745)	(1,754)
Nonsectarian	100.0%	25.7%	74.3%	90.9%	23.7%	67.3%	2.9%	0.7%	2.2%	3.9%	0.8%	3.0%	2.3%	0.6%	1.8%
	23.3%	24.4%	23.0%	23.1%	24.6%	22.6%	21.8%	17.3%	23.7%	27.8%	24.2%	29.0%	30.8%	28.1%	31.8%
	(88,246)	(22,720)	(65,524)	(80,243)	(20,888)	(59,355)	(2,548)	(590)	(1,958)	(3,398)	(748)	(2,650)	(2,055)	(494)	(1,561)

Notes:
*** Test of statistical significance compares African Americans with Whites. *** p < .001, ** p < .01, * p < .05.
+++ Test of statistical significance compares White men with White women. +++ p < .001, ++ p < .01, + p < .05.
~~~ Test of statistical significance compares African American men with African American women. ~~~ p < .001, ~~ p < .01, ~ p < .05.
Tests of statistical significance calculated using adjusted sample weight to control for influence of large sample sizes.
Source: Schools and Staffing Survey, 1993-94.

Figure 2. Distribution of Public and Private School Teachers by Urbanicity: 1993/94

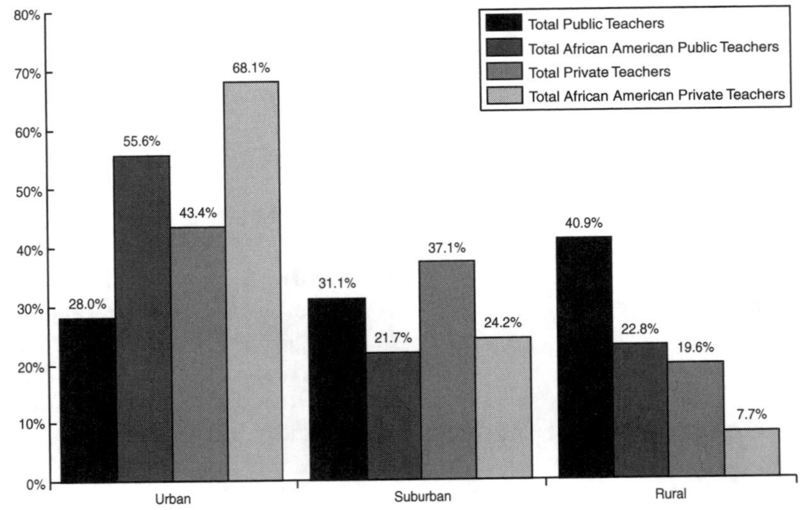

Source: Schools and Staffing Survey, 1993-94.

Table 4. Representation of Public School Teachers by Urbanicity, Race, and Sex: 1993/94
(weighted sample size in parentheses)

Urbanicity	Total	Male	Female	White, Non-Hispanic Total	Male	Female	African American, Non-Hispanic Total	Male	Female	Hispanic Total	Male	Female	Other Total	Male	Female
Total *** + ~	100.0%	27.1%	72.9%	86.5%	23.9%	62.6%	7.4%	1.5%	5.9%	4.2%	1.2%	3.0%	1.9%	0.5%	1.4%
	100.0%	100.0%	100.0%	100.0%	100.0%	100.0%	100.0%	100.0%	100.0%	100.0%	100.0%	100.0%	100.0%	100.0%	100.0%
	(2,561,294)	(694,098)	(1,867,195)	(2,216,605)	(613,178)	(1,603,426)	(188,371)	(37,233)	(151,138)	(108,744)	(30,696)	(78,048)	(47,574)	(12,991)	(34,583)
Urban	100.0%	26.5%	73.5%	74.8%	20.7%	54.1%	14.6%	3.0%	11.7%	8.3%	2.3%	6.1%	2.2%	0.6%	1.6%
	28.0%	27.4%	28.2%	24.2%	24.2%	24.2%	55.6%	56.8%	55.2%	55.0%	53.3%	55.7%	33.3%	31.7%	33.9%
	(716,313)	(189,916)	(526,397)	(536,046)	(148,281)	(387,765)	(104,644)	(21,160)	(83,484)	(59,793)	(16,354)	(43,439)	(15,830)	(4,121)	(11,709)
Suburban	100.0%	26.1%	73.9%	89.2%	23.9%	65.3%	5.1%	0.9%	4.3%	3.5%	0.8%	2.7%	2.2%	0.6%	1.6%
	31.1%	30.0%	31.5%	32.1%	31.1%	32.5%	21.7%	18.3%	22.5%	25.6%	21.5%	27.2%	36.4%	34.4%	37.2%
	(797,217)	(208,332)	(588,885)	(711,220)	(190,432)	(520,788)	(40,810)	(6,828)	(33,982)	(27,858)	(6,609)	(21,248)	(17,329)	(4,463)	(12,866)
Rural	100.0%	28.2%	71.8%	92.5%	26.2%	66.3%	4.1%	0.9%	3.2%	2.0%	0.7%	1.3%	1.4%	0.4%	1.0%
	40.9%	42.6%	40.3%	43.7%	44.8%	43.3%	22.8%	24.8%	22.3%	19.4%	25.2%	17.1%	30.3%	33.9%	28.9%
	(1,047,764)	(295,850)	(751,914)	(969,339)	(274,465)	(694,873)	(42,917)	(9,244)	(33,672)	(21,093)	(7,733)	(13,360)	(14,415)	(4,407)	(10,007)

Notes:
*** Test of statistical significance compares African Americans with Whites. *** p < .001, ** p < .01, * p < .05.
+++ Test of statistical significance compares White men with White women. +++ p < .001, ++ p < .01, + p < .05.
~~~ Test of statistical significance compares African American men with African American women. ~~~ p < .001, ~~ p < .01, ~ p < .05.
Tests of statistical significance calculated using adjusted sample weight to control for influence of large sample sizes.
Source: Schools and Staffing Survey, 1993-94.

ban schools in 1993/94, compared with 24.2% of their White counterparts.

- About 21.7% of African American teachers, but 32.1% of White teachers, worked in suburban schools.

- About 22.8% of African American teachers taught in rural public schools, compared with 43.7% of White teachers.

Private Schools

Figure 2 also shows that 43.4% of private school teachers worked in urban schools, 37.1% in suburban schools, and 19.6% in rural schools. As with public school teachers, the percentage of African American private school teachers who taught in urban schools was higher than the percentage of Whites.

- **Table 5** shows that 68.1% of African American private school teachers taught in urban areas, compared with only 41.8% of their White counterparts.

- Only 24.2% of African American private school teachers worked in suburban schools, compared with 37.7% of Whites.

- Just 7.7% of African Americans, but 20.5% of Whites, taught in rural private schools.

Representation by Geographic Region

Public Schools

Overall, more than one-third (36.9%) of all public school teachers taught in schools located in the south. Mirroring their representation in the U.S. population, **Figure 3** shows that African Americans were concentrated in the southern region.

Table 5. Representation of Private School Teachers by Urbanicity, Race, and Sex: 1993/94
(weighted sample size in parentheses)

Urbanicity	Total	Male	Female	White, Non-Hispanic Total	Male	Female	African American, Non-Hispanic Total	Male	Female	Hispanic Total	Male	Female	Other Total	Male	Female
Total *** + ~	100.0%	24.6%	75.4%	91.9%	22.4%	69.5%	3.1%	0.9%	2.2%	3.2%	0.8%	2.4%	1.8%	0.5%	1.3%
	100.0%	100.0%	100.0%	100.0%	100.0%	100.0%	100.0%	100.0%	100.0%	100.0%	100.0%	100.0%	100.0%	100.0%	100.0%
	(378,365)	(93,130)	(285,235)	(347,811)	(84,873)	(262,939)	(11,664)	(3,413)	(8,251)	(12,221)	(3,088)	(9,133)	(6,670)	(1,757)	(4,913)
Urban	100.0%	25.4%	74.6%	88.6%	22.6%	66.0%	4.8%	1.2%	3.7%	4.2%	1.1%	3.1%	2.4%	0.5%	1.9%
	43.4%	44.8%	42.9%	41.8%	43.7%	41.2%	68.1%	55.4%	73.3%	56.5%	59.7%	55.4%	58.8%	50.3%	61.8%
	(164,024)	(41,680)	(122,345)	(145,264)	(37,060)	(108,204)	(7,942)	(1,892)	(6,051)	(6,899)	(1,844)	(5,055)	(3,919)	(884)	(3,035)
Suburban	100.0%	23.2%	76.8%	93.5%	21.3%	72.2%	2.0%	0.7%	1.3%	2.9%	0.7%	2.1%	1.6%	0.5%	1.1%
	37.1%	35.0%	37.8%	37.7%	35.2%	38.5%	24.2%	30.8%	21.5%	33.0%	33.2%	33.0%	33.8%	38.9%	32.0%
	(140,276)	(32,591)	(107,685)	(131,166)	(29,834)	(101,332)	(2,820)	(1,050)	(1,770)	(4,034)	(1,025)	(3,009)	(2,256)	(683)	(1,574)
Rural	100.0%	25.5%	74.5%	96.4%	24.3%	72.1%	1.2%	0.6%	0.6%	1.7%	0.3%	1.4%	0.7%	0.3%	0.4%
	19.6%	20.3%	19.4%	20.5%	21.2%	20.3%	7.7%	13.8%	5.2%	10.5%	7.1%	11.7%	7.4%	10.8%	6.2%
	(74,065)	(18,859)	(55,206)	(71,381)	(17,979)	(53,403)	(902)	(472)	(430)	(1,288)	(219)	(1,068)	(494)	(190)	(304)

Notes:
*** Test of statistical significance compares African Americans with Whites. *** p < .001, ** p < .01, * p < .05.
+++ Test of statistical significance compares White men with White women. +++ p < .001, ++ p < .01, + p < .05.
~~~ Test of statistical significance compares African American men with African American women. ~~~ p < .001, ~~ p < .01, ~ p < .05.
Tests of statistical significance calculated using adjusted sample weight to control for influence of large sample sizes.
Source: Schools and Staffing Survey, 1993-94.

Figure 3. Representation of African American Public and Private School Teachers in Each Census Region: 1993/94

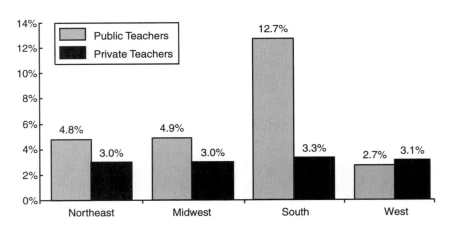

Source: Schools and Staffing Survey, 1993-94.

- African Americans represented 12.7% of public school teachers in the south, but only 4.8% of public school teachers in the northeast, 4.9% in the midwest, and 2.7% in the west.

- **Table 6** shows that nearly two-thirds (63.7%) of African American public school teachers worked in the south.

- African American women represented 5.9% of all public school teachers, but 10.4% of those in the south, 1.9% of those in the west, 3.8% of those in the northeast, and 3.8% of those in the midwest.

- African American men represented 1.5% of all public school teachers, but 2.2% of those in the south, 0.8% of those in the west, 1.0% in the northeast, and 1.1% in the midwest.

Private Schools

Table 7 shows that private school teachers were more evenly distributed by geographic region than public school teachers, with 29.9% of private school teachers in the south, 27.2% in the midwest, 25.4% in the northeast, and 17.5% in the west. African American and White private school teachers were distributed similarly by geographic region.

- **Figure 3** shows that African Americans represented 3.0% of private school teachers in the northeast, 3.0% in the midwest, 3.3% in the south, and 3.1% in the west.

Representation by Racial Composition of the Student Body

Public Schools

More than one-half (55.1%) of public school teachers worked in schools in which African Americans represented 5% or less of the student body, 16.4% in schools in which African Americans represented 6% to 20% of the student body, 11% in schools in which African Americans represented 21% to 40% of the student body, 5.9% in schools in which African Americans represented 41% to 60% of the student body, and 11.6% in schools in which African Americans represented more than 60% of the student body.

In contrast, **Figure 4** shows that African American public school teachers were concentrated in

Table 6. Representation of Public School Teachers by Census Region, School Level, Race, and Sex: 1993/94
(weighted sample size in parentheses)

Region	Total	Male	Female	White, Non-Hispanic Total	Male	Female	African American, Non-Hispanic Total	Male	Female	Hispanic Total	Male	Female	Other Total	Male	Female
Total															
Total *** +++ ~~~	100.0%	27.1%	72.9%	86.5%	23.9%	62.6%	7.4%	1.5%	5.9%	4.2%	1.2%	3.0%	1.9%	0.5%	1.4%
	100.0%	100.0%	100.0%	100.0%	100.0%	100.0%	100.0%	100.0%	100.0%	100.0%	100.0%	100.0%	100.0%	100.0%	100.0%
	(2,561,294)	(694,098)	(1,867,195)	(2,216,604)	(613,178)	(1,603,426)	(188,371)	(37,233)	(151,138)	(108,744)	(30,696)	(78,048)	(47,574)	(12,991)	(34,583)
Northeast	100.0%	30.3%	69.7%	90.1%	28.0%	62.1%	4.8%	1.0%	3.8%	4.0%	0.9%	3.1%	1.1%	0.4%	0.7%
	20.1%	22.5%	19.2%	20.9%	23.5%	20.0%	13.2%	13.9%	13.0%	18.9%	15.4%	20.3%	12.3%	15.2%	11.2%
	(515,589)	(156,280)	(359,309)	(464,324)	(144,377)	(319,947)	(24,869)	(5,190)	(19,679)	(20,562)	(4,739)	(15,823)	(5,834)	(1,974)	(3,860)
Midwest	100.0%	30.9%	69.1%	93.2%	29.1%	64.1%	4.9%	1.1%	3.8%	1.1%	0.4%	0.7%	0.8%	0.2%	0.5%
	25.0%	28.5%	23.7%	26.9%	30.4%	25.6%	16.6%	19.1%	16.0%	6.7%	9.1%	5.7%	10.5%	12.1%	9.9%
	(640,029)	(197,782)	(442,246)	(596,535)	(186,286)	(410,249)	(31,267)	(7,121)	(24,146)	(7,236)	(2,805)	(4,431)	(4,990)	(1,570)	(3,420)
South	100.0%	21.6%	78.4%	81.5%	17.7%	63.7%	12.7%	2.2%	10.4%	4.6%	1.3%	3.3%	1.3%	0.3%	0.9%
	36.9%	29.4%	39.7%	34.7%	27.3%	37.6%	63.7%	56.9%	65.3%	40.0%	40.2%	39.9%	24.9%	23.4%	25.5%
	(945,320)	(204,043)	(741,277)	(770,033)	(167,452)	(602,581)	(119,949)	(21,202)	(98,747)	(43,469)	(12,353)	(31,116)	(11,869)	(3,036)	(8,833)
West	100.0%	29.5%	70.5%	83.8%	25.0%	58.8%	2.7%	0.8%	1.9%	8.1%	2.3%	5.8%	5.4%	1.4%	4.0%
	18.0%	19.6%	17.4%	17.4%	18.8%	16.9%	6.5%	10.0%	5.7%	34.5%	35.2%	34.2%	52.3%	49.3%	53.4%
	(460,356)	(135,991)	(324,365)	(385,713)	(115,063)	(270,650)	(12,286)	(3,719)	(8,567)	(37,477)	(10,799)	(26,678)	(24,880)	(6,410)	(18,470)
Elementary															
Total *** +++ ~~~	100.0%	11.6%	88.4%	85.6%	10.0%	75.6%	7.8%	0.7%	7.2%	4.6%	0.7%	3.9%	2.0%	0.2%	1.7%
	(1,331,281)	(154,788)	(1,176,493)	(1,139,263)	(133,204)	(1,006,059)	(104,246)	(8,821)	(95,425)	(61,648)	(9,752)	(51,896)	(26,124)	(3,011)	(23,113)
Northeast	100.0%	14.7%	85.3%	88.9%	13.7%	75.1%	5.5%	0.2%	5.2%	4.6%	0.5%	4.0%	1.1%	0.2%	0.9%
	(263,727)	(38,772)	(224,955)	(234,367)	(36,183)	(198,184)	(14,422)	(630)	(13,792)	(12,002)	(1,356)	(10,646)	(2,936)	(603)	(2,333)
Midwest	100.0%	13.0%	87.0%	92.2%	11.9%	80.4%	5.9%	0.7%	5.2%	1.1%	0.3%	0.8%	0.8%	0.1%	0.7%
	(321,430)	(41,627)	(279,803)	(296,484)	(38,208)	(258,276)	(18,939)	(2,155)	(16,784)	(3,398)	(935)	(2,463)	(2,609)	(329)	(2,280)
South	100.0%	8.1%	91.9%	80.9%	6.3%	74.6%	13.1%	1.0%	12.1%	4.9%	0.7%	4.1%	1.2%	0.1%	1.1%
	(494,790)	(40,226)	(454,564)	(400,180)	(31,133)	(369,047)	(64,590)	(4,883)	(59,707)	(24,085)	(3,689)	(20,396)	(5,935)	(521)	(5,414)
West	100.0%	13.6%	86.4%	82.9%	11.0%	71.8%	2.5%	0.5%	2.0%	8.8%	1.5%	7.3%	5.8%	0.6%	5.2%
	(251,334)	(34,163)	(217,171)	(208,232)	(27,680)	(180,552)	(6,295)	(1,153)	(5,142)	(22,163)	(3,773)	(18,390)	(14,644)	(1,557)	(13,087)
Secondary															
Total *** +++ ~~~	100.0%	43.8%	56.2%	87.6%	39.0%	48.6%	6.8%	2.3%	4.5%	3.8%	1.7%	2.1%	1.7%	0.8%	0.9%
	(1,230,013)	(539,310)	(690,703)	(1,077,342)	(479,974)	(597,368)	(84,125)	(28,412)	(55,713)	(47,096)	(20,944)	(26,152)	(21,450)	(9,980)	(11,470)
Northeast	100.0%	46.7%	53.3%	91.3%	43.0%	48.3%	4.1%	1.8%	2.3%	3.4%	1.3%	2.1%	1.2%	0.5%	0.6%
	(251,861)	(117,508)	(134,354)	(229,956)	(108,193)	(121,763)	(10,447)	(4,560)	(5,887)	(8,560)	(3,383)	(5,177)	(2,899)	(1,372)	(1,527)
Midwest	100.0%	49.0%	51.0%	94.2%	46.5%	47.7%	3.9%	1.6%	2.3%	1.2%	0.6%	0.6%	0.7%	0.4%	0.4%
	(318,598)	(156,156)	(162,443)	(300,051)	(148,078)	(151,973)	(12,329)	(4,967)	(7,362)	(3,838)	(1,870)	(1,968)	(2,381)	(1,241)	(1,140)
South	100.0%	36.4%	63.6%	82.1%	30.3%	51.8%	12.3%	3.6%	8.7%	4.3%	1.9%	2.4%	1.3%	0.6%	0.8%
	(450,530)	(163,819)	(286,712)	(369,854)	(136,320)	(233,534)	(55,359)	(16,319)	(39,040)	(19,384)	(8,665)	(10,719)	(5,934)	(2,515)	(3,419)
West	100.0%	48.7%	51.3%	84.9%	41.8%	43.1%	2.9%	1.2%	1.6%	7.3%	3.4%	4.0%	4.9%	2.3%	2.6%
	(209,023)	(101,829)	(107,195)	(177,481)	(87,383)	(90,098)	(5,991)	(2,566)	(3,425)	(15,315)	(7,027)	(8,288)	(10,237)	(4,853)	(5,384)

Notes:

*** Test of statistical significance compares African Americans with Whites. *** p < .001, ** p < .01, * p < .05.

+++ Test of statistical significance compares White men with White women. +++ p < .001, ++ p < .01, + p < .05.

~~~ Test of statistical significance compares African American men with African American women. ~~~ p < .001, ~~ p < .01, ~ p < .05.

Tests of statistical significance calculated using adjusted sample weight to control for influence of large sample sizes.

Source: Schools and Staffing Survey, 1993-94.

Table 7. Representation of Private School Teachers by Census Region, Race, and Sex: 1993/94
(weighted sample size in parentheses)

Region	Total	Male	Female	White, Non-Hispanic Total	Male	Female	African American, Non-Hispanic Total	Male	Female	Hispanic Total	Male	Female	Other Total	Male	Female
Total ++	100.0%	24.6%	75.4%	91.9%	22.4%	69.5%	3.1%	0.9%	2.2%	3.2%	0.8%	2.4%	1.8%	0.5%	1.3%
	100.0%	100.0%	100.0%	100.0%	100.0%	100.0%	100.0%	100.0%	100.0%	100.0%	100.0%	100.0%	100.0%	100.0%	100.0%
	(378,365)	(93,130)	(285,235)	(347,812)	(84,873)	(262,939)	(11,664)	(3,413)	(8,251)	(12,221)	(3,088)	(9,133)	(6,670)	(1,757)	(4,913)
Northeast	100.0%	27.3%	72.7%	93.3%	25.6%	67.7%	3.0%	0.7%	2.3%	2.4%	0.7%	1.7%	1.3%	0.3%	1.0%
	25.4%	28.2%	24.5%	25.8%	29.0%	24.7%	24.5%	18.9%	26.8%	18.7%	21.2%	17.8%	19.3%	18.2%	19.6%
	(96,103)	(26,251)	(69,852)	(89,677)	(24,631)	(65,046)	(2,857)	(644)	(2,213)	(2,284)	(656)	(1,628)	(1,285)	(320)	(965)
Midwest	100.0%	23.1%	76.9%	95.3%	21.7%	73.6%	3.0%	1.0%	2.0%	1.1%	0.2%	1.0%	0.6%	0.2%	0.4%
	27.2%	25.5%	27.8%	28.2%	26.3%	28.8%	26.4%	30.5%	24.7%	9.7%	6.5%	10.8%	9.1%	10.3%	8.7%
	(103,077)	(23,779)	(79,298)	(98,210)	(22,355)	(75,855)	(3,077)	(1,041)	(2,036)	(1,184)	(202)	(982)	(606)	(181)	(425)
South	100.0%	23.4%	76.6%	90.9%	20.7%	70.2%	3.3%	1.1%	2.2%	4.9%	1.2%	3.8%	0.9%	0.4%	0.5%
	29.9%	28.4%	30.4%	29.6%	27.6%	30.2%	31.8%	37.2%	29.5%	45.7%	43.0%	46.6%	14.9%	26.0%	10.9%
	(113,079)	(26,463)	(86,615)	(102,799)	(23,410)	(79,389)	(3,707)	(1,270)	(2,437)	(5,580)	(1,327)	(4,253)	(992)	(456)	(536)
West	100.0%	25.2%	74.8%	86.4%	21.9%	64.5%	3.1%	0.7%	2.4%	4.8%	1.4%	3.4%	5.7%	1.2%	4.5%
	17.5%	17.9%	17.3%	16.4%	17.1%	16.2%	17.3%	13.4%	19.0%	26.0%	29.3%	24.9%	56.7%	45.5%	60.8%
	(66,106)	(16,638)	(49,468)	(57,125)	(14,477)	(42,648)	(2,022)	(458)	(1,564)	(3,174)	(904)	(2,270)	(3,785)	(799)	(2,986)

Notes:
*** Test of statistical significance compares African Americans with Whites. *** p < .001, ** p < .01, * p < .05.
+++ Test of statistical significance compares White men with White women. +++ p < .001, ++ p < .01, + p < .05.
~~~Test of statistical significance compares African American men with African American women. ~~~ p < .001, ~~ p < .01, ~ p < .05.
Tests of statistical significance calculated using adjusted sample weight to control for influence of large sample sizes.
Source: Schools and Staffing Survey, 1993-94.

Figure 4. Distribution of Public and Private School Teachers by Percentage of African American Students at the School: 1993/94

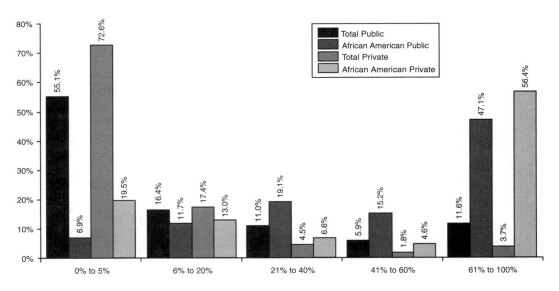

Source: Schools and Staffing Survey, 1993-94.

schools in which African Americans represented the majority of the student body.

- **Table 8** shows that nearly one-half (47.1%) of African American public school teachers taught in schools in which African Americans comprised more than 60% of the student body, compared with only 8.7% of their White counterparts.

- Only 6.9% of African American teachers worked in public schools in which 5% or fewer of the students were African American, compared with 59.2% of White teachers.

Private Schools

Figure 4 shows that nearly three-fourths (72.6%) of private school teachers worked in schools in which African Americans represented 5% or less of all students and only 3.7% worked in schools in which African Americans represented more than 60% of all students. As at public schools, African Americans were concentrated in private schools in which African Americans comprised more than 60% of the student body.

- **Table 9** shows that 56.4% of African Americans taught in private schools in which African Americans comprised more than 60% of all students.

- Among African Americans, a higher share of women than men worked in private schools in which African Americans comprised more than 60% of the student population (65.8% versus 34.4%).

Representation by School Characteristics

Public Schools

In 1993/94, public school teachers worked in schools with an average of 745.8 students, 30.2% of

Table 8. Distribution of Public School Teachers by Percentage of African American Students at School, Race, and Sex: 1993/94
(weighted sample size in parentheses)

% African American Students	Total	Male	Female	White, Non-Hispanic			African American, Non-Hispanic			Hispanic			Other		
				Total	Male	Female	Total	Male	Female	Total	Male	Female	Total	Male	Female
Total *** +++ ~~	100.0%	100.0%	100.0%	100.0%	100.0%	100.0%	100.0%	100.0%	100.0%	100.0%	100.0%	100.0%	100.0%	100.0%	100.0%
	(2,381,689)	(647,031)	(1,734,658)	(2,066,703)	(574,265)	(1,492,438)	(170,823)	(33,697)	(137,125)	(100,098)	(27,632)	(72,466)	(44,065)	(11,437)	(32,628)
0% to 5%	55.1%	59.4%	53.6%	59.2%	62.5%	58.0%	6.9%	10.5%	6.0%	50.9%	51.6%	50.7%	59.5%	62.5%	58.5%
	(1,313,467)	(384,038)	(929,428)	(1,224,486)	(359,096)	(865,390)	(11,781)	(3,545)	(8,236)	(50,966)	(14,246)	(36,720)	(26,233)	(7,151)	(19,082)
6% to 20%	16.4%	15.2%	16.9%	16.6%	15.2%	17.1%	11.7%	10.2%	12.1%	20.6%	20.5%	20.6%	16.7%	15.5%	17.1%
	(390,613)	(98,300)	(292,313)	(342,589)	(87,411)	(255,178)	(20,054)	(3,443)	(16,611)	(20,612)	(5,673)	(14,940)	(7,358)	(1,773)	(5,585)
21% to 40%	11.0%	10.5%	11.1%	10.3%	10.0%	10.4%	19.1%	16.6%	19.7%	10.6%	13.1%	9.6%	10.0%	10.3%	9.9%
	(260,910)	(67,811)	(193,099)	(213,280)	(57,417)	(155,863)	(32,638)	(5,599)	(27,039)	(10,596)	(3,614)	(6,982)	(4,396)	(1,181)	(3,215)
41% to 60%	5.9%	4.7%	6.3%	5.2%	4.1%	5.6%	15.2%	14.2%	15.4%	5.8%	6.0%	5.7%	3.5%	2.7%	3.8%
	(139,810)	(30,212)	(109,598)	(106,543)	(23,449)	(83,095)	(25,885)	(4,787)	(21,098)	(5,819)	(1,668)	(4,151)	(1,563)	(309)	(1,253)
61% to 100%	11.6%	10.3%	12.1%	8.7%	8.2%	8.9%	47.1%	48.4%	46.8%	12.1%	8.8%	13.3%	10.2%	8.9%	10.7%
	(276,889)	(66,670)	(210,219)	(179,805)	(46,892)	(132,912)	(80,465)	(16,323)	(64,141)	(12,106)	(2,432)	(9,673)	(4,514)	(1,022)	(3,492)

Notes:

*** Test of statistical significance compares African Americans with Whites. *** p < .001, ** p < .01, * p < .05.

+++ Test of statistical significance compares White men with White women. +++ p < .001, ++ p < .01, + p < .05.

~~~Test of statistical significance compares African American men with African American women. ~~~ p < .001, ~~ p < .01, ~ p < .05.

Tests of statistical significance calculated using adjusted sample weight to control for influence of large sample sizes.

Source: Schools and Staffing Survey, 1993-94.

Table 9. Distribution of Private School Teachers by Percentage of African American Students at the School, Race, and Sex: 1993/94
(weighted sample size in parentheses)

% African American Students	Total	Male	Female	White, Non-Hispanic			African American, Non-Hispanic			Hispanic			Other		
				Total	Male	Female	Total	Male	Female	Total	Male	Female	Total	Male	Female
Total *** +++ ~~~	100.0% (326,505)	100.0% (78,170)	100.0% (248,335)	100.0% (300,109)	100.0% (71,185)	100.0% (228,923)	100.0% (9,831)	100.0% (2,939)	100.0% (6,892)	100.0% (11,251)	100.0% (2,789)	100.0% (8,462)	100.0% (5,314)	100.0% (1,257)	100.0% (4,057)
0% to 5%	72.6% (237,036)	71.3% (55,718)	73.0% (181,318)	74.6% (223,807)	72.8% (51,834)	75.1% (171,973)	19.5% (1,916)	39.1% (1,149)	11.1% (767)	70.8% (7,964)	75.1% (2,094)	69.4% (5,870)	63.0% (3,349)	51.0% (641)	66.8% (2,708)
6% to 20%	17.4% (56,902)	19.7% (15,434)	16.7% (41,468)	17.4% (52,350)	19.8% (14,088)	16.7% (38,262)	13.0% (1,274)	15.1% (443)	12.1% (831)	16.5% (1,852)	19.9% (555)	15.3% (1,297)	26.8% (1,425)	27.6% (347)	26.6% (1,078)
21% to 40%	4.5% (14,784)	4.5% (3,525)	4.5% (11,259)	4.5% (13,467)	4.7% (3,314)	4.4% (10,153)	6.6% (646)	5.0% (147)	7.2% (499)	4.2% (469)	0.0% –	5.5% (469)	3.8% (203)	5.1% (64)	3.4% (138)
41% to 60%	1.8% (5,780)	2.2% (1,728)	1.6% (4,052)	1.6% (4,919)	1.9% (1,351)	1.6% (3,567)	4.6% (450)	6.4% (188)	3.8% (262)	2.8% (311)	5.0% (140)	2.0% (171)	1.9% (101)	3.9% (49)	1.3% (52)
61% to 100%	3.7% (12,003)	2.3% (1,765)	4.1% (10,238)	1.9% (5,566)	0.8% (598)	2.2% (4,968)	56.4% (5,545)	34.4% (1,011)	65.8% (4,533)	5.8% (655)	0.0% –	7.7% (655)	4.5% (237)	12.4% (156)	2.0% (81)

Notes:
" – " indicates sample size too small to estimate.
*** Test of statistical significance compares African Americans with Whites. *** p < .001, ** p < .01, * p < .05.
+++ Test of statistical significance compares White men with White women. +++ p < .001, ++ p < .01, + p < .05.
~~~Test of statistical significance compares African American men with African American women. ~~~ p < .001, ~~ p < .01, ~ p < .05.
Tests of statistical significance calculated using adjusted sample weight to control for influence of large sample sizes.
Source: Schools and Staffing Survey, 1993-94.

whom were minorities. **Figure 5** shows that African American public school teachers taught at schools with higher proportions of minority students and minority teachers than did public school teachers overall.

- **Table 10** shows that, among elementary school teachers, the average total enrollment of the schools in which they taught varied from 516.4 for Whites to 591.7 for African Americans.

- Among secondary school teachers, the average total enrollment of the schools in which they taught ranged from 954.3 for Whites to 1,049.8 for African Americans.

- Two-thirds (66.8%) of the students at schools in which African Americans taught were minorities, compared with only one-fourth (24.9%) of

the students at the public schools in which Whites taught.

Private Schools

On average, private school teachers worked at schools with 365.8 students, 19.9% of whom were minorities. **Figure 5** shows that, on average, 7.2% of the teachers at private schools were minorities. In contrast to the pattern at public schools, African American private school teachers taught at smaller schools than their White counterparts (273.4 students versus 368.4 students).

At both the elementary and secondary school levels, African American teachers worked at schools with substantially higher shares of minority students and minority teachers than White teachers.

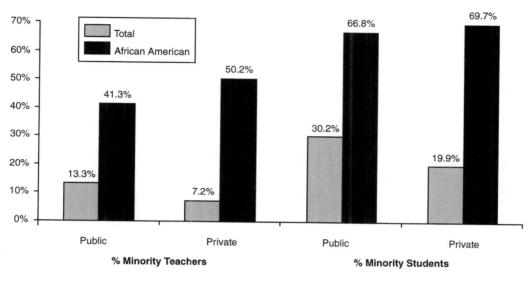

Figure 5. Racial Composition of Schools in Which Public and Private School Teachers Teach: 1993/94

Source: Schools and Staffing Survey, 1993-94.

• **Table 11** shows that, at private elementary schools, 79.3% of the students at the schools at which African American teachers worked were minorities, compared with a 17.0% minority student population at the schools with White teachers.

• At the secondary school level, about 43.8% of the students at schools in which African Americans worked were minorities, and 16.9% of the students at schools in which Whites worked were minorities.

EDUCATION AND EXPERIENCE OF AFRICAN AMERICAN TEACHERS

Highest Level of Education Attained

Public Schools

Figure 6 shows that about one-half (47.3%) of all public school teachers had attained at least a master's degree.

• **Table 12** shows that the percentage of African Americans who had earned at least a master's degree was comparable to the percentage of Whites (50.9% versus 47.6%).

• The percentage of male African American elementary school teachers who had earned at least a master's degree (37.3%) was smaller than the percentage of female African American elementary school teachers (52.3%).

Private Schools

Figure 6 shows that about one-third (34.4%) of all private school teachers had attained a degree beyond the bachelor's degree. A higher proportion of White men than of White women, African American men, or African American women had attained at least a master's degree.

• **Table 13** shows that the master's degree was the highest degree attained for 41.4% of White men, but for only 26.6% of White women, 28.9%

Table 10. Characteristics of the Schools in Which Public School Teachers Teach by School Level, Race, and Sex: 1993/94
(weighted sample size in parentheses)

Characteristic	Total	Male	Female	White, Non-Hispanic Total	White, Non-Hispanic Male	White, Non-Hispanic Female	African American, Non-Hispanic Total	African American, Non-Hispanic Male	African American, Non-Hispanic Female	Hispanic Total	Hispanic Male	Hispanic Female	Other Total	Other Male	Other Female
Total															
Total	100.0%	27.2%	72.8%	86.8%	24.1%	62.7%	7.2%	1.4%	5.8%	4.2%	1.2%	3.0%	1.9%	0.5%	1.4%
	(2,381,689)	(647,031)	(1,734,657)	(2,066,703)	(574,265)	(1,492,438)	(170,822)	(33,697)	(137,125)	(100,098)	(27,632)	(72,466)	(44,065)	(11,437)	(32,628)
Total Enrollment *** +++ ~~~ (K-12 and ungraded)	745.8	881.4	695.2	730.0	864.5	678.3	795.2	948.4	757.5	956.9	1,119.7	894.8	813.7	955.2	764.1
% Minority Teachers *** +++	13.3%	11.8%	13.8%	9.3%	8.7%	9.6%	41.3%	40.7%	41.4%	39.1%	35.0%	40.7%	30.4%	24.4%	32.5%
# Minority Teachers *** +++ ~~~	6.6	7.3	6.3	4.7	5.4	4.4	18.9	21.7	18.2	21.4	24.9	20.0	15.0	14.7	15.1
% Minority Students *** +++	30.2%	28.4%	30.8%	24.9%	24.0%	25.2%	66.8%	67.5%	66.7%	67.9%	63.9%	69.4%	51.3%	46.8%	52.8%
# Minority Students *** +++ ~~	255.8	299.5	239.5	208.8	252.7	191.8	534.3	644.4	507.3	666.4	764.4	629.0	448.3	511.2	426.2
Elementary															
Total	100.0%	11.6%	88.4%	85.7%	10.0%	75.7%	7.7%	0.7%	7.0%	4.6%	0.7%	3.9%	2.0%	0.2%	1.8%
	(1,234,469)	(142,831)	(1,091,639)	(1,058,501)	(123,555)	(934,946)	(94,939)	(8,101)	(86,838)	(56,499)	(8,692)	(47,807)	(24,531)	(2,483)	(22,048)
Total Enrollment *** ~~~ (K-12 and ungraded)	530.4	530.5	530.4	516.4	511.8	517.0	591.7	671.3	584.2	670.5	678.9	668.9	573.6	482.9	583.8
% Minority Teachers ***	14.3%	14.1%	14.3%	9.7%	9.7%	9.6%	42.0%	40.7%	42.1%	45.5%	47.4%	45.1%	34.8%	27.7%	35.6%
# Minority Teachers ***	4.9	5.1	4.9	3.2	3.4	3.2	14.3	14.2	14.3	17.4	20.9	16.7	12.6	8.9	13.0
% Minority Students ***	31.3%	30.7%	31.4%	25.4%	25.2%	25.5%	66.4%	63.2%	66.7%	73.3%	72.7%	73.4%	53.6%	49.4%	54.1%
# Minority Students ***	182.8	182.7	182.8	143.8	141.8	144.1	388.5	411.9	386.3	507.6	528.7	503.8	319.8	255.8	327.0
Secondary															
Total	100.0%	43.9%	56.1%	87.9%	39.3%	48.6%	6.6%	2.2%	4.4%	3.8%	1.7%	2.1%	1.7%	0.8%	0.9%
	(1,147,220)	(504,200)	(643,019)	(1,008,202)	(450,710)	(557,492)	(75,883)	(25,596)	(50,287)	(43,600)	(18,940)	(24,660)	(19,534)	(8,954)	(10,580)
Total Enrollment *** ~~~ (K-12 and ungraded)	977.6	980.8	975.0	954.3	961.3	948.6	1,049.8	1,036.0	1,056.8	1,328.1	1,322.0	1,332.8	1,115.3	1,086.2	1,139.9
% Minority Teachers *** +++	12.2%	11.1%	13.0%	9.0%	8.4%	9.4%	40.4%	40.7%	40.2%	30.8%	29.2%	32.1%	24.7%	23.5%	25.8%
# Minority Teachers ***	8.3	7.9	8.7	6.1	6.0	6.3	24.6	24.0	24.9	26.6	26.7	26.5	18.1	16.3	19.6
% Minority Students *** ++	28.9%	27.7%	29.9%	24.3%	23.7%	24.8%	67.4%	68.8%	66.6%	60.8%	59.8%	61.5%	48.3%	46.1%	50.1%
# Minority Students ***	334.3	332.6	335.6	276.9	283.1	272.0	716.8	718.0	716.2	872.1	872.6	871.8	609.6	582.0	632.9

Notes:
*** Test of statistical significance compares African Americans with Whites. *** p < .001, ** p < .01, * p < .05.
+++ Test of statistical significance compares White men with White women. +++ p < .001, ++ p < .01, + p < .05.
~~~ Test of statistical significance compares African American men with African American women. ~~~ p < .001, ~~ p < .01, ~ p < .05.
Tests of statistical significance calculated using adjusted sample weight to control for influence of large sample sizes.
Source: Schools and Staffing Survey, 1993-94.

Table 11. Characteristics of the Schools in Which Private School Teachers Teach, by School Level, Race, and Sex: 1993/94
(weighted sample size in parentheses)

Characteristic	Total	Male	Female	White, Non-Hispanic Total	Male	Female	African American, Non-Hispanic Total	Male	Female	Hispanic Total	Male	Female	Other Total	Male	Female
Total															
Total	100.0% (378,365)	24.6% (93,130)	75.4% (285,235)	91.9% (347,812)	22.4% (84,873)	69.5% (262,939)	3.1% (11,664)	0.9% (3,413)	2.2% (8,251)	3.2% (12,221)	0.8% (3,088)	2.4% (9,133)	1.8% (6,670)	0.5% (1,757)	1.3% (4,913)
Total Enrollment *** +++ ~~ (K-12 and ungraded)	365.8	41.8	341.5	368.6	442.8	345.1	273.4	374.5	233.4	367.8	450.3	340.5	378.0	518.8	331.8
% Minority Teachers *** + ~~~	7.2%	7.0%	7.2%	4.7%	5.1%	4.6%	50.2%	32.4%	57.2%	28.2%	26.9%	28.7%	22.3%	13.6%	25.2%
# Minority Teachers *** +++	1.9	2.5	1.7	1.5	2.2	1.2	6.5	5.6	6.9	6.6	7.2	6.3	5.6	5.1	5.8
% Minority Students *** ~~~	19.9%	19.5%	20.1%	17.0%	17.1%	16.9%	69.7%	51.7%	76.8%	44.0%	40.2%	45.3%	42.3%	37.1%	44.1%
# Minority Students *** +++	70.9	87.9	65.4	62.3	79.6	56.8	174.6	174.8	174.5	163.7	163.9	163.7	164.7	197.6	153.9
Elementary															
Total	100.0% (221,036)	11.1% (24,602)	88.9% (196,434)	91.9% (203,242)	10.1% (22,286)	81.9% (180,956)	3.7% (8,158)	0.6% (1,360)	3.1% (6,798)	2.8% (6,124)	0.3% (586)	2.5% (5,538)	1.6% (3,512)	0.2% (370)	1.4% (3,142)
Total Enrollment ** (K-12 and ungraded)	288.6	285.1	289.1	291.5	283.4	292.5	239.4	320.8	223.1	272.0	230.5	276.7	270.7	343.0	261.2
% Minority Teachers *** ~	7.8%	8.7%	7.7%	4.7%	5.2%	4.6%	57.6%	45.9%	59.9%	32.5%	45.8%	31.0%	27.9%	16.9%	29.4%
# Minority Teachers *** ++	1.5	2.0	1.5	1.1	1.6	1.0	6.8	6.2	6.9	5.4	5.6	5.3	5.9	3.6	6.2
% Minority Students ***	20.7%	21.1%	20.7%	17.0%	16.1%	17.1%	79.3%	71.4%	80.9%	47.4%	66.5%	45.3%	46.1%	49.3%	45.7%
# Minority Students ***	57.8	63.2	57.1	48.4	50.6	48.1	186.9	204.2	183.4	138.0	148.1	136.9	147.4	142.4	148.0
Secondary															
Total	100.0% (157,359)	43.5% (68,528)	56.4% (88,802)	91.9% (144,570)	39.8% (62,587)	52.1% (81,983)	2.2% (3,506)	1.3% (2,053)	0.9% (1,453)	3.9% (6,096)	1.6% (2,501)	2.3% (3,595)	2.0% (3,158)	0.9% (1,387)	1.1% (1,771)
Total Enrollment * ++ (K-12 and ungraded)	477.0	501.4	458.7	479.3	502.4	462.1	364.5	414.7	290.4	462.7	505.9	434.4	525.3	584.6	481.2
% Minority Teachers *** + ~	6.2%	6.4%	6.1%	4.7%	5.1%	4.5%	30.4%	22.3%	42.3%	24.0%	22.2%	25.2%	14.7%	12.3%	16.4%
# Minority Teachers *** +++	2.4	2.7	2.1	2.0	2.4	1.7	5.8	5.2	6.8	7.8	7.6	7.8	5.3	5.7	5.0
% Minority Students ***	18.8%	18.9%	18.8%	16.9%	17.4%	16.5%	43.8%	37.0%	53.7%	40.6%	33.5%	45.3%	37.2%	32.5%	40.7%
# Minority Students ** ++	89.7	97.3	84.0	82.3	90.4	76.1	141.6	152.7	125.1	189.2	167.9	203.2	188.6	218.3	166.5

Notes:
*** Test of statistical significance compares African Americans with Whites. *** p < .001, ** p < .01, * p < .05.
+++ Test of statistical significance compares White men with White women. +++ p < .001, ++ p < .01, + p < .05.
~~~ Test of statistical significance compares African American men with African American women. ~~~ p < .001, ~~ p < .01, ~ p < .05.
Tests of statistical significance calculated using adjusted sample weight to control for influence of large sample sizes.
Source: Schools and Staffing Survey, 1993-94.

Figure 6. Highest Degree Earned by Public and Private School Teachers: 1993/94

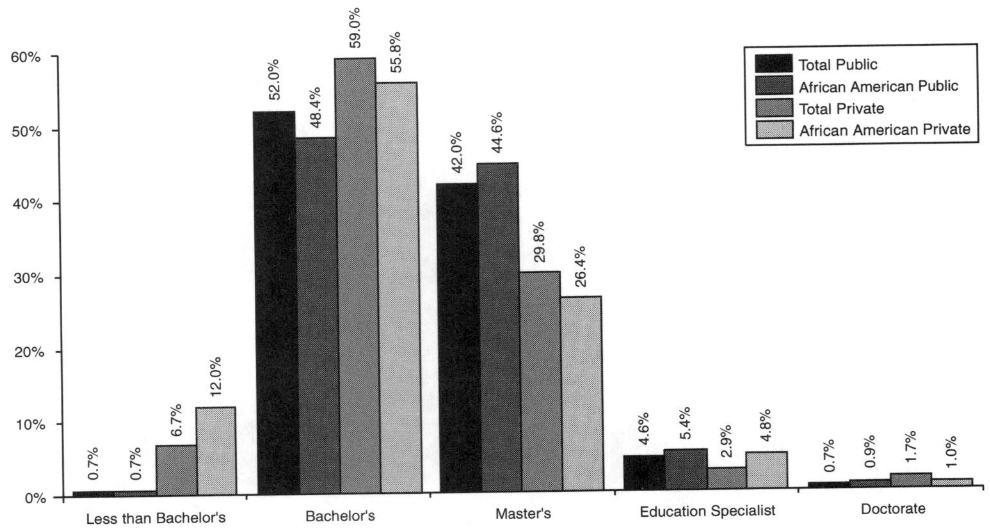

Source: Schools and Staffing Survey, 1993-94.

of African American men, and 25.3% of African American women.

- About 4.2% of White men had earned doctoral degrees, compared with 0.8% of White women, 1.4% of African American men, and 0.9% of African American women.

Teacher Certification

Public Schools

Figure 7 shows that nearly all (96.4%) public school teachers held a teaching certificate in the field of their main assignment. More than three-fourths (78.0%) held a regular or standard state certificate.

The type of certificate received varied by race and sex. **Table 14** shows that a higher percentage of African American women than of other public ele-

mentary and secondary school teachers had received an advanced professional certificate.

- Among elementary school teachers, 20.3% of African American women held advanced professional certificates, compared with 14.3% of African American men, 15.1% of White men, and 14.1% of White women.

- The percentages of secondary school teachers with an advanced professional certificate were 22.2% of African American women, 16.4% of African American men, 16.9% of White men, and 16.1% of White women.

Private Schools

Figure 7 also shows that about two-thirds (63.2%) of private school teachers held teaching certificates in their main assignment field. Overall, a

Table 12. Highest Degree Earned by Public School Teachers by School Level, Race, and Sex: 1993/94
(weighted sample size in parentheses)

Highest Degree	Total	Male	Female	White, Non-Hispanic Total	Male	Female	African American, Non-Hispanic Total	Male	Female	Hispanic Total	Male	Female	Other Total	Male	Female
Total															
Total *** +++ ~~~	100.0%	100.0%	100.0%	100.0%	100.0%	100.0%	100.0%	100.0%	100.0%	100.0%	100.0%	100.0%	100.0%	100.0%	100.0%
	(2,561,294)	(694,098)	(1,867,195)	(2,216,604)	(613,178)	(1,603,426)	(188,371)	(37,233)	(151,138)	(108,744)	(30,696)	(78,048)	(47,574)	(12,991)	(34,583)
Less Than Bachelor's Degree	0.7%	1.7%	0.4%	0.7%	1.5%	0.4%	0.7%	2.9%	0.2%	1.4%	3.0%	0.7%	1.2%	1.6%	1.0%
	(18,405)	(11,581)	(6,823)	(15,035)	(9,372)	(5,663)	(1,298)	(1,063)	(235)	(1,504)	(933)	(571)	(567)	(213)	(354)
Bachelor's Degree	52.0%	46.2%	54.1%	51.8%	44.9%	54.4%	48.4%	54.2%	46.9%	62.8%	61.1%	63.5%	51.7%	49.1%	52.6%
	(1,331,358)	(320,463)	(1,010,896)	(1,147,314)	(275,129)	(872,185)	(91,135)	(20,196)	(70,939)	(68,337)	(18,758)	(49,579)	(24,573)	(6,380)	(18,193)
Master's Degree	42.0%	45.7%	40.6%	42.5%	47.3%	40.6%	44.6%	36.0%	46.7%	29.8%	29.3%	30.0%	36.5%	39.1%	35.6%
	(1,075,074)	(317,417)	(757,657)	(941,242)	(289,930)	(651,312)	(84,045)	(13,400)	(70,645)	(32,410)	(9,009)	(23,401)	(17,377)	(5,078)	(12,299)
Education Specialist	4.6%	5.1%	4.4%	4.4%	5.1%	4.2%	5.4%	4.1%	5.7%	4.6%	5.0%	4.4%	9.4%	8.1%	9.9%
	(117,497)	(35,361)	(82,135)	(97,844)	(31,225)	(66,619)	(10,190)	(1,544)	(8,646)	(5,000)	(1,541)	(3,459)	(4,462)	(1,051)	(3,411)
Doctorate Degree	0.7%	1.3%	0.5%	0.7%	1.2%	0.5%	0.9%	2.8%	0.4%	1.4%	1.5%	1.3%	1.3%	2.1%	0.9%
	(18,960)	(9,277)	(9,682)	(15,171)	(7,523)	(7,648)	(1,702)	(1,030)	(672)	(1,491)	(455)	(1,036)	(595)	(269)	(326)
Elementary															
Total +++ +++ ~~	100.0%	100.0%	100.0%	100.0%	100.0%	100.0%	100.0%	100.0%	100.0%	100.0%	100.0%	100.0%	100.0%	100.0%	100.0%
	(1,331,280)	(154,787)	(1,176,493)	(1,139,261)	(133,203)	(1,006,058)	(104,246)	(8,821)	(95,425)	(61,649)	(9,752)	(51,897)	(26,124)	(3,011)	(23,113)
Less Than Bachelor's Degree	0.3%	0.1%	0.3%	0.3%	0.1%	0.3%	0.1%	0.0%	0.1%	0.8%	0.4%	0.9%	0.8%	0.6%	0.8%
	(3,670)	(180)	(3,490)	(2,895)	(118)	(2,777)	69.00	–	69.00	(494)	(43)	(451)	(212)	(19)	(193)
Bachelor's Degree	55.5%	51.2%	56.0%	55.5%	49.0%	56.4%	48.9%	62.8%	47.6%	65.3%	67.7%	64.9%	54.9%	62.5%	53.9%
	(738,226)	(79,248)	(658,978)	(632,629)	(65,230)	(567,399)	(50,976)	(5,538)	(45,438)	(40,275)	(6,599)	(33,676)	(14,346)	(1,881)	(12,465)
Master's Degree	39.7%	42.5%	39.3%	39.8%	44.5%	39.2%	46.0%	35.6%	46.9%	29.2%	26.4%	29.7%	34.2%	27.3%	35.0%
	(528,729)	(65,787)	(462,942)	(453,892)	(59,252)	(394,640)	(47,938)	(3,137)	(44,801)	(17,977)	(2,576)	(15,401)	(8,922)	(822)	(8,100)
Education Specialist	4.1%	5.1%	4.0%	4.0%	5.3%	3.8%	4.6%	1.7%	4.9%	3.4%	4.9%	3.2%	9.1%	6.2%	9.5%
	(55,060)	(7,917)	(47,143)	(45,752)	(7,109)	(38,643)	(4,809)	(146)	(4,663)	(2,115)	(475)	(1,640)	(2,384)	(187)	(2,197)
Doctorate Degree	4.6%	1.1%	0.3%	0.4%	1.1%	0.3%	0.4%	0.0%	0.5%	1.3%	0.6%	1.4%	1.0%	3.4%	0.7%
	(60,655)	(1,655)	(3,940)	(4,093)	(1,494)	(2,599)	(454)	–	(454)	(788)	(59)	(729)	(260)	(102)	(158)
Secondary															
Total ** +++ ~~~	100.0%	100.0%	100.0%	100.0%	100.0%	100.0%	100.0%	100.0%	100.0%	100.0%	100.0%	100.0%	100.0%	100.0%	100.0%
	(1,230,013)	(539,311)	(690,702)	(1,077,343)	(479,975)	(597,368)	(84,124)	(28,412)	(55,712)	(47,096)	(20,944)	(26,152)	(21,450)	(9,980)	(11,470)
Less Than Bachelor's Degree	1.2%	2.1%	0.5%	1.1%	1.9%	0.5%	1.5%	3.7%	0.3%	2.1%	4.2%	0.5%	1.7%	2.0%	1.4%
	(14,736)	(11,402)	(3,334)	(12,140)	(9,254)	(2,886)	(1,229)	(1,063)	(166)	(1,011)	(890)	(121)	(356)	(195)	(161)
Bachelor's Degree	48.2%	44.7%	51.0%	47.8%	43.7%	51.0%	47.7%	51.6%	45.8%	59.6%	58.1%	60.8%	47.7%	45.1%	49.9%
	(593,131)	(241,213)	(351,917)	(514,684)	(209,898)	(304,786)	(40,158)	(14,657)	(25,501)	(28,062)	(12,159)	(15,903)	(10,226)	(4,499)	(5,727)
Master's Degree	44.4%	46.7%	42.7%	45.2%	48.1%	43.0%	42.9%	36.1%	46.4%	30.7%	30.7%	30.6%	39.4%	42.6%	36.6%
	(546,344)	(251,630)	(294,715)	(487,349)	(230,678)	(256,671)	(36,107)	(10,263)	(25,844)	(14,435)	(6,434)	(8,001)	(8,454)	(4,255)	(4,199)
Education Specialist	5.1%	5.1%	5.1%	4.8%	5.0%	4.7%	6.4%	4.9%	7.1%	6.1%	5.1%	7.0%	9.7%	8.7%	10.6%
	(62,437)	(27,445)	(34,993)	(52,092)	(24,116)	(27,976)	(5,382)	(1,399)	(3,983)	(2,885)	(1,065)	(1,820)	(2,079)	(865)	(1,214)
Doctorate Degree	1.1%	1.4%	0.8%	1.0%	1.3%	0.8%	1.5%	3.6%	0.4%	1.5%	1.9%	1.2%	1.6%	1.7%	1.5%
	(13,365)	(7,622)	(5,743)	(11,078)	(6,029)	(5,049)	(1,248)	(1,030)	(218)	(703)	(396)	(307)	(336)	(167)	(169)

Notes:

" – " indicates sample size too small to estimate.

*** Test of statistical significance compares African Americans with Whites. *** p < .001, ** p < .01, * p < .05.

+++ Test of statistical significance compares White men with White women. +++ p < .001, ++ p < .01, + p < .05.

~~~Test of statistical significance compares African American men with African American women. ~~~ p < .001, ~~ p < .01, ~ p < .05.

Tests of statistical significance calculated using adjusted sample weight to control for influence of large sample sizes.

Source: Schools and Staffing Survey, 1993-94.

Table 13. Highest Degree Earned by Private School Teachers by Race and Sex: 1993/94
(weighted sample size in parentheses)

Highest Degree	Total	Male	Female	White, Non-Hispanic			African American, Non- Hispanic			Hispanic			Other		
				Total	Male	Female	Total	Male	Female	Total	Male	Female	Total	Male	Female
Total * +++	100.0%	100.0%	100.0%	100.0%	100.0%	100.0%	100.0%	100.0%	100.0%	100.0%	100.0%	100.0%	100.0%	100.0%	100.0%
	(378,365)	(93,130)	(285,235)	(347,812)	(84,873)	(262,939)	(11,660)	(3,413)	(8,251)	(12,220)	(3,088)	(9,133)	(6,670)	(1,757)	(4,913)
Less than Bachelor's Degree	6.7%	5.3%	7.1%	6.1%	5.1%	6.5%	12.0%	7.9%	13.7%	16.0%	11.1%	17.7%	8.1%	0.0%	11.0%
	(25,169)	(4,902)	(20,267)	(21,276)	(4,291)	(16,985)	(1,396)	(269)	(1,127)	(1,956)	(342)	(1,614)	(541)	–	(541)
Bachelor's Degree	59.0%	47.3%	62.8%	59.4%	46.8%	63.4%	55.8%	61.7%	53.4%	57.4%	46.7%	61.0%	46.8%	40.7%	49.0%
	(223,086)	(44,015)	(179,071)	(206,436)	(39,751)	(166,685)	(6,512)	(2,106)	(4,406)	(7,014)	(1,443)	(5,571)	(3,124)	(715)	(2,409)
Master's Degree	29.8%	40.6%	26.3%	30.2%	41.4%	26.6%	26.4%	28.9%	25.3%	19.9%	30.4%	16.3%	32.2%	41.3%	28.9%
	(112,819)	(37,829)	(74,990)	(105,167)	(35,177)	(69,990)	(3,076)	(987)	(2,089)	(2,430)	(940)	(1,490)	(2,146)	(725)	(1,421)
Education Specialist	2.9%	2.6%	3.0%	2.6%	2.4%	2.7%	4.8%	0.0%	6.8%	4.4%	5.4%	4.0%	10.1%	9.8%	10.2%
	(10,975)	(2,420)	(8,551)	(9,207)	(2,079)	(7,128)	(558)	–	(558)	(534)	(168)	(366)	(672)	(173)	(499)
Doctorate	1.7%	4.3%	0.8%	1.6%	4.2%	0.8%	1.0%	1.4%	0.9%	2.3%	6.3%	1.0%	2.8%	8.2%	0.9%
	(6,316)	(3,959)	(2,357)	(5,725)	(3,574)	(2,151)	(118)	(47)	(71)	(286)	(194)	(92)	(187)	(144)	(43)

Notes:
" – " indicates sample size too small to estimate.
*** Test of statistical significance compares African Americans with Whites. *** p < .001, ** p < .01, * p < .05.
+++ Test of statistical significance compares White men with White women. +++ p < .001, ++ p < .01, + p < .05.
~~~Test of statistical significance compares African American men with African American women. ~~~ p < .001, ~~ p < .01, ~ p < .05.
Tests of statistical significance calculated using adjusted sample weight to control for influence of large sample sizes.
Source: Schools and Staffing Survey, 1993-94.

Figure 7. Percentage of Public and Private School Teachers With Teaching Certicates: 1993/94

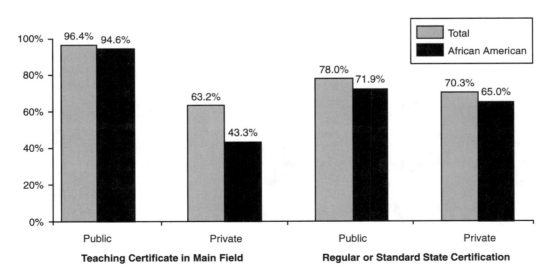

Source: Schools and Staffing Survey, 1993-94.

Table 14. Number and Percentage of Public School Teachers With Teaching Certificates by School Level, Race, and Sex: 1993/94
(weighted sample size in parentheses)

Certification	Total			White, Non-Hispanic			African American, Non-Hispanic			Hispanic			Other		
	Total	Male	Female	Total	Male	Female	Total	Male	Female	Total	Male	Female	Total	Male	Female
Total *** ~~	100.0%	100.0%	100.0%	100.0%	100.0%	100.0%	100.0%	100.0%	100.0%	100.0%	100.0%	100.0%	100.0%	100.0%	100.0%
	(2,561,294)	(694,098)	(1,867,195)	(2,216,604)	(613,178)	(1,603,426)	(188,371)	(37,233)	(151,138)	(108,744)	(30,696)	(78,048)	(47,574)	(12,991)	(34,583)
Have Teaching Certificate in Main Assignment Field	96.4%	96.3%	96.5%	96.9%	96.9%	96.9%	94.6%	92.6%	95.1%	91.1%	89.9%	91.6%	94.6%	93.8%	95.0%
	(2,470,077)	(668,454)	(1,801,623)	(2,147,731)	(594,216)	(1,553,515)	(178,243)	(34,472)	(143,771)	(99,075)	(27,586)	(71,489)	(45,028)	(12,180)	(32,848)
Type of Certificate * +++ ~~~**															
Advanced Professional Certificate	100.0%	100.0%	100.0%	100.0%	100.0%	100.0%	100.0%	100.0%	100.0%	100.0%	100.0%	100.0%	100.0%	100.0%	100.0%
	15.3%	16.2%	15.0%	15.3%	16.5%	14.8%	20.0%	15.9%	21.0%	8.1%	9.5%	7.5%	14.8%	16.1%	14.3%
	(378,915)	(108,248)	(270,668)	(328,634)	(98,207)	(230,427)	(35,644)	(5,467)	(30,177)	(7,979)	(2,612)	(5,367)	(6,659)	(1,962)	(4,697)
Regular/Standard State Certificate	78.0%	77.0%	78.4%	78.6%	77.2%	79.1%	71.9%	73.3%	71.5%	76.9%	77.5%	76.7%	77.5%	76.7%	77.7%
	(1,927,791)	(515,036)	(1,412,753)	(1,688,537)	(459,023)	(1,229,514)	(128,139)	(25,285)	(102,854)	(76,236)	(21,380)	(54,856)	(34,877)	(9,348)	(25,529)
Completed Alternative Program	0.9%	1.0%	0.8%	0.8%	1.0%	0.7%	1.0%	0.6%	1.1%	2.0%	2.1%	1.9%	1.3%	2.0%	1.1%
	(21,755)	(6,841)	(14,915)	(17,378)	(5,808)	(11,570)	(1,816)	(202)	(1,614)	(1,957)	(589)	(1,368)	(605)	(242)	(363)
Provisional/Other—Still Part of Alternative Program	2.3%	2.2%	2.4%	2.1%	2.1%	2.2%	3.7%	2.7%	4.0%	4.4%	4.6%	4.3%	1.5%	0.5%	1.8%
	(57,711)	(14,629)	(43,083)	(46,059)	(12,364)	(33,695)	(6,639)	(944)	(5,695)	(4,359)	(1,259)	(3,100)	(655)	(62)	(593)
Probationary Certificate	1.7%	1.7%	1.6%	1.7%	1.7%	1.7%	0.6%	1.6%	0.4%	2.9%	2.4%	3.1%	2.4%	2.1%	2.5%
	(41,025)	(11,428)	(29,596)	(35,948)	(9,948)	(26,000)	(1,147)	(560)	(587)	(2,846)	(664)	(2,182)	(1,083)	(256)	(827)
Temporary Certificate	1.3%	1.3%	1.2%	1.1%	1.1%	1.1%	1.9%	4.3%	1.3%	3.6%	2.5%	4.0%	1.5%	1.5%	1.6%
	(30,990)	(8,950)	(22,039)	(23,342)	(6,574)	(16,768)	(3,421)	(1,498)	(1,923)	(3,531)	(696)	(2,835)	(695)	(182)	(513)
Emergency Certificate, Waiver	0.5%	0.5%	0.5%	0.4%	0.4%	0.4%	0.8%	1.5%	0.6%	2.2%	1.4%	2.5%	1.0%	1.1%	1.0%
	(11,892)	(3,324)	(8,569)	(7,832)	(2,292)	(5,540)	(1,438)	(515)	(923)	(2,168)	(387)	(1,781)	(455)	(130)	(325)
Elementary															
Total ** +++	100.0%	100.0%	100.0%	100.0%	100.0%	100.0%	100.0%	100.0%	100.0%	100.0%	100.0%	100.0%	100.0%	100.0%	100.0%
	(1,331,281)	(154,788)	(1,176,493)	(1,139,263)	(133,204)	(1,006,059)	(104,246)	(8,821)	(95,425)	(61,648)	(9,752)	(51,896)	(26,124)	(3,011)	(23,113)
Have Teaching Certificate in Main Assignment Field	97.0%	95.7%	97.2%	97.3%	96.2%	97.5%	96.2%	95.8%	96.2%	92.4%	88.2%	93.2%	96.3%	97.2%	96.2%
	(1,291,078)	(148,070)	(1,143,007)	(1,108,694)	(128,096)	(980,598)	(100,249)	(8,450)	(91,799)	(56,971)	(8,597)	(48,374)	(25,163)	(2,927)	(22,236)
Type of Certificate * +++ ~~~**															
Advanced Professional Certificate	100.0%	100.0%	100.0%	100.0%	100.0%	100.0%	100.0%	100.0%	100.0%	100.0%	100.0%	100.0%	100.0%	100.0%	100.0%
	14.4%	15.1%	14.3%	14.2%	15.1%	14.1%	19.8%	14.3%	20.3%	7.4%	14.0%	6.3%	15.9%	20.2%	15.3%
	(185,307)	(22,304)	(163,003)	(157,242)	(19,302)	(137,940)	(19,828)	(1,211)	(18,617)	(4,238)	(1,201)	(3,037)	(3,999)	(590)	(3,409)
Regular/Standard State Certificate	79.5%	78.1%	79.7%	80.3%	78.6%	80.5%	73.4%	78.1%	73.0%	77.3%	72.8%	78.1%	77.0%	70.9%	77.8%
	(1,026,871)	(115,601)	(911,270)	(889,885)	(100,667)	(789,218)	(73,570)	(6,602)	(66,968)	(44,037)	(6,258)	(37,779)	(19,379)	(2,074)	(17,305)
Other	6.1%	6.9%	6.0%	5.6%	6.3%	5.4%	6.8%	7.5%	6.8%	15.3%	13.2%	15.6%	7.1%	9.0%	6.8%
	(78,896)	(10,164)	(68,732)	(61,566)	(8,127)	(53,439)	(6,851)	(637)	(6,214)	(8,695)	(1,138)	(7,557)	(1,784)	(262)	(1,522)
Secondary															
Total *** +++	100.0%	100.0%	100.0%	100.0%	100.0%	100.0%	100.0%	100.0%	100.0%	100.0%	100.0%	100.0%	100.0%	100.0%	100.0%
	(1,230,013)	(539,310)	(690,703)	(1,077,342)	(479,974)	(597,368)	(84,125)	(28,412)	(55,713)	(47,096)	(20,944)	(26,152)	(21,450)	(9,980)	(11,470)
Have Teaching Certificate in Main Assignment Field	95.9%	96.5%	95.4%	96.4%	97.1%	95.9%	92.7%	91.6%	93.3%	89.4%	90.7%	88.4%	92.6%	92.7%	92.5%
	(1,179,000)	(520,385)	(658,615)	(1,039,037)	(466,120)	(572,917)	(77,994)	(26,022)	(51,972)	(42,104)	(18,989)	(23,115)	(19,865)	(9,254)	(10,611)
Type of Certificate * ++ ~~**															
Advanced Professional Certificate	100.0%	100.0%	100.0%	100.0%	100.0%	100.0%	100.0%	100.0%	100.0%	100.0%	100.0%	100.0%	100.0%	100.0%	100.0%
	16.4%	16.5%	16.3%	16.5%	16.9%	16.1%	20.3%	16.4%	22.2%	8.9%	7.4%	10.1%	13.4%	14.8%	12.1%
	(193,608)	(85,944)	(107,664)	(171,392)	(78,905)	(92,487)	(15,816)	(4,256)	(11,560)	(3,740)	(1,411)	(2,329)	(2,660)	(1,372)	(1,288)
Regular/Standard State Certificate	76.4%	76.8%	76.1%	76.9%	76.9%	76.9%	70.0%	71.8%	69.0%	76.5%	79.6%	73.9%	78.0%	78.6%	77.5%
	(900,919)	(399,436)	(501,484)	(798,652)	(358,356)	(440,296)	(54,570)	(18,684)	(35,886)	(32,199)	(15,122)	(17,077)	(15,499)	(7,274)	(8,225)
Other	7.2%	6.7%	7.5%	6.6%	6.2%	7.0%	9.8%	11.8%	8.7%	14.6%	12.9%	16.0%	8.6%	6.6%	10.4%
	(84,472)	(35,005)	(49,467)	(68,992)	(28,858)	(40,134)	(7,608)	(3,082)	(4,526)	(6,165)	(2,457)	(3,708)	(1,707)	(608)	(1,099)

Notes:

*** Test of statistical significance compares African Americans with Whites. *** p < .001, ** p < .01, * p < .05.
+++ Test of statistical significance compares White men with White women. +++ p < .001, ++ p < .01, + p < .05.
~~~Test of statistical significance compares African American men with African American women. ~~~ p < .001, ~~ p < .01, ~ p < .05.
Tests of statistical significance calculated using adjusted sample weight to control for influence of large sample sizes.
Source: Schools and Staffing Survey, 1993-94.

higher share of women than men had teaching certificates in their fields (66.6% versus 52.7%). But, a smaller share of African Americans than of Whites had teaching certificates.

- **Table 15** shows that 43.3% of African American private school teachers had teaching certificates in their main assignment field, compared with 64.9% of their White counterparts.

Among those private school teachers who had teaching certificates, 70.3% had regular or standard state certificates and 7.4% had advanced professional certificates.

- A smaller proportion of African American private school teachers than of White private school teachers had regular or standard state certificates (65.0% versus 71.0%).

Table 15. Number and Percentage of Private School Teachers With Teaching Certificates by Race and Sex: 1993/94

(weighted sample size in parentheses)

Certification	Total	Male	Female	White, Not Hispanic			African American, Not Hispanic			Hispanic			Other		
				Total	Male	Female	Total	Male	Female	Total	Male	Female	Total	Male	Female
Total *** +++	100.0%	100.0%	100.0%	100.0%	100.0%	100.0%	100.0%	100.0%	100.0%	100.0%	100.0%	100.0%	100.0%	100.0%	100.0%
	(378,365)	(93,130)	(285,235)	(347,812)	(84,873)	(262,939)	(11,664)	(3,413)	(8,251)	(12,221)	(3,088)	(9,133)	(6,670)	(1,757)	(4,913)
Have Teaching Certificate in Main Assignment Field	63.2%	52.7%	66.6%	64.9%	54.2%	68.3%	43.3%	39.6%	44.9%	44.1%	28.6%	49.4%	45.3%	47.9%	44.4%
	(239,052)	(49,070)	(189,982)	(225,582)	(45,994)	(179,588)	(5,054)	(1,351)	(3,703)	(5,392)	(884)	(4,508)	(3,024)	(841)	(2,183)
Type of Certificate ***	100.0%	100.0%	100.0%	100.0%	100.0%	100.0%	100.0%	100.0%	100.0%	100.0%	100.0%	100.0%	100.0%	100.0%	100.0%
	(239,052)	(49,070)	(189,982)	(225,582)	(45,994)	(179,588)	(5,054)	(1,351)	(3,703)	(5,392)	(884)	(4,508)	(3,024)	(841)	(2,183)
Advanced Professional Certificate	7.4%	7.7%	7.4%	7.5%	8.0%	7.4%	6.5%	2.6%	7.9%	5.6%	0.0%	6.7%	5.2%	5.5%	5.1%
	(17,734)	(3,754)	(13,981)	(16,945)	(3,673)	(13,272)	(329)	(35)	(294)	(303)	–	(303)	(158)	(46)	(112)
Regular or Standard State Certificate	70.3%	67.1%	71.1%	71.0%	67.9%	71.7%	65.0%	64.0%	65.4%	55.7%	51.2%	56.5%	53.5%	44.7%	56.9%
	(167,979)	(32,932)	(135,047)	(160,075)	(31,239)	(128,836)	(3,284)	(864)	(2,420)	(3,002)	(453)	(2,549)	(1,618)	(376)	(1,242)
Full Certificate, Not From State	12.7%	15.7%	11.9%	12.4%	14.8%	11.7%	18.3%	18.9%	18.0%	13.9%	35.7%	9.6%	28.1%	34.8%	25.5%
	(30,381)	(7,682)	(22,700)	(27,863)	(6,817)	(21,046)	(923)	(256)	(667)	(747)	(316)	(431)	(849)	(293)	(556)
Completed Alternative Program	1.1%	1.3%	1.0%	1.0%	1.3%	0.9%	1.0%	0.0%	1.4%	4.0%	0.0%	4.7%	0.9%	3.3%	0.0%
	(2,561)	(626)	(1,936)	(2,269)	(598)	(1,671)	(51)	–	(51)	(214)	–	(214)	(28)	(28)	–
Provisional/Other—Still Part of Alternative Program	4.3%	3.8%	4.5%	4.4%	3.7%	4.6%	3.9%	3.5%	4.0%	3.7%	8.1%	2.8%	3.3%	7.1%	1.9%
	(10,360)	(1,868)	(8,493)	(9,866)	(1,689)	(8,177)	(195)	(47)	(148)	(199)	(72)	(127)	(101)	(60)	(41)
Probationary Certificate	1.6%	1.4%	1.7%	1.6%	1.4%	1.6%	0.0%	0.0%	0.0%	3.9%	0.0%	4.7%	4.6%	1.5%	5.8%
	(3,937)	(667)	(3,270)	(3,585)	(654)	(2,931)	–	–	–	(212)	–	(212)	(140)	(13)	(127)
Temporary Certificate	2.2%	2.5%	2.1%	2.0%	2.5%	1.8%	3.1%	3.5%	3.0%	8.4%	4.9%	9.1%	3.3%	0.0%	4.6%
	(5,152)	(1,240)	(3,913)	(4,443)	(1,150)	(3,293)	(157)	(47)	(110)	(453)	(43)	(410)	(100)	–	(100)
Emergency Certificate, Waiver	0.4%	0.6%	0.3%	0.2%	0.4%	0.2%	2.3%	7.5%	0.4%	4.9%	0.0%	5.8%	1.0%	3.0%	0.3%
	(947)	(302)	(644)	(537)	(175)	(362)	(115)	(102)	(13)	(263)	–	(263)	(31)	(25)	(6)

Notes:

" – " indicates sample size too small to estimate.

*** Test of statistical significance compares African Americans with whites. *** p < .001, ** p < .01, * p < .05.

+++ Test of statistical significance compares white men with white women. +++ p < .001, ++ p < .01, + p < .05.

~~~Test of statistical significance compares African American men with African American women. ~~~ p < .001, ~~ p < .01, ~ p < .05.

Tests of statistical significance calculated using adjusted sample weight to control for influence of large sample sizes.

Source: Schools and Staffing Survey, 1993-94.

- A higher share of African Americans than of Whites had full certification from a non-state entity (18.3% versus 12.4%).

Previous Experience

Public Schools

Figure 8 shows that the most common activity during the year prior to teaching in an elementary or secondary school was being a college student. About 72.2% of all men teachers and 74.8% of all women teachers were college students in the year prior to becoming public school teachers.

- **Table 16** shows that the percentage of African Americans who were college students in the year prior to teaching in a public school was lower than the percentage of Whites (65.4% versus 75.3%).

- Among African Americans, a smaller share of men than women were college students in the year prior to teaching (56.7% versus 67.6%).

- **Table 16** also shows that 23.9% of African American male public school teachers worked

in occupations outside the field of education in the year prior to teaching, compared with 10.5% of African American women, 14.4% of White men, and 6.5% of White women.

Private Schools

The most common primary activity in the year prior to teaching was being a college student. Similar to the pattern at public schools, a smaller percentage of African Americans than Whites were college students in the year prior to teaching.

- **Table 17** shows that 49.5% of African American private school teachers were college students in the year prior to teaching, compared with 66.6% of Whites.

More than twice the percentage of men as women worked in occupations outside the field of education in the year prior to teaching (22.0% versus 9.8% overall). But, nearly twice the proportion of African Americans as Whites of the same sex worked in other occupations prior to teaching. A higher share of African American women than of other teachers worked as substitute teachers in the year prior to teaching.

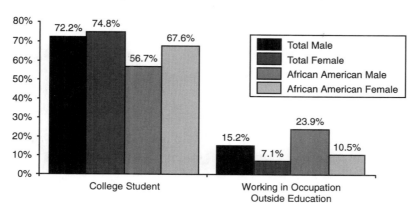

Figure 8. Main Activity in Year Before Teaching Among Public School Teachers: 1993/94

Source: Schools and Staffing Survey, 1993-94.

Table 16. Main Activity in Year Before Teaching Among Public School Teachers by Race and Sex: 1993/94
(weighted sample size in parentheses)

Activity	Total	Male	Female	White, Non-Hispanic Total	Male	Female	African American, Non-Hispanic Total	Male	Female	Hispanic Total	Male	Female	Other Total	Male	Female
Total *** +++ ~~~	100.0%	100.0%	100.0%	100.0%	100.0%	100.0%	100.0%	100.0%	100.0%	100.0%	100.0%	100.0%	100.0%	100.0%	100.0%
	(2,561,294)	(694,098)	(1,867,195)	(2,216,604)	(613,178)	(1,603,426)	(188,369)	(37,233)	(151,138)	(108,744)	(30,696)	(78,048)	(47,573)	(12,991)	(34,583)
College Student	74.1%	72.2%	74.8%	75.3%	73.8%	75.8%	65.4%	56.7%	67.6%	66.2%	59.5%	68.9%	70.8%	71.3%	70.7%
	(1,897,606)	(501,467)	(1,396,139)	(1,668,653)	(452,820)	(1,215,833)	(123,247)	(21,128)	(102,119)	(72,012)	(18,259)	(53,753)	(33,694)	(9,260)	(24,434)
Caring for Family Members	3.2%	0.2%	4.4%	3.3%	0.2%	4.5%	2.5%	0.0%	3.1%	3.1%	0.2%	4.2%	3.1%	0.0%	4.3%
	(83,176)	(1,044)	(82,132)	(73,737)	(970)	(72,767)	(4,631)	–	(4,631)	(3,318)	(74)	(3,244)	(1,490)	–	(1,490)
Substitute Teacher	7.2%	5.7%	7.7%	7.0%	5.5%	7.6%	9.0%	7.6%	9.4%	6.6%	7.2%	6.4%	6.5%	4.0%	7.5%
	(183,272)	(39,542)	(143,729)	(155,992)	(33,973)	(122,019)	(16,981)	(2,839)	(14,142)	(7,189)	(2,212)	(4,977)	(3,109)	(518)	(2,591)
Preschool Teacher	1.1%	0.1%	1.4%	1.0%	0.1%	1.3%	1.8%	0.0%	2.2%	1.2%	0.6%	1.5%	1.9%	0.3%	2.5%
	(27,298)	(727)	(26,571)	(21,647)	(474)	(21,173)	(3,417)	(17)	(3,400)	(1,331)	(193)	(1,138)	(903)	(43)	(860)
College or University Teacher	0.6%	1.0%	0.5%	0.6%	0.8%	0.5%	1.0%	2.6%	0.5%	0.9%	1.5%	0.7%	1.7%	2.2%	1.5%
	(15,952)	(6,822)	(9,129)	(12,356)	(5,095)	(7,261)	(1,791)	(979)	(812)	(987)	(457)	(530)	(817)	(291)	(526)
Work in Education Field, Not as Teacher	3.3%	2.2%	3.8%	3.0%	1.8%	3.5%	4.8%	3.4%	5.2%	7.3%	8.9%	6.6%	4.8%	3.2%	5.5%
	(85,649)	(15,328)	(70,321)	(66,331)	(10,924)	(55,407)	(9,097)	(1,257)	(7,840)	(7,921)	(2,732)	(5,189)	(2,300)	(415)	(1,885)
Work in Occupation Outside Field of Education	9.3%	15.2%	7.1%	8.7%	14.4%	6.5%	13.1%	23.9%	10.5%	13.8%	20.2%	11.3%	10.0%	16.5%	7.6%
	(237,171)	(105,506)	(131,665)	(192,641)	(88,268)	(104,373)	(24,732)	(8,902)	(15,830)	(15,030)	(6,198)	(8,832)	(4,768)	(2,138)	(2,630)
Military Service	0.9%	2.9%	0.1%	0.8%	2.9%	0.0%	1.5%	5.5%	0.5%	0.3%	0.9%	0.1%	0.5%	1.8%	0.0%
	(21,794)	(20,196)	(1,598)	(18,389)	(17,649)	(740)	(2,807)	(2,037)	(770)	(366)	(278)	(88)	(232)	(232)	–
Unemployed, Seeking Work	0.3%	0.4%	0.3%	0.3%	0.4%	0.2%	0.9%	0.1%	1.1%	0.5%	0.8%	0.3%	0.4%	0.3%	0.5%
	(8,335)	(2,777)	(5,558)	(5,985)	(2,452)	(3,533)	(1,638)	(45)	(1,593)	(510)	(245)	(265)	(202)	(35)	(167)
Retired From Another Job	0.0%	0.1%	0.0%	0.0%	0.1%	0.0%	0.0%	0.1%	0.0%	0.1%	0.2%	0.0%	0.1%	0.4%	0.0%
	(1,038)	(687)	(352)	(873)	(553)	(320)	(28)	(28)	–	(80)	(48)	(32)	(58)	(58)	–

Notes:
" – " indicates sample size too small to estimate.
*** Test of statistical significance compares African Americans with Whites. *** p < .001, ** p < .01, * p < .05.
+++ Test of statistical significance compares White men with White women. +++ p < .001, ++ p < .01, + p < .05.
~~~Test of statistical significance compares African American men with African American women. ~~~ p < .001, ~~ p < .01, ~ p < .05.
Tests of statistical significance calculated using adjusted sample weight to control for influence of large sample sizes.
Source: Schools and Staffing Survey, 1993-94.

- In the year prior to teaching, 38.9% of African American men, 21.1% of White men, 15.7% of African American women, and 9.7% of White women worked in fields other than education.

- About 11.6% of African American women were substitute teachers in the year prior to teaching, compared with 6.2% of White women, 4.1% of African American men, and 3.8% of White men.

Teaching Experience

Public Schools

Figure 9 shows that African American public school teachers had more total teaching experience than public school teachers overall (16.44 years versus 15.18 years).

At both the elementary and secondary school levels, African American women had more total

Table 17. Main Activity in Year Before Teaching Among Private School Teachers by Race and Sex: 1993/94
(weighted sample size in parentheses)

Activity	Total	Male	Female	White, Non-Hispanic			African American, Non-Hispanic			Hispanic			Other		
				Total	Male	Female	Total	Male	Female	Total	Male	Female	Total	Male	Female
Total *** +++ ~~~	100.0%	100.0%	100.0%	100.0%	100.0%	100.0%	100.0%	100.0%	100.0%	100.0%	100.0%	100.0%	100.0%	100.0%	100.0%
	(378,365)	(93,130)	(285,235)	(347,812)	(84,873)	(262,939)	(11,664)	(3,413)	(8,251)	(12,221)	(3,088)	(9,133)	(6,670)	(1,757)	(4,913)
College Student	65.5%	63.8%	66.0%	66.6%	64.7%	67.2%	49.5%	50.1%	49.2%	55.2%	59.5%	53.7%	56.1%	57.9%	55.4%
	(247,788)	(59,450)	(188,337)	(231,531)	(54,883)	(176,648)	(5,774)	(1,711)	(4,063)	(6,743)	(1,838)	(4,905)	(3,739)	(1,018)	(2,721)
Caring for Family Members	7.3%	0.1%	9.7%	7.2%	0.1%	9.5%	6.1%	0.0%	8.7%	8.5%	0.0%	11.4%	10.6%	0.0%	14.4%
	(27,642)	(95)	(27,547)	(25,181)	(95)	(25,086)	(715)	–	(715)	(1,040)	(0)	(1,040)	(706)	–	(706)
Substitute Teacher	5.7%	3.8%	6.3%	5.6%	3.8%	6.2%	9.4%	4.1%	11.6%	6.4%	3.8%	7.2%	3.3%	2.3%	3.7%
	(21,594)	(3,532)	(18,061)	(19,493)	(3,232)	(16,261)	(1,101)	(141)	(960)	(778)	(118)	(660)	(221)	(41)	(180)
Preschool Teacher	2.2%	0.2%	2.9%	2.0%	0.2%	2.5%	4.9%	0.0%	6.9%	4.2%	0.0%	5.7%	5.7%	0.0%	7.8%
	(8,354)	(212)	(8,142)	(6,886)	(212)	(6,674)	(569)	–	(569)	(518)	–	(518)	(381)	–	(381)
College or University Teacher	1.3%	2.5%	0.9%	1.2%	2.5%	0.8%	0.8%	1.3%	0.5%	2.1%	1.1%	2.5%	6.5%	9.6%	5.4%
	(5,042)	(2,362)	(2,680)	(4,265)	(2,115)	(2,150)	(88)	(46)	(42)	(257)	(33)	(224)	(432)	(168)	(264)
Work in Education Field, Not as Teacher	3.6%	4.1%	3.4%	3.4%	4.1%	3.2%	4.7%	2.7%	5.5%	7.1%	3.6%	8.2%	5.0%	7.0%	4.3%
	(13,549)	(3,819)	(9,731)	(11,811)	(3,495)	(8,316)	(544)	(91)	(453)	(863)	(110)	(753)	(332)	(123)	(209)
Work in Occupation Outside Field of Education	12.8%	22.0%	9.8%	12.4%	21.1%	9.7%	22.5%	38.9%	15.7%	14.8%	28.5%	10.2%	11.8%	22.2%	8.1%
	(48,497)	(20,480)	(28,017)	(43,282)	(17,883)	(25,399)	(2,621)	(1,328)	(1,293)	(1,806)	(879)	(927)	(788)	(390)	(398)
Military Service	0.7%	2.5%	0.1%	0.7%	2.5%	0.1%	0.8%	2.6%	0.0%	0.8%	3.2%	0.0%	0.7%	1.0%	0.6%
	(2,560)	(2,360)	(200)	(2,324)	(2,155)	(169)	(89)	(89)	(0)	(99)	(99)	–	(48)	(17)	(31)
Unemployed, Seeking Work	0.8%	0.7%	0.9%	0.8%	0.8%	0.8%	1.2%	0.0%	1.7%	0.9%	0.0%	1.2%	0.3%	0.0%	0.5%
	(3,094)	(649)	(2,445)	(2,821)	(649)	(2,172)	(144)	–	(144)	(106)	–	(106)	(23)	–	(23)
Retired from Another Job	0.1%	0.2%	0.0%	0.1%	0.2%	0.0%	0.1%	0.0%	0.1%	0.1%	0.3%	0.0%	0.0%	0.0%	0.0%
	(238)	(164)	(73)	(216)	(154)	(62)	(11)	(0)	(11)	(10)	(10)	–	–	–	–

Notes:

" – " indicates sample size too small to estimate.

*** Test of statistical significance compares African Americans with Whites. *** p < .001, ** p < .01, * p < .05.

+++ Test of statistical significance compares White men with White women. +++ p < .001, ++ p < .01, + p < .05.

~~~Test of statistical significance compares African American men with African American women. ~~~ p < .001, ~~ p < .01, ~ p < .05.

Tests of statistical significance calculated using adjusted sample weight to control for influence of large sample sizes.

Source: Schools and Staffing Survey, 1993-94.

teaching experience and had worked a greater number of years as full-time teachers in public elementary and secondary schools than African American men.

- **Table 18** shows that, on average, female African American public elementary school teachers had 17.24 years of total teaching experience, compared with 13.37 years for African American men, 14.63 for White women, and 16.40 for White men.

- Among secondary school teachers, African American women had 16.74 years of total teaching experience, compared with 14.13 years for African American men, 14.35 years for White women, and 17.40 years for White men.

Figure 9. Teaching Experience of Public School Teachers: 1993/94

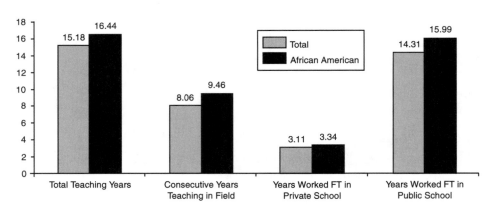

Source: Schools and Staffing Survey, 1993-94.

Private Schools

Figure 10 shows that, on average, private school teachers had 12.17 years of total teaching experience and 6.95 consecutive years of teaching.

- On average, African American teachers had about 2.52 fewer years of total teaching experience than White teachers (9.85 years versus 12.37 years).

Table 19 also shows that White women had an average of 1.35 fewer years of total teaching experience than White men, but African American women had 3.11 more years of total teaching experience than African American men.

- The number of years of total teaching experience ranged from 13.39 for White men and 12.04 for White women to 10.76 years for African American women and 7.65 years for African American men.

Age

Public Schools

In 1993/94, the average age of public school teachers was 43.05 years. **Figure 11** shows that African American public school teachers tended to be older than all public school teachers.

- **Table 20** shows that the average age of African American public school teachers was 44.68 years, compared with 43.03 years for Whites.

- A higher proportion of African American teachers than of White teachers were age 50 or older (30.9% versus 24.6%).

Private Schools

On average, private school teachers in 1993/94 were 41.6 years of age. Although, overall, men and women were comparable in age (41.5 years versus 41.7 years), African American men were about six years younger than African American women.

Table 18. Teaching Experience of Public School Teachers by School Level, Race, and Sex: 1993/94
(weighted sample size in parentheses)

Teaching Experience	Total	Male	Female	White, Non-Hispanic			African American, Non-Hispanic			Hispanic			Other		
				Total	Male	Female	Total	Male	Female	Total	Male	Female	Total	Male	Female
Total															
Total Teaching Experience *** +++ ~~~	15.18	16.74	14.60	15.26	17.18	14.53	16.44	13.95	17.06	11.93	12.61	11.66	13.81	13.82
	(2,561,294)	(694,098)	(1,867,196)	(2,216,605)	(613,178)	(1,603,427)	(188,371)	(37,233)	(151,138)	(108,744)	(30,696)	(78,048)	(47,574)	(12,991)	(34,583)
Distribution of Teaching Experience * +++ ~~~**															
Less than 4 Years Experience	12.2%	12.0%	12.3%	11.8%	10.8%	12.2%	10.9%	19.2%	8.9%	21.3%	24.2%	20.1%	16.0%	16.3%	15.8%
	(312,924)	(82,955)	(229,969)	(261,590)	(66,251)	(195,338)	(20,619)	(7,163)	(13,456)	(23,120)	(7,419)	(15,701)	(7,595)	(2,121)	(5,474)
4 to 10 Years' Experience	24.0%	20.0%	25.4%	23.9%	19.5%	25.5%	20.7%	24.4%	19.8%	29.1%	21.9%	31.9%	28.8%	28.2%	29.0%
	(613,449)	(138,983)	(474,466)	(529,023)	(119,508)	(409,515)	(39,084)	(9,094)	(29,991)	(31,634)	(6,712)	(24,923)	(13,707)	(3,669)	(10,038)
More than 10 Years' Experience	63.8%	68.0%	62.3%	64.3%	69.7%	62.3%	68.3%	56.3%	71.3%	49.6%	54.0%	48.0%	55.2%	55.4%	55.1%
	(1,634,921)	(472,161)	(1,162,760)	(1,425,992)	(427,419)	(998,573)	(128,667)	(20,976)	(107,691)	(53,990)	(16,566)	(37,424)	(26,272)	(7,200)	(19,071)
Number Consecutive Years Teaching in Field *** +++	8.06	9.47	7.64	8.02	9.65	7.53	9.49	8.83	9.60	6.77	7.42	6.55	7.45	7.37	7.48
	(691,945)	(156,880)	(535,065)	(606,293)	(139,762)	(466,531)	(45,337)	(6,559)	(38,778)	(27,482)	(6,863)	(20,619)	(12,833)	(3,696)	(9,137)
Years Worked Full-Time Teacher in Private School ++	3.11	3.43	3.03	3.07	3.38	2.98	3.34	3.39	3.33	3.55	4.24	3.38	3.89	4.27	3.71
	(294,351)	(63,452)	(230,899)	(263,909)	(57,470)	(206,439)	(14,195)	(2,256)	(11,939)	(11,458)	(2,218)	(9,240)	(4,788)	(1,508)	(3,281)
Years Worked Full-Time Teacher in Public School *** +++	14.31	16.18	13.61	14.04	16.61	13.47	15.99	13.49	16.60	11.30	12.17	10.95	12.96	13.12	12.90
	(2,561,294)	(694,098)	(1,867,196)	(2,216,605)	(613,178)	(1,603,427)	(188,371)	(37,233)	(151,138)	(108,744)	(30,696)	(78,048)	(47,574)	(12,991)	(34,583)
Elementary															
Total Teaching Experience *** +++ ~~~	14.83	15.86	14.69	14.84	16.40	14.63	16.91	13.37	17.24	11.60	11.62	11.59	13.76	12.90	13.87
	(1,331,281)	(154,788)	(1,176,493)	(1,139,263)	(133,204)	(1,006,059)	(104,246)	(8,821)	(95,425)	(61,648)	(9,752)	(51,896)	(26,124)	(3,011)	(23,113)
Number Consecutive Years Teaching in Field *** +++	7.55	8.91	7.43	7.41	9.02	7.27	9.94	11.06	9.89	6.38	6.91	6.30	7.54	6.95	7.60
	(353,023)	(28,158)	(324,865)	(307,162)	(24,372)	(282,790)	(24,824)	(1,158)	(23,665)	(14,592)	(2,053)	(12,539)	(6,446)	(575)	(5,871)
Years Worked Full-Time Teacher in Private School	3.02	2.95	3.02	2.98	2.84	2.99	3.48	4.43	3.42	3.13	3.60	3.09	3.52	4.37	3.43
	(164,217)	(14,203)	(150,014)	(146,218)	(13,015)	(133,203)	(9,491)	(542)	(8,948)	(6,526)	(469)	(6,057)	(1,982)	(177)	(1,805)
Years Worked Full-Time Teacher in Public School *** +++	13.86	15.27	13.68	13.81	15.79	13.54	16.40	12.75	16.73	11.02	11.39	10.95	12.95	12.11	13.06
	(1,331,281)	(154,788)	(1,176,492)	(1,139,263)	(133,204)	(1,006,059)	(104,246)	(8,821)	(95,425)	(61,648)	(9,752)	(51,896)	(26,124)	(3,011)	(23,113)
Secondary															
Total Teaching Experience +++ ~~~	15.56	17.00	14.44	15.71	17.40	14.35	15.86	14.13	16.74	12.37	13.07	11.80	13.88	14.09	13.69
	(1,230,013)	(539,310)	(690,703)	(1,077,342)	(479,974)	(597,368)	(84,125)	(28,412)	(55,713)	(47,096)	(20,944)	(26,152)	(21,450)	(9,980)	(11,470)
Number Consecutive Years Teaching in Field +++	8.59	9.59	7.98	8.65	9.79	7.94	8.94	8.35	9.15	7.20	7.64	6.93	7.35	7.45	7.26
	(338,922)	(128,722)	(210,199)	(299,131)	(115,390)	(183,741)	(20,513)	(5,401)	(15,113)	(12,890)	(4,810)	(8,080)	(6,387)	(3,121)	(3,266)
Years Worked Full-Time Teacher in Private School +++	3.24	3.57	3.03	3.19	3.54	2.97	3.05	3.06	3.05	4.11	4.41	3.94	4.15	4.26	4.05
	(130,134)	(49,249)	(80,885)	(117,691)	(44,455)	(73,236)	(4,705)	(1,714)	(2,991)	(4,932)	(1,749)	(3,183)	(2,806)	(1,331)	(1,476)
Years Worked Full-Time Teacher in Public School * +++ ~~~	14.79	16.45	13.50	14.91	16.84	13.36	15.48	13.72	16.37	11.66	12.53	10.96	12.97	13.42	12.58
	(1,230,013)	(539,310)	(690,703)	(1,077,342)	(479,974)	(597,368)	(84,125)	(28,412)	(55,713)	(47,096)	(20,944)	(26,152)	(21,450)	(9,980)	(11,470)

Notes:
*** Test of statistical significance compares African Americans with Whites. *** $p < .001$, ** $p < .01$, * $p < .05$.
+++ Test of statistical significance compares White men with White women. +++ $p < .001$, ++ $p < .01$, + $p < .05$.
~~~ Test of statistical significance compares African American men with African American women. ~~~ $p < .001$, ~~ $p < .01$, ~ $p < .05$.
Tests of statistical significance calculated using adjusted sample weight to control for influence of large sample sizes.
Source: Schools and Staffing Survey, 1993-94.

Figure 10. Teaching Experience of Private School Teachers: 1993/94

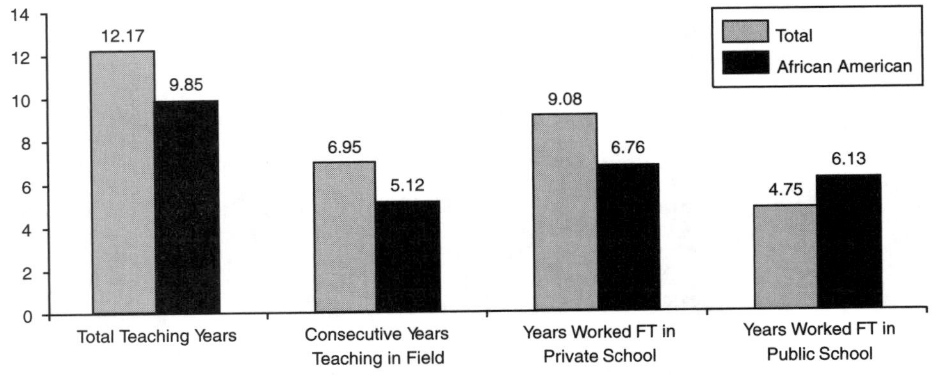

Source: Schools and Staffing Survey, 1993-94.

Table 19. Teaching Experience of Private School Teachers by Race and Sex: 1993/94
(weighted sample size in parentheses)

Teaching Experience	Total	Male	Female	White, Non-Hispanic			African American, Non-Hispanic			Hispanic			Other		
				Total	Male	Female	Total	Male	Female	Total	Male	Female	Total	Male	Female
Total	100.0%	24.6%	75.4%	91.9%	22.4%	69.5%	3.1%	0.9%	2.2%	3.2%	0.8%	2.4%	1.8%	0.5%	1.3%
	(378,365)	(93,130)	(285,235)	(347,812)	(84,873)	(262,939)	(11,664)	(3,413)	(8,251)	(12,221)	(3,088)	(9,133)	(6,670)	(1,757)	(4,913)
Total Teaching	12.17	13.02	11.89	12.37	13.39	12.04	9.85	7.65	10.76	9.61	10.46	9.32	10.13	10.09	10.15
Experience *** +++ ~~	(378,365)	(93,130)	(285,235)	(347,812)	(84,873)	(262,939)	(11,664)	(3,413)	(8,251)	(12,221)	(3,088)	(9,133)	(6,670)	(1,757)	(4,913)
Number Consecutive Years	6.95	8.51	6.56	7.07	8.73	6.66	5.12	6.36	4.80	5.65	7.08	5.23	5.80	4.48	6.35
Teaching in Field * +++	(86,151)	(17,396)	(68,755)	(79,775)	(15,902)	(63,873)	(2,014)	(421)	(1,593)	(3,144)	(718)	(2,426)	(1,218)	(355)	(863)
Years Worked Full-Time Teacher	9.08	10.56	8.60	9.28	10.93	8.74	6.76	6.09	7.04	6.72	7.33	6.52	7.44	7.51	7.42
in Private School *** +++	(378,365)	(93,130)	(285,235)	(347,812)	(84,873)	(262,939)	(11,664)	(3,413)	(8,251)	(12,221)	(3,088)	(9,133)	(6,670)	(1,757)	(4,913)
Years Worked Full-Time Teacher	4.75	5.64	4.55	4.64	5.75	4.55	6.13	4.24	6.96	6.35	11.17	5.08	5.12	3.29	5.66
in Public School ** +++	(131,830)	(23,671)	(108,160)	(121,926)	(21,547)	(100,379)	(4,431)	(947)	(3,484)	(3,614)	(752)	(2,862)	(1,859)	(424)	(1,435)

Notes:
*** Test of statistical significance compares African Americans with Whites. *** p < .001, ** p < .01, * p < .05.
+++ Test of statistical significance compares White men with White women. +++ p < .001, ++ p < .01, + p < .05.
~~~ Test of statistical significance compares African American men with African American women. ~~~ p < .001, ~~ p < .01, ~ p < .05.
Tests of statistical significance calculated using adjusted sample weight to control for influence of large sample sizes.
Source: Schools and Staffing Survey, 1993-94.

Figure 11. Distribution of Public School Teachers by Age: 1993/94

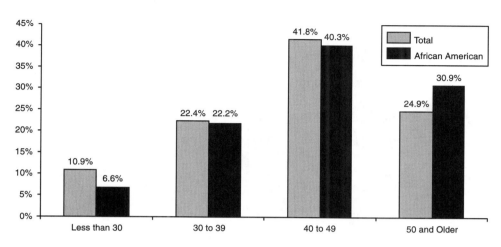

Source: Schools and Staffing Survey, 1993-94.

- **Table 21** shows that 35.0% of African American male private school teachers were under the age of 30, compared with 8.2% of African American women, 14.6% of White men, and 17.8% of White women.

- Only 11.5% of African American men were age 50 and over, compared with 25.4% of African American women, 22.8% of White men, and 23.8% of White women.

DUTIES AND RESPONSIBILITIES OF AFRICAN AMERICAN TEACHERS

Main Assignment

Public Schools

Figure 12 shows that, overall, 92.2% of all male public school teachers and 90.5% of all female public school teachers had regular full-time assignments.

- **Table 22** shows that, at the elementary school level, 96.5% of African American women were regular, full-time teachers, compared with

88.8% of African American men, 88.8% of White women, and 86.2% of White men.

Private Schools

Figure 12 also shows that, in 1993/94, 77.4% of all male private school teachers and 80.7% of all female private school teachers had regular, full-time appointments.

- **Table 23** shows that, at the elementary school level, a smaller share of African American private school teachers than of White private school teachers were regular full-time teachers (77.1% versus 81.8%).

Subject Taught

Public Schools Only

Figure 13 shows that, relative to their representation among all public school teachers (7.4%), African Americans were overrepresented among special education secondary school teachers (9.6%), general elementary teachers (8.3%), and vocational/technical teachers (8.0%). African Americans

Table 20. Age Distribution of Public School Teachers by School Level, Race, and Sex: 1993/94
(weighted sample size in parentheses)

Age	Total	Male	Female	White, Non-Hispanic Total	Male	Female	African American, Non-Hispanic Total	Male	Female	Hispanic Total	Male	Female	Other Total	Male	Female
Total															
Average Age *** +++ ~	43.05	43.86	42.75	43.03	44.02	42.65	44.68	43.98	44.86	40.81	41.29	40.62	42.70	42.24	42.88
	(2,561,294)	(694,098)	(1,867,196)	(2,216,605)	(613,178)	(1,603,427)	(188,371)	(37,232)	(151,139)	(108,743)	(30,696)	(78,047)	(47,575)	(12,992)	(34,583)
Total *** +++															
Under Age 30	10.9%	9.3%	11.6%	11.0%	9.1%	11.7%	6.6%	7.9%	6.3%	16.7%	14.9%	17.5%	12.2%	11.0%	12.7%
	(280,342)	(64,605)	(215,739)	(243,897)	(55,651)	(188,246)	(12,406)	(2,954)	(9,452)	(18,214)	(4,565)	(13,649)	(5,827)	(1,435)	(4,392)
30 to 39 Years Old	22.4%	21.2%	22.8%	22.1%	20.6%	22.7%	22.2%	23.1%	22.0%	27.7%	26.9%	28.0%	23.7%	26.9%	22.5%
	(573,444)	(146,982)	(426,462)	(490,189)	(126,596)	(363,593)	(41,854)	(8,618)	(33,236)	(30,104)	(8,269)	(21,835)	(11,297)	(3,499)	(7,798)
40 to 49 Years Old	41.8%	41.5%	41.9%	42.3%	41.7%	42.5%	40.3%	40.8%	40.1%	35.3%	37.7%	34.3%	38.6%	40.2%	38.1%
	(1,070,459)	(287,711)	(782,748)	(937,823)	(255,700)	(682,123)	(75,872)	(15,209)	(60,663)	(38,377)	(11,582)	(26,795)	(18,387)	(5,220)	(13,167)
Age 50 or Older	24.9%	28.1%	23.7%	24.6%	28.6%	23.0%	30.9%	28.1%	31.6%	20.3%	20.5%	20.2%	25.4%	21.8%	26.7%
	(637,048)	(194,800)	(442,247)	(544,696)	(175,231)	(369,465)	(58,239)	(10,451)	(47,788)	(22,048)	(6,280)	(15,768)	(12,064)	(2,838)	(9,226)
Elementary															
Average Age *** + ~	42.88	42.96	42.87	42.82	43.20	42.77	44.97	43.27	45.13	40.58	40.00	40.69	42.62	40.99	42.83
	(1,331,281)	(154,788)	(1,176,491)	(1,139,263)	(133,204)	(1,006,059)	(104,245)	(8,821)	(95,425)	(61,646)	(9,752)	(51,896)	(26,125)	(3,011)	(23,113)
Total *** + ~~~															
Under Age 30	11.5%	12.4%	11.4%	11.7%	11.6%	11.7%	5.4%	12.8%	4.7%	17.5%	21.0%	16.9%	12.3%	16.9%	11.7%
	(153,087)	(19,189)	(133,898)	(133,478)	(15,503)	(117,975)	(5,600)	(1,132)	(4,468)	(10,794)	(2,046)	(8,748)	(3,215)	(508)	(2,707)
30 to 39 Years Old	22.5%	20.5%	22.8%	22.2%	20.1%	22.5%	22.1%	20.0%	22.3%	28.8%	27.0%	29.1%	22.7%	18.0%	23.3%
	(300,056)	(31,729)	(268,327)	(253,343)	(26,788)	(226,555)	(23,032)	(1,768)	(21,264)	(17,743)	(2,630)	(15,113)	(5,938)	(543)	(5,395)
40 to 49 Years Old	42.1%	43.9%	41.9%	42.7%	44.6%	42.4%	41.3%	42.8%	41.2%	33.3%	32.2%	33.5%	40.1%	54.5%	38.2%
	(560,428)	(67,910)	(492,517)	(486,334)	(59,349)	(426,985)	(43,087)	(3,776)	(39,311)	(20,526)	(3,145)	(17,381)	(10,480)	(1,640)	(8,840)
Age 50 or Older	23.9%	23.2%	23.9%	23.4%	23.7%	23.3%	31.2%	24.3%	31.8%	20.4%	19.8%	20.5%	24.8%	10.7%	26.7%
	(317,710)	(35,960)	(281,749)	(266,108)	(31,565)	(234,543)	(32,526)	(2,144)	(30,382)	(12,583)	(1,930)	(10,653)	(6,492)	(321)	(6,171)
Secondary															
Average Age *** +++ ~	43.24	44.12	42.55	43.26	44.25	42.47	44.33	44.20	44.39	41.10	41.89	40.46	42.81	42.62	42.97
	(1,230,013)	(539,310)	(690,703)	(1,077,341)	(479,974)	(597,368)	(84,125)	(28,412)	(55,713)	(47,097)	(20,944)	(26,152)	(21,450)	(9,980)	(11,470)
Total *** +++															
Under Age 30	10.3%	8.4%	11.8%	10.2%	8.4%	11.8%	8.1%	6.4%	8.9%	15.8%	12.0%	18.7%	12.2%	9.3%	14.7%
	(127,255)	(45,415)	(81,840)	(110,417)	(40,147)	(70,270)	(6,806)	(1,822)	(4,984)	(7,420)	(2,519)	(4,901)	(2,612)	(927)	(1,685)
30 to 39 Years Old	22.2%	21.4%	22.9%	22.0%	20.8%	22.9%	22.4%	24.1%	21.5%	26.2%	26.9%	25.7%	25.0%	29.6%	21.0%
	(273,388)	(115,254)	(158,135)	(236,847)	(99,809)	(137,038)	(18,822)	(6,850)	(11,972)	(12,361)	(5,639)	(6,722)	(5,359)	(2,956)	(2,403)
40 to 49 Years Old	41.5%	40.8%	42.0%	41.9%	40.9%	42.7%	39.0%	40.2%	38.3%	37.9%	40.3%	36.0%	36.9%	35.9%	37.7%
	(510,031)	(219,802)	(290,230)	(451,490)	(196,352)	(255,138)	(32,784)	(11,433)	(21,351)	(17,851)	(8,437)	(9,414)	(7,907)	(3,580)	(4,327)
Age 50 or Older	26.0%	29.5%	23.2%	25.9%	29.9%	22.6%	30.6%	29.2%	31.2%	20.1%	20.8%	19.6%	26.0%	25.2%	26.6%
	(319,338)	(158,840)	(160,497)	(278,587)	(143,666)	(134,921)	(25,713)	(8,307)	(17,406)	(9,465)	(4,350)	(5,115)	(5,572)	(2,517)	(3,055)

Notes:
*** Test of statistical significance compares African Americans with Whites. *** p < .001, ** p < .01, * p < .05.
+++ Test of statistical significance compares White men with White women. +++ p < .001, ++ p < .01, + p < .05.
~~~ Test of statistical significance compares African American men with African American women. ~~~ p < .001, ~~ p < .01, ~ p < .05.
Tests of statistical significance calculated using adjusted sample weight to control for influence of large sample sizes.
Source: Schools and Staffing Survey, 1993-94.

Table 21. Age of Private School Teachers by Race and Sex: 1993/94
(weighted sample size in parentheses)

Age	Total	Male	Female	White, Non-Hispanic			African American, Non-Hispanic			Hispanic			Other		
				Total	Male	Female	Total	Male	Female	Total	Male	Female	Total	Male	Female
Average Age ~~~	41.6 (378,365)	41.5 (93,130)	41.7 (285,235)	41.7 (347,812)	41.8 (84,873)	41.7 (262,939)	41.0 (11,664)	36.7 (3,413)	42.7 (8,251)	39.5 (12,221)	38.9 (3,088)	39.7 (9,133)	40.2 (6,670)	40.7 (1,757)	40.0 (4,913)
Total ** +++ ~~~	100.0% (378,365)	100.0% (93,130)	100.0% (285,235)	100.0% (347,812)	100.0% (84,873)	100.0% (262,939)	100.0% (11,664)	100.0% (3,413)	100.0% (8,251)	100.0% (12,221)	100.0% (3,088)	100.0% (9,133)	100.0% (6,670)	100.0% (1,757)	100.0% (4,913)
Under 30	17.2% (65,168)	15.7% (14,661)	17.7% (50,506)	17.0% (59,230)	14.6% (12,366)	17.8% (46,864)	16.1% (1,876)	35.0% (1,196)	8.2% (680)	21.6% (2,637)	23.7% (733)	20.8% (1,904)	21.3% (1,424)	20.8% (366)	21.5% (1,058)
Aged 30 to 39	24.8% (93,999)	28.8% (26,813)	23.6% (67,187)	24.3% (84,465)	28.7% (24,393)	22.8% (60,072)	35.0% (4,080)	33.7% (1,150)	35.5% (2,930)	31.5% (3,854)	32.9% (1,016)	31.1% (2,838)	24.0% (1,601)	14.5% (254)	27.4% (1,347)
Aged 40 to 49	34.8% (131,492)	33.4% (31,062)	35.2% (100,430)	35.1% (122,118)	33.8% (28,721)	35.5% (93,397)	27.6% (3,223)	19.8% (675)	30.9% (2,548)	30.3% (3,705)	25.2% (778)	32.0% (2,927)	36.7% (2,446)	50.5% (888)	31.7% (1,558)
Aged 50 and over	23.2% (87,706)	22.1% (20,593)	23.5% (67,112)	23.6% (81,998)	22.8% (19,393)	23.8% (62,605)	21.3% (2,484)	11.5% (391)	25.4% (2,093)	16.6% (2,024)	18.1% (560)	16.0% (1,464)	18.0% (1,199)	14.2% (249)	19.3% (950)

Notes:

*** Test of statistical significance compares African Americans with Whites. *** p < .001, ** p < .01, * p < .05.

+++ Test of statistical significance compares White men with White women. +++ p < .001, ++ p < .01, + p < .05.

~~~ Test of statistical significance compares African American men with African American women. ~~~ p < .001, ~~ p < .01, ~ p < .05.

Tests of statistical significance calculated using adjusted sample weight to control for influence of large sample sizes.

Source: Schools and Staffing Survey, 1993-94.

Figure 12. Percentage of Public and Private School Teachers With Regular, Full-Time Assignments: 1993/94

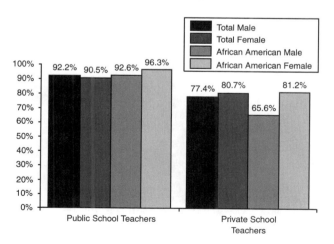

Source: Schools and Staffing Survey, 1993-94.

Table 22. Main Assignment of Public School Teachers by School Level, Race, and Sex: 1993/94
(weighted sample size in parentheses)

Main Assignment	Total	Male	Female	White, Non-Hispanic Total	White, Non-Hispanic Male	White, Non-Hispanic Female	African American, Non-Hispanic Total	African American, Non-Hispanic Male	African American, Non-Hispanic Female	Hispanic Total	Hispanic Male	Hispanic Female	Other Total	Other Male	Other Female
Total															
Total ** +++ ~~~	100.0%	100.0%	100.0%	100.0%	100.0%	100.0%	100.0%	100.0%	100.0%	100.0%	100.0%	100.0%	100.0%	100.0%	100.0%
	(2,561,294)	(694,098)	(1,867,195)	(2,216,604)	(613,178)	(1,603,426)	(188,371)	(37,233)	(151,138)	(108,744)	(30,696)	(78,048)	(47,574)	(12,991)	(34,583)
Regular Full-Time Teacher	91.0%	92.2%	90.5%	90.5%	92.1%	89.9%	95.6%	92.6%	96.3%	92.7%	92.7%	92.7%	90.6%	92.9%	89.7%
	(2,329,730)	(639,910)	(1,689,820)	(2,005,720)	(564,897)	(1,440,823)	(180,084)	(34,476)	(145,608)	(100,829)	(28,469)	(72,360)	(43,097)	(12,068)	(31,029)
Regular Part-Time Teacher	3.2%	2.1%	3.6%	3.5%	2.1%	4.0%	0.6%	1.1%	0.4%	1.7%	1.7%	1.7%	3.8%	2.1%	4.4%
	(81,924)	(14,260)	(67,663)	(77,175)	(13,063)	(64,112)	(1,070)	(397)	(673)	(1,875)	(529)	(1,346)	(1,803)	(271)	(1,532)
Itinerant Teacher	3.8%	3.5%	3.9%	4.0%	3.6%	4.2%	2.0%	2.9%	1.8%	2.2%	3.1%	1.8%	3.5%	3.0%	3.7%
	(96,624)	(24,405)	(72,221)	(88,809)	(22,008)	(66,801)	(3,771)	(1,063)	(2,708)	(2,386)	(944)	(1,442)	(1,660)	(390)	(1,270)
Long-Term Substitute	0.5%	0.5%	0.5%	0.3%	0.3%	0.4%	1.0%	2.8%	0.6%	2.2%	1.1%	2.6%	0.7%	1.0%	0.6%
	(11,970)	(3,154)	(8,815)	(7,381)	(1,648)	(5,733)	(1,893)	(1,036)	(857)	(2,346)	(345)	(2,001)	(349)	(125)	(224)
Administrator e.g., director)	0.4%	1.0%	0.2%	0.4%	1.0%	0.2%	0.2%	0.6%	0.1%	0.1%	0.1%	0.1%	0.3%	0.7%	0.1%
	(10,025)	(6,684)	(3,342)	(9,381)	(6,334)	(3,047)	(452)	(237)	(215)	(66)	(24)	(42)	(127)	(89)	(38)
Library Media Specialist or Librarian	0.3%	0.1%	0.3%	0.3%	0.1%	0.3%	0.1%	0.0%	0.1%	0.3%	0.0%	0.5%	0.2%	0.0%	0.3%
	(6,479)	(418)	(6,061)	(5,899)	(418)	(5,481)	(126)	–	(126)	(360)	–	(360)	(94)	–	(94)
Other Professional Staff (e.g., counselor)	0.9%	0.8%	1.0%	1.0%	0.8%	1.1%	0.5%	0.1%	0.6%	0.7%	1.2%	0.5%	0.9%	0.4%	1.1%
	(23,986)	(5,264)	(18,722)	(21,892)	(4,811)	(17,081)	(856)	(24)	(832)	(800)	(381)	(419)	(438)	(48)	(390)
Support Staff (e.g., secretary)	0.0%	0.0%	0.0%	0.0%	0.0%	0.0%	0.1%	0.0%	0.1%	0.1%	0.0%	0.1%	0.0%	0.0%	0.0%
	(557)	–	(546)	(348)	–	(348)	(121)	–	(121)	(77)	–	(77)	–	–	–
Elementary															
Total *** +++ ~~~	100.0%	100.0%	100.0%	100.0%	100.0%	100.0%	100.0%	100.0%	100.0%	100.0%	100.0%	100.0%	100.0%	100.0%	100.0%
	(1,331,281)	(154,788)	(1,176,493)	(1,139,263)	(133,204)	(1,006,059)	(104,246)	(8,821)	(95,425)	(61,648)	(9,752)	(51,896)	(26,124)	(3,011)	(23,113)
Regular Full-Time Teacher	89.3%	86.4%	89.6%	88.5%	86.2%	88.8%	95.9%	88.8%	96.5%	91.6%	88.5%	92.2%	88.9%	82.8%	89.6%
	(1,188,311)	(133,774)	(1,054,537)	(1,008,692)	(114,814)	(893,878)	(99,934)	(7,833)	(92,101)	(56,472)	(8,634)	(47,838)	(23,213)	(2,493)	(20,720)
Regular Part-Time Teacher	3.4%	2.5%	3.6%	3.8%	2.7%	4.0%	0.2%	0.7%	0.2%	0.9%	1.0%	0.9%	4.4%	5.0%	4.3%
	(45,734)	(3,912)	(41,822)	(43,761)	(3,606)	(40,155)	(243)	(59)	(184)	(578)	(97)	(481)	(1,152)	(150)	(1,002)
Administrator	0.2%	0.5%	0.1%	0.2%	0.6%	0.1%	0.1%	0.0%	0.1%	0.0%	0.0%	0.0%	0.0%	0.0%	0.0%
	(2,295)	(792)	(1,502)	(2,239)	(792)	(1,447)	(55)	–	(55)	–	–	–	–	–	–
Other	7.1%	10.5%	6.7%	7.4%	10.5%	7.0%	3.9%	10.5%	3.2%	7.5%	10.5%	6.9%	6.7%	12.2%	6.0%
	(94,942)	(16,310)	(78,632)	(84,570)	(13,991)	(70,579)	(4,014)	(929)	(3,085)	(4,598)	(1,022)	(3,576)	(1,760)	(368)	(1,392)
Secondary															
Total *** +++ ~	100.0%	100.0%	100.0%	100.0%	100.0%	100.0%	100.0%	100.0%	100.0%	100.0%	100.0%	100.0%	100.0%	100.0%	100.0%
	(1,230,013)	(539,310)	(690,703)	(1,077,342)	(479,974)	(597,368)	(84,125)	(28,412)	(55,713)	(47,096)	(20,944)	(26,152)	(21,450)	(9,980)	(11,470)
Regular Full-Time Teacher	92.8%	93.8%	92.0%	92.5%	93.8%	91.6%	95.3%	93.8%	96.0%	94.2%	94.7%	93.8%	92.7%	95.9%	89.9%
	(1,141,419)	(506,136)	(635,283)	(997,028)	(450,083)	(546,945)	(80,150)	(26,643)	(53,507)	(44,357)	(19,835)	(24,522)	(19,884)	(9,575)	(10,309)
Regular Part-Time Teacher	2.9%	1.9%	3.7%	3.1%	2.0%	4.0%	1.0%	1.2%	0.9%	2.8%	2.1%	3.3%	3.0%	1.2%	4.6%
	(36,190)	(10,348)	(25,842)	(33,415)	(9,457)	(23,958)	(827)	(338)	(489)	(1,296)	(432)	(864)	(652)	(121)	(531)
Administrator	0.6%	1.1%	0.3%	0.7%	1.2%	0.3%	0.5%	0.8%	0.3%	0.1%	0.1%	0.2%	0.6%	0.9%	0.3%
	(7,731)	(5,892)	(1,839)	(7,142)	(5,542)	(1,600)	(396)	(237)	(159)	(66)	(24)	(42)	(127)	(89)	(38)
Other	3.6%	3.1%	4.0%	3.7%	3.1%	4.2%	3.3%	4.2%	2.8%	2.9%	3.1%	2.8%	3.7%	2.0%	5.2%
	(44,674)	(16,935)	(27,739)	(39,759)	(14,893)	(24,866)	(2,752)	(1,194)	(1,558)	(1,375)	(653)	(722)	(788)	(195)	(593)

Notes:

" – " indicates sample size too small to estimate.

*** Test of statistical significance compares African Americans with Whites. *** p < .001, ** p < .01, * p < .05.

+++ Test of statistical significance compares White men with White women. +++ p < .001, ++ p < .01, + p < .05.

~~~ Test of statistical significance compares African American men with African American women. ~~~ p < .001, ~~ p < .01, ~ p < .05.

Tests of statistical significance calculated using adjusted sample weight to control for influence of large sample sizes.

Source: Schools and Staffing Survey, 1993-94.

Table 23. Main Assignment of Private School Teachers by School Level, Race, and Sex: 1993/94
(weighted sample size in parentheses)

Main Assignment	Total	Male	Female	White, Non-Hispanic Total	White, Non-Hispanic Male	White, Non-Hispanic Female	African American, Non-Hispanic Total	African American, Non-Hispanic Male	African American, Non-Hispanic Female	Hispanic Total	Hispanic Male	Hispanic Female	Other Total	Other Male	Other Female
Total															
Total * +++	100.0%	100.0%	100.0%	100.0%	100.0%	100.0%	100.0%	100.0%	100.0%	100.0%	100.0%	100.0%	100.0%	100.0%	100.0%
	(378,365)	(93,130)	(285,235)	(347,812)	(84,873)	(262,939)	(11,664)	(3,413)	(8,251)	(12,221)	(3,088)	(9,133)	(6,670)	(1,757)	(4,913)
Regular Full-Time Teacher	79.9%	77.4%	80.7%	80.1%	77.7%	80.8%	76.6%	65.6%	81.2%	80.7%	86.3%	78.8%	72.8%	70.7%	73.6%
	(302,165)	(72,102)	(230,063)	(278,506)	(65,957)	(212,549)	(8,938)	(2,238)	(6,700)	(9,862)	(2,665)	(7,197)	(4,859)	(1,242)	(3,617)
Regular Part-Time Teacher	14.4%	12.5%	15.0%	14.2%	11.9%	14.9%	13.6%	23.6%	9.4%	16.2%	9.5%	18.4%	25.1%	25.7%	25.0%
	(54,510)	(11,636)	(42,874)	(49,275)	(10,087)	(39,188)	(1,583)	(806)	(777)	(1,975)	(292)	(1,683)	(1,677)	(451)	(1,226)
Itinerant Teacher	0.8%	1.1%	0.7%	0.8%	1.1%	0.7%	1.2%	1.8%	1.0%	1.2%	0.0%	1.7%	1.0%	3.6%	0.0%
	(3,160)	(1,025)	(2,135)	(2,801)	(900)	(1,901)	(143)	(61)	(82)	(152)	–	(152)	(64)	(64)	–
Long-Term Substitute	0.2%	0.3%	0.1%	0.2%	0.4%	0.1%	0.7%	0.2%	0.9%	0.0%	0.0%	0.0%	0.2%	0.0%	0.3%
	(638)	(317)	(320)	(540)	(309)	(231)	(82)	(8)	(74)	–	–	–	(15)	–	(15)
Administrator (e.g., director)	3.2%	6.8%	2.0%	3.2%	7.1%	2.0%	7.0%	7.8%	6.7%	0.6%	1.3%	0.4%	0.0%	0.0%	0.0%
	(12,081)	(6,312)	(5,769)	(11,193)	(6,006)	(5,187)	(815)	(266)	(549)	(73)	(40)	(33)	–	–	–
Library Media Specialist or Librarian	0.2%	0.1%	0.3%	0.2%	0.1%	0.3%	0.0%	0.0%	0.0%	0.3%	0.0%	0.4%	0.0%	0.0%	0.0%
	(822)	(79)	(742)	(784)	(79)	(705)	–	–	–	(37)	–	(37)	–	–	–
Other Professional Staff (e.g., counselor)	1.2%	1.8%	1.1%	1.3%	1.8%	1.1%	0.9%	1.0%	0.8%	0.9%	2.9%	0.2%	0.8%	0.0%	1.1%
	(4,673)	(1,659)	(3,014)	(4,403)	(1,534)	(2,869)	(103)	(34)	(69)	(113)	(91)	(22)	(54)	–	(54)
Support Staff (e.g., secretary)	0.1%	0.0%	0.1%	0.1%	0.0%	0.1%	0.0%	0.0%	0.0%	0.1%	0.0%	0.1%	0.0%	0.0%	0.0%
	(316)	–	(316)	(308)	–	(308)	–	–	–	(8)	–	(8)	–	–	–
Elementary															
Total *** +++	100.0%	100.0%	100.0%	100.0%	100.0%	100.0%	100.0%	100.0%	100.0%	100.0%	100.0%	100.0%	100.0%	100.0%	100.0%
	(221,036)	(24,602)	(196,434)	(203,242)	(22,286)	(180,956)	(8,158)	(1,360)	(6,798)	(6,124)	(586)	(5,538)	(3,512)	(370)	(3,142)
Regular Full-Time Teacher	81.4%	75.4%	82.1%	81.8%	76.7%	82.4%	77.1%	57.9%	80.9%	77.8%	79.9%	77.5%	72.7%	55.4%	74.8%
	(179,882)	(18,562)	(161,320)	(166,278)	(17,102)	(149,176)	(6,288)	(787)	(5,501)	(4,762)	(468)	(4,294)	(2,554)	(205)	(2,349)
Regular Part-Time Teacher	14.5%	15.3%	14.4%	14.3%	14.7%	14.3%	10.7%	20.5%	8.7%	18.8%	18.9%	18.8%	23.9%	27.3%	23.5%
	(32,000)	(3,770)	(28,230)	(29,138)	(3,279)	(25,859)	(870)	(279)	(591)	(1,154)	(111)	(1,043)	(838)	(101)	(737)
Administrator	2.0%	5.5%	1.5%	1.8%	5.0%	1.4%	9.2%	17.1%	7.6%	0.0%	0.0%	0.0%	0.0%	0.0%	0.0%
	(4,371)	(1,342)	(3,022)	(3,612)	(1,109)	(2,503)	(752)	(233)	(519)	–	–	–	–	–	–
Other	2.2%	3.7%	2.0%	2.1%	3.6%	1.9%	3.0%	4.5%	2.8%	3.3%	0.0%	3.6%	3.4%	17.3%	1.8%
	(4,781)	(921)	(3,860)	(4,213)	(796)	(3,417)	(248)	(61)	(187)	(200)	–	(200)	(120)	(64)	(56)
Secondary															
Total +++	100.0%	100.0%	100.0%	100.0%	100.0%	100.0%	100.0%	100.0%	100.0%	100.0%	100.0%	100.0%	100.0%	100.0%	100.0%
	(157,329)	(68,528)	(88,802)	(144,570)	(62,587)	(81,983)	(3,506)	(2,053)	(1,453)	(6,096)	(2,501)	(3,595)	(3,158)	(1,387)	(1,771)
Regular Full-Time Teacher	77.7%	78.1%	77.4%	77.6%	78.1%	77.3%	75.6%	70.7%	82.5%	83.6%	87.8%	80.8%	73.0%	74.8%	71.6%
	(122,283)	(53,539)	(68,743)	(112,228)	(48,855)	(63,373)	(2,650)	(1,451)	(1,199)	(5,099)	(2,196)	(2,903)	(2,305)	(1,037)	(1,268)
Regular Part-Time Teacher	14.3%	11.5%	16.5%	13.9%	10.9%	16.3%	20.3%	25.7%	12.8%	13.5%	7.2%	17.8%	26.6%	25.2%	27.6%
	(22,510)	(7,866)	(14,644)	(20,137)	(6,808)	(13,329)	(713)	(527)	(186)	(821)	(181)	(640)	(839)	(350)	(489)
Administrator	4.9%	7.2%	3.1%	5.2%	7.8%	3.3%	1.8%	1.7%	2.1%	1.1%	1.3%	0.9%	0.0%	0.0%	0.0%
	(7,711)	(4,964)	(2,747)	(7,581)	(4,897)	(2,684)	(64)	(34)	(30)	(66)	(33)	(33)	–	–	–
Other	3.1%	3.2%	3.0%	3.2%	3.2%	3.2%	2.3%	2.0%	2.6%	1.8%	3.6%	0.5%	0.4%	0.0%	0.7%
	(4,825)	(2,159)	(2,666)	(4,622)	(2,026)	(2,596)	(80)	(42)	(38)	(110)	(91)	(19)	(13)	–	(13)

Notes:

" – " indicates sample size too small to estimate.

*** Test of statistical significance compares African Americans with Whites. *** p < .001, ** p < .01, * p < .05.

+++ Test of statistical significance compares White men with White women. +++ p < .001, ++ p < .01, + p < .05.

~~~ Test of statistical significance compares African American men with African American women. ~~~ p < .001, ~~ p < .01, ~ p < .05.

Tests of statistical significance calculated using adjusted sample weight to control for influence of large sample sizes.

Source: Schools and Staffing Survey, 1993-94.

Figure 13. Representation of African Americans Among Public School Teachers of Various Academic Subjects: 1993/94

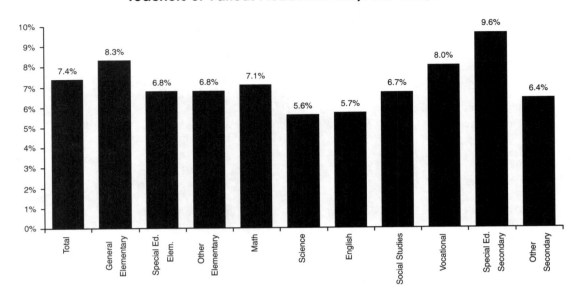

Source: Schools and Staffing Survey, 1993 -94.

were underrepresented among science (5.6%) and English (5.7%) public school teachers.

The subject taught by public school teachers also varied by sex. **Table 24** shows that men represented 27.1% of all public school teachers, but 66.0% of social studies teachers, 56.5% of science teachers, 54.2% of vocational/technical teachers, and 46.8% of mathematics teachers. Women represented 72.9% of public school teachers, but 91.1% of elementary school special education teachers and 89.8% of general elementary teachers.

Although this pattern is consistent across racial groups, African American men represented a relatively smaller share of elementary special education teachers and general elementary teachers and a relatively larger share of social studies teachers. African American women were concentrated among general elementary teachers and secondary special education teachers.

- African American men represented 1.5% of all public school teachers, but 0.4% of elementary special education teachers, 0.6% of general elementary teachers, and 3.0% of social studies teachers.

- African American women represented 5.9% of all public school teachers, but 7.7% of general elementary teachers, 7.4% of secondary special education teachers, and 3.4% of science teachers.

Chapter One Teachers

Public Schools Only

Only 7.4% of all public school teachers were Chapter One teachers in 1993/94.

- **Figure 14** shows that 17.1% of African American men were Chapter One teachers, compared

Table 24. Subject Taught by Public School Teachers by Race and Sex: 1993/94
(weighted sample size in parentheses)

Subject Taught	Total	Male	Female	White, Non-Hispanic			African American, Non-Hispanic			Hispanic			Other		
				Total	Male	Female	Total	Male	Female	Total	Male	Female	Total	Male	Female
Total *** +++ ~~~	100.0%	27.1%	72.9%	86.5%	23.9%	62.6%	7.4%	1.5%	5.9%	4.2%	1.2%	3.0%	1.9%	0.5%	1.4%
	(2,561,294)	(694,098)	(1,867,195)	(2,216,604)	(613,178)	(1,603,426)	(188,371)	(37,233)	(151,138)	(108,744)	(30,696)	(78,048)	(47,574)	(12,991)	(34,583)
General Elementary	100.0%	10.2%	89.8%	84.5%	8.6%	75.9%	8.3%	0.6%	7.7%	5.2%	0.9%	4.4%	2.1%	0.2%	1.9%
	(990,799)	(100,867)	(889,932)	(836,885)	(84,864)	(752,021)	(81,813)	(5,559)	(76,254)	(51,722)	(8,471)	(43,251)	(20,379)	(1,973)	(18,406)
Special Education Elementary	100.0%	8.9%	91.1%	88.7%	8.1%	80.6%	6.8%	0.4%	6.5%	2.5%	0.3%	2.2%	1.9%	0.2%	1.8%
	(130,548)	(11,658)	(118,890)	(115,855)	(10,626)	(105,229)	(8,939)	(476)	(8,463)	(3,222)	(354)	(2,868)	(2,532)	(202)	(2,330)
Other Elementary	100.0%	21.9%	78.1%	88.0%	19.0%	69.0%	6.8%	1.5%	5.3%	3.5%	0.7%	2.8%	1.7%	0.7%	1.0%
	(254,915)	(55,827)	(199,087)	(224,363)	(48,561)	(175,802)	(17,267)	(3,759)	(13,508)	(8,957)	(1,832)	(7,125)	(4,327)	(1,675)	(2,652)
Math	100.0%	46.8%	53.2%	88.9%	42.2%	46.7%	7.1%	2.5%	4.6%	2.3%	1.4%	0.9%	1.8%	0.7%	1.0%
	(144,423)	(67,601)	(76,822)	(128,341)	(60,907)	(67,434)	(10,187)	(3,598)	(6,589)	(3,357)	(2,071)	(1,286)	(2,538)	(1,025)	(1,513)
Science	100.0%	56.5%	43.5%	89.7%	51.5%	38.2%	5.6%	2.2%	3.4%	2.7%	1.4%	1.2%	2.0%	1.3%	0.7%
	(133,982)	(75,691)	(58,291)	(120,248)	(69,067)	(51,181)	(7,451)	(2,935)	(4,516)	(3,561)	(1,929)	(1,632)	(2,722)	(1,760)	(962)
English	100.0%	25.7%	74.3%	89.5%	23.9%	65.5%	5.7%	0.4%	5.3%	3.7%	1.1%	2.6%	1.1%	0.2%	0.9%
	(174,696)	(44,864)	(129,830)	(156,315)	(41,823)	(114,492)	(9,918)	(652)	(9,266)	(6,466)	(2,006)	(4,460)	(1,995)	(383)	(1,612)
Social Studies	100.0%	66.0%	34.0%	89.0%	60.5%	28.5%	6.7%	3.0%	3.7%	2.9%	1.7%	1.2%	1.4%	0.8%	0.6%
	(131,702)	(86,861)	(44,842)	(117,271)	(79,740)	(37,531)	(8,798)	(3,892)	(4,906)	(3,755)	(2,204)	(1,551)	(1,879)	(1,025)	(854)
Vocational/Technical	100.0%	54.2%	45.8%	87.7%	49.2%	38.5%	8.0%	2.7%	5.3%	2.5%	1.5%	1.0%	1.8%	0.9%	0.9%
	(113,807)	(61,690)	(52,115)	(99,760)	(55,945)	(43,815)	(9,106)	(3,060)	(6,046)	(2,897)	(1,712)	(1,185)	(2,042)	(973)	(1,069)
Special Education Secondary	100.0%	24.3%	75.7%	84.6%	20.0%	64.6%	9.6%	2.2%	7.4%	4.0%	1.2%	2.8%	1.7%	0.8%	0.9%
	(118,606)	(28,808)	(89,797)	(100,371)	(23,759)	(76,612)	(11,398)	(2,584)	(8,814)	(4,761)	(1,467)	(3,294)	(2,075)	(998)	(1,077)
Other Secondary	100.0%	43.6%	56.4%	86.2%	37.5%	48.7%	6.4%	2.9%	3.5%	5.5%	2.4%	3.1%	1.9%	0.8%	1.1%
	(367,818)	(160,228)	(207,591)	(317,195)	(137,885)	(179,310)	(23,492)	(10,716)	(12,776)	(20,048)	(8,651)	(11,397)	(7,084)	(2,976)	(4,108)

Notes:
*** Test of statistical significance compares African Americans with Whites. *** p < .001, ** p < .01, * p < .05.
+++ Test of statistical significance compares White men with White women. +++ p < .001, ++ p < .01, + p < .05.
~~~ Test of statistical significance compares African American men with African American women. ~~~ p < .001, ~~ p < .01, ~ p < .05.
Tests of statistical significance calculated using adjusted sample weight to control for influence of large sample sizes.
Source: Schools and Staffing Survey, 1993-94.

with 12.9% of African American women, 6.0% of all men, and 7.9% of all women.

- **Table 25** shows that a higher percentage of African Americans than Whites taught Chapter One at both the elementary (14.9% versus 8.3%) and secondary (12.2% versus 4.3%) school levels.

Chapter One teachers were concentrated in urban schools. About 40.3% of Chapter One teachers

worked in urban schools, compared with 27.0% of non-Chapter One teachers.

- **Figure 15** shows that, among African American public school teachers who taught Chapter One, more than two-thirds (68.4%) worked in urban schools.

- **Table 26** shows that only 14.8% of African American Chapter One teachers worked in sub-

Figure 14. Percentage of Public School Teachers Who Taught Chapter One: 1993/94

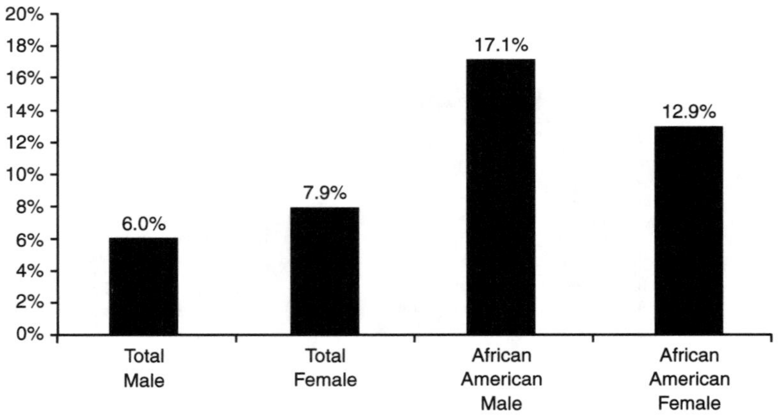

Source: Schools and Staffing Survey, 1993 -94.

urban schools (compared with 28.3% of Whites) and 16.8% in rural schools (compared with 40.0% of Whites).

Nearly one-half (45.6%) of Chapter One teachers worked in schools in which minorities represented the majority of students, compared with only 22.6% of non-Chapter One teachers. **Figure 16** shows that African American Chapter One teachers were also concentrated in schools in which minorities comprised the majority of students.

- **Table 27** shows that 83.1% of African American Chapter One teachers worked in schools in which minorities represented the majority of students, compared with only 32.7% of their White counterparts.

Organization of Teachers' Classes

Public Schools

The organization of classes varied by school level taught. For about two-thirds (62.0%) of elementary

school teachers, instruction was organized into self-contained classes. But for 84.4% of secondary school teachers, instruction was departmentalized.

The organization of classes also varied by race and sex, suggesting differences in teachers' duties and responsibilities. For example, nearly two-thirds (64.7%) of all female elementary school teachers taught self-contained classes, compared with 41.5% of males.

- **Table 28** shows that the percentage of elementary school teachers who taught self-contained classes ranged from 70.9% of African American women and 63.9% of White women to 41.4% of White men and 28.9% of African American men.

Figure 17 shows that, at the secondary school level, a smaller percentage of African Americans than of all teachers reported departmentalized instruction (78.0% versus 84.4%).

- **Table 28** shows that 8.9% of African American public secondary school teachers taught self-

Table 25. Number and Percentage of Public School Chapter One Teachers by School Level, Race, and Sex: 1993/94
(weighted sample size in parentheses)

Chapter One Teacher	Total	Male	Female	White, Non-Hispanic Total	Male	Female	African American, Non-Hispanic Total	Male	Female	Hispanic Total	Male	Female	Other Total	Male	Female
Total															
Total *** +++ ~~	100.0%	100.0%	100.0%	100.0%	100.0%	100.0%	100.0%	100.0%	100.0%	100.0%	100.0%	100.0%	100.0%	100.0%	100.0%
	(2,561,293)	(694,098)	(1,867,195)	(2,216,604)	(613,178)	(1,603,426)	(188,371)	(37,233)	(151,138)	(108,744)	(30,696)	(78,048)	(47,574)	(12,991)	(34,583)
Yes	7.4%	6.0%	7.9%	6.3%	4.7%	7.0%	13.7%	17.1%	12.9%	17.9%	15.5%	18.8%	7.6%	9.0%	7.1%
	(189,432)	(41,334)	(148,098)	(140,537)	(29,016)	(111,521)	(25,808)	(6,378)	(19,430)	(19,464)	(4,773)	(14,691)	(3,623)	(1,167)	(2,456)
No	92.6%	94.0%	92.1%	93.7%	95.3%	93.0%	86.3%	82.9%	87.1%	82.1%	84.5%	81.2%	92.4%	91.0%	92.9%
	(2,371,861)	(652,765)	(1,719,097)	(2,076,068)	(584,162)	(1,491,906)	(162,563)	(30,855)	(131,708)	(89,280)	(25,924)	(63,356)	(43,951)	(11,824)	(32,127)
Elementary															
Total *** +++ ~~	100.0%	100.0%	100.0%	100.0%	100.0%	100.0%	100.0%	100.0%	100.0%	100.0%	100.0%	100.0%	100.0%	100.0%	100.0%
	(1,331,281)	(154,788)	(1,176,493)	(1,139,263)	(133,204)	(1,006,059)	(104,246)	(8,821)	(95,425)	(61,648)	(9,752)	(51,896)	(26,124)	(3,011)	(23,113)
Yes	9.5%	7.8%	9.7%	8.3%	5.7%	8.6%	14.9%	22.3%	14.2%	23.3%	22.2%	23.5%	7.8%	11.0%	7.4%
	(126,049)	(12,101)	(113,948)	(94,089)	(7,638)	(86,451)	(15,535)	(1,970)	(13,565)	(14,379)	(2,161)	(12,218)	(2,046)	(332)	(1,714)
No	90.5%	92.2%	90.3%	91.7%	94.3%	91.4%	85.1%	77.7%	85.8%	76.7%	77.8%	76.5%	92.2%	89.0%	92.6%
	(1,205,232)	(142,687)	(1,062,545)	(1,045,174)	(125,566)	(919,608)	(88,711)	(6,851)	(81,860)	(47,269)	(7,591)	(39,678)	(24,078)	(2,679)	(21,399)
Secondary															
Total *** ~~	100.0%	100.0%	100.0%	100.0%	100.0%	100.0%	100.0%	100.0%	100.0%	100.0%	100.0%	100.0%	100.0%	100.0%	100.0%
	(1,230,013)	(539,310)	(690,702)	(1,077,342)	(479,974)	(597,368)	(84,125)	(28,412)	(55,713)	(47,095)	(20,944)	(26,151)	(21,450)	(9,980)	(11,470)
Yes	5.2%	5.4%	4.9%	4.3%	4.5%	4.2%	12.2%	15.5%	10.5%	10.8%	12.5%	9.5%	7.4%	8.4%	6.5%
	(63,384)	(29,233)	(34,150)	(46,448)	(21,378)	(25,070)	(10,273)	(4,408)	(5,865)	(5,085)	(2,612)	(2,473)	(1,577)	(835)	(742)
No	94.8%	94.6%	95.1%	95.7%	95.5%	95.8%	87.8%	84.5%	89.5%	89.2%	87.5%	90.5%	92.6%	91.6%	93.5%
	(1,166,629)	(510,077)	(656,552)	(1,030,894)	(458,596)	(572,298)	(73,852)	(24,004)	(49,848)	(42,010)	(18,332)	(23,678)	(19,873)	(9,145)	(10,728)

Notes:
*** Test of statistical significance compares African Americans with Whites. *** p < .001, ** p < .01, * p < .05.
+++ Test of statistical significance compares White men with White women. +++ p < .001, ++ p < .01, + p < .05.
~~~ Test of statistical significance compares African American men with African American women. ~~~ p < .001, ~~ p < .01, ~ p < .05.
Tests of statistical significance calculated using adjusted sample weight to control for influence of large sample sizes.
Source: Schools and Staffing Survey, 1993-94.

contained classes, compared with 5.5% of their White counterparts.

- About 8.1% of African Americans reported team teaching, compared with 4.8% of Whites.

Private Schools

About two-thirds (63.0%) of private elementary school teachers taught self-contained classes in 1993/94. Overall, a higher share of women than of

men taught self-contained classes (65.2% versus 44.7%).

- **Table 29** shows that comparable percentages of African American and White elementary school teachers taught self-contained classes (64.5% versus 63.4%).

- But, among African American elementary school teachers, only 25.9% of men, but 72.2% of women, taught self-contained classes.

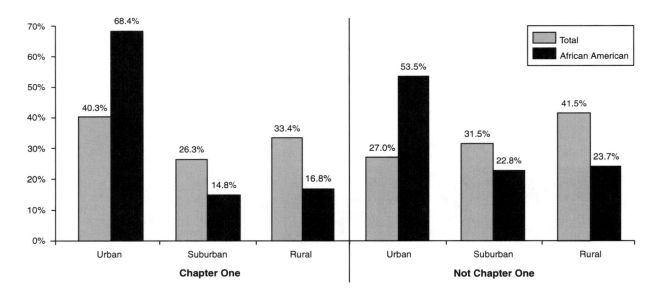

Figure 15. Distribution of Public School Chapter One
Teachers by Urbanicity: 1993/94

Source: Schools and Staffing Survey, 1993-94.

The majority (86.4%) of private secondary school teachers reported departmentalized instruction.

- A smaller proportion of African American than of White teachers reported departmentalized instruction (69.4% versus 86.6%).

Professional Development

Public Schools

Figure 18 shows that about 87.5% of all public school teachers participated in workshops or in-service programs sponsored by their school districts within the past year. The tendency to participate in particular professional development activities varied by race and sex.

- **Table 30** shows that, in 1993/94, a higher percentage of African American public school teachers than of White public school teachers participated in school-sponsored workshops or

in-service programs (85.1% versus 81.0%), committees to integrate academic skills into vocational curriculum (22.1 % versus 15.3%), education technology programs (54.3% versus 48.8%), student assessment programs (58.9% versus 50.6%), and in-depth study in their subject areas (34.0% versus 29.1%).

- A smaller percentage of African Americans than Whites participated in university extension or adult education classes (20.4% versus 25.3%) or other curriculum committees (31.5% versus 41.3%).

- A smaller percentage of African American men (75.8%) than of African American women (86.0%), White men (84.6%), and White women (89.2%) participated in school district-sponsored workshops or in-service programs.

- A higher percentage of women than men participated in professional growth activities

Table 26. Representation of Public School Chapter One Teachers by Urbanicity, Race and Sex: 1993/94
(weighted sample size in parentheses)

Urbanicity	Total	Male	Female	White, Non-Hispanic			African American, Non-Hispanic			Hispanic			Other		
				Total	Male	Female	Total	Male	Female	Total	Male	Female	Total	Male	Female
Chapter One Teacher															
Total *** ++	100.0%	100.0%	100.0%	100.0%	100.0%	100.0%	100.0%	100.0%	100.0%	100.0%	100.0%	100.0%	100.0%	100.0%	100.0%
	(189,432)	(41,334)	(148,098)	(140,537)	(29,016)	(111,521)	(25,808)	(6,378)	(19,430)	(19,464)	(4,773)	(14,691)	(3,623)	(1,167)	(2,456)
Urban	40.3%	45.6%	38.8%	31.7%	38.2%	30.0%	68.4%	64.4%	69.7%	64.1%	66.1%	63.5%	46.2%	45.7%	46.5%
	(76,339)	(18,868)	(57,471)	(44,532)	(11,073)	(33,459)	(17,649)	(4,108)	(13,541)	(12,482)	(3,154)	(9,329)	(1,676)	(533)	(1,142)
Suburban	26.3%	24.4%	26.8%	28.3%	27.1%	28.6%	14.8%	12.0%	15.7%	26.8%	23.8%	27.8%	27.1%	26.3%	27.5%
	(49,813)	(10,077)	(39,736)	(39,786)	(7,865)	(31,922)	(3,820)	(767)	(3,052)	(5,224)	(1,138)	(4,086)	(983)	(307)	(676)
Rural	33.4%	30.0%	34.4%	40.0%	34.7%	41.4%	16.8%	23.6%	14.6%	9.0%	10.1%	8.7%	26.6%	28.0%	26.0%
	(63,280)	(12,389)	(50,891)	(56,219)	(10,079)	(46,140)	(4,339)	(1,502)	(2,837)	(1,757)	(481)	(1,276)	(965)	(327)	(638)
Not a Chapter One Teacher															
Total *** ++	100.0%	100.0%	100.0%	100.0%	100.0%	100.0%	100.0%	100.0%	100.0%	100.0%	100.0%	100.0%	100.0%	100.0%	100.0%
	(2,371,861)	(652,764)	(1,719,097)	(2,076,068)	(584,162)	(1,491,906)	(162,563)	(30,855)	(131,708)	(89,280)	(25,924)	(63,356)	(43,951)	(11,824)	(32,127)
Urban	27.0%	26.2%	27.3%	23.7%	23.5%	23.7%	53.5%	55.3%	53.1%	53.0%	50.9%	53.8%	32.2%	30.3%	32.9%
	(639,974)	(171,048)	(468,926)	(491,514)	(137,208)	(354,306)	(86,995)	(17,052)	(69,943)	(47,311)	(13,201)	(34,110)	(14,155)	(3,587)	(10,567)
Suburban	31.5%	30.4%	31.9%	32.3%	31.3%	32.8%	22.8%	19.6%	23.5%	25.4%	21.1%	27.1%	37.2%	35.1%	37.9%
	(747,404)	(198,255)	(549,149)	(671,433)	(182,567)	(488,866)	(36,991)	(6,061)	(30,930)	(22,633)	(5,471)	(17,162)	(16,346)	(4,156)	(12,190)
Rural	41.5%	43.4%	40.8%	44.0%	45.3%	43.5%	23.7%	25.1%	23.4%	21.7%	28.0%	19.1%	30.6%	34.5%	29.2%
	(984,484)	(283,461)	(701,023)	(913,120)	(264,387)	(648,734)	(38,578)	(7,742)	(30,835)	(19,336)	(7,252)	(12,084)	(13,450)	(4,080)	(9,370)

Notes:

*** Test of statistical significance compares African Americans with Whites. *** p < .001, ** p < .01, * p < .05.

+++ Test of statistical significance compares White men with White women. +++ p < .001, ++ p < .01, + p < .05.

~~~ Test of statistical significance compares African American men with African American women. ~~~ p < .001, ~~ p < .01, ~ p < .05.

Tests of statistical significance calculated using adjusted sample weight to control for influence of large sample sizes.

Source: Schools and Staffing Survey, 1993-94.

sponsored by a professional organization among both African Americans (53.1% versus 46.6%) and Whites (53.0% versus 47.5%).

Private Schools

Figure 19 shows that about two-thirds of private school teachers participated in workshops or in-service programs sponsored by school districts (70.4%) or their schools (60.1%).

- **Table 31** shows that a smaller percentage of African Americans than Whites participated in workshops sponsored by school districts

(63.5% versus 70.8%) or their schools (64.9% versus 74.1%).

- A higher proportion of African American men than of African American women reported in-depth study in their subject area (39.6% versus 23.2%).

- A higher percentage of African Americans than Whites took college courses in their subject area (26.8% versus 19.5%).

- A higher share of African Americans than Whites served on committees to integrate aca-

Figure 16. Distribution of Public School Teachers by
Percentage of Minority Students Enrolled: 1993/94

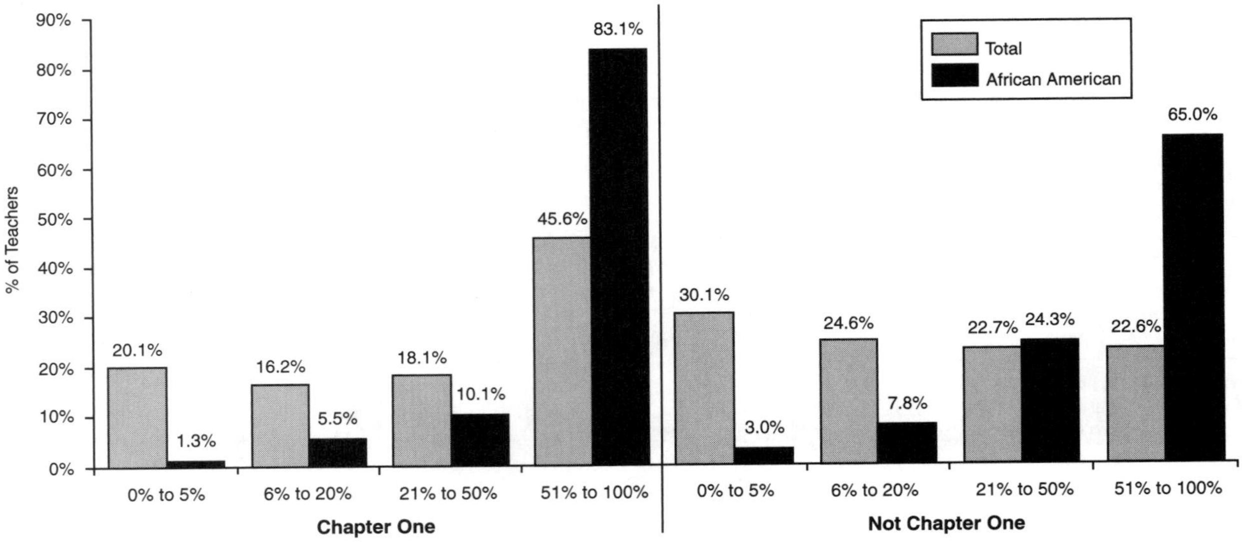

Source: Schools and Staffing Survey, 1993-94.

demic skills into vocational curricula (15.6% versus 7.7%) and student assessment programs (49.8% versus 35.8%).

SALARIES

Academic Year Base Salaries

Public Schools

In 1993/94, average salaries for African American and White public school teachers were comparable ($33,968 versus $34,247).

Private Schools

The average salary of regular, full-time private school teachers in 1993/94 was $21,898. On average, salaries were comparable for African American and White private school teachers ($20,746 versus $21,930).

Salaries by Age

Public Schools

Since age typically correlates with experience, it is not surprising to find that average base salaries were higher for older teachers than for younger teachers, regardless of race, sex, or level of school taught. For example, among elementary school teachers, average annual salaries ranged from a low of $24,897 for teachers under the age of 30 to a high of $38,896 for teachers 50 years of age and older.

After controlling for age, average salaries were comparable for African American and White public elementary school teachers.

- **Table 32** shows that average salaries were lower for African American public secondary school teachers than for their White counterparts between the ages of 40 and 49 ($33,702

Table 27. Distribution of Public School Chapter One Teachers by Percentage Minority Students at School, Race, and Sex: 1993/94
(weighted sample size in parentheses)

% Minority Students	Total	Male	Female	White, Non-Hispanic			African American, Non-Hispanic			Hispanic			Other		
				Total	Male	Female	Total	Male	Female	Total	Male	Female	Total	Male	Female
Chapter One Teacher															
Total *** ++	100.0%	100.0%	100.0%	100.0%	100.0%	100.0%	100.0%	100.0%	100.0%	100.0%	100.0%	100.0%	100.0%	100.0%	100.0%
	(171,978)	(37,812)	(134,166)	(128,046)	(26,450)	(101,597)	(22,715)	(5,980)	(16,734)	(17,822)	(4,332)	(13,490)	(3,396)	(1,051)	(2,345)
0% to 5%	20.1%	16.1%	21.3%	26.4%	22.6%	27.3%	1.3%	0.5%	1.5%	2.4%	0.8%	2.9%	4.9%	3.1%	5.7%
	(34,623)	(6,071)	(28,552)	(33,750)	(5,975)	(27,776)	(287)	(30)	(256)	(420)	(34)	(386)	(166)	(32)	(134)
6% to 20%	16.2%	16.2%	16.2%	20.4%	19.3%	20.6%	5.5%	13.1%	2.8%	1.5%	1.5%	1.5%	7.9%	17.8%	3.5%
	(27,852)	(6,125)	(21,727)	(26,058)	(5,093)	(20,965)	(1,257)	(781)	(476)	(268)	(65)	(203)	(269)	(187)	(83)
21% to 50%	18.1%	18.4%	18.0%	20.6%	21.0%	20.4%	10.1%	9.9%	10.2%	10.6%	13.7%	9.6%	17.2%	21.7%	15.2%
	(31,087)	(6,975)	(24,112)	(26,318)	(5,562)	(20,756)	(2,297)	(592)	(1,704)	(1,889)	(593)	(1,296)	(583)	(228)	(356)
51% to 100%	45.6%	49.3%	44.6%	32.7%	37.1%	31.6%	83.1%	76.5%	85.4%	85.5%	84.0%	86.0%	70.0%	57.5%	75.6%
	(78,416)	(18,641)	(59,775)	(41,920)	(9,821)	(32,099)	(18,875)	(4,577)	(14,298)	(15,244)	(3,640)	(11,605)	(2,377)	(604)	(1,772)
Not a Chapter One Teacher															
Total *** +++ ~~~	100.0%	100.0%	100.0%	100.0%	100.0%	100.0%	100.0%	100.0%	100.0%	100.0%	100.0%	100.0%	100.0%	100.0%	100.0%
	(2,209,710)	(609,219)	(1,600,492)	(1,938,657)	(547,816)	(1,390,841)	(148,108)	(27,717)	(120,391)	(82,277)	(23,300)	(58,977)	(40,669)	(10,386)	(30,283)
0% to 5%	30.1%	33.6%	28.8%	33.7%	36.4%	32.6%	3.0%	5.5%	2.4%	4.9%	8.8%	3.4%	11.1%	14.6%	9.8%
	(665,360)	(204,731)	(460,629)	(652,447)	(199,637)	(452,810)	(4,378)	(1,530)	(2,848)	(4,039)	(2,046)	(1,992)	(4,497)	(1,518)	(2,979)
6% to 20%	24.6%	24.1%	24.8%	26.7%	25.6%	27.1%	7.8%	7.3%	8.0%	9.0%	10.3%	8.4%	20.3%	19.6%	20.5%
	(544,224)	(146,905)	(397,318)	(516,997)	(140,455)	(376,542)	(11,607)	(2,010)	(9,598)	(7,374)	(2,402)	(4,972)	(8,245)	(2,039)	(6,207)
21% to 50%	22.7%	21.1%	23.3%	22.8%	21.3%	23.4%	24.3%	19.6%	25.3%	19.0%	18.9%	19.0%	20.4%	22.2%	19.8%
	(501,662)	(128,563)	(373,099)	(441,842)	(116,429)	(325,413)	(35,920)	(5,424)	(30,496)	(15,595)	(4,404)	(11,191)	(8,304)	(2,306)	(5,998)
51% to 100%	22.6%	21.2%	23.1%	16.9%	16.7%	17.0%	65.0%	67.7%	64.3%	67.2%	62.0%	69.2%	48.2%	43.6%	49.9%
	(498,465)	(129,020)	(369,445)	(327,371)	(91,295)	(236,076)	(96,203)	(18,753)	(77,449)	(55,269)	(14,448)	(40,820)	(19,623)	(4,524)	(15,099)

Notes:
*** Test of statistical significance compares African Americans with Whites. *** p < .001, ** p < .01, * p < .05.
+++ Test of statistical significance compares White men with White women. +++ p < .001, ++ p < .01, + p < .05.
~~~ Test of statistical significance compares African American men with African American women. ~~~ p < .001, ~~ p < .01, ~ p < .05.
Tests of statistical significance calculated using adjusted sample weight to control for influence of large sample sizes.
Source: Schools and Staffing Survey, 1993-94.

versus $36,670) and over the age of 50 ($37,524 versus $41,316).

- Among public secondary school teachers, average salaries were comparable for African Americans and Whites under the age of 30 ($24,031 versus $24,526) and between the ages of 30 and 39 ($29,915 versus $29,354).

- **Figure 20** shows that average salaries were comparable for African American men and women public school teachers.

Private Schools

Figure 21 shows that average salaries of private school teachers generally increased with age. Over-

Table 28. Organization of Classes Among Public School Teachers by School Level, Race, and Sex: 1993/94
(weighted sample size in parentheses)

Organization of Classes	Total	Male	Female	White, Non-Hispanic Total	White Male	White Female	African American, Non-Hispanic Total	AA Male	AA Female	Hispanic Total	Hispanic Male	Hispanic Female	Other Total	Other Male	Other Female
Total															
Total *** +++ ~~~	100.0%	100.0%	100.0%	100.0%	100.0%	100.0%	100.0%	100.0%	100.0%	100.0%	100.0%	100.0%	100.0%	100.0%	100.0%
	(2,561,294)	(694,098)	(1,867,195)	(2,216,604)	(613,178)	(1,603,426)	(188,371)	(37,233)	(151,138)	(108,744)	(30,696)	(78,048)	(47,574)	(12,991)	(34,583)
Departmentalized Instruction	44.5%	71.5%	34.4%	45.3%	72.7%	34.8%	39.8%	65.1%	33.6%	38.9%	59.2%	30.9%	38.3%	60.7%	29.8%
	(1,138,965)	(496,167)	(642,798)	(1,003,489)	(445,866)	(557,623)	(74,962)	(24,239)	(50,723)	(42,315)	(18,176)	(24,139)	(18,199)	(7,886)	(10,313)
Elementary Enrichment Class	6.4%	7.1%	6.2%	6.3%	6.8%	6.2%	6.8%	9.8%	6.1%	7.4%	9.2%	6.7%	6.7%	6.2%	6.9%
	(164,794)	(49,166)	(115,628)	(140,725)	(41,883)	(98,842)	(12,874)	(3,662)	(9,212)	(8,014)	(2,812)	(5,202)	(3,181)	(809)	(2,372)
Self-Contained Class	35.1%	13.6%	43.1%	34.2%	13.0%	42.3%	41.2%	13.8%	48.0%	41.0%	23.1%	48.0%	40.5%	19.1%	48.5%
	(899,038)	(94,148)	(804,890)	(757,552)	(79,410)	(678,142)	(77,687)	(5,154)	(72,533)	(44,538)	(7,106)	(37,432)	(19,261)	(2,478)	(16,783)
Team Teaching	7.1%	4.9%	7.9%	7.1%	4.7%	8.0%	5.8%	7.2%	5.4%	8.3%	5.2%	9.5%	9.3%	11.7%	8.4%
	(181,214)	(34,357)	(146,857)	(156,920)	(28,561)	(128,359)	(10,875)	(2,685)	(8,190)	(8,990)	(1,587)	(7,403)	(4,429)	(1,524)	(2,905)
Pull-Out Class	6.9%	2.9%	8.4%	7.1%	2.8%	8.8%	6.4%	4.0%	6.9%	4.5%	3.3%	5.0%	5.3%	2.3%	6.4%
	(177,283)	(20,260)	(157,023)	(157,919)	(17,458)	(140,461)	(11,973)	(1,493)	(10,480)	(4,887)	(1,015)	(3,872)	(2,504)	(294)	(2,210)
Elementary															
Total *** +++ ~~~	100.0%	100.0%	100.0%	100.0%	100.0%	100.0%	100.0%	100.0%	100.0%	100.0%	100.0%	100.0%	100.0%	100.0%	100.0%
	(1,331,281)	(154,788)	(1,176,493)	(1,139,263)	(133,204)	(1,006,059)	(104,246)	(8,821)	(95,425)	(61,648)	(9,752)	(51,896)	(26,124)	(3,011)	(23,113)
Departmentalized Instruction	7.6%	16.5%	6.4%	7.5%	16.4%	6.3%	8.9%	25.4%	7.4%	8.3%	12.6%	7.5%	4.4%	4.1%	4.5%
	(100,853)	(25,486)	(75,366)	(85,245)	(21,891)	(63,354)	(9,323)	(2,243)	(7,080)	(5,126)	(1,228)	(3,898)	(1,158)	(124)	(1,034)
Elementary Enrichment Class	11.1%	25.8%	9.2%	11.2%	25.8%	9.2%	10.9%	31.3%	9.0%	9.9%	21.8%	7.7%	11.3%	22.8%	9.8%
	(147,747)	(39,990)	(107,759)	(127,369)	(34,415)	(92,954)	(11,323)	(2,762)	(8,561)	(6,113)	(2,127)	(3,986)	(2,944)	(686)	(2,258)
Self-Contained Class	62.0%	41.5%	64.7%	61.3%	41.4%	63.9%	67.4%	28.9%	70.9%	64.9%	52.9%	67.1%	66.8%	46.7%	69.5%
	(825,709)	(64,261)	(761,449)	(698,053)	(55,150)	(642,903)	(70,215)	(2,546)	(67,669)	(39,979)	(5,159)	(34,820)	(17,463)	(1,406)	(16,057)
Team Teaching	8.9%	9.2%	8.9%	9.2%	9.7%	9.2%	3.9%	3.4%	3.9%	10.6%	4.1%	11.8%	10.1%	20.0%	8.8%
	(118,562)	(14,245)	(104,315)	(105,339)	(12,939)	(92,400)	(4,062)	(302)	(3,760)	(6,521)	(401)	(6,120)	(2,638)	(603)	(2,035)
Pull-Out Class	10.4%	7.0%	10.8%	10.8%	6.6%	11.4%	8.9%	11.0%	8.8%	6.3%	8.6%	5.9%	7.4%	6.4%	7.5%
	(138,409)	(10,807)	(127,603)	(123,257)	(8,810)	(114,447)	(9,323)	(968)	(8,355)	(3,909)	(837)	(3,072)	(1,921)	(192)	(1,729)
Secondary															
Total *** +++ ~	100.0%	100.0%	100.0%	100.0%	100.0%	100.0%	100.0%	100.0%	100.0%	100.0%	100.0%	100.0%	100.0%	100.0%	100.0%
	(1,230,013)	(539,310)	(690,703)	(1,077,342)	(479,974)	(597,368)	(84,125)	(28,412)	(55,713)	(47,096)	(20,944)	(26,152)	(21,450)	(9,980)	(11,470)
Departmentalized Instruction	84.4%	87.3%	82.2%	85.2%	88.3%	82.7%	78.0%	77.4%	78.3%	79.0%	80.9%	77.4%	79.4%	77.8%	80.9%
	(1,038,111)	(470,681)	(567,431)	(918,243)	(423,975)	(494,268)	(65,639)	(21,996)	(43,643)	(37,188)	(16,947)	(20,241)	(17,042)	(7,763)	(9,279)
Elementary Enrichment Class	1.4%	1.7%	1.1%	1.2%	1.6%	1.0%	1.8%	3.2%	1.2%	4.0%	3.3%	4.6%	1.1%	1.2%	1.0%
	(17,046)	(9,177)	(7,869)	(13,356)	(7,468)	(5,888)	(1,551)	(900)	(651)	(1,902)	(686)	(1,216)	(237)	(123)	(114)
Self-Contained Class	6.0%	5.5%	6.3%	5.5%	5.1%	5.9%	8.9%	9.2%	8.7%	9.7%	9.3%	10.0%	8.4%	10.7%	6.3%
	(73,329)	(29,889)	(43,441)	(59,499)	(24,261)	(35,238)	(7,474)	(2,609)	(4,865)	(4,559)	(1,947)	(2,612)	(1,798)	(1,072)	(726)
Team Teaching	5.1%	3.7%	6.2%	4.8%	3.3%	6.0%	8.1%	8.4%	8.0%	5.2%	5.7%	4.9%	8.3%	9.2%	7.6%
	(62,652)	(20,112)	(42,541)	(51,582)	(15,623)	(35,959)	(6,812)	(2,382)	(4,430)	(2,468)	(1,186)	(1,282)	(1,791)	(921)	(870)
Pull-Out Class	3.2%	1.8%	4.3%	3.2%	1.8%	4.4%	3.2%	1.8%	3.8%	2.1%	0.8%	3.1%	2.7%	1.0%	4.2%
	(38,873)	(9,453)	(29,421)	(34,662)	(8,648)	(26,014)	(2,650)	(525)	(2,125)	(979)	(178)	(801)	(583)	(102)	(481)

Notes:
*** Test of statistical significance compares African Americans with Whites. *** p < .001, ** p < .01, * p < .05.
+++ Test of statistical significance compares White men with White women. +++ p < .001, ++ p < .01, + p < .05.
~~~ Test of statistical significance compares African American men with African American women. ~~~ p < .001, ~~ p < .01, ~ p < .05.
Tests of statistical significance calculated using adjusted sample weight to control for influence of large sample sizes.
Source: Schools and Staffing Survey, 1993-94.

Figure 17. Organization of Classes Among Public Secondary School Teachers: 1993/94

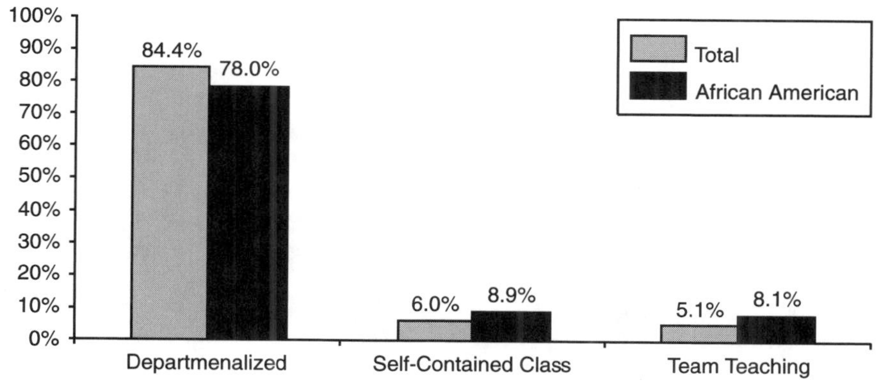

Source: Schools and Staffing Survey, 1993-94.

all, average salaries ranged from $16,944 for private school teachers under the age of 30 to $25,121 for those age 50 and over.

Average salaries were comparable for African American and White private school teachers of the same age.

- For example, **Table 33** shows that average salaries were $23,606 for African Americans and $25,260 for Whites age 50 and older.

- Among private school teachers age 50 and older, average salaries were lower for women than men among both African Americans ($20,897 versus $35,702) and Whites ($23,470 versus $31,974).

Salaries by Urbanicity

Public Schools

Average salaries were $38,318 for suburban public school teachers, $34,527 for urban public school teachers, and $30,814 for rural public school teachers.

- **Table 34** shows that African American public school teachers earned lower salaries than their White counterparts at urban ($35,501 versus $34,504), suburban ($35,893 versus $38,564), and rural ($28,354 versus $30,955) schools.

- **Figure 22** shows that average salaries were comparable for African American men and women public school teachers after controlling for urbanicity.

Private Schools

On average, private school teachers at rural schools earned $18,410, those at suburban schools earned $22,855, and those at urban schools earned $22,639.

- **Table 35** shows that, at urban private schools, African Americans earned $20,311 per year, while Whites earned $22,779.

- **Figure 23** shows that average salaries were comparable for African American and all private school teachers in suburban ($22,473 ver-

Table 29. Organization of Classes Among Private School Teachers by School Level, Race, and Sex: 1993/94
(weighted sample size in parentheses)

Organization of Classes	Total	Male	Female	White, Non-Hispanic Total	Male	Female	African American, Non-Hispanic Total	Male	Female	Hispanic Total	Male	Female	Other Total	Male	Female
Total															
Total *** +++ ~~~	100.0%	100.0%	100.0%	100.0%	100.0%	100.0%	100.0%	100.0%	100.0%	100.0%	100.0%	100.0%	100.0%	100.0%	100.0%
	(378,365)	(93,130)	(285,235)	(347,812)	(84,873)	(262,939)	(11,664)	(3,413)	(8,251)	(12,221)	(3,088)	(9,133)	(6,670)	(1,757)	(4,913)
Departmentalized Instruction	44.1%	70.9%	35.3%	44.3%	71.3%	35.6%	28.4%	56.4%	16.7%	47.3%	70.2%	39.6%	53.4%	84.3%	42.4%
	(166,720)	(66,058)	(100,661)	(154,065)	(60,483)	(93,582)	(3,307)	(1,926)	(1,381)	(5,782)	(2,168)	(3,614)	(3,565)	(1,481)	(2,084)
Elementary Enrichment Class	9.1%	7.8%	9.5%	8.9%	7.4%	9.4%	10.8%	16.0%	8.7%	13.1%	10.6%	13.9%	10.4%	8.3%	11.2%
	(34,435)	(7,277)	(27,158)	(30,882)	(6,260)	(24,622)	(1,264)	(545)	(719)	(1,596)	(327)	(1,269)	(693)	(145)	(548)
Self-Contained Class	40.1%	17.2%	47.5%	40.3%	17.7%	47.6%	49.7%	15.4%	64.0%	29.9%	12.1%	36.0%	29.3%	5.7%	37.8%
	(151,645)	(16,029)	(135,616)	(140,229)	(15,032)	(125,197)	(5,801)	(524)	(5,277)	(3,659)	(373)	(3,286)	(1,956)	(100)	(1,856)
Team Teaching	4.9%	2.6%	5.7%	4.7%	2.3%	5.5%	7.7%	7.9%	7.6%	9.2%	5.9%	10.3%	5.8%	1.7%	7.2%
	(18,702)	(2,415)	(16,286)	(16,302)	(1,935)	(14,367)	(894)	(268)	(626)	(1,121)	(182)	(939)	(384)	(30)	(354)
Pull-Out Class	1.8%	1.4%	1.9%	1.8%	1.4%	2.0%	3.4%	4.4%	3.0%	0.5%	1.2%	0.3%	1.1%	0.0%	1.4%
	(6,863)	(1,349)	(5,515)	(6,334)	(1,163)	(5,171)	(396)	(149)	(247)	(63)	(37)	(26)	(71)	–	(71)
Elementary															
Total +++ ~~~	100.0%	100.0%	100.0%	100.0%	100.0%	100.0%	100.0%	100.0%	100.0%	100.0%	100.0%	100.0%	100.0%	100.0%	100.0%
	(221,036)	(24,602)	(196,434)	(203,242)	(22,286)	(180,956)	(8,158)	(1,360)	(6,798)	(6,124)	(586)	(5,538)	(3,512)	(370)	(3,142)
Departmentalized Instruction	13.9%	23.2%	12.8%	14.2%	23.1%	13.1%	10.7%	33.5%	6.2%	8.3%	0.0%	9.2%	15.4%	30.0%	13.7%
	(30,786)	(5,716)	(25,071)	(28,862)	(5,150)	(23,712)	(874)	(455)	(419)	(511)	–	(511)	(540)	(111)	(429)
Elementary Enrichment Class	14.0%	24.3%	12.8%	13.7%	23.3%	12.5%	12.9%	25.4%	10.4%	25.0%	49.1%	22.5%	18.9%	39.2%	16.5%
	(31,043)	(5,967)	(25,077)	(27,791)	(5,188)	(22,603)	(1,054)	(346)	(708)	(1,534)	(288)	(1,246)	(665)	(145)	(520)
Self-Contained Class	63.0%	44.7%	65.2%	63.4%	46.4%	65.5%	64.5%	25.9%	72.2%	51.1%	39.8%	52.3%	54.1%	22.7%	57.8%
	(139,160)	(11,001)	(128,159)	(128,872)	(10,332)	(118,540)	(5,259)	(352)	(4,907)	(3,129)	(233)	(2,896)	(1,900)	(84)	(1,816)
Team Teaching	6.9%	5.3%	7.1%	6.6%	5.0%	6.8%	7.4%	6.1%	7.7%	15.4%	11.1%	15.8%	9.6%	8.1%	9.7%
	(15,224)	(1,296)	(13,928)	(13,339)	(1,118)	(12,221)	(607)	(83)	(524)	(942)	(65)	(877)	(336)	(30)	(306)
Pull-Out Class	2.2%	2.5%	2.1%	2.2%	2.2%	2.1%	4.5%	9.0%	3.5%	0.0%	0.0%	0.0%	2.0%	0.0%	2.3%
	(4,822)	(622)	(4,192)	(4,379)	(499)	(3,880)	(364)	(123)	(241)	–	–	–	(71)	–	(71)
Secondary															
Total *** +	100.0%	100.0%	100.0%	100.0%	100.0%	100.0%	100.0%	100.0%	100.0%	100.0%	100.0%	100.0%	100.0%	100.0%	100.0%
	(157,329)	(68,527)	(88,802)	(144,570)	(62,587)	(81,983)	(3,506)	(2,053)	(1,453)	(6,096)	(2,501)	(3,595)	(3,158)	(1,387)	(1,771)
Departmentalized Instruction	86.4%	88.1%	85.1%	86.6%	88.4%	85.2%	69.4%	71.7%	66.3%	86.5%	86.7%	86.3%	95.8%	98.8%	93.5%
	(135,934)	(60,342)	(75,592)	(125,203)	(55,333)	(69,870)	(2,434)	(1,471)	(963)	(5,272)	(2,168)	(3,104)	(3,025)	(1,370)	(1,655)
Elementary Enrichment Class	2.2%	1.9%	2.3%	2.1%	1.7%	2.5%	6.0%	9.7%	0.8%	1.0%	1.6%	0.6%	0.9%	0.0%	1.6%
	(3,392)	(1,310)	(2,081)	(3,091)	(1,072)	(2,019)	(210)	(199)	(11)	(62)	(39)	(23)	(28)	–	(28)
Self-Contained Class	7.9%	7.3%	8.4%	7.9%	7.5%	8.1%	15.5%	8.4%	25.5%	8.7%	5.6%	10.8%	1.8%	1.2%	2.2%
	(12,485)	(5,028)	(7,456)	(11,356)	(4,699)	(6,657)	(542)	(172)	(370)	(530)	(140)	(390)	(56)	(17)	(39)
Team Teaching	2.2%	1.6%	2.7%	2.1%	1.3%	2.6%	8.2%	9.0%	7.1%	2.9%	4.7%	1.7%	1.5%	0.0%	2.7%
	(3,478)	(1,120)	(2,358)	(2,964)	(818)	(2,146)	(288)	(185)	(103)	(178)	(117)	(61)	(48)	–	(48)
Pull-Out Class	1.3%	1.1%	1.5%	1.4%	1.1%	1.6%	0.7%	1.3%	0.0%	0.9%	1.5%	0.5%	0.0%	0.0%	0.0%
	(2,041)	(727)	(1,307)	(1,954)	(664)	(1,290)	(26)	(26)	–	(54)	(37)	(17)	–	–	–

Notes:

" – " indicates sample size too small to estimate.

*** Test of statistical significance compares African Americans with Whites. *** p < .001, ** p < .01, * p < .05.

+++ Test of statistical significance compares White men with White women. +++ p < .001, ++ p < .01, + p < .05.

~~~ Test of statistical significance compares African American men with African American women. ~~~ p < .001, ~~ p < .01, ~ p < .05.

Tests of statistical significance calculated using adjusted sample weight to control for influence of large sample sizes.

Source: Schools and Staffing Survey, 1993-94.

Figure 18. Percentage of Public School Teachers
Who Participated in Various Professional Development
Activities in the Past Year: 1993/94

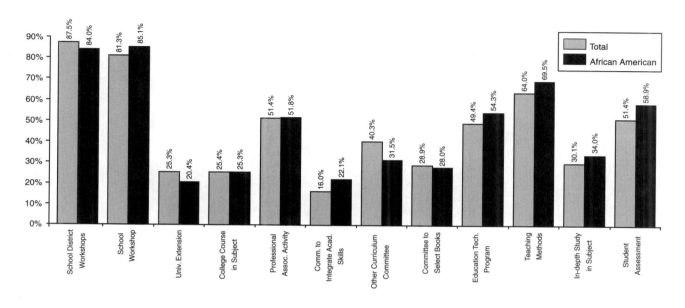

Source: Schools and Staffing Survey, 1993-94.

sus $22,855) and rural ($18,436 versus $18,410) schools.

Salaries by Region

Public Schools

Figure 24 shows that public school teachers who worked in the northeastern United States received higher salaries, on average, whereas those who worked in the south received lower salaries. **Table 36** shows that average salaries varied from $43,090 for public school teachers in the northeast, to $35,612 for those in the West, $34,142 for those in the midwest, and $28,972 for those in the south.

African American public school teachers in the midwest, west, and south received higher salaries, on average, than their White counterparts.

- **Table 36** shows that, in the northeast, average salaries were $41,076 for African Americans, compared with $43,358 for Whites.

Private Schools

Figure 25 shows that average salaries were similar for private school teachers in the south ($20,356), midwest ($20,698), northeast ($23,310), and west ($24,480).

Table 30. Number and Percentage of Public School Teachers Who Participated in Various Professional Development Activities in the Past Year by Race and Sex: 1993/94

(weighted sample size in parentheses)

Professional Development Activity	Total	Male	Female	White, Non-Hispanic Total	Male	Female	African American, Non-Hispanic Total	Male	Female	Hispanic Total	Male	Female	Other Total	Male	Female
Total	100.0% (2,561,294)	27.1% (694,098)	72.9% (1,867,195)	86.5% (2,216,604)	23.9% (613,178)	62.6% (1,603,426)	7.4% (188,371)	1.5% (37,233)	5.9% (151,138)	4.2% (108,744)	1.2% (30,696)	3.0% (78,048)	1.9% (47,574)	0.5% (12,991)	1.4% (34,583)
School-District-Sponsored In-Service Program *** +++ ~~~	87.5% (2,241,531)	83.8% (581,898)	88.9% (1,659,632)	87.9% (1,948,435)	84.6% (518,696)	89.2% (1,429,739)	84.0% (158,192)	75.8% (28,206)	86.0% (129,986)	85.9% (93,461)	79.2% (24,309)	88.6% (69,152)	87.1% (41,442)	82.3% (10,687)	88.9% (30,755)
School-Sponsored Workshop or In-Service Program *** +++ ~~~	81.3% (2,082,798)	75.9% (526,919)	83.3% (1,555,878)	81.0% (1,794,425)	75.7% (464,269)	83.0% (1,330,156)	85.1% (160,313)	78.4% (29,195)	86.8% (131,118)	81.7% (88,889)	76.2% (23,381)	83.9% (65,508)	82.3% (39,170)	77.5% (10,074)	84.1% (29,096)
University Extension or Adult Education Courses *** +++	25.3% (646,891)	23.3% (161,917)	26.0% (484,975)	25.3% (561,529)	23.1% (141,885)	26.2% (419,644)	20.4% (38,475)	21.5% (8,013)	20.2% (30,462)	29.0% (31,531)	26.0% (7,970)	30.2% (23,561)	32.3% (15,357)	31.2% (4,049)	32.7% (11,308)
College Courses in Subject +++	25.4% (651,834)	23.1% (160,288)	26.3% (491,546)	25.0% (554,367)	22.5% (138,155)	26.0% (416,212)	25.3% (47,587)	26.5% (9,858)	25.0% (37,729)	33.0% (35,914)	29.5% (9,048)	34.4% (26,866)	29.4% (13,966)	24.8% (3,227)	31.1% (10,739)
Professional Growth Activity From Prof. Assoc. +++ ~	51.4% (1,317,169)	47.4% (328,676)	52.9% (988,492)	51.5% (1,141,458)	47.5% (291,524)	53.0% (849,934)	51.8% (97,568)	46.6% (17,346)	53.1% (80,222)	47.5% (51,614)	41.5% (12,752)	49.8% (38,862)	55.8% (26,528)	54.3% (7,054)	56.3% (19,474)
Committee to Integrate Academic Skills Into Vocational Curriculum *** +++	16.0% (410,519)	19.2% (132,947)	14.9% (277,573)	15.3% (340,138)	18.9% (116,173)	14.0% (223,965)	22.1% (41,682)	21.4% (7,971)	22.3% (33,711)	17.8% (19,366)	18.5% (5,669)	17.5% (13,697)	19.6% (9,334)	24.1% (3,134)	17.9% (6,200)
Other Curriculum Committee *** +++ ~~	40.3% (1,032,198)	36.8% (255,674)	41.6% (776,524)	41.3% (914,400)	37.6% (230,402)	42.7% (683,998)	31.5% (59,361)	24.6% (9,173)	33.2% (50,188)	37.1% (40,318)	37.0% (11,359)	37.1% (28,959)	38.1% (18,119)	36.5% (4,740)	38.7% (13,379)
Committee to Select Books and Materials ~~	28.9% (740,237)	28.9% (200,583)	28.9% (539,655)	28.9% (640,998)	29.3% (179,400)	28.8% (461,598)	28.0% (52,683)	23.3% (8,658)	29.1% (44,025)	31.2% (33,898)	30.6% (9,381)	31.4% (24,517)	26.6% (12,659)	24.2% (3,144)	27.5% (9,515)
Education Technology Program *** +++	49.4% (1,264,019)	50.7% (351,937)	48.8% (912,081)	48.8% (1,081,646)	50.6% (310,200)	48.1% (771,446)	54.3% (102,214)	52.5% (19,552)	54.7% (82,662)	51.2% (55,707)	51.2% (15,707)	51.3% (40,000)	51.4% (24,451)	49.9% (6,478)	52.0% (17,973)
Teaching Methods for Subject Program *** +++ ~~~	64.0% (1,639,965)	54.1% (375,434)	67.7% (1,264,530)	63.1% (1,399,430)	53.2% (326,182)	66.9% (1,073,248)	69.5% (130,932)	59.8% (22,252)	71.9% (108,680)	71.9% (78,228)	63.8% (19,575)	75.1% (58,653)	65.9% (31,374)	57.2% (7,425)	69.3% (23,949)
In-Depth Study in Subject Program *** +++ ~	30.1% (770,686)	27.4% (190,318)	31.1% (580,369)	29.1% (646,073)	26.6% (163,008)	30.1% (483,065)	34.0% (64,022)	30.5% (11,358)	34.8% (52,664)	39.3% (42,775)	37.2% (11,406)	40.2% (31,369)	37.5% (17,817)	35.0% (4,546)	38.4% (13,271)
Student Assessment Program *** +++ ~~	51.4% (1,317,549)	45.5% (315,663)	53.7% (1,001,885)	50.6% (1,120,955)	44.7% (274,032)	52.8% (846,923)	58.9% (111,006)	53.3% (19,842)	60.3% (91,164)	54.6% (59,357)	49.9% (15,332)	56.4% (44,025)	55.1% (26,230)	49.7% (6,457)	57.2% (19,773)

Notes:

Columns do not sum to 100% as respondents may have more than one type of previous experience.

*** Test of statistical significance compares African Americans with Whites. *** p < .001, ** p < .01, * p < .05.

+++ Test of statistical significance compares White men with White women. +++ p < .001, ++ p < .01, + p < .05.

~~~ Test of statistical significance compares African American men with African American women. ~~~ p < .001, ~~ p < .01, ~ p < .05.

Tests of statistical significance calculated using adjusted sample weight to control for influence of large sample sizes.

Source: Schools and Staffing Survey, 1993-94.

Figure 19. Percentage of Private School Teachers Who Participated in Various Professional Development Activities in the Past Year: 1993/94

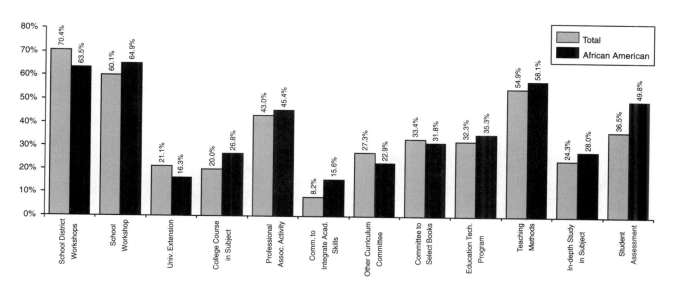

Source: Schools and Staffing Survey, 1993-94.

- **Table 37** shows that average salaries were comparable for African Americans and Whites in the northeast ($23,081 versus $23,417), midwest ($18,825 versus $20,779), and south ($20,461 versus $20,413).

- Average salaries were lower for African Americans than Whites in the west ($20,077 versus $24,436).

PROBLEMS THAT TEACHERS ASSOCIATED WITH THEIR SCHOOL

Public Schools

Tables 38, 39, and 40 indicate the aspects of school life teachers perceive to be problematic. Secondary school teachers reported a greater number of aspects of school life were a problem than elementary school teachers. For example, **Table 40**

shows that more than 90% of secondary school teachers indicated that the following items were problems: students come unprepared to learn (97.3%), student apathy (96.6%), student absenteeism (95.2%), lack of parental involvement (93.3%), students disrespectful of teachers (93.7%), parental alcoholism and drug abuse (92.6%), school tardiness (91.5%), and poverty (90.9%). **Table 39** shows that more than 90% of elementary school teachers agreed only that students coming unprepared to learn was a problem (91.1%).

Figure 26 shows that African American teachers differed from other teachers in the aspects of school life they perceived to be problems.

- A smaller percentage of African American teachers than White teachers felt that student use of alcohol was a problem at both the elementary (**Table 39:** 16.8% versus 21.0%) and

Table 31. Number and Percentage of Private School Teachers Who Participated in Various Professional Development Activities in the Past Year by Race and Sex: 1993/94
(weighted sample size in parentheses)

Professional Development Activity	Total	Male	Female	White, Non-Hispanic Total	Male	Female	African American, Non-Hispanic Total	Male	Female	Hispanic Total	Male	Female	Other Total	Male	Female
Total	100.0%	100.0%	100.0%	100.0%	100.0%	100.0%	100.0%	100.0%	100.0%	100.0%	100.0%	100.0%	100.0%	100.0%	100.0%
	(378,365)	(93,130)	(285,235)	(347,812)	(84,873)	(262,939)	(11,664)	(3,413)	(8,251)	(12,221)	(3,088)	(9,133)	(6,670)	(1,757)	(4,913)
School-District-Sponsored In-Service Program * +++	70.4%	63.4%	72.7%	70.8%	63.7%	73.1%	63.5%	54.4%	67.3%	64.2%	57.7%	66.4%	73.9%	75.6%	73.3%
	(266,400)	(59,034)	(207,364)	(246,216)	(54,067)	(192,149)	(7,406)	(1,855)	(5,551)	(7,845)	(1,783)	(6,062)	(4,931)	(1,329)	(3,602)
School-Sponsored Workshop or In-Service Program ** + +	60.1%	69.3%	74.7%	74.1%	69.9%	75.4%	64.9%	57.7%	67.9%	62.3%	64.5%	61.6%	70.1%	70.3%	70.0%
	(227,433)	(64,506)	(212,929)	(257,580)	(59,311)	(198,269)	(7,567)	(1,968)	(5,599)	(7,613)	(1,991)	(5,622)	(4,675)	(1,236)	(3,439)
University Extension or Adult Education Courses ++	21.1%	18.2%	22.0%	21.2%	18.4%	22.1%	16.3%	15.1%	16.8%	19.3%	17.1%	20.0%	25.2%	14.9%	28.9%
	(79,791)	(16,934)	(62,856)	(73,852)	(15,629)	(58,223)	(1,900)	(516)	(1,384)	(2,357)	(527)	(1,830)	(1,681)	(262)	(1,419)
College Courses in Subject ***	20.0%	20.2%	19.9%	19.5%	19.6%	19.5%	26.8%	26.7%	26.9%	23.8%	26.3%	23.0%	24.5%	26.9%	23.7%
	(75,650)	(18,836)	(56,814)	(67,974)	(16,641)	(51,333)	(3,130)	(910)	(2,220)	(2,911)	(812)	(2,099)	(1,635)	(473)	(1,162)
Professional Growth Activity From Prof. Assoc.+++	43.0%	39.7%	44.1%	42.7%	39.2%	43.8%	45.4%	38.5%	48.2%	43.0%	45.3%	42.2%	57.1%	54.7%	57.9%
	(162,797)	(36,933)	(125,864)	(148,446)	(33,258)	(115,188)	(5,293)	(1,315)	(3,978)	(5,251)	(1,399)	(3,852)	(3,807)	(961)	(2,846)
Committee to Integrate Academic Skills Into Into Vocational Curriculum ***	8.2%	7.9%	8.3%	7.7%	7.5%	7.8%	15.6%	14.4%	16.1%	13.4%	10.7%	14.3%	11.0%	11.4%	10.9%
	(31,071)	(7,383)	(23,689)	(26,876)	(6,361)	(20,515)	(1,822)	(490)	(1,332)	(1,637)	(331)	(1,306)	(737)	(201)	(536)
Other Curriculum Committee	27.3%	28.5%	26.9%	27.4%	29.0%	26.9%	22.9%	22.5%	23.1%	24.0%	23.7%	24.1%	36.8%	23.1%	41.7%
	(103,317)	(26,510)	(76,807)	(95,251)	(24,603)	(70,648)	(2,674)	(769)	(1,905)	(2,935)	(732)	(2,203)	(2,457)	(406)	(2,051)
Committee to Select Books and Materials	33.4%	32.2%	33.8%	33.8%	32.8%	34.1%	31.8%	24.9%	34.7%	27.1%	29.3%	26.3%	29.1%	24.6%	30.8%
	(126,522)	(30,030)	(96,492)	(117,558)	(27,844)	(89,714)	(3,714)	(850)	(2,864)	(3,306)	(904)	(2,402)	(1,944)	(432)	(1,512)
Education Technology Program +	32.3%	34.1%	31.7%	31.9%	33.9%	31.3%	35.3%	31.2%	36.9%	35.0%	38.9%	33.6%	41.5%	40.6%	41.8%
	(122,242)	(31,790)	(90,452)	(111,086)	(28,809)	(82,277)	(4,114)	(1,066)	(3,048)	(4,273)	(1,201)	(3,072)	(2,769)	(714)	(2,055)
Teaching Methods for Subject Program +++	54.9%	47.3%	57.4%	54.5%	46.4%	57.2%	58.1%	56.5%	58.7%	55.0%	46.3%	57.9%	67.4%	71.8%	65.8%
	(207,672)	(44,018)	(163,653)	(189,683)	(39,399)	(150,284)	(6,771)	(1,928)	(4,843)	(6,721)	(1,430)	(5,291)	(4,496)	(1,261)	(3,235)
In-depth Study in Subject Program ~~	24.3%	25.5%	24.0%	23.9%	24.1%	23.8%	28.0%	39.6%	23.2%	27.1%	34.4%	24.6%	38.7%	51.5%	34.1%
	(92,129)	(23,729)	(68,399)	(82,971)	(20,412)	(62,559)	(3,263)	(1,351)	(1,912)	(3,313)	(1,062)	(2,251)	(2,581)	(904)	(1,677)
Student Assessment Program *** +	36.5%	34.3%	37.2%	35.8%	33.6%	36.5%	49.8%	44.4%	52.0%	35.9%	31.7%	37.3%	47.1%	51.9%	45.3%
	(137,933)	(31,924)	(106,010)	(124,602)	(28,517)	(96,085)	(5,808)	(1,516)	(4,292)	(4,384)	(979)	(3,405)	(3,140)	(912)	(2,228)

Notes:

Columns do not sum to 100% as respondents may have more than one type of previous experience.

*** Test of statistical significance compares African Americans with Whites. *** p < .001, ** p < .01, * p < .05.

+++ Test of statistical significance compares White men with White women. +++ p < .001, ++ p < .01, + p < .05.

~~~ Test of statistical significance compares African American men with African American women. ~~~ p < .001, ~~ p < .01, ~ p < .05.

Tests of statistical significance calculated using adjusted sample weight to control for influence of large sample sizes.

Source: Schools and Staffing Survey, 1993-94.

Table 32. Average Annual Basic Salaries of Regular, Full-Time Public School Teachers by Age, School Level, Race, and Sex: 1993/94

(weighted sample size in parentheses)

Age	Total	Male	Female	White, Non-Hispanic Total	Male	Female	African American, Non-Hispanic Total	Male	Female	Hispanic Total	Male	Female	Other Total	Male	Female
Total Regular, Full-time Teachers	100.0% (2,329,730)	27.5% (639,910)	72.5% (1,689,820)	86.1% (2,005,720)	24.2% (564,897)	61.8% (1,440,823)	7.7% (180,084)	1.5% (34,476)	6.2% (145,608)	4.3% (100,829)	1.2% (28,469)	3.1% (72,360)	1.8% (43,097)	0.5% (12,068)	1.3% (31,029)
Total															
Total	$34,189 (2,329,730)	$36,220 (639,910)	$33,419 (1,689,820)	$34,247 (2,005,720)	$36,573 (564,897)	$33,335 (1,440,823)	$33,968 (180,084)	$33,170 (34,476)	$34,157 (145,608)	$33,113 (100,829)	$33,282 (28,469)	$33,046 (72,360)	$34,913 (43,097)	$35,332 (12,068)	$34,750 (31,029)
Under Age 30 * +++	$24,746 (255,938)	$24,199 (59,274)	$24,911 (196,664)	$24,665 (221,525)	$24,157 (50,847)	$24,816 (170,678)	$23,997 (12,096)	$24,773 (2,937)	$23,748 (9,159)	$25,847 (17,105)	$24,010 (4,189)	$26,442 (12,916)	$26,317 (5,212)	$25,171 (1,301)	$26,698 (3,911)
30 to 39 Years * ~	$29,297 (515,355)	$29,385 (135,851)	$29,265 (379,505)	$29,207 (437,638)	$29,399 (116,712)	$29,138 (320,926)	$29,892 (39,140)	$28,747 (8,162)	$30,194 (30,978)	$29,729 (28,240)	$29,523 (7,695)	$29,806 (20,545)	$29,638 (10,338)	$30,166 (3,282)	$29,392 (7,056)
40 to 49 Years *** +++	$35,781 (969,927)	$37,822 (265,148)	$35,014 (704,778)	$35,929 (846,630)	$38,208 (236,050)	$35,048 (610,580)	$34,420 (72,252)	$33,643 (13,401)	$34,597 (58,851)	$34,838 (34,615)	$34,733 (10,869)	$34,886 (23,746)	$36,150 (16,429)	$37,490 (4,828)	$35,593 (11,601)
50 Years or Older *** +++	$39,954 (588,510)	$42,992 (179,637)	$38,620 (408,873)	$40,056 (499,928)	$43,287 (161,288)	$38,517 (338,640)	$38,342 (56,596)	$38,627 (9,976)	$38,282 (46,620)	$40,787 (20,868)	$42,379 (5,716)	$40,186 (15,152)	$42,018 (11,118)	$42,764 (2,657)	$41,784 (8,461)
Elementary School															
Total	$33,553 (1,188,311)	$35,499 (133,774)	$33,307 (1,054,537)	$33,462 (1,008,692)	$35,889 (114,814)	$33,150 (893,878)	$34,560 (99,934)	$34,054 (7,833)	$34,603 (92,101)	$32,851 (56,472)	$31,782 (8,634)	$33,044 (47,838)	$34,923 (23,213)	$34,934 (2,493)	$34,921 (20,720)
Under Age 30	$24,897 (138,602)	$24,628 (16,719)	$24,934 (121,882)	$24,782 (120,080)	$24,427 (13,237)	$24,826 (106,843)	$23,955 (5,479)	$25,067 (1,132)	$23,665 (4,347)	$26,317 (10,225)	$25,514 (1,918)	$26,503 (8,307)	$26,478 (2,818)	$25,673 (432)	$26,624 (2,385)
30 to 39 Years * ++	$29,169 (262,369)	$28,065 (27,323)	$29,297 (235,047)	$29,061 (219,341)	$27,998 (22,880)	$29,185 (196,461)	$29,873 (21,316)	$29,199 (1,662)	$29,930 (19,654)	$29,809 (16,344)	$27,688 (2,278)	$30,152 (14,066)	$28,850 (5,368)	$29,113 (503)	$28,822 (4,865)
40 to 49 Years +++	$35,162 (497,145)	$38,002 (59,448)	$34,776 (437,698)	$35,207 (428,790)	$38,420 (52,171)	$34,762 (376,619)	$34,965 (41,075)	$35,649 (3,004)	$34,911 (38,071)	$34,050 (18,123)	$32,356 (2,909)	$34,374 (15,214)	$36,150 (9,156)	$39,225 (1,363)	$35,612 (7,793)
50 Years or Older +++	$38,896 (290,195)	$43,295 (30,284)	$38,383 (259,911)	$38,697 (240,480)	$43,439 (26,525)	$38,110 (213,955)	$38,969 (32,063)	$40,665 (2,035)	$38,854 (30,029)	$40,897 (11,781)	$44,644 (1,530)	$40,338 (10,251)	$42,614 (5,871)	$40,485 (195)	$42,687 (5,677)
Secondary School															
Total	$34,850 (1,141,419)	$36,411 (506,136)	$33,606 (635,283)	$35,041 (997,028)	$36,748 (450,083)	$33,637 (546,945)	$33,231 (80,150)	$32,911 (26,643)	$33,391 (53,507)	$33,447 (44,357)	$33,936 (19,835)	$33,051 (24,522)	$34,901 (19,884)	$35,435 (9,575)	$34,405 (10,309)
Under Age 30 ++	$24,567 (117,336)	$24,031 (42,554)	$24,872 (74,782)	$24,526 (101,445)	$24,062 (37,611)	$24,799 (63,834)	$24,031 (6,617)	$24,588 (1,805)	$23,823 (4,812)	$25,148 (6,880)	$22,740 (2,270)	$26,333 (4,610)	$26,126 (2,394)	$24,921 (868)	$26,812 (1,526)
30 to 39 Years ++ ~	$29,429 (252,986)	$29,718 (108,527)	$29,212 (144,459)	$29,354 (218,296)	$29,741 (93,831)	$29,063 (124,465)	$29,915 (17,824)	$28,631 (6,500)	$30,652 (11,324)	$29,620 (11,896)	$30,295 (5,417)	$29,055 (6,479)	$30,490 (4,970)	$30,357 (2,779)	$30,658 (2,191)
40 to 49 Years *** +++	$36,432 (472,783)	$37,770 (205,702)	$35,402 (267,081)	$36,670 (417,840)	$38,148 (183,879)	$35,508 (233,961)	$33,702 (31,176)	$33,063 (10,397)	$34,021 (20,779)	$35,703 (16,494)	$35,601 (7,961)	$35,798 (8,533)	$36,151 (7,273)	$36,807 (3,465)	$35,554 (3,808)
50 Years or Older *** +++	$40,984 (298,314)	$42,930 (149,353)	$39,032 (148,961)	$41,316 (259,447)	$43,257 (134,762)	$39,217 (124,685)	$37,524 (24,532)	$38,105 (7,941)	$37,246 (16,591)	$40,645 (9,088)	$41,552 (4,187)	$39,870 (4,901)	$41,352 (5,247)	$42,945 (2,463)	$39,943 (2,784)

Notes:

*** Test of statistical significance compares African Americans with Whites. *** $p < .001$, ** $p < .01$, * $p < .05$.

+++ Test of statistical significance compares White men with White women. +++ $p < .001$, ++ $p < .01$, + $p < .05$.

~~~ Test of statistical significance compares African American men with African American women. ~~~ $p < .001$, ~~ $p < .01$, ~ $p < .05$.

Tests of statistical significance calculated using adjusted sample weight to control for influence of large sample sizes.

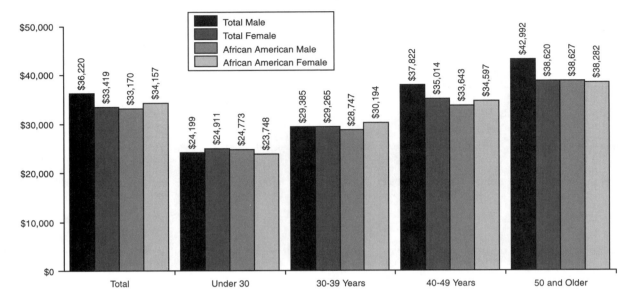

Figure 20. Average Annual Basic Salaries of Regular, Full-Time African American Public School Teachers by Age: 1993/94

Source: Schools and Staffing Survey, 1993 -94.

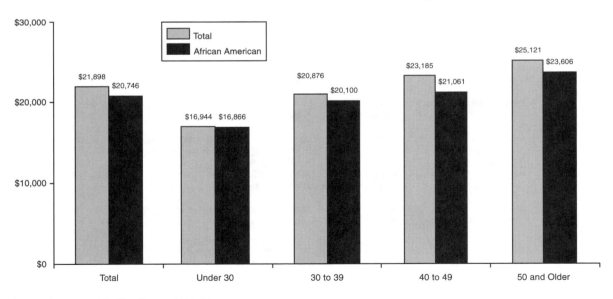

Figure 21. Average Annual Basic Salaries of Regular, Full-Time African American Private School Teachers by Age: 1993/94

Source: Schools and Staffing Survey, 1993 -94.

Table 33. Average Salaries of Regular, Full-Time Private School Teachers by Age, Race, and Sex: 1993/94
(weighted sample size in parentheses)

Age	Total	Male	Female	White, Non-Hispanic			African American, Non-Hispanic			Hispanic			Other		
				Total	Male	Female	Total	Male	Female	Total	Male	Female	Total	Male	Female
Total Regular, Full-Time Teachers	100.0% (302,165)	23.9% (72,101)	76.1% (230,065)	92.2% (278,507)	21.8% (65,957)	70.3% (212,550)	3.0% (8,938)	0.7% (2,238)	2.2% (6,700)	3.3% (9,863)	0.9% (2,665)	2.4% (7,198)	1.6% (4,858)	0.4% (1,241)	1.2% (3,617)
Total	$21,898 (302,165)	$25,978 (72,101)	$20,619 (230,065)	$21,930 (278,507)	$26,028 (65,957)	$20,659 (212,550)	$20,746 (8,938)	$25,725 (2,238)	$19,083 (6,700)	$20,513 (9,863)	$23,909 (2,665)	$19,255 (7,198)	$24,944 (4,858)	$28,215 (1,241)	$23,821 (3,617)
Under Age 30 +++	$16,944 (56,672)	$18,765 (11,823)	$16,463 (44,849)	$16,771 (52,357)	$18,666 (10,590)	$16,290 (41,767)	$16,866 (906)	$18,766 (362)	$15,603 (544)	$18,868 (2,397)	$19,492 (627)	$18,648 (1,770)	$21,408 (1,012)	$21,237 (244)	$21,463 (768)
30 to 39 Years +++ ~~	$20,876 (73,678)	$22,902 (21,617)	$20,035 (52,061)	$20,792 (65,607)	$22,740 (19,475)	$19,970 (46,132)	$20,100 (3,595)	$24,237 (931)	$18,654 (2,664)	$21,166 (3,182)	$23,651 (971)	$20,074 (2,211)	$26,605 (1,294)	$27,828 (240)	$26,326 (1,054)
40 to 49 Years +++ ~	$23,185 (102,219)	$28,649 (23,988)	$21,510 (78,231)	$23,269 (95,277)	$28,751 (22,155)	$21,608 (73,122)	$21,061 (2,693)	$26,870 (626)	$19,302 (2,067)	$20,639 (2,682)	$26,459 (605)	$18,945 (2,077)	$26,095 (1,567)	$28,936 (602)	$24,322 (965)
50 Years or Older +++ ~~	$25,121 (69,597)	$31,955 (14,673)	$23,295 (54,924)	$25,260 (65,266)	$31,974 (13,737)	$23,470 (51,529)	$23,606 (1,744)	$35,702 (319)	$20,897 (1,425)	$21,464 (1,602)	$27,110 (462)	$19,175 (1,140)	$24,562 (985)	$36,976 (155)	$22,242 (830)

Notes:
*** Test of statistical significance compares African Americans with Whites. *** p < .001, ** p < .01, * p < .05.
+++ Test of statistical significance compares White men with White women. +++ p < .001, ++ p < .01, + p < .05.
~~~ Test of statistical significance compares African American men with African American women. ~~~ p < .001, ~~ p < .01, ~ p < .05.
Tests of statistical significance calculated using adjusted sample weight to control for influence of large sample sizes.
Source: Schools and Staffing Survey, 1993-94.

secondary (**Table 40**: 79.8% versus 89.4%) school levels.

- Similar percentages of African American and White elementary (55.7% versus 52.6%) and secondary school (73.4% versus 70.8%) teachers indicated "racial tension" was a problem.

- A higher percentage of African American elementary school teachers than of their White peers indicated that the following were problems: teacher absenteeism (65.7% versus 48.4%), students possessing weapons (35.2% versus 26.7%), and students dropping out (25.7% versus 15.9%).

- A higher percentage of African American secondary school teachers than of White secondary

school teachers reported problems with students cutting class (87.5% versus 77.2%), teacher absenteeism (76.1% versus 62.3%), students possessing weapons (75.3% versus 67.9%), student pregnancy (83.3% versus 78.5%), and students dropping out (84.7% versus 78.0%).

Private Schools

The aspects of school life viewed by private school teachers as problems varied by racial group.

- **Table 41** shows that a higher share of African American than White private school teachers reported the following to be problems: teacher absenteeism (44.6% versus 31.5%), physical conflict among students (61.9% versus 49.7%),

Table 34. Average Annual Basic Salaries of Regular, Full-Time Public School Teachers by Urbanicity, School Level, Race, and Sex
(weighted sample size in parentheses)

Urbanicity	Total	Male	Female	White, Non-Hispanic Total	Male	Female	African American, Non-Hispanic Total	Male	Female	Hispanic Total	Male	Female	Other Total	Male	Female
Total Regular, Full-time Teachers	100.0% (2,329,730)	27.5% (639,910)	72.5% (1,689,820)	86.1% (2,005,720)	24.2% (564,897)	61.8% (1,440,823)	7.7% (180,084)	1.5% (34,476)	6.2% (145,608)	4.3% (100,829)	1.2% (28,469)	3.1% (72,360)	1.8% (43,097)	0.5% (12,068)	1.3% (31,029)
Total															
Total	$34,189 (2,329,730)	$36,220 (639,910)	$33,419 (1,689,820)	$34,247 (2,005,719)	$36,573 (564,897)	$33,335 (1,440,822)	$33,968 (180,084)	$33,170 (34,476)	$34,157 (145,608)	$33,113 (100,828)	$33,282 (28,468)	$33,046 (72,360)	$34,913 (43,097)	$35,332 (12,068)	$34,750 (31,029)
Urban *** +++ ~	$34,527 (662,540)	$36,433 (175,121)	$33,843 (487,419)	$34,504 (492,653)	$37,033 (136,847)	$33,531 (355,806)	$35,501 (99,785)	$34,590 (19,062)	$35,716 (80,723)	$32,882 (55,758)	$33,399 (15,346)	$32,685 (40,412)	$34,954 (14,344)	$36,301 (3,866)	$34,458 (10,478)
Suburban *** +++	$38,318 (719,843)	$41,473 (191,832)	$37,172 (528,011)	$38,564 (637,964)	$42,029 (174,335)	$37,261 (463,629)	$35,893 (39,519)	$35,212 (6,733)	$36,033 (32,786)	$36,313 (26,449)	$36,448 (6,439)	$36,270 (20,010)	$37,834 (15,911)	$36,322 (4,325)	$38,399 (11,586)
Rural *** +++	$30,814 (947,346)	$32,392 (272,956)	$30,175 (674,389)	$30,955 (875,102)	$32,577 (253,715)	$30,293 (621,387)	$28,354 (40,780)	$28,469 (8,681)	$28,322 (32,099)	$29,260 (18,621)	$29,964 (6,683)	$28,866 (11,938)	$31,246 (12,842)	$33,262 (3,877)	$30,375 (8,965)
Elementary School															
Total	$33,553 (1,188,311)	$35,499 (133,773)	$33,307 (1,054,538)	$33,462 (1,008,692)	$35,889 (114,814)	$33,150 (893,878)	$34,560 (99,933)	$34,054 (7,832)	$34,603 (92,101)	$32,851 (56,472)	$31,782 (8,634)	$33,044 (47,838)	$34,923 (23,214)	$34,934 (2,493)	$34,921 (20,721)
Urban *** +++ ~	$34,098 (360,205)	$36,013 (45,196)	$33,824 (315,009)	$33,870 (259,764)	$36,268 (34,406)	$33,503 (225,358)	$35,870 (58,863)	$37,919 (4,555)	$35,699 (54,308)	$32,751 (33,929)	$33,293 (5,362)	$32,649 (28,567)	$34,203 (7,650)	$32,729 (873)	$34,393 (6,777)
Suburban +++	$36,973 (355,484)	$38,418 (35,352)	$36,814 (320,132)	$36,983 (312,024)	$38,928 (32,056)	$36,760 (279,968)	$36,822 (20,064)	$33,641 (869)	$36,966 (19,195)	$36,362 (14,725)	$33,176 (1,595)	$36,749 (13,130)	$38,016 (8,671)	$33,831 (832)	$38,460 (7,839)
Rural *** +++	$30,566 (472,622)	$33,124 (53,226)	$30,241 (419,396)	$30,704 (436,904)	$33,606 (48,352)	$30,343 (388,552)	$28,726 (21,006)	$26,893 (2,408)	$28,964 (18,598)	$26,673 (7,818)	$25,623 (1,677)	$26,959 (6,141)	$31,830 (6,893)	$38,541 (788)	$30,964 (6,105)
Secondary School															
Total	$34,850 (1,141,418)	$36,411 (506,136)	$33,606 (635,282)	$35,041 (997,028)	$36,748 (450,083)	$33,637 (546,945)	$33,231 (80,150)	$32,911 (26,643)	$33,391 (53,507)	$33,447 (44,357)	$33,936 (19,835)	$33,051 (24,522)	$34,901 (19,883)	$35,435 (9,575)	$34,405 (10,308)
Urban +++ ~~	$35,038 (302,335)	$36,579 (129,926)	$33,877 (172,409)	$35,211 (232,890)	$37,290 (102,442)	$33,578 (130,448)	$34,970 (40,922)	$33,545 (14,507)	$35,752 (26,415)	$33,085 (21,829)	$33,457 (9,984)	$32,772 (11,845)	$35,813 (6,694)	$37,343 (2,993)	$34,577 (3,701)
Suburban *** +++	$39,630 (364,359)	$42,164 (156,480)	$37,723 (207,879)	$40,077 (325,940)	$42,727 (142,279)	$38,024 (183,661)	$34,934 (19,455)	$35,445 (5,864)	$34,714 (13,591)	$36,253 (11,724)	$37,526 (4,844)	$35,356 (6,880)	$37,617 (7,240)	$36,915 (3,493)	$38,271 (3,747)
Rural *** +++ ~	$31,061 (474,724)	$32,215 (219,730)	$30,066 (254,994)	$31,206 (438,198)	$32,335 (205,362)	$30,210 (232,836)	$27,958 (19,773)	$29,074 (6,272)	$27,439 (13,501)	$31,133 (10,804)	$31,418 (5,007)	$30,886 (5,797)	$30,570 (5,949)	$31,915 (3,089)	$29,117 (2,860)

Notes:

*** Test of statistical significance compares African Americans with Whites. *** p < .001, ** p < .01, * p < .05.

+++ Test of statistical significance compares White men with White women. +++ p < .001, ++ p < .01, + p < .05.

~~~ Test of statistical significance compares African American men with African American women. ~~~ p < .001, ~~ p < .01, ~ p < .05.

Tests of statistical significance calculated using adjusted sample weight to control for influence of large sample sizes.

Source: Schools and Staffing Survey, 1993-94.

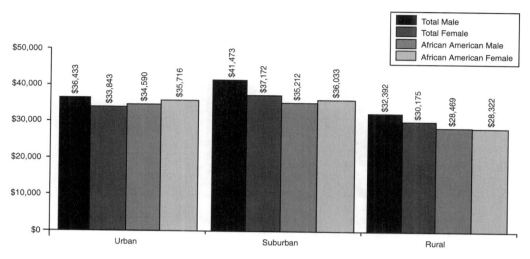

Figure 22. Average Annual Basic Salaries of Regular, Full-Time
African American Public School Teachers by Urbanicity: 1993/94

Source: Schools and Staffing Survey, 1993 -94.

Table 35. Average Salaries of Regular, Full-Time Private School Teachers by Urbanicity, Race, and Sex: 1993/94
(weighted sample size in parentheses)

Urbanicity	Total	Male	Female	White, Non-Hispanic			African American, Non-Hispanic			Hispanic			Other		
				Total	Male	Female	Total	Male	Female	Total	Male	Female	Total	Male	Female
Total Regular, Full-Time Teachers	100.0% (302,165)	23.8% (72,020)	76.2% (230,063)	92.2% (278,506)	21.8% (65,957)	70.4% (212,549)	2.9% (8,856)	0.7% (2,157)	2.2% (6,699)	3.3% (9,861)	0.9% (2,664)	2.4% (7,197)	1.6% (4,860)	0.4% (1,242)	1.2% (3,618)
Total	$21,898 (302,165)	$25,978 (72,020)	$20,619 (230,063)	$21,930 (278,506)	$26,028 (65,957)	$20,659 (212,549)	$20,746 (8,856)	$25,725 (2,157)	$19,083 (6,699)	$20,513 (9,861)	$23,909 (2,664)	$19,255 (7,197)	$24,944 (4,860)	$28,215 (1,242)	$23,821 (3,618)
Urban ** +++ ~~~	$22,639 (131,436)	$26,787 (31,902)	$21,309 (99,534)	$22,779 (116,160)	$26,858 (28,288)	$21,466 (87,872)	$20,311 (6,428)	$26,915 (1,407)	$18,461 (5,021)	$20,480 (5,930)	$23,827 (1,634)	$19,207 (4,296)	$26,587 (2,918)	$31,427 (573)	$25,405 (2,345)
Suburban +++	$22,855 (112,034)	$26,972 (25,974)	$21,612 (86,060)	$22,886 (105,272)	$27,179 (23,828)	$21,630 (81,444)	$22,473 (2,129)	$24,008 (750)	$1,639 (1,379)	$21,961 (2,948)	$24,109 (818)	$21,136 (2,130)	$22,986 (1,685)	$26,350 (578)	$21,228 (1,107)
Rural +++	$18,410 (58,613)	$22,349 (14,144)	$17,151 (44,469)	$18,442 (57,074)	$22,352 (13,841)	$17,191 (43,233)	$18,436 (299)	– –	$7,742 (299)	$16,364 (983)	$23,772 (212)	$14,326 (771)	$19,109 (257)	$19,811 (91)	$18,725 (166)

Notes:
" – " indicates sample size too small to estimate.
*** Test of statistical significance compares African Americans with Whites. *** p < .001, ** p < .01, * p < .05.
+++ Test of statistical significance compares White men with White women. +++ p < .001, ++ p < .01, + p < .05.
~~~ Test of statistical significance compares African American men with African American women. ~~~ p < .001, ~~ p < .01, ~ p < .05.
Tests of statistical significance calculated using adjusted sample weight to control for influence of large sample sizes.
Source: Schools and Staffing Survey, 1993-94.

Figure 23. Average Annual Basic Salaries of Regular, Full-Time African American Private School Teachers by Urbanicity: 1993/94

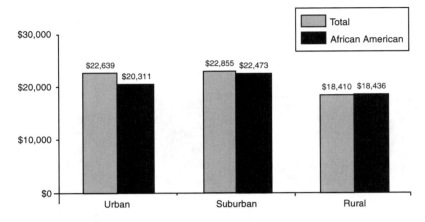

Source: Schools and Staffing Survey, 1993 -94.

Figure 24. Average Annual Basic Salaries of Regular, Full-Time African American Public School Teachers by Census Region: 1993/94

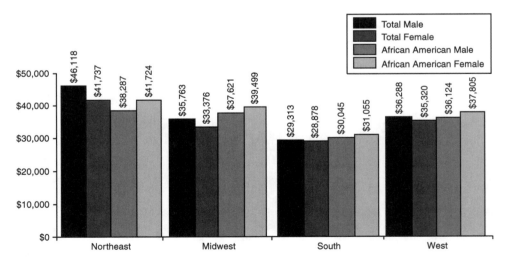

Source: Schools and Staffing Survey, 1993-94.

Table 36. Average Annual Basic Salaries of Regular, Full-Time Public School Teachers by Census Region, School Level, Race, and Sex
(weighted sample size in parentheses)

Region	Total	Male	Female	White, Non-Hispanic			African American, Non-Hispanic			Hispanic			Other		
				Total	Male	Female	Total	Male	Female	Total	Male	Female	Total	Male	Female
Total Regular, Full-time Teachers	100.0% (2,329,730)	27.5% (639,910)	72.5% (1,689,820)	86.1% (2,005,720)	24.2% (564,897)	61.8% (1,440,823)	7.7% (180,084)	1.5% (34,476)	6.2% (145,608)	4.3% (100,829)	1.2% (28,469)	3.1% (72,360)	1.8% (43,097)	0.5% (12,068)	1.3% (31,029)
Total															
Total	$34,189 (2,329,728)	$36,220 (639,909)	$33,419 (1,689,819)	$34,247 (2,005,718)	$36,573 (564,896)	$33,335 (1,440,822)	$33,968 (180,084)	$33,170 (34,476)	$34,157 (145,608)	$33,113 (100,829)	$33,282 (28,469)	$33,046 (72,360)	$34,913 (43,097)	$35,332 (12,068)	$34,750 (31,029)
Northeast *** +++ ~	$43,090 (455,950)	$46,118 (140,794)	$41,737 (315,156)	$43,358 (410,427)	$46,489 (131,108)	$41,888 (279,319)	$41,076 (23,058)	$38,287 (4,347)	$41,724 (18,711)	$38,990 (17,475)	$31,775 (3,823)	$38,254 (13,652)	$44,656 (4,990)	$47,770 (1,516)	$43,297 (3,474)
Midwest *** +++ ~	$34,142 (566,360)	$35,763 (181,618)	$33,376 (384,742)	$33,879 (525,520)	$35,692 (171,076)	$33,004 (354,444)	$39,082 (29,675)	$37,621 (6,589)	$39,499 (23,086)	$31,710 (6,728)	$29,981 (2,519)	$31,670 (4,209)	$35,931 (4,437)	$42,767 (1,434)	$32,667 (3,003)
South *** +++ ~	$28,972 (887,416)	$29,313 (190,961)	$28,878 (696,455)	$28,664 (719,578)	$29,211 (155,973)	$28,513 (563,605)	$30,880 (115,256)	$30,045 (19,920)	$31,055 (95,336)	$29,339 (42,004)	$34,481 (12,133)	$29,079 (29,871)	$27,638 (10,578)	$26,992 (2,935)	$27,886 (7,643)
West ** +++	$35,612 (420,002)	$36,288 (126,536)	$35,320 (293,466)	$35,592 (350,193)	$36,565 (106,739)	$35,166 (243,454)	$37,302 (12,095)	$36,124 (3,620)	$37,805 (8,475)	$34,997 (34,622)	$33,282 (9,994)	$35,207 (24,628)	$35,944 (23,092)	$34,516 (6,183)	$36,466 (16,909)
Elementary School															
Total	$33,553 (1,188,311)	$35,499 (133,774)	$33,606 (1,054,537)	$33,462 (1,008,692)	$35,889 (114,814)	$33,150 (893,878)	$34,560 (99,934)	$34,054 (7,833)	$34,603 (92,101)	$32,851 (56,472)	$31,782 (8,634)	$33,044 (47,838)	$34,923 (23,213)	$34,934 (2,493)	$34,921 (20,720)
Northeast +++	$42,034 (226,003)	$45,822 (31,950)	$41,411 (194,053)	$42,305 (199,907)	$46,249 (30,089)	$41,606 (169,818)	$41,087 (13,856)	$38,451 (630)	$41,213 (13,226)	$36,676 (9,794)	$34,706 (880)	$36,870 (8,914)	$46,750 (2,446)	$50,309 (351)	$46,154 (2,095)
Midwest *** +	$33,102 (277,189)	$33,832 (36,249)	$32,992 (240,941)	$32,644 (253,840)	$33,428 (33,489)	$32,525 (220,351)	$39,803 (18,025)	$41,117 (1,832)	$39,654 (16,193)	$31,117 (3,108)	$31,865 (722)	$30,891 (2,386)	$33,805 (2,217)	$41,496 (206)	$33,019 (2,011)
South *** ~~	$28,739 (457,881)	$28,447 (35,133)	$28,764 (422,750)	$28,328 (367,870)	$28,268 (26,758)	$28,333 (341,112)	$31,116 (61,819)	$28,547 (4,278)	$31,307 (57,541)	$29,384 (23,210)	$30,032 (3,646)	$29,264 (19,564)	$26,594 (4,984)	$25,306 (451)	$26,722 (4,533)
West ***	$35,369 (227,238)	$34,788 (30,444)	$35,459 (196,794)	$35,214 (187,075)	$34,852 (24,478)	$35,269 (162,597)	$39,044 (6,235)	$41,230 (1,093)	$38,579 (5,142)	$35,227 (20,361)	$32,888 (3,387)	$35,694 (16,974)	$36,032 (13,567)	$33,318 (1,486)	$36,366 (12,081)
Secondary School															
Total	$34,850 (1,141,418)	$36,411 (506,135)	$33,606 (635,283)	$35,041 (997,028)	$36,748 (450,083)	$33,637 (546,945)	$33,231 (80,150)	$32,911 (26,643)	$33,391 (53,507)	$33,447 (44,357)	$33,936 (19,835)	$33,051 (24,522)	$34,901 (19,884)	$35,435 (9,575)	$34,405 (10,309)
Northeast ** +++ ~~	$44,127 (229,947)	$46,204 (108,846)	$42,259 (121,101)	$44,358 (210,520)	$46,561 (101,019)	$42,327 (109,501)	$41,060 (9,201)	$38,260 (3,717)	$42,958 (5,484)	$41,940 (7,682)	$43,684 (2,944)	$40,857 (4,738)	$42,643 (2,544)	$47,007 (1,166)	$38,953 (1,378)
Midwest *** +++ ~	$35,138 (289,171)	$36,245 (145,369)	$34,019 (143,802)	$35,032 (271,681)	$36,243 (137,587)	$33,790 (134,094)	$37,966 (11,650)	$36,275 (4,757)	$39,134 (6,893)	$32,218 (3,620)	$31,739 (1,797)	$32,690 (1,823)	$38,053 (2,220)	$42,980 (1,228)	$31,954 (992)
South *** +++	$29,219 (429,535)	$29,508 (155,829)	$29,055 (273,706)	$29,015 (351,709)	$29,406 (129,216)	$28,788 (222,493)	$30,608 (53,438)	$30,454 (15,642)	$30,671 (37,796)	$29,284 (18,794)	$29,959 (8,487)	$28,728 (10,307)	$28,568 (5,594)	$27,297 (2,484)	$29,582 (3,110)
West +++	$35,898 (192,765)	$36,763 (96,091)	$35,038 (96,674)	$36,026 (163,118)	$37,075 (82,261)	$34,959 (80,857)	$35,449 (5,861)	$33,915 (2,527)	$36,611 (3,334)	$34,669 (14,262)	$35,298 (6,607)	$34,127 (7,655)	$35,818 (9,524)	$34,895 (4,696)	$36,716 (4,828)

Notes:

*** Test of statistical significance compares African Americans with Whites. *** p < .001, ** p < .01, * p < .05.

+++ Test of statistical significance compares White men with White women. +++ p < .001, ++ p < .01, + p < .05.

~~~ Test of statistical significance compares African American men with African American women. ~~~ p < .001, ~~ p < .01, ~ p < .05.

Tests of statistical significance calculated using adjusted sample weight to control for influence of large sample sizes.

Source: Schools and Staffing Survey, 1993-94.

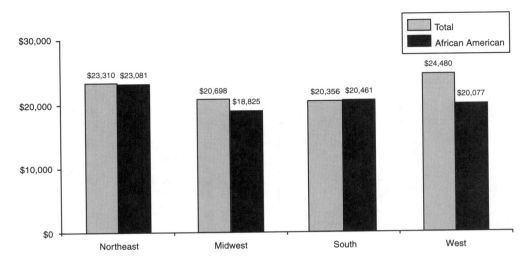

Figure 25. Average Annual Basic Salaries of Regular, Full-Time
African American Private School Teachers by Census Region: 1993/94

Source: Schools and Staffing Survey, 1993 -94.

Table 37. Average Salaries of Regular, Full-Time Private School Teachers by Region, Race, and Sex: 1993/94
(weighted sample size in parentheses)

Region	Total	Male	Female	White, Non-Hispanic			African American, Non-Hispanic			Hispanic			Other		
				Total	Male	Female	Total	Male	Female	Total	Male	Female	Total	Male	Female
Total Regular, Full-time Teachers	100.0% (302,165)	23.9% (72,103)	76.1% (230,063)	92.2% (278,508)	21.8% (65,958)	70.3% (212,550)	3.0% (8,938)	0.7% (2,238)	2.2% (6,700)	3.3% (9,861)	0.9% (2,665)	2.4% (7,196)	1.6% (4,859)	0.4% (1,242)	1.2% (3,617)
Total	$21,898 (302,165)	$25,978 (72,103)	$20,619 (230,063)	$21,930 (278,508)	$26,028 (65,958)	$20,659 (212,550)	$20,746 (8,938)	$25,725 (2,238)	$19,083 (6,700)	$20,513 (9,861)	$23,909 (2,665)	$19,255 (7,196)	$24,944 (4,859)	$28,215 (1,242)	$23,821 (3,617)
Northeast +++ ~	$23,310 (76,249)	$28,599 (19,982)	$21,431 (56,267)	$23,417 (70,836)	$28,695 (18,753)	$21,516 (52,083)	$23,081 (2,485)	$28,503 (514)	$21,668 (1,971)	$20,291 (1,902)	$27,601 (496)	$17,711 (1,406)	$22,090 (1,026)	$22,938 (219)	$21,859 (807)
Midwest +++	$20,698 (80,560)	$24,063 (18,131)	$19,721 (62,429)	$20,779 (77,249)	$24,131 (17,446)	$19,801 (59,803)	$18,825 (2,099)	$22,055 (395)	$18,077 (1,704)	$17,449 (707)	$20,269 (129)	$16,819 (578)	$20,750 (505)	$24,728 (161)	$18,891 (344)
South +++ ~~~	$20,356 (93,723)	$23,662 (21,108)	$19,395 (72,615)	$20,413 (85,290)	$23,708 (18,500)	$19,501 (66,790)	$20,461 (2,975)	$25,904 (1,015)	$17,641 (1,960)	$19,158 (4,713)	$21,264 (1,240)	$18,407 (3,473)	$20,993 (745)	$23,245 (353)	$18,968 (392)
West * +++	$24,480 (51,634)	$28,401 (12,882)	$23,177 (38,752)	$24,436 (45,133)	$28,339 (11,259)	$23,139 (33,874)	$20,077 (1,379)	$25,214 (314)	$18,561 (1,065)	$24,046 (2,539)	$26,306 (800)	$23,007 (1,739)	$28,036 (2,583)	$35,037 (509)	$26,319 (2,074)

Notes:
*** Test of statistical significance compares African Americans with Whites. *** p < .001, ** p < .01, * p < .05.
+++ Test of statistical significance compares White men with White women. +++ p < .001, ++ p < .01, + p < .05.
~~~ Test of statistical significance compares African American men with African American women. ~~~ p < .001, ~~ p < .01, ~ p < .05.
Tests of statistical significance calculated using adjusted sample weight to control for influence of large sample sizes.
Source: Schools and Staffing Survey, 1993-94.

Table 38. Number and Percentage of Public School Teachers Who Report Various Aspects of School Life to Be a "Problem" by Race and Sex: 1993/94
(weighted sample size in parentheses)

Aspect of School Life	Total	Male	Female	White, Non-Hispanic Total	Male	Female	African American, Non-Hispanic Total	Male	Female	Hispanic Total	Male	Female	Other Total	Male	Female
Total															
Total	100.0%	100.0%	100.0%	100.0%	100.0%	100.0%	100.0%	100.0%	100.0%	100.0%	100.0%	100.0%	100.0%	100.0%	100.0%
	(2,561,292)	(694,097)	(1,867,195)	(2,216,605)	(613,178)	(1,603,427)	(188,370)	(37,232)	(151,138)	(108,743)	(30,696)	(78,047)	(47,574)	(12,991)	(34,583)
Students Cut Class *** +++ ~~	49.8%	67.1%	43.4%	49.0%	66.6%	42.3%	54.4%	76.4%	49.0%	56.6%	65.4%	53.1%	55.1%	71.6%	48.9%
	(1,275,968)	(465,889)	(810,079)	(1,085,701)	(408,078)	(677,623)	(102,519)	(28,428)	(74,091)	(61,523)	(20,085)	(41,438)	(26,225)	(9,298)	(16,927)
Student Tardiness *** +++ ~	83.0%	85.7%	82.0%	82.5%	85.4%	81.4%	86.5%	89.4%	85.8%	86.7%	88.0%	86.2%	85.2%	84.5%	85.5%
	(2,126,045)	(594,853)	(1,531,192)	(1,828,296)	(523,603)	(1,304,693)	(162,956)	(33,269)	(129,687)	(94,255)	(27,000)	(67,255)	(40,538)	(10,981)	(29,557)
Student Absenteeism *** +++ ~	88.5%	91.3%	87.4%	88.1%	91.2%	86.9%	90.9%	93.1%	90.4%	90.9%	92.5%	90.3%	90.3%	90.1%	90.4%
	(2,265,704)	(633,822)	(1,631,882)	(1,952,664)	(559,058)	(1,393,606)	(171,229)	(34,659)	(136,570)	(98,843)	(28,403)	(70,440)	(42,968)	(11,702)	(31,266)
Teacher Absenteeism *** +++ ~	56.8%	59.2%	55.9%	55.1%	58.1%	54.0%	70.3%	73.9%	69.4%	66.3%	62.7%	67.8%	59.3%	62.5%	58.1%
	(1,454,584)	(411,199)	(1,043,385)	(1,221,793)	(356,304)	(865,489)	(132,431)	(27,527)	(104,904)	(72,139)	(19,248)	(52,891)	(28,221)	(8,120)	(20,101)
Verbal Abuse of Teachers +++ ~~~	76.5%	81.0%	74.8%	76.6%	80.7%	75.1%	76.5%	83.9%	74.6%	74.0%	81.9%	70.9%	76.2%	83.7%	73.4%
	(1,959,791)	(562,255)	(1,397,536)	(1,699,012)	(494,993)	(1,204,019)	(144,061)	(31,246)	(112,815)	(80,473)	(25,147)	(55,326)	(36,245)	(10,869)	(25,376)
Students Disrespectful of Teachers +++	89.1%	90.3%	88.7%	89.4%	90.4%	89.0%	88.5%	88.9%	88.4%	85.8%	90.2%	84.1%	87.4%	89.5%	86.6%
	(2,282,865)	(626,509)	(1,656,356)	(1,981,271)	(554,114)	(1,427,157)	(166,710)	(33,087)	(133,623)	(93,307)	(27,683)	(65,624)	(41,577)	(11,625)	(29,952)
Physical Conflict Among Students ***	84.7%	84.5%	84.7%	84.5%	84.1%	84.6%	87.4%	88.6%	87.2%	85.0%	87.1%	84.2%	82.8%	82.6%	82.9%
	(2,168,711)	(586,316)	(1,582,395)	(1,872,155)	(515,858)	(1,356,297)	(164,714)	(32,996)	(131,718)	(92,435)	(26,730)	(65,705)	(39,407)	(10,732)	(28,675)
Student Possession of Weapons *** +++ ~~	47.3%	56.4%	43.9%	46.7%	56.0%	43.2%	53.1%	62.7%	50.7%	49.2%	58.5%	45.6%	45.6%	51.4%	43.4%
	(1,211,122)	(391,316)	(819,806)	(1,035,833)	(343,308)	(692,525)	(100,050)	(23,358)	(76,692)	(53,533)	(17,969)	(35,564)	(21,706)	(6,681)	(15,025)
Robbery/Theft ** +++	74.2%	78.6%	72.5%	74.4%	78.9%	72.7%	72.3%	75.1%	71.6%	73.1%	78.7%	70.9%	74.4%	73.9%	74.6%
	(1,899,613)	(545,283)	(1,354,330)	(1,648,519)	(483,565)	(1,164,954)	(136,188)	(27,962)	(108,226)	(79,521)	(24,160)	(55,361)	(35,385)	(9,596)	(25,789)
Vandalism School Property +++ ~~~	77.0%	82.5%	74.9%	76.8%	82.1%	74.8%	76.4%	85.1%	74.3%	79.2%	85.6%	76.6%	82.3%	86.9%	80.6%
	(1,971,191)	(572,499)	(1,398,692)	(1,701,947)	(503,275)	(1,198,672)	(144,002)	(31,669)	(112,333)	(86,084)	(26,262)	(59,822)	(39,158)	(11,293)	(27,865)
Student Use of Alcohol *** +++ ~~~	53.1%	74.8%	45.0%	54.3%	75.9%	46.0%	44.9%	70.6%	38.6%	46.0%	61.8%	39.7%	47.1%	64.1%	40.7%
	(1,360,074)	(519,267)	(840,807)	(1,203,039)	(465,690)	(737,349)	(84,663)	(26,290)	(58,373)	(49,975)	(18,960)	(31,015)	(22,397)	(8,327)	(14,070)
Student Drug Abuse *** +++ ~~~	55.2%	75.8%	47.6%	56.1%	76.5%	48.2%	48.3%	73.0%	42.2%	52.3%	69.1%	45.7%	51.3%	67.2%	45.3%
	(1,414,603)	(526,332)	(888,271)	(1,242,419)	(469,219)	(773,200)	(90,911)	(27,174)	(63,737)	(56,890)	(21,211)	(35,679)	(24,383)	(8,728)	(15,655)
Student Pregnancy * +++ ~~~	43.8%	64.6%	36.0%	43.8%	65.0%	35.8%	46.0%	65.6%	41.2%	39.7%	57.4%	32.8%	39.5%	57.0%	33.0%
	(1,120,669)	(448,147)	(672,522)	(971,963)	(398,722)	(573,241)	(86,730)	(24,419)	(62,311)	(43,175)	(17,605)	(25,570)	(18,801)	(7,401)	(11,400)
Student Dropping Out *** +++ ~~~	46.6%	67.1%	39.0%	46.1%	66.8%	38.2%	52.0%	73.8%	46.7%	48.1%	65.8%	41.2%	48.2%	63.8%	42.3%
	(1,194,768)	(465,752)	(729,016)	(1,021,493)	(409,775)	(611,718)	(98,043)	(27,490)	(70,553)	(52,317)	(20,198)	(32,119)	(22,915)	(8,289)	(14,626)
Student Apathy *** +++ ~~~	87.4%	92.7%	85.4%	88.0%	92.9%	86.1%	82.9%	90.0%	81.1%	84.4%	93.8%	80.7%	83.3%	89.3%	81.0%
	(2,237,493)	(643,329)	(1,594,164)	(1,949,948)	(569,413)	(1,380,535)	(156,148)	(33,525)	(122,623)	(91,767)	(28,790)	(62,977)	(39,630)	(11,601)	(28,029)
Students Come Unprepared to Learn ** +++ ~~~	94.1%	95.3%	93.6%	94.1%	95.1%	93.8%	92.9%	96.0%	92.2%	95.3%	97.9%	94.2%	92.5%	94.4%	91.8%
	(2,409,213)	(661,326)	(1,747,887)	(2,086,553)	(583,260)	(1,503,293)	(175,056)	(35,740)	(139,316)	(103,610)	(30,063)	(73,547)	(43,994)	(12,263)	(31,731)
Lack of Academic Challenge +++ ~~~	69.7%	77.0%	67.0%	69.5%	76.8%	66.6%	69.3%	76.4%	67.5%	74.5%	79.5%	72.6%	72.1%	81.3%	68.6%
	(1,785,530)	(534,495)	(1,251,035)	(1,539,693)	(471,106)	(1,068,587)	(130,508)	(28,428)	(102,080)	(81,032)	(24,397)	(56,635)	(34,297)	(10,564)	(23,733)
Lack of Parental Involvement +++ ~~	87.8%	90.8%	86.7%	87.8%	90.7%	86.7%	87.5%	90.7%	86.7%	88.9%	91.7%	87.9%	87.2%	92.6%	85.2%
	(2,249,567)	(630,259)	(1,619,308)	(1,946,602)	(556,318)	(1,390,284)	(164,741)	(33,762)	(130,979)	(96,726)	(28,145)	(68,581)	(41,498)	(12,034)	(29,464)

—continued next page

Table 38.—*continued from previous page*

Aspect of School Life	Total	Male	Female	White, Non-Hispanic			African American, Non-Hispanic			Hispanic			Other		
				Total	Male	Female	Total	Male	Female	Total	Male	Female	Total	Male	Female
Parental Alcoholism or Drug Abuse *** +++ ~	88.2% (2,259,049)	90.6% (628,705)	87.3% (1,630,344)	88.7% (1,966,833)	90.9% (557,551)	87.9% (1,409,282)	82.0% (154,528)	85.6% (31,888)	81.1% (122,640)	89.2% (97,030)	90.1% (27,669)	88.9% (69,361)	85.5% (40,658)	89.3% (11,597)	84.0% (29,061)
Poverty *** ++	89.3% (2,288,164)	88.9% (617,037)	89.5% (1,671,127)	89.0% (1,972,723)	88.3% (541,547)	89.3% (1,431,176)	91.3% (171,913)	92.6% (34,495)	90.9% (137,418)	92.7% (100,822)	94.8% (29,096)	91.9% (71,726)	89.8% (42,706)	91.6% (11,899)	89.1% (30,807)
Poor Student Nutrition ** ++	82.4% (2,111,186)	81.8% (567,760)	82.7% (1,543,426)	82.4% (1,827,375)	81.6% (500,172)	82.8% (1,327,203)	80.6% (151,871)	82.9% (30,861)	80.1% (121,010)	85.2% (92,607)	84.5% (25,940)	85.4% (66,667)	82.7% (39,333)	83.0% (10,787)	82.5% (28,546)
Poor Student Health	78.3% (2,004,366)	77.9% (540,971)	78.4% (1,463,395)	78.0% (1,729,275)	77.5% (475,222)	78.2% (1,254,053)	78.2% (147,340)	80.8% (30,083)	77.6% (117,257)	82.6% (89,859)	82.3% (25,256)	82.8% (64,603)	79.6% (37,892)	80.1% (10,410)	79.5% (27,482)
Racial Tension * +++	62.1% (1,591,206)	64.0% (444,288)	61.4% (1,146,918)	61.4% (1,362,050)	63.3% (387,967)	60.8% (974,083)	63.6% (119,768)	65.8% (24,503)	63.0% (95,265)	70.0% (76,088)	73.4% (22,529)	68.6% (53,559)	70.0% (33,300)	71.5% (9,289)	69.4% (24,011)

Notes:
*** Test of statistical significance compares African Americans with Whites. *** p < .001, ** p < .01, * p < .05.
+++ Test of statistical significance compares White men with White women. +++ p < .001, ++ p < .01, + p < .05.
~~~ Test of statistical significance compares African American men with African American women. ~~~ p < .001, ~~ p < .01, ~ p < .05.
Tests of statistical significance calculated using adjusted sample weight to control for influence of large sample sizes.
Source: Schools and Staffing Survey, 1993-94.

poverty (56.1% versus 42.1%), and poor student nutrition (44.4% versus 32.1%).

- A lower share of African Americans than Whites agreed that the following aspects of school life were problems: robbery or theft (31.8% versus 40.5%), vandalism of school property (36.2% versus 46.4%), student use of alcohol (16.7% versus 32.2%), student drug abuse (16.6% versus 29.0%), and student apathy (53.1% versus 65.6%).

JOB SATISFACTION OF TEACHERS

Public Schools

Figure 27 shows that a higher percentage of women than men indicated that they would "certainly become a teacher" again if they could go back to their college days overall (40.0% versus 32.6%) and among African Americans (42.3% versus 34.5%).

Among elementary school teachers, the percentage of African Americans who were certain they would *not* become a teacher again was twice as large as the percentage of Whites (9.4% versus 4.1%).

- **Table 42** shows that, among elementary school teachers, 13.4% of African American men and 9.0% of African American women would certainly *not* become teachers again, compared with 7.2% of White men and 3.7% of White women.

Private Schools

Figure 27 shows that about one-half of all private school teachers (47.4% of all men and 53.6% of all women) indicated that they would certainly become teachers again if they could go back to their college days.

Table 43 shows similar percentages of African Americans and Whites reported that they would certainly become teachers again (60.7% versus 51.9%).

Table 39. Number and Percentage of Elementary Public School Teachers Who Report Various Aspects of School Life to Be a "Problem" by Race and Sex: 1993/94
(weighted sample size in parentheses)

Aspect of School Life	Total	Male	Female	White, Non-Hispanic			African American, Non-Hispanic			Hispanic			Other		
				Total	Male	Female	Total	Male	Female	Total	Male	Female	Total	Male	Female
Elementary															
Total	100.0%	100.0%	100.0%	100.0%	100.0%	100.0%	100.0%	100.0%	100.0%	100.0%	100.0%	100.0%	100.0%	100.0%	100.0%
	(1,331,281)	(154,788)	(1,176,493)	(1,139,263)	(133,204)	(1,006,059)	(104,246)	(8,821)	(95,425)	(61,648)	(9,752)	(51,896)	(26,124)	(3,011)	(23,113)
Students Cut Class *** +++	23.4%	26.7%	22.9%	22.3%	26.6%	21.7%	27.7%	30.8%	27.4%	33.4%	22.7%	35.4%	30.7%	31.9%	30.5%
	(311,083)	(41,375)	(269,708)	(253,604)	(35,488)	(218,116)	(28,872)	(2,714)	(26,158)	(20,597)	(2,212)	(18,385)	(8,010)	(961)	(7,049)
Student Tardiness *** +++ ~	75.2%	67.2%	76.2%	74.2%	66.0%	75.3%	80.8%	74.5%	81.4%	81.6%	75.2%	82.8%	81.4%	73.7%	82.4%
	(1,000,919)	(104,032)	(896,887)	(845,164)	(87,902)	(757,262)	(84,208)	(6,576)	(77,632)	(50,280)	(7,336)	(42,944)	(21,267)	(2,218)	(19,049)
Student Absenteeism *** ++	82.3%	79.9%	82.6%	81.6%	79.4%	81.9%	85.9%	82.1%	86.2%	86.7%	83.8%	87.3%	87.5%	85.7%	87.8%
	(1,095,342)	(123,746)	(971,596)	(929,517)	(105,748)	(823,769)	(89,499)	(7,246)	(82,253)	(53,464)	(8,173)	(45,291)	(22,862)	(2,579)	(20,283)
Teacher Absenteeism *** +	50.6%	48.7%	50.9%	48.4%	46.4%	48.6%	65.7%	62.9%	65.9%	66.2%	64.5%	66.5%	53.7%	56.7%	53.4%
	(674,124)	(75,396)	(598,728)	(550,851)	(61,851)	(489,000)	(68,446)	(5,549)	(62,897)	(40,787)	(6,289)	(34,498)	(14,040)	(1,707)	(12,333)
Verbal Abuse of Teachers ++	66.4%	64.4%	66.6%	66.5%	63.8%	66.8%	66.6%	62.9%	66.9%	63.4%	69.0%	62.3%	67.5%	77.9%	66.2%
	(883,510)	(99,647)	(783,863)	(757,398)	(85,021)	(672,377)	(69,404)	(5,551)	(63,853)	(39,071)	(6,728)	(32,343)	(17,637)	(2,347)	(15,290)
Students Disrespectful of Teachers * +++ ~~~	84.9%	82.3%	85.2%	85.3%	83.0%	85.6%	83.5%	71.3%	84.6%	80.4%	83.1%	79.9%	83.3%	84.1%	83.2%
	(1,130,185)	(127,450)	(1,002,735)	(971,814)	(110,522)	(861,292)	(87,034)	(6,289)	(80,745)	(49,574)	(8,107)	(41,467)	(21,763)	(2,532)	(19,231)
Physical Conflict Among Students * +++ ~	80.3%	76.1%	80.8%	80.1%	75.8%	80.7%	82.5%	76.8%	83.0%	80.0%	79.7%	80.0%	78.6%	75.6%	79.0%
	(1,068,624)	(117,796)	(950,828)	(912,820)	(100,971)	(811,849)	(85,964)	(6,774)	(79,190)	(49,294)	(7,774)	(41,520)	(20,546)	(2,277)	(18,269)
Student Possession of Weapons *** ++	27.5%	24.7%	27.8%	26.7%	24.0%	27.0%	35.2%	32.6%	35.4%	28.5%	27.5%	28.7%	29.1%	19.8%	30.4%
	(365,829)	(38,176)	(327,653)	(303,994)	(32,023)	(271,971)	(36,665)	(2,874)	(33,791)	(17,556)	(2,684)	(14,872)	(7,614)	(595)	(7,019)
Robbery/Theft ++	63.7%	61.8%	64.0%	63.6%	61.2%	63.9%	64.0%	57.7%	64.6%	63.2%	72.4%	61.5%	69.6%	68.8%	69.7%
	(848,517)	(95,693)	(752,824)	(724,697)	(81,475)	(643,222)	(66,695)	(5,089)	(61,606)	(38,950)	(7,056)	(31,894)	(18,175)	(2,073)	(16,102)
Vandalism School Property ~	67.5%	67.5%	67.6%	67.0%	65.5%	67.2%	68.2%	75.4%	67.5%	71.9%	81.1%	70.2%	78.7%	89.0%	77.4%
	(899,275)	(104,436)	(794,839)	(763,274)	(87,197)	(676,077)	(71,112)	(6,653)	(64,459)	(44,320)	(7,906)	(36,414)	(20,569)	(2,680)	(17,889)
Student Use of Alcohol *** +++ ~~~	20.5%	23.5%	20.1%	21.0%	24.0%	20.6%	16.8%	28.1%	15.8%	16.9%	15.7%	17.2%	19.3%	13.1%	20.1%
	(272,574)	(36,313)	(236,261)	(239,579)	(31,911)	(207,668)	(17,507)	(2,476)	(15,031)	(10,445)	(1,532)	(8,913)	(5,043)	(394)	(4,649)
Student Drug Abuse ** ++ ~~~	23.8%	27.3%	23.4%	24.1%	26.8%	23.7%	21.3%	41.1%	19.5%	23.1%	24.8%	22.8%	24.5%	18.1%	25.3%
	(317,347)	(42,250)	(275,097)	(274,451)	(35,668)	(238,783)	(22,256)	(3,622)	(18,634)	(14,243)	(2,414)	(11,829)	(6,397)	(546)	(5,851)
Student Pregnancy *** +	11.4%	12.4%	11.2%	11.0%	12.6%	10.8%	15.9%	14.4%	16.1%	10.3%	10.3%	10.2%	10.5%	5.0%	11.2%
	(151,444)	(19,194)	(132,250)	(125,766)	(16,771)	(108,995)	(16,625)	(1,269)	(15,356)	(6,320)	(1,003)	(5,317)	(2,733)	(151)	(2,582)
Student Dropping Out *** +++ ~~	17.0%	20.7%	16.6%	15.9%	19.2%	15.4%	25.7%	36.2%	24.7%	22.0%	26.7%	21.2%	22.4%	25.1%	22.0%
	(226,911)	(32,085)	(194,826)	(180,690)	(25,531)	(155,159)	(26,780)	(3,190)	(23,590)	(13,589)	(2,608)	(10,981)	(5,852)	(756)	(5,096)
Student Apathy ***	78.8%	78.9%	78.8%	79.6%	79.2%	79.7%	73.2%	69.0%	73.6%	75.7%	83.9%	74.2%	74.4%	79.5%	73.7%
	(1,049,234)	(122,131)	(927,103)	(906,826)	(105,467)	(801,359)	(76,294)	(6,083)	(70,211)	(46,679)	(8,186)	(38,493)	(19,435)	(2,395)	(17,040)
Students Come Unprepared to Learn * +++	91.1%	89.5%	91.3%	91.1%	89.1%	91.4%	89.6%	86.8%	89.9%	93.0%	97.0%	92.2%	89.2%	88.7%	89.3%
	(1,212,408)	(138,474)	(1,073,934)	(1,038,345)	(118,683)	(919,662)	(93,423)	(7,659)	(85,764)	(57,331)	(9,460)	(47,871)	(23,309)	(2,672)	(20,637)
Lack of Academic Challenge +++	60.1%	63.4%	59.7%	59.6%	62.9%	59.1%	61.0%	57.5%	61.4%	67.7%	73.5%	66.6%	61.8%	68.2%	61.0%
	(800,173)	(98,151)	(702,022)	(678,651)	(83,849)	(594,802)	(63,628)	(5,076)	(58,552)	(41,742)	(7,172)	(34,570)	(16,152)	(2,054)	(14,098)
Lack of Parental Involvement +	82.7%	81.5%	82.9%	82.6%	81.1%	82.9%	83.0%	78.4%	83.5%	84.8%	88.5%	84.1%	80.6%	85.8%	79.9%
	(1,101,485)	(126,113)	(975,372)	(941,571)	(107,979)	(833,592)	(86,569)	(6,917)	(79,652)	(52,296)	(8,635)	(43,661)	(21,049)	(2,582)	(18,467)

—continued next page

Table 39.—continued from previous page

Aspect of School Life	Total	Male	Female	White, Non-Hispanic			African American, Non-Hispanic			Hispanic			Other		
				Total	Male	Female	Total	Male	Female	Total	Male	Female	Total	Male	Female
Parental Alcoholism or Drug Abuse *** ++	84.1% (1,119,889)	82.6% (127,904)	84.3% (991,985)	84.6% (964,027)	82.6% (110,075)	84.9% (853,952)	78.1% (81,456)	80.4% (7,091)	77.9% (74,365)	86.2% (53,123)	83.7% (8,158)	86.6% (44,965)	81.5% (21,283)	85.7% (2,580)	80.9% (18,703)
Poverty * +++	87.9% (1,169,724)	84.8% (131,208)	88.3% (1,038,516)	87.4% (995,638)	83.6% (111,345)	87.9% (884,293)	89.2% (92,951)	87.6% (7,725)	89.3% (85,226)	94.3% (58,150)	96.8% (9,444)	93.9% (48,706)	88.0% (22,985)	89.5% (2,694)	87.8% (20,291)
Poor Student Nutrition *** +++	81.1% (1,079,692)	78.4% (121,402)	81.5% (958,290)	81.2% (925,267)	77.9% (103,791)	81.7% (821,476)	77.7% (80,964)	76.8% (6,775)	77.7% (74,189)	85.1% (52,476)	87.4% (8,523)	84.7% (43,953)	80.3% (20,985)	76.8% (2,313)	80.8% (18,672)
Poor Student Health +++	76.0% (1,012,126)	72.6% (112,358)	76.5% (899,768)	75.7% (862,144)	71.3% (94,986)	76.3% (767,158)	75.5% (78,748)	75.1% (6,625)	75.6% (72,123)	83.1% (51,218)	87.5% (8,536)	82.2% (42,682)	76.6% (20,016)	73.4% (2,211)	77.0% (17,805)
Racial Tension ** +++	53.5% (712,184)	49.4% (76,389)	54.0% (635,795)	52.6% (598,819)	47.5% (63,224)	53.2% (535,595)	55.7% (58,039)	59.8% (5,277)	55.3% (52,762)	63.3% (39,012)	63.3% (6,173)	63.3% (32,839)	62.4% (16,314)	57.0% (1,715)	63.2% (14,599)

Notes:

*** Test of statistical significance compares African Americans with Whites. *** p < .001, ** p < .01, * p < .05.

+++ Test of statistical significance compares White men with White women. +++ p < .001, ++ p < .01, + p < .05.

~~~ Test of statistical significance compares African American men with African American women. ~~~ p < .001, ~~ p < .01, ~ p < .05.

Tests of statistical significance calculated using adjusted sample weight to control for influence of large sample sizes.

Source: Schools and Staffing Survey, 1993-94.

Table 40. Number and Percentage of Secondary Public School Teachers Who Report Various Aspects of School Life to Be a "Problem" by Race and Sex: 1993/94
(weighted sample size in parentheses)

Aspect of School Life	Total	Male	Female	White, Non-Hispanic Total	Male	Female	African American, Non-Hispanic Total	Male	Female	Hispanic Total	Male	Female	Other Total	Male	Female
Secondary															
Total	100.0%	100.0%	100.0%	100.0%	100.0%	100.0%	100.0%	100.0%	100.0%	100.0%	100.0%	100.0%	100.0%	100.0%	100.0%
	(1,230,012)	(539,309)	(690,703)	(1,077,342)	(479,974)	(597,368)	(84,124)	(28,411)	(55,713)	(47,096)	(20,944)	(26,152)	(21,450)	(9,980)	(11,470)
Students Cut Class *** ~	78.4%	78.7%	78.2%	77.2%	77.6%	76.9%	87.5%	90.5%	86.0%	86.9%	85.3%	88.2%	84.9%	83.5%	86.1%
	(964,886)	(424,515)	(540,371)	(832,096)	(372,589)	(459,507)	(73,647)	(25,714)	(47,933)	(40,927)	(17,874)	(23,053)	(18,216)	(8,338)	(9,878)
Student Tardiness ** +	91.5%	91.0%	91.8%	91.3%	90.8%	91.6%	93.6%	94.0%	93.4%	93.4%	93.9%	93.0%	89.8%	87.8%	91.6%
	(1,125,127)	(490,821)	(634,306)	(983,132)	(435,701)	(547,431)	(78,748)	(26,693)	(52,055)	(43,976)	(19,664)	(24,312)	(19,271)	(8,763)	(10,508)
Student Absenteeism *** ++	95.2%	94.6%	95.6%	95.0%	94.4%	95.4%	97.2%	96.5%	97.5%	96.4%	96.6%	96.2%	93.7%	91.4%	95.8%
	(1,170,362)	(510,075)	(660,287)	(1,023,146)	(453,309)	(569,837)	(81,731)	(27,413)	(54,318)	(45,379)	(20,230)	(25,149)	(20,106)	(9,123)	(10,983)
Teacher Absenteeism *** +	63.5%	62.3%	64.4%	62.3%	61.3%	63.0%	76.1%	77.4%	75.4%	66.6%	61.9%	70.3%	66.1%	64.3%	67.7%
	(780,460)	(335,804)	(444,656)	(670,943)	(294,454)	(376,489)	(63,984)	(21,978)	(42,006)	(31,352)	(12,959)	(18,393)	(14,181)	(6,413)	(7,768)
Verbal Abuse of Teachers +++	87.5%	85.8%	88.8%	87.4%	85.4%	89.0%	88.7%	90.4%	87.9%	87.9%	87.9%	87.9%	86.8%	85.4%	87.9%
	(1,076,282)	(462,609)	(613,673)	(941,614)	(409,972)	(531,642)	(74,657)	(25,695)	(48,962)	(41,403)	(18,420)	(22,983)	(18,608)	(8,522)	(10,086)
Students Disrespectful of Teachers +++	93.7%	92.5%	94.6%	93.7%	92.4%	94.7%	94.7%	94.3%	94.9%	92.9%	93.5%	92.4%	92.4%	91.1%	93.5%
	(1,152,679)	(499,058)	(653,621)	(1,009,457)	(443,592)	(565,865)	(79,676)	(26,798)	(52,878)	(43,733)	(19,576)	(24,157)	(19,813)	(9,092)	(10,721)
Physical Conflict Among Students *** +++	89.4%	86.9%	91.4%	89.0%	86.4%	91.1%	93.6%	92.3%	94.3%	91.6%	90.5%	92.5%	87.9%	84.7%	90.7%
	(1,100,089)	(468,521)	(631,568)	(959,336)	(414,888)	(544,448)	(78,750)	(26,222)	(52,528)	(43,141)	(18,956)	(24,185)	(18,862)	(8,455)	(10,407)
Student Possession of Weapons *** +++ ~	68.7%	65.5%	71.3%	67.9%	64.9%	70.4%	75.3%	72.1%	77.0%	76.4%	73.0%	79.1%	65.7%	61.0%	69.8%
	(845,293)	(353,139)	(492,154)	(731,839)	(311,285)	(420,554)	(63,385)	(20,484)	(42,901)	(35,976)	(15,284)	(20,692)	(14,093)	(6,086)	(8,007)
Robbery/Theft ** +++	85.5%	83.4%	87.1%	85.8%	83.8%	87.3%	82.6%	80.5%	83.7%	86.1%	81.7%	89.7%	80.2%	75.4%	84.5%
	(1,051,095)	(449,588)	(601,507)	(923,821)	(402,089)	(521,732)	(69,492)	(22,872)	(46,620)	(40,571)	(17,104)	(23,467)	(17,211)	(7,523)	(9,688)
Vandalism School Property	87.1%	86.8%	87.4%	87.1%	86.7%	87.5%	86.6%	88.1%	85.9%	88.7%	87.6%	89.5%	86.7%	86.3%	87.0%
	(1,071,920)	(468,064)	(603,856)	(938,673)	(416,078)	(522,595)	(72,891)	(25,016)	(47,875)	(41,765)	(18,356)	(23,409)	(18,591)	(8,614)	(9,977)
Student Use of Alcohol *** +++	88.4%	89.6%	87.5%	89.4%	90.4%	88.7%	79.8%	83.8%	77.8%	83.9%	83.2%	84.5%	80.9%	79.5%	82.1%
	(1,087,499)	(482,954)	(604,545)	(963,460)	(433,779)	(529,681)	(67,156)	(23,814)	(43,342)	(39,530)	(17,428)	(22,102)	(17,353)	(7,933)	(9,420)
Student Drug Abuse *** +	89.2%	89.8%	88.8%	89.8%	90.3%	89.5%	81.6%	82.9%	81.0%	90.6%	89.7%	91.2%	83.9%	82.0%	85.5%
	(1,097,258)	(484,083)	(613,175)	(967,968)	(433,551)	(534,417)	(68,656)	(23,553)	(45,103)	(42,647)	(18,797)	(23,850)	(17,987)	(8,182)	(9,805)
Student Pregnancy *** +	78.8%	79.5%	78.2%	78.5%	79.6%	77.7%	83.3%	81.5%	84.3%	78.3%	79.3%	77.4%	74.9%	72.6%	76.9%
	(969,226)	(428,953)	(540,273)	(846,198)	(381,952)	(464,246)	(70,106)	(23,150)	(46,956)	(36,854)	(16,601)	(20,253)	(16,068)	(7,250)	(8,818)
Student Dropping Out *** +++	78.7%	80.4%	77.3%	78.0%	80.1%	76.4%	84.7%	85.5%	84.3%	82.2%	84.0%	80.8%	79.5%	75.5%	83.1%
	(967,857)	(433,668)	(534,189)	(840,803)	(384,244)	(456,559)	(71,264)	(24,301)	(46,963)	(38,727)	(17,590)	(21,137)	(17,063)	(7,533)	(9,530)
Student Apathy *** ~	96.6%	96.6%	96.6%	96.8%	96.7%	97.0%	94.9%	96.6%	94.1%	95.7%	98.4%	93.6%	94.1%	92.2%	95.8%
	(1,188,257)	(521,196)	(667,061)	(1,043,121)	(463,945)	(579,176)	(79,854)	(27,442)	(52,412)	(45,087)	(20,603)	(24,484)	(20,195)	(9,206)	(10,989)
Students Come Unprepared to Learn +++ ~~	97.3%	96.9%	97.6%	97.3%	96.8%	97.7%	97.0%	98.8%	96.1%	98.3%	98.4%	98.2%	96.4%	96.1%	96.7%
	(1,196,807)	(522,853)	(673,954)	(1,048,208)	(464,577)	(583,631)	(81,634)	(28,081)	(53,553)	(46,279)	(20,603)	(25,676)	(20,686)	(9,592)	(11,094)
Lack of Academic Challenge +	80.1%	80.9%	79.5%	79.9%	80.7%	79.3%	79.5%	82.2%	78.1%	83.4%	82.2%	84.4%	84.6%	85.3%	84.0%
	(985,356)	(436,344)	(549,012)	(861,042)	(387,257)	(473,785)	(66,879)	(23,351)	(43,528)	(39,291)	(17,226)	(22,065)	(18,144)	(8,510)	(9,634)
Lack of Parental Involvement	93.3%	93.5%	93.2%	93.3%	93.4%	93.2%	92.9%	94.5%	92.1%	94.3%	93.2%	95.3%	95.3%	94.7%	95.9%
	(1,148,083)	(504,146)	(643,937)	(1,005,031)	(448,339)	(556,692)	(78,171)	(26,845)	(51,326)	(44,431)	(19,510)	(24,921)	(20,450)	(9,452)	(10,998)

—continued next page

265

Table 40.—*continued from previous page*

Aspect of School Life	Total	Male	Female	White, Non-Hispanic			African American, Non-Hispanic			Hispanic			Other		
				Total	Male	Female	Total	Male	Female	Total	Male	Female	Total	Male	Female
Parental Alcoholism or Drug Abuse ***	92.6% (1,139,160)	92.9% (500,801)	92.4% (638,359)	93.1% (1,002,806)	93.2% (447,476)	93.0% (555,330)	86.9% (73,072)	87.3% (24,797)	86.6% (48,275)	93.2% (43,907)	93.2% (19,511)	93.3% (24,396)	90.3% (19,375)	90.4% (9,017)	90.3% (10,358)
Poverty *** +++	90.9% (1,118,440)	90.1% (485,828)	91.6% (632,612)	90.7% (977,086)	89.6% (430,202)	91.5% (546,884)	93.9% (78,961)	94.2% (26,769)	93.7% (52,192)	90.6% (42,672)	93.8% (19,652)	88.0% (23,020)	91.9% (19,721)	92.2% (9,205)	91.7% (10,516)
Poor Student Nutrition +++	83.9% (1,031,496)	82.8% (446,360)	84.7% (585,136)	83.7% (902,109)	82.6% (396,382)	84.7% (505,727)	84.3% (70,908)	84.8% (24,087)	84.0% (46,821)	85.2% (40,131)	83.2% (17,417)	86.9% (22,714)	85.5% (18,348)	84.9% (8,474)	86.1% (9,874)
Poor Student Health +++	80.7% (992,241)	79.5% (428,613)	81.6% (563,628)	80.5% (867,131)	79.2% (380,236)	81.5% (486,895)	81.5% (68,592)	82.6% (23,458)	81.0% (45,134)	82.0% (38,641)	79.8% (16,720)	83.8% (21,921)	83.3% (17,877)	82.2% (8,199)	84.4% (9,678)
Racial Tension * +++ ~~~	71.5% (879,018)	68.2% (367,897)	74.0% (511,121)	70.8% (763,231)	67.7% (324,743)	73.4% (438,488)	73.4% (61,728)	67.7% (19,225)	76.3% (42,503)	78.7% (37,075)	78.1% (16,356)	79.2% (20,719)	79.2% (16,984)	75.9% (7,573)	82.0% (9,411)

Notes:
*** Test of statistical significance compares African Americans with Whites. *** p < .001, ** p < .01, * p < .05.
+++ Test of statistical significance compares White men with White women. +++ p < .001, ++ p < .01, + p < .05.
~~~ Test of statistical significance compares African American men with African American women. ~~~ p < .001, ~~ p < .01, ~ p < .05.
Tests of statistical significance calculated using adjusted sample weight to control for influence of large sample sizes.
Source: Schools and Staffing Survey, 1993–94.

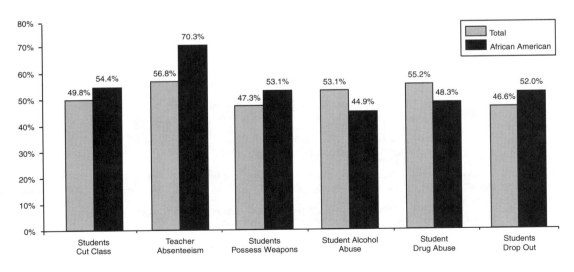

Figure 26. Percentage of Public School Teachers Who Report Various Aspects of School Life to Be a "Problem": 1993/94

Source: Schools and Staffing Survey, 1993 -94.

Table 41. Number and Percentage of Private School Teachers Who Report Various Aspects of School Life to Be a "Problem" by Race and Sex: 1993/94

(weighted sample size in parentheses)

Aspect of School Life	Total	Male	Female	White, Non-Hispanic Total	Male	Female	African American, Non-Hispanic Total	Male	Female	Hispanic Total	Male	Female	Other Total	Male	Female
Total															
Total	100.0% (378,365)	100.0% (93,130)	100.0% (285,235)	100.0% (347,812)	100.0% (84,873)	100.0% (262,939)	100.0% (11,664)	100.0% (3,413)	100.0% (8,251)	100.0% (12,221)	100.0% (3,088)	100.0% (9,133)	100.0% (6,670)	100.0% (1,757)	100.0% (4,913)
Students Cut Class +++ ~~	19.6% (73,987)	30.8% (28,638)	15.9% (45,350)	19.2% (66,656)	30.3% (25,754)	15.6% (40,902)	18.0% (2,095)	30.1% (1,028)	12.9% (1,067)	28.6% (3,495)	41.5% (1,281)	24.2% (2,214)	26.1% (1,744)	32.8% (576)	23.8% (1,168)
Student Tardiness ++	66.6% (252,026)	68.7% (63,957)	65.9% (188,068)	66.2% (230,305)	68.7% (58,296)	65.4% (172,009)	68.5% (7,994)	60.8% (2,074)	71.7% (5,920)	72.8% (8,894)	69.8% (2,154)	73.8% (6,740)	72.5% (4,834)	81.6% (1,434)	69.2% (3,400)
Student Absenteeism +++	63.2% (239,178)	67.6% (62,915)	61.8% (176,262)	62.7% (217,958)	67.1% (56,957)	61.2% (161,001)	67.7% (7,900)	63.2% (2,157)	69.6% (5,743)	69.3% (8,473)	77.4% (2,389)	66.6% (6,084)	72.7% (4,848)	80.4% (1,413)	69.9% (3,435)
Teacher Absenteeism *** ++	32.6% (123,310)	35.2% (32,791)	31.7% (90,520)	31.5% (109,686)	34.0% (28,859)	30.7% (80,827)	44.6% (5,204)	45.4% (1,551)	44.3% (3,653)	49.5% (6,045)	53.7% (1,658)	48.0% (4,387)	35.7% (2,378)	41.2% (724)	33.7% (1,654)
Verbal Abuse of Teachers ++	37.4% (141,687)	39.9% (37,161)	36.6% (104,526)	37.3% (129,652)	40.0% (33,972)	36.4% (95,680)	36.4% (4,249)	29.5% (1,007)	39.3% (3,242)	39.9% (4,872)	42.7% (1,318)	38.9% (3,554)	43.7% (2,916)	49.2% (865)	41.7% (2,051)
Students Disrespectful of Teachers	64.2% (243,008)	63.1% (58,795)	64.6% (184,214)	64.2% (223,457)	63.4% (53,785)	64.5% (169,672)	60.0% (6,996)	54.4% (1,858)	62.3% (5,138)	63.2% (7,729)	61.0% (1,884)	64.0% (5,845)	72.4% (4,829)	72.2% (1,269)	72.5% (3,560)
Physical Conflict Among Students *** +++	50.3% (190,301)	46.3% (43,137)	51.6% (147,165)	49.7% (172,873)	45.9% (38,930)	50.9% (133,943)	61.9% (7,225)	53.1% (1,813)	65.6% (5,412)	50.3% (6,143)	45.5% (1,406)	51.9% (4,737)	60.9% (4,063)	56.3% (989)	62.6% (3,074)
Student Possession of Weapons +++	9.2% (34,724)	13.0% (12,120)	7.9% (22,604)	9.0% (31,352)	12.7% (10,819)	7.8% (20,533)	9.3% (1,082)	10.5% (360)	8.8% (722)	9.6% (1,179)	15.0% (463)	7.8% (716)	16.7% (1,113)	27.3% (479)	12.9% (634)
Robbery/Theft ** +++ ~	40.7% (154,005)	51.9% (48,306)	37.1% (105,699)	40.5% (140,983)	51.6% (43,814)	37.0% (97,169)	31.8% (3,708)	40.9% (1,396)	28.0% (2,312)	49.7% (6,077)	60.1% (1,855)	46.2% (4,222)	48.6% (3,239)	70.7% (1,242)	40.6% (1,997)
Vandalism School Property ** ++	46.1% (174,500)	54.4% (50,624)	43.4% (123,875)	46.4% (161,476)	54.5% (46,284)	43.8% (115,192)	36.2% (4,222)	33.4% (1,141)	37.3% (3,081)	45.0% (5,502)	60.5% (1,867)	39.8% (3,635)	49.5% (3,301)	75.9% (1,333)	40.1% (1,968)
Student Use of Alcohol *** +++	31.9% (120,693)	52.5% (48,856)	25.2% (71,838)	32.2% (112,167)	52.9% (44,860)	25.6% (67,307)	16.7% (1,943)	32.6% (1,111)	10.1% (832)	34.3% (4,192)	63.1% (1,950)	24.5% (2,242)	35.9% (2,394)	53.3% (936)	29.7% (1,458)
Student Drug Abuse *** +++ ~	28.8% (109,140)	47.2% (43,941)	22.9% (65,200)	29.0% (100,845)	47.5% (40,335)	23.0% (60,510)	16.6% (1,932)	30.8% (1,051)	10.7% (881)	31.7% (3,869)	53.8% (1,660)	24.2% (2,209)	37.4% (2,497)	51.0% (896)	32.6% (1,601)
Student Pregnancy * +++	12.9% (48,998)	20.2% (18,775)	10.6% (30,224)	12.9% (45,009)	20.4% (17,274)	10.5% (27,735)	8.5% (994)	8.4% (287)	8.6% (707)	12.8% (1,567)	22.1% (683)	9.7% (884)	21.5% (1,431)	30.3% (532)	18.3% (899)
Student Dropping Out +++	16.8% (63,511)	25.3% (23,568)	14.0% (39,942)	16.2% (56,182)	24.9% (21,134)	13.3% (35,048)	16.7% (1,952)	18.5% (633)	16.0% (1,319)	27.9% (3,407)	34.5% (1,064)	25.7% (2,343)	29.6% (1,971)	42.0% (738)	25.1% (1,233)
Student Apathy *** +++	65.3% (247,136)	73.5% (68,429)	62.7% (178,706)	65.6% (228,241)	74.1% (62,857)	62.9% (165,384)	53.1% (6,193)	52.0% (1,776)	53.5% (4,417)	65.9% (8,052)	72.7% (2,245)	63.6% (5,807)	69.7% (4,651)	88.3% (1,552)	63.1% (3,099)
Students Come Unprepared to Learn +++	66.1% (250,267)	72.4% (67,469)	64.1% (182,798)	65.9% (229,079)	72.2% (61,285)	63.8% (167,794)	67.7% (7,894)	73.8% (2,520)	65.1% (5,374)	67.3% (8,230)	76.0% (2,348)	64.4% (5,882)	76.0% (5,066)	75.0% (1,317)	76.3% (3,749)
Lack of Academic Challenge +++	40.9% (154,651)	45.4% (42,271)	39.4% (112,379)	40.4% (140,567)	45.6% (38,731)	38.7% (101,836)	42.6% (4,971)	35.0% (1,194)	45.8% (3,777)	45.6% (5,568)	41.5% (1,283)	46.9% (4,285)	53.2% (3,546)	60.6% (1,064)	50.5% (2,482)
Lack of Parental Involvement * ++	50.8% (192,026)	55.9% (52,103)	49.1% (139,923)	50.3% (174,827)	55.8% (47,325)	48.5% (127,502)	57.7% (6,730)	52.7% (1,798)	59.8% (4,932)	51.3% (6,272)	56.9% (1,758)	49.4% (4,514)	63.0% (4,199)	69.6% (1,223)	60.6% (2,976)

—continued next page

Table 41.—*continued from previous page*

Aspect of School Life	Total	Male	Female	White, Non-Hispanic			African American, Non-Hispanic			Hispanic			Other		
				Total	Male	Female	Total	Male	Female	Total	Male	Female	Total	Male	Female
Parental Alcoholism or Drug Abuse ** +++	48.1% (182,108)	54.9% (51,157)	45.9% (130,949)	48.5% (168,579)	55.0% (46,715)	46.3% (121,864)	38.5% (4,491)	49.8% (1,700)	33.8% (2,791)	44.4% (5,423)	54.2% (1,674)	41.0% (3,749)	54.2% (3,615)	60.8% (1,069)	51.8% (2,546)
Poverty ***	42.5% (160,880)	42.6% (39,661)	42.5% (121,219)	42.1% (146,464)	42.1% (35,725)	42.1% (110,739)	56.1% (6,541)	54.8% (1,871)	56.6% (4,670)	39.0% (4,761)	41.4% (1,278)	38.1% (3,483)	46.7% (3,116)	44.8% (788)	47.4% (2,328)
Poor Student Nutrition ***	32.8% (124,072)	33.3% (31,029)	32.6% (93,043)	32.1% (111,677)	32.5% (27,550)	32.0% (84,127)	44.4% (5,175)	42.3% (1,443)	45.2% (3,732)	32.2% (3,933)	36.3% (1,120)	30.8% (2,813)	49.3% (3,289)	52.2% (917)	48.3% (2,372)
Poor Student Health *	30.7% (116,183)	31.3% (29,125)	30.5% (87,059)	30.1% (104,781)	30.4% (25,810)	30.0% (78,971)	37.5% (4,374)	35.4% (1,209)	38.4% (3,165)	29.8% (3,646)	39.6% (1,223)	26.5% (2,423)	50.7% (3,385)	50.3% (884)	50.9% (2,501)
Racial Tension +++	28.8% (108,795)	35.6% (33,162)	26.5% (75,632)	28.7% (99,848)	35.3% (30,002)	26.6% (69,846)	25.8% (3,004)	33.1% (1,130)	22.7% (1,874)	27.2% (3,328)	36.0% (1,112)	24.3% (2,216)	39.2% (2,616)	52.3% (919)	34.5% (1,697)

Notes:

*** Test of statistical significance compares African Americans with whites. *** p < .001, ** p < .01, * p < .05.

+++ Test of statistical significance compares white men with white women. +++ p < .001, ++ p < .01, + p < .05.

~~~ Test of statistical significance compares African American men with African American women. ~~~ p < .001, ~~ p < .01, ~ p < .05.

Tests of statistical significance calculated using adjusted sample weight to control for influence of large sample sizes.

Source: Schools and Staffing Survey, 1993-94.

Figure 27. Percentage of Public and Private School Teachers Who Would Certainly Become Teachers Again If They Could Go Back to Their College Days: 1993/94

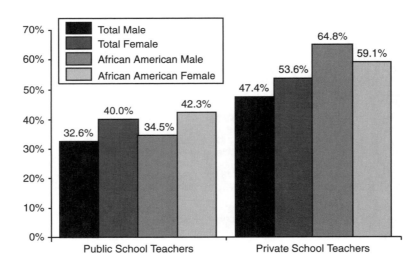

Source: Schools and Staffing Survey, 1993 -94.

Table 42. Number and Percentage of Public School Teachers Who Would Be a Teacher If They Could Go Back to Their College Days, by School Level, Race, and Sex: 1993/94
(weighted sample size in parentheses)

Become a Teacher Again	Total	Male	Female	White, Non-Hispanic			African American, Non-Hispanic			Hispanic			Other		
				Total	Male	Female	Total	Male	Female	Total	Male	Female	Total	Male	Female
Total															
Total *** +++ ~~	100.0%	100.0%	100.0%	100.0%	100.0%	100.0%	100.0%	100.0%	100.0%	100.0%	100.0%	100.0%	100.0%	100.0%	100.0%
	(2,561,294)	(694,098)	(1,867,195)	(2,216,604)	(613,178)	(1,603,426)	(188,371)	(37,233)	(151,138)	(108,744)	(30,696)	(78,048)	(47,574)	(12,991)	(34,583)
Certainly	38.0%	32.6%	40.0%	37.4%	32.4%	39.3%	40.8%	34.5%	42.3%	44.0%	34.0%	48.0%	41.3%	34.1%	44.0%
	(972,624)	(226,196)	(746,429)	(828,247)	(198,483)	(629,764)	(76,849)	(12,849)	(64,000)	(47,891)	(10,434)	(37,457)	(19,638)	(4,430)	(15,208)
Probably	26.0%	25.5%	26.2%	26.8%	25.9%	27.1%	20.8%	23.8%	20.1%	22.3%	22.7%	22.1%	21.5%	19.2%	22.4%
	(666,735)	(177,253)	(489,482)	(593,066)	(158,931)	(434,135)	(39,205)	(8,849)	(30,356)	(24,212)	(6,975)	(17,237)	(10,252)	(2,498)	(7,754)
Chances About Even	16.7%	18.8%	15.9%	16.7%	18.6%	16.0%	15.9%	18.7%	15.2%	16.6%	20.0%	15.3%	18.8%	24.1%	16.8%
	(427,871)	(130,456)	(297,416)	(370,818)	(114,201)	(256,617)	(30,023)	(6,979)	(23,044)	(18,095)	(6,141)	(11,954)	(8,936)	(3,135)	(5,801)
Probably Not	13.8%	15.4%	13.1%	14.0%	15.7%	13.3%	13.4%	13.8%	13.3%	10.7%	13.8%	9.6%	12.4%	12.5%	12.3%
	(352,376)	(106,981)	(245,395)	(309,549)	(95,995)	(213,554)	(25,241)	(5,132)	(20,109)	(11,687)	(4,225)	(7,462)	(5,899)	(1,629)	(4,270)
Certainly Not	5.5%	7.7%	4.7%	5.2%	7.4%	4.3%	9.1%	9.2%	9.0%	6.3%	9.5%	5.0%	6.0%	10.0%	4.5%
	(141,687)	(53,212)	(88,476)	(114,926)	(45,569)	(69,357)	(17,053)	(3,423)	(13,630)	(6,859)	(2,921)	(3,938)	(2,850)	(1,299)	(1,551)
Elementary															
Total *** +++ ~~~	100.0%	100.0%	100.0%	100.0%	100.0%	100.0%	100.0%	100.0%	100.0%	100.0%	100.0%	100.0%	100.0%	100.0%	100.0%
	(1,331,281)	(154,788)	(1,176,493)	(1,139,263)	(133,204)	(1,006,059)	(104,246)	(8,821)	(95,425)	(61,648)	(9,752)	(51,896)	(26,124)	(3,011)	(23,113)
Certainly	41.5%	34.1%	42.4%	41.1%	34.5%	42.0%	42.6%	36.5%	43.2%	44.6%	28.9%	47.5%	43.3%	25.8%	45.6%
	(551,902)	(52,803)	(499,101)	(468,687)	(45,988)	(422,699)	(44,443)	(3,221)	(41,222)	(27,467)	(2,818)	(24,649)	(11,307)	(776)	(10,531)
Probably	26.4%	26.3%	26.5%	27.3%	27.3%	27.3%	21.1%	22.8%	20.9%	21.9%	20.5%	22.1%	20.5%	15.5%	21.1%
	(352,013)	(40,776)	(311,236)	(311,188)	(36,303)	(274,885)	(21,999)	(2,012)	(19,987)	(13,471)	(1,995)	(11,476)	(5,354)	(466)	(4,888)
Chances About Even	15.1%	17.4%	14.8%	15.1%	16.7%	14.8%	14.0%	21.9%	13.3%	16.2%	18.3%	15.8%	19.2%	28.8%	18.0%
	(201,189)	(26,867)	(174,323)	(171,582)	(22,275)	(149,307)	(14,588)	(1,936)	(12,652)	(9,994)	(1,789)	(8,205)	(5,026)	(867)	(4,159)
Probably Not	12.3%	13.9%	12.1%	12.4%	14.3%	12.2%	12.9%	5.3%	13.6%	10.3%	15.1%	9.3%	11.8%	16.7%	11.2%
	(164,301)	(21,476)	(142,826)	(141,465)	(19,026)	(122,439)	(13,422)	(469)	(12,953)	(6,321)	(1,477)	(4,844)	(3,094)	(504)	(2,590)
Certainly Not	4.6%	8.3%	4.2%	4.1%	7.2%	3.7%	9.4%	13.4%	9.0%	7.1%	17.2%	5.2%	5.1%	13.3%	4.1%
	(61,875)	(12,868)	(49,008)	(46,341)	(9,612)	(36,729)	(9,794)	(1,183)	(8,611)	(4,397)	(1,674)	(2,723)	(1,344)	(399)	(945)
Secondary															
Total *** +++ ~	100.0%	100.0%	100.0%	100.0%	100.0%	100.0%	100.0%	100.0%	100.0%	100.0%	100.0%	100.0%	100.0%	100.0%	100.0%
	(1,230,013)	(539,310)	(690,703)	(1,077,342)	(479,974)	(597,368)	(84,125)	(28,412)	(55,713)	(47,096)	(20,944)	(26,152)	(21,450)	(9,980)	(11,470)
Certainly	34.2%	32.2%	35.8%	33.4%	31.8%	34.7%	38.5%	33.9%	40.9%	43.4%	36.4%	49.0%	38.8%	36.6%	40.8%
	(420,722)	(173,393)	(247,329)	(359,561)	(152,495)	(207,066)	(32,406)	(9,628)	(22,778)	(20,424)	(7,616)	(12,808)	(8,331)	(3,654)	(4,677)
Probably	25.6%	25.3%	25.8%	26.2%	25.5%	26.7%	20.5%	24.1%	18.6%	22.8%	23.8%	22.0%	22.8%	20.4%	25.0%
	(314,722)	(136,477)	(178,244)	(281,878)	(122,628)	(159,250)	(17,204)	(6,836)	(10,368)	(10,741)	(4,980)	(5,761)	(4,898)	(2,033)	(2,865)
Chances About Even	18.4%	19.2%	17.8%	18.5%	19.2%	18.0%	18.3%	17.7%	18.7%	17.2%	20.8%	14.3%	18.2%	22.7%	14.3%
	(226,682)	(103,590)	(123,093)	(199,236)	(91,926)	(107,310)	(15,435)	(5,043)	(10,392)	(8,102)	(4,353)	(3,749)	(3,910)	(2,268)	(1,642)
Probably Not	15.3%	15.9%	14.8%	15.6%	16.0%	15.3%	14.0%	16.4%	12.8%	11.4%	13.1%	10.0%	13.1%	11.3%	14.6%
	(188,075)	(85,505)	(102,569)	(168,083)	(76,969)	(91,114)	(11,819)	(4,663)	(7,156)	(5,367)	(2,748)	(2,619)	(2,805)	(1,125)	(1,680)
Certainly Not	6.5%	7.5%	5.7%	6.4%	7.5%	5.5%	8.6%	7.9%	9.0%	5.2%	6.0%	4.6%	7.0%	9.0%	5.3%
	(79,812)	(40,345)	(39,468)	(68,585)	(35,957)	(32,628)	(7,260)	(2,241)	(5,019)	(2,462)	(1,247)	(1,215)	(1,506)	(900)	(606)

Notes:

*** Test of statistical significance compares African Americans with whites. *** p < .001, ** p < .01, * p < .05.

+++ Test of statistical significance compares white men with white women. +++ p < .001, ++ p < .01, + p < .05.

~~~ Test of statistical significance compares African American men with African American women. ~~~ p < .001, ~~ p < .01, ~ p < .05.

Tests of statistical significance calculated using adjusted sample weight to control for influence of large sample sizes.

Source: Schools and Staffing Survey, 1993-94.

Table 43. Number and Percentage of Private School Teachers Who Would Be a Teacher If They Could Go Back to Their College Days, by Race and Sex: 1993/94
(weighted sample size in parentheses)

Become a Teacher Again	Total	Male	Female	White, Non-Hispanic			African American, Non-Hispanic			Hispanic			Other		
				Total	Male	Female	Total	Male	Female	Total	Male	Female	Total	Male	Female
Total +++	100.0%	100.0%	100.0%	100.0%	100.0%	100.0%	100.0%	100.0%	100.0%	100.0%	100.0%	100.0%	100.0%	100.0%	100.0%
	(378,365)	(93,130)	(285,235)	(347,812)	(84,873)	(262,939)	(11,664)	(3,413)	(8,251)	(12,221)	(3,088)	(9,133)	(6,670)	(1,757)	(4,913)
Certainly	52.1%	47.4%	53.6%	51.9%	47.1%	53.5%	60.7%	64.8%	59.1%	49.6%	45.1%	51.1%	49.2%	33.9%	54.7%
	(197,034)	(44,158)	(152,875)	(180,604)	(39,959)	(140,645)	(7,085)	(2,210)	(4,875)	(6,060)	(1,393)	(4,667)	(3,284)	(596)	(2,688)
Probably	26.3%	26.8%	26.1%	26.4%	27.3%	26.2%	22.9%	20.7%	23.7%	25.2%	18.9%	27.4%	26.4%	27.9%	25.8%
	(99,475)	(24,934)	(74,540)	(91,964)	(23,151)	(68,813)	(2,666)	(708)	(1,958)	(3,083)	(584)	(2,499)	(1,761)	(491)	(1,270)
Chances About Even	12.7%	15.2%	11.9%	12.8%	15.5%	12.0%	9.9%	9.2%	10.2%	11.8%	13.3%	11.2%	14.3%	16.1%	13.6%
	(48,204)	(14,181)	(34,024)	(44,662)	(13,174)	(31,488)	(1,154)	(313)	(841)	(1,437)	(411)	(1,026)	(952)	(283)	(669)
Probably Not	6.8%	7.9%	6.5%	6.8%	7.6%	6.5%	4.9%	3.9%	5.3%	10.7%	18.5%	8.1%	5.2%	8.5%	4.0%
	(25,714)	(7,311)	(18,402)	(23,490)	(6,457)	(17,033)	(567)	(133)	(434)	(1,309)	(572)	(737)	(347)	(149)	(198)
Certainly Not	2.1%	2.7%	1.9%	2.0%	2.5%	1.9%	1.6%	1.4%	1.7%	2.7%	4.1%	2.2%	4.9%	13.5%	1.8%
	(7,939)	(2,544)	(5,394)	(7,091)	(2,131)	(4,960)	(191)	(49)	(142)	(331)	(127)	(204)	(325)	(237)	(88)

Notes:
*** Test of statistical significance compares African Americans with whites. *** p < .001, ** p < .01, * p < .05.
+++ Test of statistical significance compares white men with white women. +++ p < .001, ++ p < .01, + p < .05.
~~~ Test of statistical significance compares African American men with African American women. ~~~ p < .001, ~~ p < .01, ~ p < .05.
Tests of statistical significance calculated using adjusted sample weight to control for influence of large sample sizes.
Source: Schools and Staffing Survey, 1993-94.

CHAPTER IX.
Indicators of the Quality of Elementary and Secondary School Teachers

---

What percentage of the nation's African American teachers receive their bachelor's degrees from Historically Black Colleges and Universities? How well do African Americans score on teacher certification examinations relative to their White counterparts? Is the level of education attained by African American teachers comparable to that of White teachers? What kinds of support do African Americans receive to further develop and enhance their teaching abilities? In what kinds of professional development activities do African American teachers engage?

The U.S. Department of Education's National Center for Education Statistics sponsors two surveys that provide some data describing the "quality" of America's teachers. Based upon a nationally representative sample of public school teachers, the Schools and Staffing Survey (SASS) includes the names of the institutions from which teachers received their undergraduate degrees. The National Educational Longitudinal Study of 1988 8th graders (NELS:88) includes data on the education and training of students' teachers as reported by the teachers themselves.

Standardized test data provide another indicator of teacher quality. Before granting licensure or certification to teach, many states require individuals to pass a standardized test. The PRAXIS program (known as the National Teacher's Examination [NTE] prior to 1993) has three parts: (a) Pre-Professional Skills Tests and Computer-Based Testing Program; (b) NTE Core Battery tests, Subject Assessment/Specialty Area tests, Multiple Subjects Assessment for Teachers, and Principles of Learning and Teaching test; and (c) Classroom Performance Assessment for beginning teachers. This chapter presents scores on the three tests that constitute the NTE Core Battery tests: General Knowledge, Communications Skills, and Professional Knowledge. Subject Assessment/Specialty Area test scores are not shown since these tests tend to have small numbers of cases, particularly when divided by race and ethnicity. Because the Pre-Professional Skills Tests are administered at an earlier stage in an individual's career than the NTE Core Battery tests, the NTE Core Battery tests provide a better picture of the education and training of the nation's newest teachers.

CHAPTER ORGANIZATION

This chapter examines the quality of America's school teachers from three perspectives:

1. Distribution of public school teachers nationwide in 1993/94 by the type of undergraduate institution they attended;

2. Characteristics of the teachers who taught America's 1990 10th graders; and

3. Performance of teachers on standardized tests that are required to gain licensure or certification to teach.

PART I — OVERVIEW

Historically Black Colleges and Universities (HBCUs) play a vital role in training America's African American public school teachers. More than one-half (53.4%) of African American public school teachers in 1993/94 received their undergraduate degrees from HBCUs. Interestingly, the percentage of African American public school teachers who received their undergraduate degrees from HBCUs increased with the percentage of African American students enrolled at the schools.

On average, the level of education attained by the teachers of African American 10th graders was comparable to the level attained by the teachers of White 10th graders. But, on average, African American teachers scored lower than White teachers on tests measuring general knowledge, communications skills, and professional knowledge. Moreover, the teachers of African American students have taken fewer undergraduate courses in the subject areas in which they teach than the teachers of White students.

The teachers of African American students may be restricted in their ability to acquire additional preparation, since they tend to receive less support for in-service and professional development activities than the teachers of White students. For example, less than one-fourth (22.8%) of the teachers of African Americans, but one-third (33.6%) of the teachers of Whites, received release time from teaching for in-service activities.

The educational experiences of African American students may be influenced by the types of in-service activities in which their teachers engage. Specifically, the educational interests, behaviors, and experiences of African American students may be inadequately reflected in school curricula since a smaller percentage of the teachers of African American 10th graders than of the teachers of White 10th graders participated in curriculum development committees.

PART II — DETAILED DESCRIPTIONS AND TABLES

DISTRIBUTION OF TEACHERS BY TYPE OF UNDERGRADUATE INSTITUTION ATTENDED

(Source: Schools and Staffing Survey, 1993/94)

Type of Undergraduate Institution

Figure 1 shows that about one-half (46.8%) of America's public school teachers in 1993/94 received

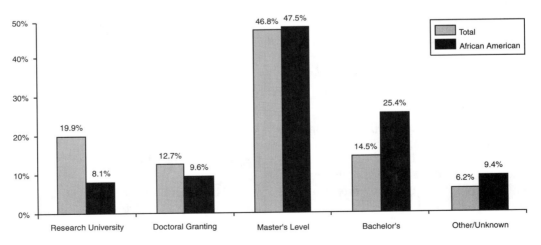

Figure 1. Distribution of 1993/94 Public School Teachers by Carnegie Classification of Their Undergraduate Institution

Source: Schools and Staffing Survey, 1993-94.

their undergraduate degrees from master's level institutions, one-fifth (19.9%) from research universities, 12.7% from doctoral granting institutions, and 14.5% from bachelor's degree institutions (also known as liberal arts colleges).

- **Table 1** shows that comparable percentages of 1993/94 African American and White public school teachers received their undergraduate degrees from master's level institutions (47.5% versus 46.5%).

- A higher share of African Americans than Whites received their undergraduate degrees from bachelor's degree institutions (25.4% versus 14.1%).

- Only 8.1% of African American public school teachers obtained their degrees from research universities, compared with 20.9% of their White counterparts.

Attendance at HBCUs

Figure 2 shows that 4.4% of public school teachers nationwide in 1993/94 earned their undergraduate degrees from HBCUs.

- **Table 2** shows that more than one-half (53.4%) of African American public school teachers received their undergraduate degrees from HBCUs, compared with less than 1% (0.4%) of their White counterparts.

Table 1. Distribution of Public School Teachers by Carnegie Classification of Their Undergraduate Institution, Race, and Sex: 1993/94
(weighted sample size in parentheses)

Carnegie Classification of Undergraduate Institution	Race and Sex of Teachers			White, Not Hispanic			African American, Non-Hispanic			Hispanic			Other		
	Total	Male	Female	Total	Male	Female	Total	Male	Female	Total	Male	Female	Total	Male	Female
Total *** +++	100.0%	100.0%	100.0%	100.0%	100.0%	100.0%	100.0%	100.0%	100.0%	100.0%	100.0%	100.0%	100.0%	100.0%	100.0%
	(2,561,294)	(694,098)	(1,867,195)	(2,216,605)	(613,178)	(1,603,426)	(188,371)	(37,233)	(151,138)	(108,744)	(30,696)	(78,048)	(47,574)	(12,991)	(34,583)
Unknown	5.9%	6.0%	5.8%	5.3%	5.5%	5.1%	8.5%	8.9%	8.4%	10.4%	9.2%	10.9%	12.9%	11.1%	13.6%
	(149,998)	(41,507)	(108,490)	(116,472)	(33,934)	(82,539)	(16,037)	(3,322)	(12,715)	(11,352)	(2,815)	(8,537)	(6,136)	(1,437)	(4,699)
Research University	19.9%	19.9%	19.9%	20.9%	20.4%	21.1%	8.1%	9.4%	7.7%	14.9%	20.1%	12.8%	31.3%	27.6%	32.7%
	(509,254)	(138,297)	(370,957)	(462,999)	(125,038)	(337,961)	(15,204)	(3,498)	(11,706)	(16,176)	(6,181)	(9,995)	(14,874)	(3,580)	(11,294)
Doctoral Institution	12.7%	12.7%	12.7%	13.0%	12.9%	13.0%	9.6%	11.0%	9.3%	12.1%	11.0%	12.5%	10.7%	10.7%	10.7%
	(324,272)	(87,866)	(236,406)	(287,922)	(79,003)	(208,919)	(18,089)	(4,086)	(14,002)	(13,176)	(3,388)	(9,788)	(5,086)	(1,389)	(3,697)
Master's Institution	46.8%	46.5%	46.9%	46.5%	46.1%	46.6%	47.5%	48.4%	47.2%	55.5%	52.9%	56.5%	37.4%	42.3%	35.6%
	(1,198,282)	(322,553)	(875,728)	(1,030,754)	(282,824)	(747,931)	(89,416)	(18,012)	(71,404)	(60,311)	(16,226)	(44,085)	(17,801)	(5,492)	(12,309)
Bachelor's Institution	14.5%	14.5%	14.5%	14.1%	14.6%	13.9%	25.4%	21.8%	26.3%	6.5%	5.6%	6.9%	7.5%	8.0%	7.3%
	(371,326)	(100,674)	(270,652)	(312,747)	(89,801)	(222,947)	(47,929)	(8,114)	(39,814)	(7,094)	(1,724)	(5,370)	(3,556)	(1,035)	(2,521)
Other	0.3%	0.5%	0.3%	0.3%	0.4%	0.2%	0.9%	0.5%	1.0%	0.6%	1.2%	0.3%	0.3%	0.5%	0.2%
	(8,163)	(3,201)	(4,962)	(5,710)	(2,579)	(3,131)	(1,697)	(201)	(1,496)	(635)	(362)	(272)	(122)	(59)	(63)

Notes:

*** Test of statistical significance compares African Americans with Whites. *** p < .001, ** p < .01, * p < .05.

+++ Test of statistical significance compares White men with White women. +++ p < .001, ++ p < .01, + p < .05.

~~~ Test of statistical significance compares African American men with African American women. ~~~ p < .001, ~~ p < .01, ~ p < .05.

Tests of statistical significance calculated using adjusted sample weight to control for influence of large sample sizes.

Source: Schools and Staffing Survey, 1993-94.

Figure 2. Percentage of 1993/94 Public School Teachers Who Attended HBCUs

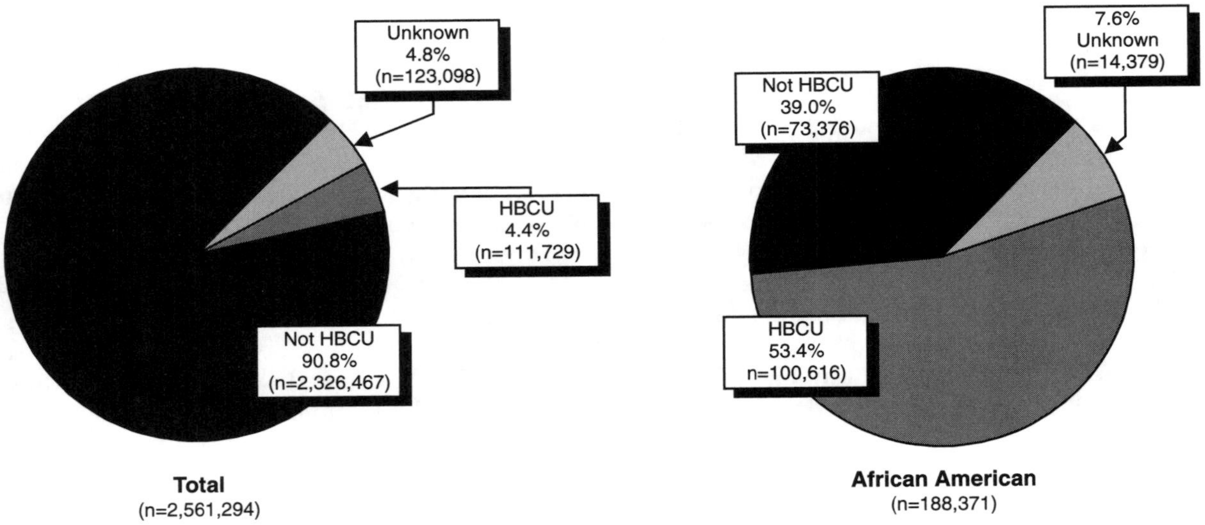

Unknown
4.8%
(n=123,098)

HBCU
4.4%
(n=111,729)

Not HBCU
90.8%
(n=2,326,467)

Total
(n=2,561,294)

7.6%
Unknown
(n=14,379)

Not HBCU
39.0%
(n=73,376)

HBCU
53.4%
n=100,616)

African American
(n=188,371)

Source: Schools and Staffing Survey, 1993-94.

Table 2. Percentage of Public School Teachers Who Attended HBCUs by Race and Sex: 1993/94
(weighted sample size in parentheses)

Attended HBCU	Race and Sex of Teachers			White, Non-Hispanic			African American, Non-Hispanic			Hispanic			Other		
	Total	Male	Female	Total	Male	Female	Total	Male	Female	Total	Male	Female	Total	Male	Female
Total *** +	100.0%	100.0%	100.0%	100.0%	100.0%	100.0%	100.0%	100.0%	100.0%	100.0%	100.0%	100.0%	100.0%	100.0%	100.0%
	(2,561,294)	(694,098)	(1,867,195)	(2,216,605)	(613,178)	(1,603,426)	(188,371)	(37,233)	(151,138)	(108,744)	(30,696)	(78,048)	(47,574)	(12,991)	(34,583)
Unknown	4.8%	5.0%	4.7%	4.2%	4.6%	4.1%	7.6%	8.0%	7.5%	8.9%	7.5%	9.4%	11.5%	10.4%	11.9%
	(123,098)	(34,670)	(88,428)	(93,591)	(28,026)	(65,565)	(14,379)	(2,973)	(11,406)	(9,641)	(2,316)	(7,325)	(5,487)	(1,355)	(4,132)
HBCU	4.4%	3.2%	4.8%	0.4%	0.5%	0.4%	53.4%	50.8%	54.1%	1.3%	1.3%	1.3%	1.4%	1.8%	1.2%
	(111,729)	(22,446)	(89,283)	(9,007)	(2,898)	(6,109)	(100,616)	(18,904)	(81,712)	(1,445)	(411)	(1,034)	(661)	(233)	(429)
Not HBCU	90.8%	91.8%	90.5%	95.4%	95.0%	95.5%	39.0%	41.2%	38.4%	89.8%	91.1%	89.3%	87.1%	87.8%	86.8%
	(2,326,467)	(636,983)	(1,689,484)	(2,114,007)	(582,254)	(1,531,753)	(73,376)	(15,356)	(58,021)	(97,658)	(27,970)	(69,688)	(41,425)	(11,403)	(30,022)

Notes:
*** Test of statistical significance compares African Americans with Whites. *** p < .001, ** p < .01, * p < .05.
+++ Test of statistical significance compares White men with White women. +++ p < .001, ++ p < .01, + p < .05.
~~~ Test of statistical significance compares African American men with African American women. ~~~ p < .001, ~~ p < .01, ~ p < .05.
Tests of statistical significance calculated using adjusted sample weight to control for influence of large sample sizes.
Source: Schools and Staffing Survey, 1993-94.

- **Table 3** shows that the percentage of African Americans who earned their undergraduate degrees from HBCUs was comparable for those teaching at elementary and secondary schools (52.6% versus 54.4%).

Figure 3 shows that the proportion of African American public school teachers who earned their undergraduate degrees from HBCUs increased with the percentage of African American students enrolled in the schools in which they taught.

Table 4 shows that 42.0% of African Americans who taught in schools in which African Americans constituted 5% or less of the student body received

their undergraduate degrees from HBCUs, compared with 60.9% of African Americans who taught in schools in which African Americans represented more than 60% of the student body.

CHARACTERISTICS OF THE TEACHERS OF 1990 10TH GRADERS

(Source: National Educational Longitudinal Study of 1988 8th graders)

Educational Attainment

Figure 4 shows that, overall, about one-half (50.4%) of the teachers of 1990 10th graders re-

Table 3. Percentage of Public School Teachers Who Attended HBCUs by Level of School Taught, Race, and Sex: 1993/94
(weighted sample size in parentheses)

Attended HBCU	Race and Sex of Teachers			White, Non-Hispanic			African American, Non-Hispanic			Hispanic			Other		
	Total	Male	Female	Total	Male	Female	Total	Male	Female	Total	Male	Female	Total	Male	Female
Elementary															
Total *** ++ ~	100.0%	100.0%	100.0%	100.0%	100.0%	100.0%	100.0%	100.0%	100.0%	100.0%	100.0%	100.0%	100.0%	100.0%	100.0%
	(1,331,281)	(154,788)	(1,176,492)	(1,139,263)	(133,204)	(1,006,059)	(104,246)	(8,821)	(95,425)	(61,648)	(9,752)	(51,896)	(26,124)	(3,011)	(23,113)
Unknown	4.7%	3.4%	4.9%	4.0%	3.0%	4.1%	8.1%	6.0%	8.3%	9.2%	4.3%	10.1%	10.6%	10.1%	10.6%
	(62,374)	(5,281)	(57,093)	(45,525)	(4,025)	(41,500)	(8,423)	(527)	(7,896)	(5,670)	(423)	(5,247)	(2,756)	(305)	(2,451)
HBCU	4.6%	4.4%	4.6%	0.4%	0.7%	0.4%	52.6%	61.9%	51.8%	1.4%	3.2%	1.1%	2.0%	5.6%	1.6%
	(60,874)	(6,821)	(54,053)	(4,603)	(873)	(3,730)	(54,857)	(5,464)	(49,393)	(881)	(315)	(566)	(534)	(169)	(364)
Not HBCU	90.7%	92.2%	90.6%	95.6%	96.3%	95.5%	39.3%	32.1%	40.0%	89.4%	92.4%	88.8%	87.4%	84.2%	87.8%
	(1,208,032)	(142,686)	(1,065,346)	(1,089,135)	(128,306)	(960,829)	(40,966)	(2,830)	(38,136)	(55,097)	(9,014)	(46,083)	(22,834)	(2,536)	(20,298)
Secondary															
Total *** ++ ~~~	100.0%	100.0%	100.0%	100.0%	100.0%	100.0%	100.0%	100.0%	100.0%	100.0%	100.0%	100.0%	100.0%	100.0%	100.0%
	(1,230,013)	(539,310)	(690,703)	(1,077,342)	(479,974)	(597,368)	(84,125)	(28,412)	(55,713)	(47,096)	(20,944)	(26,152)	(21,450)	(9,980)	(11,470)
Unknown	4.9%	5.4%	4.5%	4.5%	5.0%	4.0%	7.1%	8.6%	6.3%	8.4%	9.0%	7.9%	12.7%	10.5%	14.7%
	(60,724)	(29,389)	(31,335)	(48,066)	(24,000)	(24,065)	(5,956)	(2,446)	(3,510)	(3,971)	(1,892)	(2,079)	(2,731)	(1,050)	(1,680)
HBCU	4.1%	2.9%	5.1%	0.4%	0.4%	0.4%	54.4%	47.3%	58.0%	1.2%	0.5%	1.8%	0.6%	0.6%	0.6%
	(50,855)	(15,625)	(35,230)	(4,404)	(2,026)	(2,379)	(45,759)	(13,440)	(32,319)	(564)	(96)	(468)	(128)	(63)	(65)
Not HBCU	90.9%	91.7%	90.4%	95.1%	94.6%	95.6%	38.5%	44.1%	35.7%	90.4%	90.5%	90.3%	86.7%	88.8%	84.8%
	(1,118,435)	(494,296)	(624,138)	(1,024,872)	(453,948)	(570,924)	(32,411)	(12,526)	(19,885)	(42,561)	(18,956)	(23,605)	(18,591)	(8,866)	(9,725)

Notes:
*** Test of statistical significance compares African Americans with Whites. *** p < .001, ** p < .01, * p < .05.
+++ Test of statistical significance compares White men with White women. +++ p < .001, ++ p < .01, + p < .05.
~~~ Test of statistical significance compares African American men with African American women. ~~~ p < .001, ~~ p < .01, ~ p < .05.
Tests of statistical significance calculated using adjusted sample weight to control for influence of large sample sizes.

Figure 3. Percentage of 1993/94 Public School Teachers Who Attended HBCUs by Percentage of African American Students at the Schools in Which They Teach

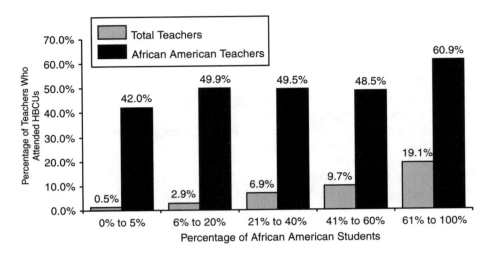

Source: Schools and Staffing Survey, 1993-94.

ported a master's degree as their highest degree. For 45.5% of their teachers, the highest degree was a bachelor's.

- **Table 5** shows that, on average, 50.9% of the full-time teachers of African American students and 50.5% of the full-time teachers of White students reported the master's degree as their highest level of education.

- About 2.3% of African American students' teachers and 1.6% of White students' teachers held doctoral degrees.

Base Salaries

The lowest salaries paid to the teachers of 1990 10th graders averaged $19,834 whereas the highest averaged $38,421. The average lowest and highest salaries were about 4% higher for the teachers of African American 10th graders than for the teachers of White 10th graders.

- **Table 5** also shows that the lowest salaries paid to the teachers of African American 10th graders averaged $20,280 regardless of the teachers' racial group, compared with $19,558 for the teachers of White 10th graders.

- The highest salaries paid to teachers of African American 1990 10th graders averaged $39,434, compared with $37,759 for Whites.

Teacher Certification

The majority (91.5%) of 1990 10th graders' teachers held standard teaching certificates. Only 2.5% of 10th graders' teachers were not certified.

Table 4. Percentage of Public School Teachers Who Attended HBCUs by Percentage of African American Students at the Schools in Which They Teach, Race, and Sex: 1993/94
(weighted sample size in parentheses)

Type of Institution Attended by Teachers	Race and Sex of Teachers			White, Non-Hispanic			African American, Non-Hispanic			Hispanic			Other		
	Total	Male	Female	Total	Male	Female	Total	Male	Female	Total	Male	Female	Total	Male	Female
0% to 5% African American Student Enrollment															
Total ***	100.0%	100.0%	100.0%	100.0%	100.0%	100.0%	100.0%	100.0%	100.0%	100.0%	100.0%	100.0%	100.0%	100.0%	100.0%
	(1,313,467)	(384,038)	(929,428)	(1,224,486)	(359,096)	(865,390)	(11,781)	(3,545)	(8,236)	(50,966)	(14,246)	(36,720)	(26,233)	(7,151)	(19,082)
Unknown	4.1%	4.0%	4.2%	3.9%	3.9%	3.9%	6.5%	5.1%	7.2%	6.5%	5.0%	7.1%	8.7%	5.3%	9.9%
	(54,350)	(15,214)	(39,136)	(47,997)	(13,938)	(34,059)	(771)	(182)	(589)	(3,313)	(716)	(2,597)	(2,269)	(378)	(1,891)
HBCU	0.5%	0.5%	0.6%	0.2%	0.1%	0.2%	42.0%	40.6%	42.6%	0.2%	0.2%	0.1%	0.1%	0.1%	0.1%
	(6,949)	(1,787)	(5,163)	(1,885)	(305)	(1,580)	(4,950)	(1,441)	(3,509)	(80)	(34)	(47)	(34)	(6)	(27)
Not HBCU	95.3%	95.6%	95.2%	95.9%	96.0%	95.9%	51.4%	54.2%	50.2%	93.3%	94.7%	92.8%	91.2%	94.6%	89.9%
	(1,252,167)	(367,038)	(885,130)	(1,174,604)	(344,852)	(829,752)	(6,061)	(1,922)	(4,138)	(47,572)	(13,497)	(34,076)	(23,930)	(6,767)	(17,164)
6% to 20% African American Student Enrollment															
Total *** ++	100.0%	100.0%	100.0%	100.0%	100.0%	100.0%	100.0%	100.0%	100.0%	100.0%	100.0%	100.0%	100.0%	100.0%	100.0%
	(390,613)	(98,300)	(292,313)	(342,589)	(87,411)	(255,178)	(20,054)	(3,443)	(16,611)	(20,612)	(5,673)	(14,940)	(7,358)	(1,773)	(5,585)
Unknown	5.2%	5.7%	5.0%	4.4%	5.0%	4.2%	6.3%	9.5%	5.6%	15.6%	12.0%	16.9%	12.6%	16.6%	11.3%
	(20,325)	(5,635)	(14,690)	(14,926)	(4,332)	(10,594)	(1,262)	(326)	(935)	(3,214)	(683)	(2,531)	(924)	(294)	(630)
HBCU	2.9%	2.3%	3.1%	0.4%	0.8%	0.3%	49.9%	43.2%	51.3%	0.0%	0.0%	0.0%	0.0%	0.0%	0.0%
	(11,389)	(2,218)	(9,172)	(1,376)	(721)	(655)	(10,004)	(1,488)	(8,517)	–	–	–	–	–	–
Not HBCU	91.9%	92.0%	91.8%	95.2%	94.2%	95.6%	43.8%	47.3%	43.1%	84.4%	87.8%	83.1%	87.4%	83.4%	88.7%
	(358,899)	(90,447)	(268,452)	(326,286)	(82,358)	(243,929)	(8,788)	(1,629)	(7,159)	(17,390)	(4,981)	(12,409)	(6,434)	(1,479)	(4,956)
21% to 40% African American Student Enrollment															
Total ***	100.0%	100.0%	100.0%	100.0%	100.0%	100.0%	100.0%	100.0%	100.0%	100.0%	100.0%	100.0%	100.0%	100.0%	100.0%
	(260,910)	(67,811)	(193,099)	(213,280)	(57,417)	(155,863)	(32,638)	(5,599)	(27,039)	(10,596)	(3,614)	(6,982)	(4,396)	(1,181)	(3,215)
Unknown	6.2%	7.4%	5.8%	4.7%	5.7%	4.4%	12.0%	17.1%	11.0%	12.0%	14.5%	10.7%	21.3%	23.6%	20.5%
	(16,213)	(5,051)	(11,162)	(10,087)	(3,289)	(6,798)	(3,921)	(960)	(2,962)	(1,268)	(524)	(744)	(938)	(279)	(658)
HBCU	6.9%	5.4%	7.4%	0.6%	0.8%	0.6%	49.5%	50.9%	49.2%	3.9%	8.9%	1.3%	1.2%	4.4%	0.0%
	(17,948)	(3,674)	(14,275)	(1,331)	(449)	(882)	(16,152)	(2,852)	(13,300)	(414)	(321)	(93)	(52)	(52)	–
Not HBCU	86.9%	87.1%	86.8%	94.6%	93.5%	95.1%	38.5%	31.9%	39.9%	84.1%	76.6%	88.0%	77.5%	72.0%	79.5%
	(226,748)	(59,086)	(167,662)	(201,862)	(53,679)	(148,183)	(12,565)	(1,788)	(10,777)	(8,915)	(2,769)	(6,146)	(3,407)	(850)	(2,557)
41% to 60% African American Student Enrollment															
Total ***	100.0%	100.0%	100.0%	100.0%	100.0%	100.0%	100.0%	100.0%	100.0%	100.0%	100.0%	100.0%	100.0%	100.0%	100.0%
	(139,810)	(30,212)	(109,598)	(106,543)	(23,449)	(83,095)	(25,885)	(4,787)	(21,098)	(5,819)	(1,668)	(4,151)	(1,563)	(309)	(1,253)
Unknown	6.0%	6.8%	5.8%	5.4%	6.8%	5.0%	7.5%	7.4%	7.5%	8.1%	5.9%	9.0%	18.7%	3.7%	22.4%
	(8,436)	(2,047)	(6,389)	(5,731)	(1,583)	(4,149)	(1,940)	(355)	(1,585)	(473)	(98)	(375)	(292)	(12)	(280)
HBCU	9.7%	9.7%	9.7%	0.8%	0.6%	0.8%	48.5%	58.3%	46.3%	3.2%	0.0%	4.5%	0.0%	0.0%	0.0%
	(13,575)	(2,921)	(10,653)	(831)	(132)	(699)	(12,557)	(2,789)	(9,767)	(187)	–	(187)	–	–	–
Not HBCU	84.3%	83.6%	84.5%	93.8%	92.7%	94.2%	44.0%	34.3%	46.2%	88.7%	94.1%	86.5%	81.3%	96.3%	77.6%
	(117,799)	(25,244)	(92,556)	(99,981)	(21,734)	(78,247)	(11,389)	(1,643)	(9,746)	(5,159)	(1,570)	(3,590)	(1,271)	(298)	(973)

—continued next page

Table 4. —continued from previous page

Type of Institution Attended by Teachers	Race and Sex of Teachers			White, Non-Hispanic			African American, Non-Hispanic			Hispanic			Other		
	Total	Male	Female	Total	Male	Female	Total	Male	Female	Total	Male	Female	Total	Male	Female
61% to 100% African American Student Enrollment															
Total *** ++ ~~	100.0%	100.0%	100.0%	100.0%	100.0%	100.0%	100.0%	100.0%	100.0%	100.0%	100.0%	100.0%	100.0%	100.0%	100.0%
	(276,889)	(66,670)	(210,219)	(179,805)	(46,892)	(132,912)	(80,465)	(16,323)	(64,141)	(12,106)	(2,432)	(9,673)	(4,514)	(1,022)	(3,492)
Unknown	5.6%	6.4%	5.3%	5.0%	6.5%	4.4%	6.9%	4.8%	7.5%	2.4%	4.9%	1.7%	15.5%	30.4%	11.1%
	(15,468)	(4,276)	(11,192)	(8,914)	(3,067)	(5,848)	(5,571)	(779)	(4,791)	(285)	(119)	(166)	(698)	(311)	(387)
HBCU	19.1%	15.3%	20.3%	1.4%	2.2%	1.1%	60.9%	54.8%	62.5%	6.2%	2.0%	7.3%	12.5%	16.6%	11.3%
	(52,795)	(10,178)	(42,618)	(2,456)	(1,015)	(1,441)	(49,019)	(8,945)	(40,073)	(755)	(48)	(708)	(565)	(169)	(396)
Not HBCU	75.3%	78.3%	74.4%	93.7%	91.3%	94.5%	32.2%	40.4%	30.1%	91.4%	93.1%	91.0%	72.0%	53.0%	77.6%
	(208,626)	(52,217)	(156,409)	(168,434)	(42,811)	(125,624)	(25,875)	(6,599)	(19,276)	(11,065)	(2,265)	(8,800)	(3,251)	(542)	(2,709)

Notes:
" – " indicates sample size too small to estimate.
*** Test of statistical significance compares African Americans with Whites. *** p < .001, ** p < .01, * p < .05.
+++ Test of statistical significance compares White men with White women. +++ p < .001, ++ p < .01, + p < .05.
~~~ Test of statistical significance compares African American men with African American women. ~~~ p < .001, ~~ p < .01, ~ p < .05.
Tests of statistical significance calculated using adjusted sample weight to control for influence of large sample sizes.
Source: Schools and Staffing Survey, 1993-94.

Figure 4. Highest Level of Education Attained by 1990 10th Graders' Teachers

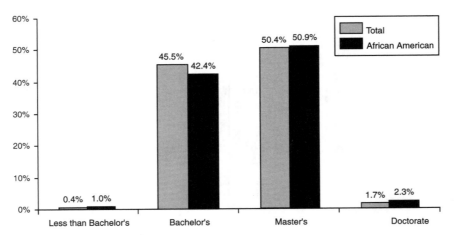

Source: National Educational Longitudinal Study of 1988 Eighth Graders, First (1990) Follow-Up.

- **Table 6** shows that the percentage of students who had teachers with standard teaching certificates was similar for African American and White students (92.0% versus 91.9%).

- Only 2.4% of African American 10th graders' teachers and 2.3% of White 10th graders' teachers did not have teaching certificates.

Undergraduate and Graduate Coursework in the Assigned Subject

Figure 5 shows that nearly three-fourths of the teachers of 1990 10th graders had taken at least eight undergraduate courses in the subject area in which they taught (71.0% of math teachers, 71.6% of science teachers, and 74.0% of English teachers). About one-third had taken eight or more courses at the graduate level (33.4% of math teachers, 38.8% of science teach-

ers, and 36.5% of English teachers). But, in all three subject areas, less than two-thirds of African American students' teachers had taken at least eight courses at the undergraduate level.

- **Table 7** shows that only 61.1% of African American 10th graders' math teachers had taken at least eight undergraduate math courses, compared with 72.2% of their White counterparts' teachers.

- **Table 8** shows that only 63.8% of African American 10th graders' science teachers, but 72.5% of White 10th graders' science teachers, had taken at least eight undergraduate science courses.

- **Table 9** shows that 63.3% of African American students' English teachers had taken at least

Table 5. Education Attained and Salaries Received by 1990 10th Graders' Teachers by Students' Race and Sex: 1990
(weighted sample size in parentheses)

Characteristic of Teachers	Race and Sex of Students			White, Non-Hispanic			African American, Non-Hispanic			Hispanic			Other		
	Total	Male	Female	Total	Male	Female	Total	Male	Female	Total	Male	Female	Total	Male	Female
% Full-Time Teachers With Less Than Bachelor ***	0.4% (1,781,657)	0.4% (892,554)	0.3% (889,103)	0.3% (1,364,542)	0.3% (682,017)	0.2% (682,524)	1.0% (195,611)	1.3% (94,887)	0.8% (100,724)	0.8% (131,662)	1.1% (66,641)	0.5% (65,021)	0.3% (89,843)	0.3% (49,009)	0.3% (40,834)
%Full-Time Teachers With Bachelor's Degree ***	45.5% (1,630,008)	45.4% (818,839)	45.6% (811,169)	45.9% (1,249,825)	45.9% (625,201)	45.9% (624,624)	42.4% (179,509)	42.4% (88,247)	42.4% (91,262)	46.4% (115,593)	46.2% (59,088)	46.6% (56,505)	44.9% (85,081)	42.7% (46,303)	46.0% (38,778)
% Full-Time Teachers With Master's Degree	50.4% (1,630,008)	50.1% (818,839)	50.7% (811,169)	50.5% (1,249,825)	50.3% (625,201)	50.8% (624,624)	50.9% (179,509)	49.8% (88,247)	52.0% (91,262)	46.9% (115,593)	46.5% (59,088)	47.4% (56,505)	50.5% (85,081)	52.4% (46,303)	50.0% (38,778)
% Full-Time Teachers With Ed.D. or Ph.D. ***	1.7% (1,673,261)	1.6% (841,050)	1.8% (832,211)	1.6% (1,283,146)	1.5% (643,719)	1.6% (639,427)	2.3% (184,630)	2.2% (90,140)	2.3% (94,490)	2.2% (119,108)	1.4% (60,236)	2.9% (58,872)	1.8% (86,377)	1.8% (46,955)	1.8% (39,422)
Lowest Salary Paid to Full-Time Teachers *** +	$19,834 (1,893,372)	$19,917 (936,277)	$19,753 (957,095)	$19,558 (1,443,379)	$19,657 (713,369)	$19,461 (730,010)	$20,280 (205,133)	$20,185 (97,581)	$20,366 (107,552)	$20,966 (143,670)	$21,001 (72,748)	$20,930 (70,922)	$21,262 (101,190)	$21,451 (52,579)	$21,069 (48,611)
Highest Salary Paid to Full-Time Teachers *** ++ ~~	$38,421 (1,877,656)	$38,770 (930,450)	$38,077 (947,206)	$37,759 (1,433,155)	$38,032 (709,906)	$37,491 (723,249)	$39,434 (203,861)	$40,178 (96,787)	$38,762 (107,074)	$41,280 (141,593)	$41,775 (71,466)	$40,774 (70,127)	$41,661 (99,047)	$42,077 (52,291)	$41,534 (46,756)

Notes:

*** Test of statistical significance compares African Americans with Whites. *** p < .001, ** p < .01, * p < .05.
+++ Test of statistical significance compares White men with White women. +++ p < .001, ++ p < .01, + p < .05.
~~~ Test of statistical significance compares African American men with African American women. ~~~ p < .001, ~~ p < .01, ~ p < .05.
Tests of statistical significance calculated using adjusted sample weight to control for influence of large sample sizes.
Source: National Educational Longitudinal Study of 1988 Eighth Graders, First (1990) Follow-Up.

Table 6. Type of Teaching Certificate Held by 1990 10th Graders' Teachers by Students' Race and Sex: 1990
(weighted sample size in parentheses)

Type of Certificate Held by Teachers	Race and Sex of Students			White, Non-Hispanic			African American, Non-Hispanic			Hispanic			Other		
	Total	Male	Female	Total	Male	Female	Total	Male	Female	Total	Male	Female	Total	Male	Female
Total ** ++	100.0%	100.0%	100.0%	100.0%	100.0%	100.0%	100.0%	100.0%	100.0%	100.0%	100.0%	100.0%	100.0%	100.0%	100.0%
	(2,070,270)	(1,028,660)	(1,041,610)	(1,550,485)	(771,761)	(778,724)	(239,019)	(114,161)	(124,858)	(179,346)	(91,000)	(88,346)	(101,420)	(51,737)	(49,682)
Standard Certificate	91.5%	92.0%	91.0%	91.9%	92.8%	91.1%	92.0%	92.0%	92.0%	88.0%	87.1%	88.9%	90.0%	88.3%	91.8%
	(1,894,174)	(946,147)	(948,027)	(1,425,329)	(716,253)	(709,075)	(219,799)	(104,983)	(114,816)	(157,756)	(79,246)	(78,510)	(91,290)	(45,664)	(45,626)
Probationary	2.9%	2.8%	2.9%	2.6%	2.6%	2.7%	3.8%	4.3%	3.4%	3.4%	2.2%	4.7%	2.8%	4.0%	1.6%
	(59,030)	(28,905)	(30,125)	(40,917)	(19,968)	(20,950)	(9,164)	(4,878)	(4,286)	(6,084)	(1,968)	(4,115)	(2,865)	(2,091)	(774)
Temporary	3.1%	3.0%	3.2%	3.1%	2.8%	3.5%	1.8%	1.4%	2.2%	5.2%	7.5%	2.8%	2.3%	1.9%	2.7%
	(64,723)	(31,165)	(33,558)	(48,805)	(21,827)	(26,979)	(4,341)	(1,559)	(2,781)	(9,251)	(6,791)	(2,460)	(2,326)	(988)	(1,338)
Not Certified	2.5%	2.2%	2.9%	2.3%	1.8%	2.8%	2.4%	2.4%	2.4%	3.5%	3.3%	3.7%	4.9%	5.8%	3.9%
	(52,343)	(22,443)	(29,900)	(35,434)	(13,714)	(21,721)	(5,715)	(2,741)	(2,974)	(6,255)	(2,995)	(3,261)	(4,939)	(2,994)	(1,945)

Notes:
*** Test of statistical significance compares African Americans with Whites. *** p < .001, ** p < .01, * p < .05.
+++ Test of statistical significance compares White men with White women. +++ p < .001, ++ p < .01, + p < .05.
~~~ Test of statistical significance compares African American men with African American women. ~~~ p < .001, ~~ p < .01, ~ p < .05.
Tests of statistical significance calculated using adjusted sample weight to control for influence of large sample sizes.
Source: National Educational Longitudinal Study of 1988 Eighth Graders, First (1990) Follow-Up.

eight undergraduate English courses, compared with 75.5% White students' English teachers.

- **Table 7** shows that comparable percentages of African American and White students' math teachers had taken at least eight graduate courses in math (35.2% versus 32.6%).

- **Table 8** shows that 38.0% of African American and 38.8% of White students' science teachers had taken at least eight graduate courses in science.

- **Table 9** shows that similar percentages of African American and White students' English teachers had taken at least eight graduate courses in English (38.6% versus 36.5%)

Self-Reported Preparation for Teaching the Assigned Subject

Figure 6 shows that more than one-half of 1990 10th graders' teachers in math (64.0%), science (58.8%), and English (60.9%) felt well prepared to teach the subject.

- **Table 10** shows that comparable percentages of African American and White students' mathematics (65.3% versus 63.6%), science (55.1% versus 60.5%), and English (60.4% versus 61.4%) teachers felt well prepared to teach these subjects.

Professional Development Activities

Figure 7 shows that nearly three-fourths (72.5%) of 1990 10th graders' teachers reported attending

Figure 5. Number of Undergraduate and Graduate Courses Taken by 1990 10th Graders' Teachers in Their Subject Area

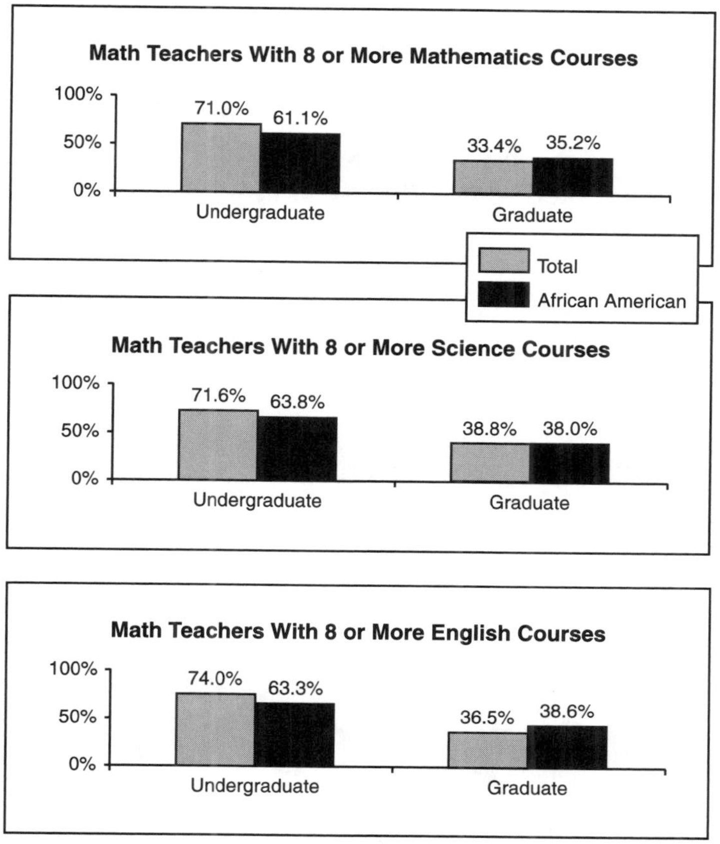

Math Teachers With 8 or More Mathematics Courses

Undergraduate: 71.0% (Total), 61.1% (African American)
Graduate: 33.4% (Total), 35.2% (African American)

Legend: Total, African American

Math Teachers With 8 or More Science Courses

Undergraduate: 71.6% (Total), 63.8% (African American)
Graduate: 38.8% (Total), 38.0% (African American)

Math Teachers With 8 or More English Courses

Undergraduate: 74.0% (Total), 63.3% (African American)
Graduate: 36.5% (Total), 38.6% (African American)

Source: National Educational Longitudinal Study of 1988 Eighth Graders, First (1990) Follow-Up.

in-service workshops during the school year. Other common in-service activities were in-department curriculum committees (49.5%), committee work or special assignment (37.8%), and professional growth activities (36.5%). About one-half (48.1%) of 1990 10th graders' teachers received no support for in-service activities. On average, a smaller percentage of African American than White 10th graders' teach-

ers received support for professional development activities.

- **Table 11** shows that a smaller share of African American than White students' teachers participated in in-department curriculum committees (40.1% versus 51.6%), committee work or special assignments (33.9% versus 38.4%), and

Table 7. Number of Undergraduate and Graduate Math Courses Taken by 1990 10th Graders' Math Teachers by Student's Race and Sex
(weighted sample size in parentheses)

Number of Courses Taken by Teachers	Race and Sex of Students			White, Non-Hispanic			African American, Non-Hispanic			Hispanic			Other		
	Total	Male	Female	Total	Male	Female	Total	Male	Female	Total	Male	Female	Total	Male	Female
Undergraduate Courses in Mathematics															
Total *** ~	100.0%	100.0%	100.0%	100.0%	100.0%	100.0%	100.0%	100.0%	100.0%	100.0%	100.0%	100.0%	100.0%	100.0%	100.0%
	(784,637)	(392,771)	(391,866)	(606,677)	(302,459)	(304,218)	(82,566)	(39,130)	(43,436)	(60,002)	(31,749)	(28,253)	(35,392)	(19,433)	(15,959)
Don't Remember	9.1%	9.2%	9.1%	8.9%	8.8%	9.1%	14.2%	16.1%	12.5%	3.7%	2.9%	4.7%	10.5%	11.6%	9.2%
	(71,784)	(35,978)	(35,806)	(54,095)	(26,475)	(27,620)	(11,729)	(6,319)	(5,410)	(2,246)	(932)	(1,315)	(3,713)	(2,252)	(1,461)
None	1.8%	2.0%	1.6%	1.9%	1.9%	1.9%	0.8%	0.9%	0.7%	1.9%	3.3%	0.3%	2.3%	3.8%	0.5%
	(14,174)	(7,831)	(6,343)	(11,599)	(5,711)	(5,888)	(638)	(339)	(299)	(1,123)	(1,049)	(74)	(814)	(732)	(81)
2 to 4 Courses	9.5%	10.2%	8.8%	8.9%	9.9%	7.9%	13.1%	13.8%	12.5%	10.7%	8.2%	13.4%	9.9%	10.6%	9.0%
	(74,600)	(40,016)	(34,584)	(53,838)	(29,922)	(23,916)	(10,854)	(5,411)	(5,442)	(6,409)	(2,618)	(3,791)	(3,499)	(2,064)	(1,435)
5 to 7 Courses	8.5%	9.1%	8.0%	8.1%	8.1%	8.1%	10.7%	15.1%	6.8%	8.4%	9.4%	7.4%	10.4%	11.6%	8.9%
	(66,871)	(35,641)	(31,230)	(49,259)	(24,493)	(24,765)	(8,874)	(5,918)	(2,956)	(5,063)	(2,979)	(2,084)	(3,676)	(2,251)	(1,425)
8 or More Courses	71.0%	69.6%	72.4%	72.2%	71.4%	73.0%	61.1%	54.0%	67.5%	75.3%	76.1%	74.3%	66.9%	62.4%	72.4%
	(557,209)	(273,306)	(283,903)	(437,886)	(215,857)	(222,029)	(50,472)	(21,143)	(29,329)	(45,161)	(24,172)	(20,989)	(23,690)	(12,133)	(11,557)
Graduate Courses in Mathematics															
Total +	100.0%	100.0%	100.0%	100.0%	100.0%	100.0%	100.0%	100.0%	100.0%	100.0%	100.0%	100.0%	100.0%	100.0%	100.0%
	(663,882)	(333,977)	(329,905)	(524,882)	(264,560)	(260,322)	(63,668)	(29,419)	(34,249)	(44,339)	(22,527)	(21,812)	(30,993)	(17,471)	(13,522)
Don't Remember	6.1%	6.1%	6.1%	6.2%	6.3%	6.1%	8.3%	8.0%	8.7%	3.6%	3.7%	3.4%	3.6%	3.3%	4.0%
	(40,431)	(20,366)	(20,065)	(32,426)	(16,619)	(15,807)	(5,315)	(2,340)	(2,975)	(1,587)	(839)	(748)	(1,103)	(568)	(535)
None	15.5%	15.9%	15.0%	15.5%	16.0%	15.0%	12.9%	10.8%	14.7%	16.7%	16.3%	17.0%	18.1%	21.8%	13.4%
	(102,618)	(53,123)	(49,495)	(81,398)	(42,455)	(38,943)	(8,207)	(3,183)	(5,024)	(7,401)	(3,683)	(3,718)	(5,612)	(3,802)	(1,810)
2 to 4 Courses	27.5%	29.1%	25.9%	27.7%	29.7%	25.7%	25.4%	27.7%	23.5%	27.5%	26.5%	28.5%	28.2%	25.2%	32.0%
	(182,588)	(97,195)	(85,393)	(145,482)	(78,674)	(66,808)	(16,180)	(8,146)	(8,034)	(12,197)	(5,976)	(6,222)	(8,729)	(4,400)	(4,329)
5 to 7 Courses	17.6%	17.1%	18.1%	18.0%	17.8%	18.2%	18.2%	15.5%	20.4%	13.5%	12.1%	14.9%	14.7%	14.5%	14.9%
	(116,637)	(57,034)	(59,603)	(94,550)	(47,209)	(47,341)	(11,561)	(4,569)	(6,991)	(5,973)	(2,725)	(3,249)	(4,553)	(2,532)	(2,021)
8 or More Courses	33.4%	31.8%	35.0%	32.6%	30.1%	35.1%	35.2%	38.0%	32.8%	38.8%	41.3%	36.1%	35.5%	35.3%	35.7%
	(221,608)	(106,258)	(115,350)	(171,026)	(79,604)	(91,422)	(22,405)	(11,180)	(11,225)	(17,182)	(9,305)	(7,877)	(10,995)	(6,169)	(4,826)

Notes:
*** Test of statistical significance compares African Americans with whites. *** p < .001, ** p < .01, * p < .05.
+++ Test of statistical significance compares white men with white women. +++ p < .001, ++ p < .01, + p < .05.
~~~ Test of statistical significance compares African American men with African American women. ~~~ p < .001, ~~ p < .01, ~ p < .05.
Tests of statistical significance calculated using adjusted sample weight to control for influence of large sample sizes.
Source: National Educational Longitudinal Study of 1988 Eighth Graders, First (1990) Follow-Up.

Table 8. Number of Undergraduate and Graduate Science Courses Taken by 1990 10th Graders' Science Teachers by Students' Race and Sex: 1990

(weighted sample size in parentheses)

Number of Courses Taken by Teachers	Race and Sex of Students			White, Non-Hispanic			African American, Non-Hispanic			Hispanic			Other		
	Total	Male	Female	Total	Male	Female	Total	Male	Female	Total	Male	Female	Total	Male	Female
Undergraduate Courses in Science															
	100.0%	100.0%	100.0%	100.0%	100.0%	100.0%	100.0%	100.0%	100.0%	100.0%	100.0%	100.0%	100.0%	100.0%	100.0%
	(675,618)	(329,127)	(346,491)	(514,605)	(251,884)	(262,721)	(67,308)	(32,139)	(35,169)	(57,869)	(29,531)	(28,338)	(35,836)	(15,573)	(20,263)
Don't Remember	9.3%	9.1%	9.5%	8.8%	9.0%	8.7%	13.4%	10.9%	15.8%	8.9%	6.3%	11.5%	9.1%	12.3%	6.6%
	(62,960)	(29,970)	(32,990)	(45,535)	(22,678)	(22,856)	(9,049)	(3,503)	(5,546)	(5,131)	(1,871)	(3,260)	(3,245)	(1,917)	(1,328)
None	1.8%	1.5%	2.1%	1.7%	1.5%	1.9%	3.3%	3.6%	3.0%	0.0%	0.0%	0.0%	3.5%	0.0%	6.2%
	(12,335)	(4,911)	(7,424)	(8,844)	(3,739)	(5,105)	(2,225)	(1,171)	(1,054)	–	–	–	(1,266)	–	(1,266)
2 to 4 Courses	7.5%	7.1%	7.9%	7.4%	6.6%	8.1%	8.6%	9.4%	7.9%	9.7%	9.4%	10.1%	3.7%	5.3%	2.4%
	(50,676)	(23,232)	(27,443)	(37,955)	(16,630)	(21,325)	(5,772)	(3,007)	(2,765)	(5,627)	(2,770)	(2,858)	(1,321)	(825)	(496)
5 to 7 Courses	9.8%	10.0%	9.6%	9.6%	10.0%	9.2%	10.9%	13.4%	8.6%	10.1%	7.0%	13.4%	9.9%	8.1%	11.2%
	(65,991)	(32,768)	(33,223)	(49,278)	(25,157)	(24,121)	(7,331)	(4,292)	(3,039)	(5,839)	(2,055)	(3,784)	(3,542)	(1,264)	(2,278)
8 or More Courses	71.6%	72.4%	70.8%	72.5%	72.9%	72.1%	63.8%	62.7%	64.7%	71.3%	77.3%	65.1%	73.8%	74.3%	73.5%
	(483,657)	(238,247)	(245,410)	(372,992)	(183,679)	(189,314)	(42,931)	(20,165)	(22,766)	(41,272)	(22,836)	(18,436)	(26,462)	(11,567)	(14,895)
Graduate Courses in Science															
Total	100.0%	100.0%	100.0%	100.0%	100.0%	100.0%	100.0%	100.0%	100.0%	100.0%	100.0%	100.0%	100.0%	100.0%	100.0%
	(586,969)	(283,670)	(303,299)	(449,045)	(216,447)	(232,599)	(62,045)	(28,285)	(33,760)	(42,925)	(23,558)	(19,367)	(32,953)	(15,381)	(17,573)
Don't Remember	7.0%	6.9%	7.1%	6.6%	6.8%	6.4%	11.0%	9.6%	12.0%	6.4%	4.2%	9.1%	6.2%	7.9%	4.7%
	(41,105)	(19,636)	(21,469)	(29,512)	(14,699)	(14,813)	(6,796)	(2,729)	(4,066)	(2,750)	(992)	(1,758)	(2,047)	(1,216)	(830)
None	14.1%	13.9%	14.3%	14.2%	14.2%	14.2%	11.7%	12.0%	11.4%	14.8%	15.2%	14.4%	16.9%	11.9%	21.2%
	(82,804)	(39,457)	(43,346)	(63,642)	(30,669)	(32,973)	(7,235)	(3,381)	(3,854)	(6,362)	(3,570)	(2,791)	(5,565)	(1,837)	(3,728)
2 to 4 Courses	25.1%	24.4%	25.7%	25.2%	24.4%	26.0%	25.3%	21.8%	28.2%	22.1%	20.1%	24.6%	26.3%	35.5%	18.2%
	(147,136)	(69,122)	(78,014)	(113,313)	(52,760)	(60,553)	(15,671)	(6,165)	(9,506)	(9,497)	(4,742)	(4,755)	(8,656)	(5,455)	(3,201)
5 to 7 Courses	15.0%	15.2%	14.8%	15.2%	15.2%	15.3%	14.1%	14.3%	14.0%	12.3%	14.4%	9.7%	16.9%	18.6%	15.4%
	(88,040)	(43,229)	(44,812)	(68,435)	(32,942)	(35,493)	(8,758)	(4,038)	(4,721)	(5,279)	(3,394)	(1,886)	(5,568)	(2,856)	(2,712)
8 or More Courses	38.8%	39.6%	38.1%	38.8%	39.4%	38.2%	38.0%	42.3%	34.4%	44.4%	46.1%	42.2%	33.7%	26.1%	40.4%
	(227,884)	(112,226)	(115,658)	(174,143)	(85,377)	(88,766)	(23,585)	(11,972)	(11,612)	(19,037)	(10,860)	(8,177)	(11,118)	(4,017)	(7,102)

Notes:
" – " indicates sample size too small to estimate.
*** Test of statistical significance compares African Americans with Whites. *** p < .001, ** p < .01, * p < .05.
+++ Test of statistical significance compares White men with White women. +++ p < .001, ++ p < .01, + p < .05.
~~~ Test of statistical significance compares African American men with African American women. ~~~ p < .001, ~~ p < .01, ~ p < .05.
Tests of statistical significance calculated using adjusted sample weight to control for influence of large sample sizes.
Source: National Educational Longitudinal Study of 1988 Eighth Graders, First (1990) Follow-Up.

Table 9. Number of Undergraduate and Graduate English Courses Taken by 1990 10th Graders' English Teachers by Students' Race and Sex: 1990

(weighted sample size in parentheses)

Number of Courses Taken by Teachers	Race and Sex of Students			White, Non-Hispanic			African American, Non-Hispanic			Hispanic			Other		
	Total	Male	Female	Total	Male	Female	Total	Male	Female	Total	Male	Female	Total	Male	Female
Undergraduate Courses in English															
	100.0%	100.0%	100.0%	100.0%	100.0%	100.0%	100.0%	100.0%	100.0%	100.0%	100.0%	100.0%	100.0%	100.0%	100.0%
	(959,746)	(470,799)	(488,947)	(728,226)	(360,269)	(367,957)	(103,256)	(47,428)	(55,827)	(82,515)	(41,838)	(40,677)	(45,749)	(21,263)	(24,486)
Don't Remember	10.1%	10.6%	9.7%	9.7%	10.2%	9.3%	15.4%	17.4%	13.7%	6.3%	4.8%	7.8%	11.5%	14.1%	9.2%
	(97,207)	(49,902)	(47,305)	(70,896)	(36,644)	(34,252)	(15,886)	(8,260)	(7,626)	(5,174)	(2,000)	(3,174)	(5,251)	(2,999)	(2,252)
None	1.2%	1.3%	1.1%	1.3%	1.3%	1.2%	0.9%	0.7%	1.1%	1.7%	2.5%	0.9%	0.2%	0.0%	0.5%
	(11,625)	(6,025)	(5,600)	(9,135)	(4,623)	(4,513)	(963)	(339)	(624)	(1,413)	(1,064)	(349)	(114)	–	(114)
2 to 4 Courses	7.9%	7.4%	8.3%	7.5%	7.5%	7.4%	11.2%	7.7%	14.1%	9.2%	8.0%	10.3%	4.4%	3.8%	4.8%
	(75,489)	(35,004)	(40,485)	(54,401)	(27,190)	(27,211)	(11,546)	(3,665)	(7,880)	(7,552)	(3,343)	(4,209)	(1,991)	(806)	(1,185)
5 to 7 Courses	6.8%	7.3%	6.4%	6.1%	6.3%	5.8%	9.2%	11.8%	7.0%	8.0%	7.6%	8.4%	11.8%	13.1%	10.7%
	(65,672)	(34,216)	(31,456)	(44,156)	(22,650)	(21,507)	(9,510)	(5,591)	(3,919)	(6,599)	(3,180)	(3,419)	(5,407)	(2,795)	(2,612)
8 or More Courses	74.0%	73.4%	74.5%	75.5%	74.7%	76.2%	63.3%	62.4%	64.1%	74.9%	77.1%	72.6%	72.1%	69.0%	74.8%
	(709,753)	(345,652)	(364,101)	(549,638)	(269,164)	(280,474)	(65,351)	(29,573)	(35,778)	(61,777)	(32,251)	(29,526)	(32,987)	(14,663)	(18,323)
Graduate Courses in English															
Total **	100.0%	100.0%	100.0%	100.0%	100.0%	100.0%	100.0%	100.0%	100.0%	100.0%	100.0%	100.0%	100.0%	100.0%	100.0%
	(835,174)	(407,952)	(427,223)	(643,905)	(317,440)	(326,464)	(88,740)	(39,575)	(49,166)	(60,908)	(31,135)	(29,773)	(41,621)	(19,802)	(21,820)
Don't Remember	7.0%	7.3%	6.7%	6.9%	7.4%	6.4%	10.7%	11.4%	10.1%	5.3%	4.1%	6.5%	3.9%	3.7%	4.0%
	(58,440)	(29,883)	(28,557)	(44,173)	(23,368)	(20,804)	(9,458)	(4,510)	(4,948)	(3,200)	(1,271)	(1,929)	(1,610)	(733)	(877)
None	13.7%	13.8%	13.6%	14.0%	14.3%	13.8%	10.3%	10.5%	10.1%	15.0%	14.4%	15.6%	14.2%	12.4%	15.8%
	(114,572)	(56,453)	(58,119)	(90,460)	(45,392)	(45,069)	(9,096)	(4,148)	(4,949)	(9,116)	(4,469)	(4,647)	(5,900)	(2,446)	(3,454)
2 to 4 Courses	25.7%	25.3%	26.2%	26.2%	25.7%	26.7%	22.6%	22.0%	23.1%	23.3%	22.7%	24.0%	28.7%	29.5%	28.1%
	(214,913)	(103,115)	(111,799)	(168,697)	(81,505)	(87,192)	(20,046)	(8,712)	(11,334)	(14,209)	(7,060)	(7,149)	(11,962)	(5,838)	(6,124)
5 to 7 Courses	17.1%	17.5%	16.7%	17.2%	17.9%	16.5%	17.9%	15.8%	19.6%	13.6%	13.3%	14.0%	18.4%	21.5%	15.7%
	(142,546)	(71,386)	(71,160)	(110,659)	(56,727)	(53,932)	(15,913)	(6,255)	(9,658)	(8,309)	(4,155)	(4,154)	(7,665)	(4,248)	(3,417)
8 or More Courses	36.5%	36.1%	36.9%	35.7%	34.8%	36.6%	38.6%	40.3%	37.2%	42.8%	45.5%	40.0%	34.8%	33.0%	36.4%
	(304,702)	(147,115)	(157,587)	(229,915)	(110,448)	(119,468)	(34,228)	(15,950)	(18,278)	(26,074)	(14,180)	(11,894)	(14,485)	(6,537)	(7,948)

Notes:

" – " indicates sample size too small to estimate.

*** Test of statistical significance compares African Americans with Whites. *** p < .001, ** p < .01, * p < .05

+++ Test of statistical significance compares White men with White women. +++ p < .001, ++ p < .01, + p < .05

~~~ Test of statistical significance compares African American men with African American women. ~~~ p < .001, ~~ p < .01, ~ p < .05

Tests of statistical significance calculated using adjusted sample weight to control for influence of large sample sizes.

Source: National Educational Longitudinal Study of 1988 Eighth Graders, First (1990) Follow-Up.

Figure 6. Percentage of 1990 10th Graders Whose Teachers Report That They Are Very Well Prepared to Teach the Assigned Subject: 1990

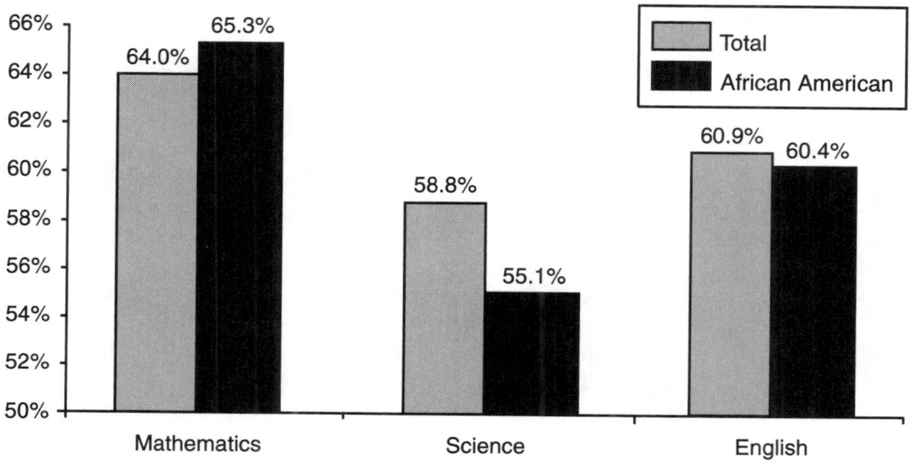

Source: National Educational Longitudinal Study of 1988 Eighth Graders, First. (1990) Follow-Up.

other professional growth activities (32.4% versus 37.7%).

- About 53.0% of African American students' teachers received no support for in-service activities, compared with 47.7% of their White counterparts.

- Only 22.8% of African American 10th graders' teachers, but 33.6% of White 10th graders' teachers, received release time for in-service activities.

- About 10.3% of African American 10th graders' teachers, but 17.7% of White 10th graders' teachers, received reimbursement for expenses associated with in-service programs.

Allocation of Time

About three-fourths (76.1%) of 1990 10th graders' teachers spent some amount of time maintaining order in their classrooms. About two-thirds (60.5%) of students' teachers dedicated some amount, but less than 10%, of their time to maintaining classroom order. **Figure 8** shows that more than one-third (37.1%) of 1990 10th graders' teachers reported that maintaining classroom discipline and order was extremely important.

- **Table 12** shows that a higher percentage of African American 10th graders' teachers than of White 10th graders' teachers spent some amount of time maintaining order in their classrooms (81.8% versus 75.5%).

Table 10. Percentage of 1990 10th Graders Whose Teachers Report That They Are Prepared to Teach the Assigned Subject by Students' Race and Sex: 1990

(weighted sample size in parentheses)

Teachers' Preparation	Race and Sex of Students — Total	Male	Female	White, Non-Hispanic — Total	Male	Female	African American, Non-Hispanic — Total	Male	Female	Hispanic — Total	Male	Female	Other — Total	Male	Female
Mathematics															
Total ~	100.0% (935,737)	100.0% (468,885)	100.0% (466,852)	100.0% (718,323)	100.0% (358,337)	100.0% (359,986)	100.0% (98,227)	100.0% (46,474)	100.0% (51,753)	100.0% (76,689)	100.0% (40,686)	100.0% (36,003)	100.0% (42,498)	100.0% (23,387)	100.0% (19,110)
Very Well Prepared	64.0% (598,489)	63.4% (297,407)	64.5% (301,082)	63.6% (456,640)	63.8% (228,720)	63.3% (227,920)	65.3% (64,172)	61.9% (28,787)	68.4% (35,386)	64.3% (49,339)	62.5% (25,419)	66.4% (23,920)	66.7% (28,338)	61.9% (14,481)	72.5% (13,857)
Well Prepared	18.8% (175,562)	18.6% (87,039)	19.0% (88,523)	18.9% (135,907)	18.0% (64,504)	19.8% (71,403)	16.7% (16,403)	18.5% (8,586)	15.1% (7,817)	19.5% (14,941)	20.0% (8,137)	18.9% (6,804)	19.6% (8,311)	24.9% (5,812)	13.1% (2,499)
Adequately Prepared	4.3% (40,374)	3.9% (18,126)	4.8% (22,249)	4.4% (31,939)	4.0% (14,420)	4.9% (17,520)	3.7% (3,621)	1.7% (805)	5.4% (2,816)	5.5% (4,206)	6.7% (2,709)	4.2% (1,497)	1.4% (609)	0.8% (192)	2.2% (417)
Somewhat Unprepared	1.3% (11,895)	1.6% (7,466)	0.9% (4,428)	1.2% (8,627)	1.3% (4,611)	1.1% (4,015)	0.5% (520)	0.8% (364)	0.3% (157)	1.8% (1,354)	2.7% (1,098)	0.7% (256)	3.3% (1,394)	6.0% (1,394)	0.0% –
Very Unprepared	11.7% (109,417)	12.6% (58,847)	10.8% (50,570)	11.9% (85,210)	12.9% (46,082)	10.9% (39,128)	13.8% (13,511)	17.1% (7,933)	10.8% (5,578)	8.9% (6,849)	8.2% (3,323)	9.8% (3,526)	9.1% (3,846)	6.5% (1,509)	12.2% (2,338)
Science															
Total +	100.0% (819,002)	100.0% (396,840)	100.0% (422,162)	100.0% (612,709)	100.0% (297,567)	100.0% (315,142)	100.0% (88,422)	100.0% (42,942)	100.0% (45,480)	100.0% (72,599)	100.0% (36,141)	100.0% (36,458)	100.0% (45,271)	100.0% (20,190)	100.0% (25,081)
Very Well Prepared	58.8% (481,263)	56.5% (224,370)	60.9% (256,892)	60.5% (370,576)	58.1% (172,919)	62.7% (197,657)	55.1% (48,727)	53.1% (22,798)	57.0% (25,929)	52.9% (38,369)	52.3% (18,898)	53.4% (19,471)	52.1% (23,590)	48.3% (9,755)	55.2% (13,835)
Well Prepared	20.7% (169,491)	20.7% (82,031)	20.7% (87,460)	20.0% (122,251)	20.4% (60,632)	19.6% (61,619)	24.9% (22,018)	24.0% (10,324)	25.7% (11,694)	21.8% (15,837)	20.5% (7,403)	23.1% (8,434)	20.7% (9,385)	18.2% (3,671)	22.8% (5,714)
Adequately Prepared	6.1% (49,785)	6.9% (27,263)	5.3% (22,523)	5.5% (33,918)	6.3% (18,793)	4.8% (15,125)	6.9% (6,091)	8.5% (3,640)	5.4% (2,451)	7.1% (5,155)	7.0% (2,529)	7.2% (2,626)	10.2% (4,622)	11.4% (2,300)	9.3% (2,321)
Somewhat Unprepared	2.4% (19,267)	2.7% (10,644)	2.0% (8,622)	2.2% (13,750)	2.5% (7,467)	2.0% (6,284)	2.6% (2,333)	2.3% (988)	3.0% (1,345)	3.0% (2,151)	4.4% (1,589)	1.5% (562)	2.3% (1,033)	3.0% (601)	1.7% (431)
Very Unprepared	12.1% (99,196)	13.2% (52,531)	11.1% (46,665)	11.8% (72,214)	12.7% (37,756)	10.9% (34,458)	10.5% (9,253)	12.1% (5,192)	8.9% (4,062)	15.3% (11,088)	15.8% (5,721)	14.7% (5,366)	14.7% (6,641)	19.1% (3,862)	11.1% (2,779)
English															
Total	100.0% (1,177,351)	100.0% (580,717)	100.0% (596,634)	100.0% (877,184)	100.0% (438,412)	100.0% (438,772)	100.0% (137,271)	100.0% (61,580)	100.0% (75,691)	100.0% (105,282)	100.0% (53,856)	100.0% (51,426)	100.0% (57,614)	100.0% (26,869)	100.0% (30,745)
Very Well Prepared	60.9% (716,640)	60.0% (348,319)	61.7% (368,321)	61.4% (538,410)	61.0% (267,216)	61.8% (271,194)	60.4% (82,926)	56.6% (34,884)	63.5% (48,042)	56.3% (59,237)	55.1% (29,687)	57.5% (29,549)	62.6% (36,067)	61.5% (16,532)	63.5% (19,536)
Well Prepared	20.5% (241,215)	20.6% (119,608)	20.4% (121,607)	20.5% (180,229)	20.1% (88,109)	21.0% (92,121)	20.3% (27,879)	22.8% (14,024)	18.3% (13,855)	20.4% (21,493)	22.4% (12,073)	18.3% (9,420)	20.2% (11,614)	20.1% (5,403)	20.2% (6,211)
Adequately Prepared	4.0% (47,235)	4.0% (22,957)	4.1% (24,278)	3.6% (31,850)	3.8% (16,559)	3.5% (15,291)	5.1% (7,034)	4.3% (2,626)	5.8% (4,408)	4.4% (4,599)	4.1% (2,197)	4.7% (2,401)	6.5% (3,752)	5.9% (1,574)	7.1% (2,177)
Somewhat Unprepared	1.6% (18,388)	1.7% (9,981)	1.4% (8,408)	1.4% (12,459)	1.5% (6,785)	1.3% (5,674)	1.7% (2,360)	1.9% (1,153)	1.6% (1,207)	2.8% (2,924)	3.1% (1,660)	2.5% (1,263)	1.1% (646)	1.4% (383)	0.9% (263)
Very Unprepared	13.1% (153,873)	13.8% (79,852)	12.4% (74,021)	13.0% (114,237)	13.6% (59,744)	12.4% (54,493)	12.4% (17,071)	14.4% (8,892)	10.8% (8,178)	16.2% (17,030)	15.3% (8,238)	17.1% (8,792)	9.6% (5,535)	11.1% (2,978)	8.3% (2,557)

Notes:
" – " indicates sample size too small to estimate.

*** Test of statistical significance compares African Americans with Whites. *** $p < .001$, ** $p < .01$, * $p < .05$.

+++ Test of statistical significance compares White men with White women. +++ $p < .001$, ++ $p < .01$, + $p < .05$.

~~~ Test of statistical significance compares African American men with African American women. ~~~ $p < .001$, ~~ $p < .01$, ~ $p < .05$.

Tests of statistical significance calculated using adjusted sample weight to control for influence of large sample sizes.

Source: National Educational Longitudinal Study of 1988 Eighth Graders, First (1990) Follow-Up.

Figure 7. Participation in In-Service Training by
1990 10th Graders' Teachers and Support They Received: 1990

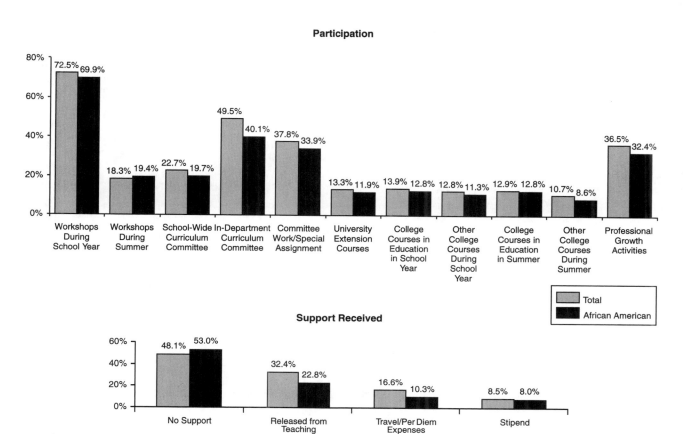

Source: National Educational Longitudinal Study of 1988 Eighth Graders, First (1990) Follow-Up.

Table 11. Participation in In-Service Training by 1990 10th Graders' Teachers by Students' Race and Sex: 1990
(weighted sample size in parentheses)

Teachers' In-Service Training	Race and Sex of Students			White, Non-Hispanic			African American, Non-Hispanic			Hispanic			Other		
	Total	Male	Female	Total	Male	Female	Total	Male	Female	Total	Male	Female	Total	Male	Female
Participation in In-Service	100.0%	100.0%	100.0%	100.0%	100.0%	100.0%	100.0%	100.0%	100.0%	100.0%	100.0%	100.0%	100.0%	100.0%	100.0%
	(1,577,228)	(785,138)	(792,090)	(1,201,869)	(596,943)	(604,926)	(171,238)	(82,875)	(88,364)	(127,633)	(67,063)	(60,570)	(76,488)	(38,258)	(38,230)
Workshops During School Year + ~	72.5%	72.5%	72.6%	73.1%	72.7%	73.4%	69.9%	73.9%	66.2%	72.2%	71.7%	72.8%	70.0%	66.5%	73.5%
	(1,143,744)	(568,873)	(574,871)	(878,323)	(434,121)	(444,202)	(119,731)	(61,228)	(58,503)	(92,141)	(48,069)	(44,072)	(53,549)	(25,455)	(28,094)
Workshops During Summer	18.3%	17.9%	18.8%	18.3%	17.8%	18.7%	19.4%	19.6%	19.2%	19.0%	20.0%	17.9%	16.0%	11.2%	20.8%
	(289,180)	(140,432)	(148,749)	(219,455)	(106,449)	(113,006)	(33,224)	(16,255)	(16,968)	(24,260)	(13,438)	(10,822)	(12,242)	(4,290)	(7,952)
School-Wide Curriculum Committee *	22.7%	22.3%	23.1%	23.5%	23.4%	23.7%	19.7%	17.8%	21.4%	20.3%	20.2%	20.5%	20.7%	18.1%	23.2%
	(358,391)	(175,045)	(183,345)	(282,900)	(139,798)	(143,103)	(33,742)	(14,791)	(18,951)	(25,942)	(13,537)	(12,405)	(15,806)	(6,919)	(8,887)
In-Department Curriculum Committee ***	49.5%	49.2%	49.9%	51.6%	52.2%	51.1%	40.1%	38.3%	41.8%	42.4%	40.4%	44.6%	49.4%	41.3%	57.5%
	(781,344)	(386,171)	(395,173)	(620,762)	(311,479)	(309,283)	(68,676)	(31,773)	(36,904)	(54,099)	(27,100)	(26,998)	(37,807)	(15,819)	(21,989)
Committee Work/ Special Assignment **	37.8%	38.1%	37.4%	38.4%	39.3%	37.5%	33.9%	34.2%	33.5%	38.9%	36.8%	41.2%	34.6%	30.9%	38.2%
	(595,551)	(299,261)	(296,290)	(461,475)	(234,382)	(227,092)	(57,988)	(28,360)	(29,628)	(49,647)	(24,684)	(24,962)	(26,442)	(11,835)	(14,607)
University Extension Courses	13.3%	13.8%	12.8%	13.3%	13.8%	12.8%	11.9%	13.3%	10.5%	12.8%	12.2%	13.5%	17.1%	17.8%	16.5%
	(209,521)	(108,370)	(101,151)	(159,769)	(82,366)	(77,403)	(20,313)	(11,056)	(9,257)	(16,342)	(8,157)	(8,185)	(13,098)	(6,791)	(6,307)
College Courses in Ed. During School Year	13.9%	14.2%	13.6%	13.7%	13.9%	13.5%	12.8%	14.9%	10.9%	16.9%	15.6%	18.4%	15.3%	15.4%	15.1%
	(219,637)	(111,714)	(107,923)	(164,432)	(83,023)	(81,409)	(21,955)	(12,351)	(9,604)	(21,569)	(10,439)	(11,130)	(11,682)	(5,901)	(5,781)
Other College Courses During School Year ~	12.8%	13.0%	12.7%	13.2%	13.1%	13.3%	11.3%	13.6%	9.1%	12.2%	12.3%	12.0%	11.9%	11.3%	12.5%
	(202,553)	(102,131)	(100,422)	(158,567)	(78,261)	(80,306)	(19,326)	(11,281)	(8,045)	(15,548)	(8,259)	(7,289)	(9,112)	(4,329)	(4,782)
College Courses in Ed. During Summer	12.9%	13.6%	12.2%	12.8%	13.4%	12.1%	12.8%	13.8%	11.9%	15.0%	15.0%	15.1%	11.4%	12.8%	10.0%
	(203,102)	(106,577)	(96,525)	(153,268)	(80,223)	(73,045)	(21,938)	(11,419)	(10,519)	(19,191)	(10,039)	(9,151)	(8,706)	(4,896)	(3,810)
Other College Courses During Summer *	10.7%	10.3%	11.0%	10.7%	10.4%	11.1%	8.6%	8.6%	8.5%	11.9%	12.0%	11.8%	12.3%	10.8%	13.7%
	(168,135)	(81,215)	(86,920)	(128,848)	(61,875)	(66,973)	(14,677)	(7,140)	(7,537)	(15,226)	(8,049)	(7,177)	(9,385)	(4,150)	(5,234)
Other Professional Growth Activities **	36.5%	36.0%	37.1%	37.7%	36.9%	38.5%	32.4%	32.2%	32.6%	31.2%	33.5%	28.7%	35.5%	33.7%	37.3%
	(576,094)	(282,523)	(293,570)	(453,604)	(220,499)	(233,105)	(55,501)	(26,654)	(28,847)	(39,839)	(22,479)	(17,360)	(27,149)	(12,891)	(14,258)
None of the Above ** +	6.5%	5.8%	7.2%	5.9%	5.2%	6.7%	8.9%	7.1%	10.5%	7.8%	8.1%	7.4%	8.0%	8.4%	7.6%
	(102,663)	(45,545)	(57,118)	(71,404)	(30,967)	(40,437)	(15,193)	(5,897)	(9,296)	(9,935)	(5,459)	(4,475)	(6,132)	(3,222)	(2,910)
Support for In-Service Total	100.0%	100.0%	100.0%	100.0%	100.0%	100.0%	100.0%	100.0%	100.0%	100.0%	100.0%	100.0%	100.0%	100.0%	100.0%
	(2,050,613)	(1,018,046)	(1,032,567)	(1,541,137)	(766,269)	(774,868)	(234,859)	(112,156)	(122,703)	(174,467)	(88,864)	(85,603)	(100,149)	(50,757)	(49,392)
Received No Support **	48.1%	47.9%	48.3%	47.7%	48.3%	47.2%	53.0%	50.8%	55.1%	45.4%	44.0%	46.8%	47.7%	43.7%	51.9%
	(987,184)	(488,146)	(499,038)	(735,610)	(369,843)	(365,767)	(124,554)	(56,988)	(67,566)	(79,201)	(39,144)	(40,057)	(47,819)	(22,171)	(25,648)
Released From Teaching ***	32.4%	32.4%	32.4%	33.6%	32.9%	34.3%	22.8%	23.5%	22.1%	34.0%	36.1%	31.9%	34.4%	38.6%	30.0%
	(665,244)	(330,201)	(335,043)	(518,054)	(252,175)	(265,879)	(53,449)	(26,366)	(27,083)	(59,338)	(32,060)	(27,277)	(34,403)	(19,600)	(14,803)
Travel/Per Diem *** Expenses	16.6%	17.0%	16.2%	17.7%	18.0%	17.4%	10.3%	10.1%	10.5%	15.4%	16.4%	14.3%	16.9%	18.2%	15.5%
	(340,996)	(173,257)	(167,738)	(273,052)	(138,173)	(134,879)	(24,218)	(11,275)	(12,943)	(26,819)	(14,551)	(12,268)	(16,906)	(9,258)	(7,648)
Received Stipend	8.5%	8.6%	8.3%	8.4%	8.3%	8.5%	8.0%	8.9%	7.3%	9.5%	9.7%	9.3%	8.4%	10.9%	5.9%
	(173,381)	(87,408)	(85,974)	(129,515)	(63,298)	(66,216)	(18,861)	(9,963)	(8,897)	(16,563)	(8,595)	(7,968)	(8,443)	(5,551)	(2,891)

Notes:
*** Test of statistical significance compares African Americans with Whites. *** p < .001, ** p < .01, * p < .05.
+++ Test of statistical significance compares White men with White women. +++ p < .001, ++ p < .01, + p < .05.
~~~ Test of statistical significance compares African American men with African American women. ~~~ p < .001, ~~ p < .01, ~ p < .05.
Tests of statistical significance calculated using adjusted sample weight to control for influence of large sample sizes.
Source: National Educational Longitudinal Study of 1988 Eighth Graders, First (1990) Follow-Up.

Figure 8. 1990 10th Grade Teachers' Ratings of Importance of Maintaining Discipline in the Classroom: 1990

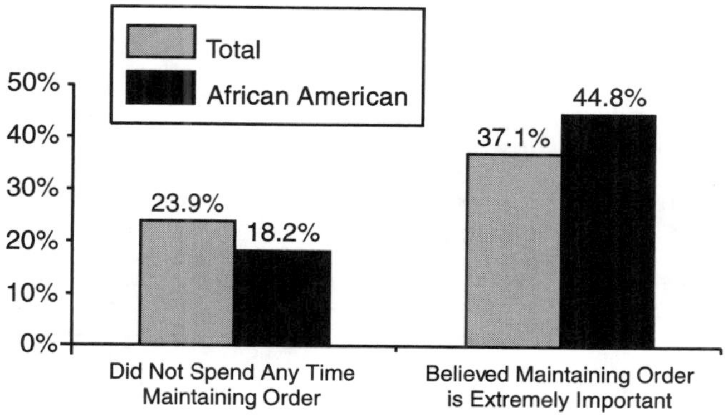

Source: National Educational Longitudinal Study of 1988 Eighth Graders, First (1990) Follow-Up.

- A higher percentage of African American students' teachers than of White students' teachers felt that maintaining order and discipline in the classroom was extremely important (44.8% versus 36.2%).

STANDARDIZED TEST PERFORMANCE

(Source: PRAXIS Program of Educational Testing Service)

Representation of African Americans

The extent to which the 50 states require prospective teachers to take the PRAXIS examination varies. Because of this variation, determining whether African Americans are appropriately represented nationally on any part of the Core Battery is difficult.

Nonetheless, relative to their representation in the U.S. population, African Americans were underrepresented among PRAXIS test takers in 1995/96.

Regardless of race group, the majority of PRAXIS test takers were women.

- **Table 13** shows that, since examinees did not necessarily take all three Core Battery tests, the percentage of African Americans varied between 8.5% for the Test of Professional Knowledge and 9.5% for the Test of General Knowledge.

- The percentage of PRAXIS test takers who were female was similar for African Americans (72% to 74%) and Whites (74% to 75%).

Note: National historical comparisons are problematic (and are not presented here) since the states that require the PRAXIS test vary from year to year. For example, use of the NTE has recently increased in the western states. As a result, an apparent decline in the representation of African Americans among examinees would be an artifact of the states requiring the examination rather than a change in the number of African American examinees.

Table 12. 1990 10th Grade Teachers' Ratings of Importance of Maintaining Discipline in the Classroom by Students' Race and Sex: 1990

(weighted sample size in parentheses)

Maintaining Order	Race and Sex of Students			White, Non-Hispanic			African American, Non-Hispanic			Hispanic			Other		
	Total	Male	Female	Total	Male	Female	Total	Male	Female	Total	Male	Female	Total	Male	Female
Time Spent Maintaining Order															
Total *** +++ ~~~	100.0%	100.0%	100.0%	100.0%	100.0%	100.0%	100.0%	100.0%	100.0%	100.0%	100.0%	100.0%	100.0%	100.0%	100.0%
	(1,986,249)	(987,010)	(999,239)	(1,495,107)	(744,712)	(750,396)	(220,497)	(104,709)	(115,788)	(172,614)	(88,469)	(84,145)	(98,030)	(49,120)	(48,910)
None	23.9%	22.8%	25.1%	24.5%	23.4%	25.7%	18.2%	15.4%	20.8%	24.1%	24.5%	23.6%	26.9%	26.1%	27.7%
	(474,905)	(224,593)	(250,312)	(366,836)	(173,980)	(192,857)	(40,175)	(16,084)	(24,091)	(41,536)	(21,706)	(19,830)	(26,358)	(12,825)	(13,534)
Some Time Maintaining Order	76.1%	77.2%	74.9%	75.5%	76.6%	74.3%	81.8%	84.6%	79.2%	75.9%	75.5%	76.4%	73.1%	73.9%	72.3%
	(1,511,344)	(762,417)	(748,927)	(1,128,271)	(570,732)	(557,539)	(180,322)	(88,625)	(91,697)	(131,079)	(66,764)	(64,315)	(71,672)	(36,296)	(35,376)
Amount of Time Maintaining Order															
Some Time Maintaining Order	100.0%	100.0%	100.0%	100.0%	100.0%	100.0%	100.0%	100.0%	100.0%	100.0%	100.0%	100.0%	100.0%	100.0%	100.0%
	(1,511,344)	(762,417)	(748,927)	(1,128,271)	(570,732)	(557,539)	(180,322)	(88,625)	(91,697)	(131,079)	(66,764)	(64,315)	(71,672)	(36,296)	(35,376)
Less than 10%	79.5%	78.6%	80.5%	81.4%	80.7%	82.1%	72.4%	69.6%	75.1%	72.6%	72.3%	73.0%	80.9%	77.6%	84.3%
	(1,202,143)	(598,924)	(603,219)	(918,374)	(460,836)	(457,537)	(130,564)	(61,667)	(68,897)	(95,203)	(48,240)	(46,963)	(58,002)	(28,181)	(29,822)
10% to 24%	12.3%	11.9%	12.7%	11.8%	11.2%	12.3%	14.8%	15.1%	14.5%	15.0%	14.4%	15.6%	9.9%	10.7%	9.1%
	(186,128)	(90,762)	(95,366)	(132,706)	(63,868)	(68,838)	(26,666)	(13,407)	(13,259)	(19,649)	(9,607)	(10,042)	(7,106)	(3,880)	(3,227)
25% to 49%	4.1%	4.9%	3.1%	3.1%	4.1%	2.0%	8.4%	8.7%	8.1%	6.5%	7.7%	5.3%	4.0%	4.4%	3.6%
	(61,266)	(37,721)	(23,545)	(34,701)	(23,278)	(11,423)	(15,150)	(7,723)	(7,427)	(8,570)	(5,139)	(3,431)	(2,844)	(1,581)	(1,263)
50% to 74%	1.8%	1.8%	1.8%	1.8%	1.7%	1.8%	1.4%	1.4%	1.5%	2.9%	3.2%	2.6%	2.0%	3.1%	0.9%
	(27,720)	(14,093)	(13,627)	(19,879)	(9,628)	(10,251)	(2,588)	(1,223)	(1,366)	(3,800)	(2,112)	(1,687)	(1,453)	(1,130)	(323)
75% to 100%	2.3%	2.7%	1.8%	2.0%	2.3%	1.7%	3.0%	5.2%	0.8%	2.9%	2.5%	3.4%	3.2%	4.2%	2.1%
	(34,087)	(20,917)	(13,171)	(22,611)	(13,122)	(9,489)	(5,353)	(4,605)	(748)	(3,857)	(1,665)	(2,192)	(2,266)	(1,525)	(741)
Importance of Maintaining Discipline & Order															
Total *** +++	100.0%	100.0%	100.0%	100.0%	100.0%	100.0%	100.0%	100.0%	100.0%	100.0%	100.0%	100.0%	100.0%	100.0%	100.0%
	(1,574,492)	(782,761)	(791,732)	(1,199,783)	(595,674)	(604,108)	(169,971)	(81,540)	(88,431)	(128,230)	(67,299)	(60,931)	(76,508)	(38,247)	(38,261)
Not Important	1.3%	0.6%	2.1%	1.4%	0.5%	2.2%	0.7%	0.2%	1.1%	0.7%	0.5%	0.9%	3.6%	1.8%	5.5%
	(21,248)	(4,396)	(16,852)	(16,469)	(3,225)	(13,244)	(1,168)	(193)	(974)	(837)	(303)	(534)	(2,775)	(674)	(2,100)
Somewhat Important	14.7%	15.3%	14.2%	15.0%	15.9%	14.2%	10.5%	9.5%	11.5%	15.3%	17.5%	12.9%	18.7%	14.7%	22.6%
	(231,958)	(119,669)	(112,289)	(180,128)	(94,532)	(85,596)	(17,911)	(7,743)	(10,168)	(19,632)	(11,762)	(7,871)	(14,287)	(5,633)	(8,654)
Very Important	46.8%	47.7%	45.9%	47.4%	48.4%	46.4%	44.0%	41.6%	46.2%	47.9%	48.0%	47.8%	42.6%	49.3%	35.9%
	(737,243)	(373,503)	(363,740)	(568,463)	(288,445)	(280,019)	(74,753)	(33,900)	(40,853)	(61,425)	(32,297)	(29,128)	(32,601)	(18,861)	(13,740)
Extremely Important	37.1%	36.4%	37.7%	36.2%	35.2%	37.3%	44.8%	48.7%	41.2%	36.1%	34.1%	38.4%	35.1%	34.2%	36.0%
	(584,044)	(285,193)	(298,850)	(434,723)	(209,473)	(225,250)	(76,140)	(39,704)	(36,435)	(46,336)	(22,938)	(23,398)	(26,846)	(13,079)	(13,767)

Notes:

*** Test of statistical significance compares African Americans with Whites. *** p < .001, ** p < .01, * p < .05.

+++ Test of statistical significance compares White men with White women. +++ p < .001, ++ p < .01, + p < .05.

~~~ Test of statistical significance compares African American men with African American women. ~~~ p < .001, ~~ p < .01, ~ p < .05.

Tests of statistical significance calculated using adjusted sample weight to control for influence of large sample sizes.

Source: National Educational Longitudinal Study of 1988 Eighth Graders, First (1990) Follow-Up.

Test Scores

Figure 9 shows that, on average, mean scores for African Americans were lower than the mean scores for Whites on each of the three Core Battery tests.

- **Table 13** shows that the average score for African Americans was 14 points lower than the

average score for Whites on the Test of General Knowledge (647 versus 661), 12 points lower on the Test of Communication Skills (651 versus 663), and 12 points lower on the Test of Professional Knowledge (651 versus 663).

Table 13. Summary Information for PRAXIS Core Battery Tests: 1995/96

Test Type	White	African American	Hispanic	Asian American/ Pacific Islander	American Indian/ Alaskan Native	Other
Test of General Knowledge						
Number of Tests	53,344	6,025	1,557	794	320	1,639
%of Total Test Takers	83.8%	9.5%	2.4%	1.2%	0.5%	2.6%
Mean Score	661	647	652	658	653	657
Standard Deviation	11	11	12	12	14	15
%Female	75%	73%	77%	78%	76%	70%
Test of Communication Skills						
Number of Tests	45,540	5,111	1,274	692	308	1,367
%of Total Test Takers	83.9%	9.4%	2.3%	1.2%	0.6%	2.5%
Mean Score	663	651	655	657	654	658
Standard Deviation	10	12	14	13	13	15
%Female	74%	72%	76%	76%	75%	69%
Test of Professional Knowledge						
Number of Tests	60,097	5,996	1,448	897	375	1,504
%of Total Test Takers	85.5%	8.5%	2.1%	1.3%	0.5%	2.1%
Mean Score	663	651	655	658	656	658
Standard Deviation	9	11	13	12	13	14
%Female	75%	74%	75%	77%	75%	66%

Notes:

Score Scale: 600 to 695 by 1 point increments.

Numbers do not include repeat test takers.

Source: Summary Statistics for Praxis Tests Taken Testing Year 1995-96 (ETS: Oct. 1996).

Figure 9. Mean Scores of PRAXIS Core Battery Tests in 1995/96

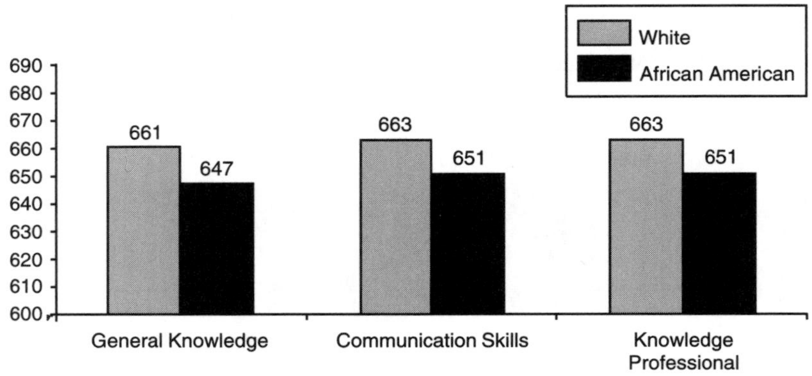

Source: Summary Statistics for Praxis Tests Taken Testing Year 1995-96 Educational Testing Service, October 1996.

CHAPTER X.
Characteristics of Public and Private School Principals

How well are African Americans represented among the nation's public and private school principals? How does the experience and training of African American principals compare with that received by their White counterparts? Do African American and White principals receive comparable salaries? What aspects of their schools and student bodies do African American principals perceive to be problematic?

The School Administrator Survey of the Schools and Staffing Survey (SASS) collects the background characteristics and employment experiences of public and private school principals nationwide at both the elementary and the secondary school levels. Sponsored by the U.S. Department of Education's National Center for Education Statistics, this survey also provides information on the educational qualifications and working conditions of the nation's principals. The most recent (1993/94) SASS data are used for the analyses presented in this chapter.

CHAPTER ORGANIZATION

To facilitate comparisons among principals who work in public and private schools, the data have been arranged under common headings, with the public sector information preceding the private. The data are organized into four sections:

1. Representation of African Americans among public and private school principals by school characteristics, including school level, affiliation, urbanicity, geographic region, racial composition of the student body, and other school characteristics;

2. Education and experience of public and private school principals, including the highest level of education attained, their previous positions, age, professional experience, and training received;

3. Average salaries overall and by age, urbanicity, region, and months employed; and

4. Aspects of their schools that principals define as problems.

PART I — OVERVIEW

Representation

African Americans are underrepresented among America's public and private school principals relative to their share of school-age children nationwide (16.0%). Like their representation among public and private school students, African Americans are better represented among public (10.1%) than among private (4.2%) school principals. Nonetheless, the share of African American principals exceeds their representation as teachers in both public (10.1% of principals versus 7.4% of teachers) and private (4.2% of principals and 3.1% of teachers) schools.

Overall, women constituted only 34.5% of public school principals (but 72.9% of all teachers). In contrast, African American women made up a higher share than African American men of both public and private school principals. But among both African Americans and Whites at public and private schools, a higher share of women than men were principals of elementary rather than secondary schools.

African American principals were concentrated in urban public and private schools. More than one-half of African American public school principals and private school principals worked in urban areas. African American principals were also concentrated in schools with high percentages of minority students and teachers.

Mirroring the regional distribution of African Americans throughout the United States, about one-half of African American public school principals worked in the South. In contrast, the distribution of African American private school principals appeared to be unrelated to region, with only 30.8% of African American private school principals working in the South.

Education and Experience

The career paths of public and private school principals appeared to vary by race and sex. For example, a higher percentage of African Americans than Whites worked as assistant principals prior to becoming public school principals. A higher share of African American women than of other public school principals had once served as curriculum coordinators. Only one-fifth of African Americans, but one-third of Whites, worked as department heads prior to becoming private school principals.

African American public school principals tended to be older than their White counterparts. But, on average, African Americans had fewer years of experience as public school principals than Whites. Female public school principals had less experience than men among both African Americans and Whites. Although African American and White private school principals had comparable levels of experience as principals, African Americans had less teaching experience than Whites, on average.

Some programs appear to be working to increase the representation of African Americans among America's principals. Among both public and private school principals a higher percentage of African Americans than Whites received administrative internships, and training and development for aspiring principals.

Annual Salaries

Overall, average salaries were about one-half as high for private school principals as for public school principals ($29,714 versus $54,858). Salaries for African American and White public school principals appeared to be comparable, on average, for those who were employed 12 months of the year.

The small number of African American private school principals in the sample limits the conclusions that may be drawn about differences in salaries by race and sex.

Aspects of School Life Perceived to Be Problems

African American principals tended to face different challenges than their White counterparts. For example, school poverty was perceived to be a problem by a higher percentage of African American than White public and private school principals. But student use of alcohol appeared to be a problem for a smaller proportion of African American principals than for White principals in both public and private schools.

PART II — DETAILED DESCRIPTIONS AND TABLES

REPRESENTATION OF PRINCIPALS

Representation of Principals by School Level

Public Schools

Although more than 2.56 million individuals worked as teachers in America's public schools in 1993/94, only about 80,000 worked as principals. African Americans were better represented among public school principals than among public school teachers, since African Americans constituted 10.1%

of all public school principals (**Figure** 1) but 7.4% of all public school teachers (see Chapter VIII). The greater representation of African Americans among public school principals than among public school teachers is attributable primarily to the greater representation of African American men among principals than among teachers. Although still underrepresented relative to their representation in the U.S. population, African American men represented 4.3% of all public school principals but only 1.5% of all public school teachers.

- **Table 1** shows that African Americans comprised 10.8% of all public elementary school principals, 7.3% of all secondary school principals, and 6.3% of all elementary/secondary combined school principals. These shares are

conservative estimates, since African Americans represented 14.1% of those for whom school level was unknown.

Overall, women were underrepresented among public school principals, particularly at secondary schools. Although women represented 72.9% of all public school teachers, they represented 34.5% of all public school principals, 41.1% of elementary school principals, and 13.8% of secondary school principals.

- **Table 1** shows that 27.0% of African American male and 30.7% of White male public school principals worked at secondary schools, compared with only 8.9% of African American women and 9.2% of White women.

Figure 1. Distribution of Public School Principals by Race and Sex: 1993/94

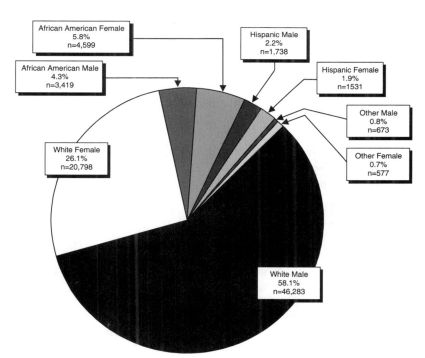

Source: Schools and Staffing Survey, 1993-94.

Table 1. School Level of Public School Principals by Race, and Sex: 1993/94
(weighted sample size in parentheses)

School Level	Total	Male	Female	White, Non-Hispanic Total	Male	Female	African American, Non-Hispanic Total	Male	Female	Hispanic Total	Male	Female	Other Total	Male	Female
Total Weighted Sample	100.0%	65.5%	34.5%	84.3%	58.1%	26.1%	10.1%	4.3%	5.8%	4.1%	2.2%	1.9%	1.6%	0.8%	0.7%
	(79,618)	(52,113)	(27,505)	(67,081)	(46,283)	(20,798)	(8,018)	(3,419)	(4,599)	(3,269)	(1,738)	(1,531)	(1,250)	(673)	(577)
Totals*** +++ ~~~	100.0%	100.0%	100.0%	100.0%	100.0%	100.0%	100.0%	100.0%	100.0%	100.0%	100.0%	100.0%	100.0%	100.0%	100.0%
(row %)	100.0%	65.5%	34.5%	84.3%	58.1%	26.1%	10.1%	4.3%	5.8%	4.1%	2.2%	1.9%	1.6%	0.8%	0.7%
	(79,618)	(52,113)	(27,505)	(67,081)	(46,283)	(20,798)	(8,018)	(3,419)	(4,599)	(3,269)	(1,738)	(1,531)	(1,250)	(673)	(577)
Elementary	67.4%	60.7%	80.2%	66.4%	60.3%	79.9%	72.6%	61.6%	80.8%	73.9%	68.2%	80.3%	73.4%	60.6%	88.2%
(row %)	100.0%	58.9%	41.1%	83.0%	52.0%	31.0%	10.8%	3.9%	6.9%	4.5%	2.2%	2.3%	1.7%	0.8%	0.9%
	(53,684)	(31,616)	(22,069)	(44,533)	(27,916)	(16,617)	(5,820)	(2,106)	(3,714)	(2,415)	(1,186)	(1,229)	(917)	(408)	(509)
Secondary	22.9%	30.2%	9.1%	24.0%	30.7%	9.2%	16.6%	27.0%	8.9%	18.0%	24.3%	10.8%	18.6%	30.3%	5.0%
(row %)	100.0%	86.2%	13.8%	88.2%	77.8%	10.5%	7.3%	5.0%	2.2%	3.2%	2.3%	0.9%	1.3%	1.1%	0.2%
	(18,262)	(15,750)	(2,513)	(16,111)	(14,202)	(1,909)	(1,332)	(922)	(410)	(587)	(422)	(165)	(233)	(204)	(29)
Combined	3.5%	4.0%	2.4%	3.6%	4.1%	2.6%	2.1%	2.9%	1.6%	2.0%	2.4%	1.6%	4.8%	5.3%	4.2%
(row %)	100.0%	76.0%	24.0%	89.1%	69.6%	19.5%	6.3%	3.6%	2.7%	2.4%	1.5%	0.9%	2.2%	1.3%	0.9%
	(2,747)	(2,088)	(659)	(2,448)	(1,912)	(536)	(172)	(98)	(74)	(67)	(42)	(25)	(60)	(36)	(24)
Unknown	6.2%	5.1%	8.2%	5.9%	4.9%	8.3%	8.7%	8.6%	8.7%	6.1%	5.1%	7.3%	3.2%	3.7%	2.6%
(row %)	100.0%	54.0%	46.0%	81.0%	45.8%	35.3%	14.1%	6.0%	8.1%	4.1%	1.8%	2.3%	0.8%	0.5%	0.3%
	(4,923)	(2,659)	(2,264)	(3,989)	(2,253)	(1,736)	(694)	(293)	(401)	(200)	(88)	(112)	(40)	(25)	(15)

Notes:

*** Test of statistical significance compares African Americans with Whites. *** p < .001, ** p < .01, * p < .05.

+++ Test of statistical significance compares White men with White women. +++ p < .001, ++ p < .01, + p < .05.

~~~ Test of statistical significance compares African American men with African American women. ~~~ p < .001, ~~ p < .01, ~ p < .05.

Tests of statistical significance calculated using adjusted sample weight to control for influence of large sample sizes.

Source: Schools and Staffing Survey, 1993-94.

- More than three-fourths of African American women (80.8%) and White women (79.9%) worked at elementary schools, compared with less than two-thirds of African American men (61.6%) and White men (60.3%).

Private Schools

In 1993/94, the ratio of private school teachers to private school principals was about 15:1, since 378,000 individuals were employed as teachers (see Chapter VIII) and 25,000 as principals in America's private schools. African Americans were slightly better represented among private school principals than among private school teachers, since African Americans represented 4.2% of private school principals and 3.1% of private school teachers. Nonetheless, African Americans were underrepresented among both principals and teachers relative to their 12.1% representation in the U. S. population in 1993/94.

Overall, women represented a smaller share of private school principals than private school teachers (53.6% versus 75.4%). Among African Americans, more than twice as many women as men were private school principals in 1993/94 (713 women versus 347 men).

- **Figure 2** shows that, in 1993/94, African American women represented 2.9% and African American men represented 1.4% of all private school principals.

Figure 2. Distribution of Private School Principals by Race and Sex: 1993/94

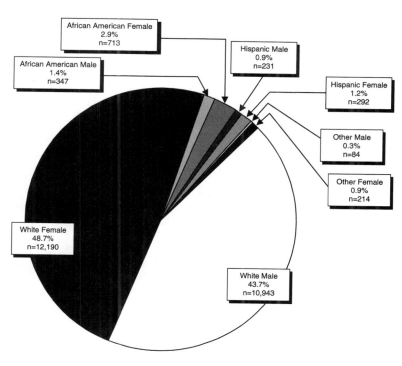

African American Female
2.9%
n=713

African American Male
1.4%
n=347

Hispanic Male
0.9%
n=231

Hispanic Female
1.2%
n=292

Other Male
0.3%
n=84

Other Female
0.9%
n=214

White Female
48.7%
n=12,190

White Male
43.7%
n=10,943

Source: Schools and Staffing Survey, 1993-94.

More than one-half of private school principals (53.4%) worked in elementary schools. Overall, women were overrepresented among private elementary school principals and underrepresented among private secondary school principals; women represented 67.7% of elementary school principals but 34.1% of secondary school principals.

- **Table 2** shows that African American women represented 4.1% of elementary school principals but only 0.5% of secondary school principals.

- The distribution of African American men by school level is unclear, given that school level is unknown for 42.1% of African American males.

Representation of Principals by School Affiliation

Private Schools Only

Nearly one-half (45.4%) of private school principals worked in non-Catholic religious schools, about one-third (33.3%) in Catholic schools, and one-fifth (21.3%) in nonsectarian schools. Relative to their representation among private school principals (4.2%), African Americans were overrepresented among principals at non-Catholic religious schools (5.6%).

Overall, women were concentrated at Catholic schools and nonsectarian schools, rather than at non-Catholic religious schools. **Table 3** shows that overall, women represented 76.1% of principals at Catholic schools and 68.1% of principals at nonsectarian

Table 2. School Level of Private School Principals by Race and Sex: 1993/94
(weighted sample size in parentheses)

School Level	Total	Male	Female	White, Non-Hispanic			African American, Non-Hispanic			Hispanic			Other		
				Total	Male	Female	Total	Male	Female	Total	Male	Female	Total	Male	Female
Total Weighted Sample	100.0%	46.4%	53.6%	92.5%	43.7%	48.7%	4.2%	1.4%	2.9%	2.1%	0.9%	1.2%	1.2%	0.3%	0.9%
	(25,015)	(11,605)	(13,409)	(23,133)	(10,943)	(12,190)	(1,060)	(347)	(713)	(523)	(231)	(292)	(298)	(84)	(214)
Total *** +++ ~	100.0%	100.0%	100.0%	100.0%	100.0%	100.0%	100.0%	100.0%	100.0%	100.0%	100.0%	100.0%	100.0%	100.0%	100.0%
(row %)	100.0%	46.4%	53.6%	92.5%	43.7%	48.7%	4.2%	1.4%	2.9%	2.1%	0.9%	1.2%	1.2%	0.3%	0.9%
	(25,015)	(11,605)	(13,409)	(23,133)	(10,943)	(12,190)	(1,060)	(347)	(713)	(523)	(231)	(292)	(298)	(84)	(214)
Elementary	53.4%	37.2%	67.4%	52.6%	37.1%	66.4%	63.0%	34.9%	76.7%	54.1%	41.1%	64.4%	80.9%	45.2%	94.9%
(row %)	100.0%	32.3%	67.7%	91.1%	30.4%	60.7%	5.0%	0.9%	4.1%	2.1%	0.7%	1.4%	1.8%	0.3%	1.5%
	(13,355)	(4,317)	(9,038)	(12,163)	(4,063)	(8,100)	(668)	(121)	(547)	(283)	(95)	(188)	(241)	(38)	(203)
Secondary	9.2%	13.0%	5.8%	9.6%	13.3%	6.3%	3.3%	6.6%	1.7%	9.2%	17.3%	2.7%	0.0%	0.0%	0.0%
(row %)	100.0%	65.9%	34.1%	96.4%	63.1%	33.3%	1.5%	1.0%	0.5%	2.1%	1.7%	0.3%	0.0%	0.0%	0.0%
	(2,297)	(1,513)	(784)	(2,214)	(1,450)	(764)	(35)	(23)	(12)	(48)	(40)	(8)	–	–	–
Combined	27.1%	37.3%	18.2%	27.8%	37.9%	18.8%	12.0%	16.4%	9.8%	30.8%	37.2%	25.7%	15.1%	47.6%	2.3%
(row %)	100.0%	63.9%	36.1%	95.1%	61.2%	33.9%	1.9%	0.8%	1.0%	2.4%	1.3%	1.1%	0.7%	0.6%	0.1%
	(6,772)	(4,329)	(2,443)	(6,439)	(4,146)	(2,293)	(127)	(57)	(70)	(161)	(86)	(75)	(45)	(40)	(5)
Unknown	10.4%	12.5%	8.5%	10.0%	11.7%	8.5%	21.7%	42.1%	11.8%	5.9%	4.3%	7.2%	4.0%	7.1%	2.8%
(row %)	100.0%	55.8%	44.2%	89.5%	49.6%	39.9%	8.9%	5.6%	3.2%	1.2%	0.4%	0.8%	0.5%	0.2%	0.2%
	(2,590)	(1,446)	(1,144)	(2,317)	(1,284)	(1,033)	(230)	(146)	(84)	(31)	(10)	(21)	(12)	(6)	(6)

Notes:
" – " indicates sample size too small to estimate.
*** Test of statistical significance compares African Americans with Whites. *** p < .001, ** p < .01, * p < .05.
+++ Test of statistical significance compares White men with White women. +++ p < .001, ++ p < .01, + p < .05.
~~~ Test of statistical significance compares African American men with African American women. ~~~ p < .001, ~~ p < .01, ~ p < .05.
Tests of statistical significance calculated using adjusted sample weight to control for influence of large sample sizes.
Source: Schools and Staffing Survey, 1993-94.

schools, but only 30.3% of principals at non-Catholic religious schools.

- African Americans represented 5.6% of principals at non-Catholic religious schools, 3.3% of principals at nonsectarian schools, and 3.0% of principals at Catholic schools.

Representation of Principals by Urbanicity

Public Schools

About one-half (48.8%) of all public school principals worked at rural schools, 27.3% at suburban schools and 23.9% at urban schools. **Figure 3** shows

that African American principals were concentrated in urban public schools.

- **Table 4** shows that 57.7% of African American public school principals worked at urban schools, compared with only 18.5% of Whites.

- Only 18.5% of African American public school principals, but 54.0% of Whites, worked in rural schools.

- African Americans represented 24.3% of all public school principals working in urban schools but only 8.8% of all suburban public

Table 3. Representation of Private School Principals by School Affiliation, Race, and Sex: 1993/94
(weighted sample size in parentheses)

Affiliation	Total	Male	Female	White, Non-Hispanic			African American, Non-Hispanic			Hispanic			Other		
				Total	Male	Female	Total	Male	Female	Total	Male	Female	Total	Male	Female
Total Weighted Sample	100.0%	46.4%	53.6%	92.5%	43.7%	48.7%	4.2%	1.4%	2.9%	2.1%	0.9%	1.2%	1.2%	0.3%	0.9%
	(25,015)	(11,605)	(13,409)	(23,133)	(10,943)	(12,190)	(1,060)	(347)	(713)	(523)	(231)	(292)	(298)	(84)	(214)
Total ** +++	100.0%	100.0%	100.0%	100.0%	100.0%	100.0%	100.0%	100.0%	100.0%	100.0%	100.0%	100.0%	100.0%	100.0%	100.0%
(row %)	100.0%	46.4%	53.6%	92.5%	43.7%	48.7%	4.2%	1.4%	2.9%	2.1%	0.9%	1.2%	1.2%	0.3%	0.9%
	(25,015)	(11,605)	(13,409)	(23,133)	(10,943)	(12,190)	(1,060)	(347)	(713)	(523)	(231)	(292)	(300)	(84)	(214)
Catholic	33.3%	17.1%	47.2%	33.5%	16.8%	48.6%	23.3%	19.0%	25.4%	50.3%	34.6%	62.7%	19.0%	10.7%	22.4%
(row %)	100.0%	23.9%	76.1%	93.2%	22.0%	71.2%	3.0%	0.8%	2.2%	3.2%	1.0%	2.2%	0.7%	0.1%	0.6%
	(8,323)	(1,988)	(6,335)	(7,756)	(1,833)	(5,923)	(247)	(66)	(181)	(263)	(80)	(183)	(57)	(9)	(48)
Other Religious	45.4%	68.2%	25.7%	45.6%	69.1%	24.6%	60.3%	69.5%	55.8%	14.3%	24.2%	6.5%	29.3%	70.2%	13.6%
(row %)	100.0%	69.7%	30.3%	92.9%	66.6%	26.4%	5.6%	2.1%	3.5%	0.7%	0.5%	0.2%	0.8%	0.5%	0.3%
	(11,362)	(7,918)	(3,444)	(10,560)	(7,562)	(2,998)	(639)	(241)	(398)	(75)	(56)	(19)	(88)	(59)	(29)
Non-Sectarian	21.3%	14.6%	27.1%	20.8%	14.1%	26.8%	16.4%	11.2%	18.9%	35.4%	41.1%	30.8%	51.7%	20.2%	64.5%
(row %)	100.0%	31.9%	68.1%	90.4%	29.0%	61.3%	3.3%	0.7%	2.5%	3.5%	1.8%	1.7%	2.9%	0.3%	2.6%
	(5,331)	(1,699)	(3,632)	(4,817)	(1,548)	(3,269)	(174)	(39)	(135)	(185)	(95)	(90)	(155)	(17)	(138)

Notes:

*** Test of statistical significance compares African Americans with Whites. *** p < .001, ** p < .01, * p < .05.

+++ Test of statistical significance compares White men with White women. +++ p < .001, ++ p < .01, + p < .05.

~~~ Test of statistical significance compares African American men with African American women. ~~~ p < .001, ~~ p < .01, ~ p < .05.

Tests of statistical significance calculated using adjusted sample weight to control for influence of large sample sizes.

Source: Schools and Staffing Survey, 1993-94.

school principals and 3.8% of all rural public school principals.

Private Schools

Figure 3 also shows that 38.7% of private school principals worked in urban schools, 33.9% in suburban schools, and 27.4% in rural schools. **Table 5** shows that African American private school principals were also concentrated in urban schools.

- About 82.8% of African American private school principals worked in urban schools, compared with 36.1% of their White counterparts.

- Only 9.8% of African Americans, but 35.0% of Whites, worked in suburban private schools.

- About 7.4% of African Americans, but 28.9% of Whites, worked in rural private schools.

- African Americans represented 9.1% of all private school principals in urban schools, but only 1.2% of all suburban private school principals and 1.1% of all rural private school principals.

Representation of Principals by Geographic Region

Public Schools

Table 6 shows that about 33.0% of all public school principals worked in the southern region of the United States, 29.1% in the Midwest, 21.0% in the West, and 16.9% in the Northeast. African Americans were overrepresented among principals in the South and underrepresented among principals in the West.

- **Figure 4** shows that African Americans represented 15.5% of all principals in the South, 8.3% in the Midwest, 8.2% in the Northeast, and 5.4% in the West.

Figure 3. Distribution of African American Public and Private School Principals by Urbanicity: 1993/94

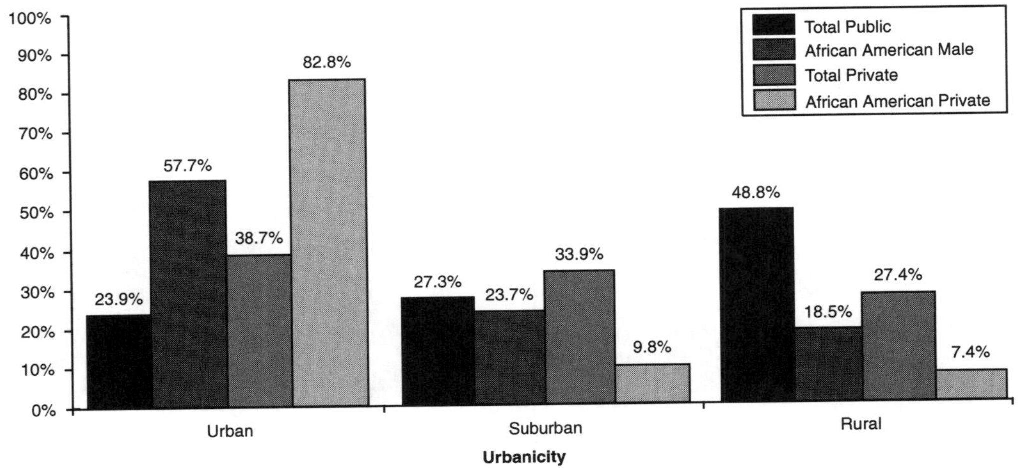

Source: Schools and Staffing Survey, 1993-94.

Table 4. Representation of Public School Principals by Urbanicity, Race, and Sex: 1993/94
(weighted sample size in parentheses)

Urbanicity	Total	Male	Female	White, Non-Hispanic Total	Male	Female	African American, Non-Hispanic Total	Male	Female	Hispanic Total	Male	Female	Other Total	Male	Female
Total *** +++ ~~~	100.0%	100.0%	100.0%	100.0%	100.0%	100.0%	100.0%	100.0%	100.0%	100.0%	100.0%	100.0%	100.0%	100.0%	100.0%
(row %)	100.0%	65.5%	34.5%	84.3%	58.1%	26.1%	10.1%	4.3%	5.8%	4.1%	2.2%	1.9%	1.6%	0.8%	0.7%
	(79,618)	(52,114)	(27,505)	(67,081)	(46,283)	(20,798)	(8,018)	(3,419)	(4,599)	(3,269)	(1,738)	(1,531)	(1,250)	(673)	(577)
Urban	23.9%	19.2%	32.8%	18.5%	15.7%	24.8%	57.7%	51.5%	62.4%	48.2%	47.3%	49.2%	30.8%	22.7%	40.1%
(row %)	100.0%	52.6%	47.4%	65.4%	38.3%	27.1%	24.3%	9.2%	15.1%	8.3%	4.3%	4.0%	2.0%	0.8%	1.2%
	(19,027)	(10,016)	(9,010)	(12,437)	(7,282)	(5,155)	(4,630)	(1,759)	(2,871)	(1,575)	(822)	(753)	(385)	(153)	(231)
Suburban	27.3%	24.7%	32.2%	27.5%	25.0%	32.9%	23.7%	22.3%	24.8%	29.9%	19.8%	41.3%	31.4%	25.4%	38.4%
(row %)	100.0%	59.2%	40.8%	84.9%	53.3%	31.6%	8.8%	3.5%	5.2%	4.5%	1.6%	2.9%	1.8%	0.8%	1.0%
	(21,700)	(12,855)	(8,845)	(18,429)	(11,577)	(6,852)	(1,902)	(763)	(1,139)	(977)	(345)	(632)	(393)	(171)	(222)
Rural	48.8%	56.1%	35.1%	54.0%	59.3%	42.3%	18.5%	26.2%	12.8%	21.9%	32.9%	9.5%	37.8%	51.9%	21.5%
(row %)	100.0%	75.2%	24.8%	93.1%	70.5%	22.6%	3.8%	2.3%	1.5%	1.8%	1.5%	0.4%	1.2%	0.9%	0.3%
	(38,891)	(29,242)	(9,649)	(36,215)	(27,424)	(8,791)	(1,486)	(897)	(589)	(717)	(572)	(145)	(473)	(349)	(124)

Notes:
*** Test of statistical significance compares African Americans with Whites. *** p < .001, ** p < .01, * p < .05.
+++ Test of statistical significance compares White men with White women. +++ p < .001, ++ p < .01, + p < .05.
~~~ Test of statistical significance compares African American men with African American women. ~~~ p < .001, ~~ p < .01, ~ p < .05.
Tests of statistical significance calculated using adjusted sample weight to control for influence of large sample sizes.
Source: Schools and Staffing Survey, 1993-94.

Table 5. Representation of Private School Principals by Urbanicity, Race, and Sex: 1993/94
(weighted sample size in parentheses)

Urbanicity	Total	Male	Female	White, Non-Hispanic			African American, Non-Hispanic			Hispanic			Other		
				Total	Male	Female	Total	Male	Female	Total	Male	Female	Total	Male	Female
Total *** ++	100.0%	100.0%	100.0%	100.0%	100.0%	100.0%	100.0%	100.0%	100.0%	100.0%	100.0%	100.0%	100.0%	100.0%	100.0%
(row %)	100.0%	46.4%	53.6%	92.5%	43.7%	48.7%	4.2%	1.4%	2.9%	2.1%	0.9%	1.2%	1.2%	0.3%	0.9%
	(25,015)	(11,606)	(13,410)	(23,133)	(10,943)	(12,190)	(1,060)	(347)	(713)	(524)	(231)	(292)	(299)	(84)	(214)
Urban	38.7%	36.6%	40.6%	36.1%	35.5%	36.8%	82.8%	74.8%	86.8%	47.2%	30.8%	60.2%	69.2%	47.5%	77.7%
(row %)	100.0%	43.9%	56.1%	86.3%	40.0%	46.2%	9.1%	2.7%	6.4%	2.6%	0.7%	1.8%	2.1%	0.4%	1.7%
	(9,693)	(4,251)	(5,442)	(8,361)	(3,881)	(4,480)	(878)	(259)	(619)	(247)	(71)	(176)	(207)	(40)	(167)
Suburban	33.9%	32.3%	35.2%	35.0%	32.6%	37.1%	9.8%	18.7%	5.4%	41.7%	44.2%	39.8%	19.2%	16.9%	20.1%
(row %)	100.0%	44.3%	55.7%	95.5%	42.1%	53.4%	1.2%	0.8%	0.5%	2.6%	1.2%	1.4%	0.7%	0.2%	0.5%
	(8,469)	(3,750)	(4,719)	(8,089)	(3,569)	(4,521)	(103)	(65)	(39)	(219)	(102)	(116)	(57)	(14)	(43)
Rural	27.4%	31.1%	24.2%	28.9%	31.9%	26.2%	7.4%	6.6%	7.8%	11.0%	25.0%	0.0%	11.6%	35.6%	2.1%
(row %)	100.0%	52.6%	47.4%	97.5%	51.0%	46.5%	1.1%	0.3%	0.8%	0.8%	0.8%	0.0%	0.5%	0.4%	0.1%
	(6,854)	(3,604)	(3,249)	(6,683)	(3,494)	(3,189)	(79)	(23)	(56)	(58)	(58)	–	(35)	(30)	(5)

Notes:

" – " indicates sample size too small to estimate.

*** Test of statistical significance compares African Americans with Whites. *** p < .001, ** p < .01, * p < .05.

+++ Test of statistical significance compares White men with White women. +++ p < .001, ++ p < .01, + p < .05.

~~~ Test of statistical significance compares African American men with African American women. ~~~ p < .001, ~~ p < .01, ~ p < .05.

Tests of statistical significance calculated using adjusted sample weight to control for influence of large sample sizes.

Source: Schools and Staffing Survey, 1993-94.

Table 6. Census Region of Public School Principals by Race and Sex: 1993/94
(weighted sample size in parentheses)

Census Region	Total	Male	Female	White, Non-Hispanic			African American, Non-Hispanic			Hispanic			Other		
				Total	Male	Female	Total	Male	Female	Total	Male	Female	Total	Male	Female
Total Weighted Sample	100.0%	65.5%	34.5%	84.3%	58.1%	26.1%	10.1%	4.3%	5.8%	4.1%	2.2%	1.9%	1.6%	0.8%	0.7%
	(79,618)	(52,113)	(27,505)	(67,081)	(46,283)	(20,798)	(8,018)	(3,419)	(4,599)	(3,269)	(1,738)	(1,531)	(1,250)	(673)	(577)
Total *** +++ ~~~	100.0%	100.0%	100.0%	100.0%	100.0%	100.0%	100.0%	100.0%	100.0%	100.0%	100.0%	100.0%	100.0%	100.0%	100.0%
(row %)	100.0%	65.5%	34.5%	84.3%	58.1%	26.1%	10.1%	4.3%	5.8%	4.1%	2.2%	1.9%	1.6%	0.8%	0.7%
	(79,618)	(52,113)	(27,505)	(67,081)	(46,283)	(20,798)	(8,018)	(3,419)	(4,599)	(3,269)	(1,738)	(1,531)	(1,250)	(673)	(577)
Northeast	16.9%	17.7%	15.4%	18.0%	18.7%	16.5%	13.7%	13.5%	13.9%	6.7%	5.0%	8.6%	5.6%	5.9%	5.2%
(row %)	100.0%	68.6%	31.4%	89.7%	64.2%	25.5%	8.2%	3.4%	4.8%	1.6%	0.6%	1.0%	0.5%	0.3%	0.2%
	(13,469)	(9,234)	(4,235)	(12,080)	(8,647)	(3,433)	(1,100)	(460)	(640)	(219)	(87)	(132)	(70)	(40)	(30)
Midwest	29.1%	31.6%	24.2%	31.0%	33.4%	25.7%	24.1%	21.8%	25.7%	6.7%	8.5%	4.7%	14.8%	19.8%	9.0%
(row %)	100.0%	71.2%	28.8%	89.9%	66.8%	23.1%	8.3%	3.2%	5.1%	0.9%	0.6%	0.3%	0.8%	0.6%	0.2%
	(23,144)	(16,481)	(6,663)	(20,810)	(15,455)	(5,355)	(1,930)	(746)	(1,184)	(219)	(147)	(72)	(185)	(133)	(52)
South	33.0%	31.7%	35.5%	30.9%	29.7%	33.8%	51.0%	57.9%	45.8%	35.4%	39.0%	31.4%	25.2%	22.9%	27.9%
(row %)	100.0%	62.8%	37.2%	78.9%	52.2%	26.7%	15.5%	7.5%	8.0%	4.4%	2.6%	1.8%	1.2%	0.6%	0.6%
	(26,308)	(16,533)	(9,774)	(20,748)	(13,723)	(7,025)	(4,086)	(1,979)	(2,107)	(1,158)	(677)	(481)	(315)	(154)	(161)
West	21.0%	18.9%	24.8%	20.0%	18.3%	24.0%	11.3%	6.9%	14.5%	51.2%	47.6%	55.3%	54.3%	51.4%	57.7%
(row %)	100.0%	59.1%	40.9%	80.5%	50.7%	29.9%	5.4%	1.4%	4.0%	10.0%	5.0%	5.1%	4.1%	2.1%	2.0%
	(16,698)	(9,866)	(6,832)	(13,443)	(8,458)	(4,985)	(903)	(235)	(668)	(1,673)	(827)	(846)	(679)	(346)	(333)

Notes:

*** Test of statistical significance compares African Americans with Whites. *** p < .001, ** p < .01, * p < .05.

+++ Test of statistical significance compares White men with White women. +++ p < .001, ++ p < .01, + p < .05.

~~~ Test of statistical significance compares African American men with African American women. ~~~ p < .001, ~~ p < .01, ~ p < .05.

Tests of statistical significance calculated using adjusted sample weight to control for influence of large sample sizes.

Source: Schools and Staffing Survey, 1993-94.

Figure 4. Representation of African American Public and Private School Principals in Each Census Region: 1993/94

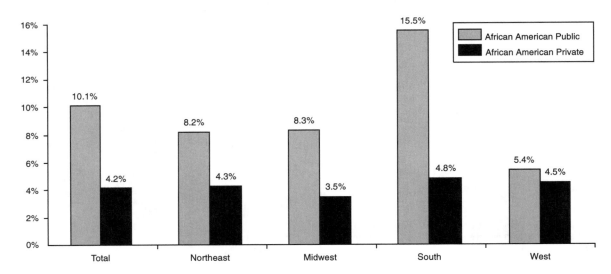

Source: Schools and Staffing Survey, 1993-94.

- About one-half (51.0%) of all African American public school principals worked in the South, compared with only 30.9% of their White counterparts.

Private Schools

The distribution of private school principals across geographic regions mirrored the distribution of private school teachers. In 1993/94, 27.1% of principals worked in private schools in the South, 29.2% in the Midwest, 23.8% in the Northeast, and 19.9% in the West. **Table 7** shows that, unlike the distribution for public school principals, the regional distribution of private school principals was comparable for African Americans and Whites.

- **Figure 4** shows that African Americans represented 3.5% of all principals in the Midwest, 4.3% in the Northeast, 4.5% in the West, and 4.8% in the South.

- Similar percentages of African American and White private school principals worked in the South (30.8% versus 27.0%).

Representation of Principals by Racial Composition of the Student Body

Public Schools

Figure 5 shows, overall, that nearly two-thirds (61.0%) of public school principals in 1993/94 worked in schools in which African Americans comprised 5% or less of the student body and 10.4% worked in schools in which African Americans comprised more than 60% of the student body.

- **Table 8** shows that 52.8% of African American public school principals worked in schools in which African Americans comprised more than 60% of students, compared with only 5.7% of their White counterparts.

Table 7. Census Region of Private School Principals by Race and Sex: 1993/94
(weighted sample size in parentheses)

Census Region	Total	Male	Female	White, Non-Hispanic			African American, Non-Hispanic			Hispanic			Other		
				Total	Male	Female	Total	Male	Female	Total	Male	Female	Total	Male	Female
Total Weighted Sample	100.0%	46.4%	53.6%	92.5%	43.7%	48.7%	4.2%	1.4%	2.9%	2.1%	0.9%	1.2%	1.2%	0.3%	0.9%
	(25,015)	(11,605)	(13,409)	(23,133)	(10,943)	(12,190)	(1,060)	(347)	(713)	(523)	(231)	(292)	(298)	(84)	(214)
Total +++ ~	100.0%	100.0%	100.0%	100.0%	100.0%	100.0%	100.0%	100.0%	100.0%	100.0%	100.0%	100.0%	100.0%	100.0%	100.0%
(row %)	100.0%	46.4%	53.6%	92.5%	43.7%	48.7%	4.2%	1.4%	2.9%	2.1%	0.9%	1.2%	1.2%	0.3%	0.9%
	(25,015)	(11,605)	(13,409)	(23,133)	(10,943)	(12,190)	(1,060)	(347)	(713)	(523)	(231)	(292)	(298)	(84)	(214)
Northeast	23.8%	20.3%	26.9%	24.2%	19.9%	28.1%	24.0%	35.7%	18.2%	15.9%	21.6%	11.3%	5.4%	0.0%	7.5%
(row %)	100.0%	39.4%	60.5%	94.0%	36.5%	57.5%	4.3%	2.1%	2.2%	1.4%	0.8%	0.6%	0.3%	0.0%	0.3%
	(5,966)	(2,352)	(3,610)	(5,609)	(2,178)	(3,431)	(254)	(124)	(130)	(83)	(50)	(33)	(16)	–	(16)
Midwest	29.2%	32.4%	26.4%	29.6%	33.1%	26.6%	24.0%	22.8%	24.5%	30.0%	24.7%	34.2%	11.1%	7.1%	12.6%
(row %)	100.0%	51.5%	48.5%	93.9%	49.6%	44.3%	3.5%	1.1%	2.4%	2.2%	0.8%	1.4%	0.5%	0.1%	0.4%
	(7,302)	(3,762)	(3,540)	(6,858)	(3,620)	(3,238)	(254)	(79)	(175)	(157)	(57)	(100)	(33)	(6)	(27)
South	27.1%	29.4%	25.1%	27.0%	29.3%	24.9%	30.8%	33.7%	29.5%	21.0%	24.7%	18.2%	30.9%	38.1%	28.0%
(row %)	100.0%	50.4%	49.6%	92.2%	47.4%	44.8%	4.8%	1.7%	3.1%	1.6%	0.8%	0.8%	1.4%	0.5%	0.9%
	(6,777)	(3,417)	(3,359)	(6,247)	(3,211)	(3,036)	(327)	(117)	(210)	(110)	(57)	(53)	(92)	(32)	(60)
West	19.9%	17.9%	21.6%	19.1%	17.7%	20.4%	21.2%	7.8%	27.8%	32.9%	28.6%	36.3%	51.7%	52.4%	51.4%
(row %)	100.0%	41.7%	58.3%	88.9%	38.9%	50.0%	4.5%	0.5%	4.0%	3.5%	1.3%	2.1%	3.1%	0.9%	2.2%
	(4,971)	(2,072)	(2,899)	(4,420)	(1,935)	(2,485)	(225)	(27)	(198)	(172)	(66)	(106)	(154)	(44)	(110)

Notes:

" – " indicates sample size too small to estimate.

*** Test of statistical significance compares African Americans with Whites. *** p < .001, ** p < .01, * p < .05.

+++ Test of statistical significance compares White men with White women. +++ p < .001, ++ p < .01, + p < .05.

~~~ Test of statistical significance compares African American men with African American women. ~~~ p < .001, ~~ p < .01, ~ p < .05.

Tests of statistical significance calculated using adjusted sample weight to control for influence of large sample sizes.

Source: Schools and Staffing Survey, 1993-94.

- Only 7.4% of African American principals worked in schools in which 5% or less of all students were African Americans, compared with 67.1% of White principals.

Private Schools

More than two-thirds (69.0%) of private school principals worked in schools in which 5% or less of all students were African American. Only 5.6% worked in schools in which more than 60% of all students were African American.

- **Table 9** shows that the majority (76.5%) of African American private school principals worked in schools in which African Americans represented more than 60% of the student body, compared with only 2.4% of their White counterparts.

Representation of Principals by School Characteristics

Public Schools

On average, public school principals worked at schools with 516.4 students, 28.1% of whom were minorities, and 4.3 (or 12.3%) minority teachers. **Table 10** shows that, compared with male principals, female principals tended to work at smaller schools (505.4 students versus 522.0 students) and at schools with a larger proportion of minority students (36.0% versus 24.0%) and minority teachers (16.4% versus 10.3%).

Figure 5. Distribution of African American Public School Principals by the Percentage of African American Students at the School: 1993/94

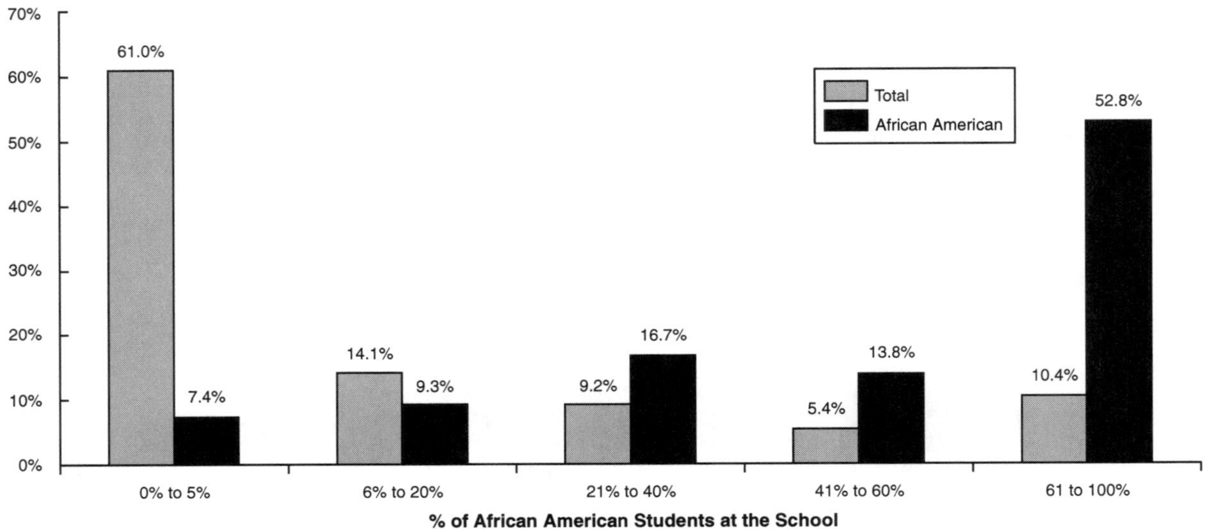

Table 8. Distribution of Public School Principals by Percentage African American Students at School, Race, and Sex: 1993/94
(weighted sample size in parentheses)

% African American Students	Total	Male	Female	White, Non-Hispanic Total	Male	Female	African American, Non-Hispanic Total	Male	Female	Hispanic Total	Male	Female	Other Total	Male	Female
Total *** +++	100.0%	100.0%	100.0%	100.0%	100.0%	100.0%	100.0%	100.0%	100.0%	100.0%	100.0%	100.0%	100.0%	100.0%	100.0%
	(74,693)	(49,455)	(25,240)	(63,092)	(44,030)	(19,062)	(7,323)	(3,126)	(4,197)	(3,069)	(1,650)	(1,419)	(1,211)	(649)	(562)
0% to 5%	61.0%	65.2%	52.6%	67.1%	69.2%	62.3%	7.4%	6.6%	7.9%	59.6%	67.4%	50.5%	68.2%	70.9%	65.1%
	(45,531)	(32,249)	(13,282)	(42,336)	(30,469)	(11,866)	(540)	(207)	(333)	(1,830)	(1,112)	(717)	(825)	(460)	(366)
6% to 20%	14.1%	12.9%	16.4%	14.1%	13.0%	16.7%	9.3%	9.7%	9.0%	24.0%	16.7%	32.4%	18.1%	14.2%	22.7%
	(10,533)	(6,387)	(4,147)	(8,899)	(5,716)	(3,183)	(679)	(303)	(376)	(735)	(276)	(459)	(220)	(92)	(127)
21% to 40%	9.2%	8.5%	10.6%	8.6%	8.1%	9.6%	16.7%	13.8%	18.9%	5.7%	6.5%	4.7%	7.0%	12.4%	0.8%
	(6,891)	(4,205)	(2,686)	(5,407)	(3,584)	(1,822)	(1,225)	(432)	(793)	(174)	(108)	(66)	(85)	(81)	(5)
41% to 60%	5.4%	5.2%	5.7%	4.6%	4.7%	4.2%	13.8%	14.2%	13.5%	2.7%	2.0%	3.4%	2.1%	0.0%	4.5%
	(3,999)	(2,553)	(1,446)	(2,878)	(2,074)	(803)	(1,011)	(443)	(568)	(82)	(33)	(49)	(25)	–	(25)
61% to 100%	10.4%	8.2%	14.6%	5.7%	5.0%	7.3%	52.8%	55.7%	50.7%	8.1%	7.3%	9.0%	4.2%	1.8%	6.9%
	(7,739)	(4,060)	(3,680)	(3,573)	(2,186)	(1,387)	(3,868)	(1,741)	(2,127)	(248)	(120)	(127)	(51)	(12)	(39)

Notes:
" – " indicates sample size too small to estimate.
*** Test of statistical significance compares African Americans with Whites. *** p < .001, ** p < .01, * p < .05.
+++ Test of statistical significance compares White men with White women. +++ p < .001, ++ p < .01, + p < .05.
~~~ Test of statistical significance compares African American men with African American women. ~~~ p < .001, ~~ p < .01, ~ p < .05.
Tests of statistical significance calculated using adjusted sample weight to control for influence of large sample sizes.
Source: Schools and Staffing Survey, 1993-94.

Table 9. Distribution of Private School Principals by Percentage of African American Students at School, Race, and Sex: 1993/94
(weighted sample size in parentheses)

% African American Students	Total	Male	Female	White, Non-Hispanic			African American, Non-Hispanic			Hispanic			Other		
				Total	Male	Female	Total	Male	Female	Total	Male	Female	Total	Male	Female
Total *** ++	100.0%	100.0%	100.0%	100.0%	100.0%	100.0%	100.0%	100.0%	100.0%	100.0%	100.0%	100.0%	100.0%	100.0%	100.0%
	(21,436)	(9,644)	(11,791)	(19,849)	(9,157)	(10,692)	(826)	(201)	(625)	(473)	(202)	(271)	(288)	(84)	(203)
0% to 5%	69.0%	69.5%	68.6%	72.0%	71.6%	72.3%	9.9%	10.4%	9.8%	62.0%	45.9%	73.9%	45.6%	40.7%	47.6%
	(14,789)	(6,703)	(8,086)	(14,283)	(6,555)	(7,728)	(82)	(21)	(61)	(293)	(93)	(200)	(131)	(34)	(97)
6% to 20%	17.2%	18.7%	16.0%	17.5%	18.6%	16.5%	7.4%	11.3%	6.1%	13.1%	19.5%	8.3%	32.8%	42.3%	28.9%
	(3,683)	(1,801)	(1,882)	(3,466)	(1,703)	(1,763)	(61)	(23)	(38)	(62)	(39)	(22)	(94)	(36)	(59)
21% to 40%	5.5%	5.4%	5.6%	5.4%	5.0%	5.7%	3.4%	0.0%	4.5%	8.5%	19.2%	0.0%	9.7%	17.1%	6.6%
	(1,173)	(517)	(656)	(1,075)	(461)	(614)	(28)	(28)	(40)	(39)	–	(28)	(14)	(13)	0.0%
41% to 60%	2.7%	3.3%	2.3%	2.7%	3.5%	2.1%	2.2%	0.0%	2.9%	0.0%	0.0%	0.0%	6.6%	0.0%	9.3%
	(584)	(320)	(265)	(546)	(318)	(228)	(18)	–	(18)	–	–	–	(19)	–	(19)
61% to 100%	5.6%	3.2%	7.6%	2.4%	1.3%	3.4%	76.5%	76.1%	76.6%	16.6%	15.4%	17.5%	5.4%	0.0%	7.6%
	(1,206)	(304)	(902)	(480)	(120)	(359)	(632)	(153)	(479)	(79)	(31)	(47)	(15)	–	(15)

Notes:
" – " indicates sample size too small to estimate.
*** Test of statistical significance compares African Americans with Whites. *** p < .001, ** p < .01, * p < .05.
+++ Test of statistical significance compares White men with White women. +++ p < .001, ++ p < .01, + p < .05.
~~~ Test of statistical significance compares African American men with African American women. ~~~ p < .001, ~~ p < .01, ~ p < .05.
Tests of statistical significance calculated using adjusted sample weight to control for influence of large sample sizes.
Source: Schools and Staffing Survey, 1993-94.

Table 10. Characteristics of Public School Principals' Schools by Race and Sex: 1993/94
(weighted sample size in parentheses)

Characteristic	Total	Male	Female	White, Non-Hispanic			African American, Non-Hispanic			Hispanic			Other		
				Total	Male	Female	Total	Male	Female	Total	Male	Female	Total	Male	Female
Total Weighted Sample	100.0%	65.5%	34.5%	84.3%	58.1%	26.1%	10.1%	4.3%	5.8%	4.1%	2.2%	1.9%	1.6%	0.8%	0.7%
	(79,618)	(52,113)	(27,505)	(67,081)	(46,283)	(20,798)	(8,018)	(3,419)	(4,599)	(3,269)	(1,738)	(1,531)	(1,250)	(673)	(577)
Total Respondents	100.0%	66.2%	33.8%	84.5%	58.9%	25.5%	9.8%	4.2%	5.6%	4.1%	2.2%	1.9%	1.6%	0.9%	0.8%
	(74,693)	(49,453)	(25,240)	(63,092)	(44,030)	(19,062)	(7,323)	(3,126)	(4,197)	(3,069)	(1,650)	(1,419)	(1,209)	(647)	(562)
Total Enrollment *** + ~~~ (K-12 & ungraded)	516.4	522.0	505.4	501.4	507.8	486.4	578.8	641.8	531.9	663.1	652.9	674.9	550.0	572.1	524.6
% Minority Teachers *** +++	12.3%	10.3%	16.4%	7.5%	6.8%	9.1%	41.3%	42.8%	40.2%	35.9%	33.4%	38.8%	27.8%	26.8%	29.0%
Number Minority Teachers *** +++ ~~~	4.3	3.8	5.5	2.7	2.4	3.2	14.2	16.2	12.7	13.2	13.4	12.9	10.0	9.8	10.2
% Minority Students *** +++	28.1%	24.0%	36.0%	21.0%	19.3%	25.1%	70.0%	68.2%	71.4%	64.4%	58.2%	71.6%	49.2%	47.4%	51.3%
Number Minority Students *** +++	166.3	146.6	204.9	122.0	113.8	140.8	406.0	432.4	386.3	454.3	414.6	500.5	294.4	309.7	276.9

Notes:
*** Test of statistical significance compares African Americans with Whites. *** p < .001, ** p < .01, * p < .05.
+++ Test of statistical significance compares White men with White women. +++ p < .001, ++ p < .01, + p < .05.
~~~ Test of statistical significance compares African American men with African American women. ~~~ p < .001, ~~ p < .01, ~ p < .05.
Tests of statistical significance calculated using adjusted sample weight to control for influence of large sample sizes.
Source: Schools and Staffing Survey, 1993-94.

- African American principals worked at larger schools than White principals (578.8 students versus 501.4 students overall) and schools with higher proportions of both minority students and minority teachers.

- More than two-thirds (70.0%) of the students at schools with African American principals were minorities, compared with only one-fifth (21.0%) of the students at the schools with White principals.

- **Figure 6** shows that the percentage of minority teachers was more than three times higher for African American principals than for all principals (41.3% versus 12.3%).

Private Schools

On average, private school principals worked in schools with 195.8 enrolled students, 22.2% of whom were minorities. **Table 11** shows that, overall,

women worked in schools with fewer enrolled students than men.

- Total enrollment ranged from 112.6 students for African American women principals, to 189.6 for White women and 208.0 for White men, to 227.0 for African American men.

Regardless of sex, African American principals worked in schools with substantially higher percentages of minority students and minority teachers than White principals.

- **Figure 6** shows that, on average, 83.0% of the students at schools in which African American principals worked were minorities, compared with only 22.2% of the students for all principals.

- About two-thirds (67.4%) of the teachers at schools in which African American principals worked were minorities, compared with only 5.8% of the teachers for White principals.

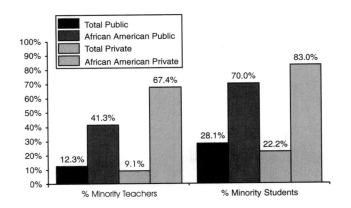

Figure 6. Racial Composition of the Schools in Which African American Public and Private School Principals Work: 1993/94

Source: Schools and Staffing Survey, 1993-94.

Table 11. Characteristics of Private School Principals' Schools by Race and Sex: 1993/94
(weighted sample size in parentheses)

Characteristic	Total	Male	Female	White, Non-Hispanic			African American, Non-Hispanic			Hispanic			Other		
				Total	Male	Female	Total	Male	Female	Total	Male	Female	Total	Male	Female
Total Weighted Sample	100.0% (25,015)	46.4% (11,605)	53.6% (13,409)	92.5% (23,133)	43.7% (10,943)	48.7% (12,190)	4.2% (1,060)	1.4% (347)	2.9% (713)	2.1% (523)	0.9% (231)	1.2% (292)	1.2% (298)	0.3% (84)	0.9% (214)
Total Respondents	100.0% (22,430)	45.3% (10,165)	54.7% (12,265)	92.8% (20,816)	43.1% (9,659)	49.7% (11,157)	3.7% (830)	0.9% (201)	2.8% (629)	2.2% (492)	1.0% (221)	1.2% (271)	1.3% (292)	0.4% (84)	0.9% (208)
Total Enrollment ** + ~~ (K-12 & ungraded)	195.8	208.4	185.3	198.2	208.0	189.6	140.3	227.0	112.6	206.5	176.6	230.9	164.3	297.2	110.5
% Minority Teachers ***	9.1%	7.4%	10.4%	5.8%	5.6%	6.0%	67.4%	67.6%	67.3%	33.8%	30.0%	36.8%	31.2%	9.9%	39.9%
Number Minority Teachers *** ~~	1.2	1.1	1.2	0.8	0.9	0.8	6.0	8.7	5.1	4.5	5.0	4.1	3.8	3.6	3.9
% Minority Students *** +++	22.2%	18.5%	25.3%	18.8%	16.5%	20.8%	83.0%	79.9%	84.0%	53.8%	45.8%	60.3%	41.6%	34.1%	44.7%
Number Minority Students *** ~	44.1	40.6	47.0	39.0	35.9	41.7	120.9	191.1	98.4	109.8	83.9	130.9	77.9	106.3	66.4

Notes:

*** Test of statistical significance compares African Americans with Whites. *** p < .001, ** p < .01, * p < .05.

+++ Test of statistical significance compares White men with White women. +++ p < .001, ++ p < .01, + p < .05.

~~~ Test of statistical significance compares African American men with African American women. ~~~ p < .001, ~~ p < .01, ~ p < .05.

Tests of statistical significance calculated using adjusted sample weight to control for influence of large sample sizes.

Source: Schools and Staffing Survey, 1993-94.

EDUCATION AND EXPERIENCE OF PUBLIC SCHOOL PRINCIPALS

Highest Level of Education Attained by Principals

Public Schools

Table 12 shows that only 1.4% of all public school principals in 1993/94 had not attained a degree higher than a bachelor's degree. Nearly two-thirds (63.4%) of principals had attained a master's degree; one-fourth (25.8%), an education specialist degree; and about one in ten (9.3%), a doctorate.

- Figure 7 shows that similar percentages of African American and all public school principals earned doctorates (11.9% versus 9.3%).

Private Schools

Figure 7 shows that about one-third (34.3%) of all private school principals had earned no more than a bachelor's degree. The average level of education attained by private school principals was comparable for African Americans and Whites.

- Table 13 shows that about 4.6% of African American and 5.8% of White private school principals had earned a doctorate.

Previous Position Held by Principals

Public Schools

More than three-fourths (78.6%) of all public school principals held some other school position

Table 12. Highest Degree Earned by Public School Principals by Race and Sex: 1993/94
(weighted sample size in parentheses)

Highest Degree	Total	Male	Female	White, Non-Hispanic			African American, Non-Hispanic			Hispanic			Other		
				Total	Male	Female	Total	Male	Female	Total	Male	Female	Total	Male	Female
Total Weighted Sample	100.0% (79,618)	65.5% (52,113)	34.5% (27,505)	84.3% (67,081)	58.1% (46,283)	26.1% (20,798)	10.1% (8,018)	4.3% (3,419)	5.8% (4,599)	4.1% (3,269)	2.2% (1,738)	1.9% (1,531)	1.6% (1,250)	0.8% (673)	0.7% (577)
Total ** +++	100.0% (79,618)	100.0% (52,114)	100.0% (27,504)	100.0% (67,081)	100.0% (46,283)	100.0% (20,798)	100.0% (8,018)	100.0% (3,420)	100.0% (4,598)	100.0% (3,269)	100.0% (1,738)	100.0% (1,531)	100.0% (1,250)	100.0% (673)	100.0% (577)
No More Than Bachelor's	1.4% (1,146)	1.1% (594)	2.0% (553)	1.5% (1,004)	1.0% (477)	2.5% (527)	0.1% (7)	0.2% (7)	0.0% –	2.7% (88)	4.2% (73)	1.0% (15)	3.8% (48)	5.5% (37)	1.9% (11)
Master's Degree	63.4% (50,469)	65.1% (33,901)	60.2% (16,568)	62.8% (42,144)	64.8% (29,983)	58.5% (12,161)	64.3% (5,158)	64.1% (2,192)	64.5% (2,966)	74.5% (2,436)	73.4% (1,276)	75.8% (1,160)	58.5% (731)	66.9% (450)	48.7% (281)
Education Specialist	25.8% (20,573)	24.7% (12,893)	27.9% (7,680)	26.5% (17,794)	25.2% (11,674)	29.4% (6,120)	23.7% (1,898)	23.5% (802)	23.8% (1,096)	17.3% (567)	17.1% (297)	17.6% (270)	25.1% (314)	17.8% (120)	33.6% (194)
Doctorate	9.3% (7,431)	9.1% (4,728)	9.8% (2,703)	9.2% (6,140)	9.0% (4,150)	9.6% (1,990)	11.9% (955)	12.3% (419)	11.7% (536)	5.5% (179)	5.4% (93)	5.6% (86)	12.6% (157)	9.8% (66)	15.8% (91)

Notes:
" – " indicates sample size too small to estimate.
*** Test of statistical significance compares African Americans with Whites. *** p < .001, ** p < .01, * p < .05.
+++ Test of statistical significance compares White men with White women. +++ p < .001, ++ p < .01, + p < .05.
~~~ Test of statistical significance compares African American men with African American women. ~~~ p < .001, ~~ p < .01, ~ p < .05.
Tests of statistical significance calculated using adjusted sample weight to control for influence of large sample sizes.
Source: Schools and Staffing Survey, 1993-94.

**Figure 7. Highest Degree Earned by African American
Public and Private School Principals: 1993/94**

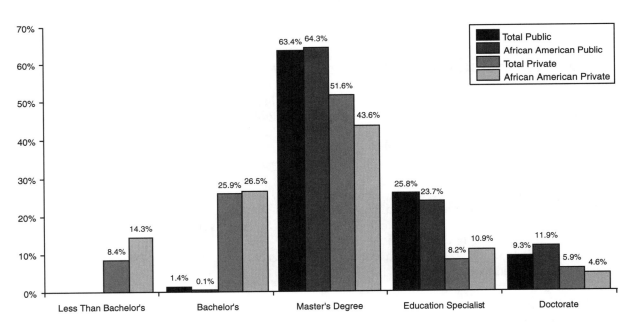

Source: Schools and Staffing Survey, 1993-94.

Table 13. Highest Degree Earned by Private School Principals by Race and Sex: 1993/94
(weighted sample size in parentheses)

Highest Degree	Total	Male	Female	White, Non-Hispanic			African American, Non-Hispanic			Hispanic			Other		
				Total	Male	Female	Total	Male	Female	Total	Male	Female	Total	Male	Female
Total Weighted Sample	100.0%	46.4%	53.6%	92.5%	43.7%	48.7%	4.2%	1.4%	2.9%	2.1%	0.9%	1.2%	1.2%	0.3%	0.9%
	(25,015)	(11,605)	(13,409)	(23,133)	(10,943)	(12,190)	(1,060)	(347)	(713)	(523)	(231)	(292)	(298)	(84)	(214)
Total +++	100.0%	100.0%	100.0%	100.0%	100.0%	100.0%	100.0%	100.0%	100.0%	100.0%	100.0%	100.0%	100.0%	100.0%	100.0%
	(25,015)	(11,605)	(13,409)	(23,133)	(10,943)	(12,190)	(1,060)	(347)	(713)	(524)	(231)	(292)	(296)	(84)	(214)
Less than Bachelor's	8.4%	11.3%	6.0%	8.4%	11.4%	5.6%	14.3%	17.3%	12.9%	0.0%	0.0%	0.0%	7.8%	0.0%	10.7%
	(2,110)	(1,307)	(803)	(1,935)	(1,247)	(688)	(152)	(60)	(92)	–	–	–	(23)	–	(23)
Bachelor's Degree	25.9%	23.1%	28.3%	25.6%	22.3%	28.6%	26.5%	32.0%	23.8%	34.5%	37.2%	32.5%	31.8%	54.8%	22.4%
	(6,480)	(2,685)	(3,795)	(5,924)	(2,442)	(3,482)	(281)	(111)	(170)	(181)	(86)	(95)	(94)	(46)	(48)
Master's Degree	51.6%	49.6%	53.3%	52.1%	50.4%	53.6%	43.6%	41.8%	44.5%	43.9%	29.0%	55.8%	51.7%	32.1%	58.9%
	(12,899)	(5,757)	(7,142)	(12,054)	(5,518)	(6,536)	(462)	(145)	(317)	(230)	(67)	(163)	(153)	(27)	(126)
Education Specialist	8.2%	6.8%	9.4%	8.1%	6.8%	9.2%	10.9%	6.3%	13.2%	9.4%	8.7%	9.9%	5.1%	0.0%	7.0%
	(2,050)	(785)	(1,265)	(1,870)	(743)	(1,127)	(116)	(22)	(94)	(49)	(20)	(29)	(15)	–	(15)
Doctorate	5.9%	9.2%	3.0%	5.8%	9.1%	2.9%	4.6%	2.6%	5.6%	12.2%	25.5%	1.7%	3.7%	13.1%	0.0%
	(1,474)	(1,072)	(402)	(1,350)	(993)	(357)	(49)	(9)	(40)	(64)	(59)	(5)	(11)	(11)	–

Notes:

" – " indicates sample size too small to estimate.

*** Test of statistical significance compares African Americans with Whites. *** p < .001, ** p < .01, * p < .05.

+++ Test of statistical significance compares White men with White women. +++ p < .001, ++ p < .01, + p < .05.

~~~ Test of statistical significance compares African American men with African American women. ~~~ p < .001, ~~ p < .01, ~ p < .05.

Tests of statistical significance calculated using adjusted sample weight to control for influence of large sample sizes.

Source: Schools and Staffing Survey, 1993-94.

---

prior to becoming principal. A higher percentage of African Americans than of Whites had held some other school position prior to becoming principal (87.1% versus 77.0%).

- **Table 14** shows that a higher share of African American than of White public school principals were assistant principals or program directors before becoming principals (81.9% versus 66.1%).

Figure 8 shows that the percentage of all men who were athletic coaches before becoming principals (48.7%) was substantially higher than the percentage of African American men (27.1%), all women (7.0%), and African American women (2.9%).

- A higher percentage of African American women than of all principals were curriculum

specialists or coordinators before becoming principals (46.1% versus 22.1%).

Private Schools

About one-half (53.3%) of private school principals had held some school position prior to becoming principal.

- Similar percentages of African Americans and Whites had held some other school position prior to becoming private school principals (46.1% versus 53.1%).

- **Table 15** shows that about one-third (33.3%) of White principals had served as sponsors for student clubs, compared with only 11.2% of African Americans.

Table 14. Previous Position Held by Public School Principals by Race and Sex: 1993/94
(weighted sample size in parentheses)

Previous Position	Total	Male	Female	White, Non-Hispanic Total	Male	Female	African American, Non-Hispanic Total	Male	Female	Hispanic Total	Male	Female	Other Total	Male	Female
Total Weighted Sample	100.0% (79,618)	65.5% (52,113)	34.5% (27,505)	84.3% (67,081)	58.1% (46,283)	26.1% (20,798)	10.1% (8,018)	4.3% (3,419)	5.8% (4,599)	4.1% (3,269)	2.2% (1,738)	1.9% (1,531)	1.6% (1,250)	0.8% (673)	0.7% (577)
Total ***	100.0% (79,618)	100.0% (52,113)	100.0% (27,505)	100.0% (67,081)	100.0% (46,283)	100.0% (20,798)	100.0% (8,018)	100.0% (3,419)	100.0% (4,599)	100.0% (3,269)	100.0% (1,738)	100.0% (1,531)	100.0% (1,250)	100.0% (673)	100.0% (577)
Held Other School Position BEFORE Principal	78.6% (62,589)	77.5% (40,388)	80.7% (22,201)	77.0% (51,654)	76.7% (35,490)	77.7% (16,164)	87.1% (6,980)	85.3% (2,916)	88.4% (4,064)	87.4% (2,857)	81.5% (1,416)	94.1% (1,441)	87.8% (1,098)	84.1% (566)	92.2% (532)
Total Respondents Total	100.0% (62,589)	100.0% (40,388)	100.0% (22,201)	100.0% (51,654)	100.0% (35,490)	100.0% (16,164)	100.0% (6,980)	100.0% (2,916)	100.0% (4,064)	100.0% (2,857)	100.0% (1,416)	100.0% (1,441)	100.0% (1,098)	100.0% (566)	100.0% (532)
Department Head ++ ~	24.9% (15,580)	26.3% (10,637)	22.3% (4,942)	25.0% (12,924)	26.1% (9,273)	22.6% (3,651)	24.9% (1,741)	29.2% (851)	21.9% (890)	21.1% (603)	23.2% (328)	19.1% (275)	28.3% (311)	32.7% (185)	23.7% (126)
Curriculum Specialist or Coordinator *** +++ ~~~	22.1% (13,820)	14.0% (5,637)	36.9% (8,183)	19.7% (10,157)	13.3% (4,723)	33.6% (5,434)	34.3% (2,392)	17.8% (518)	46.1% (1,874)	37.4% (1,068)	21.3% (301)	53.2% (767)	18.5% (203)	16.8% (95)	20.3% (108)
Assistant Principal or Program Director *** ++ ~~	68.8% (43,083)	69.5% (28,066)	67.6% (15,017)	66.1% (34,138)	67.4% (23,925)	63.2% (10,213)	81.9% (5,715)	86.8% (2,531)	78.3% (3,184)	86.0% (2,456)	85.0% (1,204)	86.9% (1,252)	70.5% (774)	71.7% (406)	69.2% (368)
Guidance Counselor	9.7% (6,083)	9.7% (3,922)	9.7% (2,161)	9.2% (4,777)	9.4% (3,332)	8.9% (1,445)	10.9% (764)	10.6% (308)	11.2% (456)	14.0% (400)	15.5% (220)	12.5% (180)	12.9% (142)	11.0% (62)	15.0% (80)
Library Specialist +++	1.8% (1,100)	0.9% (369)	3.3% (731)	1.6% (831)	0.9% (326)	3.1% (505)	2.0% (138)	0.9% (26)	2.8% (112)	3.3% (95)	0.6% (9)	6.0% (86)	3.3% (36)	1.4% (8)	5.3% (28)
Athletic Coach *** +++ ~~~	33.9% (21,201)	48.7% (19,654)	7.0% (1,546)	37.7% (19,471)	51.0% (18,113)	8.4% (1,358)	13.0% (906)	27.1% (789)	2.9% (117)	18.3% (524)	35.5% (503)	1.5% (21)	27.2% (299)	44.0% (249)	9.4% (50)
Sponsor for Student Clubs +++	35.4% (22,184)	38.9% (15,721)	29.1% (6,464)	35.7% (18,438)	39.4% (13,969)	27.6% (4,469)	33.7% (2,350)	33.2% (969)	34.0% (1,381)	35.6% (1,017)	39.1% (554)	32.1% (463)	34.6% (380)	40.5% (229)	28.4% (151)
Other Position *** +++ ~~	27.3% (17,057)	24.3% (9,799)	32.7% (7,257)	26.5% (13,695)	24.0% (8,524)	32.0% (5,171)	34.2% (2,390)	28.8% (840)	38.1% (1,550)	21.3% (608)	21.4% (303)	21.2% (305)	33.1% (363)	23.3% (132)	43.4% (231)

Notes:

Columns do not sum to 100% as respondents may have more than one type of previous experience.

*** Test of statistical significance compares African Americans with Whites. *** p < .001, ** p < .01, * p < .05.

+++ Test of statistical significance compares White men with White women. +++ p < .001, ++ p < .01, + p < .05.

~~~ Test of statistical significance compares African American men with African American women. ~~~ p < .001, ~~ p < .01, ~ p < .05.

Tests of statistical significance calculated using adjusted sample weight to control for influence of large sample sizes.

Source: Schools and Staffing Survey, 1993-94.

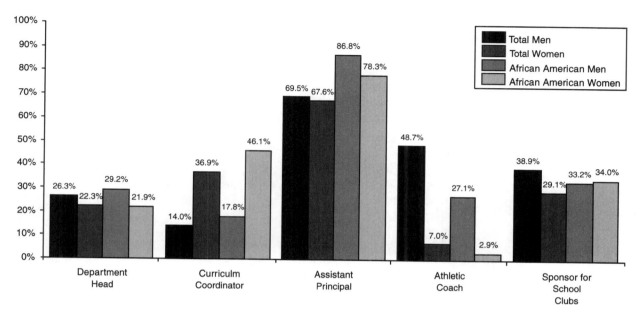

Figure 8. Previous Position Held by African American
Public School Principals: 1993/94

Source: Schools and Staffing Survey, 1993-94.

- A smaller proportion of African Americans than Whites were once department heads (22.3% versus 35.8%).

- Only 8.0% of African American private school principals were athletic coaches prior to becoming principal, compared with 30.0% of their White counterparts.

Age of Principals

Public Schools

On average, public school principals were 48.7 years of age. **Figure 9** shows that African Americans tended to be older than all public school principals.

- **Table 16** shows that 25.2% of African American public school principals were age 55 and older, compared with only 18.1% of Whites.

Private Schools

On average, private school principals were 48.1 years of age in 1993/94. **Figure 9** shows that African American principals tended to be younger than all private school principals.

- **Table 17** shows that more than one-fourth (29.2%) of African Americans were under the age of 40, compared with only 18.6% of Whites.

Professional Experience of Principals

Public Schools

Public school principals in 1993/94 had been principals for an average of 8.7 years. In general, principal experience increased with age for African Americans and Whites and men and women. **Figure 10** shows that, among both African American

Table 15. Previous Position of Private School Principals Who Held a School Position Before Becoming Principal by Race and Sex: 1993/94
(weighted sample size in parentheses)

Previous Position	Total	Male	Female	White, Non-Hispanic Total	White, Non-Hispanic Male	White, Non-Hispanic Female	African American, Non-Hispanic Total	African American, Non-Hispanic Male	African American, Non-Hispanic Female	Hispanic Total	Hispanic Male	Hispanic Female	Other Total	Other Male	Other Female
Total Weighted Sample	100.0% (25,015)	46.4% (11,605)	53.6% (13,409)	92.5% (23,133)	43.7% (10,943)	48.7% (12,190)	4.2% (1,060)	1.4% (347)	2.9% (713)	2.1% (523)	0.9% (231)	1.2% (292)	1.2% (298)	0.3% (84)	0.9% (214)
Total	100.0% (25,015)	100.0% (11,605)	100.0% (13,409)	100.0% (23,133)	100.0% (10,943)	100.0% (12,190)	100.0% (1,060)	100.0% (347)	100.0% (713)	100.0% (523)	100.0% (231)	100.0% (292)	100.0% (298)	100.0% (84)	100.0% (214)
Held Other School Position BEFORE Principal	53.3% (13,334)	53.2% (6,178)	53.4% (7,157)	53.1% (12,279)	52.9% (5,791)	53.2% (6,488)	46.1% (489)	40.3% (140)	48.9% (349)	70.2% (367)	83.1% (192)	59.9% (175)	67.1% (200)	65.5% (55)	67.8% (145)
Total	100.0% (13,334)	100.0% (6,178)	100.0% (7,157)	100.0% (12,279)	100.0% (5,791)	100.0% (6,488)	100.0% (489)	100.0% (140)	100.0% (349)	100.0% (367)	100.0% (192)	100.0% (175)	100.0% (200)	100.0% (55)	100.0% (145)
Department Head * ~	35.1% (4,681)	36.8% (2,275)	33.6% (2,408)	35.8% (4,394)	36.6% (2,120)	35.0% (2,274)	22.3% (109)	42.9% (60)	14.0% (49)	34.1% (125)	38.5% (74)	29.1% (51)	37.7% (55)	37.7% (21)	23.2% (34)
Curriculum Specialist or Coordinator +++	24.8% (3,307)	19.4% (1,201)	29.4% (2,106)	24.6% (3,025)	19.4% (1,125)	29.3% (1,900)	22.5% (154)	22.5% (31)	35.2% (123)	24.0% (88)	13.0% (25)	36.0% (63)	35.7% (40)	35.7% (20)	14.0% (20)
Assistant Principal or Program Director +++	54.4% (7,257)	60.8% (3,758)	48.9% (3,499)	54.5% (6,695)	60.5% (3,503)	49.2% (3,192)	51.6% (207)	51.6% (72)	38.7% (135)	73.8% (271)	82.8% (159)	64.0% (112)	43.3% (84)	43.3% (24)	41.6% (60)
Guidance Counselor +++	11.8% (1,580)	15.2% (937)	9.0% (644)	11.8% (1,453)	15.2% (879)	8.8% (574)	7.5% (57)	7.5% (11)	13.3% (46)	15.3% (56)	19.3% (37)	10.9% (19)	17.6% (15)	17.6% (10)	3.4% (5)
Library Specialist ++	2.2% (295)	0.9% (54)	3.4% (242)	2.4% (296)	0.9% (54)	3.7% (242)	0.0% –	0.0% –	0.0% –	0.0% –	0.0% –	0.0% –	0.0% –	0.0% –	0.0% –
Athletic Coach *** +++	29.2% (3,893)	53.8% (3,323)	8.0% (571)	30.0% (3,685)	54.6% (3,163)	8.0% (522)	8.0% (39)	17.1% (24)	4.3% (15)	35.4% (130)	59.9% (115)	8.6% (15)	20.0% (40)	38.2% (21)	13.1% (19)
Sponsor for Student Clubs ** ++	32.4% (4,325)	35.9% (2,220)	29.4% (2,105)	33.3% (4,090)	36.9% (2,139)	30.1% (1,951)	11.2% (55)	15.0% (21)	9.7% (34)	35.7% (131)	16.1% (31)	57.1% (100)	52.8% (49)	52.8% (29)	13.8% (20)
Other Position	35.8% (4,774)	34.1% (2,106)	37.3% (2,667)	35.1% (4,306)	33.8% (1,958)	36.2% (2,348)	40.7% (199)	35.0% (49)	43.0% (150)	51.0% (187)	40.6% (78)	62.3% (109)	38.6% (81)	38.6% (21)	41.1% (60)

Notes:

Columns do not sum to 100% as respondents may have more than one type of previous experience.

" – " indicates sample size too small to estimate.

*** Test of statistical significance compares African Americans with Whites. *** p < .001, ** p < .01, * p < .05.

+++ Test of statistical significance compares White men with White women. +++ p < .001, ++ p < .01, + p < .05.

~~~ Test of statistical significance compares African American men with African American women. ~~~ p < .001, ~~ p < .01, ~ p < .05.

Tests of statistical significance calculated using adjusted sample weight to control for influence of large sample sizes.

Source: Schools and Staffing Survey, 1993-94.

Figure 9. Distribution of African American Public and
Private School Principals by Age: 1993/94

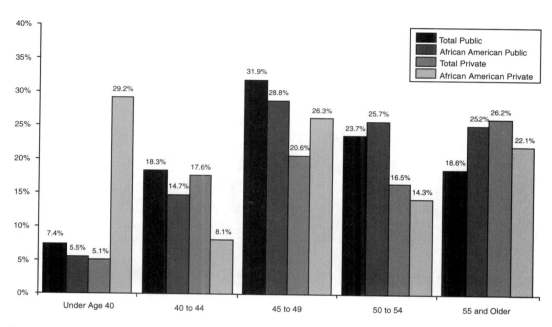

Source: Schools and Staffing Survey, 1993-94.

and all public school principals, men had more experience as principals than women of the same age.

- **Table 18** shows that African Americans had less experience as principals than Whites of the same age, on average (7.1 years versus 9.0 years overall).

- The average number of years of principal experience ranged from 5.8 years for African American women and 5.6 years for White women to 8.7 years for African American men and 10.5 years for White men.

- Among public school principals age 55 and older, African Americans had an average of 11.2 years of principal experience, but Whites had 16.0 years.

- Women age 55 and older had fewer years of experience than their male counterparts among both African Americans (9.4 years versus 13.0 years) and Whites (9.3 years versus 18.8 years).

Private Schools

On average, private school principals in 1993/94 had been principals for 8.8 years and teachers for 14.3 years. African American private school principals averaged similar amounts of principal experience as Whites (8.3 years versus 8.7 years), but fewer years of teaching experience (12.6 years versus 14.4 years).

- **Table 19** shows that African Americans age 55 and older averaged 18.6 years of teaching experience, compared with 20.0 years for their White counterparts.

Table 16. Age of Public School Principals by Race and Sex: 1993/94
(weighted sample size in parentheses)

Age	Total	Male	Female	White, Non-Hispanic Total	Male	Female	African American, Non-Hispanic Total	Male	Female	Hispanic Total	Male	Female	Other Total	Male	Female
Total Weighted Sample	100.0% (79,618)	65.5% (52,113)	34.5% (27,505)	84.3% (67,081)	58.1% (46,283)	26.1% (20,798)	10.1% (8,018)	4.3% (3,419)	5.8% (4,599)	4.1% (3,269)	2.2% (1,738)	1.9% (1,531)	1.6% (1,250)	0.8% (673)	0.7% (577)
Average Age *** + ~~	48.7 (79,618)	48.8 (52,113)	48.5 (27,505)	48.6 (67,080)	48.7 (46,282)	48.3 (20,798)	50.0 (8,018)	50.7 (3,419)	49.5 (4,599)	47.8 (3,271)	48.4 (1,740)	47.1 (1,531)	48.1 (1,251)	48.4 (674)	47.6 (577)
Total *** ~	100.0% (79,618)	100.0% (52,113)	100.0% (27,505)	100.0% (67,080)	100.0% (46,282)	100.0% (20,798)	100.0% (8,018)	100.0% (3,419)	100.0% (4,599)	100.0% (3,271)	100.0% (1,740)	100.0% (1,531)	100.0% (1,251)	100.0% (674)	100.0% (577)
Under Age 35	1.6% (1,287)	1.7% (901)	1.5% (410)	1.8% (1,217)	1.8% (833)	1.8% (384)	1.0% (81)	1.6% (55)	0.6% (26)	0.2% (5)	0.3% (5)	0.0% –	0.6% (8)	1.2% (8)	0.0% –
35 to 39 Years	5.8% (4,626)	5.8% (3,042)	5.8% (1,584)	6.0% (4,022)	6.0% (2,772)	6.0% (1,250)	4.5% (364)	4.1% (140)	4.9% (224)	4.7% (155)	3.9% (67)	5.7% (88)	6.8% (85)	9.3% (63)	3.8% (22)
40 to 44 Years	18.3% (14,572)	17.8% (9,272)	19.3% (5,300)	18.1% (12,155)	17.8% (8,246)	18.8% (3,909)	14.7% (1,179)	12.9% (441)	16.0% (738)	28.7% (940)	24.7% (429)	33.4% (511)	23.8% (298)	23.1% (156)	24.6% (142)
45 to 49 Years	31.9% (25,429)	31.9% (16,624)	32.0% (8,805)	32.4% (21,726)	32.2% (14,921)	32.7% (6,805)	28.8% (2,313)	27.6% (943)	29.8% (1,370)	29.7% (971)	33.7% (586)	25.1% (385)	33.5% (419)	25.8% (174)	42.5% (245)
50 to 54 Years	23.7% (18,868)	23.4% (12,216)	24.2% (6,652)	23.6% (15,806)	23.6% (10,909)	23.5% (4,897)	25.7% (2,062)	23.8% (813)	27.2% (1,249)	25.3% (826)	24.0% (418)	26.6% (408)	13.9% (174)	11.3% (76)	17.0% (98)
55 and Older	18.6% (14,817)	19.3% (10,061)	17.3% (4,756)	18.1% (12,155)	18.6% (8,601)	17.1% (3,554)	25.2% (2,021)	30.1% (1,028)	21.6% (993)	11.4% (374)	13.5% (235)	9.1% (139)	21.3% (267)	29.2% (197)	12.1% (70)

Notes:

" – " indicates sample size too small to estimate.

*** Test of statistical significance compares African Americans with Whites. *** p < .001, ** p < .01, * p < .05.

+++ Test of statistical significance compares White men with White women. +++ p < .001, ++ p < .01, + p < .05.

~~~ Test of statistical significance compares African American men with African American women. ~~~ p < .001, ~~ p < .01, ~ p < .05.

Tests of statistical significance calculated using adjusted sample weight to control for influence of large sample sizes.

Source: Schools and Staffing Survey, 1993-94.

Training Received by Principals

Public Schools

More than one-third (38.9%) of all 1993/94 public school principals had received training and development for aspiring principals.

- **Figure 11** shows that more than one-half (58.0%) of African Americans had received such training and development prior to becoming principals, compared with only one-third (38.9%) of all public school principals.

A higher percentage of African American men than of African American women, White men, and White women had had training in management techniques.

- **Table 20** shows that 82.5% of African American men had had training in management techniques, compared with 77.1% of African American women, 74.7% of White men, and 71.8% of White women.

- Comparable shares of African American and White public school principals had received

Table 17. Age of Private School Principals by Race and Sex: 1993/94
(weighted sample size in parentheses)

Age	Total	Male	Female	White, Non-Hispanic			African American, Non-Hispanic			Hispanic			Other		
				Total	Male	Female	Total	Male	Female	Total	Male	Female	Total	Male	Female
Total Weighted Sample	100.0%	46.4%	53.6%	92.5%	43.7%	48.7%	4.2%	1.4%	2.9%	2.1%	0.9%	1.2%	1.2%	0.3%	0.9%
	(25,015)	(11,605)	(13,409)	(23,133)	(10,943)	(12,190)	(1,060)	(347)	(713)	(523)	(231)	(292)	(298)	(84)	(214)
Average Age +++ ~~	48.1	46.7	49.4	48.1	46.8	49.4	47.3	43.2	49.3	49.1	50.2	48.2	49.5	48.1	50.0
	(25,015)	(52,113)	(13,409)	(23,133)	(10,943)	(12,190)	(1,061)	(347)	(4,599)	(526)	(231)	(292)	(298)	(84)	(214)
Total ** +++	100.0%	100.0%	100.0%	100.0%	100.0%	100.0%	100.0%	100.0%	100.0%	100.0%	100.0%	100.0%	100.0%	100.0%	100.0%
	(25,015)	(11,605)	(13,409)	(23,133)	(10,943)	(12,190)	(1,061)	(347)	(713)	(526)	(231)	(292)	(298)	(84)	(214)
Under Age 40	5.1%	23.2%	15.7%	18.6%	22.8%	14.8%	29.2%	35.4%	26.2%	23.2%	18.2%	27.4%	21.8%	35.7%	16.4%
	(1,287)	(2,687)	(2,107)	(4,297)	(2,492)	(1,805)	(310)	(123)	(187)	(122)	(42)	(80)	(65)	(30)	(35)
40 to 44 Years	17.6%	19.3%	16.1%	18.4%	19.9%	17.1%	8.1%	9.8%	7.3%	8.0%	10.4%	6.2%	3.7%	3.6%	3.7%
	(4,403)	(2,241)	(2,162)	(4,264)	(2,180)	(2,084)	(86)	(34)	(52)	(42)	(24)	(18)	(11)	(3)	(8)
45 to 49 Years	20.6%	20.6%	20.5%	20.3%	20.5%	20.1%	26.3%	23.1%	27.9%	19.4%	25.5%	14.7%	24.8%	11.9%	29.9%
	(5,144)	(2,389)	(2,755)	(4,689)	(2,240)	(2,449)	(279)	(80)	(199)	(102)	(59)	(43)	(74)	(10)	(64)
50 to 54 Years	16.5%	13.2%	19.3%	16.6%	13.2%	19.6%	14.3%	22.5%	10.4%	13.9%	3.9%	21.9%	22.8%	10.7%	27.6%
	(4,122)	(1,536)	(2,586)	(3,829)	(1,440)	(2,389)	(152)	(78)	(74)	(73)	(9)	(64)	(68)	(9)	(59)
55 and Older	26.2%	23.7%	28.3%	26.2%	23.7%	28.4%	22.1%	8.9%	28.5%	35.6%	42.9%	30.1%	26.5%	38.1%	22.0%
	(6,554)	(2,753)	(3,801)	(6,054)	(2,591)	(3,463)	(234)	(31)	(203)	(187)	(99)	(88)	(79)	(32)	(47)

Notes:

*** Test of statistical significance compares African Americans with Whites. *** p < .001, ** p < .01, * p < .05.

+++ Test of statistical significance compares White men with White women. +++ p < .001, ++ p < .01, + p < .05.

~~~ Test of statistical significance compares African American men with African American women. ~~~ p < .001, ~~ p < .01, ~ p < .05.

Tests of statistical significance calculated using adjusted sample weight to control for influence of large sample sizes.

Source: Schools and Staffing Survey, 1993-94.

in-service training in evaluation and supervision (88.2% versus 86.0%).

- The percentage of African Americans who had had an administrative internship was higher than the percentage of Whites (45.1% versus 40.0%).

Private Schools

Figure 11 shows that the share of private school principals who had had training and development for aspiring principals was comparable to the share of public school principals (38.5% versus 38.9%). But,

Table 21 shows that, among private school principals, a higher share of African American women than of all principals received such training.

- About 57.4% of African American women had received training and development for aspiring principals, compared with only 32.9% of African American men, 34.8% of White men, and 39.8% of White women.

- **Table 21** shows that 76.3% of African Americans had participated in in-service training in evaluation and supervision, compared with 64.0% of Whites.

**Figure 10. Years of Principal Experience Among
Public School Principals by Age: 1993/94**

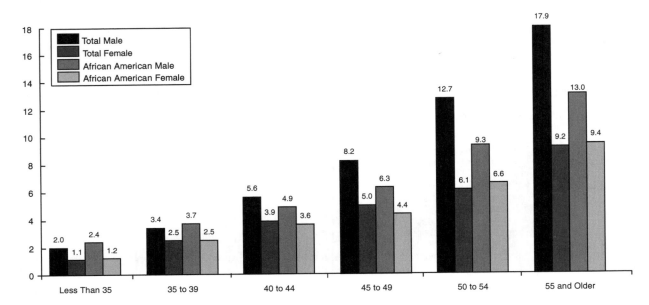

Source: Schools and Staffing Survey, 1993-94.

- Similarly, 73.6% of African Americans had had training in management techniques, compared with 56.1% of Whites.

- About one-third (33.5%) of African American principals had had administrative internships, compared with only 20.8% of White principals.

ACADEMIC-YEAR BASE SALARIES OF PRINCIPALS

On average, public school principals received annual salaries of $54,858 in 1993/94 (**Table 22**). Average salaries for private school principals ($29,714) were about one-half as high as those received by public school principals (**Table 23**).

Average Salaries by Principals' Age

Public Schools

Even after controlling for age, average salaries of African American public school principals appeared to be higher than those of their White counterparts. But when only principals employed 12 months of the year are considered, the difference in the average salaries of African Americans and Whites of the same age disappears. **Figure 12** shows that, on average, men and women of the same age received comparable salaries overall and among African Americans.

- **Table 22** shows that, among all public school principals age 55 and older, average salaries

Table 18. Professional Experience of Public School Principals by Age, Race, and Sex: 1993/94
(weighted sample size in parentheses)

Professional Experience	Total	Male	Female	White, Non-Hispanic			African American, Non-Hispanic			Hispanic			Other		
				Total	Male	Female	Total	Male	Female	Total	Male	Female	Total	Male	Female
Total Weighted Sample	100.0%	65.5%	34.5%	84.3%	58.1%	26.1%	10.1%	4.3%	5.8%	4.1%	2.2%	1.9%	1.6%	0.8%	0.7%
	(79,618)	(52,113)	(27,505)	(67,081)	(46,283)	(20,798)	(8,018)	(3,419)	(4,599)	(3,269)	(1,738)	(1,531)	(1,250)	(673)	(577)
Total Principal Experience															
Total *** +++ ~~~	8.7	10.3	5.6	9.0	10.5	5.6	7.1	8.7	5.8	6.3	7.7	4.8	6.9	8.6	5.0
[Age: *** +++ ~~~]	(79,619)	(52,114)	(27,505)	(67,081)	(46,283)	(20,798)	(8,018)	(3,419)	(4,599)	(3,269)	(1,738)	(1,531)	(1,250)	(673)	(577)
Under Age 35	1.7	2.0	1.1	1.7	2.0	1.1	2.0	2.4	1.2	–	–	–	–	–	–
	(1,311)	(901)	(410)	(1,217)	(833)	(384)	(81)	(55)	(26)	–	–	–	–	–	–
35 to 39 years old	3.1	3.4	2.5	3.1	3.4	2.5	2.9	3.7	2.5	2.4	2.3	2.4	3.8	4.5	1.9
	(4,626)	(3,042)	(1,584)	(4,022)	(2,772)	(1,250)	(364)	(140)	(224)	(155)	(67)	(88)	(85)	(63)	(22)
40 to 44 years old	5.0	5.6	3.9	5.2	5.7	4.2	4.1	4.9	3.6	3.5	4.3	2.8	4.5	6.6	2.3
	(14,572)	(9,272)	(5,300)	(12,155)	(8,246)	(3,909)	(1,179)	(441)	(738)	(940)	(429)	(511)	(298)	(156)	(142)
45 to 49 years old	7.1	8.2	5.0	7.4	8.4	5.2	5.2	6.3	4.4	6.0	6.9	4.6	6.3	7.2	5.6
	(25,429)	(16,624)	(8,805)	(21,726)	(14,921)	(6,805)	(2,313)	(943)	(1,370)	(971)	(586)	(385)	(419)	(174)	(245)
50 to 54 years old	10.3	12.7	6.1	10.8	13.0	5.9	7.7	9.3	6.6	8.6	10.1	7.1	7.6	10.2	5.6
	(18,868)	(12,216)	(6,652)	(15,806)	(10,909)	(4,897)	(2,062)	(813)	(1,249)	(826)	(418)	(408)	(174)	(76)	(98)
55 or older	15.2	17.9	9.2	16.0	18.8	9.3	11.2	13.0	9.4	10.9	13.3	6.9	11.4	12.5	8.2
	(14,817)	(10,061)	(4,756)	(12,155)	(8,601)	(3,554)	(2,021)	(1,028)	(993)	(374)	(235)	(139)	(267)	(197)	(70)
Total Teaching Experience															
Total *** +++ ~~~	12.6	11.9	14.0	12.5	11.9	13.8	14.0	12.7	15.0	12.4	11.9	13.1	11.8	11.0	12.8
[Age: *** +++ ~~~]	(79,619)	(52,114)	(27,505)	(67,081)	(46,283)	(20,798)	(8,018)	(3,419)	(4,599)	(3,269)	(1,738)	(1,531)	(1,250)	(673)	(577)
Under Age 35	6.7	6.5	6.9	6.7	6.6	7.0	5.7	5.5	6.0	6.0	6.0	–	4.4	4.4	–
	(1,311)	(901)	(410)	(1,217)	(833)	(384)	(81)	(55)	(26)	(5)	(5)	–	(8)	(8)	–
35 to 39 years old	9.3	8.9	10.1	9.5	9.1	10.2	8.7	6.5	10.2	7.2	7.1	7.3	7.4	6.1	10.9
	(4,626)	(3,042)	(1,584)	(4,022)	(2,772)	(1,250)	(364)	(140)	(224)	(155)	(67)	(88)	(85)	(63)	(22)
40 to 44 years old	11.3	10.7	12.3	11.3	10.8	12.4	11.9	11.8	11.9	11.1	9.7	12.2	10.5	9.4	11.8
	(14,571)	(9,271)	(5,300)	(12,155)	(8,246)	(3,909)	(1,179)	(441)	(738)	(940)	(429)	(511)	(298)	(156)	(142)
45 to 49 years old	12.6	12.1	13.4	12.5	12.1	13.4	13.8	12.8	14.4	12.2	12.1	12.3	12.5	14.6	10.9
	(25,429)	(16,624)	(8,805)	(21,726)	(14,921)	(6,805)	(2,313)	(943)	(1,370)	(971)	(586)	(385)	(419)	(174)	(245)
50 to 54 years old	13.4	12.2	15.6	13.2	12.2	15.5	15.4	13.2	16.8	12.3	12.2	12.4	13.0	9.6	15.7
	(18,868)	(12,216)	(6,652)	(15,806)	(10,909)	(4,897)	(2,062)	(813)	(1,249)	(826)	(418)	(408)	(174)	(76)	(98)
55 or older	14.5	13.6	16.5	14.3	13.6	16.0	15.4	13.8	17.1	18.8	15.8	23.8	13.2	11.4	18.2
	(14,817)	(10,061)	(4,756)	(12,155)	(8,601)	(3,554)	(2,021)	(1,028)	(993)	(374)	(235)	(139)	(267)	(197)	(70)

Notes:
" – " indicates sample size too small to estimate.
*** Test of statistical significance compares African Americans with Whites. *** p < .001, ** p < .01, * p < .05.
+++ Test of statistical significance compares White men with White women. +++ p < .001, ++ p < .01, + p < .05.
~~~ Test of statistical significance compares African American men with African American women. ~~~ p < .001, ~~ p < .01, ~ p < .05.
Tests of statistical significance calculated using adjusted sample weight to control for influence of large sample sizes.
Source: Schools and Staffing Survey, 1993-94.

Table 19. Professional Experience of Private School Principals by Age, Race, and Sex: 1993/94
(weighted sample size in parentheses)

Professional Experience	Total	Male	Female	White, Non-Hispanic Total	Male	Female	African American, Non-Hispanic Total	Male	Female	Hispanic Total	Male	Female	Other Total	Male	Female
Total Weighted Sample	100.0% (25,015)	46.4% (11,605)	53.6% (13,409)	92.5% (23,133)	43.7% (10,943)	48.7% (12,190)	4.2% (1,060)	1.4% (347)	2.9% (713)	2.1% (523)	0.9% (231)	1.2% (292)	1.2% (298)	0.3% (84)	0.9% (214)
Total Principal Experience															
Total + ~~ [Age: *** +++ ~~~]	8.8 (25,015)	9.0 (11,605)	8.6 (13,411)	8.7 (23,133)	9.0 (10,943)	8.5 (12,190)	8.3 (1,061)	5.7 (347)	9.6 (713)	10.1 (526)	11.8 (231)	8.8 (292)	10.1 (297)	5.9 (84)	11.8 (214)
Under Age 40	3.5 (4,794)	3.9 (2,687)	2.9 (2,107)	3.6 (4,297)	4.1 (2,492)	2.9 (1,805)	3.2 (310)	1.2 (123)	4.5 (187)	3.2 (122)	6.2 (42)	1.6 (80)	1.5 (65)	1.5 (30)	1.6 (35)
40 to 44 Years Old	5.3 (4,403)	6.4 (2,241)	4.1 (2,162)	5.3 (4,264)	6.4 (2,180)	4.1 (2,084)	5.8 (86)	9.9 (34)	3.0 (52)	5.4 (42)	3.0 (24)	8.5 (18)	2.2 (11)	–	–
45 to 50 Years Old	8.4 (5,144)	9.9 (2,389)	7.0 (2,755)	8.4 (4,689)	10.1 (2,240)	6.8 (2,449)	7.0 (279)	4.8 (80)	7.9 (199)	8.3 (102)	8.9 (59)	7.6 (43)	11.4 (74)	7.5 (10)	12.0 (64)
50 to 54 Years Old	9.6 (4,120)	10.7 (1,535)	8.9 (2,586)	9.6 (3,829)	10.9 (1,440)	8.8 (2,389)	10.9 (152)	8.5 (78)	13.5 (74)	6.2 (73)	–	4.5 (64)	12.5 (68)	–	14.0 (59)
55 or older	14.8 (6,553)	14.2 (2,753)	15.2 (3,801)	14.6 (6,054)	14.1 (2,591)	15.0 (3,463)	15.9 (234)	14.3 (31)	16.1 (203)	18.2 (187)	17.4 (99)	19.1 (88)	15.1 (79)	10.2 (32)	18.4 (47)
Total Teaching Experience															
Total * +++ [Age: *** +++ ~~~]	14.3 (25,015)	13.4 (11,606)	15.2 (13,411)	14.4 (23,133)	13.5 (10,943)	15.2 (12,190)	12.6 (1,061)	11.1 (347)	13.4 (713)	15.5 (526)	14.0 (231)	16.6 (292)	13.4 (299)	11.9 (84)	14.0 (214)
Under Age 40	7.8 (4,794)	7.5 (2,687)	8.1 (2,107)	7.8 (4,297)	7.6 (2,492)	8.1 (1,805)	5.4 (310)	3.9 (123)	6.3 (187)	11.9 (122)	10.1 (42)	12.8 (80)	4.9 (65)	8.3 (30)	2.1 (35)
40 to 44 Years Old	11.3 (4,403)	12.3 (2,241)	10.3 (2,162)	11.3 (4,264)	12.4 (2,180)	10.2 (2,084)	10.1 (86)	12.2 (34)	8.8 (52)	12.5 (42)	–	–	–	–	–
45 to 50 Years Old	14.8 (5,144)	16.1 (2,389)	13.7 (2,755)	14.9 (4,689)	15.9 (2,240)	14.1 (2,449)	14.2 (279)	21.8 (80)	11.1 (199)	15.3 (102)	16.5 (59)	13.6 (43)	10.7 (74)	–	9.4 (64)
50 to 54 Years Old	15.7 (4,120)	15.5 (1,536)	15.8 (2,586)	15.7 (3,829)	15.9 (1,440)	15.6 (2,389)	16.9 (152)	10.0 (78)	24.1 (74)	17.9 (73)	–	18.5 (64)	10.9 (68)	–	12.2 (59)
55 or older	20.0 (6,553)	16.5 (2,753)	22.4 (3,801)	20.0 (6,054)	16.6 (2,591)	22.5 (3,463)	18.6 (234)	–	19.4 (203)	17.7 (187)	15.5 (99)	20.2 (88)	25.5 (79)	15.1 (32)	32.4 (47)

Notes:
" – " indicates sample size too small to estimate.
*** Test of statistical significance compares African Americans with Whites. *** p < .001, ** p < .01, * p < .05.
+++ Test of statistical significance compares White men with White women. +++ p < .001, ++ p < .01, + p < .05.
~~~ Test of statistical significance compares African American men with African American women. ~~~ p < .001, ~~ p < .01, ~ p < .05.
Tests of statistical significance calculated using adjusted sample weight to control for influence of large sample sizes.
Source: Schools and Staffing Survey, 1993-94.

Figure 11. Training Received by Public and Private School Principals: 1993/94

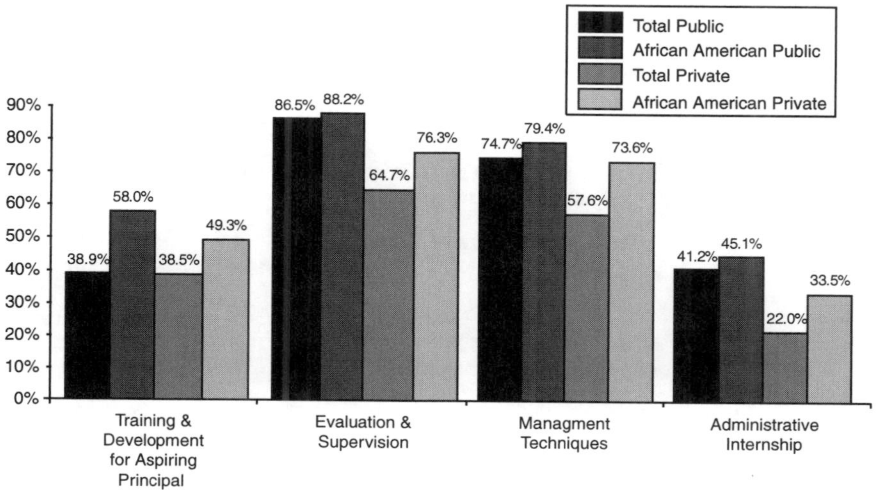

Legend:
- Total Public
- African American Public
- Total Private
- African American Private

Training & Development for Aspiring Principal: 38.9%, 58.0%, 38.5%, 49.3%
Evaluation & Supervision: 86.5%, 88.2%, 64.7%, 76.3%
Managment Techniques: 74.7%, 79.4%, 57.6%, 73.6%
Administrative Internship: 41.2%, 45.1%, 22.0%, 33.5%

Source: Schools and Staffing Survey, 1993-94.

Table 20. Training Received by Public School Principals by Race and Sex: 1993/94
(weighted sample size in parentheses)

Training for Current Position	Total	Male	Female	White, Non-Hispanic Total	Male	Female	African American, Non-Hispanic Total	Male	Female	Hispanic Total	Male	Female	Other Total	Male	Female
Total Weighted Sample	100.0% (79,618)	65.5% (52,113)	34.5% (27,505)	84.3% (67,081)	58.1% (46,283)	26.1% (20,798)	10.1% (8,018)	4.3% (3,419)	5.8% (4,599)	4.1% (3,269)	2.2% (1,738)	1.9% (1,531)	1.6% (1,250)	0.8% (673)	0.7% (577)
Training for Current Position															
Total *** +++	100.0% (79,618)	100.0% (52,113)	100.0% (27,505)	100.0% (67,081)	100.0% (46,283)	100.0% (20,798)	100.0% (8,018)	100.0% (3,419)	100.0% (4,599)	100.0% (3,269)	100.0% (1,738)	100.0% (1,531)	100.0% (1,250)	100.0% (673)	100.0% (577)
Prior to Principal, Training and Development for ASPIRING Principal	38.9% (30,974)	35.6% (18,577)	45.1% (12,397)	35.4% (23,761)	33.2% (15,376)	40.3% (8,385)	58.0% (4,651)	59.0% (2,016)	57.3% (2,635)	57.6% (1,883)	53.0% (922)	62.8% (961)	54.3% (679)	39.1% (263)	72.1% (416)
In-Service Training in Evaluation & Supervision ~~	86.5% (68,844)	86.8% (45,229)	85.9% (23,615)	86.0% (57,718)	86.3% (39,948)	85.4% (17,770)	88.2% (7,070)	91.8% (3,140)	85.5% (3,930)	90.3% (2,953)	87.1% (1,513)	94.1% (1,440)	88.2% (1,103)	93.3% (628)	82.3% (475)
Training in Management Techniques *** ++ ~	74.7% (59,494)	75.6% (39,403)	73.0% (20,091)	73.8% (49,525)	74.7% (34,594)	71.8% (14,931)	79.4% (6,368)	82.5% (2,820)	77.1% (3,548)	78.9% (2,578)	80.3% (1,396)	77.2% (1,182)	81.8% (1,023)	88.1% (593)	74.5% (430)
Administrative Internship ** +++	41.2% (32,788)	38.9% (20,259)	45.6% (12,530)	40.0% (26,855)	38.1% (17,611)	44.4% (9,244)	45.1% (3,613)	44.7% (1,527)	45.4% (2,086)	52.2% (1,705)	47.0% (817)	58.0% (888)	49.3% (616)	45.2% (304)	54.1% (312)
Had None of These for Current Position + ~	7.5% (6,006)	7.2% (3,747)	8.2% (2,259)	7.8% (5,257)	7.4% (3,432)	8.8% (1,825)	6.3% (504)	3.9% (135)	8.0% (369)	6.0% (196)	9.0% (156)	2.6% (40)	3.9% (49)	3.6% (24)	4.3% (25)

Notes:
*** Test of statistical significance compares African Americans with Whites. *** p < .001, ** p < .01, * p < .05.
+++ Test of statistical significance compares White men with White women. +++ p < .001, ++ p < .01, + p < .05.
~~~ Test of statistical significance compares African American men with African American women. ~~~ p < .001, ~~ p < .01, ~ p < .05.
Tests of statistical significance calculated using adjusted sample weight to control for influence of large sample sizes.
Source: Schools and Staffing Survey, 1993-94.

Table 21. Training Received by Private School Principals by Race and Sex: 1993/94
(weighted sample size in parentheses)

Training for Current Position	Total	Male	Female	White, Non-Hispanic			African American, Non-Hispanic			Hispanic			Other		
				Total	Male	Female	Total	Male	Female	Total	Male	Female	Total	Male	Female
Total Weighted Sample	100.0%	46.4%	53.6%	92.5%	43.7%	48.7%	4.2%	1.4%	2.9%	2.1%	0.9%	1.2%	1.2%	0.3%	0.9%
	(25,015)	(11,605)	(13,409)	(23,133)	(10,943)	(12,190)	(1,060)	(347)	(713)	(523)	(231)	(292)	(298)	(84)	(214)
Training for Current Position															
Total * + ~	100.0%	100.0%	100.0%	100.0%	100.0%	100.0%	100.0%	100.0%	100.0%	100.0%	100.0%	100.0%	100.0%	100.0%	100.0%
	(25,015)	(11,605)	(13,409)	(23,133)	(10,943)	(12,190)	(1,060)	(347)	(713)	(523)	(231)	(292)	(298)	(84)	(214)
Prior to Principal, Training and Development for ASPIRING Principal	38.5%	35.3%	41.4%	37.5%	34.8%	39.8%	49.3%	32.9%	57.4%	52.0%	49.8%	53.8%	61.4%	65.5%	59.8%
	(9,642)	(4,097)	(5,545)	(8,664)	(3,813)	(4,851)	(523)	(114)	(409)	(272)	(115)	(157)	(183)	(55)	(128)
In-Service Training in Evaluation & Supervision **	64.7%	62.8%	66.3%	64.0%	62.6%	65.2%	76.3%	69.7%	79.5%	67.3%	55.4%	76.7%	71.1%	82.1%	66.8%
	(16,177)	(7,293)	(8,884)	(14,804)	(6,854)	(7,950)	(809)	(242)	(567)	(352)	(128)	(224)	(212)	(69)	(143)
Training in Management Techniques **	57.6%	56.3%	58.8%	56.1%	55.3%	56.9%	73.6%	62.5%	79.0%	79.5%	91.3%	70.2%	79.2%	66.7%	84.1%
	(14,419)	(6,538)	(7,881)	(12,987)	(6,054)	(6,933)	(780)	(217)	(563)	(416)	(211)	(205)	(236)	(56)	(180)
Administrative Internship ** +++	22.0%	18.4%	25.1%	20.8%	17.4%	23.9%	33.5%	35.4%	32.5%	40.3%	42.9%	38.4%	43.3%	23.8%	50.9%
	(5,508)	(2,141)	(3,367)	(4,813)	(1,899)	(2,914)	(355)	(123)	(232)	(211)	(99)	(112)	(129)	(20)	(109)
Had None of These for Current Position ** ~	25.3%	25.9%	24.7%	26.3%	26.5%	26.1%	13.6%	24.8%	8.1%	9.8%	4.8%	13.7%	14.1%	14.3%	14.0%
	(6,321)	(3,009)	(3,313)	(6,085)	(2,900)	(3,185)	(144)	(86)	(58)	(51)	(11)	(40)	(42)	(12)	(30)

Notes:
*** Test of statistical significance compares African Americans with Whites. *** p < .001, ** p < .01, * p < .05.
+++ Test of statistical significance compares White men with White women. +++ p < .001, ++ p < .01, + p < .05.
~~~ Test of statistical significance compares African American men with African American women. ~~~ p < .001, ~~ p < .01, ~ p < .05.
Tests of statistical significance calculated using adjusted sample weight to control for influence of large sample sizes.
Source: Schools and Staffing Survey, 1993-94.

were $61,512 for African Americans and $57,227 for Whites.

- **Table 22** also shows that, among principals who worked 12 months of the year and who were age 55 or older, average salaries were $62,876 for African Americans and $62,018 for Whites.

Private Schools

After controlling for age, average salaries for African American and White private school principals appeared to be similar.

- For example, **Table 23** shows that, among private school principals between the ages of 45

and 49, average salaries were $37,679 for African Americans and $32,339 for Whites.

Principals' Annual Salaries by Urbanicity

Public Schools

Figure 13 shows that public school principals employed at suburban and urban schools tended to average higher salaries than their counterparts at rural schools. **Table 24** shows that, on average, suburban public school principals earned $61,810, urban public school principals earned $58,023, and rural public school principals earned $49,430 per year.

Table 22. Annual Salaries of Public School Principals by Age, Months Employed, Race, and Sex: 1993/94
(weighted sample size in parentheses)

Age	Total	Male	Female	White, Non-Hispanic			African American, Non-Hispanic			Hispanic			Other		
				Total	Male	Female	Total	Male	Female	Total	Male	Female	Total	Male	Female
Total Weighted Sample	100.0%	65.5%	34.5%	84.3%	58.1%	26.1%	10.1%	4.3%	5.8%	4.1%	2.2%	1.9%	1.6%	0.8%	0.7%
	(79,618)	(52,113)	(27,505)	(67,081)	(46,283)	(20,798)	(8,018)	(3,419)	(4,599)	(3,269)	(1,738)	(1,531)	(1,250)	(673)	(577)
Annual Salary by Age—All Principals															
Total *** +	$54,858	$54,922	$54,736	$54,466	$54,701	$53,942	$57,669	$57,658	$57,677	$55,862	$55,046	$56,789	$55,245	$55,912	$54,465
[Age: *** +++ ~~~]	(79,618)	(52,114)	(27,505)	(67,081)	(46,283)	(20,798)	(8,018)	(3,419)	(4,599)	(3,269)	(1,738)	(1,531)	(1,250)	(673)	(577)
Under age 35	$42,897	$43,813	$40,882	$42,706	$43,652	$40,654	$45,819	$46,518	$44,324	–	–	–	–	–	–
	(1,311)	(901)	(410)	(1,217)	(833)	(384)	(80)	(55)	(26)	–	–	–	–	–	–
35 to 39 Years Old	$47,574	$48,236	$46,302	$47,120	$47,955	$45,270	$50,618	$57,353	$46,402	$51,744	$44,065	$57,596	$48,431	$44,793	$59,075
	(4,625)	(3,042)	(1,584)	(4,022)	(2,772)	(1,250)	(364)	(140)	(224)	(155)	(67)	(88)	(85)	(63)	(22)
40 to 44 Years Old	$52,038	$51,986	$52,130	$51,639	$51,524	$51,882	$54,331	$56,925	$52,781	$54,363	$55,417	$53,479	$51,927	$53,024	$50,728
	(14,571)	(9,272)	(5,300)	(12,155)	(8,246)	(3,909)	(1,179)	(441)	(738)	(939)	(429)	(511)	(298)	(156)	(142)
45 to 49 Years Old	$55,423	$55,211	$55,823	$55,272	$55,153	$55,532	$56,454	$55,050	$57,421	$55,431	$55,844	$54,803	$57,546	$58,934	$56,563
	(25,427)	(16,624)	(8,805)	(21,726)	(14,921)	(6,805)	(2,312)	(943)	(1,370)	(970)	(586)	(385)	(419)	(174)	(245)
50 to 54 Years Old	$56,559	$56,470	$56,724	$56,182	$56,470	$55,543	$58,875	$57,660	$59,665	$58,955	$55,202	$62,793	$51,984	$50,707	$52,964
	(18,868)	(12,216)	(6,652)	(15,806)	(10,909)	(4,897)	(2,062)	(813)	(1,249)	(826)	(418)	(408)	(174)	(76)	(98)
55 or Older	$57,826	$58,287	$56,849	$57,227	$57,963	$55,445	$61,512	$60,994	$62,049	$55,838	$55,567	$56,297	$59,948	$61,544	$55,421
	(14,817)	(10,062)	(4,755)	(12,155)	(8,601)	(3,554)	(2,021)	(1,028)	(993)	(374)	(235)	(139)	(267)	(197)	(70)
Annual Salary by Age—Principals who work 12 months of year															
Total	$58,399	$58,492	$58,195	$58,311	$58,401	$58,073	$58,836	$58,882	$58,794	$59,597	$60,750	$58,623	$56,935	$57,968	$55,541
[Age: *** +++ ~]	(36,759)	(25,246)	(11,513)	(30,871)	(22,395)	(8,476)	(4,050)	(1,954)	(2,096)	(1,365)	(625)	(740)	(473)	(272)	(201)
Under age 35	$49,962	$50,762	$46,379	$50,132	$50,905	$46,628	$48,956	$49,900	–	–	–	–	–	–	–
	(379)	(310)	(69)	(324)	(265)	(59)	(55)	(44)	–	–	–	–	–	–	–
35 to 39 Years Old	$49,744	$50,361	$48,518	$49,101	$49,635	$47,823	$52,411	$62,063	$44,836	$60,810	$49,785	–	$42,712	$42,712	–
	(1,967)	(1,308)	(659)	(1,646)	(1,160)	(485)	(220)	(97)	(123)	(66)	(15)	–	(36)	(36)	–
40 to 44 Years Old	$55,443	$55,343	$55,644	$55,261	$55,018	$55,867	$56,515	$58,161	$55,060	$56,997	$59,293	$54,979	$52,152	$47,672	$55,904
	(6,990)	(4,674)	(2,316)	(5,695)	(4,069)	(1,626)	(632)	(296)	(336)	(525)	(246)	(280)	(138)	(63)	(75)
45 to 49 Years Old	$58,872	$58,413	$59,922	$58,921	$58,420	$60,247	$58,150	$56,794	$59,350	$58,693	$60,253	$56,240	$61,325	$65,117	$57,445
	(11,720)	(8,155)	(3,565)	(10,176)	(7,386)	(2,790)	(1,127)	(529)	(597)	(270)	(165)	(105)	(148)	(75)	(73)
50 to 54 Years Old	$59,643	$59,732	$59,449	$59,562	$59,850	$58,742	$59,386	$57,838	$60,495	$63,559	$61,805	$64,614	$48,608	$55,996	–
	(9,392)	(6,446)	(2,946)	(7,874)	(5,826)	(2,048)	(1,133)	(473)	(660)	(346)	(130)	(216)	(39)	(17)	–
55 or Older	$62,148	$63,175	$59,861	$62,018	$63,102	$59,295	$62,876	$62,578	$63,292	$60,595	$67,424	$55,186	$64,584	$66,696	$59,068
	(6,310)	(4,354)	(1,957)	(5,158)	(3,689)	(1,469)	(884)	(515)	(369)	(158)	(70)	(88)	(111)	(80)	(31)

Notes:

" – " indicates sample size too small to estimate.

*** Test of statistical significance compares African Americans with Whites. *** p < .001, ** p < .01, * p < .05.

+++ Test of statistical significance compares White men with White women. +++ p < .001, ++ p < .01, + p < .05.

~~~ Test of statistical significance compares African American men with African American women. ~~~ p < .001, ~~ p < .01, ~ p < .05.

Tests of statistical significance calculated using adjusted sample weight to control for influence of large sample sizes.

Source: Schools and Staffing Survey, 1993-94.

Table 23. Annual Salaries of Private School Principals by Age, Race, and Sex: 1993/94
(weighted sample size in parentheses)

Age	Total	Male	Female	White, Non-Hispanic			African American, Non-Hispanic			Hispanic			Other		
				Total	Male	Female	Total	Male	Female	Total	Male	Female	Total	Male	Female
Total Weighted Sample	100.0%	46.4%	53.6%	92.5%	43.7%	48.7%	4.2%	1.4%	2.9%	2.1%	0.9%	1.2%	1.2%	0.3%	0.9%
	(25,015)	(11,605)	(13,409)	(23,133)	(10,943)	(12,190)	(1,060)	(347)	(713)	(523)	(231)	(292)	(298)	(84)	(214)
Annual Salary by Age—All Principals															
Total +++	$29,714	$32,039	$27,701	$29,725	$31,860	$27,808	$28,836	$34,091	$26,283	$31,101	$35,844	$27,348	$29,536	$36,368	$26,848
[Age: *** +++ ~]	(25,015)	(11,605)	(13,410)	(23,133)	(10,943)	(12,190)	(1,061)	(347)	(713)	(525)	(231)	(293)	(299)	(84)	(214)
Under age 40	$24,427	$22,201	$27,264	$23,562	$21,490	$26,423	$31,684	$28,014	$34,106	$34,790	$40,456	$31,849	$27,601	–	$23,738
	(4,794)	(2,687)	(2,107)	(4,297)	(2,492)	(1,805)	(310)	(123)	(187)	(122)	(42)	(80)	(65)	–	(35)
40 to 44 Years Old	$29,373	$33,881	$24,702	$29,229	$33,936	$24,307	$28,270	$29,678	$27,336	$27,081	$25,028	$29,757	–	–	–
	(4,403)	(2,241)	(2,162)	(4,264)	(2,180)	(2,084)	(86)	(34)	(52)	(42)	(24)	(18)	–	–	–
45 to 49 Years Old	$32,691	$35,315	$30,416	$32,339	$34,459	$30,399	$37,679	$50,486	$32,514	$32,884	$42,619	$19,539	$35,984	–	$31,820
	(5,144)	(2,389)	(2,755)	(4,689)	(2,240)	(2,449)	(279)	(80)	(199)	(102)	(59)	(43)	(74)	–	(64)
50 to 54 Years Old	$35,096	$43,306	$30,219	$36,070	$44,163	$31,192	$24,305	$28,524	$19,849	$24,416	–	$20,819	$15,641	–	$13,953
	(4,121)	(1,535)	(2,586)	(3,829)	(1,440)	(2,389)	(152)	(78)	(74)	(72)	–	(64)	(68)	–	(59)
55 or Older	$28,090	$31,015	$25,971	$28,411	$31,006	$26,469	$17,664	$34,671	$15,045	$31,217	$31,148	$31,294	$26,961	$27,735	$26,440
	(6,554)	(2,753)	(3,801)	(6,054)	(2,591)	(3,463)	(234)	(31)	(203)	(187)	(99)	(88)	(79)	(32)	(47)

Notes:
" – " indicates sample size too small to estimate.
*** Test of statistical significance compares African Americans with Whites. *** p < .001, ** p < .01, * p < .05.
+++ Test of statistical significance compares White men with White women. +++ p < .001, ++ p < .01, + p < .05.
~~~ Test of statistical significance compares African American men with African American women. ~~~ p < .001, ~~ p < .01, ~ p < .05.
Tests of statistical significance calculated using adjusted sample weight to control for influence of large sample sizes.
Source: Schools and Staffing Survey, 1993-94.

- At rural public schools, African American principals salaries averaged 8.7% lower than White principals ($45,317 versus $49,646).

- At urban public schools, African American principals salaries were 3.6% higher than their White counterparts ($59,536 versus $57,451).

- At suburban public schools, African American and White public school principals received comparable salaries, averaging $62,775 for African Americans and $61,923 for Whites.

Private Schools

Table 25 shows that suburban private school principals averaged $32,568, urban private school

principals averaged $31,822, and rural private school principals averaged $23,206 per year.

- Average salaries for African American and White private school teachers appeared to be similar after controlling for school urbanicity. The failure to find statistically significant differences may be attributable to the small number of African American private school principals.

Principals' Annual Salaries by Region

Public Schools

Figure 14 shows that average salaries for public school principals ranged from $65,188 in the North-

Figure 12. Annual Salaries of Public School Principals
by Age: 1993/94

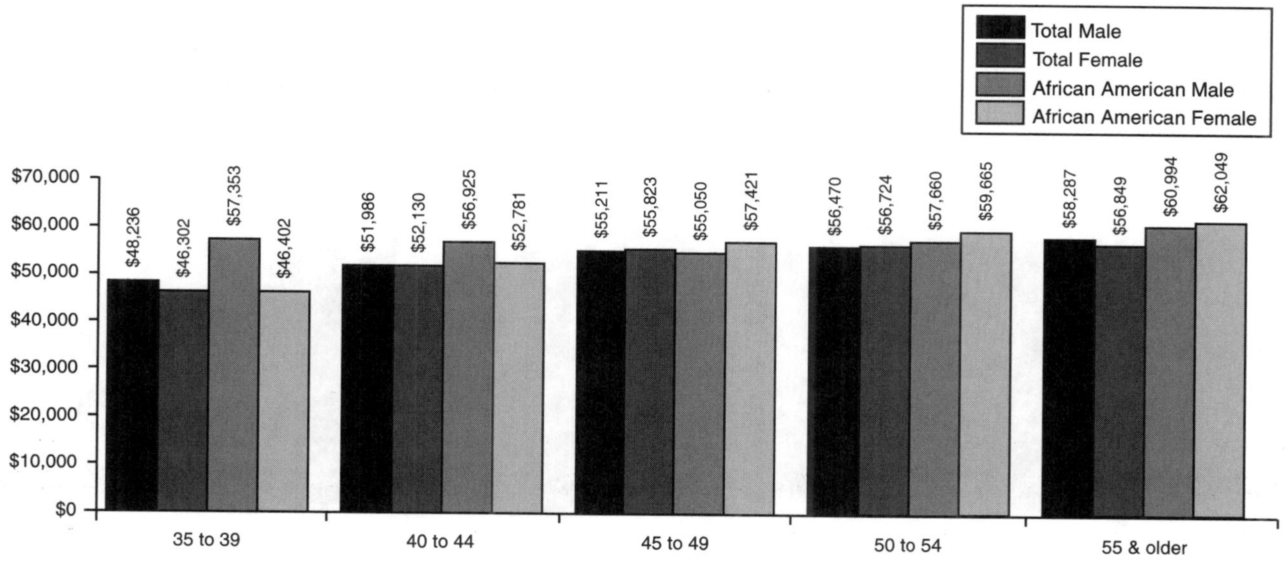

Legend:
- Total Male
- Total Female
- African American Male
- African American Female

Source: Schools and Staffing Survey, 1993-94.

east to $56,971 in the West to $53,061 in the Midwest to $49,808 in the South.

- **Table 26** shows that African American principals received higher average salaries than their White counterparts in the Northeast ($70,416 versus $64,612), West ($63,017 versus $56,533), Midwest ($60,674 versus $52,244), and South ($51,636 versus $49,447).

Private Schools

Table 27 shows that average salaries for private school principals were $30,936 in the Northeast, $30,472 in the West, $29,566 in the South, and $28,337 in the Midwest. Differences in salaries by race and sex across geographic region must be interpreted with caution because of the small number of male and female African American men and women principals.

Annual Salaries by Months Employed as Principal

Public Schools

About one-half (46.2%) of all public school principals were employed 12 months of the year. **Figure 15** shows that a smaller percentage of women than of men were employed 12 months of the year among both African Americans (45.6% versus 57.2%) and overall (41.9% versus 48.4%).

- **Table 28** shows that a higher percentage of African American than White public school principals were employed 12 months of the year (50.5% versus 46.0%).

As expected, average salaries increased with the number of months of the year employed and ranged from $45,381 for principals employed nine or fewer

Figure 13. Annual Salaries of Public School Principals by Urbanicity: 1993/94

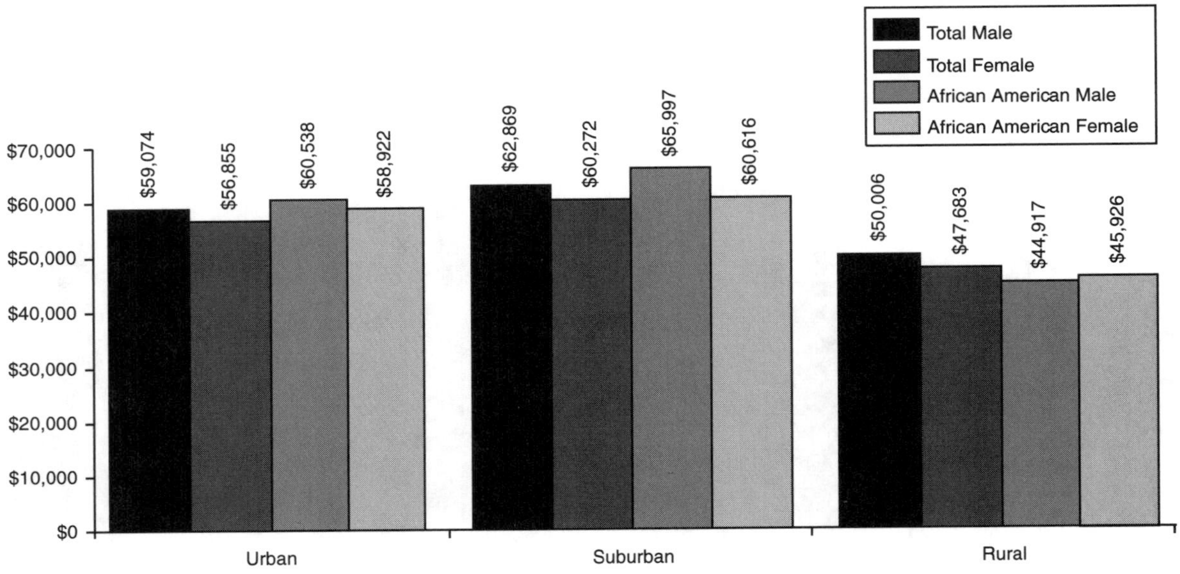

Source: Schools and Staffing Survey, 1993-94.

Table 24. Annual Salaries of Public School Principals by Urbanicity, Race, and Sex: 1993/94
(weighted sample size in parentheses)

Urbanicity	Total	Male	Female	White, Non-Hispanic			African American, Non-Hispanic			Hispanic			Other		
				Total	Male	Female	Total	Male	Female	Total	Male	Female	Total	Male	Female
Total Weighted Sample	100.0%	65.5%	34.5%	84.3%	58.1%	26.1%	10.1%	4.3%	5.8%	4.1%	2.2%	1.9%	1.6%	0.8%	0.7%
	(79,618)	(52,113)	(27,505)	(67,081)	(46,283)	(20,798)	(8,018)	(3,419)	(4,599)	(3,269)	(1,738)	(1,531)	(1,250)	(673)	(577)
Total *** ++	$54,858	$54,922	$54,736	$54,466	$54,701	$53,942	$57,669	$57,658	$57,677	$55,862	$55,046	$56,789	$55,245	$55,912	$54,465
[Urbanicity: *** +++ ~~~	[79,618)	(52,113)	(27,505)	(67,081)	(46,283)	(20,798)	(8,018)	(3,419)	(4,599)	(3,269)	(1,738)	(1,531)	(1,250)	(673)	(577)
Urban	$58,023	$59,074	$56,855	$57,451	$58,665	$55,735	$59,536	$60,538	$58,922	$58,088	$58,678	$57,444	$58,048	$63,810	$54,235
	(19,026)	(10,016)	(9,010)	(12,437)	(7,282)	(5,155)	(4,630)	(1,759)	(2,871)	(1,575)	(822)	(753)	(384)	(153)	(231)
Suburban	$61,810	$62,869	$60,272	$61,923	$62,817	$60,412	$62,775	$65,997	$60,616	$58,160	$58,201	$58,138	$60,928	$61,812	$60,248
	(21,701)	(12,856)	(8,845)	(18,429)	(11,577)	(6,852)	(1,902)	(763)	(1,139)	(977)	(345)	(632)	(393)	(171)	(222)
Rural	$49,430	$50,006	$47,683	$49,646	$50,222	$47,848	$45,317	$44,917	$45,926	$47,845	$47,927	$47,524	$48,249	$49,563	$44,540
	(38,891)	(29,242)	(9,649)	(36,215)	(27,424)	(8,791)	(1,486)	(897)	(589)	(717)	(572)	(145)	(473)	(349)	(124)

Notes:
*** Test of statistical significance compares African Americans with Whites. *** p < .001, ** p < .01, * p < .05.
+++ Test of statistical significance compares White men with White women. +++ p < .001, ++ p < .01, + p < .05.
~~~ Test of statistical significance compares African American men with African American women. ~~~ p < .001, ~~ p < .01, ~ p < .05.
Tests of statistical significance calculated using adjusted sample weight to control for influence of large sample sizes.
Source: Schools and Staffing Survey, 1993-94.

Table 25. Annual Salaries of Private School Principals by Urbanicity, Race, and Sex: 1993/94
(weighted sample size in parentheses)

Urbanicity	Total	Male	Female	White, Non-Hispanic			African American, Non-Hispanic			Hispanic			Other		
				Total	Male	Female	Total	Male	Female	Total	Male	Female	Total	Male	Female
Total Weighted Sample	100.0%	46.4%	53.6%	92.5%	43.7%	48.7%	4.2%	1.4%	2.9%	2.1%	0.9%	1.2%	1.2%	0.3%	0.9%
	(25,015)	(11,605)	(13,409)	(23,133)	(10,943)	(12,190)	(1,060)	(347)	(713)	(523)	(231)	(292)	(298)	(84)	(214)
Total +++	$29,714	$32,039	$27,701	$29,725	$31,860	$27,808	$28,836	$34,091	$26,283	$31,101	$35,844	$27,348	$29,536	$36,368	$26,848
[Urbanicity: *** +++]	(25,015)	(11,606)	(13,410)	(23,134)	(10,944)	(12,190)	(1,061)	(347)	(714)	(523)	(231)	(292)	(299)	(84)	(210)
Urban	$31,822	$35,298	$29,106	$32,446	$35,532	$29,774	$26,725	$31,205	$24,849	$31,652	$36,087	$29,854	$28,401	$37,721	$26,162
	(9,693)	(4,251)	(5,442)	(8,361)	(3,881)	(4,480)	(878)	(259)	(619)	(247)	(71)	(176)	(207)	(40)	(167)
Suburban	$32,568	$36,090	$29,770	$32,607	$36,206	$29,766	$35,117	$28,446	$46,254	$29,429	$36,110	$23,558	$34,445	$41,413	$32,139
	(8,469)	(3,750)	(4,719)	(8,090)	(3,569)	(4,521)	(104)	(65)	(39)	(218)	(102)	(116)	(57)	(14)	(43)
Rural	$23,206	$23,981	$22,346	$22,831	$23,343	$22,270	$44,178	$82,910	$28,339	$35,072	$35,072	–	$28,169	$32,165	–
	(6,854)	(3,604)	(3,249)	(6,683)	(3,494)	(3,189)	(79)	(23)	(56)	(58)	(58)	–	(35)	(30)	–

Notes:

" – " indicates sample size too small to estimate.

*** Test of statistical significance compares African Americans with Whites. *** p < .001, ** p < .01, * p < .05.

+++ Test of statistical significance compares White men with White women. +++ p < .001, ++ p < .01, + p < .05.

~~~ Test of statistical significance compares African American men with African American women. ~~~ p < .001, ~~ p < .01, ~ p < .05.

Tests of statistical significance calculated using adjusted sample weight to control for influence of large sample sizes.

Source: Schools and Staffing Survey, 1993-94.

Figure 14. Annual Salaries of Public School Principals by Census Region: 1993/94

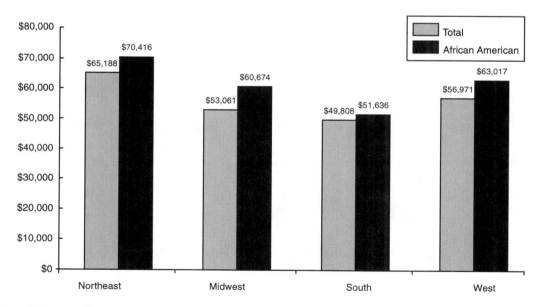

Source: Schools and Staffing Survey, 1993-94.

Table 26. Annual Salaries of Public School Principals by Census Region, Race, and Sex: 1993/94
(weighted sample size in parentheses)

Census Region	Total	Male	Female	White, Non-Hispanic			African American, Non-Hispanic			Hispanic			Other		
				Total	Male	Female	Total	Male	Female	Total	Male	Female	Total	Male	Female
Total Weighted Sample	100.0%	65.5%	34.5%	84.3%	58.1%	26.1%	10.1%	4.3%	5.8%	4.1%	2.2%	1.9%	1.6%	0.8%	0.7%
	(79,618)	(52,113)	(27,505)	(67,081)	(46,283)	(20,798)	(8,018)	(3,419)	(4,599)	(3,269)	(1,738)	(1,531)	(1,250)	(673)	(577)
Total *** ++	$54,858	$54,922	$54,736	$54,466	$54,701	$53,942	$57,669	$57,658	$57,677	$55,862	$55,046	$56,789	$55,245	$55,912	$54,465
[Region: *** +++ ~~~]	(79,618)	(52,114)	(27,505)	(67,081)	(46,283)	(20,798)	(8,018)	(3,419)	(4,599)	(3,269)	(1,738)	(1,531)	(1,250)	(673)	(577)
Northeast	$65,188	$65,851	$63,742	$64,612	$65,274	$62,944	$70,416	$73,363	$68,299	$68,635	$78,594	$62,079	$71,680	$76,693	$65,084
	(13,469)	(9,234)	(4,235)	(12,080)	(8,647)	(3,433)	(1,100)	(460)	(640)	(219)	(87)	(132)	(70)	(40)	(30)
Midwest	$53,061	$53,071	$53,037	$52,244	$52,457	$51,630	$60,674	$63,678	$58,781	$59,684	$56,676	$65,860	$57,717	$60,938	$49,493
	(23,144)	(16,481)	(6,663)	(20,810)	(15,455)	(5,355)	(1,930)	(746)	(1,184)	(219)	(147)	(72)	(185)	(133)	(52)
South	$49,808	$49,618	$50,129	$49,447	$49,431	$49,479	$51,636	$50,979	$52,254	$51,405	$51,115	$51,813	$44,000	$42,264	$45,660
	(26,307)	(16,533)	(9,774)	(20,748)	(13,723)	(7,025)	(4,086)	(1,979)	(2,107)	(1,158)	(677)	(481)	(315)	(154)	(161)
West	$56,971	$56,673	$57,402	$56,533	$56,542	$56,517	$63,017	$64,062	$62,650	$56,780	$55,504	$58,028	$58,086	$57,655	$58,535
	(16,698)	(9,866)	(6,832)	(13,443)	(8,458)	(4,985)	(903)	(235)	(668)	(1,673)	(827)	(846)	(679)	(346)	(333)

Notes:
*** Test of statistical significance compares African Americans with Whites. *** p < .001, ** p < .01, * p < .05.
+++ Test of statistical significance compares White men with White women. +++ p < .001, ++ p < .01, + p < .05.
~~~ Test of statistical significance compares African American men with African American women. ~~~ p < .001, ~~ p < .01, ~ p < .05.
Tests of statistical significance calculated using adjusted sample weight to control for influence of large sample sizes.
Source: Schools and Staffing Survey, 1993-94.

Table 27. Annual Salaries of Private School Principals by Census Region, Race, and Sex: 1993/94
(weighted sample size in parentheses)

Census Region	Total	Male	Female	White, Non-Hispanic			African American, Non-Hispanic			Hispanic			Other		
				Total	Male	Female	Total	Male	Female	Total	Male	Female	Total	Male	Female
Total Weighted Sample	100.0%	46.4%	53.6%	92.5%	43.7%	48.7%	4.2%	1.4%	2.9%	2.1%	0.9%	1.2%	1.2%	0.3%	0.9%
	(25,015)	(11,605)	(13,409)	(23,133)	(10,943)	(12,190)	(1,060)	(347)	(713)	(523)	(231)	(292)	(298)	(84)	(214)
Total +++	$29,714	$32,039	$27,701	$29,725	$31,860	$27,808	$28,836	$34,091	$26,283	$31,101	$35,844	$27,348	$29,536	$36,368	$26,848
[Region: ++]	(25,015)	(11,605)	(13,409)	(23,134)	(10,944)	(12,190)	(1,060)	(347)	(713)	(524)	(230)	(292)	(299)	(84)	(214)
Northeast	$30,936	$36,802	$27,109	$30,860	$37,011	$26,956	$30,295	$29,452	$31,097	$34,244	$42,210	$22,106	–	–	–
	(5,965)	(2,355)	(3,610)	(5,609)	(2,178)	(3,431)	(254)	(124)	(130)	(83)	(50)	(33)	–	–	–
Midwest	$28,337	$28,855	$27,786	$27,889	$28,924	$26,732	$36,526	$23,859	$42,210	$29,985	$29,169	$30,452	–	–	–
	(7,302)	(3,761)	(3,541)	(6,858)	(3,620)	(3,238)	(254)	(79)	(175)	(157)	(57)	(100)	–	–	–
South	$29,566	$30,960	$28,147	$29,736	$30,751	$28,662	$28,732	$38,395	$23,352	$30,356	$29,275	$31,530	$20,041	–	–
	(6,776)	(3,417)	(3,359)	(6,247)	(3,211)	(3,036)	(327)	(117)	(210)	(110)	(57)	(53)	(92)	–	–
West	$30,472	$34,185	$27,819	$31,117	$33,397	$29,342	$18,656	–	–	$31,081	$42,482	$23,961	$28,542	–	$25,376
	(4,971)	(2,072)	(2,899)	(4,420)	(1,935)	(2,485)	(225)	–	–	(172)	(66)	(106)	(154)	–	(110)

Notes:
" – " indicates sample size too small to estimate.
*** Test of statistical significance compares African Americans with Whites. *** p < .001, ** p < .01, * p < .05.
+++ Test of statistical significance compares White men with White women. +++ p < .001, ++ p < .01, + p < .05.
~~~ Test of statistical significance compares African American men with African American women. ~~~ p < .001, ~~ p < .01, ~ p < .05.
Tests of statistical significance calculated using adjusted sample weight to control for influence of large sample sizes.
Source: Schools and Staffing Survey, 1993-94.

Figure 15. Distribution of Public School Principals by Number of Months per Year Employed: 1993/94

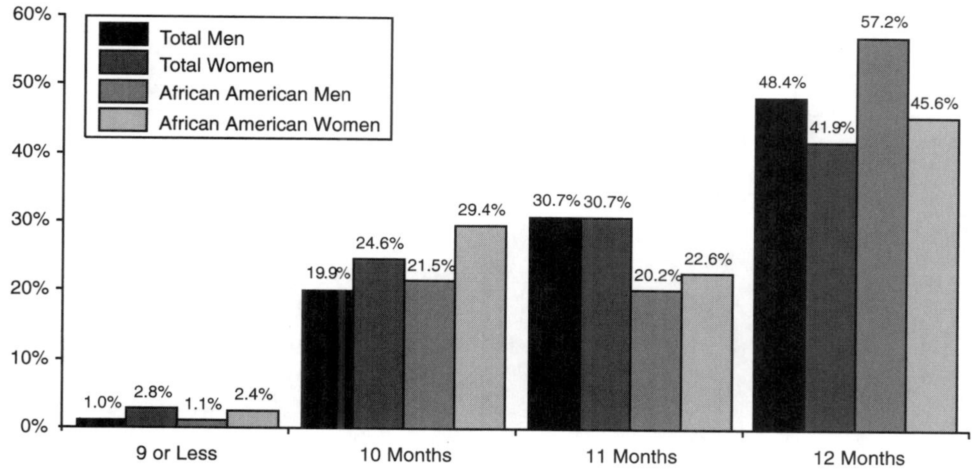

Source: Schools and Staffing Survey, 1993-94.

months of the year to $58,399 for principals employed the entire year. Among principals employed for 12 months of the year, the average salaries of African Americans and Whites were comparable ($58,836 for African Americans and $58,311 for Whites). But among principals employed for fewer than 11 months of the year, average salaries of African Americans appeared to be higher than the salaries of their White counterparts.

- Average salaries were higher for African Americans than for Whites among those employed nine or fewer months ($60,258 versus $43,643) or 10 months ($58,208 versus $49,183) of the year.

Private Schools

Table 29 shows that about two-thirds (65.3%) of private school principals were employed for 12 months of the year. Overall, a higher percentage of

men than women were employed for the entire year (72.3% versus 59.3%).

- Comparable percentages of African Americans and Whites were employed for the entire year (65.5% versus 65.7%).

- But a higher percentage of African Americans than Whites were employed for nine or fewer months of the year (10.8% versus 4.9%).

When only principals who were employed for 12 months of the year were considered, average salaries for African Americans appeared to be similar to those received by Whites. Nonetheless, this finding may be attributable to the small number of African American private school principals.

- Considering only principals employed for 12 months of the year, average salaries were $27,846 for African Americans and $32,510 for Whites.

Table 28. Annual Salaries of Public School Principals by Months Employed, Race, and Sex: 1993/94
(weighted sample size in parentheses)

Number of Months	Total	Male	Female	White, Non-Hispanic			African American, Non-Hispanic			Hispanic			Other		
				Total	Male	Female	Total	Male	Female	Total	Male	Female	Total	Male	Female
Total Weighted Sample	100.0%	65.5%	34.5%	84.3%	58.1%	26.1%	10.1%	4.3%	5.8%	4.1%	2.2%	1.9%	1.6%	0.8%	0.7%
	(79,618)	(52,113)	(27,505)	(67,081)	(46,283)	(20,798)	(8,018)	(3,419)	(4,599)	(3,269)	(1,738)	(1,531)	(1,250)	(673)	(577)
Total *** +++ ~~	100.0%	100.0%	100.0%	100.0%	100.0%	100.0%	100.0%	100.0%	100.0%	100.0%	100.0%	100.0%	100.0%	100.0%	100.0%
	(79,618)	(52,113)	(27,505)	(67,081)	(46,283)	(20,798)	(8,018)	(3,419)	(4,599)	(3,269)	(1,738)	(1,531)	(1,250)	(673)	(577)
9 or less	1.6%	1.0%	2.8%	1.6%	1.0%	2.8%	1.9%	1.1%	2.4%	1.3%	0.2%	2.5%	3.6%	0.3%	7.5%
	(1,287)	(505)	(781)	(1,049)	(462)	(587)	(150)	(38)	(112)	(42)	(3)	(39)	(45)	(2)	(43)
10	21.5%	19.9%	24.6%	20.9%	19.6%	23.9%	26.0%	21.5%	29.4%	19.2%	22.4%	15.6%	31.6%	29.9%	33.6%
	(17,139)	(10,384)	(6,756)	(14,030)	(9,057)	(4,973)	(2,086)	(736)	(1,350)	(629)	(390)	(239)	(395)	(201)	(194)
11	30.7%	30.7%	30.7%	31.5%	31.0%	32.5%	21.6%	20.2%	22.6%	37.7%	41.5%	33.5%	27.0%	29.6%	24.1%
	(24,433)	(15,979)	(8,454)	(21,130)	(14,368)	(6,762)	(1,731)	(691)	(1,040)	(1,234)	(721)	(513)	(338)	(199)	(139)
12	46.2%	48.4%	41.9%	46.0%	48.4%	40.8%	50.5%	57.2%	45.6%	41.8%	36.0%	48.3%	37.8%	40.4%	34.8%
	(36,759)	(25,246)	(11,513)	(30,871)	(22,395)	(8,476)	(4,050)	(1,954)	(2,096)	(1,365)	(625)	(740)	(473)	(272)	(201)
Annual Salary by Months of Year Employed as Principal															
Total *** +	$54,858	$54,922	$54,736	$54,466	$54,701	$53,942	$57,669	$57,658	$57,677	$55,862	$55,046	$56,789	$55,245	$55,912	$54,465
[Months: *** +++ ~~~]	(79,618)	(52,114)	(27,505)	(67,081)	(46,283)	(20,798)	(8,018)	(3,419)	(4,599)	(3,269)	(1,738)	(1,531)	(1,250)	(673)	(577)
9 or less	$45,381	$48,846	$43,142	$43,643	$48,109	$40,127	$60,258	$57,111	$61,326	$37,800	–	$36,962	$43,148	–	$42,403
	(1,287)	(505)	(781)	(1,049)	(462)	(587)	(150)	(38)	(112)	(42)	–	(39)	(45)	–	(43)
10	$50,457	$49,579	$51,806	$49,183	$48,925	$49,653	$58,208	$56,397	$59,195	$50,841	$49,166	$53,569	$54,185	$54,934	$53,409
	(17,139)	(10,384)	(6,756)	(14,030)	(9,057)	(4,973)	(2,086)	(736)	(1,350)	(629)	(390)	(239)	(395)	(201)	(194)
11	$53,117	$52,946	$53,439	$52,893	$52,787	$53,120	$54,061	$55,570	$53,059	$54,898	$53,299	$57,146	$55,719	$54,043	$58,127
	(24,433)	(15,979)	(8,454)	(21,130)	(14,368)	(6,762)	(1,731)	(691)	(1,040)	(1,234)	(721)	(513)	(338)	(199)	(139)
12	$58,399	$58,492	$58,195	$58,311	$58,401	$58,073	$58,836	$58,882	$58,794	$59,597	$60,750	$58,623	$56,935	$57,968	$55,541
	(36,759)	(25,246)	(11,513)	(30,871)	(22,395)	(8,476)	(4,050)	(1,954)	(2,096)	(1,365)	(625)	(740)	(473)	(272)	(201)

Notes:

" – " indicates sample size too small to estimate.

*** Test of statistical significance compares African Americans with Whites. *** p < .001, ** p < .01, * p < .05.

+++ Test of statistical significance compares White men with White women. +++ p < .001, ++ p < .01, + p < .05.

~~~ Test of statistical significance compares African American men with African American women. ~~~ p < .001, ~~ p < .01, ~ p < .05.

Tests of statistical significance calculated using adjusted sample weight to control for influence of large sample sizes.

Source: Schools and Staffing Survey, 1993-94.

Table 29. Annual Salaries of Private School Principals by Months Employed, Race, and Sex: 1993/94
(weighted sample size in parentheses)

Number of Months	Total	Male	Female	White, Non-Hispanic			African American, Non-Hispanic			Hispanic			Other		
				Total	Male	Female	Total	Male	Female	Total	Male	Female	Total	Male	Female
Total Weighted Sample	100.0%	46.4%	53.6%	92.5%	43.7%	48.7%	4.2%	1.4%	2.9%	2.1%	0.9%	1.2%	1.2%	0.3%	0.9%
	(25,015)	(11,605)	(13,409)	(23,133)	(10,943)	(12,190)	(1,060)	(347)	(713)	(523)	(231)	(292)	(298)	(84)	(214)
Total ** +++	100.0%	100.0%	100.0%	100.0%	100.0%	100.0%	100.0%	100.0%	100.0%	100.0%	100.0%	100.0%	100.0%	100.0%	100.0%
	(25,015)	(11,605)	(13,409)	(23,133)	(10,943)	(12,190)	(1,060)	(347)	(713)	(523)	(231)	(292)	(298)	(84)	(214)
9 or less	5.1%	5.7%	4.5%	4.9%	5.9%	4.1%	10.8%	5.2%	13.6%	0.8%	1.7%	0.0%	1.7%	0.0%	2.3%
	(1,266)	(665)	(601)	(1,142)	(643)	(499)	(115)	(18)	(97)	(4)	(4)	–	(5)	–	(5)
10	15.8%	12.5%	18.6%	15.6%	12.0%	18.9%	17.1%	20.7%	15.3%	20.8%	31.2%	12.7%	16.4%	0.0%	22.9%
	(3,946)	(1,452)	(2,493)	(3,606)	(1,308)	(2,298)	(181)	(72)	(109)	(109)	(72)	(37)	(49)	–	(49)
11	13.8%	9.4%	17.7%	13.7%	9.1%	17.9%	6.5%	0.0%	9.7%	30.2%	33.3%	27.7%	18.5%	31.0%	13.6%
	(3,462)	(1,095)	(2,367)	(3,180)	(992)	(2,188)	(69)	–	(69)	(158)	(77)	(81)	(55)	(26)	(29)
12	65.3%	72.3%	59.3%	65.7%	73.1%	59.1%	65.5%	73.8%	61.4%	48.2%	33.8%	59.6%	63.4%	69.0%	61.2%
	(16,342)	(8,392)	(7,948)	(15,205)	(8,000)	(7,205)	(694)	(256)	(438)	(252)	(78)	(174)	(189)	(58)	(131)
Annual Salary by Months of Year Employed as Principal															
Total ++ ~~	$29,714	$32,039	$27,701	$29,725	$31,860	$27,808	$28,836	$34,091	$26,283	$31,101	$35,844	$27,348	$29,536	$36,368	$26,848
	(25,015)	(11,605)	(13,409)	(23,133)	(10,943)	(12,190)	(1,060)	(347)	(713)	(523)	(231)	(292)	(298)	(84)	(214)
12	$32,288	$34,205	$30,265	$32,510	$33,959	$30,902	$27,846	$39,024	$21,319	$33,149	$44,567	$28,031	$29,597	$32,934	$28,120
	(16,342)	(8,392)	(7,948)	(15,205)	(8,000)	(7,205)	(694)	(256)	(438)	(252)	(78)	(174)	(189)	(58)	(131)

Notes:

" – " indicates sample size too small to estimate.

*** Test of statistical significance compares African Americans with Whites. *** p < .001, ** p < .01, * p < .05.

+++ Test of statistical significance compares White men with White women. +++ p < .001, ++ p < .01, + p < .05.

~~~ Test of statistical significance compares African American men with African American women. ~~~ p < .001, ~~ p < .01, ~ p < .05.

Tests of statistical significance calculated using adjusted sample weight to control for influence of large sample sizes.

Source: Schools and Staffing Survey, 1993-94.

"PROBLEMS" ASSOCIATED WITH PRINCIPALS' SCHOOLS

Public Schools

Figure 16 shows that about 86.4% of public school principals agreed that "students coming unprepared to learn" was a "problem" at school.

- **Table 30** shows that similar proportions of African Americans and Whites reported that racial tension was a problem (43.1% versus 40.9%).

The percentages of African Americans and Whites who reported various aspects of school life to be problematic differed in some instances, suggesting that African American principals and White principals face different types of daily challenges.

- A higher percentage of African Americans than Whites reported that student possession of weapons (35.9% versus 26.8%) and poverty (88.0% versus 84.6%) were problems.

- A smaller percentage of African Americans than Whites reported that student use of alcohol (20.9% versus 37.6%), student drug abuse (24.7% versus 36.6%), and parental alcoholism and drug abuse (71.1% versus 80.4%) were problems.

Figure 16. Percentage of Public School Principals Who Report Various Aspects of School Life to Be a "Problem": 1993/94

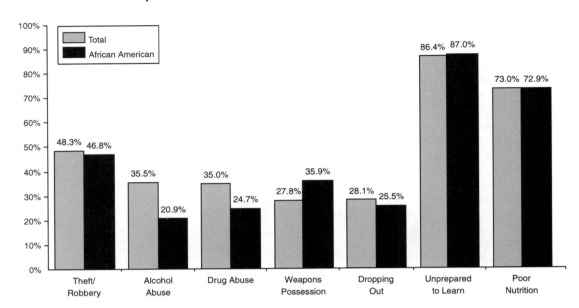

Source: Schools and Staffing Survey, 1993-94.

Private Schools

A higher share of African American principals than White principals felt that students dropping out, poverty, poor student nutrition, and poor student health were problems at their schools.

- **Table 31** shows the differences between African American principals and White principals

on the following problems: students dropping out (17.3 % versus 10.2%), poverty (55.1% versus 41.6%), poor student nutrition (35.5% versus 26.2%), and poor student health (31.2% versus 22.4%).

- A smaller percentage of African American principals than White principals viewed student use of alcohol as a problem (6.4% versus 15.3%).

Table 30. Number and Percentage of Public School Principals Who Report Various Aspects of School Life to Be a "Problem" by Race and Sex: 1993/94

(weighted sample size in parentheses)

Aspect of School Life	Total	Male	Female	White, Non-Hispanic Total	Male	Female	African American, Non-Hispanic Total	Male	Female	Hispanic Total	Male	Female	Other Total	Male	Female
Total Weighted Sample	100.0% (79,618)	65.5% (52,113)	34.5% (27,505)	84.3% (67,081)	58.1% (46,283)	26.1% (20,798)	10.1% (8,018)	4.3% (3,419)	5.8% (4,599)	4.1% (3,269)	2.2% (1,738)	1.9% (1,531)	1.6% (1,250)	0.8% (673)	0.7% (577)
Total Respondents															
Total	100.0% (79,618)	100.0% (52,113)	100.0% (27,505)	100.0% (67,081)	100.0% (46,283)	100.0% (20,798)	100.0% (8,018)	100.0% (3,419)	100.0% (4,599)	100.0% (3,269)	100.0% (1,738)	100.0% (1,531)	100.0% (1,250)	100.0% (673)	100.0% (577)
Robbery/Theft +++	48.3% (38,454)	51.5% (26,834)	42.2% (11,620)	48.6% (32,626)	51.9% (24,014)	41.4% (8,612)	46.8% (3,755)	48.5% (1,657)	45.6% (2,098)	43.5% (1,421)	44.5% (774)	42.3% (647)	52.2% (652)	57.8% (389)	45.6% (263)
Vandalism of School Property	55.9% (44,512)	56.1% (29,224)	55.6% (15,288)	55.5% (37,215)	56.2% (26,008)	53.9% (11,207)	54.9% (4,400)	53.3% (1,821)	56.1% (2,579)	66.1% (2,161)	56.9% (989)	76.6% (1,172)	58.9% (736)	60.3% (406)	57.2% (330)
Student Pregnancy +++ ~~~	28.8% (22,895)	36.1% (18,831)	14.8% (4,065)	28.9% (19,377)	35.9% (16,608)	13.3% (2,769)	28.1% (2,250)	40.7% (1,390)	18.7% (860)	30.0% (981)	35.8% (622)	23.4% (359)	23.0% (288)	31.4% (211)	13.3% (77)
Student Use of Alcohol *** +++ ~~~	35.5% (28,257)	44.2% (23,011)	19.1% (5,246)	37.6% (25,217)	45.3% (20,983)	20.4% (4,234)	20.9% (1,678)	31.6% (1,080)	13.0% (598)	30.4% (993)	38.5% (669)	21.2% (324)	29.5% (369)	41.5% (279)	15.6% (90)
Student Drug Abuse *** +++ ~~~	35.0% (27,880)	42.8% (22,329)	20.2% (5,551)	36.6% (24,524)	43.6% (20,168)	20.9% (4,356)	24.7% (1,977)	36.5% (1,247)	15.9% (730)	31.3% (1,024)	37.5% (652)	24.3% (372)	28.4% (355)	38.9% (262)	16.1% (93)
Student Possession of Weapons *** ++ ~~	27.8% (22,138)	29.0% (15,088)	25.6% (7,050)	26.8% (18,000)	27.9% (12,910)	24.5% (5,090)	35.9% (2,878)	41.5% (1,418)	31.7% (1,460)	30.0% (981)	32.5% (565)	27.2% (416)	22.3% (279)	29.0% (195)	14.6% (84)
Student Dropping Out +++ ~~~	28.1% (22,366)	34.7% (18,088)	15.6% (4,279)	28.3% (18,996)	34.6% (15,992)	14.4% (3,004)	25.5% (2,044)	39.0% (1,333)	15.5% (711)	30.6% (1,000)	31.0% (539)	30.1% (461)	26.2% (327)	33.3% (224)	17.9% (103)
Lack of Parental Involvement +++	76.4% (60,845)	78.2% (40,761)	73.0% (20,083)	76.2% (51,132)	78.3% (36,226)	71.7% (14,906)	78.1% (6,265)	79.0% (2,702)	77.5% (3,563)	74.6% (2,438)	75.5% (1,313)	73.5% (1,125)	80.7% (1,009)	77.3% (520)	84.7% (489)
Parental Alcoholism or Drug Abuse *** +++ ~~	79.5% (63,270)	80.6% (42,020)	77.3% (21,250)	80.4% (53,949)	81.7% (37,813)	77.6% (16,136)	71.1% (5,703)	65.8% (2,250)	75.1% (3,453)	78.3% (2,560)	80.3% (1,396)	76.0% (1,164)	84.6% (1,058)	83.4% (561)	86.1% (497)
Poverty ** +	85.2% (67,840)	85.5% (44,548)	84.7% (23,291)	84.6% (56,754)	85.3% (39,461)	83.1% (17,293)	88.0% (7,057)	86.9% (2,972)	88.8% (4,085)	91.0% (2,975)	89.5% (1,556)	92.7% (1,419)	84.2% (1,053)	83.1% (559)	85.6% (494)
Racial Tension +++	41.5% (33,042)	39.8% (20,720)	44.8% (12,324)	40.9% (27,459)	39.0% (18,071)	45.1% (9,388)	43.1% (3,458)	45.8% (1,565)	41.2% (1,893)	45.9% (1,500)	42.3% (735)	50.0% (765)	50.2% (627)	51.9% (349)	48.2% (278)
Students Come Unprepared to Learn +++	86.4% (68,763)	87.2% (45,460)	84.7% (23,303)	86.3% (57,889)	87.4% (40,459)	83.8% (17,430)	87.0% (6,976)	85.1% (2,908)	88.5% (4,068)	84.1% (2,750)	85.0% (1,477)	83.1% (1,273)	91.8% (1,148)	91.5% (616)	92.2% (532)
Poor Student Nutrition	73.0% (58,096)	72.9% (37,993)	73.1% (20,103)	72.7% (48,755)	72.6% (33,619)	72.8% (15,136)	72.9% (5,848)	71.5% (2,443)	74.0% (3,405)	75.0% (2,451)	78.1% (1,357)	71.5% (1,094)	83.4% (1,042)	85.3% (574)	81.1% (468)
Poor Student Health	65.4% (52,091)	65.0% (33,872)	66.2% (18,221)	64.7% (43,415)	64.2% (29,718)	65.9% (13,697)	67.4% (5,403)	68.9% (2,357)	66.2% (3,046)	73.1% (2,391)	74.7% (1,299)	71.3% (1,092)	70.7% (884)	74.0% (498)	66.9% (386)

Notes:

*** Test of statistical significance compares African Americans with Whites. *** p < .001, ** p < .01, * p < .05.

+++ Test of statistical significance compares White men with White women. +++ p < .001, ++ p < .01, + p < .05.

~~~ Test of statistical significance compares African American men with African American women. ~~~ p < .001, ~~ p < .01, ~ p < .05.

Tests of statistical significance calculated using adjusted sample weight to control for influence of large sample sizes.

Source: Schools and Staffing Survey, 1993-94.

Table 31. Number and Percentage of Private School Principals Who Report Various Aspects of School Life to Be "Problem" by Race and Sex: 1993/94
(weighted sample size in parentheses)

Aspect of School Life	Total	Male	Female	White, Non-Hispanic Total	White, Non-Hispanic Male	White, Non-Hispanic Female	African American, Non-Hispanic Total	African American, Non-Hispanic Male	African American, Non-Hispanic Female	Hispanic Total	Hispanic Male	Hispanic Female	Other Total	Other Male	Other Female
Total Weighted Sample	100.0% (25,015)	46.4% (11,605)	53.6% (13,409)	92.5% (23,133)	43.7% (10,943)	48.7% (12,190)	4.2% (1,060)	1.4% (347)	2.9% (713)	2.1% (523)	0.9% (231)	1.2% (292)	1.2% (298)	0.3% (84)	0.9% (214)
Total Respondents															
Total	100.0% (25,015)	100.0% (11,605)	100.0% (13,409)	100.0% (23,133)	100.0% (10,943)	100.0% (12,190)	100.0% (1,060)	100.0% (347)	100.0% (713)	100.0% (523)	100.0% (231)	100.0% (292)	100.0% (298)	100.0% (84)	100.0% (214)
Robbery/Theft ++ ~	20.7% (5,174)	23.9% (2,779)	17.8% (2,393)	20.2% (4,672)	22.9% (2,508)	17.8% (2,164)	23.0% (244)	35.2% (122)	17.1% (122)	26.8% (140)	50.6% (117)	7.9% (23)	38.9% (116)	38.1% (32)	39.3% (84)
Vandalism of School Property	31.1% (7,776)	33.4% (3,875)	29.1% (3,900)	30.7% (7,100)	32.4% (3,548)	29.1% (3,552)	32.0% (339)	38.9% (135)	28.6% (204)	37.5% (196)	63.6% (147)	16.8% (49)	47.0% (140)	53.6% (45)	44.4% (95)
Student Pregnancy ++	7.3% (1,834)	9.2% (1,071)	5.7% (761)	7.5% (1,737)	9.1% (992)	6.1% (745)	3.3% (35)	7.8% (27)	1.1% (8)	10.5% (55)	20.8% (48)	2.4% (7)	1.7% (5)	4.8% (4)	0.5% (1)
Student Use of Alcohol ** +++ ~	14.9% (3,720)	20.7% (2,397)	9.9% (1,323)	15.3% (3,549)	20.6% (2,253)	10.6% (1,296)	6.4% (68)	13.8% (48)	2.8% (20)	12.8% (67)	26.0% (60)	2.4% (7)	12.1% (36)	42.9% (36)	0.0% –
Student Drug Abuse +++	12.5% (3,128)	16.2% (1,882)	9.3% (1,243)	12.7% (2,942)	16.1% (1,760)	9.7% (1,182)	7.5% (79)	13.8% (48)	4.3% (31)	12.0% (63)	24.2% (56)	2.4% (7)	13.8% (41)	21.4% (18)	10.7% (23)
Student Possession of Weapons ~	4.2% (1,042)	5.2% (602)	3.3% (438)	3.9% (909)	4.3% (473)	3.6% (436)	2.8% (30)	8.1% (28)	0.3% (2)	18.4% (96)	41.6% (96)	0.0% –	1.7% (5)	6.0% (5)	0.0% –
Student Dropping Out * +++	10.9% (2,718)	16.9% (1,960)	5.7% (758)	10.2% (2,353)	16.2% (1,770)	4.8% (583)	17.3% (183)	24.8% (86)	13.6% (97)	16.6% (87)	37.7% (87)	0.0% –	31.9% (95)	20.2% (17)	36.4% (78)
Lack of Parental Involvement +++	44.6% (11,158)	50.5% (5,858)	39.5% (5,299)	44.0% (10,189)	50.2% (5,488)	38.6% (4,701)	44.6% (473)	45.5% (158)	44.2% (315)	56.8% (297)	68.8% (159)	47.3% (138)	66.4% (198)	63.1% (53)	67.8% (145)
Parental Alcoholism or Drug Abuse ~	37.6% (9,398)	36.5% (4,239)	38.5% (5,157)	37.1% (8,576)	35.6% (3,899)	38.4% (4,677)	36.7% (389)	50.4% (175)	30.0% (214)	54.9% (287)	52.4% (121)	56.8% (166)	48.3% (144)	52.4% (44)	46.7% (100)
Poverty ** + ~~	42.7% (10,680)	45.4% (5,265)	40.4% (5,415)	41.6% (9,624)	43.7% (4,777)	39.8% (4,847)	55.1% (584)	74.9% (260)	45.4% (324)	64.6% (338)	74.9% (173)	56.5% (165)	45.0% (134)	65.5% (55)	36.9% (79)
Racial Tension ~~~	15.1% (3,785)	16.6% (1,921)	13.9% (1,863)	15.1% (3,502)	15.4% (1,690)	14.9% (1,812)	9.0% (95)	23.1% (80)	2.1% (15)	23.3% (122)	45.9% (106)	5.5% (16)	21.8% (65)	53.6% (45)	9.3% (20)
Students Come Unprepared to Learn +++	48.7% (12,190)	56.1% (6,511)	42.4% (5,679)	48.6% (11,233)	56.1% (6,134)	41.8% (5,099)	44.9% (476)	49.6% (172)	42.6% (304)	62.7% (328)	68.4% (158)	58.2% (170)	51.3% (153)	56.0% (47)	49.5% (106)
Poor Student Nutrition * ~	27.1% (6,772)	28.9% (3,359)	25.4% (3,412)	26.2% (6,068)	27.6% (3,019)	25.0% (3,049)	35.5% (376)	48.7% (169)	29.0% (207)	45.9% (240)	61.0% (141)	33.9% (99)	29.2% (87)	35.7% (30)	26.6% (57)
Poor Student Health * ~~~	23.3% (5,818)	24.4% (2,826)	22.3% (2,991)	22.4% (5,183)	22.5% (2,460)	22.3% (2,723)	31.2% (331)	52.7% (183)	20.8% (148)	41.1% (215)	61.0% (141)	25.3% (74)	29.5% (88)	50.0% (42)	21.5% (46)

Notes:

" – " indicates sample size too small to estimate.

Columns do not sum to 100% as respondents may have more than one type of previous experience.

*** Test of statistical significance compares African Americans with Whites. *** p < .001, ** p < .01, * p < .05.

+++ Test of statistical significance compares White men with White women. +++ p < .001, ++ p < .01, + p < .05.

~~~ Test of statistical significance compares African American men with African American women. ~~~ p < .001, ~~ p < .01, ~ p < .05.

Tests of statistical significance calculated using adjusted sample weight to control for influence of large sample sizes.

Source: Schools and Staffing Survey, 1993-94.

CHAPTER XI.
Parents' Involvement
in Their Children's Schools

How involved are the parents of African American students in their schools? To what extent do African American students' parents choose the schools their children attend? Do African American students' parents participate in activities at their children's schools at the same rates as their White counterparts? How frequently do African American students' parents talk with their children about school events?

One source for determining the extent of parental involvement is the 1993 School Safety and Discipline component of the National Household Education Survey (NHES). In addition to focusing on parents' and students' perceptions of their schools' safety, this survey includes a number of items describing parents' involvement in their children's schools.

The NHES differs from other data collection initiatives sponsored by the U.S. Department of Education's National Center for Education Statistics in that data are collected from households rather than from schools or students. Interviews for the School Safety and Discipline Component were conducted with the parents of 12,680 children in grades 3 through 12 and with 6,504 students in grades 6 through 12.

CHAPTER ORGANIZATION

This chapter examines racial group differences in parents' involvement in their children's schools, as reported by parents, by focusing upon two behaviors:

1. The choice of school their children to attend;

2. Their participation in activities at their children's schools.

Four levels of school choice are considered:

1. Choosing to attend a private rather than a public school;

2. Attending the public school of their choice;

3. Choosing a residence based on the quality of the local public schools; and

4. Not choosing (i.e., attending the assigned public school).

PART I — OVERVIEW

Data revealed in this chapter offer few comforts to those who believe that parental involvement can ultimately make a difference in both a child's education and the quality of the school district. While more African American students than Whites appear to be attending public schools of their choice, this may be due more to desegregation policies than to any particular selectivity of their parents.

As one might expect, attendance at private schools increased with family income and parents' educational attainment for both African Americans and Whites. Nonetheless, a smaller share of African Americans than Whites attend private schools regardless of their family incomes and mother's highest level of education. African Americans who attended private schools generally lived in urban rather than in suburban or rural areas.

Low family incomes also appear to limit participation in school activities for both African American and White parents. The gap between African American and White levels of parental participation persists even after controlling for mother's employment status, child's grade level, the poverty level of the community, and urbanicity.

Communication about school events appears to be weakest between African American boys and their parents. Comparable proportions of African American girls and White boys talk with their parents about school events. Communication appears to be most common between White girls and their parents.

PART II — DETAILED DESCRIPTIONS AND TABLES

SCHOOL CHOICE

Figure 1 shows that about 8.8% of students in grades 3 to 12 attended private schools in 1993. An additional 10.9% attended the public schools of their choice. Among students who attended their assigned public schools, less than one-half of the students' parents (39.2% of all students) indicated that they had chosen their residence based upon the quality of local public schools and less than one-half (41.2%) had not.

Figure 1. Distribution of Students in Grades 3 to 12 by Type of School Attended: 1993

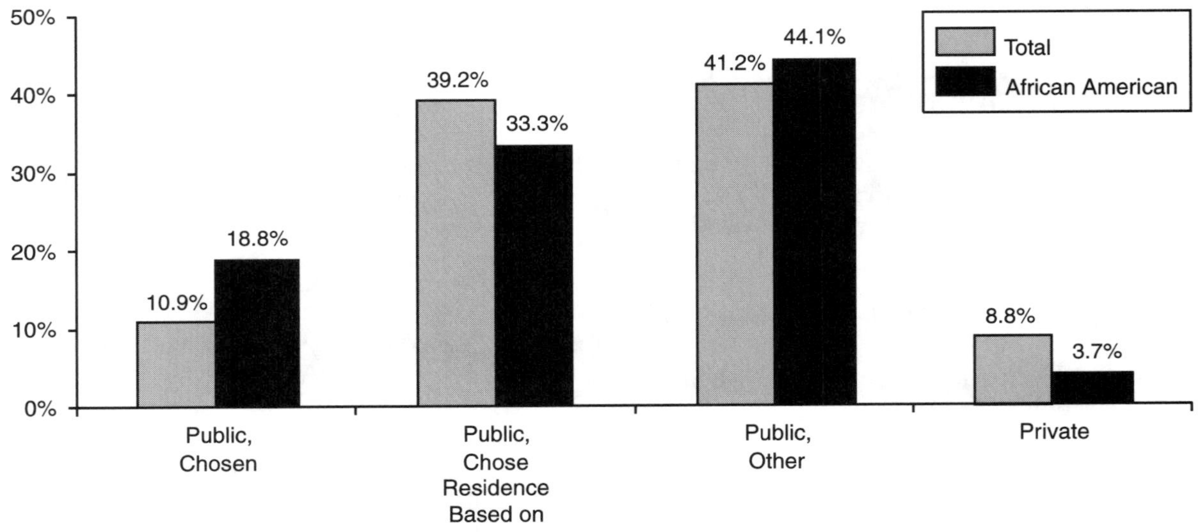

Source: National Household Education Survey, 1993 School Safety & Discipline Component.

- **Table 1** shows that a smaller percentage of African Americans than of Whites attended private schools in 1993 (3.7% versus 10.1%).

- A higher percentage of African Americans than Whites attended the public schools of their choice (18.8% versus 8.4%).

Among those who attended assigned public schools, **Table 1** shows that a smaller percentage of African American students' parents than of White students' parents chose their residences based on the local public schools.

- About 33.3% of African American students attended public schools in areas selected by their parents based on the quality of the local schools, compared with 41.7% of White students.

Choice by Family Income

Figure 2 shows that, for African Americans and for all students, the percentage who attended private schools increased with family income. Only 3.2% of students with family incomes below $15,000 attended private schools, compared with 15.6% of students with family incomes above $50,000.

The percentage of students who attended the public schools of their choice did not appear to vary by income. Regardless of income, a higher percentage of African Americans than Whites attended the public schools of their choice.

- **Table 2** shows that, among those with family incomes below $15,000, 17.4% of African Americans and 10.9% of Whites attended the public schools of their choice.

- Among those with incomes above $50,000, 20.6% of African Americans and 7.5% of Whites attended the public schools of their choice.

A higher percentage of students with family incomes above $50,000 than of students with lower family incomes attended assigned public schools located in areas chosen because of the public school quality. About one-half (47.6%) of students with fam-

Table 1. Percentage of Students in Grades 3 to 12 Who Attended a Chosen or Assigned School by Race and Sex: 1993
(weighted sample size in parentheses)

Type of School	Total	Male	Female	White, Non-Hispanic Total	Male	Female	African American, Non-Hispanic Total	Male	Female	Hispanic Total	Male	Female	Other Total	Male	Female
Total *** ++	100.0%	100.0%	100.0%	100.0%	100.0%	100.0%	100.0%	100.0%	100.0%	100.0%	100.0%	100.0%	100.0%	100.0%	100.0%
	(34,815,050)	(17,727,500)	(17,087,550)	(24,121,178)	(12,276,126)	(11,845,052)	(5,479,502)	(2,825,600)	(2,653,903)	(3,907,155)	(1,979,180)	(1,927,975)	(1,307,214)	(646,595)	(660,620)
Public, Chosen	10.9%	10.6%	11.1%	8.4%	8.2%	8.6%	18.8%	17.8%	19.9%	13.6%	13.6%	13.7%	14.4%	15.7%	13.1%
	(3,783,072)	(1,884,225)	(1,898,847)	(2,031,730)	(1,011,465)	(1,020,265)	(1,031,241)	(502,436)	(528,805)	(532,378)	(269,026)	(263,352)	(187,723)	(101,299)	(86,425)
Private	8.8%	8.3%	9.3%	10.1%	9.6%	10.7%	3.7%	3.9%	3.5%	6.7%	6.0%	7.5%	12.2%	11.0%	13.3%
	(3,065,939)	(1,475,558)	(1,590,380)	(2,440,345)	(1,175,608)	(1,264,738)	(203,155)	(109,583)	(93,572)	(263,097)	(119,103)	(143,994)	(159,342)	(71,265)	(88,077)
Public, Chose Residence Based Upon School	39.2%	41.0%	37.3%	41.7%	43.4%	39.9%	33.3%	35.3%	31.3%	32.2%	33.9%	30.4%	38.3%	40.9%	35.7%
	(13,639,518)	(7,262,791)	(6,376,726)	(10,055,200)	(5,330,597)	(4,724,604)	(1,826,058)	(996,545)	(829,514)	(1,258,170)	(671,351)	(586,818)	(500,089)	(264,299)	(235,790)
Public, Other	41.2%	40.1%	42.3%	39.8%	38.8%	40.8%	44.1%	43.1%	45.3%	47.4%	46.5%	48.4%	35.2%	32.4%	37.9%
	(14,326,522)	(7,104,925)	(7,221,596)	(9,593,903)	(4,758,457)	(4,835,446)	(2,419,048)	(1,217,036)	(1,202,012)	(1,853,511)	(919,700)	(933,811)	(460,060)	(209,733)	(250,327)

Notes:
*** Test of statistical significance compares African Americans with Whites. *** p < .001, ** p < .01, * p < .05.
+++ Test of statistical significance compares White boys with White girls. +++ p < .001, ++ p < .01, + p < .05.
~~~ Test of statistical significance compares African American boys with African American girls. ~~~ p < .001, ~~ p < .01, ~ p < .05.
Tests of statistical significance calculated using adjusted sample weight to control for influence of large sample sizes.
Source: National Household Education Survey, 1993 School Safety & Discipline Component.

Figure 2. Distribution of Students in Grades 3 to 12 by Type of School Attended and Family Income: 1993

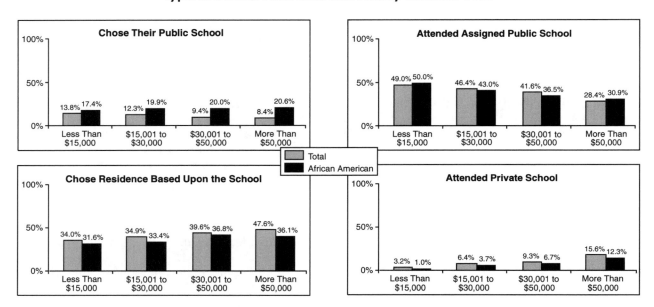

Source: National Household Education Survey, 1993 School Safety & Discipline Component.

ily incomes above $50,000 attended assigned public schools in areas chosen because of school quality, compared with 34.0% of those with family incomes less than $15,000, 34.9% of those with incomes between $15,000 and $30,000, and 39.6% of those with incomes between $30,000 and $50,000.

A smaller percentage of African Americans than of Whites appeared to attend public schools in residential areas chosen because of public school quality.

- **Table 2** shows that, among those with family incomes above $50,000, 36.1% of African Americans attended assigned public schools in chosen residential areas, compared with 48.8% of Whites.

- Among those with incomes below $15,000, 31.6% of African Americans attended assigned public schools in chosen residential areas, compared with 38.4% of Whites.

Choice by Parents' Education

Figures 3 and 4 suggest that, regardless of race, the percentage of students who attended private schools in 1993 increased with their parents' level of education. For example, **Table 3** shows that only 4.0% of students whose fathers had not graduated from high school attended private schools, compared with 17.6% of students whose fathers had earned advanced degrees.

- **Table 3** shows that 2.9% of African American students whose fathers earned high school diplomas attended private schools, compared with 20.1% of African American students whose fathers earned advanced degrees.

The percentage of students who attended the public schools of their choice did not appear to be related to parents' education. **Table 3** shows that the percentages of students who attended public schools

Table 2. Percentage of Students in Grades 3 to 12 Who Attended a Chosen or Assigned School by Family Income, Race, and Sex: 1993

(weighted sample size in parentheses)

Family Income	Total	Male	Female	White, Non-Hispanic Total	Male	Female	African American, Non-Hispanic Total	Male	Female	Hispanic Total	Male	Female	Other Total	Male	Female
Less than $15,000 ***	100.0%	100.0%	100.0%	100.0%	100.0%	100.0%	100.0%	100.0%	100.0%	100.0%	100.0%	100.0%	100.0%	100.0%	100.0%
	(7,643,835)	(4,012,868)	(3,630,967)	(3,202,481)	(1,654,930)	(1,547,551)	(2,550,116)	(1,409,263)	(1,140,854)	(1,610,762)	(794,147)	(816,615)	(280,476)	(154,528)	(125,948)
Public, Chosen	13.8%	12.5%	15.3%	10.9%	9.8%	12.1%	17.4%	15.1%	20.2%	12.7%	10.0%	15.3%	21.4%	31.2%	9.4%
	(1,057,186)	(503,379)	(553,807)	(349,215)	(162,588)	(186,627)	(443,681)	(213,151)	(230,531)	(204,166)	(79,376)	(124,790)	(60,125)	(48,265)	(11,860)
Private	3.2%	2.7%	3.7%	5.0%	4.4%	5.6%	1.0%	1.0%	1.0%	3.0%	3.0%	3.1%	3.3%	0.0%	7.4%
	(243,046)	(109,934)	(133,112)	(158,964)	(72,267)	(86,697)	(25,752)	(14,201)	(11,551)	(48,952)	(23,466)	(25,486)	(9,377)	–	(9,377)
Public, Chose Residence Based upon School	34.0%	36.2%	31.6%	38.4%	39.0%	37.7%	31.6%	34.8%	27.5%	28.7%	32.8%	24.7%	36.4%	35.2%	37.9%
	(2,598,333)	(1,451,910)	(1,146,424)	(1,229,125)	(646,068)	(583,057)	(804,932)	(491,084)	(313,848)	(462,226)	(260,397)	(201,829)	(102,050)	(54,360)	(47,689)
Public, Other	49.0%	48.5%	49.5%	45.8%	46.8%	44.7%	50.0%	49.0%	51.3%	55.6%	54.3%	56.9%	38.8%	33.6%	45.3%
	(3,745,269)	(1,947,645)	(1,797,624)	(1,465,177)	(774,007)	(691,170)	(1,275,750)	(690,827)	(584,923)	(895,417)	(430,908)	(464,509)	(108,924)	(51,903)	(57,021)
$15,001 to $30,000 * ++**	100.0%	100.0%	100.0%	100.0%	100.0%	100.0%	100.0%	100.0%	100.0%	100.0%	100.0%	100.0%	100.0%	100.0%	100.0%
	(9,008,808)	(4,552,927)	(4,455,881)	(5,836,777)	(3,009,540)	(2,827,236)	(1,573,512)	(740,273)	(833,239)	(1,261,542)	(625,119)	(636,423)	(336,977)	(177,995)	(158,982)
Public, Chosen	12.3%	12.6%	12.0%	9.7%	9.3%	10.2%	19.9%	23.1%	17.0%	14.6%	17.6%	11.7%	12.5%	6.9%	18.7%
	(1,108,615)	(574,046)	(534,569)	(568,937)	(280,673)	(288,265)	(313,031)	(171,132)	(141,899)	(184,529)	(109,896)	(74,634)	(42,117)	(12,346)	(29,772)
Private	6.4%	6.3%	6.5%	7.0%	7.2%	6.7%	3.7%	3.9%	3.5%	5.0%	3.2%	6.7%	14.7%	12.9%	16.6%
	(575,995)	(287,227)	(288,768)	(405,921)	(215,272)	(190,649)	(57,902)	(28,944)	(28,958)	(62,768)	(20,003)	(42,766)	(49,404)	(23,009)	(26,395)
Public, Chose Residence Based upon School	34.9%	37.6%	32.2%	36.1%	40.1%	31.8%	33.4%	32.2%	34.5%	31.3%	30.8%	31.8%	34.7%	41.4%	27.3%
	(3,143,118)	(1,710,199)	(1,432,919)	(2,105,293)	(1,206,265)	(899,028)	(525,896)	(238,061)	(287,835)	(394,838)	(192,230)	(202,609)	(117,090)	(73,643)	(43,447)
Public, Other	46.4%	43.5%	49.4%	47.2%	43.4%	51.3%	43.0%	40.8%	45.0%	49.1%	48.5%	49.7%	38.1%	38.8%	37.3%
	(4,181,080)	(1,981,456)	(2,199,625)	(2,756,625)	(1,307,331)	(1,449,295)	(676,684)	(302,137)	(374,547)	(619,406)	(302,991)	(316,415)	(128,365)	(68,997)	(59,368)
$30,001 to $50,000 ***	100.0%	100.0%	100.0%	100.0%	100.0%	100.0%	100.0%	100.0%	100.0%	100.0%	100.0%	100.0%	100.0%	100.0%	100.0%
	(9,362,721)	(4,678,432)	(4,684,289)	(7,488,322)	(3,729,890)	(3,758,433)	(845,214)	(427,308)	(417,905)	(643,560)	(346,235)	(297,325)	(385,625)	(174,999)	(210,626)
Public, Chosen	9.4%	9.5%	9.3%	7.3%	7.7%	6.9%	20.0%	16.8%	23.3%	15.4%	15.5%	15.2%	16.6%	17.0%	16.2%
	(879,317)	(443,856)	(435,461)	(547,402)	(288,780)	(258,622)	(169,132)	(71,645)	(97,488)	(98,795)	(53,669)	(45,126)	(63,987)	(29,762)	(34,226)
Private	9.3%	9.6%	9.1%	9.5%	9.9%	9.1%	6.7%	7.0%	6.4%	11.1%	11.0%	11.1%	9.4%	6.7%	11.7%
	(874,254)	(449,516)	(424,738)	(710,130)	(369,779)	(340,351)	(56,644)	(29,721)	(26,923)	(71,120)	(38,211)	(32,909)	(36,361)	(11,806)	(24,555)
Public, Chose Residence Based upon School	39.6%	40.0%	39.3%	40.3%	39.9%	40.7%	36.8%	41.0%	32.4%	37.5%	39.2%	35.5%	37.0%	41.8%	33.0%
	(3,710,949)	(1,871,496)	(1,839,453)	(3,016,085)	(1,487,413)	(1,528,672)	(310,649)	(175,086)	(135,563)	(241,502)	(135,888)	(105,613)	(142,714)	(73,108)	(69,605)
Public, Other	41.6%	40.9%	42.4%	42.9%	42.5%	43.4%	36.5%	35.3%	37.8%	36.1%	34.2%	38.2%	37.0%	34.5%	39.0%
	(3,898,202)	(1,913,565)	(1,984,637)	(3,214,706)	(1,583,918)	(1,630,788)	(308,789)	(150,857)	(157,932)	(232,144)	(118,467)	(113,676)	(142,563)	(60,323)	(82,240)

—continued next page

Table 2.—continued from previous page

Family Income	Total	Male	Female	White, Non-Hispanic Total	Male	Female	African American, Non-Hispanic Total	Male	Female	Hispanic Total	Male	Female	Other Total	Male	Female
$50,001 or More * + +**	100.0%	100.0%	100.0%	100.0%	100.0%	42.2%	100.0%	100.0%	100.0%	100.0%	100.0%	100.0%	100.0%	100.0%	100.0%
	(8,799,686)	(4,483,273)	(4,316,413)	(7,593,598)	(3,881,766)	(3,711,832)	(510,660)	(248,756)	(261,904)	(391,291)	(213,679)	(177,612)	(304,137)	(139,073)	(165,064)
Public, Chosen	8.4%	8.1%	8.7%	7.5%	7.2%	7.7%	20.6%	18.7%	22.5%	11.5%	12.2%	10.6%	7.1%	7.9%	6.4%
	(737,954)	(362,945)	(375,009)	(566,175)	(279,424)	(286,752)	(105,396)	(46,509)	(58,887)	(44,889)	(26,086)	(18,803)	(21,494)	(10,926)	(10,568)
Private	15.6%	14.0%	17.2%	15.3%	13.4%	17.4%	12.3%	14.8%	10.0%	20.5%	17.5%	24.1%	21.1%	26.2%	16.8%
	(1,372,644)	(628,882)	(743,762)	(1,165,330)	(518,290)	(647,040)	(62,857)	(36,718)	(26,140)	(80,256)	(37,423)	(42,833)	(64,200)	(36,450)	(27,750)
Public, Chose Residence Based upon School	47.6%	49.7%	45.4%	48.8%	51.3%	46.2%	36.1%	37.1%	35.2%	40.8%	38.8%	43.2%	45.5%	45.4%	45.5%
	(4,187,118)	(2,229,187)	(1,957,931)	(3,704,698)	(1,990,850)	(1,713,847)	(184,582)	(92,313)	(92,268)	(159,603)	(82,837)	(76,767)	(138,236)	(63,187)	(75,049)
Public, Other	28.4%	28.2%	28.7%	28.4%	28.2%	28.7%	30.9%	29.4%	32.3%	27.2%	31.5%	22.1%	26.4%	20.5%	31.3%
	(2,501,970)	(1,262,259)	(1,239,711)	(2,157,394)	(1,093,201)	(1,064,193)	(157,825)	(73,215)	(84,609)	(106,544)	(67,334)	(39,210)	(80,207)	(28,509)	(51,698)

Notes:

Student's residence determined by ZIP code. An Urbanized Area (UA) comprises a place (e.g., city, village) and adjacent densely settled surrounding territory that together have a population of at least 50,000.

"Urban, outside Urbanized Area" includes incorporated and unincorporated places outside of UA with population of at least 2,500.

"Rural" represents all other places.

"–" indicates sample size too small to estimate.

*** Test of statistical significance compares African Americans with Whites. *** p < .001, ** p < .01, * p < .05.

+++ Test of statistical significance compares White boys with White girls. +++ p < .001, ++ p < .01, + p < .05.

~~~ Test of statistical significance compares African American boys with African American girls. ~~~ p < .001, ~~ p < .01, ~ p < .05.

Tests of statistical significance calculated using adjusted sample weight to control for influence of large sample sizes.

Source: National Household Education Survey, 1993 School Safety & Discipline Component.

---

of choice were 8.6% for those whose fathers had less than a high school education, 9.7% for those whose fathers had only high school diplomas, 7.8% for those whose fathers had bachelor's degrees, and 9.5% for those whose fathers had advanced degrees. Regardless of their parents' education, a higher percentage of African American students than of White students attended the public schools of their choice.

- Among students whose fathers had only a high school diploma, 19.8% of African American students and 7.9% of White students attended public schools of their choice.

- Among students whose fathers had advanced degrees, 19.4% of African Americans and 8.4% of Whites attended public schools of their choice.

Overall, the percentage of students who attended assigned public schools in areas chosen based on public school quality increased with their parents' level of education. For example, **Figure 4** shows that about 37.9% of students whose mothers earned only a high school diploma and 45.7% of students whose mothers earned advanced degrees attended assigned schools located in areas chosen for the public schools' quality.

- **Table 4** shows that only 27.9% of African Americans whose mothers had advanced degrees attended public schools in chosen residential areas, compared with 47.2% of their White peers.

Choice by Urbanicity

Figure 5 shows that, regardless of school location, a smaller share of African American students than of students overall attended private schools. African Americans who attended private schools appeared to be concentrated in urban areas.

- **Table 5** shows that, in urban areas, only 4.8% of African American students attended private schools, compared with 14.0% of White students.

Figure 3. Distribution of Students in Grades 3 to 12 by Father's Highest Level of Education and Type of School Attended: 1993

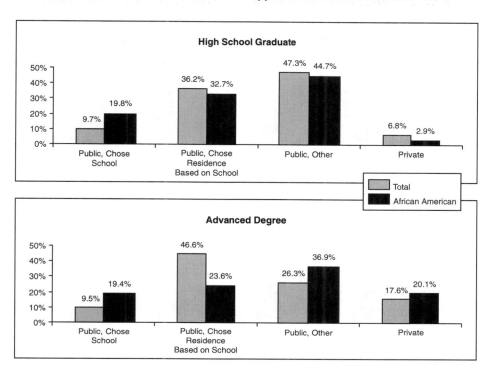

Source: National Household Education Survey, 1993 School Safety & Discipline. Component.

- Only 0.7% of African Americans but 6.1% of Whites attended private schools in suburban areas.

- Virtually no African Americans attended private schools in rural areas, compared with 5.8% of Whites.

- Comparable percentages of African American and White students in suburban (6.0% versus 7.2%) and rural (5.4% versus 6.3%) areas attended public schools of their choice.

- But in urban areas, the proportion of African American students who attended public schools of their choice was more than twice as large as the proportion of White students (22.9% versus 10.1%).

Choice by Census Region

Figure 6 shows that private school attendance was more common in the Northeast (13.0%) than in the Midwest (9.7%), West (7.4%), and South (6.8%).

- **Table 6** shows that a smaller percentage of African Americans than Whites attend private schools in the Northeast (8.0% versus 14.3%), South (1.8% versus 8.5%), and Midwest (5.1% versus 10.5%).

- In the West, 5.2% of African Americans and 7.8% of Whites attend private schools.

Regardless of census region, a higher proportion of African Americans than Whites attended public schools of their choice. The gap was smaller among

Figure 4. Distribution of Students in Grades 3 to 12 by Mother's Highest Level of Education and Type of School Attended: 1993

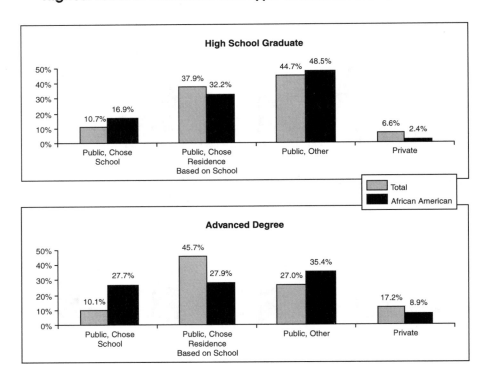

Source: National Household Education Survey, 1993 School Safety & Discipline Component.

students in the South, where 13.0% of African Americans and 9.6% of Whites attend public schools of their choice.

- About 25.0% of African Americans and 5.9% of Whites in the Northeast, 27.7% of African Americans and 7.0% of Whites in the Midwest, and 25.4% of African Americans and 11.2% of Whites in the West attended public schools of their choice.

PARTICIPATION IN SCHOOL ACTIVITIES

In 1993, about two-thirds (62.5%) of the parents of students in grades 3 to 12 reported that they had engaged in two or more of the following activities at their schools: attended a general school meeting, at-

tended a school or class event, and volunteered at the school or served on a school committee.

- **Table 7** shows that only one-half (50.4%) of African American students' parents but two-thirds (67.6%) of White students' parents participated in school activities.

Parental participation in school activities tended to decline with their children's grade level. About three-fourths (73.8%) of the parents of students in grades 3 to 5 participated in school activities, compared with 62.2% of parents of students in grades 6 to 8, and 53.1% of parents of students in grades 9 to 12.

Figure 7 shows that, among African Americans and overall, the percentage of students whose par-

Table 3. Percentage of Students in Grades 3 to 12 Who Attended a Chosen or Assigned School by Father's Education, Race, and Sex: 1993

(weighted sample size in parentheses)

Father's Education	Total	Male	Female	White, Non-Hispanic Total	Male	Female	African American, Non-Hispanic Total	Male	Female	Hispanic Total	Male	Female	Other Total	Male	Female
Less than High School	100.0% (3,606,070)	100.0% (1,948,035)	100.0% (1,658,035)	100.0% (1,910,883)	100.0% (1,030,077)	100.0% (880,805)	100.0% (509,800)	100.0% (307,298)	100.0% (202,502)	100.0% (1,078,246)	100.0% (567,519)	100.0% (510,727)	100.0% (107,141)	100.0% (43,140)	100.0% (64,001)
Public, Chosen	8.6% (310,332)	9.3% (180,817)	7.8% (129,516)	6.7% (127,248)	7.1% (73,056)	6.2% (54,192)	8.8% (44,624)	11.0% (33,697)	5.4% (10,928)	10.7% (115,656)	10.8% (61,165)	10.7% (54,492)	21.3% (22,804)	29.9% (12,900)	15.5% (9,904)
Private	4.0% (144,518)	3.4% (65,362)	4.8% (79,156)	3.7% (71,216)	3.2% (32,654)	4.4% (38,562)	2.4% (12,305)	3.7% (11,481)	0.4% (824)	3.7% (39,466)	3.7% (21,228)	3.6% (18,239)	20.1% (21,531)	0.0% –	33.6% (21,531)
Public, Chose Residence Based upon School	34.0% (1,225,299)	37.2% (723,898)	30.2% (501,400)	36.9% (705,438)	39.3% (404,843)	34.1% (300,595)	35.7% (181,854)	38.5% (118,461)	31.3% (63,394)	27.9% (301,315)	33.0% (187,483)	22.3% (113,832)	34.2% (36,691)	30.4% (13,111)	36.8% (23,580)
Public, Other	53.4% (1,925,921)	50.2% (977,958)	57.2% (947,963)	52.7% (1,006,981)	50.4% (519,525)	55.3% (487,456)	53.2% (271,016)	46.7% (143,660)	62.9% (127,356)	57.7% (621,809)	52.4% (297,643)	63.5% (324,166)	24.4% (26,115)	39.7% (17,129)	14.0% (8,986)
High School ***	100.0% (8,158,564)	100.0% (4,182,302)	100.0% (3,976,262)	100.0% (6,449,285)	100.0% (3,293,261)	100.0% (3,156,024)	100.0% (799,723)	100.0% (400,770)	100.0% (398,953)	100.0% (644,973)	100.0% (334,290)	100.0% (310,683)	100.0% (264,583)	100.0% (153,981)	100.0% (110,602)
Public, Chosen	9.7% (795,043)	10.0% (418,200)	9.5% (376,843)	7.9% (507,052)	7.6% (251,630)	8.1% (255,422)	19.8% (158,143)	22.0% (88,322)	17.5% (69,821)	14.9% (96,023)	17.5% (58,662)	12.0% (37,361)	12.8% (33,825)	12.7% (19,586)	12.9% (14,239)
Private	6.8% (558,224)	6.6% (277,135)	7.1% (281,089)	7.4% (474,659)	7.2% (236,549)	7.5% (238,110)	2.9% (23,116)	3.4% (13,633)	2.4% (9,484)	7.9% (50,692)	7.5% (25,032)	8.3% (25,660)	3.7% (9,756)	1.2% (1,921)	7.1% (7,835)
Public, Chose Residence Based upon School	36.2% (2,950,125)	37.3% (1,561,189)	34.9% (1,388,936)	37.2% (2,398,706)	38.4% (1,265,829)	35.9% (1,132,877)	32.7% (261,363)	33.3% (133,370)	32.1% (127,994)	32.0% (206,154)	29.3% (97,787)	34.9% (108,367)	31.7% (83,901)	41.7% (64,203)	17.8% (19,698)
Public, Other	47.3% (3,855,172)	46.0% (1,925,778)	48.5% (1,929,394)	47.6% (3,068,868)	46.7% (1,539,253)	48.5% (1,529,615)	44.7% (357,100)	41.3% (165,446)	48.0% (191,654)	45.3% (292,104)	45.7% (152,809)	44.8% (139,295)	51.8% (137,101)	44.3% (68,271)	62.2% (68,830)
Some College ***	100.0% (6,991,717)	100.0% (3,555,587)	100.0% (3,436,130)	100.0% (5,625,327)	100.0% (2,848,711)	100.0% (2,776,616)	100.0% (534,253)	100.0% (262,663)	100.0% (271,590)	100.0% (595,870)	100.0% (331,274)	100.0% (264,596)	100.0% (236,267)	100.0% (112,939)	100.0% (123,329)
Public, Chosen	9.6% (672,002)	8.8% (313,052)	10.4% (358,950)	8.0% (448,932)	7.5% (212,985)	8.5% (235,947)	17.6% (93,978)	13.8% (36,180)	21.3% (57,798)	14.6% (86,928)	12.0% (39,711)	17.8% (47,217)	17.8% (42,164)	21.4% (24,176)	14.6% (17,988)
Private	11.0% (771,883)	11.2% (398,293)	10.9% (373,590)	11.9% (669,066)	12.0% (341,631)	11.8% (327,435)	6.4% (34,333)	7.3% (19,158)	5.6% (15,175)	8.5% (50,655)	9.3% (30,866)	7.5% (19,788)	7.5% (17,829)	5.9% (6,638)	9.1% (11,191)
Public, Chose Residence Based upon School	40.6% (2,836,038)	41.7% (1,482,026)	39.4% (1,354,011)	41.5% (2,336,069)	42.7% (1,217,647)	40.3% (1,118,422)	35.4% (189,212)	36.3% (95,305)	34.6% (93,907)	39.3% (234,033)	41.8% (138,505)	36.1% (95,529)	32.5% (76,723)	27.1% (30,570)	37.4% (46,154)
Public, Other	38.8% (2,711,794)	38.3% (1,362,215)	39.3% (1,349,579)	38.6% (2,171,259)	37.8% (1,076,447)	39.4% (1,094,812)	40.6% (216,730)	42.6% (112,020)	38.6% (104,710)	37.6% (224,253)	36.9% (122,192)	38.6% (102,061)	42.1% (99,552)	45.6% (51,556)	38.9% (47,996)
Bachelor's Degree **	100.0% (3,167,379)	100.0% (1,608,691)	100.0% (1,558,689)	100.0% (2,749,281)	100.0% (1,401,121)	100.0% (1,348,161)	100.0% (150,810)	100.0% (93,421)	100.0% (57,389)	100.0% (137,315)	100.0% (62,311)	100.0% (75,004)	100.0% (129,973)	100.0% (51,838)	100.0% (78,135)
Public, Chosen	7.8% (247,863)	7.9% (127,570)	7.7% (120,293)	6.9% (190,612)	6.9% (96,575)	7.0% (94,037)	19.7% (29,768)	17.0% (15,910)	24.1% (13,858)	9.6% (13,199)	10.8% (6,752)	8.6% (6,447)	11.0% (14,284)	16.1% (8,333)	7.6% (5,950)
Private	14.9% (470,869)	12.8% (206,060)	17.0% (264,809)	15.3% (420,130)	13.3% (186,996)	17.3% (233,134)	4.8% (7,228)	5.2% (4,898)	4.1% (2,330)	13.3% (18,204)	11.0% (6,825)	15.2% (11,379)	19.5% (25,307)	14.2% (7,341)	23.0% (17,965)
Public, Chose Residence Based upon School	47.7% (1,509,829)	49.7% (800,003)	45.5% (709,825)	48.3% (1,326,955)	49.4% (692,683)	47.0% (634,272)	49.2% (74,127)	53.5% (49,995)	42.0% (24,132)	46.4% (63,650)	47.0% (29,294)	45.8% (34,355)	34.7% (45,097)	54.1% (28,031)	21.8% (17,066)
Public, Other	29.6% (938,819)	29.5% (475,058)	29.8% (463,761)	29.5% (811,584)	30.3% (424,867)	28.7% (386,718)	26.3% (39,687)	24.2% (22,618)	29.7% (17,069)	30.8% (42,262)	31.2% (19,439)	30.4% (22,822)	34.8% (45,286)	15.7% (8,133)	47.5% (37,153)

—continued next page

Table 3.—continued from previous page

Father's Education	Total	Male	Female	White, Non-Hispanic			African American, Non-Hispanic			Hispanic			Other		
				Total	Male	Female	Total	Male	Female	Total	Male	Female	Total	Male	Female
**Advanced Degree ** **	100.0%	100.0%	100.0%	100.0%	100.0%	100.0%	100.0%	100.0%	100.0%	100.0%	100.0%	100.0%	100.0%	100.0%	100.0%
	(3,581,391)	(1,804,711)	(1,776,681)	(3,044,558)	(1,538,468)	(1,506,091)	(164,094)	(78,915)	(85,179)	(141,394)	(73,449)	(67,945)	(231,345)	(113,879)	(117,465)
Public, Chosen	9.5%	9.0%	10.1%	8.4%	7.7%	9.1%	19.4%	16.2%	22.5%	19.5%	17.3%	22.0%	11.6%	15.8%	7.5%
	(341,650)	(162,214)	(179,436)	(255,320)	(118,780)	(136,540)	(31,888)	(12,761)	(19,127)	(27,588)	(12,671)	(14,917)	(26,855)	(18,002)	(8,853)
Private	17.6%	16.5%	18.6%	17.1%	15.7%	18.4%	20.1%	18.4%	21.6%	20.4%	9.4%	32.2%	20.4%	29.8%	11.4%
	(628,647)	(297,629)	(331,018)	(519,618)	(242,302)	(277,316)	(32,911)	(14,496)	(18,415)	(28,812)	(6,907)	(21,904)	(47,306)	(33,923)	(13,383)
Public, Chose Residence Based upon School	46.6%	48.9%	44.3%	48.0%	51.2%	44.8%	23.6%	24.8%	22.4%	34.1%	37.9%	29.9%	52.4%	41.6%	62.7%
	(1,670,475)	(882,842)	(787,633)	(1,462,505)	(788,013)	(674,492)	(38,690)	(19,598)	(19,092)	(48,153)	(27,808)	(20,344)	(121,127)	(47,422)	(73,705)
Public, Other	26.3%	25.6%	26.9%	26.5%	25.3%	27.7%	36.9%	40.6%	33.5%	26.1%	35.5%	15.9%	15.6%	12.8%	18.3%
	(940,619)	(462,026)	(478,594)	(807,116)	(389,373)	(417,743)	(60,605)	(32,059)	(28,546)	(36,842)	(26,062)	(10,780)	(36,057)	(14,532)	(21,525)

Notes:

Student's residence determined by ZIP code. An Urbanized Area (UA) comprises a place (e.g., city, village) and adjacent densely settled surrounding territory that together have a population of at least 50,000.

"Urban, outside Urbanized Area" includes incorporated and unincorporated places outside of UA with population of at least 2,500.

"Rural" represents all other places.

*** Test of statistical significance compares African Americans with Whites. *** p < .001, ** p < .01, * p < .05.

+++ Test of statistical significance compares White boys with White girls. +++ p < .001, ++ p < .01, + p < .05.

~~~ Test of statistical significance compares African American boys with African American girls. ~~~ p < .001, ~~ p < .01, ~ p < .05.

Tests of statistical significance calculated using adjusted sample weight to control for influence of large sample sizes.

Source: National Household Education Survey, 1993 School Safety & Discipline Component.

ents participated in school activities generally increased with family income. The percentage of African American participants ranged from 42.1% of those with family incomes below $15,000 to 70.7% of those with family incomes of more than $50,000. Even after controlling for family income, African American students' parents participated at a lower rate than White students' parents.

- **Table 7** shows that, among those with family incomes below $15,000, 42.1% of African American students' parents but 47.1% of White students' parents participated in school activities.

- Among those with family incomes above $50,000, 70.7% of African American students' parents participated compared with 79.8% of White students' parents.

Table 7 shows that the percentage of students whose parents participated in school activities ranged from 69.6% for those whose mothers worked part-time to 63.6% for those whose mothers worked full-time to 58.3% for those whose mothers were not in the labor force to 54.6% for those whose mothers were unemployed.

- Parental participation ranged from 39.5% for African American students whose mothers were not in the labor force to 65.6% for their White peers.

- One-half (55.3%) of African American students whose mothers worked full-time had parents who were involved with school activities, compared with 67.3% of their White peers.

Table 4. Percentage of Students in Grades 3 to 12 Who Attended a Chosen or Assigned School by Mother's Education, Race, and Sex: 1993

(weighted sample size in parentheses)

Mother's Education	Total	Male	Female	White, Non-Hispanic Total	Male	Female	African American, Non-Hispanic Total	Male	Female	Hispanic Total	Male	Female	Other Total	Male	Female
Less than High School * ++**	100.0%	100.0%	100.0%	100.0%	100.0%	100.0%	100.0%	100.0%	100.0%	100.0%	100.0%	100.0%	100.0%	100.0%	100.0%
	(5,314,520)	(2,666,835)	(2,647,685)	(2,256,239)	(1,161,623)	(1,094,616)	(1,106,211)	(524,532)	(581,679)	(1,708,137)	(855,499)	(852,638)	(243,933)	(125,181)	(118,752)
Public, Chosen	13.0%	12.9%	13.1%	9.5%	10.5%	8.5%	19.1%	16.0%	21.8%	13.2%	13.8%	12.6%	16.4%	16.7%	16.0%
	(690,969)	(345,051)	(345,918)	(215,088)	(122,165)	(92,923)	(210,877)	(83,924)	(126,953)	(225,048)	(118,015)	(107,033)	(39,956)	(20,947)	(19,009)
Private	2.2%	2.2%	2.1%	2.8%	3.2%	2.3%	0.5%	1.1%	0.0%	2.4%	1.8%	3.0%	2.4%	0.8%	4.1%
	(115,380)	(59,919)	(55,461)	(62,280)	(37,631)	(24,649)	(5,635)	(5,635)	–	(41,515)	(15,601)	(25,915)	(5,950)	(1,053)	(4,897)
Public, Chose Residence Based upon School	32.1%	35.1%	29.1%	37.1%	42.1%	31.8%	32.6%	35.3%	30.2%	24.7%	25.8%	23.6%	35.8%	33.2%	38.6%
	(1,706,466)	(936,085)	(770,381)	(837,152)	(489,144)	(348,008)	(360,711)	(185,101)	(175,610)	(421,300)	(220,322)	(200,978)	(87,303)	(41,518)	(45,785)
Public, Other	52.7%	49.7%	55.7%	50.6%	44.1%	57.5%	47.8%	47.6%	48.0%	59.7%	58.6%	60.8%	45.4%	49.3%	41.3%
	(2,801,705)	(1,325,780)	(1,475,925)	(1,141,719)	(512,684)	(629,036)	(528,988)	(249,872)	(279,116)	(1,020,274)	(501,561)	(518,712)	(110,724)	(61,664)	(49,061)
High School ***	100.0%	100.0%	100.0%	100.0%	100.0%	100.0%	100.0%	100.0%	100.0%	100.0%	100.0%	100.0%	100.0%	100.0%	100.0%
	(12,205,419)	(6,213,370)	(5,992,049)	(8,718,586)	(4,393,854)	(4,324,732)	(2,132,696)	(1,128,625)	(1,004,071)	(1,052,082)	(540,532)	(511,550)	(302,055)	(150,359)	(151,696)
Public, Chosen	10.7%	11.1%	10.3%	8.7%	9.2%	8.1%	16.9%	17.3%	16.4%	13.7%	12.4%	15.0%	16.1%	13.8%	18.4%
	(1,308,406)	(689,232)	(619,173)	(755,941)	(405,809)	(350,132)	(359,941)	(195,469)	(164,472)	(143,811)	(67,224)	(76,587)	(48,713)	(20,731)	(27,983)
Private	6.6%	6.1%	7.2%	7.4%	6.8%	8.1%	2.4%	2.1%	2.6%	7.7%	9.7%	5.6%	9.6%	1.1%	18.0%
	(809,061)	(378,681)	(430,380)	(648,493)	(300,260)	(348,233)	(50,156)	(24,131)	(26,024)	(81,380)	(52,575)	(28,806)	(29,032)	(1,715)	(27,317)
Public, Chose Residence Based upon School	37.9%	39.0%	36.8%	39.5%	40.9%	38.2%	32.2%	31.7%	32.8%	38.3%	40.0%	36.5%	30.5%	35.3%	25.8%
	(4,628,838)	(2,423,610)	(2,205,227)	(3,446,408)	(1,796,191)	(1,650,216)	(687,286)	(358,180)	(329,106)	(403,021)	(216,196)	(186,825)	(92,124)	(53,043)	(39,081)
Public, Other	44.7%	43.8%	45.7%	44.4%	43.1%	45.7%	48.5%	48.8%	48.3%	40.3%	37.8%	42.9%	43.8%	49.8%	37.8%
	(5,459,115)	(2,721,847)	(2,737,268)	(3,867,744)	(1,891,593)	(1,976,151)	(1,035,314)	(550,845)	(484,469)	(423,871)	(204,538)	(219,332)	(132,186)	(74,870)	(57,316)
Some College ***	100.0%	100.0%	100.0%	100.0%	100.0%	100.0%	100.0%	100.0%	100.0%	100.0%	100.0%	100.0%	100.0%	100.0%	100.0%
	(10,200,540)	(5,280,746)	(4,919,794)	(7,588,506)	(3,968,661)	(3,619,845)	(1,538,287)	(767,492)	(770,795)	(756,381)	(357,614)	(398,767)	(317,366)	(186,980)	(130,387)
Public, Chosen	10.7%	9.5%	12.0%	8.0%	6.8%	9.3%	21.6%	19.3%	23.9%	14.4%	14.3%	14.5%	13.0%	16.2%	8.4%
	(1,090,224)	(501,091)	(589,133)	(607,496)	(271,056)	(336,439)	(332,298)	(148,403)	(183,895)	(109,167)	(51,274)	(57,893)	(41,264)	(30,358)	(10,906)
Private	10.5%	9.9%	11.1%	11.4%	11.1%	11.7%	5.5%	5.3%	5.7%	10.7%	7.0%	14.0%	12.0%	9.4%	15.7%
	(1,067,682)	(522,711)	(544,971)	(864,830)	(439,767)	(425,063)	(84,074)	(40,408)	(43,667)	(80,823)	(25,011)	(55,811)	(37,955)	(17,525)	(20,431)
Public, Chose Residence Based upon School	40.7%	42.7%	38.6%	42.3%	43.7%	40.9%	34.4%	39.5%	29.2%	34.7%	36.6%	32.9%	45.9%	45.4%	46.5%
	(4,149,984)	(2,253,218)	(1,896,765)	(3,213,416)	(1,733,836)	(1,479,580)	(528,639)	(303,449)	(225,190)	(262,351)	(131,031)	(131,320)	(145,577)	(84,903)	(60,674)
Public, Other	38.2%	37.9%	38.4%	38.3%	38.4%	38.1%	15.2%	35.9%	41.3%	40.2%	42.0%	38.6%	29.2%	29.0%	29.4%
	(3,892,651)	(2,003,727)	(1,888,924)	(2,902,764)	(1,524,001)	(1,378,763)	(593,276)	(275,233)	(318,044)	(304,041)	(150,298)	(153,742)	(92,570)	(54,194)	(38,375)
Bachelor's Degree *	100.0%	100.0%	100.0%	100.0%	100.0%	100.0%	100.0%	100.0%	100.0%	100.0%	100.0%	100.0%	100.0%	100.0%	100.0%
	(3,225,094)	(1,584,666)	(1,640,428)	(2,592,704)	(1,295,844)	(1,296,860)	(279,050)	(152,650)	(126,400)	(130,207)	(64,682)	(65,525)	(223,133)	(71,489)	(151,643)
Public, Chosen	9.1%	9.0%	9.2%	8.4%	7.4%	9.3%	15.9%	21.0%	9.8%	8.8%	13.3%	4.4%	8.8%	7.5%	9.3%
	(292,293)	(141,981)	(150,313)	(216,794)	(95,942)	(120,852)	(44,489)	(32,092)	(12,396)	(11,483)	(8,591)	(2,892)	(19,528)	(5,355)	(14,172)
Private	16.9%	17.8%	16.0%	16.9%	17.5%	16.2%	11.7%	14.2%	8.8%	13.9%	4.8%	23.0%	25.6%	43.4%	17.2%
	(545,022)	(282,125)	(262,896)	(437,044)	(226,393)	(210,652)	(32,747)	(21,633)	(11,115)	(18,161)	(3,086)	(15,075)	(57,069)	(31,014)	(26,056)
Public, Chose Residence Based upon School	45.8%	47.6%	44.1%	47.2%	48.2%	46.3%	41.8%	42.0%	41.7%	51.7%	59.2%	44.2%	31.0%	37.3%	28.1%
	(1,478,348)	(754,216)	(724,133)	(1,225,017)	(625,141)	(599,876)	(116,774)	(64,124)	(52,649)	(67,289)	(38,305)	(28,985)	(69,268)	(26,646)	(42,622)
Public, Other	28.2%	25.6%	30.7%	27.5%	26.9%	28.2%	30.5%	22.8%	39.7%	25.6%	22.7%	28.3%	34.6%	11.9%	45.4%
	(909,431)	(406,345)	(503,086)	(713,848)	(348,369)	(365,480)	(85,040)	(34,801)	(50,239)	(33,274)	(14,700)	(18,574)	(77,268)	(8,475)	(68,793)

—continued next page

Table 4.—continued from previous page

Mother's Education	Total	Male	Female	White, Non-Hispanic			African American, Non-Hispanic			Hispanic			Other		
				Total	Male	Female	Total	Male	Female	Total	Male	Female	Total	Male	Female
Advanced Degree ***	100.0%	100.0%	100.0%	100.0%	100.0%	100.0%	100.0%	100.0%	100.0%	100.0%	100.0%	100.0%	100.0%	100.0%	100.0%
	(2,652,447)	(1,308,501)	(1,343,946)	(2,151,902)	(1,024,540)	(1,127,362)	(206,353)	(107,526)	(98,828)	(139,418)	(85,882)	(53,536)	(154,774)	(90,554)	(64,220)
Public, Chosen	10.1%	10.2%	9.9%	8.5%	9.3%	7.7%	27.7%	20.9%	35.1%	6.8%	6.1%	8.0%	11.4%	11.7%	11.0%
	(266,613)	(133,931)	(132,682)	(182,148)	(95,529)	(86,618)	(57,254)	(22,522)	(34,732)	(9,529)	(5,244)	(4,285)	(17,681)	(10,635)	(7,046)
Private	17.2%	15.6%	18.8%	17.8%	15.6%	19.8%	8.9%	6.9%	11.1%	23.2%	19.8%	28.7%	15.5%	22.0%	6.2%
	(457,230)	(203,935)	(253,296)	(382,481)	(159,551)	(222,930)	(18,440)	(7,455)	(10,985)	(32,351)	(16,970)	(15,381)	(23,958)	(19,959)	(3,999)
Public, Chose Residence Based upon School	45.7%	46.9%	44.4%	47.2%	48.4%	46.2%	27.9%	31.6%	23.9%	42.4%	39.4%	47.4%	50.5%	55.9%	42.9%
	(1,211,374)	(614,177)	(597,197)	(1,016,377)	(495,686)	(520,691)	(57,608)	(34,018)	(23,590)	(59,167)	(33,813)	(25,355)	(78,221)	(50,660)	(27,561)
Public, Other	27.0%	27.2%	26.8%	26.5%	26.7%	26.4%	35.4%	40.5%	29.9%	27.5%	34.8%	15.9%	22.6%	10.3%	39.9%
	(717,230)	(356,459)	(360,771)	(570,896)	(273,773)	(297,122)	(73,050)	(43,530)	(29,521)	(38,370)	(29,855)	(8,514)	(34,914)	(9,301)	(25,614)

Notes:

Student's residence determined by ZIP code. An Urbanized Area (UA) comprises a place (e.g., city, village) and adjacent densely settled surrounding territory that together have a population of at least 50,000.

"Urban, outside Urbanized Area" includes incorporated and unincorporated places outside of UA with population of at least 2,500.

"Rural" represents all other places.

*** Test of statistical significance compares African Americans with Whites. *** p < .001, ** p < .01, * p < .05.

+++ Test of statistical significance compares White boys with White girls. +++ p < .001, ++ p < .01, + p < .05.

~~~ Test of statistical significance compares African American boys with African American girls. ~~~ p < .001, ~~ p < .01, ~ p < .05.

Tests of statistical significance calculated using adjusted sample weight to control for influence of large sample sizes.

Source: National Household Education Survey, 1993 School Safety & Discipline. Component.

The percentage of students whose parents participated in school activities declined as the poverty level of their community increased. Overall, parental participation rates ranged from 69.6% for those who lived in areas with less than 5% of children living in poverty to 46.0% for those who lived in areas with between 20% and 24% of children living in poverty. Regardless of poverty level, a smaller percentage of African American students' parents than of White students' parents participated in school activities.

- **Table 7** shows that, among those in areas with less than 5% of children living in poverty, 60.8% of African American students' parents participated in school activities, compared with 71.3% of White students' parents.

- A smaller percentage of African American students' parents participated in school activities than of White students' parents in urban areas (49.8% versus 68.9%), suburban areas (47.9% versus 64.7%), and rural areas (55.6% versus 66.9%).

COMMUNICATION BETWEEN PARENTS AND THEIR CHILDREN ABOUT SCHOOL EVENTS

In 1993, about three-fourths (74.5%) of students in grades 6 through 12 reported that they had talked with their parents about school events.

- **Table 8** shows that the percentage of girls who talked with their parents about school events was higher than the percentage of boys among African Americans (72.6% versus 63.2%) and Whites (82.7% versus 72.2%).

- But, a smaller percentage of African American students than of White students talked with

Figure 5. Distribution of Students in Grades 3 to 12 by Type of School Attended and Urbanicity: 1993

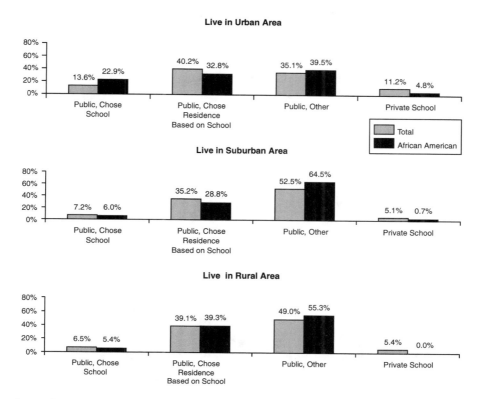

Source: National Household Education Survey, 1993 School Safety & Discipline Component.

their parents about school events (68.0% versus 77.4%).

Overall, the percentage of students who talked with their parents about school events did not appear to vary by school level, type, size, or location. At public schools; school levels above the elementary level; schools with less than 1,000 students; schools in urban, suburban, and rural areas; and schools in all regions, a smaller share of African American students than of White students talked with their parents about school events.

- **Table 8** shows that a smaller percentage of African American students than of White students talked with their parents about school events at middle and junior high schools (69.3% versus 78.5%), high schools (65.6% versus 76.0%), and combination schools (61.7% versus 80.0%).

- **Table 8** shows that about two-thirds of African Americans at public, assigned schools (67.8%) and public, chosen schools (65.9%) talked with their parents about school events, compared

Table 5. Percentage of Students in Grades 3 to 12 Who Attended a Chosen or Assigned School by Place of Residence, Race, and Sex: 1993

(weighted sample size in parentheses)

Urbanicity	Total	Male	Female	White, Non-Hispanic Total	Male	Female	African American, Non-Hispanic Total	Male	Female	Hispanic Total	Male	Female	Other Total	Male	Female
Urban * +**	100.0%	100.0%	100.0%	100.0%	100.0%	100.0%	100.0%	100.0%	100.0%	100.0%	100.0%	100.0%	100.0%	100.0%	100.0%
	(20,864,232)	(10,486,949)	(10,377,283)	(12,597,395)	(6,404,155)	(6,193,240)	(4,189,173)	(2,109,784)	(2,079,389)	(3,090,127)	(1,525,772)	(1,564,355)	(987,537)	(447,238)	(540,299)
Public, Chosen	13.6%	13.3%	13.9%	10.1%	10.0%	10.3%	22.9%	22.4%	23.4%	15.5%	14.8%	16.2%	13.1%	13.6%	12.7%
	(2,842,199)	(1,398,617)	(1,443,582)	(1,274,600)	(638,959)	(635,642)	(958,524)	(472,546)	(485,978)	(479,491)	(226,232)	(253,259)	(129,585)	(60,881)	(68,704)
Private	11.2%	10.2%	12.1%	14.0%	12.7%	15.3%	4.8%	5.0%	4.5%	7.1%	6.1%	8.2%	14.7%	13.6%	15.5%
	(2,327,722)	(1,072,253)	(1,255,469)	(1,762,524)	(812,539)	(949,985)	(199,696)	(106,124)	(93,572)	(220,536)	(92,593)	(127,943)	(144,966)	(60,996)	(83,970)
Public, Chose Residence Based upon School	40.2%	42.2%	38.1%	45.2%	46.9%	43.4%	32.8%	35.2%	30.4%	30.4%	32.4%	28.5%	38.1%	41.3%	35.5%
	(8,381,073)	(4,426,280)	(3,954,793)	(5,690,134)	(3,004,547)	(2,685,587)	(1,374,181)	(742,586)	(631,596)	(940,663)	(494,612)	(446,051)	(376,095)	(184,536)	(191,559)
Public, Other	35.1%	34.2%	35.9%	30.7%	30.4%	31.0%	39.5%	37.4%	41.8%	46.9%	46.7%	47.1%	34.1%	31.5%	36.3%
	(7,313,237)	(3,589,799)	(3,723,438)	(3,870,136)	(1,948,110)	(1,922,026)	(1,656,771)	(788,528)	(868,244)	(1,449,437)	(712,335)	(737,102)	(336,892)	(140,825)	(196,067)
Suburban * ~~**	100.0%	100.0%	100.0%	100.0%	100.0%	100.0%	100.0%	100.0%	100.0%	100.0%	100.0%	100.0%	100.0%	100.0%	100.0%
	(5,092,369)	(2,741,345)	(2,351,024)	(3,912,517)	(2,070,972)	(1,841,545)	(527,450)	(300,825)	(226,625)	(490,276)	(275,931)	(214,345)	(162,125)	(93,617)	(68,509)
Public, Chosen	7.2%	7.0%	7.3%	7.2%	7.4%	6.9%	6.0%	1.0%	12.7%	6.3%	8.8%	3.1%	13.6%	12.2%	15.6%
	(365,181)	(192,502)	(172,679)	(280,400)	(153,796)	(126,604)	(31,623)	(2,920)	(28,703)	(31,087)	(24,398)	(6,689)	(22,071)	(11,387)	(10,683)
Private	5.1%	5.5%	4.7%	6.1%	6.3%	5.9%	0.7%	1.1%	0.0%	3.3%	5.3%	0.7%	1.5%	2.5%	0.0%
	(261,176)	(151,743)	(109,434)	(239,304)	(131,353)	(107,951)	(3,459)	(3,459)	–	(16,040)	(14,557)	(1,483)	(2,374)	(2,374)	–
Public, Chose Residence Based upon School	35.2%	34.5%	36.0%	35.8%	34.3%	37.4%	28.8%	32.2%	24.3%	34.3%	33.0%	36.1%	43.0%	49.3%	34.4%
	(1,790,852)	(945,424)	(845,428)	(1,400,790)	(711,347)	(689,443)	(151,959)	(96,895)	(55,063)	(168,360)	(91,025)	(77,335)	(69,743)	(46,157)	(23,586)
Public, Other	52.5%	53.0%	52.0%	50.9%	51.9%	49.8%	64.5%	65.7%	63.0%	56.0%	52.9%	60.1%	41.9%	36.0%	50.0%
	(2,675,160)	(1,451,676)	(1,223,484)	(1,992,024)	(1,074,477)	(917,547)	(340,410)	(197,550)	(142,859)	(274,789)	(145,951)	(128,839)	(67,938)	(33,699)	(34,239)
Rural * ++**	100.0%	100.0%	100.0%	100.0%	100.0%	100.0%	100.0%	100.0%	100.0%	100.0%	100.0%	100.0%	100.0%	100.0%	100.0%
	(8,858,449)	(4,499,207)	(4,359,242)	(7,611,266)	(3,800,998)	(3,810,267)	(762,879)	(414,991)	(347,888)	(326,752)	(177,477)	(149,275)	(157,552)	(105,740)	(51,812)
Public, Chosen	6.5%	6.5%	6.5%	6.3%	5.8%	6.8%	5.4%	6.5%	4.1%	6.7%	10.4%	2.3%	22.9%	27.5%	13.6%
	(575,692)	(293,106)	(282,586)	(476,729)	(218,710)	(258,020)	(41,094)	(26,970)	(14,124)	(21,801)	(18,396)	(3,405)	(36,068)	(29,030)	(7,038)
Private	5.4%	5.6%	5.2%	5.8%	6.1%	5.4%	0.0%	0.0%	0.0%	8.1%	6.7%	9.8%	7.6%	7.5%	7.9%
	(477,040)	(251,563)	(225,477)	(438,517)	(231,716)	(206,801)	–	–	–	(26,521)	(11,953)	(14,568)	(12,002)	(7,895)	(4,107)
Public, Chose Residence Based upon School	39.1%	42.0%	36.2%	38.9%	42.5%	35.4%	39.3%	37.8%	41.1%	45.6%	48.3%	42.5%	34.4%	31.8%	39.8%
	(3,467,593)	(1,891,087)	(1,576,505)	(2,964,277)	(1,614,703)	(1,349,574)	(299,918)	(157,063)	(142,855)	(149,146)	(85,715)	(63,432)	(54,251)	(33,606)	(20,645)
Public, Other	49.0%	45.9%	52.2%	49.0%	45.7%	52.4%	55.3%	55.7%	54.9%	39.6%	34.6%	45.5%	35.1%	33.3%	38.6%
	(4,338,124)	(2,063,451)	(2,274,674)	(3,731,742)	(1,735,870)	(1,995,872)	(421,867)	(230,958)	(190,910)	(129,284)	(61,414)	(67,870)	(55,231)	(35,209)	(20,022)

Notes:

Student's residence determined by ZIP code. An Urbanized Area (UA) comprises a place (e.g., city, village) and adjacent densely settled surrounding territory that together have a population of at least 50,000.

"Urban, outside Urbanized Area" includes incorporated and unincorporated places outside of UA with population of at least 2,500.

"Rural" represents all other places.

"–" indicates sample size too small to estimate.

*** Test of statistical significance compares African Americans with Whites. *** $p < .001$, ** $p < .01$, * $p < .05$.

+++ Test of statistical significance compares White boys with White girls. +++ $p < .001$, ++ $p < .01$, + $p < .05$.

~~~ Test of statistical significance compares African American boys with African American girls. ~~~ $p < .001$, ~~ $p < .01$, ~ $p < .05$.

Tests of statistical significance calculated using adjusted sample weight to control for influence of large sample sizes.

Source: National Household Education Survey, 1993 School Safety & Discipline Component.

Figure 6. Distribution of Students in Grades 3 to 12 by Type of School Attended and Census Region: 1993

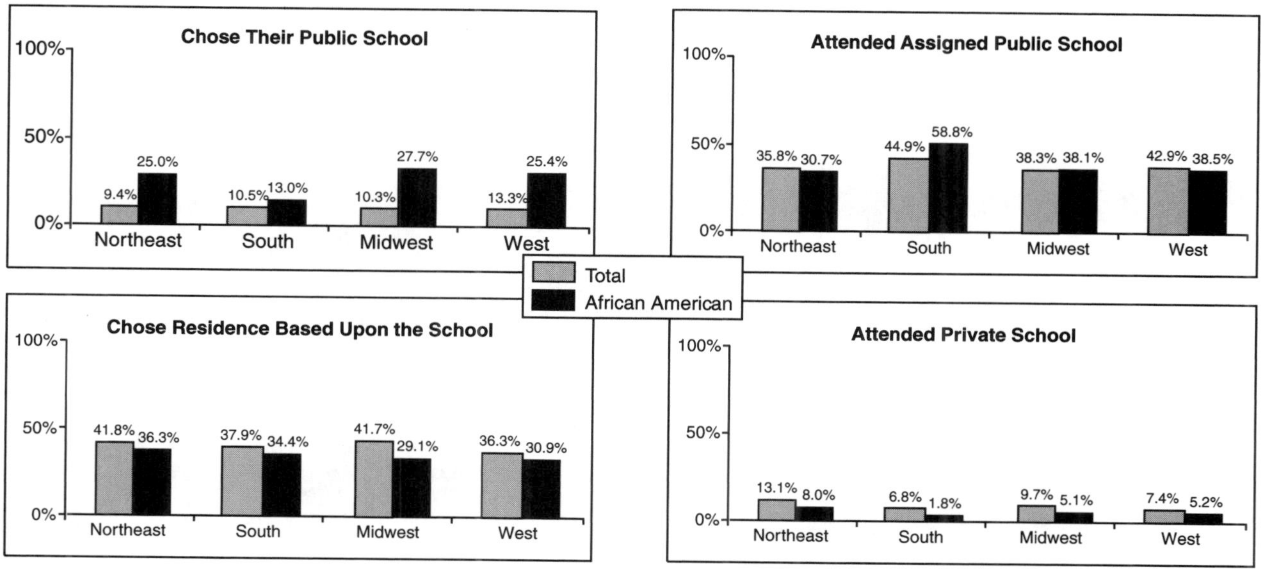

Chose Their Public School

	Northeast	South	Midwest	West
Total	9.4%	10.5%	10.3%	13.3%
African American	25.0%	13.0%	27.7%	25.4%

Attended Assigned Public School

	Northeast	South	Midwest	West
Total	35.8%	44.9%	38.3%	42.9%
African American	30.7%	58.8%	38.1%	38.5%

Total
African American

Chose Residence Based Upon the School

	Northeast	South	Midwest	West
Total	41.8%	37.9%	41.7%	36.3%
African American	36.3%	34.4%	29.1%	30.9%

Attended Private School

	Northeast	South	Midwest	West
Total	13.1%	6.8%	9.7%	7.4%
African American	8.0%	1.8%	5.1%	5.2%

Source: National Household Education Survey, 1993 School Safety & Discipline Component.

with more than three-fourths of their White peers (77.0% and 79.9%, respectively).

- **Figure 8** shows that 71.8% of African Americans at schools with 1,000 or more students talked with their parents about school events, compared with only about two-thirds (64.8%) of African

Americans at schools with fewer than 1,000 students.

- **Table 8** shows that only 58.0% of African Americans in rural schools talked with their parents about school events, compared with 77.0% of Whites.

Table 6. Percentage of Students in Grades 3 to 12 Who Attended a Chosen or Assigned School by Census Region, Race, and Sex: 1993

(weighted sample size in parentheses)

Region	Total	Male	Female	White, Non-Hispanic Total	Male	Female	African American, Non-Hispanic Total	Male	Female	Hispanic Total	Male	Female	Other Total	Male	Female
Northeast ***	100.0% (6,399,271)	100.0% (3,326,622)	100.0% (3,072,649)	100.0% (4,810,512)	100.0% (2,542,964)	100.0% (2,267,548)	100.0% (819,891)	100.0% (415,627)	100.0% (404,264)	100.0% (470,717)	100.0% (221,641)	100.0% (249,076)	100.0% (298,152)	100.0% (146,390)	100.0% (151,762)
Public, Chosen	9.4% (603,310)	9.3% (310,106)	9.5% (293,204)	5.9% (283,019)	5.8% (146,453)	6.0% (136,566)	25.0% (204,621)	27.6% (114,564)	22.3% (90,057)	16.2% (76,053)	9.3% (20,642)	22.2% (55,411)	13.3% (39,617)	19.4% (28,446)	7.4% (11,171)
Private	13.0% (835,044)	12.9% (430,378)	13.2% (404,666)	14.3% (686,927)	13.2% (336,415)	15.5% (350,513)	8.0% (65,674)	7.9% (32,754)	8.1% (32,920)	13.0% (61,122)	20.1% (44,647)	6.6% (16,475)	7.2% (21,321)	11.3% (16,563)	3.1% (4,759)
Public, Chose Residence Based upon School	41.8% (2,672,150)	42.1% (1,401,341)	41.4% (1,270,809)	44.3% (2,132,658)	45.7% (1,161,036)	42.8% (971,622)	36.3% (297,791)	37.1% (154,362)	35.5% (143,429)	24.6% (115,987)	17.5% (38,679)	31.0% (77,308)	42.2% (125,713)	32.3% (47,264)	51.7% (78,449)
Public, Other	35.8% (2,288,767)	35.6% (1,184,796)	35.9% (1,103,970)	35.5% (1,707,907)	35.4% (899,060)	35.7% (808,847)	30.7% (251,805)	27.4% (113,946)	34.1% (137,858)	46.2% (217,555)	53.1% (117,673)	40.1% (99,882)	37.4% (111,500)	37.0% (54,117)	37.8% (57,383)
South ***	100.0% (12,263,375)	100.0% (6,170,043)	100.0% (6,093,332)	100.0% (7,698,708)	100.0% (3,814,415)	100.0% (3,884,293)	100.0% (3,067,082)	100.0% (1,630,277)	100.0% (1,436,806)	100.0% (1,226,144)	100.0% (608,226)	100.0% (617,919)	100.0% (271,441)	100.0% (117,126)	100.0% (154,315)
Public, Chosen	10.5% (1,284,151)	10.5% (648,742)	10.4% (635,409)	9.6% (738,709)	9.7% (368,732)	9.5% (369,976)	13.0% (398,028)	11.8% (192,845)	14.3% (205,182)	9.0% (110,356)	11.5% (69,677)	6.6% (40,679)	13.7% (37,059)	14.9% (17,487)	12.7% (19,572)
Private	6.8% (834,079)	6.5% (403,927)	7.1% (430,152)	8.5% (656,302)	8.7% (332,677)	8.3% (323,624)	1.8% (55,342)	2.1% (34,915)	1.4% (20,427)	6.0% (73,306)	3.9% (23,683)	8.0% (49,623)	18.1% (49,129)	10.8% (12,652)	23.6% (36,477)
Public, Chose Residence Based upon School	37.9% (4,644,199)	39.5% (2,437,597)	36.2% (2,206,602)	39.3% (3,028,117)	40.2% (1,533,296)	38.5% (1,494,821)	34.4% (1,054,834)	37.6% (612,722)	30.8% (442,112)	37.6% (461,126)	39.7% (241,663)	35.5% (219,463)	36.9% (100,122)	42.6% (49,916)	32.5% (50,207)
Public, Other	44.9% (5,500,946)	43.4% (2,679,778)	46.3% (2,821,169)	42.5% (3,275,581)	41.4% (1,579,709)	43.7% (1,695,871)	50.8% (1,558,879)	48.4% (789,794)	53.5% (769,084)	47.4% (581,357)	44.9% (273,203)	49.9% (308,154)	31.4% (85,130)	31.7% (37,071)	31.1% (48,059)
Midwest *** +	100.0% (8,532,932)	100.0% (4,344,488)	100.0% (4,188,444)	100.0% (6,930,725)	100.0% (3,510,225)	100.0% (3,420,500)	100.0% (1,058,794)	100.0% (537,685)	100.0% (521,109)	100.0% (363,750)	100.0% (177,478)	100.0% (186,272)	100.0% (179,663)	100.0% (119,101)	100.0% (60,562)
Public, Chosen	10.3% (879,639)	10.7% (466,628)	9.9% (413,010)	7.0% (483,643)	7.5% (262,283)	6.5% (221,360)	27.7% (293,278)	27.0% (145,252)	28.4% (148,026)	18.4% (66,808)	18.7% (33,206)	18.0% (33,603)	20.0% (35,910)	21.7% (25,887)	16.5% (10,022)
Private	9.7% (829,461)	8.7% (376,253)	10.8% (453,208)	10.5% (731,001)	9.1% (318,779)	12.1% (412,223)	5.1% (54,212)	5.9% (31,523)	4.4% (22,689)	5.9% (21,316)	3.3% (5,914)	8.3% (15,403)	12.8% (22,932)	16.8% (20,038)	4.8% (2,894)
Public, Chose Residence Based upon School	41.7% (3,558,776)	43.2% (1,875,852)	40.2% (1,682,924)	43.8% (3,038,853)	46.0% (1,613,914)	41.7% (1,424,939)	29.1% (308,398)	25.4% (136,385)	33.0% (172,014)	35.0% (127,453)	38.8% (68,829)	31.5% (58,624)	46.8% (84,072)	47.6% (56,725)	45.2% (27,347)
Public, Other	38.3% (3,265,056)	37.4% (1,625,755)	39.1% (1,639,301)	38.6% (2,677,229)	37.5% (1,315,250)	39.8% (1,361,979)	38.1% (402,906)	41.8% (224,525)	34.2% (178,381)	40.7% (148,172)	39.2% (69,529)	42.2% (78,643)	20.5% (36,749)	13.8% (16,451)	33.5% (20,299)

—continued next page

Table 6.—continued from previous page

Region	Total	Male	Female	White, Non-Hispanic			African American, Non-Hispanic			Hispanic			Other		
				Total	Male	Female	Total	Male	Female	Total	Male	Female	Total	Male	Female
West * +**	100.0%	100.0%	100.0%	100.0%	100.0%	100.0%	100.0%	100.0%	100.0%	100.0%	100.0%	100.0%	100.0%	100.0%	100.0%
	(7,619,472)	(3,886,347)	(3,733,125)	(4,681,233)	(2,408,522)	(2,272,712)	(533,736)	(242,011)	(291,724)	(1,846,543)	(971,836)	(874,708)	(557,959)	(263,978)	(293,981)
Public, Chosen	13.3%	11.8%	14.9%	11.2%	9.7%	12.9%	25.4%	20.6%	29.3%	15.1%	15.0%	15.3%	13.5%	11.2%	15.5%
	(1,015,972)	(458,749)	(557,223)	(526,360)	(233,996)	(292,363)	(135,314)	(49,774)	(85,540)	(279,161)	(145,501)	(133,660)	(75,138)	(29,478)	(45,659)
Private	7.4%	6.8%	8.1%	7.8%	7.8%	7.8%	5.2%	4.3%	6.0%	5.8%	4.6%	7.1%	11.8%	8.3%	14.9%
	(567,354)	(265,000)	(302,354)	(366,115)	(187,737)	(178,378)	(27,927)	(10,392)	(17,536)	(107,352)	(44,859)	(62,493)	(65,960)	(22,012)	(43,948)
Public, Chose Residence Based upon School	36.3%	39.8%	32.6%	39.6%	42.4%	36.7%	30.9%	38.5%	24.7%	30.0%	33.2%	26.5%	34.1%	41.8%	27.1%
	(2,764,393)	(1,548,001)	(1,216,392)	(1,855,573)	(1,022,351)	(833,222)	(165,035)	(93,075)	(71,960)	(553,604)	(322,181)	(231,423)	(190,181)	(110,394)	(79,787)
Public, Other	42.9%	41.5%	44.4%	41.3%	40.0%	42.6%	38.5%	36.7%	40.0%	49.1%	47.3%	51.1%	40.6%	38.7%	42.4%
	(3,271,752)	(1,614,596)	(1,657,156)	(1,933,186)	(964,437)	(968,748)	(205,459)	(88,770)	(116,689)	(906,427)	(459,295)	(447,132)	(226,680)	(102,094)	(124,587)

Notes:

*** Test of statistical significance compares African Americans with Whites. *** p < .001, ** p < .01, * p < .05.

+++ Test of statistical significance compares White boys with White girls. +++ p < .001, ++ p < .01, + p < .05.

~~~ Test of statistical significance compares African American boys with African American girls. ~~~ p < .001, ~~ p < .01, ~ p < .05.

Tests of statistical significance calculated using adjusted sample weight to control for influence of large sample sizes.

Source: National Household Education Survey, 1993 School Safety & Discipline Component.

Table 7. Percentage of Students in Grades 3 to 12 Whose Parents Reported That They Had Participated in Two or More School Activities by School Characteristic, Race, and Sex: 1993

(weighted sample size in parentheses)

Characteristic	Total	Male	Female	White, Non-Hispanic Total	Male	Female	African American, Non-Hispanic Total	Male	Female	Hispanic Total	Male	Female	Other Total	Male	Female
Total *** +++	100.0%	100.0%	100.0%	100.0%	100.0%	100.0%	100.0%	100.0%	100.0%	100.0%	100.0%	100.0%	100.0%	100.0%	100.0%
	(34,815,050)	(17,727,500)	(17,087,550)	(24,121,178)	(12,276,126)	(11,845,052)	(5,479,502)	(2,825,600)	(2,653,903)	(3,907,155)	(1,979,180)	(1,927,975)	(1,307,214)	(646,595)	(660,620)
Parents Participated in	62.5%	59.9%	65.2%	67.6%	64.6%	70.7%	50.4%	48.8%	52.1%	50.0%	47.8%	52.3%	57.3%	56.9%	57.7%
2 or More Activities	(21,767,552)	(10,620,349)	(11,147,202)	(16,302,739)	(7,928,647)	(8,374,092)	(2,760,952)	(1,377,702)	(1,383,250)	(1,954,753)	(946,050)	(1,008,703)	(749,108)	(367,950)	(381,158)
Child's Grade															
Grades 3 to 5 *** +++	73.8%	70.5%	77.2%	79.3%	75.4%	83.4%	60.7%	58.9%	62.9%	60.4%	59.9%	61.0%	70.7%	65.4%	75.3%
	(8,137,573)	(3,971,371)	(4,166,202)	(5,965,031)	(2,901,472)	(3,063,559)	(1,053,003)	(558,545)	(494,457)	(795,670)	(373,216)	(422,454)	(323,869)	(138,138)	(185,731)
Grades 6 to 8 *** +	62.2%	59.6%	65.0%	67.2%	64.9%	69.6%	52.0%	49.8%	54.3%	50.1%	44.0%	57.2%	51.1%	53.6%	48.6%
	(6,829,530)	(3,346,920)	(3,482,610)	(5,084,567)	(2,494,070)	(2,590,498)	(890,504)	(438,377)	(452,126)	(645,757)	(306,140)	(339,617)	(208,702)	(108,333)	(100,369)
Grades 9 to 12 *** ++	53.1%	51.0%	55.2%	58.1%	55.2%	61.1%	40.2%	38.2%	42.2%	39.5%	40.4%	38.4%	49.2%	52.1%	45.8%
	(6,800,449)	(3,302,058)	(3,498,391)	(5,253,140)	(2,533,105)	(2,720,035)	(817,446)	(380,780)	(436,666)	(513,327)	(266,695)	(246,632)	(216,536)	(121,479)	(95,058)
Family Income															
Less than $15,000 * ++	43.9%	41.4%	46.6%	47.1%	43.0%	51.6%	42.1%	41.5%	42.8%	39.6%	35.9%	43.2%	47.3%	51.7%	41.9%
	(3,353,646)	(1,661,333)	(1,692,314)	(1,508,828)	(710,956)	(797,872)	(1,074,079)	(585,443)	(488,636)	(638,091)	(284,994)	(353,097)	(132,649)	(79,940)	(52,709)
$15,001 to $30,000 *** ++	55.6%	53.8%	57.4%	59.1%	56.2%	62.3%	49.1%	46.2%	51.7%	49.4%	51.0%	47.8%	47.7%	54.2%	40.3%
	(5,007,370)	(2,447,840)	(2,559,530)	(3,450,869)	(1,690,377)	(1,760,492)	(772,801)	(341,876)	(430,926)	(623,072)	(319,053)	(304,019)	(160,628)	(96,535)	(64,093)
$30,001 to $50,000 ++	69.2%	66.2%	72.3%	70.5%	67.5%	73.6%	65.4%	63.3%	67.6%	66.3%	62.3%	70.8%	57.4%	52.0%	61.8%
	(6,483,534)	(3,095,178)	(3,388,356)	(5,282,880)	(2,517,881)	(2,764,999)	(553,085)	(270,526)	(282,559)	(426,370)	(215,727)	(210,643)	(221,198)	(91,044)	(130,155)
$50,001 or More ** ++	78.7%	76.2%	81.2%	79.8%	77.5%	82.2%	70.7%	72.3%	69.2%	68.3%	59.1%	79.4%	77.1%	72.2%	81.3%
	(6,923,002)	(3,415,999)	(3,507,003)	(6,060,162)	(3,009,433)	(3,050,729)	(360,987)	(179,858)	(181,129)	(267,220)	(126,276)	(140,944)	(234,632)	(100,432)	(134,201)
Mother's Work Status															
No Mom in Household ~	47.8%	41.7%	55.3%	51.4%	46.6%	56.9%	44.1%	36.1%	60.2%	30.2%	32.3%	26.8%	46.9%	14.8%	63.1%
	(581,175)	(280,737)	(300,438)	(418,040)	(201,025)	(217,015)	(95,654)	(52,254)	(43,400)	(36,516)	(24,206)	(12,309)	(30,965)	(3,251)	(27,713)
Work Full-Time *** +++ ~	63.6%	61.0%	66.3%	67.3%	64.3%	70.4%	55.3%	51.9%	58.6%	53.6%	52.9%	54.4%	58.6%	62.2%	55.2%
	(10,243,745)	(5,022,744)	(5,221,002)	(7,532,228)	(3,689,573)	(3,842,656)	(1,541,047)	(725,005)	(816,042)	(822,618)	(427,758)	(394,860)	(347,852)	(180,408)	(167,444)
Work Part-Time *** ++	69.6%	66.7%	72.6%	73.6%	70.9%	76.4%	51.5%	49.7%	53.4%	59.3%	56.2%	62.8%	55.4%	42.7%	67.2%
	(4,932,343)	(2,423,263)	(2,509,080)	(4,079,185)	(2,014,621)	(2,064,564)	(380,320)	(188,946)	(191,374)	(361,699)	(178,385)	(183,314)	(111,139)	(41,311)	(69,828)
Looking for Work	54.6%	52.2%	57.2%	60.4%	61.2%	59.5%	52.1%	47.6%	56.9%	45.1%	36.8%	53.2%	49.7%	50.9%	48.0%
	(865,926)	(423,458)	(442,467)	(460,514)	(236,779)	(223,736)	(238,742)	(113,065)	(125,677)	(137,994)	(56,091)	(81,902)	(28,676)	(17,523)	(11,152)
Not in Labor Force *** +++ ~	58.3%	56.4%	60.3%	65.6%	62.0%	69.2%	39.5%	44.8%	33.8%	44.6%	41.5%	47.3%	59.2%	61.8%	56.4%
	(5,144,363)	(2,470,148)	(2,674,215)	(3,812,772)	(1,786,650)	(2,026,122)	(505,188)	(298,432)	(206,757)	(595,926)	(259,609)	(336,317)	(230,477)	(125,457)	(105,020)
Percent Under 18 Below Poverty Line															
Less than 5% *** +++	69.6%	66.4%	72.8%	71.3%	68.1%	74.7%	60.8%	56.6%	64.9%	59.5%	56.0%	62.7%	62.7%	60.1%	64.9%
	(9,105,132)	(4,375,773)	(4,729,359)	(7,768,528)	(3,768,053)	(4,000,475)	(464,167)	(214,083)	(250,084)	(508,955)	(227,923)	(281,032)	(363,482)	(165,713)	(197,768)
5% to 9% *** +++	62.9%	60.1%	65.8%	66.7%	63.6%	70.0%	50.8%	47.1%	54.9%	49.6%	51.0%	48.1%	51.3%	48.5%	54.1%
	(6,925,071)	(3,401,238)	(3,523,833)	(5,628,330)	(2,749,752)	(2,878,578)	(578,223)	(283,235)	(294,988)	(528,941)	(279,811)	(249,129)	(189,577)	(88,439)	(101,137)
10% to 19% *** +	56.9%	55.7%	58.2%	61.6%	58.8%	64.5%	52.0%	52.1%	51.8%	49.6%	49.4%	49.7%	51.4%	63.8%	36.9%
	(4,217,193)	(2,133,054)	(2,084,139)	(2,535,885)	(1,219,944)	(1,315,941)	(963,516)	(505,330)	(458,185)	(582,995)	(317,498)	(265,497)	(134,797)	(90,282)	(44,515)
20% to 24% **	46.0%	43.1%	48.9%	54.7%	55.3%	54.0%	43.8%	42.8%	44.8%	41.3%	31.7%	49.8%	63.9%	50.0%	77.4%
	(1,520,156)	(710,284)	(809,872)	(369,996)	(190,898)	(179,098)	(755,046)	(375,054)	(379,992)	(333,862)	(120,817)	(213,045)	(61,252)	(23,515)	(37,737)

—continued next page

Table 7.—continued from previous page

Characteristic	Total	Male	Female	White, Non-Hispanic			African American, Non-Hispanic			Hispanic			Other		
				Total	Male	Female	Total	Male	Female	Total	Male	Female	Total	Male	Female
Urbanicity															
Urban *** +++	61.6%	58.6%	64.6%	68.9%	65.5%	72.4%	49.8%	47.4%	52.2%	49.2%	46.0%	52.2%	57.2%	56.2%	58.0%
	(12,846,215)	(6,146,731)	(6,699,484)	(8,678,308)	(4,193,705)	(4,484,604)	(2,084,222)	(999,525)	(1,084,697)	(1,518,982)	(702,261)	(816,721)	(564,702)	(251,240)	(313,461)
Suburban *** +	60.6%	58.2%	63.5%	64.7%	61.6%	68.1%	47.9%	48.4%	47.3%	47.0%	48.3%	45.2%	45.7%	42.4%	50.3%
	(3,088,261)	(1,594,914)	(1,493,347)	(2,530,894)	(1,276,119)	(1,254,774)	(252,870)	(145,746)	(107,124)	(230,336)	(133,349)	(96,987)	(74,161)	(39,700)	(34,461)
Rural *** +	65.8%	64.0%	67.8%	66.9%	64.7%	69.1%	55.6%	56.0%	55.0%	62.9%	62.2%	63.6%	70.0%	72.8%	64.1%
	(5,833,076)	(2,878,704)	(2,954,372)	(5,093,537)	(2,458,823)	(2,634,714)	(423,860)	(232,432)	(191,428)	(205,435)	(110,439)	(94,995)	(110,245)	(77,010)	(33,235)

Notes:

Activities include attending a general school meeting, attending a school or class event, and acting as a volunteer at the school or serving on a school committee.
Student's residence determined by ZIP code. An Urbanized Area (UA) comprises a place (e.g., city, village) and adjacent densely settled surrounding territory that together have a population of at least 50,000.

"Urban, outside Urbanized Area" includes incorporated and unincorporated places outside of UA with population of at least 2,500.

"Rural" represents all other places.

*** Test of statistical significance compares African Americans with Whites. *** p < .001, ** p < .01, * p < .05.

+++ Test of statistical significance compares White boys with White girls. +++ p < .001, ++ p < .01, + p < .05.

~~~ Test of statistical significance compares African American boys with African American girls. ~~~ p < .001, ~~ p < .01, ~ p < .05.

Tests of statistical significance calculated using adjusted sample weight to control for influence of large sample sizes.

Source: National Household Education Survey, 1993 School Safety & Discipline Component.

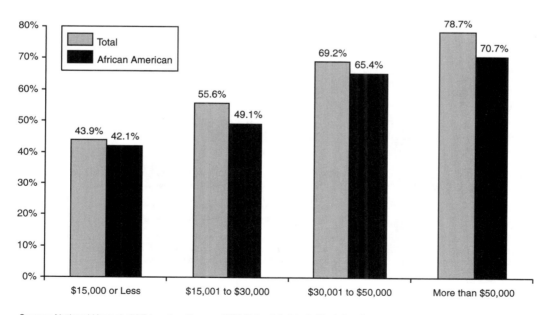

Figure 7. Percentage of Students in Grades 3 to 12 Whose Parents Reported They Had Participated in 2 or More School Activities by Family Income: 1993

Source: National Household Education Survey, 1993 School Safety & Discipline Component.

Table 8. Percentage of Students in Grades 6 to 12 Who Reported Talking With Their Parents About School Events by School Characteristics, Race, and Sex: 1993

(weighted sample size in parentheses)

School Characteristic	Total	Male	Female	White, Non-Hispanic Total	White, Non-Hispanic Male	White, Non-Hispanic Female	African American, Non-Hispanic Total	African American, Non-Hispanic Male	African American, Non-Hispanic Female	Hispanic Total	Hispanic Male	Hispanic Female	Other Total	Other Male	Other Female
Total *** +++ ~~	100.0%	100.0%	100.0%	100.0%	100.0%	100.0%	100.0%	100.0%	100.0%	100.0%	100.0%	100.0%	100.0%	100.0%	100.0%
	(23,810,309)	(11,926,918)	(11,883,391)	(16,721,186)	(8,353,179)	(8,368,007)	(3,745,525)	(1,860,254)	(1,885,271)	(2,598,884)	(1,359,295)	(1,239,589)	(744,714)	(354,190)	(390,524)
Talk to Parents about School Events	74.5%	69.6%	79.4%	77.4%	72.2%	82.7%	68.0%	63.2%	72.6%	63.8%	61.1%	66.8%	77.8%	74.7%	80.7%
	(17,733,421)	(8,301,951)	(9,431,470)	(12,949,386)	(6,030,528)	(6,918,858)	(2,546,144)	(1,176,605)	(1,369,539)	(1,658,266)	(830,255)	(828,011)	(579,625)	(264,563)	(315,062)
School Level															
Elementary +	78.4%	75.3%	81.7%	78.4%	74.8%	82.3%	78.0%	76.5%	79.6%	73.9%	72.0%	75.8%	97.6%	100.0%	96.4%
	(2,074,308)	(1,019,408)	(1,054,900)	(1,379,237)	(684,729)	(694,509)	(313,827)	(160,265)	(153,562)	(277,516)	(138,829)	(138,687)	(103,727)	(35,585)	(68,143)
Middle/Junior High *** +++	75.6%	70.3%	81.3%	78.5%	73.2%	84.0%	69.3%	65.1%	74.3%	67.2%	62.0%	74.0%	79.5%	75.3%	83.0%
	(5,607,149)	(2,707,666)	(2,899,483)	(3,944,987)	(1,862,003)	(2,082,984)	(910,560)	(466,358)	(444,202)	(581,846)	(305,614)	(276,233)	(169,756)	(73,691)	(96,064)
High School *** +++ ~	72.2%	66.5%	77.5%	76.0%	69.6%	81.9%	65.6%	60.9%	69.6%	57.5%	54.8%	60.2%	69.8%	62.8%	76.8%
	(8,191,908)	(3,640,804)	(4,551,105)	(6,101,182)	(2,716,618)	(3,384,564)	(1,174,933)	(497,147)	(677,785)	(687,084)	(325,285)	(361,799)	(228,709)	(101,753)	(126,956)
Combination ** ~~	77.4%	74.9%	80.1%	80.0%	77.4%	82.8%	61.7%	45.2%	77.7%	68.8%	75.9%	61.9%	79.6%	91.4%	61.7%
	(1,860,055)	(934,074)	(925,981)	(1,523,979)	(767,178)	(756,801)	(146,824)	(52,834)	(93,990)	(111,820)	(60,527)	(51,293)	(77,433)	(53,535)	(23,898)
School Type															
Public, Assigned *** +++ ~	74.1%	68.9%	79.5%	77.0%	71.0%	82.9%	67.8%	64.2%	71.6%	62.5%	60.5%	64.9%	77.3%	72.4%	81.6%
	(14,363,828)	(6,710,283)	(7,653,544)	(10,793,339)	(4,961,842)	(5,831,497)	(1,872,029)	(904,467)	(967,563)	(1,293,593)	(667,945)	(625,649)	(404,866)	(176,030)	(228,836)
Public, Chosen *** ~	73.9%	69.7%	78.0%	79.9%	77.2%	82.5%	65.9%	57.7%	73.1%	71.3%	65.5%	77.3%	75.2%	79.8%	70.8%
	(1,911,052)	(886,090)	(1,024,962)	(996,916)	(485,104)	(511,811)	(544,676)	(224,682)	(319,994)	(268,119)	(124,378)	(143,741)	(101,341)	(51,926)	(49,416)
Private, Religious	77.6%	74.2%	80.7%	78.5%	75.9%	81.2%	84.0%	75.7%	87.8%	62.5%	58.0%	65.6%	82.2%	71.9%	93.4%
	(1,191,777)	(544,784)	(646,993)	(936,726)	(454,719)	(482,006)	(110,371)	(31,551)	(78,820)	(92,554)	(34,823)	(57,731)	(52,126)	(23,690)	(28,436)
Private, Non-Religious +	84.5%	91.4%	75.8%	86.4%	95.2%	76.6%	67.5%	73.5%	47.9%	57.6%	51.4%	100.0%	92.7%	100.0%	83.4%
	(266,764)	(160,794)	(105,970)	(222,405)	(128,862)	(93,544)	(19,067)	(15,905)	(3,162)	(4,000)	(3,109)	(891)	(21,292)	(12,918)	(8,374)
School Enrollment															
Less than 300 Students *	73.8%	70.9%	76.7%	76.8%	74.3%	79.2%	64.8%	60.3%	70.2%	51.6%	46.9%	56.1%	100.0%	100.0%	100.0%
	(1,916,466)	(904,221)	(1,012,245)	(1,540,829)	(726,286)	(814,543)	(151,071)	(76,095)	(74,975)	(141,430)	(62,324)	(79,106)	(83,136)	(39,516)	(43,621)
300 to 599 Students *** +++ ~	75.1%	70.2%	80.2%	77.4%	72.0%	83.0%	66.9%	61.4%	73.3%	73.1%	72.4%	73.8%	71.2%	70.9%	71.5%
	(5,834,077)	(2,789,772)	(3,044,305)	(4,274,015)	(2,023,608)	(2,250,407)	(827,028)	(405,530)	(421,497)	(567,712)	(274,913)	(292,799)	(165,323)	(85,721)	(79,602)
600 to 999 Students *** +++	75.3%	72.0%	78.6%	78.5%	74.1%	82.7%	65.4%	63.1%	67.4%	64.4%	68.2%	59.3%	92.5%	88.0%	95.0%
	(4,617,681)	(2,175,026)	(2,442,655)	(3,424,643)	(1,592,818)	(1,831,825)	(677,436)	(311,385)	(366,051)	(363,780)	(219,021)	(144,760)	(151,822)	(51,803)	(100,019)
1,000 or More Students +++ ~	73.3%	66.5%	80.1%	76.8%	69.9%	83.7%	71.8%	66.1%	76.9%	59.5%	52.1%	68.0%	67.7%	64.9%	70.5%
	(5,365,196)	(2,432,932)	(2,932,264)	(3,709,899)	(1,687,816)	(2,022,083)	(890,609)	(383,594)	(507,015)	(585,344)	(273,998)	(311,346)	(179,344)	(87,524)	(91,820)
Urbanicity															
Urban *** +++ ~~~	74.3%	69.8%	78.7%	78.3%	73.6%	83.0%	70.1%	63.8%	76.1%	63.2%	61.9%	64.6%	75.6%	71.0%	79.3%
	(10,350,733)	(4,839,192)	(5,511,541)	(6,654,506)	(3,136,016)	(3,518,491)	(1,999,617)	(885,841)	(1,113,776)	(1,294,845)	(647,378)	(647,467)	(401,765)	(169,958)	(231,807)
Suburban * ++	74.2%	69.0%	79.7%	75.8%	71.3%	80.8%	66.0%	63.9%	67.6%	67.4%	56.6%	82.9%	80.3%	67.0%	92.2%
	(2,642,348)	(1,276,835)	(1,365,513)	(2,086,272)	(1,031,916)	(1,054,355)	(236,158)	(95,323)	(140,835)	(232,840)	(115,123)	(117,717)	(87,079)	(34,473)	(52,606)
Rural *** +++	75.1%	69.6%	80.5%	77.0%	70.4%	83.1%	58.0%	60.5%	54.1%	63.5%	61.6%	65.6%	86.9%	95.1%	74.3%
	(4,740,340)	(2,185,924)	(2,554,415)	(4,208,608)	(1,862,596)	(2,346,012)	(310,369)	(195,441)	(114,928)	(130,581)	(67,754)	(62,827)	(90,781)	(60,133)	(30,648)

—continued next page

Table 8.—continued from previous page

School Characteristic	Total	Male	Female	White, Non-Hispanic			African American, Non-Hispanic			Hispanic			Other		
				Total	Male	Female	Total	Male	Female	Total	Male	Female	Total	Male	Female
Census Region															
Northeast * +++	73.1%	66.7%	80.1%	74.9%	67.1%	84.0%	66.3%	66.4%	66.3%	61.4%	58.6%	64.5%	82.2%	75.8%	89.2%
	(3,180,036)	(1,505,771)	(1,674,265)	(2,511,882)	(1,208,773)	(1,303,109)	(332,936)	(132,576)	(200,360)	(208,919)	(103,705)	(105,214)	(126,299)	(60,717)	(65,582)
South *** +++	72.6%	68.6%	76.5%	75.8%	71.8%	79.7%	68.1%	64.5%	71.9%	63.7%	58.5%	68.2%	65.5%	59.5%	70.6%
	(6,103,716)	(2,851,154)	(3,252,562)	(4,045,637)	(1,893,453)	(2,152,183)	(1,467,578)	(711,202)	(756,376)	(482,252)	(201,306)	(280,946)	(108,248)	(45,192)	(63,056)
Midwest * +++	78.3%	73.1%	83.4%	79.1%	73.2%	84.7%	72.0%	66.3%	78.4%	76.5%	86.2%	67.7%	87.6%	89.9%	84.9%
	(4,596,572)	(2,096,335)	(2,500,237)	(3,807,376)	(1,698,799)	(2,108,578)	(526,641)	(255,379)	(271,262)	(162,656)	(86,966)	(75,690)	(99,899)	(55,192)	(44,707)
West *** + ~~	74.4%	70.0%	78.9%	80.2%	77.1%	83.2%	61.2%	44.9%	76.4%	62.4%	59.5%	66.3%	78.6%	75.6%	81.0%
	(3,853,097)	(1,848,691)	(2,004,406)	(2,584,491)	(1,229,502)	(1,354,989)	(218,988)	(77,448)	(141,541)	(804,439)	(438,278)	(366,161)	(245,178)	(103,463)	(141,716)

Notes:

Student's residence determined by ZIP code. An Urbanized Area (UA) comprises a place (e.g., city, village) and adjacent densely settled surrounding territory that together have a population of at least 50,000.

"Urban, outside Urbanized Area" includes incorporated and unincorporated places outside of UA with population of at least 2,500.

"Rural" represents all other places.

*** Test of statistical significance compares African Americans with whites. *** p < .001, ** p < .01, * p < .05.

+++ Test of statistical significance compares white boys with white girls. +++ p < .001, ++ p < .01, + p < .05.

~~~ Test of statistical significance compares African American boys with African American girls. ~~~ p < .001, ~~ p < .01, ~ p < .05.

Tests of statistical significance calculated using adjusted sample weight to control for influence of large sample sizes.

Source: National Household Education Survey, 1993 School Safety & Discipline Component.

Figure 8. Percentage of Students in Grades 6 to 12 Who Reported Talking With Their Parents About School Events by Number of Students Enrolled at Their Schools: 1993

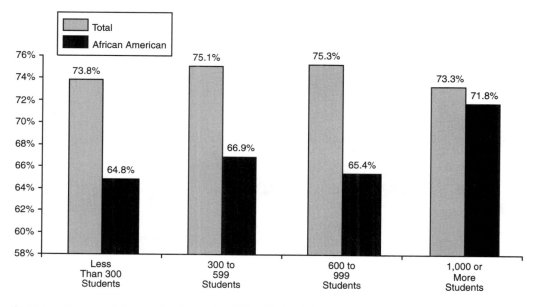

Source: National Household Education Survey, 1993 School Safety & Discipline Component.

CHAPTER XII.
Conclusion

This compilation of data about the educational status and achievement of African Americans in preschool through high school is intended to be of use to the general population as well as to particular groups of individuals. For all readers, this Data Book provides a single source of data and information describing the preschool, elementary, and secondary education of African Americans. At each level, indicators of progress and challenges are presented. We hope that this compilation will cause readers to raise questions about the additional types of data that need to be collected at the national, state, and institutional levels in order to develop a more complete understanding about the progress achieved by and the challenges continuing to face African Americans.

Like Volume I, this Volume of the Data Book reveals several gaps in our knowledge base. In some instances, the data are not available from existing national databases to completely understand the status and condition of African Americans. For example, while educators may be encouraged by African Americans' relatively high rates of participation in Head Start and other types of preschool, these analyses are limited by the absence of important contextual data. Missing from this discussion is important evidence about the quality of the experiences of preschoolers, including the curricula, the personnel, and the educational focus of the preschool exposures. In addition, the small number of African American private school principals in the sample limits the conclusions that may be drawn about differences between their experiences and the experiences of their majority counterparts.

The data included in this, Volume II, are also intended to provide preschool, elementary, and sec-ondary school teachers and administrators with the baseline of facts describing the current status of African American students. Educators and administrators can then use these facts to identify areas in their plans for improvements and necessary changes in existing policies and practices.

This Data Book also raises a number of important questions that warrant further attention by educational researchers. Among the questions of greatest importance to researchers at the Frederick D. Patterson Research Institute are the following:

PRESCHOOLERS

- What are the effects of participation in prekindergarten programs such as Head Start, Chapter One prekindergarten, and school or district-sponsored prekindergarten programs on students' readiness for school, achievement, progress, high school completion, and postsecondary activities?

- What strategies are needed to raise the vocabulary test scores of African American preschoolers to the level of their white counterparts?

ELEMENTARY AND SECONDARY SCHOOL STUDENTS

- What actions are needed to ensure that the levels of enthusiasm for school that are exhibited by African American preschoolers are maintained through later years rather than dissipate into absenteeism, tardiness, and opting-out of school activities?

- What new policies and practices are needed to increase the representation of African American students in America's private schools?

- What strategies are needed to raise the test scores of African American students on national assessments of reading, writing, history, geography, and mathematics to the proficient level?

- What actions are needed to increase feelings of personal safety and security at school, on school grounds, and traveling to and from school among African American students?

- What policies and practices are needed to reduce the presence of fighting gangs, weapons, and drug dealers in America's elementary and secondary schools?

- What lessons can be learned about the lower use of alcohol, marijuana, and cocaine among African American high school seniors than among their white counterparts?

- What are the effects of participation in community service activities upon their postsecondary activities?

ELEMENTARY AND SECONDARY SCHOOL TEACHERS AND PRINCIPALS

- What new policies and practices are needed to increase the representation of African Americans, particularly African American men, among America's public and private school teachers and principals?

- What strategies are needed to increase the number of African American teachers who receive their undergraduate degrees from research universities?

What lessons can be learned from the success of historically black colleges and universities (HBCUs) in preparing African American elementary and secondary school teachers?

- Why does the share of African American public school teachers who have received their undergraduate degrees from HBCUs increase with the representation of African American students in the schools in which they teach?

- What policies and practices are needed to increase school support for in-service and other professional development activities for African American school teachers and principals?

What strategies are needed to raise the level of preparation of African American school teachers, as evidenced by scores on tests measuring general knowledge, communications skills, and professional knowledge?

PARENTAL INVOLVEMENT IN THEIR CHILDREN'S SCHOOLS

- What policies and practices are needed to reduce the negative effects of poverty upon the participation of the parents of African American students in their children's education?

- What strategies are needed to increase the level of communication between African American boys and their parents about school-related activities and events?

Glossary

African American: The African American racial group includes U.S. citizens who are not-Hispanic and who are classified as "black" by the Bureau of the Census. African Americans include individuals descending from any of the black racial groups of Africa.

Bachelor's degree: Bachelor's degrees are awarded for successfully completing a baccalaureate program. Typically these programs require the equivalent of four-years of full-time study.

Catholic school: A private school that is controlled by and/or subsidized in part by a Roman Catholic church group, such as a parish, group of parishes, diocese, or Catholic religious order.

Chapter One: Now known as Title I of the Elementary and Secondary Schools Act.

Combined elementary and secondary school: A school that provides instruction at both the elementary and secondary school levels. Combined elementary and secondary schools start with grade 6 or below and end with grade 9 or above.

Doctoral Degree: Doctoral degrees include Doctor of Education (Ed.D.), Doctor of Public Health, and Doctor of Philosophy (Ph.D.) in any field

Educational Attainment: Educational attainment refers to the highest level of education completed by an individual.

Elementary school: A school comprised of any span of grades not above the eighth grade. A preschool or kindergarten school is classified as an elementary school if it is an essential part of an elementary school or a regularly established school system.

Enrollment: Total number of students registered in a particular school at a given point in time (typically the fall of a year).

Extracurricular activities: Activities that are offered outside of the regular course of study and that are not required as part of the curriculum. Extracurricular activities may be sponsored by both schools (e.g., varsity athletics, academic subject clubs) and community groups (e.g., girl and boy scouts, hobby clubs).

First-Professional Degree: First-professional degree programs require a total of at least six academic years, including at least two years of college-level work prior to beginning the program. First-professional degrees are awarded in the following fields: dentistry (D.D.S. or D.M.D.), medicine (M.D.), optometry (O.D.), osteopathic medicine (D.O.), pharmacy (D.Phar.), podiatric medicine (D.P.M.), veterinary medicine (D.V.M.), chiropractic (D.C. or D.C.M.), law (J.D.), and theological professions (M.Div. or M.H.L.).

Hispanic: The Hispanic racial group includes U.S. citizens who are classified as "Hispanic" by the Bureau of the Census. The Hispanic racial group includes people of Puerto Rico, Mexico, Cuba, Central and South American, and other Spanish culture or orgin, regardless of race.

Historically Black Colleges and Universities (HBCUs): HBCUs include colleges and universities that were founded prior to 1964 and that have as their primary mission the education of African Americans. The majority of HBCUs are four-year institutions and are located in southern, midwestern, and mid-Atlantic regions of the United States, but HBCUs include both two- and four-year institutions as well as public and private institutions. In 1996, there were a total of 103 HBCUs: 40 public four-year, 10 public two-year, 49 private four-year, and 4 private two-year.

IQ Tests: Standardized tests used to measure ability. Examples of IQ tests at the preschool level include the Peabody Picture Vocabulary Test and the Test of Social/Motor Development.

Master's Degree: Master's degrees are awarded for completing academic programs that typically require one or two years of full-time academic work beyond the baccalaureate. Master's degrees are awarded in both liberal arts and sciences, such as the Master of Arts (M.A.) and the Master of Science (M.S.) as well as in more professionally-oriented fields, such as the Master of Education (M.Ed.), Master of Business Administration (M.B.A.), Master of Fine Arts (M.F.A.), Master of Music (M.M.), Master of Public Policy (M.P.P.), and Master of Social Work (M.S.W.). Master's degrees are also awarded for completing programs beyond the first-professional degree, such as the Master of Laws (LL.M.).

National Assessment Governing Board (NAGB) Achievement Levels: The National Assessment Governing Board (NAGB) has defined standards for reporting the results of the National Assessment of Educational Progress (NAEP). The three achievement levels are: basic, proficient, and advanced. These levels correspond to expected levels of student knowledge and performance in particular subject areas.

Basic: Basic signifies partial mastery of the knowledge and skills that are essential for proficient work at the fourth, eighth, and twelfth grade levels.

Proficient: Proficient denotes solid academic performance for the grade level tested. Students have displayed competency over challenging subject material and are ready for the next level of schooling.

Advanced: Advanced represents superior performance above the proficient level at grades 4, 8, and 12.

National Assessment of Educational Progress (NAEP): A congressionally mandated study funded by the U.S. Department of Education's Office of Educational Research and Improvement. Initially implemented in 1969, NAEP is designed to assess the nation's progress in education. NAEP has tested the educational levels of 9-, 13-, and 17-year old students (and more recently, students in grades 4, 8, and 12) in 10 learning areas. As of 1980/81, different learning areas are assessed biennially. Learning areas are reassessed periodically to measure changes over time in educational achievement.

National School Lunch Program: A federal program under which low-income families with school aged children may be eligible to receive free or reduced-price school lunches.

PRAXIS Examination: Many states require individuals to pass a standardized test before granting licensure or certification to teach. The PRAXIS program (known as the National Teacher's Examination prior to 1993) has three parts: 1) Pre-Professional Skills Tests and Computer-Based Testing Program; 2) NTE Core Battery tests, Subject Assessment/Specialty Area tests, Multiple Subjects Assessment for Teachers, and Principles of Learning and Teaching test; and 3) Classroom Performance Assessment for beginning teachers. Three tests comprise the NTE Core Battery tests: General Knowledge, Communications Skills, and Professional Knowledge. Subject Assessment/Specialty Area tests are also administered.

Preschool: Preschool refers to the years before kindergarten and is synonymous with nursery school and pre-kindergarten. Preschool age children are typically three and four years old.

Secondary school: A school encompassing any span of grades beginning with the next grade following an elementary or middle-school (typically 7, 8, or 9) and ending with or below grade 12. Secondary schools include both junior and senior high schools.

Socioeconomic status: Socioeconomic status is a composite that summarizes family income, father's education, mother's education, father's occupation, mother's occupation, and items in the home (e.g., dishwasher, two or more vehicles, computer).

Urbanicity: Urbanicity is a summary term including urban, suburban, and rural.

Urban: Within a central city of a Metropolitan Statistical Area (MSA). MSAs are designated by the Office of Management and Budget and are defined based upon population, commuting patterns, and metropolitan charater. MSAs typically include a city, its entire urban area, and the re-

mainder of the county or counties in which the urban area is located.

Suburban: Within an MSA, but outside of the central city area.

Rural: Outside of an MSA.

White: The White racial group includes U.S. citizens who are not-Hispanic and who are classified as "White" by the Bureau of the Census. The White racial group includes individuals descending from the orginal people of Europe, North Africa, and the Middle East.

Index

___